REGISTRATION AND RECOGNITION

PROCEEDINGS OF THE BRITISH ACADEMY • 182

REGISTRATION AND RECOGNITION

Documenting the Person in World History

Edited by
KEITH BRECKENRIDGE
AND
SIMON SZRETER

Published for THE BRITISH ACADEMY
by OXFORD UNIVERSITY PRESS

Oxford University Press, Great Clarendon Street, Oxford OX2 6DP

First edition published in 2012

British Library Cataloguing in Publication Data
Data available

Library of Congress Cataloging in Publication Data
Data available

Typeset by
Keystroke, Station Road, Codsall, Wolverhampton

Printed in Great Britain by
TJ International Ltd, Padstow, Cornwall

ISBN 978–0–19–726531–4

FSC
www.fsc.org
MIX
Paper from responsible sources
FSC® C013056

Contents

Foreword by C. A. Bayly ix
Acknowledgements xv
Notes on Contributors xvii

Editors' Introduction: Recognition and Registration: The Infrastructure of Personhood in World History 1
SIMON SZRETER AND KEITH BRECKENRIDGE

PART I: REGISTRATION, STATES AND LEGAL PERSONHOOD

1. Household Registration, Property Rights, and Social Obligations in Imperial China: Principles and Practices 39
RICHARD VON GLAHN

2. Registration of Identities in Early Modern English Parishes and amongst the English Overseas 67
SIMON SZRETER

3. Too Much Information? Too Little Coordination? (Civil) Registration in Nineteenth-Century Germany 93
ANDREAS FAHRMEIR

4. Japan's Civil Registration Systems Before and After the Meiji Restoration 113
OSAMU SAITO AND MASAHIRO SATO

5. Civil Status and Identification in Nineteenth-Century France: A Matter of State Control? 137
PAUL-ANDRÉ ROSENTAL

PART II: REGISTRATION AS NEGOTIATED RECOGNITION

6. Identity Registration in the Classical Mediterranean World 169
REBECCA FLEMMING

7. Naming, Identifying and Authorizing Movement in Early Modern Spain and Spanish America 191
TAMAR HERZOG

8. Establishing and Registering Identity in the Dutch Republic 211
HENK LOOIJESTEIJN AND MARCO H. D. VAN LEEUWEN

9. The Identity Thieves of the Indian Ocean: Forgery, Fraud and the Origins of South African Immigration Control, 1890s–1920s 253
ANDREW MACDONALD

10. Parish Baptism Registers, Vital Registration and Fixing Identities in Uganda 277
SHANE DOYLE

PART III: EMPIRES AND REGISTRATION

11. Identity Registration in India During and After the Raj 299
RAVINDRAN GOPINATH

12. Monitoring the Abolition of the International Slave Trade: Slave Registration in the British Caribbean 323
STANLEY L. ENGERMAN

13. Birth of the 'Secular' Individual: Medical and Legal Methods of Identification in Nineteenth-Century Egypt 335
KHALED FAHMY

14. No Will to Know: The Rise and Fall of African Civil Registration in Twentieth-Century South Africa 357
KEITH BRECKENRIDGE

15. Voting, Welfare and Registration: The Strange Fate of the État-Civil in French Africa, 1945–1960 385
FREDERICK COOPER

PART IV: REGISTRATION, RECOGNITION AND HUMAN RIGHTS

16. Uruguay's Child Rights Approach to Health: What Role for Civil Registration? 415
ANNE-EMANUELLE BIRN

17. Birth Registration and the Promotion of Children's Rights in the Interwar Years: The Save the Children International Union's Conference on the African Child, and Herbert Hoover's American Child Health Association 449
DOMINIQUE MARSHALL

18. Children, Citizenship and Child Support: The Child Support Grant in Post-Apartheid South Africa 475
FRANCIE LUND

19. What Comes After the Social? Historicizing the Future of Social Assistance and Identity Registration in Africa 495
JAMES FERGUSON

Index 517

Foreword

BY C. A. BAYLY

It is a pleasure to have been asked to introduce this fascinating and original collection of essays. I write as a colonial and more specifically Indian historian, and the approach taken in the Introduction and many of the chapters represents a rather different way of looking at the registration and counting of persons than has been common in my field. Broadly, in the work of scholars such as Nicholas Dirks, Bernard Cohn and even Susan Bayly on South Asia or Frederick Cooper on Africa, the census and more local forms of registration have been seen as instrumental intrusions into, or even 'epistemic violence' on society perpetrated by colonial states intent on extracting revenue or classifying people into tribes or castes for political purposes or for the coercion of labour. The 'person' registered, from the Thugee and Dacoity (bandit) registrations of India in the 1830s, through to registration of dissident villages in the Mau Mau rebellion in Kenya in the 1950s, was an insurgent or troublesome collective, though individual leaders were sometimes mentioned. The themes of the early Foucault and modern governmentality hang heavily over this literature.

Individuals were only registered spasmodically because there was little concern with the person of the colonial subject as such. For this reason, mortality from famines, disease or local ethnic conflict, could never be adequately assessed. Yet even in British and European historiography, a wide range of historians from neo-Marxists to conservatives have tended to assume that registration proceeded from the desire of the elites to monitor the 'dangerous classes', as in Gareth Stedman Jones's London of the 1870s, for instance, or to gauge the extent of crime and degeneration among slum-dwellers in the 1920s and 1930s, as recently emphasised in Richard Overy's study of eugenic theorists in his recent book, *The Morbid Age*. Indeed, personal experience tends to confirm me in my own suspicion of registration and 'marking the person', even for apparently benign purposes. At the age of eight, I was measured, photographed in the nude, plucked from my family and sent to a Thomas Mann-like sanatorium on the bracing Kentish coast full of London slum children. The bizarre medical theory proposed to justify this was that the ozone gusting along the coast would prevent incipient lung disease.

The Introduction and several of the papers take a rather different perspective: that the registration of persons is an essential, if contingent precursor to social provision, equality and welfare. The Editors argue that registration is fundamental to recognition and so to entitlement. What the registration of slaves in Stanley Engerman's paper, for instance, was directed to was halting the illegal slave trade and gave ammunition to groups and individuals seeking to abolish slavery altogether. Contemporary societies with the most elaborate and coherent system of lifetime registration and monitoring, such as the Netherlands and Scandinavia, certainly have the highest scores for social equality. Ravindran Gopinath's chapter similarly reveals that the most highly educated states in India in the recent past were also those with the highest scores for the registration of births: Tamilnadu, Kerala and, to a lesser extent, West Bengal. The state that comes out worst in his analysis is Bihar, still almost a byword for inequality, low literacy and 'caste-ism'.

One great success of this collection is that it moderates the conflict between this image of the domineering, instrumentalist, counting state and these contingently benign features of the registration of persons. Clearly, the ideological predisposition of the state in question must immediately be brought into the picture: registration could evidently function either as an instrument of gross oppression, as in Nazi Europe, or, to a lesser extent in Communist East Germany, or equally, as an instrument to promote liberation and equality. It all depended on the political and ideological context.

A second general point concerns the density of forms of registration of persons and the identity of the registering agent. Emerging state projects of registration, as in early modern England, were set within a dense matrix of local and non-state forms: church records of births, marriages and deaths; manorial records of individual property; urban property registers, and so on. Religious groups, and not only Christian ones, registered their adherents. Among the first Asians to have lifelong accounting in colonial provinces, were Indian, Chinese and Vietnamese Christians, for instance, because they were registered in churches, even if often segregated off during religious services. But equally, it is possible, to get some sense of the size of congregations or adherents from the records of *madrasah*s and Sufi *khanqah*s in the Islamic world, or even the *akhara*s, or the records of establishments of Hindu 'renouncers' in India, which have recently and somewhat dubiously, been used to assess deaths during the Rebellion of 1857. Some years ago ancient personalised records of Hindu priests at the holy bathing sites were supposedly appropriated by Mormons with a view to 'converting' those recorded.

Some questions arise. How far, I wonder, can the idea of identity registration be expanded? How far should the comparative approach to personal registration take account of the different forms of state, local and familial power and recognition of and meaning of 'the person' in different world societies? What, ultimately, are the theoretical boundaries of a collection such as this? Khaled Fahmy's chapter sets the beginning of registration of persons in Mehmed Ali's Egypt in a very broad context: the emergence of the modern state in the Middle East and the move he charts, following Foucault, from state as sovereign to state as instrumental governmentality. I'm sure a broad approach such as his will bring enormous benefits to students of registration. But it will be difficult to stop it merging into a catch-all social and political history of the world. And, as the editors are well aware, the studies assembled here suggest there may be limits to the invocation of Foucault as a kind of Holy Spirit blessing all social sciences through all time.

Among other, more general points to bear in mind in this debate, it seems to me that a critical issue is, first: in Lenin's phrase, who is doing what to whom? What is registration and what is a person? We can distinguish between registration by high state authority, as in the colonial and Euro-American censuses, for instance, and local forms of registration by authoritative agencies loosely related to the rulers. I am sure that Ravindran Gopinath and Khaled Fahmy are both correct to argue that broad state censuses were specifically features of modernity, however defined, and that they were only broadly characteristic of the period after 1800. The Mughals' great accounting of their realm, the *Ain-i-Akbari*, was in Fahmy's terms, an expression of sovereignty, not a reflection of centralised governmentality. Equally, Pre-Napoleonic Mameluke Egypt or Ottoman Turkey certainly produced 'descriptions of the people', but there was no census in a modern sense.

At the same time, these societies *did* produce dense systems of local registration connected with the payment of tax and rent in cash whose origins stretched back into the Middle Ages or even antiquity. Their consequences could be quite significant in these early periods: not least the purported birth of God on earth as a result of Caesar Augustus's census. In fact, the spectre lying behind the registration of persons in most societies was often the tax collector. Indian historians, for instance, are aware of the existence of village accountants (*patwaris*) even in pre-colonial polities. These recorded taxes, landholdings and dues, though mostly in the form of 'collective persons', i.e. local brotherhoods or caste groups. Something similar seems to be true of the Ottoman Empire, including Egypt, and more distantly the *pao-chia* in Ming and Qing China and parallel local forms of accounting for people through family groups in Tokugawa Japan.

Local disputes over inheritance and privileges also empowered the expansion of quite dense systems of local registration, perhaps similar to European manorial records. In western India, for instance, the historian Narendra Wagle has spent years ploughing through the dense records of the Peshwa Daftar (the archive of the Poona ruler). He finds the records of local bodies of arbitration called *panchayats*. Representatives of the state authorities were present at these gatherings, but rather than controlling the proceedings, their role was to get 'the sense of the neighbourhood'. These bodies may well have something in common with Rebecca Flemming's Athens, where status was created outside, but registered in the assembly. Most striking is the fact that the personal names of the local leaders of castes and brotherhoods present were appended to these documents, according to Wagle. The persons registered here validated the judicial outcome. This raises another general question about agency in registration. This was a case of self-registration in the context of local governmentality, rather than simple registration by the state. It is not surprising that in the nineteenth century, Indians – perhaps erroneously – took this to be evidence of the existence of a tradition of democracy. A general question arising from the volume is: what is the relationship between self-registration and the development of representative and democratic forms of government?

A further comparative question arises: was it more difficult in societies where cash-revenue, defined landholdings and complex systems of local authority were not so clearly developed, for the modern state, with its own superordinate systems of personal registration, to take root in the longer run? I am thinking here of African examples. We hear of the 'exit option' of African farmers, who in pre-colonial polities could literally up-sticks and disappear if they didn't like the terms of their agrarian relationships with local power-holders. There is a pervasive argument among African historians that this partly explains the relative superficiality of pre-colonial African polities, which were often mere 'gatekeepers' for migrant groups. In some analyses, this argument suggests that African farmers were less open to subjugation than many of their European or Asian contemporaries, who were subject to local registration for labour services or cash-revenue payments. Here we are pushed back to the issue of whether registration was a 'good' or a 'bad' thing, though my view would be that this depended on the ideology, power and aims of the rulers in question.

So who did the registration to whom and what was recorded: individuals, community leaders or group persons, i.e. castes, tribes or religious communities (like the Iberian Moriscos, for instance)? At what point does the centralised, modern state come in, and to what purpose? Fahmy's broad account shows decisively how fear of epidemic disease, the need for military labour and, latterly, various types of Islamic juridical activity set the scene for the widespread registration of persons in nineteenth-century Egypt. Yet with growing population pressure, colonial incursions and the destruction of Egypt's emerging small-scale industries by European free-traders, it is not clear how far the more benign corollaries of registration were ever realised in Egypt.

One thing I would like to point to, however, is the way in which emerging nationalist and humanitarian movements could use state statistics to argue for better governance even in dire situations like this. By the time of the rule of Lord Cromer in the 1890s, Egyptian patriots were compiling a range of charges against colonial governance and local landholders based on Mehmed Ali's and Ibrahmim Pasha's registrations or censuses and British blue books.

Equally, even if the Indian census paid little attention to the welfare of persons, being merely a massive exercise of counting for revenue and police purposes, nevertheless, people whom I call 'statistical liberals' were using the census and other forms of British accounting and registration to attack the colonial state as early as the 1860s. R. C. Dutt and Dadabhai Naoroji were among the foremost among them. Dutt recorded the income and expenditure of individual cultivators. This did not go unnoticed among more conservative groups in Indian society who felt their interests were being threatened by registration. In the mid-1850s the British in Bengal began to try to require the registration of tenants by the local landed classes. This was not, at root, a humanitarian exercise: the British were worried by the prevalence of agrarian riots in the countryside around indigo production and also looking for new sources of revenue. But the local newspaper working in the interests of the landlords, the *Hindoo Patriot*, was adamantly opposed to registration of tenants. It would impose enormous cost and hardship on the unfortunate landholders, an editorial said. Moreover, the landlords would not allow tenants to register voluntarily because 'registration is not a custom of the country'.

Understandably, registration by the modern state – and increasingly full-life personal registration – is a major topic in the volume. But it is worth pointing out that the rise of the registering state was also accompanied by a massive expansion of non-state registering bodies and bodies using state data for their own purposes: perhaps a key, but underplayed aspect of the emergence of Habermas's public sphere itself. Stanley Engerman's slave registration registers were used by abolitionists. And the issue of slaves reminds us that diasporas, forced or voluntarily, and particularly those crossing jurisdictions, were at the cutting edge of registration.

Contemporary parallels to slave registration included the registration of *lascars* – East Indian seamen. British owners began the move to register them when discontented seamen set fire to their vessels or the Chinese or Dutch authorities imprisoned British Indian seamen in Canton or Batavia. Yet the cause was soon taken up by British and Indian liberals, notably James Silk Buckingham, anti-slaver, opponent of the East India Company, Methodist, teetotaller and, later, town planner. Buckingham and his co-actors were genuinely concerned with the welfare of sailors. He deplored the incarceration of Indian seamen in what he called a 'kennel in the Isle of Dogs', near the Port of London. He put this down to the fact that the Indians might see the poverty and depravity of London with their own eyes and pass on the news to their discontented countrymen in India. The registration of indentured labourers across the world had similar consequences. This 'new system of slavery', in the words popularised by Hugh Tinker, soon attracted the attention of reformers.

Finally, I return to the questions: who did the registration; what was the 'person' being registered; was the person merely being counted, or was there regular lifelong periodic assessment; what were the longer-term consequences of registration for different societies, both progressive and malign? How did registration relate to the expansion of the cash-economy, global diasporas and labour requirements? The following chapters go a long way to answering these important historical questions.

Acknowledgements

All the authors of the chapters in this volume met together at a workshop that took place during 7–10 September 2010 in St John's College, Cambridge, which was supported by a British Academy conference grant to the two editors. Edited volumes – like registration systems – can be bad-tempered affairs, with scholars of different enthusiasms tied to a common project that can only proceed at the pace of the slowest member. The speed of the appearance of this large book, in just over two years since that meeting in Cambridge, is testimony not only to the remarkable efficiency of the British Academy and OUP, to whom we are all most grateful, but also to the fact that the production of this book has been a remarkably mutually supportive process and a highly enjoyable one for the two editors. We would like to thank all of the authors for their professional and good-humoured cooperation. We would also like to thank all the participants in the workshop that was held at St John's College, especially the several discussants for their excellent commentaries and those who contributed papers that do not appear in this volume. Those present comprised: Ross Anderson, Claudine Dardy, Eddy Higgs, Peter Kitson, Philip Kreager, Karl Jacob Krogness, Pier Larson, Gayle Lonergan, Jelle van Lottum, David Lyon, Susan Pearson, Pierre Piazza, Richard Smith, Catherine Sumnall, Stephen Thompson, Sarah Walters, Michael Woolcock, and Tony Wrigley.

The staff of the British Academy, particularly James Rivington and Brigid Hamilton-Jones, have provided us with invaluable advice and assistance. Sarah Pearsall was an unflappable, quick and careful copy-editor, and her professionalism and generosity made the last stages of production quick and pleasant. We would also like to thank Kyla O'Neill, who provided invaluable editorial assistance for several of the chapters.

Keith Breckenridge would like to thank his current and former colleagues in Durban and at WISER and, especially, Catherine Burns, for her assistance and encouragement. Similarly, Simon Szreter would like to acknowledge Hilary Cooper. He would also like to express his general gratitude to the Cambridge History Faculty and to the Master and Fellows of St John's College for the supportive scholarly environments they provide, and to the college staff for their customary courtesy and efficiency during the workshop. His work has also been supported and stimulated during the last three years by the Wellcome Trust 5-year Strategic Award to Cambridge University, 'Generation to Reproduction', and by colleagues and staff at www.historyandpolicy.org.

HISTORY & POLICY
Connecting historians, policymakers and the media

Notes on Contributors

Anne-Emanuelle Birn is Professor and Canada Research Chair in International Health at the University of Toronto, with appointments in International Development Studies and the Dalla Lana School of Public Health. Her research explores the history of public health in Latin America and the history and politics of international health, with particular emphases on child health and global health philanthropy – and perspectives ranging from the scatological to the ideological. Her books include: *Marriage of Convenience: Rockefeller International Health and Revolutionary Mexico* (2006), *Textbook of International Health: Global Health in a Dynamic World*, 3rd edn (2009; with co-authors Yogan Pillay and Timothy Holtz) and the forthcoming *Comrades in Health: US Health Internationalists, Abroad and at Home* (with co-editor Theodore Brown).

Keith Breckenridge is an Associate Professor at WISER, the Wits Institute for Social and Economic Research, in Johannesburg. He has written extensively on the social and cultural history of the mining industry and on the making of the state in South Africa. Over the last five years he has focused especially on the very elaborate forms of biometric registration that have been developed in South Africa over the last century.

Frederick Cooper is Professor of History at New York University and a specialist in the history of Africa, of colonization and decolonization, and of empires more generally. He is the author of a trilogy of books on labour and society in East Africa and more recently of *Decolonization and African Society: The Labor Question in French and British Africa* (1996), *Africa Since 1940: The Past of the Present* (2002), *Colonialism in Question: Theory, Knowledge, History* (2005) and, with Jane Burbank, *Empires in World History: Power and the Politics of Difference* (2010). He is currently writing about citizenship in France and French Africa between 1945 and 1960.

Shane Doyle was educated at Cambridge and SOAS. Currently Senior Lecturer in African History at the University of Leeds, he was previously a British Academy Post-Doctoral Fellow at the Cambridge Group for the History of Population and Social Structure, and before that Assistant Director of the British Institute in Eastern Africa. His current research on the history of sexuality, identity and demographic change in East Africa has been funded by the AHRC, the British Academy and the ESRC.

Stanley L. Engerman is John H. Munro Professor of Economics and Professor of

History at the University of Rochester, New York. His most recent books are *Economic Development of the Americas Since 1500: Institutions and Endowments* (co-authored with Kenneth L. Sokoloff) and *The Cambridge World History of Slavery, Volume 3, AD1420 to AD1804* (co-edited with David Eltis).

Khaled Fahmy is a Professor and Chair of the History Department at the American University in Cairo. He is the author of *All the Pasha's Men: Mehmed Ali, His Army and the Making of Modern Egypt* (1997) and *Mehmed Ali: From Ottoman Governor to Ruler of Egypt* (2009). His current research interests include the social and cultural history of modern Egypt with an emphasis on the history of law, medicine and urban planning.

Andreas Fahrmeir studied at the universities of Frankfurt and Cambridge and McGill University in Montreal. After researching and teaching in London, Frankfurt and Cologne, he was appointed Professor of Modern History at Goethe University in 2006, where he also co-edits the *Historische Zeitschrift*. His research interests include the history of citizenship and immigration policies (*Citizenship: The Rise and Fall of a Modern Concept*, 2007), the general history of nineteenth-century Europe (*Revolutionen und Reformen*, 2010) and, more recently, corruption (*Geld – Geschenke – Politik*, co-edited, 2009).

James Ferguson is Susan S. and William H. Hindle Professor of Anthropology at Stanford University. He also holds honorary appointments in the Department of Sociology and Social Anthropology at Stellenbosch University and the Department of Social Anthropology at the University of Cape Town. He is the author or editor of several books, including *Global Shadows: Africa in the Neoliberal World Order* (2006). His current work on distribution and social assistance will appear as a forthcoming book, with the provisional title, *Give a Man a Fish: Reflections on the New Politics of Distribution*.

Rebecca Flemming is Senior Lecturer in Ancient History at the University of Cambridge, and a Fellow of Jesus College, Cambridge. Her research focuses on the society and culture of the Roman world.

Richard von Glahn has taught Chinese history and world history at the University of California, Los Angeles, since 1987. His primary field of research is the economic and social history of premodern China, with a particular focus on monetary history and the relationship between China and the world economy. He has published three monographs on Chinese history, edited several other books, and co-authored a world history textbook, *Crossroads and Cultures: A History of the World's Peoples* (2012).

Ravindran Gopinath is Professor of History and currently the Head of the Department of History and Culture, Jamia Millia Islamia University, New Delhi. He specializes in historical demography and economic history.

Tamar Herzog is Professor of History at Stanford University. She earned her Ph.D. at the École des Hautes Études en Sciences Sociales, Paris. Her work centres on the relationship between Spain, Portugal and Portuguese and Spanish America and the ways in which Iberian societies changed as a result of their involvement in a colonial project. Among her publications are *Upholding Justice: State, Law and the Penal System in Quito* (2004; published in Spanish 1995 and in French 2001), *Defining Nations: Immigrants and Citizens in Early Modern Spain and Spanish America* (2003; Spanish translation 2006), *Ritos de control, prácticas de negociación: las relaciones entre Quito y Madrid (1650–1750)* (2000; French translation forthcoming), and *Mediación, archivos y ejercicio: los escribanos de Quito (siglo XVII–XVIII)* (1996).

Marco H. D. van Leeuwen is Professor of Historical Sociology at Utrecht University and Honorary Fellow at the International Institute of Social History in Amsterdam. He studies social inequality from 1500 to the present. He has recently published on early modern philanthropy, guild welfare and residential segregation. He also studies social mobility: see www.hisma.org and www.towardsopen societies.org.

Henk Looijesteijn studied Early Modern History at Amsterdam University and obtained his doctorate from the European University Institute in Florence. Since 2009, he has been Postdoctoral Researcher at the International Institute of Social History in Amsterdam. His research interests include the history of the Dutch Republic in a global perspective, and he has published in the fields of intellectual and social history.

Francie Lund is Senior Research Associate in the School of Built Environment and Development Studies at the University of KwaZulu-Natal. She specializes in social policy, and especially in the impacts of state social spending on poverty and inequality. She was involved in social policy reforms at the time of the transition from apartheid to democracy, and this included chairing the Lund Committee on Child and Family Support in 1995 and 1996. She is Director of the Social Protection Programme of the global research and advocacy network, WIEGO – Women in Informal Employment: Globalizing and Organizing.

Andrew MacDonald recently completed a Ph.D. at St John's College, Cambridge and is now a postdoctoral fellow at the Centre for Indian Studies in Africa at the University of Witwatersrand, South Africa. His contribution in this volume forms part of a larger study on the making and unmaking of South Africa's international borders in the early twentieth century.

Dominique Marshall teaches Canadian and Quebec history at Carleton University. She researches the history of poverty and welfare, families and childhood, state formation and political economy, as well as the transnational history of humanitarian aid. She has written about the history of the Canadian welfare state, the history of children's rights and the Child Welfare Committee of the League of Nations. Her current research is about the Conference on the African Child of 1931, and the early history of Oxfam in Africa and Canada. Her book, *Aux origines sociales de l'État providence* (1998; available in English as *The Social Origins of the Welfare State*, 2006), received the Jean-Charles Falardeau Prize from the Canadian Federation for the Humanities and Social Sciences.

Paul-André Rosental is a full professor at Sciences Po and a fellow scholar at the Institut National d'Études Démographiques in Paris. He has created and leads the research team ESOPP, devoted to the interdisciplinary analysis of social, demographic and health policies (http://esopp.ehess.fr/). His books include *L'intelligence démographique: Sciences et politiques des populations en France (1930–1960)* (2003), and he has edited several thematic journal issues, including 'Histoire Politique des Populations' (*Annales HSS*, 2006, 1) and 'Health and Safety at Work: A Transnational History' (*Journal of Modern European History*, 2009, 2). He currently works on the history of migrants' social rights and post-World War II eugenics, and has been awarded a European Research Council Advanced Grant for the study of the transnational history of silicosis.

Osamu Saito is Professor Emeritus, Hitotsubashi University. He has written widely on both economic history and historical demography.

Masahiro Sato is Professor in the Research Centre for Information and Statistics in Social Science, Hitotsubashi University, and is a specialist on the history of census taking in Japan, Korea and Taiwan.

Simon Szreter is Professor of History and Public Policy in the History Faculty, University of Cambridge, and Fellow of St John's College, Cambridge. He is a founder of the History and Policy Network and Managing Editor of its electronic journal, www.historyandpolicy.org. He teaches modern British economic and social history since 1700 and the comparative history of population, development and environment in Britain, Africa, India and China. His main fields of research are demographic and social history, the history of empirical and official social science, and the relationship between history, development and contemporary public policy. In 2009 he was awarded the Arthur Viseltear Prize by the American Public Health Association for distinguished contributions to the history of public health.

Editors' Introduction

Recognition and Registration: The Infrastructure of Personhood in World History

SIMON SZRETER AND KEITH BRECKENRIDGE

Introduction

AROUND THE WORLD STATES REQUIRE that their citizens register as tax-payers, property owners, school students, patients, drivers, welfare recipients, and insured workers. The modern state seems almost to have become a registering machine, with the act of registration replacing taxation as the citizen's most common encounter with the state. This is because registration lies at the centre of the process of 'textually mediated organisation' that Giddens (following Weber and many others) has observed as the *raison d'être* of the modern state (Giddens 1985, 2: 185; Sankar 1992, 9). Civil registration – the administrative recording of the birth, death, and marital status of individual citizens – is the linchpin of this web of obligations and rights. The significance of birth registration, in particular, as the 'foundation for the fulfillment of other rights' is reflected in Article 7 of the 1989 UN Convention on the Rights of the Child, which places the right to a name and nationality immediately after the primary right that children have to life itself (Szreter 2007, 68; Mackenzie 2008, 534).

Yet many people, perhaps as many as half of the global population, live out their lives unrecorded by any state system of civil registration: Unicef (2005, 3) estimated that 36 per cent of births worldwide went unregistered. This is an even more disabling birthright lottery than the inequalities that go with registration, as expounded by Shachar (2009). These undocumented peoples exist on the margins of all societies, but the largest contiguous blocks of unregistered populations live in South Asia and on the African continent, where, until very recently, national systems of civil registration have not succeeded in recording even a majority of births (Setel *et al.* 2007, 1570; Kwankye 1999, 430; Jewkes and Wood 1998). This situation is changing rapidly as universal systems of civil registration, often complemented by biometric identification schemes aimed at adults, are being fostered by donor aid oriented towards meeting the Millennium Development Goals and other statistically-measured public health projects. One non-governmental organization in particular,

Plan International, has been driving a global campaign for universal birth registration. The results, to date, are impressive, with significant improvements in the scope of birth registration in countries like Angola and Ghana (Mackenzie 2008, 522).

The implementation of universal civil registration is difficult and expensive everywhere, but it has been Herculean in Africa and in South Asia, where the colonial state in the nineteenth and early twentieth century showed little enthusiasm for the long-term effort required to build the necessary administrative infrastructure. One consequence of this informational void is that administrators in Africa and South Asia have begun to opt for biometric population registers that will allow them to identify the current generation of adult citizens. The most ambitious of these national population registration schemes is the biometric Unique Identity Authority currently under development in India (Economist 2012), but almost identical projects (often with the publicly announced objective of increasing the size of the banking population) are under way in most developing countries.

These biometric registration systems, which primarily target adult citizens, promise to bypass the difficulties of building a birth and death registration infrastructure. Typically they involve a single government tender for a paperless and automated registration process which is delivered, managed and maintained by one of the global corporations, such as Sagem, Accenture, NEC or De La Rue, that dominate the field of biometric administration. In comparison the work of delivering a national system of birth and death registration may involve the opening of hundreds of offices and the training of thousands, often tens of thousands, of officials – an expensive official commitment that will last for decades. Yet the political and economic effects of the relatively cheap and efficient biometric population registers have still to be assessed. They may strengthen the workings and effects of the civil registry, or undermine it. As has been acknowledged recently by some of the leading epidemiological and demographic experts involved in designing them, earlier attempts from the 1960s onwards to substitute for the absence of full civil registration schemes, such as sample registration and indirect estimation techniques, may unfortunately have turned what were supposed to be only interim measures for analytical purposes into cheap alternatives to proper citizen registration (Hill *et al.* 2007). Rather than consigning civil registration systems to the dustbin of history, these novel schemes heighten the urgency of exploring the social and political effects of the older systems.

Establishing an understanding of the social and economic value of civil registration is especially important because of the tenacity required to make these systems work in the absence of a supporting state infrastructure. After several years of initial enthusiasm for universal population registration, the advocates of these schemes have begun to wilt in the face of the costs and administrative difficulties of deploying a nationwide registration system and enrolling a sometimes unenthusiastic population. In Ghana and Nigeria – which both inherited very limited birth registration systems from colonial rule (see Kuczynski 1948) – national projects of population registration have foundered after several months of energetic delivery, leaving officials and citizens wondering what the effort of civil registration is actually meant to produce (Breckenridge 2010, 2011).

This book aims to explore this question – examining the work of registration in societies around the world through the last millennium and more. In the process the volume opens up the politics of registration as a major new topic for historical and comparative research. The individual studies of regional practices of registration gathered here, although widely separated in time and space, address a set of themes that allow us to bring into a common framework of analysis societies that have typically been treated as dissimilar. Perhaps because it is one of the basic activities of state-making, the problem of registration, like class, gender or the state itself, provides a conceptual vocabulary that supports illuminating global comparisons.

Considered together the chapters that follow present several points of argument of wide significance. Scholars, and historians in particular, have tended to explain registration as part of an often vaguely conceived technology of writing tightly associated with the rise of state power. We show here that it is possible, and productive, to disaggregate the different types and functions of registration. Similarly, there have been many non-state agents of registration typically associated with the provision and policing of different kinds of welfare. The global trajectories of registration are much more complicated and contested than much social science theory currently allows, such that many societies, including those with elaborate administrations like modern Spain or the nineteenth-century United States, have dismantled or resisted the creation of such systems. Performative, or oral, challenges to the capacities of the written documents of registration have been tenacious and they have remained dominant in many societies into the twenty-first century (Sadiq 2009). Viewed globally, societies, and the individuals within them, seem to be very variably shaped by what we might call cultures of registration; some like the Netherlands and Japan have exalted the authority of the registry over the reputation of individuals, while others, like the Spanish territories, India and most African states, have relied on the social and oral authorities as arbiters of identification. Finally, it is important for our social science to recognize that the Chinese state, and its mandarinate neighbours (Woodside 2006), had in place a registration order, aimed at measuring and preserving the well-being of its population, at least one millennium before the nineteenth-century processes that scholars have explored as key elements in the 'science of population' (see Chapters 1 and 4). As our readers can probably perceive, viewed in combination these arguments present a challenge to some of the simplifying effects of Foucault's arguments about the emergence of biopower and governmentality.

What is registration?

Registration, in its most basic form, is the act of producing a written record. In Chinese (and the Japanese script derived from it) the word has such immense time-depth that its etymology is impossible to discern. The earliest uses of the word *registrum* in medieval European history, as Clanchy has shown, referred to the recording, usually in a book or a scroll, of copies of the contents of other important documents such as land-titles or letters. Registers provided fragile documents a measure of security for posterity but they were also, from the beginning, tools for abstracting from a larger body of information. Registration produced the capacity to generate selective lists, often, like Domesday, sorted by the name of the title-holder or the correspondent. These lists also served as tests of authenticity after the twelfth century as the ascendancy of written documents of entitlement placed an increasing premium on forgery (Clanchy 1979, 11, 55, 75, 92, 266; McCrank 1993).

List-making is an intrinsic feature of registers wherever they have been found. This may not be quite as banal as it seems. Goody and Ong have both claimed that lists were impossible in societies without writing (Goody 1986, 52–111; Ong 2002, 96). These sorts of binary claims about the epistemological rupture between written and oral cultures have mostly not survived the detailed research on literacy in Africa, and we should probably treat them with some scepticism (Halverson 1992; Hawkins 2002). But the indexing function of registers does seem particularly important. In this volume, for example, von Glahn shows that the twelfth-century Chinese texts we call household registers took three different forms: one was organized by the location of land, identifying its owner or tenant; another was ordered by the households' surnames, providing an inventory of their property; and a third, called 'rat-tail registers', listed all the households in each district according to the size of the tax-assessment levied on them (see Chapter 1, p. 54, note 17).

Registration seems always to involve multiple obligations and rights, although some of these mutually constructed implications may have been more convincing than others. Colonial officials in South Africa, for instance, routinely attempted to justify the requirement that black people were subjected to an onerous pass regime by suggesting, rather morbidly, that the passes were indispensable in the identification of dead bodies (Wilson 1912). A very common example of these interlocking obligations was the connection between the security of property holding and the liability for tax which were products of the medieval chancellery registers. Another more recent, and perhaps even more typical, example was the Maoist state's stipulation of officially sanctioned marriage registration as a condition for successful registration as an urban resident (Diamant 2001, 459).

A further feature of registers, which follows in part from their intrinsically multi-functional character, is a strong tendency towards reproduction and proliferation. Registers were instrumental in the slow and contested ascendancy of writing, which Clanchy traces from the royal chancellery out into the English countryside in the two centuries after the drawing up of the Domesday survey. 'Once the idea of copying documents into books for greater security and convenience became familiar,' he notes, 'the practice took many forms' (Clanchy 1979, 93). These registers were important because they had a dual character as collections of other documents and as instruments of administrative power in their own right. This double-sided power, especially after chancellery registers of correspondence began from the twelfth century to be viewed as the equivalent of the original documents, made them, as Clanchy acknowledges, instruments of archival government and the 'best measure of the rate of episcopal record-making' (Clanchy 1979, 67). Nor was the proliferation of registers confined to England; Groebner, for example, has claimed that Emperor Frederick II's use of paper for his chancellery register in the mid-thirteenth century 'marked nothing less than the beginning of the history of bureaucracy in Europe' (Groebner 2007, 158; for the same processes in Spain and in the Roman Church, see McCrank 1993, 262, 264). One result of this proliferation of usages is that the problem of researching registration is complicated, as Cooper and Brubaker (2000) showed, by the problematic ambiguities of the word 'identity'. This disabling confusion, as they suggest, makes it all the more important for researchers to give careful attention to the history of the ways in which almost invisible processes of identification and apparatuses of registration have produced the infrastructure of what we now conventionally think of as individuals' identities (Scott *et al.* 2002).

One of the most interesting features of registration, in Europe and in Asia, was its intrinsically religious character and function. The intense forms of village household registration that Saito and Sato describe for modern Japan have their origins in a seventeenth-century religious survey that the Tokugawan state used to expel Christianity (see Chapter 4). In China, as von Glahn shows, registration took on similar ritual and religious functions in extending the rights and powers of village lineages. Similarly, the best evidence we have, from Europe, shows that registration spread out from royal chancelleries into forms of parish government during the late Middle Ages, and that from the sixteenth century it was religious registration, by state-supported and dissenting congregations, that set up the widespread systems of registration in northern Europe. What is clear is that registration, especially of new individuals soon after birth, carried much of the cultural and ritual authority of the church wherever it was implemented (Clanchy 1979, 126; Ong 2002, 102; Loveman 2007, 21; and see Chapter 2 in this volume). Ironically, as Gorski has shown, this intermingling of clerical and religious work in the building of the northern European bureaucracies required a much more significant dependence on ascetic Protestantism than even Weber allowed, whose account of the autonomous and rule-bound bureaucracy placed its emphasis on the demands of capitalist firms and democratic political parties. (For the Prussian case, see Wilke 2004; and for the ascetic revolution in the Protestant states, see Gorski 1993.)

Registration in theory

Registration of property and people is often accorded a key role in theoretical explanations of the administrative elevation of writing, but it has never been properly investigated. In these accounts registration is typically the agent of the direct and unqualified ascendancy of written bureaucracy, driven by the administrative benefits that accrue to the state from the record-keeping technologies of writing. Two contentions – the technological ascendancy of writing over oral forms of authority; and the simplification of social relationships that apparently derives from it – have been very influential. A third sometimes implicit claim might be described as a misplaced certainty about the universality of the will to know; and a fourth is an unjustifiable preoccupation with developments in Europe in the modern period. In the focused studies of registration that follow almost all of these theoretical claims are systematically challenged.

The title of Jack Goody's book – *The Logic of Writing and the Organization of Society* – aptly summarizes the existing theoretical argument of the effects of literary bureaucracy on society. Writing in these accounts is the state's instrument for reaching into the domestic world of its subjects, primarily as a means to raise taxes (Goody 1986, 63). A key result of the work of registration in Goody's very influential synthesis is the reduction of the thicket of relationships that existed in a world of oral relationships. 'When registration of title takes place . . . complex arrangements often have to be summed up in a single entry in the register that attempts to allocate "ownership" (that is, the total nexus of rights) to one individual rather than specifying all the claims of kith and kin', Goody writes. Adopting Wordsworth's criticism of the book, he argues that 'writing strips the social relationships of its complicating context and "murders to dissect"' ('The Tables Turned', in Wordsworth 1888; Goody 1986, 155). This argument – of the simplification that follows from written registration – has been very important, most notably in James Scott's *Seeing Like a State* (Scott 1998).

Goody presented his account of the political consequences of writing as a supplement to Foucault's account of the rise of governmentality. He suggested that, like the growth of statistics that Foucault saw underpinning the science of population, the rules and practices of written government supported a new kind of power: 'The increase in knowledge by the state represented an increase in its power to govern.' This will to know, he suggests, was carried by the British to India and Africa where 'knowability meant governability, and both entailed the extensive use of the written word' (Goody 1986, 116). This claim, which continues to have strong contemporary scholarly influence in the search for governmentality in colonial Africa and India, seems especially mistaken, as several of the chapters here show (see Chapters 9, 10, 14 and 15). These studies confirm the thrust of Stoler's (2009) reinterpretation of the Dutch colonial archive in Indonesia, showing that African colonial governments, and their modern heirs, typically lacked the resources, long-term administrative tenacity and local political agents required to make civil registration work outside of the scattered cities on the continent.

Foucault's account of the emergence of the science of population as the goal, and justification, of government stresses the European and modern origins of the bureaucratic science of population. 'We live in the era of a "governmentality"', Foucault writes, 'first discovered in the eighteenth century' (Foucault 1991, 103). Under this new form of state power in Europe a new kind of sovereignty developed, derived, not from the possession of territory or the personality of the sovereign, but from the well-being of the population. Power, Foucault suggested, ceased to be an end itself and became instead an instrument for, and product of, the well-being of the population (Foucault 1991, 100).

In a similar vein Foucault describes a will to truth emerging over centuries in European history, sometimes breaking into its modern form 'at the turn of the sixteenth century (and particularly in England)' (Foucault 1981, 54), at others in the eighteenth (Foucault and Gordon 1980, 100; Foucault 1977, 1991, 100). A key part of his argument, drawing playfully from Nietzsche, is that power and knowledge are mutually constituted. 'There is no power relation without the correlative constitution of a field of knowledge', he writes in *Discipline and Punish*, 'nor any knowledge that does not presuppose and constitute at the same time power relations' (Foucault 1977, 27). This claim has encouraged many scholars to overstate the bureaucratic enthusiasm for information gathering and it has discouraged research into the limits of bureaucratic knowledge. As many of the chapters in this volume show (see Chapters 2, 5, 7, 10, 14 and 15), states frequently sought to restrict, abandon or devolve registration, without any direct effect on their authority and power. This is because registration, unlike enumeration (see below for more on this distinction), is often more valuable, or at least as useful, to individual citizens, as to the state. It has the potential to provide a legal technology and resource for individuals which strengthens civic society: a strong state which creates a registration system can be legally empowering of its citizens, rather than disempowering; and this diffused power in the hands of citizens does not equate with any particular form of knowledge sought by or useful to the state.

Written registration plays a similarly key but obscure part in the institutional order that Foucault traces in *Discipline and Punish*. He repeatedly stresses its special significance in the organization of what he calls the power of writing. 'The procedures of examination were accompanied at the same time by a system of intense registration and of documentary accumulation', Foucault writes (1977, 189). And he suggests that the hospitals of the eighteenth century were laboratories for the 'scriptuary and documentary methods' that allowed institutions to isolate and capture the features of individual subjects in '"ignoble" archives' (Foucault 1977, 190). 'Surveillance', he argues, 'is based on a system of permanent registration' (Foucault 1977, 196). But, aside from these very general observations about the importance of registration, Foucault – like Goody – pays little attention to the actual workings of registration, in any of its forms.

A similar thinly conceived but significant emphasis on registration as the motor of state power can be found in Corrigan and Sayer's very influential and important study of the long-wave cultures of authority in England. Drawing on Clanchy's work, they argue that state-making in England involved a peculiar combination of very old Anglo-Saxon forms of local authority tied to the centralized administration of parliament through the expansion of writing. They explain the rise of the English state – and of English capitalism – as a cultural movement, with the instruments of writing binding ancient local elites to London after the twelfth century. Parish registration, and especially the recording of marriages after 1538, gave the state-church a hold on the most mundane cultural activities (Corrigan and Sayer 1985, 22–23). And Corrigan and Sayer continue this stress on the importance of registration, and the wider obsession with documentary government, in their discussion of the 'moral revolution of the nineteenth century' (1985, 124–135, quotation 124).

In these very influential studies by Goody, Foucault, Giddens, and Corrigan and Sayer there is a powerful tendency to regard highly elaborated documentary government, and extensive systems of local registration in particular, as distinctively European. In their discussion of the increase in the administrative capacity of the English ruling classes after the twelfth century, Corrigan and Sayer, for example, claim that the '"official documentary system" is unparalleled in its coverage, continuity and comprehensiveness' (Corrigan and Sayer 1985, 21). Chapter 1 by von Glahn and Chapter 4 by Saito and Sato on the workings of Chinese and Japanese household registration, and the studies by Szreter (Chapter 2) and Herzog (Chapter 7) on the limits of registration in the Spanish and English empires, suggest that these claims of European distinctiveness are misconceived at best.

The concept that currently has the most powerful explanatory traction in the study of the state may be James Scott's notion of legibility (Scott 1998; Diamant 2001; Loveman 2007; on the influence of Scott's term, see Caplan 2009). Like the scholars who have approached this subject before him, Scott arrives at the problem of registration from a surprising direction. His interest is primarily in map-making, and, in particular, in the conflicts between the dense thickets of customary forms of land tenure and the bureaucratic urge for the simplification of spaces, human relationships and mobility. His analysis was chiefly metaphorical, interpreting the bureaucratic interest in a fixed address as the 'state's attempt to make a society legible, to arrange the population in ways that simplified the classic state functions of taxation, conscription, and prevention of rebellion' (Scott 1998, 2). He does examine, briefly, the administrative arrangements in early-modern Tuscany and in the mid-nineteenth-century Philippines, but the great influence of his study is derived much more from its elegance than his interest in the complexity of the processes of registration he is describing (Scott 1998, 66–69, see also 372, n.42). Scott's emphasis on 'authoritarian high-modernism' as the source of the grand project of social engineering has also encouraged the notion that legibility was a product of the late nineteenth century, and was primarily European.

In his recent history of the 100 million people who live in the highland territories of Southeast Asia, *The Art of Not Being Governed*, Scott's theory of legibility has changed in significant ways (Scott 2009). Gone now is the emphasis on European authoritarian modernism; it is replaced by the long-wave power of the rice-growing states of Southeast Asia. Legibility remains an all-purpose description of knowing, typically derived metaphorically. Grain farming, especially rice-growing, he argues, was much more 'legible to the state' than the production of root crops (Scott 2009, 41). But the idea is also distinguished by the very long history of literary state-building in Asia. This prompts an entirely new, and important, emphasis on the history and politics of Asian state-making. 'Nonliterate peoples in the Southeast Asian massif', he argues, 'have for more than two thousand years lived in contact with one or more states with small literate minorities, texts, and written records. They have had to position themselves vis-à-vis such states' (Scott 2009, 221). Registration, once again, is attributed a critical, but in fact empirically largely unexamined, role in the development of these states. 'It is hard to conceive', Scott writes, 'of a padi state without cadastral maps of taxable land, registration lists for corvée labor, receipts, record keeping, royal decrees, legal codes, specific agreements and contracts, and lists, lists, lists – in short, without writing' (Scott 2009, law 228).

What is particularly provocative about Scott's new argument is his claim that the peoples of the hills have deliberately crafted their own marginalization from the padi states, and that the key instrument of their independence was illiteracy, a conscious rejection or abandonment of writing. For these hill societies – which Scott describes as democratic, economically unhierarchical and 'egalitarian in gender terms' (2009, 218) – the technologies of the documentary state are a threat; 'the world of literacy and writing', he writes, was 'a clear and present danger' (Scott 2009, 229).[1]

Scott's writing resonates with a pervasive academic scepticism about bureaucracy and state-driven development in the international social sciences, which affects the way the social sciences have approached registration. There are certainly well-established grounds, dating back to the 1930s, to view the developmental promises of the state in Africa and India with mistrust, and to doubt the beneficial effects that officials and experts profess in the design of development programmes (Ferguson 1990, 1999, 1–81, 234–254; Cooper 1996, esp. 57–170, 2002, 38–65, 85–132; Ferguson and Gupta 2002). A major part of this international scholarly

[1] Scott intends this study to have broader significance than a local account of the hill peoples of Southeast Asia. He suggests that similar processes were at work in the makings of the independence of the Cossacks of the Ukrainian steppe and the scattered highland peoples of Africa. And there is certainly power in his suggestive discussions of the effects of terrain on states' abilities to project their power. In southern Africa, the independence of the highland people of Swaziland and Lesotho (or the Berg-Dama of Namibia) was certainly aided by the difficulties that both white and black forces faced in the nineteenth century entering their terrain. But there is, in the present at least, little of the political virtue that Scott perceives in the societies of the hill peoples. Quite apart from their fiercely patriarchal and undemocratic social order, both Swaziland and Lesotho have paid a terrible price for their administrative independence. Life expectancy at birth in both countries has collapsed to the low-thirties in the face of the AIDS epidemic, and large numbers of people in both countries have called for the abolition of their independence because the state is unable to provide basic services (Smith 2010).

cynicism about the possibility of the state ever providing meaningful remedies for the poor derives from the very widespread rejection of nationalism and communism amongst Indian scholars in the wake of the 1975 Emergency (Guha 2008; Menon 2005, 2006, x). A similar mood of angry disillusion has become common in many African countries (Ake 1987; Thiong'o 2007). Nor is the state the only villain in the social science of this development predicament. Historians have re-examined the role of expert knowledge (Mitchell 2002; Hodge 2007), and anthropologists have looked closely at the de-politicizing effects of the campaigns of donor-funded human rights organizations (Englund 2006; Brown 2004).

Yet there are also good contemporary grounds to be cautious about the dismissive inclination that follows from viewing registration, as Scott and many others have, as intrinsically coercive. The most obvious is that there seems to be a performative contradiction at work between the glorification of escape and marginality for the poor while the wealthy in the industrial democracies (including many social scientists) scramble to secure access for their families to state-supported schools, well-policed neighbourhoods, properties, hospitals and universities (all of which function on the basis of civil registration systems). Another only apparently trivial reason is that the determined Nietzschean scepticism about the intellectual aims of the modern state can, and probably will, very quickly dissolve into a glorification of the unregulated (because unregistered) market, or provide an inadvertent rationalization for the preservation of an inequitable status quo.

But the most important reason to re-examine the politics of registration is that it highlights the very different state form that exists in many of the regions of the world with weak or non-existent infrastructures for recording their citizens' vital events. African historians have called this state, which is typical of both the colony and its successor, the 'gatekeeper'. Fred Cooper, who has analysed its character and limits in many works, shows that African gatekeeper states 'had weak instruments for entering the social and cultural realm' and, critically, that they survived by standing 'astride the intersection of the colonial territory and the outside world' (Cooper 2002, 5, 1996, 465–466). Far from an oppressive and ubiquitous will to know, African states were built in an informational void without the ability to 'track the individual body or understand the dynamics of the social body' (Cooper 1996, 335). Many important studies have discussed the forms of cheap indirect rule, blind tax-farming and skeletal physical and administrative infrastructure that characterized the colonial state (Berry 1993, 22–42; Herbst 2000, 161–170; Mamdani 1996, 37–61; Young 1994, 100–129; Rodney 1982, 208–209; Ake 1991, 38). Typically the colonial state in Africa was built to control the railway, a harbour, or the city, and it relied heavily on revenues from the export of a single commodity. This has changed little in the post-colonial era, with only the state's ability to 'defend the gate' undergoing any significant variation. The chapters here by Doyle (Chapter 10), Breckenridge (Chapter 14), Cooper (Chapter 15) and Lund (Chapter 18) examine efforts to extend the infrastructure of states in Africa by adopting systems of universal registration. These studies suggest some of the possibilities and the limits of the very influential rights-based approach to development policy.

In development economics, political science, and policy making, Amartya Sen's effort to combine the statistical insights of economics with the normative calculus of philosophy may be the most influential body of scholarly work that currently exists (Sen 1982, 1999; Dreze and Sen 1989). Key to the new 'human science of development' that Sen has pioneered is the idea that remedies for poverty are political, organized around the recognition of entitlements. As many of the chapters here show, much of the ability to couch claims about entitlements, or secondary rights, to land, welfare, education, and health in a process of 'open public reasoning' has typically depended on the infrastructure of an existing system of civil registration (Sen 2004, 356; see also Nancy Fraser's discussion of needs-talk in the welfare state (Fraser 1989, 161–183)). Certainly, as Lund's study here of the South African Child Support Grant shows, large-scale systems of social assistance require working civil registration (see Chapter 18). One of the key questions that Ferguson examines in his chapter on the history and theory of welfare in Africa is whether the new biometric technologies will support new kinds of universally distributed secondary rights without requiring an elaborate, and onerous, administrative infrastructure (see Chapter 19).

There are, of course, many critics of these rights-based arguments for development policy, especially in Africa and particularly where the rights at issue are liberal or first-order freedoms. A long time ago Claude Ake pointed out that most Africans face a 'totally consuming struggle' that leaves them little time or interest in freedoms of speech or assembly. 'There is', as he put it, 'no freedom for hungry people' (Ake 1987). Other scholars have suggested that human rights arguments may actually be an 'antipolitical politics of suffering' generating new forms of undemocratic institutional power and avenues for elite accumulation (Brown 2004, 461). This is the conclusion also of Englund's ethnography of non-governmental human rights in contemporary Malawi (Englund 2006).

Yet some of the most thoughtful commentators on the politics of contemporary Africa have suggested that it is only in the provision of an infrastructure of second-order rights that the African poor can begin to reverse the ongoing decline in quality of life on the continent. Even Ake has argued that if 'a bill of rights is to make any sense, it must include among others, a right to work and to a living wage, a right to shelter, to health, to education' (Ake 1987, 10). And the eminent Ugandan legal scholar, Joe Oloka-Onyango, has argued that 'without a strategy that combines both the aspirations for political liberation with the imperatives of economic sustenance and empowerment, any gains will quickly disintegrate' (Oloka-Onyango 1995). In South Africa, much of the political debate of the last decade has been focused on the question of how these rights, enshrined in the 1994 constitution, can actually be secured. Chapter 19 by Ferguson examines how these difficult struggles coalesced in the demand for, and debates around, a Basic Income Grant; Chapter

18 by Lund looks at the project of secondary rights that was implemented by a committee she chaired that made recommendations for a new form of support for poor children. This Child Support Grant is an important part of a more comprehensive set of welfare benefits that are received by one-third of the South African population and serves as a global model for addressing poverty.

Birth, death and marriage registration systems may, then, be the most extensive, and important, of the informational infrastructures that have been highlighted by Bowker and Starr (1999). They are, like almost all similar systems, shot through with standards and categories whose historical evolution is often obscured in a paradoxically undocumented provenance, stretching deep into the past, as this volume shows; and, like most such infrastructures, they are practically invisible, until they break down or face well-organized political opposition.

When critics of Sen's argument about the necessity of extending secondary rights to the world's poor question its feasibility as compared to the liberal, first-order rights which are 'not difficult to institute' (Maurice Cranston, cited in Sen 2004, 348), they are, in effect, pointing to the difficulty of building a currently non-existent infrastructure of documentary registration that would be vital, in the first instance, to ensure recognition to the very existence of all of the individuals of the human population on the planet. Many of the chapters here show that it has been registration – despite its many onerous features – that has been the crucial primary instrument for realizing entitlements and secondary rights wherever they exist, by providing this fundamental condition of recognition. (For contemporary rights, mostly of basic security, see Powell 1980; Setel *et al.* 2007.) It is possible to discern a great range of political effects flowing from these systems of registration. They may, as Setel *et al.* have recently argued, demonstrate the state's political determination to adopt the role of 'stewardship' towards their populace and also the equally important matter of 'reciprocal trust in their government by the registered population' (Setel *et al.* 2007, 1575). A more likely outcome, however, may be a bad-tempered embrace between those with property and income and those without.

Of course, registration, as Kafka would insist, may also contribute very significantly to the inflated, and exasperating, self-authorizing powers of bureaucracy. It can encourage, as Fahrmeir's study of Prussia (Chapter 3) suggests, open-ended and probably fruitless exercises of information gathering, something which was already present in seventeenth-century England (Slack 2004, 57) and which certainly seems to be a significant problem of the contemporary British state today, which has adopted the role of global outrider in the development of intrusive databases (Anderson *et al.* 2009). Commonly, onerous and coercive systems of registration can create conditions for subversion and opportunities for rent-seeking that defeat the ends that officials have in mind (as Chapter 9 by MacDonald shows). But registration systems can also collapse or become stagnant or partial operations surviving among only some parts of a population (as Chapter 2 by Szreter notes of several US states); they may (as von Glahn shows in Chapter 1) construct an alienated administrative representation that bears little or no relationship with the world of living human beings; or they may be subordinated (as Herzog shows in Chapter 7) to other legal and reputational practices. The point, surely, is that there are very significant grounds to examine and conceptualize these contingent histories much more carefully than scholars have managed to date.

Registration in history

In the broader historical accounts of twentieth-century state formation, as in the theory, registration appears only indirectly and fleetingly. Theda Skocpol's study of the paradoxical interaction of democratic politics, gender and reform in the distinctive history of the welfare state in the US is a good example of this approach (Skocpol 1992). She shows that in the 1920s women's organizations were able to use the reformers' fear of the corrupting effects of pensions for Civil War veterans, and the multi-layered architecture of the US Federal system, to foster the development of the Federal Children's Bureau and pensions for needy (and deserving) mothers. A key tool in the feminist organizations' campaign for mothers' pensions, and also in the activities of the short-lived Federal Children's Bureau, was the effort to improve the scope and accuracy of birth registration. By the end of the 1920s both political parties had lost their earlier concern for explicitly women's issues. The Depression provided the fiscal context required for the American Medical Association to re-establish private doctors' responsibility for birth registration, and the abolition of the Children's Bureau and mothers' pensions. While Skocpol shows that registration campaigns were key in both women's mobilization and the implementation of the new forms of social welfare, especially for black and Hispanic populations, her massive study offers little more than a mention of this fact, with the details of the diverse practices of birth registration left to the reader's imagination (Skocpol 1992, 511, 513; and see Chapter 17 by Marshall in this volume for further information).

For the social historians who have confronted registration directly as a tool of segregation, it is the meticulous administrative arrangements of twentieth-century genocide that have loomed ominously in the analytical background. The most influential study in this vein in English is Gareth Stedman Jones's *Outcast London*, which highlighted middle-class reformers' enthusiasm for registration as part of an ambitious and coercive (but mostly unrealized) project of segregating the irredeemably poor urban residuum (Jones 1971, 331, 334–335). This theme, of the register as a threat to the social body, has remained very powerful in historiography; it can be seen, for example, in Overy's recent study of England in the inter-war years, which highlights the popular appeal of the eugenicists' interest in Galtonian registers of the able and the unfit well into the 1930s (Overy 2009 109–114).

Amongst twentieth-century historians, the study by Aly and Roth on the bewildering array of population registers in the racial order of the Third Reich is the most systematic study of registration as a tool of genocide (Aly and Roth 2000). Their book, which provided much of the empirical material for Black's popular *IBM and the Holocaust* (2001), also shows that the Nazi state's ambitions for the orderly gathering of individualized racial statistics were mostly undone by the costs of registration and the chaos of war. And, perhaps most importantly for our purposes here, they show that the blunt tool of the census was more valuable to the Nazi state in the selection of its Jewish victims than the fine-grained individual data in the many registers (Aly and Roth 2000, 119–120; Luebke and Milton 1994; Seltzer 1998). The European genocide does provide at least one instance in which individualized registration served as an invaluable tool of genocide, and this is the infamous case of the annihilation of the Jews of the Netherlands with the aid of a sophisticated population register (though a centralized national population register is, of course, a different technology from a system of civil registration) (de Jong 1995, 5: 422–430).

The theme of the register – especially the police register – as an instrument of marginalization is common to many societies of the Atlantic (see the essays in Caplan and Torpey 2001; Cole 2001; Sankar 1992; Sekula 1986). And it has very deep historical roots. Valentin Groebner's recent book on the history of identification shows that the church and municipalities were using registers to record the names and behaviour of suspect populations long before the rise of centralized government. Groebner tracks, often on the basis of limited evidence, the church's use of registers and certificates in the monitoring of confessions from the early thirteenth century, and the municipalities' use of registers to track migrants, debtors and criminals. By the sixteenth century Groebner describes a pervasive concern to 'register everyone and everything' which affected officials, travellers, migrants, and the urban poor (Groebner 2007, 200).

This interest in registration as an instrument of an expanding and centralizing state power has also been influential in the study of Empire. Much research has been focused on the colonial census and scholars have casually blurred the distinction between enumeration and registration in the debate over the political effects of census categories. Cohn and Dirks, for example, in their 1988 essay on colonial technologies of power argue that the 'state documentation project . . . individualizes and controls through such seemingly neutral activities as assigning census numbers, birth and marriage certificates, draft cards, drivers' licenses' (Cohn and Dirks 1988, 225). While the colonial state in India adopted its predecessor's interest in the census as an instrument of government and taxation, neither body had the capacity for a mass programme of either household or individual registration (for an overview, see Chapter 11 by Gopinath; Guha 2003, 148–151).

Registration in colonial India (see Chapter 11) was actually very limited in comparison with nineteenth-century Egypt, eleventh-century China, or seventeenth-century England, as the chapters by Fahmy (Chapter 13), von Glahn (Chapter 1) and Szreter (Chapter 2) show. The police, especially during the period of Edward Henry's tenure as Commissioner of Police in Bengal in the 1890s, were responsible for the development of the most influential forms of fingerprint registration directed at criminals (Sengoopta 2003). Yet for much of the nineteenth century the colonial state relied on crude and brutal forms of body marking, and officials continued to argue for the preservation of tattooing into the 1870s (Singha 2000; Anderson 2004, 15–42). This familiarity with marking the body and the absence of a workable system of registration were key motivations behind the interest in bertillonage in India. And even after Henry's fingerprinting system had become official policy, day-to-day transactions (as Gandhi often complained in his conflict with the Transvaal state) were simply authenticated by means of a single finger-print that was not recorded in a government register (Singha 2000, 183).

The colonial society that has experienced the most systematic and enduring forms of individual registration is unmistakably South Africa. By the high-water mark of apartheid, some seventy years after the British occupation of the Transvaal initiated the grand schemes that have shaped South African society, the Native Affairs Department's obsession with registration was simply astonishing (Posel 2000, 132). Labour registration, usually targeting male migrants to the diamond, sugar and gold industries, was the heart of this order, but it expanded outward to produce an elaborate web of centralized national record-sets, culminating in the 1950s in the national Population Register, the linchpin of racial classification (Kahn 1949; Chanock 2001, 410–422; Harries 1994, 18–46; van Onselen 1985; Breckenridge 2005; Bowker and Starr 1999, 195–225; Cole 1967; Savage 1986). Yet even the South African state showed little enthusiasm before 1995 for the project of maintaining a system of civil registration for the vast majority of its people. And, as Lund shows in Chapter 18, the Population Register, formally stripped of its racial categories, has provided the democratic state with the means to deliver welfare grants to over a third of the national population.

In general, historians, even in South Africa, have discussed registration at a polite distance, and there are strikingly few detailed histories of civil registration in particular. As a study of Maoist China has observed, 'an exhaustive search of the social science and historical literature uncovered only one article dealing with marriage registration in the context of state building'. This was, predictably, Posel's study of African marriage registration in South Africa (Diamant 2001, 449; Posel 1995; on the same point, see Loveman 2007, 9). The entire body of published work in English by historians dealing with civil registration directly, reviewed here, amounts to little more than a handful of studies. This is intriguing in the light of the significance of these acts of registration both for the form of the state and for the individuals being registered. One of the reasons may be that civil registration has many inter-related social effects and historians have tended to approach the subject indirectly using a lens adopted from the subject of state documentation, illegitimacy, marriage, welfare, or social statistics.

Where historians have properly examined the development of the large-scale registers of the precocious English state directly, they have been struck by their beneficial quality. The largest and most effective government registers all provided citizens with regulated access to social goods that were provided or protected by the state. Higgs has shown that the Victorian General Register's Office worked mainly as a tool for the resolution of disputes over inherited property. In the twentieth century the largest database of identification, and the '*de facto* identity card', was a product of the registration of drivers' licences. Even the project of building a Universal Population Register, which has recently collapsed yet again in the face of widespread popular anxiety, worked in this way. Initially a product of Milner and Kitchener's concern to maximize recruitment, the National Register had administrative roots in the earlier National Insurance Register and it was fostered by its functions as a ration card (Agar 2003, 121–142; Higgs 2004, 134–143).

There is good evidence to suggest that large systems of registration, whether of people or of things, tend to work only when they provide an obvious benefit to the people being targeted. Coercive systems, like the Nazi-era *Volkskartei* and the apartheid *Bewysburo*, seem sufficiently vulnerable to subversion and escape to defeat their intended purposes (Aly and Roth 2000, 119–131; Breckenridge 2005). More importantly, as Szreter's study of the introduction of compulsory registration of subjects of the Crown in England in 1538 shows, this system of registration worked because it provided the means for the poor to make claims on the law, a direct good that seems to have produced many indirect benefits (Szreter 2007). Rosental also emphasizes the importance of consent, offering a complementary revisionist account of the evolution of the importance of the juridical and administrative concept of civil status (*état civil*) in nineteenth-century and early twentieth-century France (see Chapter 5). He argues that French historiography since Foucault has been preoccupied with the policing aspects of identity information and the theme of state control over individuals. Consequently it has neglected to listen to the voices of French citizens from this period who were focused primarily on the importance to them of being able to create certainty of their legal identities for pursuit of their commercial activities in the market economy. Chapter 15 by Cooper confirms that by 1951 the value of the *état civil* was so pervasively understood in this way that in contemplating how to 'develop' French Africa on the model of the metropole it was self-evident to the French minister concerned that this required a commitment to create and fund a universal identity registration, since for him, 'French citizens have a right to an état-civil and the right to certain identification'.

Registration and recognition

As Flemming's chapter on the classical world emphasizes, registration is derivative from the more fundamental and universal need of human individuals in groups for mutual recognition, as among the Athenian and Roman citizenry (see Chapter 6). Acknowledgement of membership in a collectivity and of one's publicly known place within it can be – and often in history was – achieved by a variety of performed rituals. Initiation rites have been studied throughout the world by anthropologists and found to be manifold in their diversity. In the medieval world, performance of witnessed oaths of fealty, usually sworn on the bible, a sacred object, was the standard practice for publicly affirming political and military membership, while in the Catholic church, after the fourth Lateran council of 1215 emphasis was increasingly laid on personal attendance at the annual Easter service, for verbal affirmation witnessed by a priest, as defining and confirming one's continuing membership of the flock (Reynolds 2001, 488; see Chapter 2 by Szreter, note 8). Most of these rituals were performative and did not involve documentation but their aim was the same as that of registration, namely to fix a record in the collective memory of the individual's identity and place within a group. As Rosental argues in Chapter 5, this has, for instance, been one of the crucial functions of the process of identification by civil status for both individuals and their families throughout the last two centuries in modern France. It is also simultaneously the case that publicly affirming membership of a defined group typically establishes some form of obligation towards the other members and the shared authority structure of the group; and reciprocally it is also perceived by the individuals to offer them some valued benefits (non-exclusion, at the least). The nature of this mix of obligations and benefits engenders various reasons why certain rules about membership and participation usually arise, and why, as many of the chapters here show, they are subject to much negotiation, as circumstances and the interests of individuals, families and the various registering authorities are all subject to change. They define criteria of inclusion and exclusion in relation to the larger universe of 'other' individuals, with whom the group may be in communication and with whom they may share or contest a physical and socio-cultural environment. While there has been much historical study of the processes and consequences of exclusion, inclusion also needs to be problematized by historical research into the agencies involved and the diversity of forms that result.

Thus, that central aspect of registration which concerns public recognition may well constitute an eternal and universal characteristic of all human communities, with or without literacy or a technology of written records. However, this diverse history of a community registration of its members' mutual recognition often only becomes available for us to study in detail when it occurred in societies which documented their recognition processes and where written records have survived, in the form of registers. There is likely therefore to be a profound bias in the documented comparative historical record, which provides us mainly with a history of registration which appears to be strongly tied to those most powerful, persisting state-like forms of government which generated and archived most efficiently the records of their processes of registration. This has perhaps misled earlier, pioneering and influential scholars such as Foucault, Goody and Scott to over-emphasize the extent to which the registration of any and all information about persons and their properties is indicative primarily of the powers of states and their interests, expressed in the seminal historiographical concepts of 'governmentality' and 'legibility'.

Yet, as a number of the studies in the following chapters show, in early modern Europe it was less nation states, and more likely to be the established church (the Roman Catholic Church in Spain and France), congregational denominations (in the Netherlands, and the Quakers in England), parishes and communities (among the English in England and overseas; and among the Germans with their *Ortsippbucheren*), towns and cities (in colonial and republican North America), or civic associations (the Orphan books in Amsterdam) which attempted to maintain comprehensive (for their purposes) forms of registration (and, for the significance of baptismal registration in Russia and in Brazil, see Steinwedel 2001; Loveman 2007). As Saito and Sato show in Chapter 4, very similar local imperatives were also key to the workings of registration in Japan. Often the purposes of the registers were related to the need of these communities, organizations and networks legally and practically to regulate access to forms of collectively-provided assistance, benefits or privileges. Only much later – typically during the course of the nineteenth century – did nation states create the civil, criminal and other registration systems which served their purposes (Caplan 2001). The influence of Foucault's writings has been to obscure these and other distinctions by wrapping all these activities up as part of grandiose concepts of governmentality and biopower, where the various practices of human accounting are subsumed together as variant manifestations of a single 'modernizing' historical trend, variously dated in his writings either from the eighteenth or the sixteenth century, whereby states create certain characteristic forms of official and legal knowledge about their citizens (Sekula 1986, 10–13; Chakrabarty 2002, 82–86).

The conflation of all registering activity with the purposes of the state leads to a tendency in the historical and social science literature to fail to make any significant distinction between registration and enumeration, and the respective records they create (Cohn and Dirks 1988, 225). As a result historians appear to have been too often content to assume that the many interesting historical studies that have been published of the census activities and classification systems of national and colonial governments, and the political ideologies and projects which they can be shown to project, tell us everything we need to know about the processes of documentation of individuals in history and their relationships with institutions of government or governance. Both enumeration and registration can be viewed, from a state perspective, as just different forms of human accounting; and it is true that states have often created and used registers – for their own tax and enlistment purposes for instance, though these are typically only partial registers – often relatively uninterested in female identities, as the chapters here on ancient and early modern Rome, China and Japan all demonstrate.

However, the diverse history of registration reveals the potential which the concept also contains for quite different usages and practices, which may have almost nothing directly to do with states, their powers and interests (on the ways that families can use registration to make claims on more affluent kin, see, in addition to Chapters 4 and 7 in this volume, Diamant 2001, 4; Mackenzie 2008, 527). Registration can involve quite the opposite process to the command and control logic of enumeration. Enumeration and all census-like activities (including the making by authorities of certain kinds of lists of named individuals which are often called 'registers', such as the twentieth-century population registers of the Netherlands) are, by definition, unilateral interventions by governmental agencies to extract defined items of information for administrative and policy purposes. By contrast, that form of registration involved in the process of determining inclusion or exclusion of recognition of membership in a defined collectivity can entail – and often has entailed – a much more bilateral process, in which the aims and interests of the person being registered may play a significant role. This is, first, in terms of the motive for the process to happen at all with respect to the individual in question: such registration systems frequently fail to persist without the voluntary cooperation of those being registered, as has been seen in many African, Asian and Latin American countries, as well as the eighteenth- and nineteenth-century USA. Second, this is in terms of negotiating – or even determining – what kind of identity information is registered as the outcome of the process, as Herzog (Chapter 7) and Doyle (Chapter 10) clearly show. To view registration exclusively as something imposed by the state or by a superordinate group on a populace of subordinate individuals is an unhelpfully limiting assumption.

Thus, in conformity with its central, age-old function of providing the service of mutual recognition, the act of registration has an irreducible performative and dialectical element to it, which has less scope – or is almost entirely lacking – where enumeration is concerned. Negotiation and performativity are almost ubiquitously part of the processes of human interaction, deposition and enquiry, which comprise the primary activity, whereby an act of registration occurs – and is agreed to have occurred – by the parties involved in recording it. This authorizing and performative background to registration, and the widespread suspicion of written documents, is well described in the chapters by Flemming (Chapter 6), Herzog (Chapter 7), Fahmy (Chapter 13) and Cooper (Chapter 15) (on the long-contested struggle over the authority of written documents, see also Clanchy 1979, 7; Ong 2002, 105). The information created in the process of registration is typically a 'representational' production. In this negotiated process the possibly diverging interests and aims of the registering and registered agents can provide a dynamic of dialectic. In general the registering agent has tended to be interested in capturing fixed identities, reflecting certain analytic or legal status categories of use to the registering authorities. Registering individuals may wish to fix upon themselves different identities from those perceived as valid by the registering agent; or they may wish to deliberately give 'false' identities or to be able to preserve the possibility of multiple or changed identities, for instance (exemplified in Chapters 7, 8,

9 and 10). The process of registration must always therefore entail some form of dialectical tension between the legalistic fiction or convention of fixed, defined or stated identities, and the more messy social and cultural reality of individuals' capacities for having multiple attributed, aspirational, or imagined relations of identity and goals for their self-representation.

This may not always be obvious from the surviving documents which appear to record information merely in fairly standardized forms, but through historical research we can sometimes recover an understanding of the representational performances being recorded at registration. For instance, the entries in Domesday Book were understood at the time as the record of a performative legal process involving the adjudication of sworn affirmations between competing protagonists over title to land and movable property ownership, which occurred in many local contests held before commissioners holding court around the country (Baxter 2012). As several of the chapters here exemplify and eloquently demonstrate, the information in identity registration documents can be the outcome of a strongly performative and highly negotiated process. Chapter 7 by Herzog on the Spanish in early modern Spain and colonial Latin America, Chapter 9 by MacDonald on Indian Ocean migrants seeking entry to South Africa, Chapter 10 by Doyle on those migrants making choices of the names they wished to register in twentieth-century Uganda in order best to assimilate, and the opening and closing story presented by Looijesteijn and van Leeuwen (Chapter 8), each skilfully demonstrate and document these processes of negotiation, which are not usually available for us to see in the written record. However, as all of these chapters also make clear in their diverse contexts, that performative negotiation is in fact a ubiquitous option – albeit often a surreptitious and therefore hidden one – whenever official and legal categories are registered. Some individuals amass great legal competence and dialectic skill in dealing with official procedures and the registering technologies they confronted, to achieve the representational outcomes for registration that they wanted (Sadiq 2009).

Identity registration systems can provide several valued services at once to different constituencies, so that even when it can be shown that a central state created any particular system for a specific purpose – perhaps even a repressive purpose – that does not necessarily exhaust its historical importance and cultural significance for the registering populace in question. As shown in the chapters on England and Japan, it seems most plausible that identity registration systems were set up in each of these two early modern states with the motive to flush-out and suppress religious unorthodoxy. But in both cases the technologies persisted because they were found useful by officials and subjects for a number of further reasons. Notably in England and Wales parish records of baptisms, burials and marriages, registered for free by the church's ministers and maintained for consultation in Diocesan archives, provided an invaluable practical tool for the efficient operation of the law in relation to property transfers between individuals and also for settling disputes over legal rights to relief (the absolute entitlement of all subjects of the Crown in England and Wales to material support from their parish of settlement, as recently shown by Charlesworth (2010)). However this was not the case, for instance, in early modern France. Here, despite a royal edict to establish parish registers almost simultaneous with Henry VIII's innovation in sixteenth-century England, the French registers failed to attract the full participation of the populace to become an established and well-maintained nationwide system as they did in England and Wales. In his chapter on France, Rosental notes that there the state's efforts prioritized the systematic registration of property, rather than people, delegating this crucial tax-related function primarily to notaries and a separate state Registry, not to parish priests and their parochial registers (see Chapter 5). There never developed in France a mechanism tightly linking registration to demotic welfare rights. Thus, parish registration in England and Wales – but not in France – has, since its origins, had a crucial role to play in the sphere of law and of subjects' and citizens' social security and economic rights within the law.

Registration and legal empowerment

This relates to a further major limitation in the historiographical inheritance from Foucault and Scott. This has been the tendency of their sweeping historical interpretations to flatten distinctions between the province of law and that of the state. Scott's notion of an 'authoritarian high modernism', exemplified in the notorious usage of population registers in the twentieth century for thoroughgoing state planning – and worse – by the totalitarian Nazi, Soviet and East European 'communist' regimes, along with the labour and migration-regulating registers of imperialist powers such as the British in East and South Africa, has contributed to the strong impression in this area of scholarship that, where identity registration is concerned, state and law are synonymous. The state makes the laws according to its plans and supervises the resulting information systems for its own purposes. According to this viewpoint the primary task of historical scholarship is to demonstrate the many ways in which legal forms of identity documentation reflect the power and will to knowledge of the state, a perspective apparent in many of the pioneering contributory chapters in Caplan and Torpey (2001).

However the sphere of law is not at all necessarily one and the same thing as the sphere of state policy and legislation, at least not in the Anglo-Saxon common law legal tradition, which, via the USA and the British Empire, has been adapted into the legal systems of many parts of the world. For instance, the identity registration systems provided by the parish and non-conformists' registers played such a valued role for propertied citizens in their legal transactions in early modern England and Wales, that, as Szreter shows in Chapter 2, laws creating such legal services for all were passed by English communities, including dissenters, wherever they settled overseas in North America and the Caribbean during the seventeenth and early eighteenth centuries. Indeed, while in England, by the end of the seventeenth century, the dissenting Quakers had created their own efficient registers, the extraordinary evidence presented in Chapter 8 by Looijesteijn and van Leeuwen shows the proliferation at this time of non-state registering bodies for a host of different purposes in the Netherlands. It could therefore be argued that both in England and in Holland, arguably the two most militarily, fiscally and commercially effective states of the late seventeenth and early eighteenth centuries, the strong state, itself supporting systems of registration for its own purposes, was not expanding its information-processing apparatus at the expense of civil society, but rather that a rich and self-registering civil society was partly piggy-backing on the state's systems and partly creating its own commercial and legal information systems in parallel, as the two – strong state and strong civil society – operated in synergy (see Higgs 2004 for the English history of this process).

The essential point here is that, unlike census and other enumerative exercises, identity registration systems, including those sponsored and maintained by the state, represent a *legal* technology and resource which can be empowering and of high economic and social utility to individuals, by enabling their legally-recognized personhoods to pursue their own self-interested purposes, completely independently of the state's policies and plans. Accessible registration systems can provide an important service which reduces transaction costs and facilitates security and confidence in the way in which the rule of law mediates economic and social life, thereby contributing to the expansion and vigour of civic society, quite independently of the activities of the state. In the terminology of law, identity registration systems have been crucial practical tools which have facilitated the endowing of all individuals with legal personhood, which is defined as the entity to which rights and duties are ascribed in law. This is true today of human rights, which mean little in practice if they are not conferred on identified and self-identifiable individuals with recognized membership of a national jurisdiction – this is a practical condition for the individual to enjoy actionable legal personhood. Registration – official recognition of existence and an identity – is the grounding and basis for personhood and human rights.

Whether, however, registration systems do, in fact, come to play such a role, empowering individual subjects and citizens in this way or, alternatively, disempowering and controlling them, according to the more historiographically familiar accounts of the state's uses of such systems, is a historically contingent matter, related to many diverse influences. The scholarly contributions in the chapters collected here document many rich examples of that historical diversity and enable us to discern the nature of some of these important influences on the form that registration has taken, resulting in such different outcomes.

Obviously the ideological predisposition of the state and its rulers and the nature of the political context mattered enormously. However, it is not necessarily the case that we can expect to read-off simple equations between imperialist states with extractive ideologies and the creation and deployment of registration systems for repressive, disempowering purposes imposed on alien peoples. Two contrasting examples of the interaction between the British state and registration at the same point in time in the early nineteenth century illustrate this. As Engerman shows in Chapter 12, as part of one of the most surprising episodes of the triumph of humanitarian moral sentiment over short-term powerful financial vested interests, abolitionists within British civil society contrived to use officially-created slave registers to serve their purposes to secure immensely costly legislation from the British state to emancipate the registered slaves, the most subordinate of peoples in the colonial Caribbean islands. (See Draper (2009) on the subsequent importance of the slave registers for facilitating the detailed calculations required for the machinery of compensation enabling a 'fair' distribution of the spoils of 20 million pounds among the slave-owners – compensation was not, of course, paid to the slaves.) However, by contrast, the same British state in Westminster made no effort to endow the Catholic peasants of Ireland with the civil registration system created for England and Wales in 1836, despite the 1801 Act of Union having politically integrated Ireland into the United Kingdom. Consequently the brand new Irish Poor Law created in 1838 lacked the essential registration infrastructure (not created for Ireland until 1864), which had enabled the English Poor Law to function so effectively as to have protected the English poor from any dearth-related famine mortality for over two centuries (Szreter 2007). The consequence of creating a mere simulacrum of a Poor Law in Ireland, lacking both a recognized legal right to relief in one's attested parish of settlement and also the associated information system of registration – necessary to record settlement rights – was that the single most disastrous episode of mass death by starvation in British imperial history occurred, not in the colonies, but within the United Kingdom itself (all of Ireland was an integral part of the United Kingdom following the Act of Union of 1801), and as recently as 1846–1849, at a time when the British state represented the most economically advanced and resourceful imperial power on the face of the earth (Charlesworth 2010, 175–180).

Foucauldians have emphasized the disciplinary (and sometimes genocidal) purposes of modern state information systems in moulding the subjectivity of their own citizens (Scott 1998; Burchell *et al.* 1991; Dean 1999; Rose 1991, 1999; Ferguson and Gupta 2002; for the intrinsically genocidal character of biopower, see Agamben 1998, 119–159). However the Irish famine indicates that an even worse fate may befall those in the modern world of market economies who are not recorded at all in such official registers and consequently have no practical legal rights since, as both legal persons and recognized individuals, they do not exist. As Cooper (Chapter 15) and Breckenridge (Chapter 14) show here, both the French and the South African states, at different times in the twentieth century, assessed the costs and benefits of registration for Africans and intentionally chose to abandon their existing plans for granting such recognition – remaining in ignorance of African individuals may not have been ideal for the colonial authorities but it was perceived to be less expensive to know them only indirectly and work with the headmen. There are also new forms of administrative desolation. Recently Ferguson has pointed to the increasingly common forms of enclave development, especially on the African continent, where all the key elements of government – security, health care, sanitation – are provided by privately owned companies for the sole benefit of multinational mineral firms and their labour forces. Under those circumstances the general poor bear the costs of industrial development, without being able to derive any meaningful entitlements from the companies or the state (Ferguson 2006, 194–210).

Registration and the modern state?

The extraordinary chapter by von Glahn (Chapter 1) drives a coach and horses through another Foucauldian canard, that the registering, planning and controlling state is a product of European modernity somewhere between the sixteenth and eighteenth centuries (see the essays in Burchell *et al.* 1991). Von Glahn narrates a long, complex and continuous history of fully-documented enumeration and registration, articulated at village, prefectural and state levels in China throughout a period of a thousand years or more before the flowering of 'governmentality' or 'biopower' in the west. He documents familiar motives of preserving social order throughout a large empire, but this was not simply for the sake of control and repression (though there was certainly plenty of that, notably through the ingenious and callous device of imposing collective tax responsibility on all families within a community, as von Glahn shows). Successive Chinese regimes used registers to tax and raise a military levy for external defence, but were equally aware of the need to use population information to promote the food and social security of their peasant populations to ensure internal security. Thus, registration is not, as Foucauldians have supposed, a paradigm exemplification of the novelty of an exclusively western 'modernity' intimately associated with the liberal nation-state project of governmentality and western imperialism.

China, for so much longer than anywhere else a continuously politically unified society based, throughout extensive though fluctuating parts of its territory, on a relatively densely settled agrarian economy, was probably among the first to address the informational needs that result from a relatively high labour–land ratio. Such relatively high ratios were also true of Golden Age Holland and early modern southern England and also Japan at the same time in the seventeenth century, where the *koseki* household registration forms were introduced and then widely retained (see Chapter 4). Here, perhaps, we come to another powerful, general influence on the comparative history of identity registrations systems, quite distinct from – though undoubtedly mediated through – politics, culture and ideology: the land–labour ratio.

Goody tracked this association between carefully established land titles (and tax registration) from the first written records in Mesopotamia, and it is a dynamic that informs almost all of the regional studies published here (Goody 1986, 47, 63).

It is striking, given the precocity of Chinese investment in diverse forms of registration of individuals, how contrastingly late to develop and invest in such systems were the peoples of sub-Saharan Africa and North America. Large parts of the African continent and tracts of the United States were equally without effective registration of persons in the period *circa* 1880–1914, a time when registration was relatively ubiquitous in Western Europe, the economic peer of the USA and the effective ruler of much of Africa. Even though they were at that time at opposite poles in terms of commercial and economic development, much of the USA and sub-Saharan Africa did however share an almost equally low land–labour ratio. Egypt, by contrast, the one part of Africa with a long history of population registration since Classical times, always had a much higher land–labour ratio along the banks of the Nile and an island-like accessibility of its population to its rulers owing to their proximity to the communication channel of the Nile. It may be that in some times and places, such as the western and mid-western USA until the 1920s, despite having become part of a commercially vigorous continental economy, well-developed land registers satisfactorily performed one of the key functions of an identity registration system, thereby reducing any economic incentives among the population to perceive an urgent need for a personal identity registration system (De Soto 2000). There are echoes here of the situation in early modern France where a well-developed Registry of property went alongside a more partial and less efficient parish register system. While an identity-bearing information system can serve several purposes, it is also true that systems providing functional identity registration can exist in many forms and can be created both by central and local governments as well as by commercial, religious and other civic organizations. We cannot study the comparative history and uses of registration without taking into account all extant systems of identity information in each society, rather than privileging just one type, such as the census or, indeed, civic registration.

The incomplete and absent nature of personal registration systems for individuals at birth in many of the states of the union became the focus for a reforming campaign spearheaded by public health and census officials in the USA in the opening decades of the twentieth century. One of its protagonists, Cressy Wilbur, Chief Statistician at the Federal Census Bureau in Washington, reviewing the geographical pattern in 1907, was of the view that 'lack of sufficient density of population is one of the most obvious reasons for failure of extension of adequate registration methods in the United States' (Wilbur 1907, 398). Chapter 17 by Marshall documents how, as part of this campaign, later in the 1920s the American Child Health Association connected its own primary mission to build a network of institutions to promote child welfare with the need to extend US systems of birth registration. Marshall's chapter intriguingly demonstrates how similar to this were the arguments of the links between the two, child welfare and birth registration, which were made at the innovative 1931 Conference on the African Child organized by Save the Children International. Furthermore, Birn also uncovers this political and ideological linkage between welfare and registration in her chapter which argues that Uruguay, the first state in Latin America to pioneer a drive to full vital registration in the late nineteenth century – partly in response to concerns at its low birth rate – may have a claim to have passed the first national legislation which specified the importance of all children's right to a name and to familial identification in its Children's Code of 1934 (see Chapter 16).

After the Second World War under the aegis of the United Nations there was to emerge the famous UN Statement of Human Rights. However, curiously this did not include the right to registration we here see adumbrated in the deliberations and international conferences of various philanthropic voluntary organizations focusing their attentions on child welfare in the USA and Africa, and in the policies of the Uruguayan government during the 1930s. There is an account yet to be fully uncovered (see Chapter 16, note 40) of why such a clause was omitted in 1948 and was not to appear in UN documents until a decade later, finally appearing as Principle 3 of the 1959 Declaration of the Rights of the Child and subsequently as article 24, clause 2 of the ICCPR Covenant of 1966. This was a covenant which did not enter into force, however, until 1976 when thirty-five states had ratified it. By this time, most unfortunately, the incipient and partial registration systems of the many ex-colonial countries, including those in sub-Saharan Africa and the Indian sub-continent, had fallen into all but complete disrepair. The call for action at Geneva in 1931 had never been carried through, as Kuczynski documented in his survey (Kuczynski 1948, 1949). Furthermore, unlike in Latin American Uruguay, such systems of population registration often only had negative associations for the newly-independent nations and their governments in South Asia and in Africa (which emerged during the two decades of decolonization after the Second World War), connected as they were with past systems of colonial taxation or labour and migration control, such as the *kipandi* and Pass systems in Africa. Once again we see here the long-term influence on the comparative history of the infrastructure of registration – both its presence and its absence – of politics and ideology.

Registration and the technologies of recognition and representation

Finally the history of technology is also another important influence on the possibilities available to a group for affirming recognition among its members. For registration to acquire the characteristics of a system, four linked processes are involved: registering; recording; archiving; and accessing (or retrieval). These four technical components can each, independently or interactively, be subject to technological innovations; and their characteristics – and any changes in their character – in turn, imply and require varying forms of social capabilities and cultural resources, both in the registering organizations and among the registering populace. Thus, when we say that today there are no registration systems in many parts of sub-Saharan Africa, and in parts of South Asia and South and Central America, we mean that the groups, networks and communities living in these areas rely mainly on non-literacy-based oral or performative ritual methods for establishing mutual recognition, rights and obligations among themselves. All four processes of registration in fact occur but they do so through the most fundamental technology: oral, performative and mnemonic. There can be only very limited communication or exchange of services between the poor and their national governments in such circumstances.

By contrast, those citizens who live today in one of the economically-advanced OECD countries – the liberal democracies recognizing the rule of law and human rights – interact with many literacy- and numeracy-based registration systems operated by government, commercial, religious and civil organizations. Indeed, the literacy and numeracy technology has become digitalized and computer-automated in these countries and these organizations have access to large, electronically searchable databases of identities, along with a variety of associated information on the registered individuals (Bennett and Lyon 2008). Individuals in these societies typically have rich commerce with their national and local governments, exchanging their tax payments for a range of valued services, while also interacting with many other organizations and networks of individuals, most of whom, in theory, they have chosen to engage with for commercial or vocational reasons (though there is an increasingly sensitive legal issue whenever individuals believe they have not consented to their identity appearing on such a database). Thirdly, there is a diversity of further countries between these two polar types of locally and orally registering versus poly-registering, densely cyber-networked societies. This is where the central government, either *de jure* or *de facto*, holds a virtual monopoly of the more extensive literacy-based and IT registration systems on the population and where these systems exist primarily because the central state has found them to be of use for planning, policy and security purposes. This was the case in the USSR and the Comecon countries before 1989 and remains largely true in the important case of China today, though the Chinese state is struggling to retain a monopoly on such systems in the face of the countervailing attractiveness of the internet to its nation of would-be consumers and the many commercial and other organizations able to use the internet to build large registers of customers and members.

This volume's contributions show, however, that this wide variation in registration practices and implications across the world today is only equal in its diversity to the enormous variety found during the last two millennia. Both contemporary and historic diversity demonstrate not only that changes in technology and in forms of economic exchange produce differences in the registration systems prevailing in different societies, but also that these factors interact with distinctive ideologies and the political contexts in which states operate. Consequently, as these historical essays document, there has existed and can exist a profusion of distinct 'registration cultures'. In those communities without literacy-based technologies – but equally in those in which colonial or one-party states hold virtual monopolies of registration – there is likely to be a more limited scope for individuals to enjoy and exploit a diversity of forms of self-representation of their identities and selective association with others, except through their skill in illegally manipulating the rigid system, as the chapters by Herzog (Chapter 7) and MacDonald (Chapter 9) exemplify. Societies which are relatively rich in registering resources offer quite different opportunities for their citizens to deploy their own performative and negotiating skills to become legally adept in arranging their diverse memberships to best suit their various commercial and civic needs. Golden Age Holland of the late sixteenth and seventeenth centuries seems to have been a startling example of this proliferation of a Habermasian public sphere of multiple associations by recognition, subsequently emulated in this density of representational and registering possibilities by the 'polite and commercial' urban associational society of eighteenth- and nineteenth-century Britain (Morris 1990). These were registration-rich societies of poly-registering individuals, extra-empowered with their access to and use of multiple networks for representing their identities and recording their mutual recognition in a diversity of commercial and other associations.

A registration crisis? History and policy

This volume provides an intellectual resource of comparative historical knowledge with which to judge whether there may, indeed, currently be a crisis of registration approaching and what form that crisis will take. Biometric identification systems originated as ways to create a non-archival register of criminal identification with tattooing, branding and amputation (Groebner 2007; Higgs 2010). Fingerprinting for sub-sections of the population defined as criminal became the first biometric archival method. Using the pretext since 9/11 of defence against global terrorism, it is proposed, through iris-recognition technology, to apply a fully archival biometrics comprehensively to democratic and non-criminal populations across the world, to confer upon them a security from external threats and also, with the emergence of basic income grants, their internal social security and positive rights (see Chapter 19; Bennett and Lyon 2008). The interaction of this official registering technology with the application of computerized searchable and potentially linkable database information systems, and also with the emerging trend of commercial supply and delivery of these systems to states, has created an extraordinary conjuncture in the history of identity registration that should be of concern to all citizens.

The interaction of these technologies with both state security interests and commercial logics poses significant questions about the necessary regulations required, which citizens, their elected governments and their judiciaries should wish to consider. Is there, for instance, a question of 'ownership' that should be considered in relation to the right to use information about a person's identity, once that information has been created and verified as authentic? The popular notion of 'identity theft' would appear to suggest that there is such a sense in common understanding, but does this also amount to a legally defensible concept in practice? If 'ownership' is not quite the appropriate concept for legal purposes, what perhaps of a law reflecting principles of permissive 'informed consent' governing the use of such identity information by third parties or commercial organizations (including those companies increasingly bidding for and charged with the contracts to collect the information in the first place)? If such a right can be defended against a commercial corporation, can it also be defended against a sovereign state, in particular the state which also provides the institutional resources and the authorizing and verifying procedures for the registration system itself? What is the relationship between the individual and the state over the question of the right to control or change a registered identity? The individual cannot be a self-authorizing and self-verifying agency in relation to his/her identity. The state and its archiving and legal systems are ultimately necessary to provide this verification and authorization role. There are therefore irreducibly at least two distinct parties with an approximately equal, or at least complementary or reciprocal, stake and claim in creating what we refer to as a legally-valid and enforceable personal identity: the individual in question and the verifying and recording state – or, at least, its devolved legal registration agency. Each such state currently issues passports, for instance – documents which epitomize this duality. If it is considered important that an individual is to have the right to exercise personal choice in changing aspects of his or her legally-recognized identity (gender for instance), then there would need to be agreed and easily-accessible (though secure) procedures for doing this, which could satisfy the state's function as guarantor of the registration of identities. Some states deny or resist the possibility for individuals to vary by choice their identity once the state has made an original determination, which is then treated as permanent. Is this rule simply for the convenience of the state, or because it is claimed to uphold an ethical, legal or security principle of vital importance?

Can history assist with providing a perspective on these current predicaments concerning the future of registration, due to this intense set of international, technological, commercial and political developments that have all come together during the last ten years? At the moment we face these issues as a citizenry and set of experts who are equally uninformed of the rich and deep comparative history of the technologies of representation and recognition. This book provides a set of empirically-researched historical resources with which to address these contemporary problems. There are chapters here which uncover the rich but previously largely invisible histories of the evolution of these important infrastructures of social rights in European, American and Asian societies. There are many chapters which explore the history of registration in Africa, as well as in India and China, the three greatest population centres of the poor in the world today, where registration is a highly contentious issue affecting a large proportion of the world's populace. There are chapters which explore the curious absence of direct relationship between the modern history of identity registration and the emergence of the international human rights agenda. And there are several contributions which explicitly link the diversity of historical information presented to the highly contemporary policy questions of the future of identity registration in a biometric and commercialized global context preoccupied with internal and external security.

Conclusion: the concept of registration in the humanities

The novelty of registration as a subject of study lies in its differentiation from the previously-studied topics which have addressed other aspects of the history of identifying and accounting for individuals, often within a Foucauldian framework: enumeration and censuses; identification systems developed for policing, labour migration and border control purposes; and the study of vital statistics for public health, demographic and economic uses.

The form of registration which is the subject of study in this volume is the registration of persons for purposes of conferring public recognition of their legal personhood and status. Registration in this sense confers acknowledged rights and obligations in relation to other members of the community of mutual recognition. This might be termed 'civil registration'. However, that term has only previously been used of the administrative practices supposedly originating in post-Enlightenment 'western' liberal, secular democratic polities of the nineteenth and twentieth centuries. The studies collected here indicate the existence of 'registration as recognition' as a fundamental feature of human life in groups – and therefore occurring ubiquitously in a wide variety of other contexts and time periods throughout human history, even though the earliest records of written, documented forms of registration are only available with the rise of literate and powerful state and imperial bureaucracies.

'Registration' has previously been hidden from analytical view to historians and social scientists because of its superficial similarity to several other purely documentary practices requiring the registering and rendering legible of individuals for various governmental purposes. But in fact registration, in the form that has provided the focus for the studies presented in this volume, is an entirely distinct and separable concept.

It is a central argument of this collection of studies that the subject of registration itself needs to be 'registered' in the academic world. Registration needs to be recognized and explicitly acknowledged as a critical concept with the capacity to illuminate comparative historical study in the humanities, as is illustrated by the many and diverse contributions to this volume. In due course we believe that the concept of registration will require – and sustain – further elucidation and comparative study in its own right, in the way that such other critical concepts as class, gender, the state and community command entire historiographies of historical research in the humanities and theoretical debate in the social sciences. Registration, ultimately, is a conceptual tool for approaching the comparative study of recognition and representation of individual persons in relation to their wider communities and the protean constitution of these crucial relationships throughout human history.

References

Agamben, Giorgio. 1998. *Homo Sacer: Sovereign Power and Bare Life*. Berkeley: University of California Press.

Agar, Jon. 2003. *The Government Machine: A Revolutionary History of the Computer*. Cambridge, MA: MIT Press.

Ake, Claude. 1987. 'The African Context of Human Rights.' *Africa Today* 34(1): 5–12.

—— 1991. 'Rethinking African Democracy.' *Journal of Democracy* 2(1): 32–44.

Aly, Gotz and Karl Heinz Roth. 2000. *The Nazi Census: Identification and Control in the Third Reich*. Philadelphia, PA: Temple University Press.

Anderson, Clare. 2004. *Legible Bodies: Race, Criminality and Colonialism in South Asia*. Oxford: Berg.

Anderson, Ross, Ian Brown, Terri Dowty, Philip Inglesant, William Heath and Angela Sasse. 2009. *Database State*. York: Joseph Rowntree Reform Trust.

Baxter, Stephen. 2012. 'Domesday Book and the Languages of Lordship.' In *Conceptualizing Multilingualism in England, 800–1250*, ed. Elizabeth Tyler. Begijnhof, Belgium: Brepols, 271–308.

Bennett, Colin J. and David Lyon. 2008. *Playing the Identity Card: Surveillance, Security and Identification in Global Perspective*. London: Routledge.

Berry, S. 1993. *No Condition Is Permanent: The Social Dynamics of Agrarian Change in Sub-Saharan Africa*. Madison: University of Wisconsin Press.

Black, Edwin. 2001. *IBM and the Holocaust: The Strategic Alliance between Nazi Germany and America's Most Powerful*. New York: Little Brown.

Bowker, Geoffrey and Susan Leigh Starr. 1999. *Sorting Things Out: Classification and Its Consequences*. Cambridge, MA: MIT Press.

Breckenridge, Keith. 2005. 'Verwoerd's Bureau of Proof: Total Information in the Making of Apartheid.' *History Workshop Journal* 59: 83–109.

—— 2010. 'The World's First Biometric Money: Ghana's e-Zwich and the Contemporary Influence of South African Biometrics.' *Africa: The Journal of the International African Institute* 80(4): 642–662.

—— 2011. 'Capitaliser sur les pauvres: les enjeux de l'adoption de services financiers biométriques au Nigeria.' In *L'identification Biométrique: Champs, Acteurs, Enjeux et Controverses*, ed. Ayse Cehan amd Pierre Piazza. Paris: Éditions de la Maison des sciences de l'homme.

Brown, W. 2004. '"The Most We Can Hope For . . .": Human Rights and the Politics of Fatalism.' *South Atlantic Quarterly* 103(2): 451.

Burchell, Peter, Colin Gordon and Peter Miller, eds. 1991. *The Foucault Effect: Studies in Governmentality with Two Lectures by and an Interview with Michel Foucault*. London: Harvester Wheatsheaf.

Caplan, Jane. 2001. '"This or That Particular Person": Protocols of Identification in Nineteenth-Century Europe.' In *Documenting Individual Identity: The Development of State Practices in the Modern World*, ed. Jane Caplan and John Torpey. Princeton, NJ: Princeton University Press, 49–66.

—— 2009. 'Illegibility: Reading and Insecurity in History, Law and Government.' *History Workshop Journal* 68(1): 99–121.

Caplan, Jane and John C. Torpey, eds. 2001. *Documenting Individual Identity: The Development of State Practices in the Modern World*. Princeton, NJ: Princeton University Press.

Chakrabarty, Dipesh. 2002. *Habitations of Modernity: Essays in the Wake of Subaltern Studies*. Chicago: University of Chicago Press.

Chanock, Martin. 2001. *The Making of South African Legal Culture, 1902–1936: Fear, Favour and Prejudice*. Cambridge: Cambridge University Press.

Charlesworth, Lorie. 2010. *Welfare's Forgotten Past: A Socio-Legal History of the Poor Law*. London: Routledge.

Clanchy, M. T. 1979. *From Memory to Written Record, England 1066–1307*. London: Edward Arnold.

Cohn, Bernard S. and Nicholas B. Dirks. 1988. 'Beyond the Fringe: The Nation State, Colonialism, and the Technologies of Power.' *Journal of Historical Sociology* 1(2): 224–229.

Cole, Ernest. 1967. *House of Bondage by Ernest Cole (A South African Black Man Exposes in His Own Pictures and Words the Bitter Life of His Homeland Today)*, ed. Thomas Flaherty. New York: Random House.

Cole, Simon A. 2001. *Suspect Identities: A History of Fingerprinting and Criminal Identification*. Cambridge, MA: Harvard University Press.

Cooper, Frederick. 1996. *Decolonization and African Society: The Labor Question in French and British Africa*. Cambridge: Cambridge University Press.

—— 2002. *Africa Since 1940: The Past of the Present*. Cambridge: Cambridge University Press.

Cooper, Frederick and Rogers Brubaker. 2000. 'Beyond "Identity".' *Theory and Society* 29: 1–47.

Corrigan, Philip Richard D. and Derek Sayer. 1985. *The Great Arch: English State Formation as Cultural Revolution*. Oxford: Blackwell.

Dean, M. 1999. *Governmentality: Power and Rule in Modern Society*. London: Sage.

De Soto, H. 2000. *The Mystery of Capital: Why Capitalism Triumphs in the West and Fails Everywhere Else*. New York: Basic Books.

Diamant, N. J. 2001. 'Making Love "Legible" in China: Politics and Society during the Enforcement of Civil Marriage Registration, 1950–1966.' *Politics and Society* 29(3): 447–480.

Draper, Nick. 2009. *The Price of Emancipation: Slave-Ownership, Compensation and British Society at the End of Slavery*. Cambridge: Cambridge University Press.

Dreze, Jean and Amartya Sen. 1989. *Hunger and Public Action*. New York: Oxford University Press.

Economist. 2012. Leader 'India's Identity Scheme.' *Economist*, 14 January. www.economist.com/node/21542763?fsrc=nlw|hig|1-12-2012|editors_highlights.

Englund, Harri. 2006. *Prisoners of Freedom: Human Rights and the African Poor*. Berkeley: University of California Press.

Ferguson, James. 1990. *The Anti-Politics Machine: 'Development,' Depoliticization, and Bureaucratic Power in Lesotho*. Cambridge: Cambridge University Press.

—— 1999. *Expectations of Modernity: Myths and Meanings of Urban Life on the Zambian Copperbelt*. Berkeley: University of California Press.

—— 2006. *Global Shadows: Africa in the Neoliberal World Order*. Durham, NC: Duke University Press.

Ferguson, James and Anil Gupta. 2002. 'Spatializing States: Toward an Ethnography of Neoliberal Governmentality.' *American Ethnologist* 29(4): 981–1002.

Foucault, Michel. 1977. *Discipline and Punish: The Birth of the Prison*. London: Penguin.

—— 1981. 'The Order of Discourse: Inaugural Lecture at the Collège de France, given 2 December 1970.' In *Untying the Text*, ed. Robert Young. Boston: Routledge & Kegan Paul, 48–78.

—— 1991. 'Governmentality.' In *The Foucault Effect: Studies in Governmentality with Two Lectures by and an Interview with Michel Foucault*, ed. Peter Burchell, Colin Gordon and Peter Miller. London: Harvester Wheatsheaf, 87–104.

Foucault, Michel and Colin Gordon. 1980. *Power/Knowledge: Selected Interviews and Other Writings, 1972–1977*. New York: Pantheon.

Fraser, N. 1989. *Unruly Practices: Power, Discourse and Gender in Contemporary Social Theory*. Minneapolis: Minnesota University Press.

Giddens, A. 1985. *The Nation-State and Violence: A Contemporary Critique of Historical Materialism*. Berkeley: University of California Press.

Goody, Jack. 1977. *The Domestication of the Savage Mind*. Cambridge: Cambridge University Press.

—— 1986. *The Logic of Writing and the Organization of Society*. Oxford: Oxford University Press.

Gorski, Philip S. 1993. 'The Protestant Ethic Revisited: Disciplinary Revolution and State Formation in Holland and Prussia.' *American Journal of Sociology* 99(2): 265–316.

Groebner, Valentin. 2007. *Who Are You? Identification, Deception, and Surveillance in Early Modern Europe*. New York: Zone Books.

Guha, Sumit. 2003. 'The Politics of Identity and Enumeration in India c. 1600–1990.' *Comparative Studies in Society and History* 45(2): 148–167.

Guha, Ramachandra. 2008. *India After Gandhi*. London: Pan Macmillan.

Halverson, John. 1992. 'Goody and the Implosion of the Literacy Thesis.' *Man*, 27(2): 301–317.

Harries, Patrick. 1994. *Work, Culture and Identity: Migrant Labourers in Mozambique and South Africa, c 1860–1910*. Johannesburg: Witwatersrand University Press.

Hawkins, Sean. 2002. *Writing and Colonialism in Northern Ghana: The Encounter between the LoGagaa and the 'World on Paper'*. Toronto: University of Toronto Press.

Herbst, J. 2000. *States and Power in Africa: Comparative Lessons in Authority and Control*. Princeton, NJ: Princeton University Press.

Higgs, Edward. 2004. *The Information State in England: The Central Collection of Information on Citizens since 1500*. New York: Palgrave Macmillan.

—— 2010. 'Fingerprints and Citizenship: The British State and the Identification of Pensioners in the Interwar Period.' *History Workshop Journal* 69: 52–67.

Hill, Kenneth, Alan D. Lopez, Kenji Shibuya and Prabat Jha. 2007. 'Interim Measures for Meeting Needs for Health Sector Data: Births, Deaths and Causes of Death.' *The Lancet* 370(9600): 1726–1735.

Hodge, Joseph Morgan. 2007. *Triumph of the Expert: Agrarian Doctrines of Development and the Legacies of British Colonialism*. Athens: Ohio University Press.

Jones, G. S. 1971. *Outcast London: A Study in the Relationship between the Classes in Victorian Society*. New York: Pantheon.

Jewkes, Rachel and Katherine Wood. 1998. 'Competing Discourses of Vital Registration and Personhood: Perspectives from Rural South Africa.' *Social Science and Medicine* 46(8): 1043–1056.

de Jong, Louis. 1995. *Het Koninkrijk der Nederlanden in de Tweede Wereldoorlog*, vol. 5. Amsterdam: Rijksinstituut voor Oorlogsdocumentatie.

Kahn, E. 1949. 'The Pass Laws.' *Handbook of Race Relations in South Africa*. Johannesburg: Race Relations Institute, 275–291.

Kuczynski, Robert René. 1948. *Demographic Survey of the British Colonial Empire. Volume I. West Africa*. London: Oxford University Press.

—— 1949. *Demographic Survey of the British Colonial Empire. Volume II. South Africa High Commission Territories, East Africa, Mauritius, Seychelles*. London: Oxford University Press.

Kwankye, S. O. 1999. 'The Vital Registration System in Ghana: A Relegated Option for Demographic Data Collection.' In *The African Population in the 21st Century*. Durban: Popline.

Loveman, Mara. 2007. 'Blinded Like a State: The Revolt against Civil Registration in Nineteenth-Century Brazil.' *Comparative Studies in Society and History* 49(1): 5–39.

Luebke, David Martin and Sybil Milton. 1994. 'Locating the Victim: An Overview of Census-Taking, Tabulation Technology, and Persecution in Nazi Germany.' *IEEE Annals of the History of Computing* 16(3): 25.

Mackenzie, Y. 2008. 'Campaign for Universal Birth Registration in Latin America: Ensuring All Latin American Children's Inherent Right to Life and Survival by First Guaranteeing Their Right to a Legal Identity.' *Georgia Journal of International and Comparative Law* 37: 519–554.

Mamdani, Mahmood. 1996. *Citizen and Subject: Contemporary Africa and the Legacy of Late Colonialism*. Cape Town: James Currey.

McCrank, Lawrence. 1993. 'Documenting Reconquest and Reform: The Growth of Archives in the Medieval Crown of Aragon.' *American Archivist* 56(1): 256–318.

Menon, Dilip M. 2005. 'Things Fall Apart: The Cinematic Rendition of Agrarian Landscape in South India.' *Journal of Peasant Studies* 32(2): 304–334.

—— 2006. 'Introduction.' In *Cultural History of Modern India*. New Delhi: Social Science Press, ix–xxii.

Mitchell, Timothy. 2002. *Rule of Experts: Egypt, Techno-Politics, Modernity*. Berkeley: University of California Press.

Morris, R. J. 1990. 'Clubs, Societies and Associations.' In *The Cambridge Social History of Britain 1750–1950*, vol. 3, ed. F. M. L. Thompson. Cambridge: Cambridge University Press, 395–443.

Oloka-Onyango, J. 1995. 'Beyond the Rhetoric: Reinvigorating the Struggle for Economic and Social Rights in Africa.' *California Western International Law Journal* 26: 1.

Ong, W. J. 2002. *Orality and Literacy: The Technologizing of the Word*. London: Routledge.

van Onselen, Charles. 1985. 'Crime and Total Institutions in the Making of Modern South Africa: The Life of "Nongoloza" Mathebula, 1867–1948.' *History Workshop Journal* 19: 62–81.

Overy, R. J. 2009. *The Morbid Age: Britain Between the Wars*. London: Allen Lane.

Posel, Deborah. 1995. 'State, Power, and Gender: Conflict over the Registration of African Customary Marriage in South Africa, 1910–1970.' *Journal of Historical Sociology* 8(3): 223–256.

—— 2000. 'A Mania for Measurement: Statistics and Statecraft in the Transition to Apartheid.' In *Science and Society in Southern Africa*, ed. Saul Dubow. Manchester: Manchester University Press, 116–142.

Powell, Nora. 1980. *Human Rights and Registration of Vital Events*. Technical Report. International Institute for Vital Registration and Statistics.

Reynolds, Susan. 2001. 'Medieval Law.' In *The Medieval World*, ed. Peter Linehan and Janet Laughland Nelson. London: Routledge, 485–502.

Rodney, Walter. 1982. *How Europe Underdeveloped Africa*. Washington, DC: Howard University Press.

Rose, Nikolas. 1991. 'Governing by Numbers: Figuring out Democracy.' *Accounting, Organizations and Society* 16(7): 673–692.

—— 1999. *Governing the Soul: The Shaping of the Private Self*. London: Free Association Books.

Sadiq, Kamal. 2009. *Paper Citizens. How Illegal Immigrants Acquire Citizenship in Developed Countries*. Oxford: Oxford University Press.

Sankar, P. 1992. 'State Power and Record-Keeping: The History of Individualized Surveillance in the United States, 1790–1935.' Unpublished Ph.D. dissertation, University of Pennsylvania.

Savage, Michael. 1986. 'The Imposition of Pass Laws on the African Population in South Africa 1916–1984.' *African Affairs* 85(339): 181–205.

Scott, James C. 1998. *Seeing Like a State: How Certain Schemes to Improve the Human Condition Have Failed*. New Haven, CT: Yale University Press.

—— 2009. *The Art of Not Being Governed: An Anarchist History of Upland Southeast Asia*. New Haven, CT: Yale University Press.

Scott, James C., John Tehranian and Jeremy Mathias. 2002. 'The Production of Legal Identities Proper to States: The Case of the Permanent Family Surname.' *Comparative Studies in Society and History* 44(1): 4–44.

Sekula, Allan. 1986. 'The Body and the Archive.' *October* 39: 3–64.

Seltzer, William. 1998. 'Population Statistics, the Holocaust, and the Nuremberg Trials.' *Population and Development Review* 24(3): 511–552.

Sen, Amartya. 1982. *Poverty and Famines: An Essay on Entitlement and Deprivation*. New York: Oxford University Press.

—— 1999. *Development as Freedom*. Oxford: Oxford University Press.

—— 2004. 'Elements of a Theory of Human Rights.' *Philosophy and Public Affairs* 32(4): 315–356.

Sengoopta, Chandak. 2003. *Imprint of the Raj: How Fingerprinting Was Born in Colonial India*. London: Macmillan.

Setel, Philip W., Sarah B. Macfarlane, Simon Szreter, Lene Mikkelsen, Prabhat Jha, Susan Stout and Carla AbouZahr. 2007. 'A Scandal of Invisibility: Making Everyone Count by Counting Everyone.' *The Lancet* 370(9598): 1569–1577.

Shachar, Ayelet. 2009. *The Birthright Lottery: Citizenship and Global Inequality*. Cambridge, MA: Harvard University Press.

Singha, Radhika. 2000. 'Settle, Mobilize, Verify: Identification Practices in Colonial India.' *Studies in History* 16(2): 151–198.

Skocpol, Theda. 1992. *Protecting Soldiers and Mothers: The Political Origins of Social Policy in the United States*. Cambridge, MA: Belknap Press of Harvard University Press.

Slack, Paul. 2004. 'Government and Information in Seventeenth-Century England.' *Past and Present* 184(1): 33–68.

Smith, Alex Duval. 2010. 'Lesotho's People Plead with South Africa to Annex Their Troubled Country.' *Guardian*, 6 June. www.guardian.co.uk/world/2010/jun/06/lesotho-independence-south-africa.

Steinwedel, Charles. 2001. 'Making Social Groups, One Person at a Time: The Identification of Individuals by Estate, Religious Confession, and Ethnicity in Late Imperial Russia.' In *Documenting Individual Identity: The Development of State Practices in the Modern World*, ed. Jane Caplan and John Torpey. Princeton, NJ: Princeton University Press, 61–82.

Stoler, Ann Laura. 2009. *Along the Archival Grain: Epistemic Anxieties and Colonial Common Sense*. Princeton, NJ: Princeton University Press.

Szreter, Simon. 2007. 'The Right of Registration: Development, Identity Registration, and Social Security: A Historical Perspective.' *World Development* 35(1): 67–86.

Thiong'o, Ngugi wa. 2007. *Wizard of the Crow*. New York: Anchor.

Unicef. 2005. *The 'Rights' Start to Life: A Statistical Analysis of Birth Registration*. New York: UNICEF.

Wilbur, Cressy L. 1907. 'The Outlook for a General System of Registration of Vital Statistics in the United States.' *Publications of the American Statistical Association* 10(80): 395–420.

Wilke, Jürgen. 2004. 'From Parish Register to the "Historical Table": The Prussian Population Statistics in the 17th and 18th Centuries.' *The History of the Family* 9(1): 63–79.

Wilson, Edward. Acting Chief Pass Officer, Native Affairs Department, Johannesburg. 1912. 'The Employment in the Union of South Africa of the System of Identification by Finger Impressions.' Chamber of Mines Archive, Assaults on European Women by Natives, 1912 (1).

Woodside, Alexander. 2006. *Lost Modernities: China, Vietnam, Korea, and the Hazards of World History*. Cambridge, MA: Harvard University Press.

Wordsworth, William. 1888. 'The Tables Turned.' In *The Complete Poetical Works*. London: Macmillan and Co. www.bartleby.com/145/.

Young, M. Crawford. 1994. *The African Colonial State in Comparative Perspective*. New Haven, CT: Yale University Press.

Part I

REGISTRATION, STATES AND LEGAL PERSONHOOD

1

Household Registration, Property Rights, and Social Obligations in Imperial China: Principles and Practices

RICHARD VON GLAHN

CIVIL REGISTRATION FOR THE PURPOSES OF SOCIAL CONTROL and the mobilization of labour and other resources was a cornerstone of the Chinese imperial state. Likewise, the *hukou* household registration system has been one of the key institutions governing social life and work in the People's Republic of China (PRC). The hukou system is a product of the transition to a socialist economy in the mid-1950s, and its immediate antecedent was the passbook system inaugurated in the USSR in concert with its strategy of economic development through rapid industrialization. But the hukou system of civil registration also represents a culmination of principles and practices of governance and state–society relations in China that date back more than 2,000 years. This essay traces the origins and historical development of the civil registration system of imperial China in order to clarify its ideological and institutional evolution. Like any system of social control, civil registration imposed constraints on the population but also created opportunities. In late imperial China, for example, local elites manipulated the civil registration system to solidify property rights and entrench their power over local society. Before considering the institutional evolution of Chinese civil registration, I will briefly sketch the main features of the hukou system in contemporary China to serve as a frame of reference for the following historical survey.

Civil registration in contemporary China

War with Japan and the subsequent civil war between the Communists and Nationalists caused enormous population displacement in China from 1937 to 1949. In the early 1950s, as part of its initial efforts at restoring stability, the fledgling PRC government began to define and register the urban population in terms of native residence, education, and occupation. Household registers were issued for the first time following the national census of 1953. Although the constitution

Proceedings of the British Academy **182**, 39–66. © The British Academy 2012.

enacted by the PRC in 1954 nominally guaranteed freedom of residence and movement to its citizens, over the next several years the government adopted policies that severely curtailed internal migration, especially migration from the countryside to the cities.

With the launch of its first Five-Year Plan in 1953, the PRC embraced the Soviet-style model of economic development, which devoted maximum effort to rapid expansion of urban heavy industries such as steel, chemicals, and producer goods. As in the USSR, the PRC state assumed total control of urban areas, guaranteeing not only employment to urban residents but also vital goods and services such as food, housing, education, and medical care. The collectivization of agriculture that took place at the same time did not extend similar services and welfare entitlements to the rural population, however. The initial push for industrialization was accompanied by extensive labour recruitment by municipal governments and industrial enterprises. But already in 1954 the central government began to curb migration from the countryside to the cities and to return unemployed urban residents to their home villages. In 1955 the PRC issued a series of directives that created the formal hukou system, which restricted residence to a person's registered domicile and mandated a highly restrictive application process for transfer of registered domicile, especially relocation to the cities. By the end of 1956 private housing in the cities had been eliminated, and housing, along with grain rations and other vital services, was allocated strictly on the basis of hukou status. Rural-to-urban migration came to a virtual halt. In January 1958 the National People's Congress established the hukou registration system on a nationwide basis (Cheng and Selden 1994).

Before the economic liberalization of urban industrial enterprises in the 1990s the hukou system acted as a powerful instrument of social control.[1] Possession of an urban hukou was an absolute necessity to gain access to jobs, housing, schools, and other services in cities. Children inherited their hukou status from their mother. Although this policy may seem an aberration in the context of China's strongly patriarchal and patrilineal traditions, it served to restrict the pool of those eligible for urban hukou, since most urban workers were male. At the same time the hukou system tightly linked hukou registration to the work unit (*danwei*). An urban danwei (literally, 'unit') – which might be a factory, school, store, office, or government agency – typically had its own residential compound (often walled), forming a community of intense social interaction that extended from the workplace into all corners of private life.[2] Thus workplace supervisors and Communist Party committees at the work unit acquired effective control over the lives of their employees. Administration of the hukou system and the application procedures

[1] The most comprehensive study of the hukou system prior to 2002 is Wang (2005).

[2] For a study of the danwei system that emphasizes its continuities with the spatial structures and socio-economic institutions of pre-revolutionary China, see Bray (2005).

for relocation were entrusted to the Public Security Bureau and delegated to its more than 30,000 local police stations.

The hukou system enabled the PRC government to prevent the rampant rural-to-urban migration and the emergence of mega-cities with vast pools of unemployed slum dwellers that became common in many developing countries during the second half of the twentieth century. At the same time the system created and perpetuated a hierarchy of privilege that relegated rural residents to the status of second-class citizens. The major avenues for acquiring urban hukou were admission to specialized secondary schools and universities or Communist Party membership. But rural residents were at a marked disadvantage in pursuit of these objectives; urban residents were far more likely to gain admission to institutions of higher education and party membership. Thus the privileges and economic benefits obtained from urban hukou became self-reinforcing (Wu and Treiman 2004). The hukou system also contributed to the political domination of the cities over the countryside. In the mid-1990s, over 10 per cent of urban hukou holders were party members, in contrast to less than 2 per cent of the rural population (Wang 2005, 115). Hukou restrictions have also been a major factor in widening the growing inequalities in income and wealth (as measured, for example, by home values) between urban and rural residents (Whalley and Zhang 2004).

The hukou system also enhanced the state's capacity for surveillance and political repression. Even before the formal creation of hukou the state's registration procedures identified individuals belonging to 'targeted populations'. In 1950 six categories of targeted populations were established (spies, local tyrants, bandits, cadres of reactionary groups, and leaders of secret societies or 'superstitious' religious sects). During the high tide of Maoism from the mid-1950s to the mid-1970s, 'class enemies' were designated as the main targeted population. After 1980 the class enemy labels were dropped, and the targeted population category was focused primarily on criminals and political dissidents. In recent years, however, the targeted population has been expanded to include a variety of politically suspect groups, such as Muslim separatists and Falungong activists (Wang 2004).

The piecemeal abandonment of the socialist economy since the 1980s has resulted in the withdrawal of the guarantees of goods and services for urban residents. Urban workers have been liberated from the tyranny of their danwei supervisors, and immigrants from rural areas can now obtain food, housing, etc. through the market. Consequently the utility of the hukou system as an instrument of social control has diminished, and since 1997 the PRC has begun to make major modifications in the hukou system. Beginning in 1998, children were allowed to choose to inherit hukou status from either their father or mother. Permission for relocation was liberally granted to elderly parents, children, and skilled workers. In 2001–2002, the coastal provinces that had enjoyed extremely high rates of economic growth – and consequently attracted large numbers of immigrants from the countryside and the interior provinces – experimented with abolishing the urban/rural distinction altogether and allowing persons with 'stable' residences and sources of income to obtain urban hukou. However, the national government stepped in and rescinded these initiatives (Wang 2004, 121). Without question, however, the rich, the well-educated, and the politically-connected can readily obtain an urban hukou (for example, anyone with a Ph.D. degree is allowed to move to the city of their choice). In essence, the hukou has become a market commodity rather than a socialist good.

But lack of an urban hukou no longer serves as an effective impediment to internal migration. The 'floating population' – defined as those who have been absent from their registered domicile for more than six months – swelled to an estimated 148 million people (more than 10 per cent of the total population) by 2005 (Fan 2008a). Still, the demand for cheap labour has enabled China's cities to absorb rural migrants without engendering the severe social dislocation and poverty typical of many developing countries. Moreover, hukou policies continue to play a crucial role in furthering the state's economic development strategy of labour-intensive industrialization and targeted urban growth. Government policy has created a migrant labour regime that confines rural migrants to specific sectors of the urban economy. Many rural households have adopted a split-household strategy – often split along gender lines – to take maximum advantage of both rural and urban work opportunities. At the same time, the out-migration of women from rural areas has accelerated, and mobility rates among men and women are roughly equal (Fan 2008b).

Despite increasing public pressure to modify the hukou system and its own embrace of the cause of hukou reform, the PRC leadership has taken only small steps. Relocation to small and medium-sized cities has become easier, and peasants can now exchange land rights for urban hukou.[3] In 2010 provincial and municipal governments initiated their own reforms, such as introducing scoring systems to enable migrant workers to earn urban hukou.[4] But no breakthrough has come for the great tide of migrant workers in large cities who suffer the most from the

[3] In early 2010 the Chinese government leaders announced that hukou reform was a top priority, triggering bold appeals for meaningful reforms and even outright abolition of the system. But the central government has only endorsed minimal changes, such as broadening access to urban hukou in small and medium-sized cities. See Kam Wing Chan, 'Making Real Hukou Reform in China', posted 3 March 2010. www.eastasiaforum.org/2010/03/03/making-real-hukou-reform-in-china/.

[4] Guangdong province, with a floating population estimated at 26 million, introduced a scoring system in July 2010 based on documented length of stay, educational level, technical skills, payment of social insurance fees, public security records (including conformity to family planning rules), and participation in charitable activities such as donating blood. See '"Hukou" Scoring System Quickens China's Pace Toward Urbanization', *People's Daily Online*, 12 November 2010, http://english.peopledaily.com.cn/90001/90776/90882/7197897.html. A similar but more stringent scoring system was adopted in Shanghai – where approximately one-third of 19 million residents lack a Shanghai hukou – in 2009. However, critics have complained that the threshold for obtaining urban hukou, especially in the major cities, has been set too high, and only a tiny fraction of migrants can achieve eligibility.

inequities stemming from the hukou system. Although the hukou system is by no means obsolete, its purposes have changed. Its function as a means of controlling internal migration has been diminished, but the hukou system still perpetuates regional inequality and imbalances in resource allocation – not only of public goods, but also skilled and educated workers and foreign capital investment. It also remains part of the apparatus of political control by the state and its police forces. In this respect the hukou system continues to adhere to the original purposes of the earliest forms of civil registration in ancient China.

Origins of household registration in China

The fragmentary evidence at our disposal suggests that the use of written population registers dates back to the sixth century BCE, a period of transformative political and social change.[5] The kings of the Zhou dynasty, founded in the eleventh century BCE, had awarded hundreds of domains to kinfolk and vassals. These domains took the form of agrarian city-states, consisting of a capital city where the ruling lineage dwelled and adjoining rural settlements whose inhabitants worked the land under serf-like conditions. From the mid-eighth century BCE onward the Zhou kings were reduced to mere figureheads, while chronic warfare among the vassals caused the extinction and annexation of numerous domains. During the sixth century BCE a series of sweeping changes transformed the Zhou socio-political order. The precisely-graded ranking of the nobility broke down. Stratification within the ruling class intensified, resulting in a vast disparity in wealth and power between the rulers and the rest of the nobility. A group of roughly a dozen states emerged as the dominant contenders for power.

The next several centuries witnessed the destruction of the old noble lineages and the largely autarchic estate economies under their dominion. The patrimonial order of the early Zhou, in which political authority was broadly shared among noble lineages, was eclipsed by autocratic states in which power and economic resources were concentrated in the hands of an exalted ruler. Rulers asserted direct control over the land, which they awarded to farming families in return for tax payments, labour service, and military service. The nobility's hereditary rights to office were abrogated, and rulers instead established bureaucratic forms of government in which officials served at the ruler's pleasure. The widespread diffusion of iron metallurgy at this time also prompted a revolution in warfare. Chariot warfare conducted by nobles under strict rules of chivalry was replaced by far more bloody conflicts fought by massive infantry armies conscripted from the agrarian population and equipped with iron weapons, including powerful

[5] This section draws principally on Sato (1967), Hori (1994, 1996), and especially Du (1990). Some of these issues are also touched on in Lewis (2006).

crossbows. This transformation of the state and the relationship between rulers and subjects prompted the development of written registers to record information about individuals, households, and property. The earliest references to population registration, dating from the sixth century BCE, indicate that its main purpose was military conscription.

The most detailed information on population registration comes from the state of Qin. The far-reaching political reforms carried out in Qin under the aegis of Shang Yang (prime minister of Qin from 361 to 338 BCE) made it the most powerful of the contending states and paved the way for a Qin king to found the first unified empire (221–206 BCE). Shang Yang's reforms created a multi-tiered administrative hierarchy connecting subjects to rulers through a military-style chain of command. The entire population was organized into units of five families (known as *wu*) that served as the basis for taxation and conscription. The wu groupings were based on residential proximity rather than kinship connections. In addition, the five families of a wu shared joint legal liability for the actions of all of its members. If one person committed a crime, the entire wu group was deemed culpable and would suffer the same punishment as the miscreant. This doctrine of mutual implication, which used surveillance and peer pressure among neighbours as an instrument of social control, became a cardinal feature of law and government under China's first empires.

The Qin system of household registration thus applied a military model of hierarchical organization and discipline to civil governance. The conjugal household became the basic unit of production, taxation, and social reproduction.[6] Shang Yang's reforms prohibited co-residence of fathers and adult sons; instead, each son was to be given his share of the family patrimony in order to live apart as a separate household. Each household was required to provide both statutory labour service and military service on a regular basis. The household also became the basic unit for distribution of social services. For example, the Qin state lent seed and ploughing oxen to farmers and distributed famine relief to the needy based on the population registers. The conjugal family also became the property-owning unit, and property was transmitted through the patriline from fathers to sons, who formed separate patrilines.

The fundamental ethos of the Qin population registration system was summed up by the guiding principle of *bianhu qimin*: 'register households in order to make the people equal'. It eliminated the special status and privileges of the nobility, reducing the whole free population to common and equal status as subjects of the

[6] Among the enduring reforms enacted by the Qin was the principle of equal inheritance: all sons were entitled to an equal share of the household property. The Qin deliberately repudiated the earlier principle of primogeniture in order to undermine the concentration of landownership in the hands of the old nobility – and its own new office-holding elite as well. Equal inheritance remained the foundation of inheritance laws in China down to modern times.

ruler.[7] A philosophical treatise attributed to Shang Yang emphasizes that it is only by knowing the names of his subjects and fixing their residence that the ruler can gather the resources he requires and the people can obtain the lands and dwellings they need for their subsistence. This work singles out merchants and itinerants as 'vermin' whose mobility – and their ability to hide their wealth – threatens to subvert the state. The subsequent Han dynasty (202 BCE–220 CE) compiled separate registers for merchants and artisans which were used to requisition goods and also to impose certain legal discriminations (for example, merchants and artisans at times were forbidden to hold government office, or to own arable land). Moreover, unauthorized change of residence was deemed a heinous crime, punishable by brutal convict labour servitude. Numerous treatises on political philosophy written in this period describe a world in which the state had spun a tightly-meshed net of surveillance from which scarcely anyone could escape.

No actual population registers from the Qin period survive. The oldest extant specimens, which date from the early Han dynasty (second century BCE), are registers for soldiers stationed at Juyan, the key garrison town on the northwestern frontier of the Han Empire.[8] The basic information contained in these registers included the soldier's name, assignment classification, military rank, registered domicile, height, and complexion ('colour'). The Qin dynasty began to require that men report their age only from 231 BCE. Previously, liability for military service was determined by height rather than age, no doubt testifying to the limited reliability of birth records in the population registers prior to this time. Certain prescriptive texts – which employ archaic terms that suggest they reflect the circumstances of the sixth century BCE – state that military service was required of inhabitants of the capital who were 7 chi tall (161 cm) and under the age of 60, and rural inhabitants who were 6 chi (138 cm) and not yet 65 years old. In the Qin period the height requirement for military conscription was 7.1 chi (163 cm); the average height of soldiers recorded in the Juyan documents was 168 cm. In the Han period, males became liable for military service at age 20 and were required to serve two year-long tours: one year as a common infantryman and a second year in a more specialized role in the cavalry, crossbow corps, carriage drivers, etc.

[7] Slavery existed in China, but slaves constituted only a small fraction of the population. Several categories of slavery were recognized in imperial law, but in general only war captives and certain classes of convicted criminals could be enslaved. Thus the state itself was the principal owner of slaves, although meritorious officials and soldiers were often rewarded with gifts of slaves, and slave markets existed at least by the third century BCE. Slaves constituted an important part of the labour force in government workshops and mines under the early empires, but played a negligible role in the private economy. See Yates (2002).

[8] The Juyan documents, like other texts dating from this era, were written with brush and ink on strips of wood. More commonly during this era texts were written on strips of bamboo, but bamboo did not grow in the arid northwestern region in which Juyan was located. The invention of paper in the first century CE resulted in a shift to paper records. Unfortunately for the historian, however, paper is more fragile than bamboo and no paper documents dating before the seventh century have survived.

Some of the Juyan documents take the form of property registers, detailing the lands, buildings, vehicles, slaves, livestock, and property (measured in coin) owned by the soldier but omitting any information about family members. Other Juyan documents – for example, lists for allocating grain rations – also record the wife and children of the soldier, specifying their names, ages, and taxation status. Under Han law, all persons aged 7 and above were assessed for a poll tax known as *kouqian*. Persons aged 15 and above – men and women alike – were liable for labour service as well as a more substantial poll tax (*suanfuqian*).[9] The poll taxes and labour service levies – the main sources of government revenue during the Han dynasty – thus required extensive documentation of the age and gender of all members of the household. The Juyan registers carefully recorded liability for labour service (which varied by age) and military service (which varied by age and gender).

The fullest description of the registration process has been preserved in the Rituals of Zhou (Zhouli), a prescriptive text describing the government of the autocratic state which probably reflects the circumstances of the fourth to third centuries BCE. According to this text, local officials at the canton[10] level were obliged 'to apply the state's assessment rules and periodically investigate the numbers of individuals in each household; to distinguish the household's elderly and young, noble and base, lame and infirm, and its livestock resources; and to determine who is liable for labour service and who should be exempted'. Parallel passages add that the household surveys also registered weapons in the family's possession.[11] The Rituals of Zhou dictates that a 'minor assessment' (*xiaobi*) should be conducted on an annual basis – in the eighth lunar month, during the slack agricultural season – for the purpose of recording changes (births/deaths, age) and reallocating labour service and poll tax obligations. In addition, officials at higher levels of the state administration conducted a 'major assessment' (*dabi*) every three years. The major assessment accumulated aggregate information about population and resources which was forwarded to the central government. The major assess-

[9] The term of labour service for persons aged 15–17 or 60-plus was half that of an able-bodied adult.

[10] The canton (*xiang*) – generally defined as a unit of 1,000 households – was the basic unit of local government. Each *xiang* encompassed ten or more villages (which generally contained from 20 to 100 households). Census records from the Han dynasty indicate that the average household size was between 4.5 and 5.0 persons. According to the Rituals of Zhou, children were recorded in the household registers once they reached the age of 'teething' (defined as 8 months for boys, 7 months for girls), a reflection of the high infant mortality within the first six months of birth common to all premodern populations.

[11] Given the dramatic militarization of society during this period, the registration of weapons is hardly surprising. But the major polities adopted different policies toward private possession of weapons. In the southern Chu state, where weapons are wholly absent from tombs before the fifth century BCE, roughly half of all male tombs from this era contain weapons along with other artifacts that were the personal possessions of the individual. Qin tombs, by contrast, contain no weapons at all. Apparently the Qin officials kept weapons secured in state arsenals and distributed them to soldiers only when they were on active duty.

ment also served as a basis for evaluating the performance of local officials and rewarding or penalizing them accordingly.

In the absence of actual population registers from the Han it is difficult to determine to what extent the blueprint for population registration laid out in the Rituals of Zhou was realized in practice. But the available evidence suggests that it was. There are frequent references in Han texts to the annual household surveys. Household surveys (corresponding to the 'minor assessment') were conducted in the eighth lunar month, and local officials relayed aggregate information to the central government through a procedure referred to as 'submitted accounts' (*shangji*; corresponding to the 'major assessment') in the third lunar month. None of the Juyan documents – which, we must keep in mind, comprise a special case since they are registers of soldiers and officers stationed at a frontier garrison – are household registers, but, as noted above, collectively they do contain all of the data that is specified in the Rituals of Zhou.

By the second century CE, however, the Han government began to lose effective control over its population and resources. The heavy burden of taxation and labour service compelled many farmers to seek refuge under the umbrella of a powerful class of landowning families known as the Great Clans who dominated the Han civil service and were able to use their political clout to shield their properties from taxation. Much of the population was reduced to the status of bondservants who owed service to their masters but were no longer independent households and thus shed their public duties. The small family farm economy gave way to a far more autarchic manorial economy. The rise of the manorial order also curtailed the vibrant commercial exchange of the early Han period, and the circulation of money fell dramatically. In the mid-second century CE the Han state introduced a new household tax collected in cloth, and in 198 it repealed the poll tax and made the household cloth tax the centrepiece of a new tax system known as the 'household levy' (*hudiao*). The hudiao system on one hand acknowledged the diminished use of coin in both state finance and private exchange, while shifting the basis of taxation from the individual to the household on the other. Unable to conduct thorough censuses of individuals and property ownership, the state sought to levy taxes and labour services on the household as a collective unit.

State landownership and the emergence of the Equal Field system

The Han dynasty fell in 220, ushering in an era of political disunion, foreign invasion, and constant warfare that would last until the end of the sixth century. China was briefly unified under the Western Jin dynasty (280–317), which immediately conducted a census as a first step toward rebuilding the fiscal system. The census of 280 counted only 2.46 million households, however, less than a quarter of the 10.68 million households in the last national census of the Han in

157. Population losses from a century of civil war certainly exacted an enormous toll. But the reduced figures also reflected the disappearance of much of the population into bond-servitude under the dominion of the Great Clans. The Jin attempted to reverse this trend by offering land allocations (*ketian*) of 50 mu (2.3 ha) for each able-bodied adult male and 20 mu for adult women. The purpose of this law was to provide a minimum level of subsistence to allow farming families an independent livelihood. The extent to which the ketian policy was actually implemented remains unclear. In any case, the Jin capital of Luoyang was overrun by nomad invaders in the early fourth century and the court was forced to flee southward to the Yangzi Delta region. Although the Jin dynasty survived, imperial authority was reduced to a mere shell under which the Great Clans gained dominion over the population and economic resources.

Chinese rule was preserved in south China during the next several centuries under the Jin and a series of successor dynasties, but the balance of power swung in favour of nomad conquerors from central Asia who gained control of the traditional Chinese heartland of the Yellow River valley. The Tuoba confederation – cousins of the Turks – created a powerful military state in north China and took the Chinese dynastic title of Northern Wei (386–534). The consolidation of Northern Wei rule restored some measure of order, although the Tuoba monarchs relied on military clientage rather than a civil bureaucracy to govern local society.

Emperor Xiaowen (r. 471–499) undertook a series of bold initiatives aimed at remaking the Northern Wei into a centralized bureaucratic empire in the Chinese mould. Xiaowen sought to create a single ruling class by promoting intermarriage between the Tuoba nobility and select Chinese aristocratic clans. Xiaowen also encouraged the Tuoba to adopt Chinese language, dress, and customs. In 480 Xiaowen moved the Northern Wei capital from Pingcheng along the Great Wall frontier to the former Jin capital of Luoyang. More than a symbolic gesture, the relocation of the capital epitomized Xiaowen's commitment to building a settled agrarian empire.

While Xiaowen sought to woo Chinese aristocrats to participate actively in his government, he was also determined to solidify the fiscal foundations of the state. In 485 Xiaowen launched a new land allocation policy known as the Equal Field (*juntian*) system. Under the Equal Field system each household received lands in proportion to its labour power, divided into two types of tenure: permanent lands, which included lands planted with mulberry trees, fruit orchards, and other timber resources; and personal share lands, consisting of arable fields. An adult male would receive 20 mu of permanent lands and 40 mu of personal share lands (and adult women half that amount), with additional lands awarded to households with slaves or ploughing oxen. The personal share lands would be doubled or tripled in areas where the land was less fertile or the population sparse. In principle, the permanent lands passed on to the household head's heirs, while the personal share lands reverted to the state for reallocation after the holder's death. Sale of land was forbidden. Land allocations would be adjusted annually to account for changes in the size of the household and its number of oxen.

Although the Equal Field system harked back to the ancient Confucian ideal of an egalitarian division of lands among the people, its immediate goals were more practical: to maximize the amount of land under cultivation and ensure a stable revenue base for the state. The allocation of lands based on the labour power of the household rather than its consumption needs served more to equalize tax obligations than to guarantee a minimum level of subsistence. The 485 land law was also accompanied by a revised tax code in which the amounts of grain, cloth, and labour service owed to the state were directly proportional to the land allocation the household received. The permanent share allocation, intended for cultivation of the mulberry trees necessary for sericulture, was premised on the fact that households paid a substantial portion of their tax obligation in the form of silk yarn and cloth.

The Equal Field system obviously posed a direct challenge to the Great Clan aristocracy. Although the land allocations were supposed to be administered through a new network of village and hamlet heads, ultimately implementation of the Equal Field system depended on the cooperation of the aristocrats who dominated the state bureaucracy. It is unlikely, therefore, that the 485 land law encroached on the existing landholdings of powerful aristocratic families. Instead, the lands allocated under the Equal Field system consisted of abandoned fields or uncultivated wilderness. Land allocations most likely were carried out in less populated areas where land remained relatively abundant. The only direct evidence for the operation of the Equal Field system comes from land and household registers compiled at the frontier garrison town of Dunhuang in 547, during the Western Wei dynasty. These documents depict the Equal Field system functioning according to its original design, with lands regularly repossessed from deceased householders and reallocated to new ones. The successful implementation of the land allocation policy in an area of acute land scarcity far from the capital is even more remarkable. We must also keep in mind, however, that Dunhuang was a key military garrison, and military conscription was an especially crucial component of the Equal Field system there. It is likely that the Northern Wei and its successors monitored the operation of the land allocation policy in such areas with special diligence.

Rent by divisions among its tribal leaders, the Northern Wei collapsed in 534. But one of its successor regimes in north China, the Sui dynasty (581–618), conquered the south and re-established a unified empire in 589. The Sui retained the Equal Field system of the northern dynasties, but introduced some modifications. Extra land allotments for households owning slaves and oxen were eliminated, a change that adversely affected more affluent families. In an effort to inculcate loyalty among its officials, the Sui awarded substantial land grants based on bureaucratic rank. Most importantly, the Sui sought to merge its militias with the Equal Field system. The militias were assigned to local jurisdictions, mostly in the northwest, and received lands allocated through the Equal Field system. Although the Sui intended to extend the Equal Field system to the entire empire, it is unlikely that the land allocation procedures were widely applied in the territories of the former southern dynasties. Rice agriculture required heavy investments of capital and labour to build and maintain irrigation systems, but periodic reallocation of lands would greatly diminish the incentive for making such investments. Moreover, the development of the south's agricultural potential had largely come at the initiative of powerful landholding families who had staunchly resisted any attempts by the rulers of the southern dynasties to restrict their landholdings.

The short-lived Sui dynasty was soon displaced by the Tang (618–907) imperial house, which was also descended from the hybrid Tuoba-Chinese aristocracy cultivated by the Northern Wei. The Equal Field system of land tenure was renewed as the law of the land, though as noted above it probably was not enforced in the rice-growing regions of the south. Population growth and the pressure it placed on the land also hindered full application of land allocations in north China. Land and population registers from the frontier oasis towns of Dunhuang and Turfan dating from the period 690–769 reveal that households received their full allotment of permanent field lands (intended for the cultivation of mulberry orchards and fibre crops), but only a fraction of the statutory amounts of the personal share lands that reverted to the state upon the death of the holder. Although the personal share lands were reallocated as required by statute, clearly most land was held as permanent property of the household, indicating a shift toward *de facto* private ownership.

In 624 the Tang introduced a taxation system premised on the Equal Field system of land tenure, known as *zu-yong-diao* after its three principal components: taxes paid in grain (*zu*) and cloth (*diao*) and a requirement of labour service (*yong*). In contrast to previous practice, in which the conjugal pair of husband and wife (or 'bed') was the unit of taxation, the Tang shifted the basis to the adult male (*kekou* or *ding*). Since in theory each adult male possessed an equal amount of land, the rate of taxation was uniform: two shi (119 litres) of grain, two zhang (6.22 metres) of cloth (increased by 20 per cent if paid in hemp rather than silk), and twenty days of statutory labour. Labour service was often commuted to an additional payment of cloth, as was the zu grain tax in some southern provinces. Although the zu-yong-diao taxes were levied on individual adult men, taxes were paid by the head of the household. Women were exempt from paying taxes, although presumably they produced most of the cloth that was the principal item of taxation.

The fiscal structure of the Tang Empire – and the Equal Field landownership system in particular – suffered a mortal blow after the outbreak of the devastating An Lushan rebellion in 755. By the time the rebellion was quelled in 763 the rich agricultural heartland of the North China Plain lay in ruin and hundreds of thousands had perished. The Tang polity emerged from the rebellion a mere shadow of its former self, its basic institutions irreparably broken. The registered population fell by more than three-quarters, and the central government exercised effective authority only in the southern provinces where the Equal Field system had failed to take root. Consequently the Tang ministers were compelled to devise a new fiscal system. In 779 the chancellor Yang Yan launched a sweeping reform of the tax system which sought to restore direct taxation as the main source of state revenue.

Yang Yan's reform acknowledged that the Equal Field system of landownership was defunct, and along with it the zu-yong-diao tax system. Yang's plan formally abolished the zu-yong-diao assessments and created a new tax structure that came to be known as the Twice-a-Year Tax (*liangshuifa*). Households were ranked into nine property grades and assessed for a tax denominated in coin. Given the endemic shortage of coin, however, the household tax was generally commuted to commodities, primarily cloth. In addition, each household was required to pay a separate tax in grain based on the amount of land it owned. The household tax was collected in late summer and the land tax after the autumn harvest; hence the name Twice-a-Year Tax.

The Twice-a-Year Tax marked a fundamental and lasting change in economic philosophy. The principle of equity that underlay the Equal Field system and earlier measures to restrict the concentration of landholding was abandoned, never to be resurrected in any serious way before the PRC's socialist land reforms of the 1950s. Instead the state and its cadre of Confucian officials, conceding the reality of the uneven distribution of landownership, focused on implementing progressive taxation based on household wealth.

The development of the household ranking system in the Song dynasty

The Song dynasty (960–1276) is regarded as a transformational epoch in Chinese history that reshaped the fundamental social and political institutions of imperial China. Among the key features of this transformation were the decisive triumph of civil governance over military rule and the displacement of the aristocratic Great Clans as the dominant political and social elite by a more fluid scholar-official class steeped in Confucian education (Kuhn 2009). The changes in Chinese society and culture inaugurated during the Song period largely endured throughout the remainder of China's imperial era, which lasted until the early years of the twentieth century.

But the Song state was also beset by perpetual military crisis. From the time of the dynasty's founding, the Song had to contend with the powerful and hostile rival states of Liao and Xia on its northern frontiers. Humiliating defeats at the hands of both Liao and Xia over the course of the eleventh century were followed by the invasion of the upstart Manchurian state of Jin and the loss of north China, including the original Song capital of Kaifeng, in 1127. The Song dynasty survived and even flourished in south China, but in the 1270s it was finally overwhelmed by Mongol conquerors, who for the first time brought all of China under foreign rule. The military predicament of the Song required the mobilization of enormous resources to defend the empire's frontiers. In contrast to earlier dynasties which had relied on conscription of ordinary subjects into military service, however, the Song mustered large standing armies of professional soldiers – more than a million men at arms in total at their peak. The cost of maintaining these armies along frontiers that extended for thousands of kilometres imposed enormous fiscal and logistical burdens on the Song state.

At the same time, however, the Song presided over an economy enjoying a prodigious expansion unprecedented not only in Chinese history but perhaps in world history as well. This period witnessed the full flowering of intensive rice cultivation, technological innovations in metallurgy, textiles, and ceramics, and a sustained rise in labour productivity that fed growth in industry and commerce as well as agriculture. The population of the empire doubled and cities swelled along with the ranks of merchants and artisans, producing a vibrant and distinctively urban culture. A dynamic and highly competitive market economy burst through the flimsy constraints imposed by the state. Although Confucian learning, success in the civil service examinations, and careers in the imperial bureaucracy supplanted aristocratic pedigree as the source of social status and political power, wealth also reshaped the social hierarchy and became a key marker of social distinction.

The Equal Field system of landownership had been premised on the allocation of lands to families in proportion to their labour power and consumption needs. Thus tax rates were relatively uniform; in principle, every adult male had the same tax and labour service obligations to the state. With the demise of the Equal Field system and its replacement by the Twice-a-Year tax in the late Tang the basis of taxation shifted from adult males to the wealth – especially landholdings – of the household. But taxes were not levied directly on land or wealth. Instead, the Song dynasty devised a household ranking system that became the basis for direct taxation and by extension for civil registration.[12]

The origins and early development of the household ranking system are unclear; in some form it probably existed from the time that the Twice-a-Year taxes were instituted in the late eighth century. By the early eleventh century the Song enacted an empire-wide registration system that graded property-owning households into a set of ranks – five ranks in the countryside and ten ranks in the cities.[13] Property-owning households were registered as 'host households' (*zhuhu*), while propertyless

[12] This section is based primarily on Yanagida (1986). McKnight (1971) highlights some of the important institutional changes in the labour service system.

[13] One category of affluent families excluded from the regular ranking system was the so-called *xingshi hu* or 'influential households', a term designating families of active or retired officials who enjoyed generous exemptions from labour service. One official, writing in 1020, estimated that 'influential households' on average comprised 3–7 per cent of all the households in a given locality. See Yanagida (1986, 35).

households were designated 'guest households' (*kehu*) and exempt from most taxes. 'Host households' accounted for two-thirds of all registered households, and a much higher proportion in more economically developed regions such as the Lower Yangzi River Basin.

An edict of 994 ordered that labour service duties as village officers were to be assigned to first and second rank households; the ranking in turn was based on the number of able-bodied adult males (ding) and 'economic assets' (*wuli*) of each household (a nine-rank system for labour service assignments – in which the bottom five ranks were exempt from service duties – had been created in 980). In 1033 the court ordered the compilation of 'Five-Rank Ding and Property Registers' (*wudeng dingchan bu*). Although the registers recorded the names and vital information for the entire population, aggregate statistics were compiled at higher administrative levels only for numbers of households and ding; figures for women and minors usually went unreported. Heads of households prepared self-reports (*shoushi*) which they turned in to the village officers. The village officers were responsible for checking the veracity of these self-reports and compiling the Five-Rank Registers.

The registration system underwent significant modification in the 1070s, when the Song government enacted fiscal reforms to replace in-kind payment of taxes (such as the land tax collected in grain and cloth) and labour services with money payments. The Song also created a new system for local policing called *baojia* modelled on the five-family mutual responsibility units of the Qin-Han empires. In addition to the Five-Rank Registers used to calculate tax and service obligations, the state created a parallel registry for assignment of baojia duties, known as 'Fish-Scale Registers' (*yulin ce*) – apparently in reference to the maps accompanying the registers, on which the boundaries of small plots of land resembled fish scales – based on residential location. Despite its formal similarity to the ancient mutual responsibility units of the early empires, the baojia system did not entail the same kind of legal liabilities. Although primarily intended to provide police services, the baojia units gradually took over civil responsibilities such as tax collection from the village officers. By the beginning of the Southern Song period both civil and military control on the village level was entrusted to the baojia officers. At the same time many of the local labour service duties formerly discharged by drafting taxpayers were now performed by hired workers. The baojia headmen, conscripted from the affluent first and second rank households, were compelled to shoulder a heavy burden of responsibilities, including making good on shortfalls in tax payments by households within their jurisdiction.[14] The onerous duties and obligations of the office prompted village elites to shirk appointments as baojia headmen.

[14] The most important unit of local administration in the Southern Song was the *dubao*, which generally encompassed 1,000–2,000 households. The *dubao* headmen, who served annual terms on a ten-year rotation, were the pivotal figures in local administration.

The choice of criteria for ranking households varied among different regions. The amount of arable land seems to have been the most prevalent criterion, but tax quotas, the amount of seed sown, and total economic assets were also used. According to a census conducted in 1033, ranks 1 and 2, comprising 13 per cent of all 'host households', owned more than 100 mu (5.6 ha) of land, while 54 per cent of landowners were placed in rank 5 (fewer than 20 mu of land).[15] The technical problems of ranking households were even more acute in the towns. Generally urban residents were ranked according to the amount of rent collected on urban real estate (*linqian*), the volume of business income (*yingyunqian*), or their economic assets (*wuli*). The more finely-graded scale for urban households (ten ranks instead of the five used for rural inhabitants) suggests a greater concern with the accuracy of assessments in the absence of a readily measurable standard such as arable land. But after the reforms of the 1070s the ding unit (able-bodied adult males) ceased to be factored into the determination of household rankings. This change marked a key shift in the basis of the imperial system of social control from individual adult males (who bore equal responsibilities) to households graded according to wealth. In effect the state condoned a social hierarchy determined by wealth.

By statute the registers were supposed to be updated every three years, but this requirement often went unheeded. More commonly, registers were updated when properties changed hands. In 1142, a decade after the Song government relocated to the southern capital of Hangzhou following the Jin conquest of the north, a universal cadastral survey was decreed for all of the territories remaining under its control.[16] The property ownership information produced by this survey – including maps indicating the location, size, and boundaries of each parcel of land – was recorded on 'Mortar Stone Registers' (*zhenjibu*).[17] The trend in the Southern Song, both in rural and urban areas, was to calculate the monetary value of family property (*jiayeqian*), including land, 'movables', and cash. Critics warned that the rich tended to hold a relatively smaller portion of their economic assets in arable land; thus determining household ranks solely on the basis of landholdings tended to penalize the less affluent. It was also observed that basing labour service duties and tax payments strictly on household rank created inequities, especially in the upper ranks. For example, well-to-do landowners with 300 mu of property – which placed them in the top rank – were liable for the same obligations as great landowners who owned ten times as much property.

[15] At this time the average size of a family farm in the rice-growing region of the Lower Yangzi Delta was 40 mu (2.25 ha). See Li (2003). Most families owned some land and also rented additional land.

[16] For a detailed study of the 1142 cadastral survey and its consequences see He (1998, 11–37).

[17] From this time onward it became common practice to compile three types of land registers: (1) 'fish-scale registers', which were organized by location of the property and specified the name of the owner (and tenant farmer, if applicable); (2) 'name-sorted registers' (*leixingbu*), which listed households by surname and recorded all of their property, regardless of location; and (3) 'rat-tail registers' (*shuweibu*), which listed households in a given locality in order from largest to smallest tax assessment.

First and foremost, the Song state used household rankings to assess taxes and labour service duties. Village officers were drafted from the top two ranks, while the lower ranks provided servicemen who performed menial tasks such as couriers, jailers, and labourers. After 1070 actual service was replaced by cash payments for the lower rank households. Extraordinary levies, such as 'harmonious purchases' (*hemai*; mandatory sales of grain to the state at fixed prices, or sometimes without any compensation at all), likewise were apportioned on the basis of household rank. Household rankings were also used for a wide number of purposes besides tax payments and labour services. The government regularly granted tax remissions during years of harvest failures, based on household ranks. The amount of grain one could borrow or receive free as charity from public granaries during times of dearth was also calculated according to household rank. Generally speaking such relief measures were directed at the fourth and fifth rank households (sixth rank and below in the cities). The use of household ranking to determine welfare entitlements anticipated some features of the modern hukou system, although in the latter case such entitlements were awarded based on residence rather than economic status.

The Song household ranking institution reflected crucial changes taking place in Chinese society and economy. The emergence of a dynamic market economy propelled a shift from labour power to wealth as the basis of taxation. Military and labour service occupied a much diminished role in the state's system of extraction: the Song relied on paid standing armies rather than military conscription, and many labour services were commuted to money payments. Wealth itself was increasingly measured in money rather than landholdings. The graded household ranking system introduced some measure of progressivity into the tax system. The household (the conjugal family) became firmly entrenched as the fundamental economic unit in both the private economy and the state fiscal system.[18] The original goals of population registration expressed in the *bianhu qimin* formula – 'to register households in order to make the people equal' – had been eclipsed by a new doctrine of equity that acknowledged the marked disparities in the distribution of wealth.

Rise and demise of the Lijia system in Ming-Qing China

The Mongol-ruled Yuan dynasty (1271–1368) preserved many features of Song political administration and social legislation. However, the founder of the Ming dynasty (1368–1644), Emperor Hongwu (r. 1368–1398), was determined to

[18] Song law and social practice went to unusual lengths to uphold the principle of inheritance through the patriline, for example by according widows rather than agnatic male kin control over the household's property until a male heir (minor or adopted sons) could formally inherit. See Ebrey (1984) and McKnight (1992).

eradicate the stain of Mongol rule from Chinese culture and revive what he believed to be the 'classical' principles of Confucian governance. Although Hongwu's policies evolved over his thirty-year reign, his basic goals remained constant: to restore the autarchic village economy of the idealized past as envisioned by Mencius and other Confucian philosophers, and to minimize (if not eliminate) the market economy and the inequalities it was believed to engender. In pursuit of this agenda the emperor formulated fiscal policies predicated on a return to unilateral in-kind payments to the state, conscripted labour service, a self-sufficient system of military farms, and payments to officials and soldiers in the form of goods rather than money. From the outset Hongwu established strong personal control over his bureaucracy. The early Ming model of government was characterized by strong autocratic rule at the top and the delegation of many of the functions of civil governance to village leaders at the bottom.

Initially Hongwu sought the cooperation of the local landowning elite in his imperial project. The revenue system he enacted in 1371 designated the wealthiest landowners in each county as tax captains (*liangzhang*) with responsibility for collecting and delivering grain taxes to the capital. By 1380, however, Hongwu became convinced that powerful landowners, in their capacities as both government officials and private agents, were thwarting his goals. He then reversed course, purging thousands of officials and confiscating the property of many great landowners. Hongwu refined his vision of social reform: the greatest priority, as he now saw it, was to free peasant farmers from exploitation by powerful landowners, corrupt officials and clerks, and the vicissitudes of the money economy.

In 1381 Hongwu introduced a new institutional framework of rural control known as *lijia*.[19] The lijia system organized rural society into uniform groups (*li*) of 110 households under the leadership of the ten wealthiest landowners, who served in rotation as head of the li over a ten-year period. The li headmen were entrusted with broad responsibility for local governance, including policing the village, adjudicating legal disputes, collecting taxes, and assigning duties for communal public works projects such as flood control and irrigation systems as well as corvée labour services owed to the state. Despite Hongwu's antipathy toward the Mongols, his government also followed the Yuan precedent of registering the population into four hereditary occupational groups. Civilian households, the great majority of the population, were liable for taxes levied in grain and other goods as well as corvée labour service; military households were stationed at garrisons and given lands to farm when not engaged in military duties; artisan and saltern[20] households

[19] The basic elements of this system had already been established at least in the Yangzi River Basin region beginning in 1370. See Luan (2007, 16–20). For an introduction to the Ming lijia system and its evolution, see Heijdra (1998).

[20] The salt monopoly was one of the major sources of government revenue. In order to discourage smuggling, the Ming state (following Yuan precedent) made employment at the salt works a hereditary occupation.

were obligated to provide either labour services or goods to the government. Land and population surveys carried out in 1387 and 1393 provided the benchmarks for refining the lijia system and establishing permanent tax quotas.

The Ming state conducted decennial household surveys, the results of which were recorded on 'yellow registers' (*huangce*). Each household submitted its own affidavit to the local li headman, who in turn forwarded the registers to the county, the lowest level of the imperial field administration.[21] The county registrar was required to check the individual household registers for accuracy, and then make four copies of the certified register (stamped with the registrar's seal): one was returned to the household, one was kept in the county record office, a third was sent to the prefectural government, and the fourth was delivered to the Ming national archive in Nanjing. An early seventeenth-century source reports that the national archive held 2 million volumes of yellow registers from the twenty-odd censuses that had been conducted by that date. However, only a small number of yellow registers (as well as some household affidavits and tax receipts) survive, nearly all from Huizhou prefecture in Anhui province (Luan 2007).

The yellow registers were divided into four sections: information from the previous census report; additions; subtractions; and current information. The registers recorded the name, gender, age, and corvée status of each household member (only males were liable for corvée) and the family property. Family property was defined primarily in terms of landholdings, which were separated into four categories – arable, uncultivated land (i.e. for dwellings), wilderness, and irrigation ponds – and itemized by each parcel of land and its tax quota. Draft animals, boats, and dwellings (including the number of rooms and whether the roof was tiled or thatch) were also recorded under household property. The main purpose of the yellow registers was to allocate corvée service duties and taxes for each household. The registers also stipulated the order for the rotation of li headman duties for the next ten years.

Despite the thoroughness of its recording procedures, the lijia system suffered from several fatal flaws. The 110-household units – subdivided into ten units of ten households (known as *jia*), plus the ten headmen – were artificial constructions that did not correspond to natural villages or even geographically contiguous areas. Even more significantly, the lijia system was premised on a static social order in which the number of households and their relative wealth persisted unchanged over time. The lijia units remained fixed at 110 households (usually with only minor

[21] Village officers included scribes (*lishu*) who were responsible for compiling the yellow registers, tax receipts, and other documents. This office was often combined with *li* headman duties. Widespread complaints about their abuse of power suggest that scribes wielded considerable power within local society (Luan 2007, 350–353). Although we still know little about the extent of popular literacy in late imperial China (the claim in Rawski (1979) that as many as 30–45 per cent of adult males were literate has been widely disputed), a wide range of written materials circulated at the village level. See Hayes (1985).

variations) and the number of adult males liable for corvée service (a unit known as *ding*) remained constant as well. Thus the Ming censuses repeatedly reported almost the exact same number of ding over a time span of 250 years.[22] Military, artisan, and saltern households were not permitted to divide under Ming law, and some of these households had grown to number several hundred members by the late Ming period. Thus lijia registration and tax quotas remained basically unchanged after 1393, and bore increasingly little resemblance to social and economic reality. The economic fortunes of individual households fluctuated; some families became extinct for lack of heirs, while others divided their property among numerous heirs; and the population itself was highly mobile.[23]

The tax captain system collapsed during the fifteenth century, and tax collection was absorbed into the tasks of the li headmen. The onerous burden of lijia responsibilities encouraged evasion on the part of the prosperous landowning class liable for duty as headmen. Local experiments in commuting service duties to money payments culminated in 1488 with the establishment of a national programme of 'equalized service' (*junyao*) that converted many forms of corvée labour to silver payments. Labour service became an individual rather than collective responsibility, and the lijia system in many respects was reduced to a mere paper relic. The number of registered households remained static, or in some areas actually fell, over time. Nonetheless, compilation of yellow registers and assignment of li headman duties were still carried out at the prescribed ten-year intervals throughout the Ming dynasty. Although it no longer played a meaningful role as an instrument of self-government, the lijia institution continued to function as a system of tax allocation.

In the Pearl River Delta region of Guangdong, for example, the li headship became a tax account unit (referred to as 'designated households' (*chenghu*) or 'amalgamated households' (*zonghu*)), with the headmen responsible for submitting taxes for the whole village or group of villages encompassed by the li unit (Katayama 1982; Faure 2007). This practice provided a strong impetus for the development of one of the most striking features of the social landscape of coastal south China, namely the single-lineage village. The li headship (actually called *tu* headship in Guangdong) typically was assumed by lineage heads, and the two institutions tended to merge into one. This merger was reinforced by the practice of combining the officially-prescribed community rituals (by which the Ming

[22] The number of registered households also remained constant, or even fell, beginning in the late sixteenth century as labour services increasingly became converted into money taxes assessed on households rather than *ding*. Although Ming censuses regularly counted adult (married) females, after 1450 no records of minor females were kept, even at the level of the li units – a reflection, perhaps, of the ritual principle that women lacked genuine social identity until they were incorporated into a husband's household.

[23] Yellow registers from Huizhou – a highly commercialized region, to be sure – show that 15–25 per cent of landholdings changed hands during any given ten-year period in the late sixteenth to early seventeenth century. See Luan (2007, 202–206).

founder, Hongwu, intended to strengthen communal solidarity at the village level) with ancestral sacrifices regularly conducted at the lineage hall. Indeed, the collection of taxes from individual households in many cases was conducted at the lineage hall. The zonghu 'no longer defined a residential group but rather a tax account as well as a property-holding entity' (Faure 2007, 8).

The tax account system enabled lineage leaders to exercise considerable control over private landowning as well as lineage estates.[24] Local officials in nineteenth-century Guangdong observed that the recorded names of the zonghu – colloquially referred to as the 'old households' (*laohu*) – had not changed for 300 years. Landownership rights were still invested in the zonghu; no change of ownership was recorded when lands were sold or inherited.[25] Those who purchased lands were required to submit their taxes to the zonghu, who then forwarded the tax receipts to the local government. The actual owners/taxpayers became known as 'child households' (*zihu*), an allusion to their subordinate relationship to the patriarchal zonghu. Not all lineages had zonghu; property-owners without corporate lineages became 'orphans' who had to attach themselves to the zonghu of another lineage in order to make their tax payments. Thus the power to collect taxes – and the informal leverage over local society that went along with it – became the hereditary property of the dominant lineages (Katayama 1982).

In neighbouring Fujian province lijia registration likewise retained important utility because of the legal privileges and landownership rights it entailed. Here as elsewhere the lijia system ceased to bear any relationship to actual households by the sixteenth century. The empire-wide land survey conducted by the Ming state in 1581–1582 acknowledged this new reality by shifting the focus of control from households to land. But landownership rights remained tied to the original lijia registration. New landowners had to acquire rights from the registered households. Even though a household might become defunct (for lack of male heirs), it still existed as a registration account. As a result a market for household registration developed in which new landowners sought to secure their legal standing by purchasing household registration (regardless of whether the household registration had any connection to the specific property). In his study of this phenomenon in Fujian, Michael Szonyi discovered a case from 1708 in which thirteen lineages

[24] Another distinctive feature of the Pearl River Delta region was the dominant position of corporate lineage estates as landowners. Surveys conducted in the 1930s found that lineage estates held 20–60 per cent of lands in the various counties of the delta (Ye and Tan 1985). Since corporate estates were not subject to the principle of partible inheritance they provided a means for preserving family property intact over time.

[25] In imperial China, property ownership was verified by sale contracts and tax receipts rather than by titles recorded with the local government. Strictly speaking, land sale contracts were supposed to be verified and endorsed by local government officials, but the substantial stamp taxes (which at different times ranged from 5 to 15 per cent) discouraged most from doing so. The lack of an official stamp did not lessen the validity of a contract in the eyes of most magistrates, however.

pooled funds to buy a household registration that was divided among 114 separate property owners, with the tax obligations apportioned according to the actual amount of land the individual owner possessed (Szonyi 2002, 78). This competition for land rights became an incentive for lineage formation, as lineages could provide a more stable institutional base for preserving these rights over time. Depending on the immediate social context, lineages might operate on principles of exclusivity (in order to concentrate rights and privileges in the hands of a few powerful families) or inclusivity (sharing rights with a larger group of families to build up their collective power).

In the wake of the demise of the lijia system as a functioning system of local self-government, then, the registered household became a fiscal unit that bore little relationship to actual households or kinship units. Under the subsequent Qing dynasty (1644–1911), the imperial state eventually halted household registration altogether.

The Qing dynasty never conducted a universal land survey, nor did it update earlier records in any comprehensive way. Instead, the Qing continued to rely on the Ming land survey of 1581–1582 in allocating tax quotas. By the end of the Ming most labour service obligations had been converted to payments in silver, although these payments continued to be assessed on individual adult males (ding). In 1712 the Qing established permanent quotas for the ding labour service levy based on the 1711 census returns, and in 1729 the ding levy was formally merged into the land tax on an empire-wide scale. Henceforth individual landowners paid a single lump-sum tax in silver. This step completed the process of shifting taxation (and by extension the state's control over local society) from households to land.

The early Qing tax reforms obviated the need to compile detailed information about the composition of households. Indeed, the household itself was no longer a unit of taxation. In 1668 the Qing suspended the compilation of yellow registers, which had served as the basis of the Ming land and labour taxes. In their place local officials were expected to conduct quinquennial surveys known as *bianshen*. Unlike the yellow registers, which were supposed to include data on all members of the household, the bianshen surveys merely gathered information on those liable for the ding labour service levy. The merging of the ding levy into the land tax in 1729 rendered the bianshen surveys obsolete, although they were formally ended only in 1772 (Hsiao 1960, 88–91).

Lijia units continued to exist in name under the Qing dynasty, but the primary mechanism of rural social control was a revamped baojia system of local policing modelled on the earlier Song institution. As in the Song, the Qing baojia system gradually absorbed tax collection duties and other civil responsibilities (such as famine relief). In 1740 the government officially transferred responsibility for population registration from the lijia units to the baojia headmen. But since the population registers no longer had any fiscal purpose, compiling population data became an empty bureaucratic exercise. As Skinner (1986) has shown, from the early nineteenth century local officials simply adjusted older figures with routine additions (since a growing population was taken as a sign of prosperity), leading to vastly inflated population statistics by the end of the century.

Most scholars regard the Qing baojia system as largely ineffective. Hsiao Kung-ch'uan (1960, 43–83), the standard authority on the subject, concluded that the baojia system deteriorated markedly over the course of the eighteenth century, inevitably doomed by the logistical constraints of a premodern bureaucracy confronted with the challenge of governing a massive empire undergoing prodigious population growth. William Rowe (1979) likewise has acknowledged that the communal ethos of the baojia units dissipated early on, although he insists that the baojia headmen retained some local importance as semi-professional police functionaries.

Although the Qing state undertook a far more activist agenda in social and economic welfare than contemporary European states (Wong 1997), in comparison to the earlier Han and Song dynasties its presence at the village level was minimal. The Qing imperial government wielded at best indirect control over local society, relying on mediation by local elites, especially by the local gentry (scholar-officials exercising informal leadership in their places of residence). The Qing period also witnessed the proliferation of a wide range of new intermediate social institutions – including merchant and artisan guilds, native-place societies, communal water control leagues, and an array of religious, fraternal, and philanthropic associations as well as the corporate lineages mentioned earlier – to which the imperial state delegated managerial responsibilities within local society (Rowe 2002). Although the nuclear family remained the fundamental socio-economic institution in Chinese society, it had achieved unprecedented autonomy from the attenuated reach of the imperial state.

Conclusion

Household registration underwent dramatic changes in purpose and practice over the two millennia of China's imperial history. The origins of household registration probably date back to the sixth century BCE, when rule by a panoply of noble lineages – and the tightly regulated kinship order that undergirded them – was being supplanted by newly rising autocratic states. The initial purpose of household registration was to transfer to aggrandizing princes the obligations formerly owed to the noble lords. Most importantly, autocratic rulers employed household registration for military conscription, raising massive infantry armies in pursuit of conquest of the Chinese world. Household registration enabled rulers to impose military-style organization and discipline on society as a whole. The legal doctrine of mutual implication – which rendered individuals liable for the crimes of their neighbours – epitomized the draconian nature of this form of social discipline.

Household registration also became a mechanism for equalizing the legal status of all subjects under the ruler's dominion and eliminating the privileges of the nobility. In order for these policies to be effective, rulers needed to root their subjects to their registered domicile and to curb geographic mobility. Here again household registration provided an essential tool of social control.

Not surprisingly, this rigid system underwent dramatic changes over the course of imperial history. Residence remained the basic principle of civil registration, but this legal principle failed to deter geographic mobility. After the final breakdown of the Equal Field landownership system in the eighth century, the imperial state essentially abandoned efforts to circumscribe geographic mobility. The demise of the Equal Field system also fostered the emergence of a dynamic market economy, and by extension a high degree of social mobility. Social hierarchy was increasingly based on disparities in the distribution of wealth rather than hereditary rank.[26] Consequently the imperial state shifted its focus toward graduated taxes assessed on land and property, although the household and the able-bodied adult male (ding) remained the basic units of civil registration. Universal military conscription disappeared after the fall of the Han dynasty in the third century CE. Subsequent dynasties mostly resorted to creating a class of hereditary military households (registered separately from the civilian population) to man their armies, although at times – most notably during the Song dynasty – armies were recruited from paid professional soldiers. Labour service, however, remained a salient duty of the civilian population and a principal focus of civil registration down to the end of the Ming dynasty.

The founding of the Ming dynasty in 1368 led to a renewed effort to restore an imagined 'classical' social order premised on an immobile and relatively egalitarian social order and village self-government. The lijia system embodied these principles of social organization and state–society relations. But the lijia system was ill-suited to a society undergoing dynamic social and economic change. By the second half of the fifteenth century fundamental contradictions in the principles of the lijia system had seriously eroded its utility as a means of social control. The lijia system combined two principles of registration – one based on common residence, and the other on landownership. Yet geographic mobility and oscillations in socio-economic fortunes brought these principles increasingly into conflict with each other. By the late Ming the registered members of a li might be widely scattered; in the words of one observer, 'members of the same li do not recognize each other

[26] The full flowering of Neo-Confucian social theories and political institutions from the eleventh century (Song dynasty) onward abetted this trend. Although Confucian philosophy was deeply opposed to the profit motive and economic aggrandizement, it condoned a social hierarchy based on 'merit' rather than heredity. This principle of merit was incorporated into the civil service examinations used to choose imperial officials in late imperial China, and the examinations themselves became the major barrier to the reconstitution of a permanent aristocracy.

by sight, and members of the same jia (ten-household unit) never tread on the same ground' (quoted in Luan 2007, 260). Labour service requisitions had been premised on assumptions of equity among households, and consequently became an onerous burden for the poor. The Ming state was slow to depart from the precedents of the dynastic founder, but in piecemeal fashion reforms were adopted that merged labour services into the land tax. Consequently civil registration shifted to registering property rather than households. The extant yellow registers – which provide accurate information on property ownership but not on people – confirm this change in priorities.

The full consolidation of labour service into the land tax (along with the freezing of the land tax quotas in perpetuity) did not come until the early eighteenth century. Thereafter civil registration became superfluous in the eyes of the state, and the population records of the late Qing dynasty are largely fictitious. But the old lijia registration system was not completely defunct; it endured as a means of validating legal rights to property ownership. It also became a crucial institution in the formation of corporate lineages, which in certain parts of south China exercised social and economic dominance over local society. Thus in the end the original purpose of civil registration had been turned on its head: rather than serving the state's interest in imposing legal and economic equality on its subjects, it was manipulated by powerful lineages to usurp public power and strengthen the importance of kinship ties in the allocation of social goods. Such was the power of bureaucratic inscription in Chinese culture – it conjured into existence social institutions that superficially conformed to state-sanctioned prescriptions of social order while at the same time undermining the state's direct authority over local society.[27]

The hukou system of contemporary China was spawned from motives markedly different from those of the imperial state. Whereas the imperial state envisioned civil registration as a means to create legal and economic equality within an agrarian society, the incipient socialist state of the 1950s sought to create a spatial hierarchy that redefined the relationship between city and country and privileged rapid urban industrial development. Geographic immobility had been a key goal of civil registration in the early empires, just as it was an essential component of the PRC's socialist development strategy. But the imperial state lacked the monopoly over social goods – such as food rations, housing, education, and medical care – that has made the hukou system an effective means of constraining geographic mobility. Instead, from the Song period onward the imperial state shifted the focus of civil registration away from direct control of the population (and its labour power) to

[27] Here I would dispute the analysis of Dutton (1988), who contends that the family and the household were coterminous under imperial registration systems and that the baojia system successfully served the state's goal of nurturing a sense of moral community that enhanced the state's control over local society.

equitable allocation of the tax burden through graduated property taxes. One consequence of this shift was to transform household registration (and the legal rights attached to it) into a marketable commodity in ways that presaged the utility of the hukou in contemporary China.

Finally, we should note that until recently the hukou system also served the more subtle socialist goal of separating the individual from the family by tying registration to the work unit (danwei) and transmitting hukou status from mothers (rather than fathers) to children. Civil registration in the imperial era, by contrast, was premised on the conjugal household as the fundamental social unit. There is little doubt that the household registration systems contributed to the perpetuation of the family farm as the dominant socio-economic institution throughout China's imperial history. The economic transformation that has taken place in China since the 1990s has both diminished the significance of hukou as an instrument of social control and strengthened family solidarity. Economic growth has alleviated some of the scarcity of goods and welfare rights that had made the hukou a potent instrument of social planning, but it still remains an indispensable fixture of social life and economic livelihood. Reforms in the hukou system have stabilized the family institution, which has recovered much of its former significance as the keystone of Chinese social and economic life. Today, as in the past, Chinese do not simply passively submit to the civil registration regime imposed by the state. Rather, civil registration provides the institutional framework within which households develop strategies to secure their economic welfare and a stable foothold in the social order.

References

Bray, D. 2005. *Social Space and Governance in Urban China: The Danwei System from Origins to Reform*. Stanford, CA: Stanford University Press.

Cheng, T. and M. Selden. 1994. 'The Origins and Social Consequences of China's Hukou System.' *The China Quarterly* 139: 644–668.

Du, Zhengsheng. 1990. *Bianhu qimin: chuantong zhengzhi shehui jiegou zhi xingcheng [Register the Population to Make the People Equal: The Formation of the Political and Social Structure of Traditional China]*. Taipei: Lianjing chuban gongsi.

Dutton, Michael. 1988. 'Policing the Chinese Household: A Comparison of Modern and Ancient Forms.' *Economy and Society* 17(2): 195–224.

Ebrey, Patricia Buckley. 1984. *Family and Property in Sung China: Yüan Tsai's Precepts for Social Life*. Princeton, NJ: Princeton University Press.

Fan, C. Cindy. 2008a. 'Migration, Hukou, and the Chinese City.' In *China Urbanizes: Consequences, Strategies, and Policies*, ed. Shahid Yusuf and Anthony Saich. Washington, DC: World Bank Publications.

—— 2008b. *China on the Move: Migration, the State, and the Household*. London: Routledge.

Faure, D. 2007. *Emperor and Ancestor: State and Lineage in South China*. Stanford, CA: Stanford University Press.

Hayes, James. 1985. 'Specialists and Written Materials in the Village World.' In *Popular Culture in Late Imperial China*, ed. David Johnson, Andrew J. Nathan and Evelyn S. Rawksi. Berkeley: University of California Press.

He, Bingdi. 1998. *Zhongguo gujin tudi shuzide kaoshi he pingjia [An Exegesis and Evaluation of Land Figures in China in Ancient and Modern Times]*. Beijing: Zhongguo shehui kexue chubanshe.

Heijdra, Martin. 1998. 'The Socio-economic Development of Rural China during the Ming.' In *The Cambridge History of China* 8(2): 417–578, ed. Denis Twitchett. Cambridge: Cambridge University Press.

Hori, Toshikazu. 1994. 'Chūgoku kodai no henkosei: tokuni shūryaku no hensen' [Household Registration in Ancient China, with Special Attention to Settlement Change]. In Toshikazu Hori, *Chūgoku kodaishi no shiten [Perspectives on Ancient Chinese History]*. Tokyo: Kyūko shoin, 271–303.

—— 1996. *Chūgoku kodai no ie to shūryaku [Family and Settlement in Ancient China]*. Tokyo: Kyūko shoin.

Hsiao, Kung-ch'uan. 1960. *Rural China: Imperial Control in the Late 19th Century*. Seattle: University of Washington Press.

Katayama, Tsuyoshi. 1982. '"Shindai Kōtōshō shūkō deruta no zukasei ni tsuite"' [The Tujia System in the Pearl River Delta of Guangdong Province during the Qing Dynasty]. *Tōyō gakuhō* 63(3–4): 233–266.

Kuhn, D. 2009. *The Age of Confucian Rule: The Song Transformation of China*. Cambridge, MA: Belknap Press of Harvard University Press.

Lewis, M. E. 2006. *The Construction of Space in Early China*. Albany: State University of New York Press.

Li, Bozhong. 2003. 'Was There a "Fourteenth-Century Turning Point"? Population, Land, Technology, and Farm Management.' In *The Song-Yuan-Ming Transition in Chinese History*, ed. P. J. Smith and R. Von Glahn. Cambridge, MA: Harvard University Asia Center, 135–175.

Luan, Chengxian. 2007. *Mingdai huangce yanjiu [A Study of the Yellow Registers of the Ming Dynasty]*, 2nd edn. Beijing: Zhongguo shehui kexue chubanshe.

McKnight, Brian E. 1971. *Village and Bureaucracy in Southern Sung China*. Chicago: University of Chicago Press.

—— 1992. *Law and Order in Sung China*. Cambridge: Cambridge University Press.

Rawski, Evelyn Sakakida. 1979. *Education and Popular Literacy in Ch'ing China*. Ann Arbor: University of Michigan Press.

Rowe, William T. 1979. 'Urban Control in Late Imperial China: The Pao-chia System in Hankow.' In *Perspectives on a Changing China*, ed. Joshua A. Fogel and William T. Rowe. Boulder, CO: Westview Press, 89–112.

— 2002. 'Social Stability and Social Change.' In *The Cambridge History of China* 9(1): 473–562, ed. Willard Peterson. Cambridge: Cambridge University Press.

Sato, Taketoshi. 1967. 'Kandai no jinkō chōsa' [Population Censuses in the Han Dynasty]. *Shūkan tōyōgaku* 18: 1–27.

Skinner, G. W. 1986. 'The Population of Sichuan in the Nineteenth Century: Lessons from Disaggregated Data.' *Late Imperial China* 7(2): 1–79.

Szonyi, M. 2002. *Practicing Kinship: Lineage and Descent in Late Imperial China*. Stanford, CA: Stanford University Press.

Wang, Fei-Ling. 2004. 'Reformed Migration Control and New Targeted People: China's Hukou System in the 2000s.' *The China Quarterly* 177: 115–132.
—— 2005. *Organizing through Division and Exclusion: China's Hukou System*. Stanford, CA: Stanford University Press.
Whalley, J. and S. Zhang. 2004. *Inequality Change in China and (Hukou) Labour Mobility Restrictions*. Cambridge, MA: National Bureau of Economic Research.
Wong, R. B. 1997. *China Transformed: Historical Change and the Limits of European Experience*. Ithaca, NY: Cornell University Press.
Wu, X. and D. J. Treiman. 2004. 'The Household Registration System and Social Stratification in China: 1955–1996.' *Demography* 41(2): 363–384.
Yanagida, Setsuko. 1986. *Sō Gen gōsonsei no kenkyū [Studies in Rural Social Organization during the Song and Yuan Dynasties]*. Tokyo: Sōbunsha.
Yates, R. D. S. 2002. 'Slavery in Early China: A Socio-Cultural Approach.' *Journal of East Asian Archaeology* 3(1–2): 283–331.
Ye, Xian'en and Dihua Tan. 1985. 'Lun Zhujiang sanjiaozhoude zutian' [Lineage Estates in the Pearl River Delta]. In *Ming Qing Guangdong shehui jingji xingtai yanjiu [Studies on the Social and Economic Formation of Guangdong in Ming-Qing Times]*. Guangzhou: Guangdong renmin chubanshe, 22–64.

2

Registration of Identities in Early Modern English Parishes and amongst the English Overseas

SIMON SZRETER

Introduction: Thomas Cromwell's founding injunction of 1538

On 5 September 1538, under the newly-Protestant monarch, Henry VIII, his Vicar-General and the most powerful man in the kingdom after Henry himself, Thomas Cromwell, issued an official injunction to every parish incumbent (parson, vicar, curate or rector) in England and Wales to make a written record in a book of every christening, wedding and burial ceremony conducted in the parish.[1]

Careful attention was given in Cromwell's instruction to a set of four crucial, practical issues: first, the question of the accuracy of the record; second, its safe-keeping; third, its security from being tampered with or altered; and fourth, how to ensure compliance with the injunction from the parish officials.

To ensure accuracy, the entries were to be made regularly each Sunday, after the community's attendance at weekly service, by the minister of the church in the presence of at least one other official witness – one of the parish's two churchwardens (a parish office originating in the twelfth to fourteenth centuries, whose primary function was to ensure the maintenance of the church fabric).

Secondly, the parish was to provide for the safe-keeping of the register book in a 'sure coffer'. Thirdly, for security this sure coffer, or safe, was to have two locks, with the parson having charge of one key and the two churchwardens the other. Thus the book was not to be available to any single person alone, offering the opportunity for tampering with its contents.

Finally, to ensure compliance, there was to be a penalty of 3s 4d (one sixth of a pound sterling, a very large amount corresponding to about a good week's wages for a labourer) for failure of an official to undertake the recording of the ceremony, with the funds so generated going to the churchwardens' primary tasks of repairing

[1] The following details are drawn from Tate (1969, 44).

the church, presumably giving them an additional incentive to keep the incumbent to his new task.

To our eyes today there appears to be one apparent design weakness in Cromwell's set of safeguards to ensure the system's completeness and integrity. There is an absence in Cromwell's careful set of provisions of any fines or penalties imposed on the lay population for failing to register a vital event, although there were, at least, no fees or taxes attached to the process, which could have been a deterrent, especially to the poor. As I will argue in the next section, in fact this may not have been an oversight at all but, rather, a vital clue to understanding one of Cromwell's most cherished intentions for the scheme and, indeed, those of his Tudor successors, most significantly Elizabeth I and her advisers, architects of the English nation's extraordinary innovative national social security system, the Poor Laws.

Parish registration in early modern England and Wales, 1538–1794: the creation of a system of civil rights by an exclusionary confessional state

During the next sixty years Cromwell's initiative was considered to be sufficiently important that the injunction was repeated by all three of Henry's Tudor successors, first by Edward VI in 1547, who added a modification that the proceeds of all fines were to be allocated to the parish's poor. During the five-year reign of Mary, 1553–1558, when there was an attempt by the Crown to bring England back to the Catholic faith, the practice of keeping the parish registers in the manner set out by Thomas Cromwell was continued. The only modification to the registration system during this intermission of official Catholicism was attempted by Cardinal Pole in 1555 and again in 1557 when he required his bishops to ensure that the names of sponsors (godparents) were entered in the baptismal registers, an issue of particular interest to the Catholic church (Tate 1969, 45).[2] This stipulation was promptly

[2] By 1557 Pole had become Archbishop of Canterbury, in succession to Thomas Cranmer, who was burnt at the stake by Mary for heresy. Pole's effort would appear to reflect a direct influence of Catholic practices established in parts of Spain, following Mary's marriage to Philip II in 1554. Granville Edge reports that Cardinal Ximenes, as Archbishop of Toledo, had attempted to introduce written parish registers in 1497, and Edge speculated that Thomas Cromwell might have conceived the idea of such written parish registers for England in emulation (Edge 1928, 354–355). My colleague at St John's, Dr Peter Linehan, scholar of the Spanish late medieval church, traces Cardinal Ximenes's initiative to an original innovation of written registers made in Spain half a century earlier by Bishop Alfonso of Burgos in the record of his Diocesan Synod (gathering of the clergy) of 17 May 1443. It is recorded that he there gave as an Instruction, 'That priests write the names of godfathers and godmothers of the baptised infant and keep it safe in a book in the cupboard in the sacristy, with a penalty of one week's wages for non-compliance', also stipulating that at the baptism there should not be more than one 'padrino' or 'madrino' (male and female sponsors). This account is from the record of Burgos Synodal Compilation of 1503–1511, item 262, in García y García (1997, 195). This focus on the recording of godparents, as

dropped by Elizabeth I when she re-issued in 1559, under her new Protestant authority, Cromwell's original registration edict.

After four decades of further operation of the registers, towards the end of her reign Elizabeth I approved the proposals of her ecclesiastical hierarchy meeting at Canterbury in 1597 to institute a significant upgrading in the various practical arrangements to ensure the fidelity of the registers' information and to safeguard their permanence. From 1598 it was ordered that the originals of the registers in each parish church should now be entered on superior quality parchment to be purchased at the expense of each parish. Furthermore, all the old entries in the cheaper paper registers were now to be copied into the new high quality registers to preserve them. Secondly, the weekly entries were now to be made by the minister in the presence of both churchwardens and all three officials were to sign the foot of each page in the register to attest to its accuracy. Consequently the 'sure coffer' of safe-keeping was now to have three separate locks and three keys. Thirdly, a new method of 'quality control' by the community was introduced, in that the entries of each previous week were to be read out to the congregation after the Sunday service allowing public scrutiny of the accuracy of the entries. Finally, another important innovation was the provision that the churchwardens would be responsible for transmitting once a year to the diocesan registry a complete transcript of all the preceding year's entries, thereby greatly ensuring the preservation of the records by institutionalizing an archived duplicate, while also establishing the facility for magistrates and legal practitioners of a single location within each diocese for consulting all its historic parish registers (Tate 1969, 45).

Of course we recognize in all this a very contemporary theme of the central state dreaming up a whole set of time-consuming tasks for local officials to carry out. Given that the role of churchwarden, though ubiquitous, was an unpaid voluntary role taken on often in rotation by respected members of the local community, and that the curate gained no fee for making entries in the register, it is an intriguing testimony to the authority and vigour of the youthful post-Reformation state and its new, Anglican church (according to the *Oxford English Dictionary* the term's first recorded use was in 1598 by the future James I) that a large proportion – several thousand – of the sixteenth-century registers of England's 10,000 parishes survive to the present day, indicating a high degree of compliance in 1598 (Wrigley and Schofield 1981, 2).

However, there were also other compelling reasons, beyond that of simple obedience to their religious leaders by the clergy of the established church and their

in Cardinal Pole's efforts to modify the English registers, relates to a long-standing preoccupation of the Catholic church with policing rules and customs about who and how many persons could be appointed as a child's godparents. This related also to its laws of incest and the seven degrees of affinity (which were reduced to four degrees at the Fourth Lateran Council of 1215 – on which, see also below, note 8), since appointed godparents, like those persons within the degrees of affinity, were also barred from marrying their ward. For theological explication, see Bossy (1985, 14–16).

flocks, for the populace's willing cooperation with compiling the registers – and for their careful preservation and historic survival. As can be seen from the foregoing, the central state and the church's hierarchy were going to a lot of trouble – and were prepared to give orders that implied considerable inconvenience and effort for local officials – apparently in order to ensure that the parish records of christenings, marriages and burials were kept as accurately and securely as possible. One major reason for all this was that from their instigation Thomas Cromwell had deliberately created the parish registers to serve as legal documents which would be valid in a court of law, stand up to hostile cross-examination and so provide security of title to property and to the intergenerational transmission of property for that substantial proportion of the nation's community who had items of value, even if not land itself, to pass on to widows, children and other relatives. Why? As I have argued elsewhere it is likely that there was genuine demand for this service (Szreter 2011, 337). The English populace probably enjoyed the most widely diffused ownership of modest amounts of individually alienable property in Europe at this time, rendering the issue of inheritance legally problematic for a much greater proportion of the populace than throughout much of the continent, where property was subject to stronger customs of patrimonial ownership and transmission.

In containing this legal, indeed civic, rationale as a motive in their design, the early modern parish registers of England (and Wales) constitute, I think, a historic innovation in law and government of some magnitude. They may well represent the first general registration system in history created to serve the civil and legal needs of a populace (Chapter 8 in this volume by Looijesteijn and van Leeuwen describes a wide range of such systems in Holland at this time but none of them general to the whole populace, due to Holland's confessionally-divided population, partly a consequence of its systemic economic reliance on immigrant labour). This novelty has perhaps been obscured from view until recently by the fact that the registers were maintained by ecclesiastics, parish incumbents and their bishops, not by secular civil servants. With their ecclesiastical administrative structure of collection and compilation, the English parish registration system appears to resemble the other *ancien régime* parish registers established by the Catholic church in the previous century by Archbishop Ximenes in Toledo and also by the French Catholic state almost contemporaneously with Cromwell's initiative, through the Villers-Cotterêt Ordinance, 1539. However in both these Catholic cases the documented motive for creating the register of communicants is believed to have been primarily ecclesiastical, not legal-civil. A key difference, therefore, was the equal attention given to burial registration in the English scheme, a neglected feature of the Catholic systems.[3] In contrast, in the English case we have a clear and public

[3] Lacking the English design as a system to facilitate inheritance, there was no equivalent strong motive for recording burials accurately and hence it has been a curse for French historical demographers that most of their parish registers fail to record deaths efficiently before the late seventeenth century (Wrigley

statement issued by Cromwell to the Justices of the Peace in every county explaining that the primary function of the parish registers was to provide individuals with attested family and kinship records with which to avoid or settle legal inheritance disputes. The registers were: 'for the avoiding of sundry strifes and processes and contentions arising from age, lineal descent, title of inheritance, legitimation of bastardy, and for knowledge, whether any person is our subject or no'.[4]

Our conventional framework of historical periodization for thinking about the history of censuses, registration systems and the political and ideological relations between governors and governed in general envisages the period from the late seventeenth century through the eighteenth century as a crucial watershed era, encompassing the rise of Enlightenment and secular reason, scepticism at received religious doctrines, growing state toleration for religious diversity, and the emergence of a commercial and civic society and of an accompanying liberal theory of citizens' rights. Thus, Lynn Hunt has recently published a book titled *Inventing Human Rights* (2007), which, she argues, occurred during the later eighteenth and early nineteenth centuries.[5] Yet here we have, over two and a half centuries before most of the texts discussed by Hunt, an early sixteenth-century European monarchical and confessional state endowing all its non-voting subjects with the practical basis for the effective exercise of their individual human rights in relation to the fundamental issue of personal property rights, through a state-sanctioned legal identity registration system. Furthermore, before Elizabeth I's reign was over the Tudor state had also proceeded to endow all subjects with a 'legal personally enforceable right to relief' (Charlesworth 2010, 5, 35) through a universal social security system, the Poor Law, thereby also equipping them with the basis of that set of social and economic rights enshrined in the late-twentieth-century UN Covenant

and Schofield 1981, 2). In France the recording of baptisms was said to be in order to determine correct age of candidates to serve in ecclesiastical office. The innovation of parish registration was also an integral part of an expansive reforming package introduced by the French head of state to bolster the powers of the Crown at the expense of the church. Through articles 110 and 111 of the 192-article major reform legislation of Francis I, the French state attempted to prescribe uniform use of French in all judicial acts, notarized contracts and official legislation. In attempting to wean the clergy off Latin, burials and baptisms entered in French were now to be signed off by notaries. On fifteenth- and sixteenth-century Spain, see above, note 2. The Council of Trent in 1563 ruled that all Catholic parish priests should keep records of baptisms and marriages but was silent on burials.

[4] Cromwell issued his circular to Justices with this explanation in order to scotch rumours circulating that the parish registers would be used for tax-raising purposes (a use to which they were never put by either the Tudors or the Stuarts) (Elton 1985, 259–260).

[5] Probably the most influential general study of these matters, reproducing such a chronology, has been Benedict Anderson's *Imagined Communities* (1991). See also Bayly (2004). Though never producing a study as carefully documented and chronologically precise as these three historians' works, the influence of Michel Foucault's thesis of the rise of a state focus on 'biopower' has also been conducive to viewing the century of the Enlightenment as a crucial watershed in government practices, as also further elaborated by the historian of statistics, Ian Hacking (Foucault 2007, 311–358; Hacking 1991, 181–195).

on Economic, Social and Cultural Rights, which remain today a dream for the citizens of many of the Covenant's democratic signatory states. How could it be that an early modern monarchy and confessional state could have not only conceived but implemented such a system – as a practical, governmental, social and economic reality, whose constitutional and philosophical principles, the historians of political ideas tell us, were not going to be invented for a further quarter millennium?

It is also of course the case that we tend to define as civil registration systems those which were created from the nineteenth century onwards, in contradistinction to the earlier systems of ecclesiastical registration found in many European countries. A distinguishing feature of such 'modern' civil registration systems is supposedly that they register the biological events of birth and death, not the religious rites of baptism and burial, and that, by acts of liberal nation states in the nineteenth century, they were deliberately created to be 'secular', applying to all citizens regardless of religious faith. It would seem to be particularly anachronistic, or perverse, therefore to claim that a state-sponsored system registering the ceremonies of the established church, administered by its parish incumbents in the middle of the century of the religious wars of reformation and counter-reformation, could possibly be characterized as a civil registration system. However, perhaps we touch here upon a further and much more subtle politico-ideological purpose, which also lay behind Cromwell's injunction, something which even Geoffrey Elton, despite his suspicions and for all his intimate acquaintance with the Tudor governing elite, does not seem to have considered.

Was Cromwell's innovative institution in fact also a measure whose ingenious design was intended, in the long term, to act to disenfranchise from their dynastic property and wealth all subjects who would not voluntarily consent to have their marriages conducted according to the Protestant liturgy of the established church, who would not have their children christened by the Church of England's ministers, and who would not consent to be buried according to its rites? For such recusants and dissenters there would be no legally-valid set of records created to ensure their legal inheritance in the brave new world of the Church of England. Thus, I would suggest Thomas Cromwell's political motive lay lurking in the final, apparently casual clause of his statement to the Justices of the Peace, explaining that the new registration system would also give 'knowledge whether any person is our subject or no'. Given that the English monarch was also head of the established church, whether a person was 'our subject or no' in this context in 1538 really meant 'whether Catholic or no', a meaning which would not have been lost on the contemporary magistrates who received the message from the king's Vicar-General.[6] Cromwell had thus created a brilliant, subtle, insidious and long-acting

[6] This also perhaps partly explains why no effort was made under the Tudors or Stuarts to extend the combined institutions of registration and Poor Law to Ireland or Scotland – because they were not Anglican. Whereas the established church in Wales was the Church of England, since the successful

weapon which used individuals' voluntary inclusion or exclusion of themselves and their families in the registers of the established church as a means to acquire or forfeit recognition of their legal status and civil rights to transmit property. If a correct inference, this then would explain the surprising lack of any clauses compelling the populace to register, mentioned at the outset above as an uncharacteristic, apparent lapse in Cromwell's failsafe design for the system's operation. Cromwell was quite happy to allow those rejecting the new universal faith of the established church to exclude themselves from the new registers, which were so carefully constructed to be public records of permanent legal validity. This was to place themselves, their families and their property outside the legal registration system and at a permanent economic disadvantage to all others in society.[7]

I think, then, that this line of reasoning may provide us with a plausible political motivation, appropriate to its proper historical context. This motive was not dissimilar to that of the Catholic church's attempts, since the Fourth Lateran Council of 1215, to devise forms of parish registration as a means to distinguish between the faithful communicants and heretics.[8] Nevertheless, as so often happens in history, the institution which Cromwell launched in part to achieve his subtle political and ideological aim of gradually extinguishing the resources of dissenting families, also provided an important basis and model for English subjects, during the course of the next two centuries or so, to enjoy many of the civic virtues and legal services that only the much later civil registration systems of the nineteenth

constitutional absorption of Wales into the kingdom of England by Henry VIII through the Laws in Wales Acts of 1536 and 1543, by contrast in Ireland, though Henry VIII was declared head of the church in Ireland, the majority of the population and their priests remained staunchly Catholic and the importation of Protestant settler landlords only further ingrained popular Catholicism. Scotland, meanwhile, though also becoming officially Protestant, adopted a distinctively Calvinist variant of Presbyterianism, with the formation of the Scottish Kirk in 1560. It also, of course, remained a separate sovereign state throughout the period until its accession into the United Kingdom in 1707, and therefore the issue of whether or not to extend the English registration and Poor Law systems to Scotland did not arise in either the sixteenth or seventeenth centuries. With thanks to Paul Slack for Poor Law advice.

[7] There is an intriguing long-term historical analogy here with William the Conqueror's strategy in creating the Domesday Book, using the power of written record in documents designed to register a legal decision in enduring form to both create and then maintain in perpetuity the desired form of polity, with some individuals and their issue economically included and others excluded (see Hyams 1987, 127–141; Baxter 2012). I am grateful to Urvesh Shelat for drawing my attention to this and to Dr Stephen Baxter for these references.

[8] The policy of 'registering' in some way the baptized and communicant members of the church, through an annual review at Easter confession and for receiving communion, was originally conceived as long ago as the Fourth Lateran Council of 1215. In a predominantly oral culture and with a largely illiterate clergy the Lateran Council of 1215 envisaged 'registration' to take a spoken form of affirmation, through personal presentation before a clerical 'witness'. Clause 21 prescribed that, 'on reaching the age of discernment', the faithful should present themselves individually to their own parish priest for confession and absolution at least once a year at Easter, or else be debarred from entering their church and be denied a Christian burial (Tanner 1990, 245). I am grateful to Dr Peter Linehan, for this reference.

century were to provide in the rest of Europe for the citizens of liberal nation states in the post-Enlightenment period.

Once created, the parish registration system subsequently flourished and developed into a comprehensive and efficient system, which persisted not just for decades but for centuries. This is a remarkable historical fact, given not only the modest literacy rates in the populace,[9] but also the radically devolved and essentially voluntary nature of the scheme. In order to explain the popularity of registration and the consent of the populace to continue to use parish registration in a nation that in the course of the seventeenth century became, first, religiously bitterly divided to the point of civil war and then religiously plural as a statutorily-recognized fact (the Act of Toleration of 1689), we need to understand how certain crucial further legal and social developments provided important incentives for all to participate. Constitutional and legal developments came to amplify yet further the importance and value of the parish registration system for English subjects of all kinds, rich, middling and poor. It was this almost universal appeal and genuine functional value of the parish registration system to virtually all persons, in their variety of economic circumstances – not just those with property to dispose of – which probably accounted for the persistence and survival of parish registration as a universal practice, despite the practical awkwardness of maintaining it in a society of relatively limited literacy, growing religious diversity, and widespread (if not as widespread as elsewhere) poverty.

If we return now to the narrative history of successive legislative modifications, we can explain how the Henrician and Elizabethan parish registration system acquired its widespread social appeal and how it managed to survive the turmoil of England's century of constitutional and religious revolution, the literal decapitation of the head of the Anglican church, Charles I, and the decade, 1649–1660, of parliamentary Commonwealth and Puritan rule under Oliver Cromwell's Protectorate.

In 1598 when Elizabeth I supported her bishops' efforts to upgrade further all aspects of the registration system to give its records the legal virtues of accuracy and permanence, this was also the year in which her government promulgated the first of two epochal statutes which established the legal basis of a comprehensive national social security system for England and Wales of a sort which had never been seen before. These were the Poor Law statutes of 1598 and 1601, which followed a number of earlier attempts, notably in 1536, 1547 and 1572, to devise a satisfactory administrative solution to the perennial problems for the poor of periodic high prices, unemployment, illness, old age and orphanhood (Slack 1988, 1990). A crucial, innovative feature of the Poor Law from 1601 onwards was that all property-owners in every parish were compelled to contribute to a fund to support the poor of their parish. For the next two centuries every householder in the parish was rated

[9] In 1540 male literacy has been estimated at 20 per cent, female literacy at 10 per cent (Cressy 1980, 177).

in proportion to the value of their property holdings to contribute to the parish fund, and every individual with a legal settlement in that parish had an entitlement to support from the fund in times of hardship. Justices of the Peace, holding their appointments at the pleasure of the Crown – not at the behest of the local elites – scrutinized the annual rating list each year to ensure it was fair and adequate. The fund had no limit – a plea of lack of funds in the parish was not admissible in law. Poor individuals, if refused relief, had a well-recognized right to approach a magistrate (Justice of the Peace), in his court, even in his home or on the hunting field, state their destitution, explain that aid had been refused and ask for help. The Justices could, and often did, make an Order that relief must be given. This was not an appeals procedure; it represented a long-standing personal right that was eventually given a procedural formality in the terms of an Act of 1714. Parish officials were bound to assist the pauper and obey the magistrate's Order; failure to do so was contempt of court and officials incurred a personal liability (Charlesworth 2010).

Thus, not only did property-owning individuals now have a powerful interest in the efficient working of the parish registers to provide them and their heirs with uncontested legal title to their property, but so, too, did the parish's propertyless poor. Entitlement to a share of the parish's funds in times of difficulty was a right, and therefore a quasi-property, well worth having for oneself and one's children. An essential step to ensure this right was registration of all baptized children in the parish register, since the place of birth conferred any individual's primary right of entitlement (known as a person's 'settlement') in that parish, though for all women a correct marriage registration was equally significant, since on marriage a woman's parish of 'settlement' became that of her husband. It was possible to change one's place of settlement during the course of a lifetime, especially if moving to take up long-term paid work in another parish, but it was strictly observed by all officials administering the Poor Law that any individual could only possess one parish of settlement at a time.[10] Much of our historical knowledge of the Poor Law has been generated from documentation of legal disputes between parish overseers of the Poor Law concerning which parish was financially liable to support various mobile individuals, with the production of parish register evidence often playing a role in this (Snell 1987; Hindle 2004).[11]

[10] On the laws of settlement in their administrative practice, see Taylor (1989, *passim*); and on pre-1662 practice, see Hindle (2004, 306–325, 403–405, 431–432).

[11] The Poor Law of 1598 included a specific provision that vagabonds (those of no fixed abode) could be sent back to their place of birth, which presupposes of course the availability of the information on place of baptism contained in the parish registers for the use of Poor Law officials (Slack 1990, 61). While historians have not systematically studied the use of parish registers in relation to the Poor Law, see Snell's comments cited in Szreter (2007, n.17). Lorie Charlesworth's view, from her expert knowledge of the historical records of case law is: 'For settlement so far as I can tell, it is straightforward; the registers are accepted as proof of baptism, and therefore ok for settlement by birth proof. . . . I can find them mentioned in lots of cases . . . without any challenge' (personal communication).

Given the importance therefore of accurate registration to everybody in the parish, rich and poor, now that all were bound together by the Poor Law in this system of reciprocal financial obligations and entitlements, the declaration of a Puritan Commonwealth after the defeat of the king in the English Civil War required ideologically appropriate adjustment, if this scheme was to continue under the new regime. Consequently during 1653 and 1654, by executive ordinances of government, custody of the registers was taken out of the hands of ministers and placed with a new secular official, the 'Parish Register' (*sic*), elected by all ratepayers in a parish and approved by a magistrate. Justices of the Peace were also now entrusted with the solemnization of marriages, in place of ministers of the Anglican church, and civil marriages were legalized. Placing all registration functions in the hands of civil officials thus raised the problem of how to pay for their labour, now that the Anglican church and its clergy were no longer employed in this work by a confessional state as a free service. Consequently registration now attracted fees, set at 12 pence (equal to one shilling, one twentieth of a pound) per birth and baptism, and 4 pence per death and burial (Tate 1969, 46–47).[12] Thus, note also that a shift in terminology, from the ecclesiastical registering of ceremonies of the Anglican church of baptism or christening and of funeral rites to the civil registering of the biological events of birth and death, first occurs (but only temporarily until the Restoration of an Anglican monarch in 1660) in ordinances of the Commonwealth and Protectorate, for the obvious reason that the monopoly of the Anglican church was no longer official policy of the nation's government.

Not surprisingly, perhaps, given this novel financial disincentive of having to pay fees to register, the parish register records of the Interregnum decade are considered by historians to be the least well-kept or reliable before the late eighteenth century (when rapid urban and dissenter growth disrupted the accuracy of many) (Tate 1969, 47). Although the Interregnum registration ordinances became void with the Restoration of the monarchy in 1660 and Anglican ministers resumed their unpaid roles, three decades later, under William and Mary, an even greater financial disincentive to registration was put on the statute books when for the first time Parliament granted the Crown the right to levy a tax on the registers, 'for carrying on the war against France', of two shillings (2/-) per birth, 2/6 per marriage and 4/- per burial (Tate 1969, 48). Given its fiscal aims, for the first time it was therefore necessary also to provide penalties for non-compliance, a colossal £2 fine (40 shillings) for a birth not notified to the vicar within five days. Vicars were now to earn 6 pence from their customers for each registration entered in their books, or also face a £2 penalty as a sanction on them to ensure they policed the unpopular Act (which, however, they often neglected to do). The experiment in using parish registration for fiscal purposes ended after its five-year period of parliamentary

[12] Tate does not mention a fee for marriages.

licence expired in 1699 and was not again repeated for almost 100 years until 1783 (Tate 1969, 49–50). Again this was unpopular, and passed at a time when the Anglican hierarchy was already becoming extremely concerned at the failure of parish clergy to maintain their registers properly in the face of rapid population growth and the proliferation of dissenting congregations, and again the experiment was repealed in 1794 (Basten 2006, 43).

Parish registration among the English in North America in the early modern period, 1583–1800

Some dissenters, most particularly the Quakers (also the Methodists and some Catholic ministers), were keeping their own legally-valid registers from the late seventeenth century onwards in the new 'tolerant' English state ushered in by the Act of Toleration of 1689.[13] The Quaker registers perfectly exemplify how Cromwell's innovative institution, designed in part to exclude Catholic recusants from civil and legal privileges, was in fact coming to provide the model for a universal system. The common people in England appreciated the value to themselves of an identity registration system, and, as has been pointed out above, the creation of the Poor Laws added an additional, crucial dimension to the functional importance of registration in people's lives.[14]

However, there is also available to us as historians an interesting comparative methodology for evaluating further and refining the interpretation that has been put forward so far. During the century following Elizabeth I's consolidation of the parish registration system in 1598 and before the Act of Toleration in 1689, groups of Englishmen of various religious persuasions and with diverse motives left the land of their birth, with its Anglican registers, and went to settle in various trading posts and colonies, which subsequently coalesced, through the course of much conflict with the governments of the other European colonizing powers of the seventeenth and eighteenth centuries (principally Holland and France, respectively), into the British empire of the nineteenth century. It is thus possible to review the early histories of settlement in these diverse islands and territories to examine whether and for what reasons identity registration systems were considered at all important by the early modern English when they settled in lands lacking such ecclesiastical

[13] The Quakers were the first to start keeping their own registers – practically from their origins in the late 1640s onwards, exhorted to do so by their founder, George Fox (Vann and Eversley 1992, 15). The Act of Toleration of 1689 established that although the Anglican church continued to be the nation's established church, there was to be freedom of worship for dissenting Protestants such as Quakers, Congregationalists and Baptists (though not as yet for Catholics), subject to individuals giving an oath of allegiance to the Crown and their exclusion from holding public offices.

[14] Quaker registration was also linked to their own system of welfare funds. See Szreter (2007, 78).

systems of legal record, providing something of a laboratory for studying the circumstances under which registration systems of varying kinds were created.

The beginnings of the history of the formal British empire are often dated to Sir Humphrey Gilbert's claiming of Newfoundland for the Crown in 1583. However, throughout most of the early modern period not only was there no official interest in settling Newfoundland, but it was positively discouraged as a wasteful activity, since it was not viewed as a valuable producer of agricultural commodities but only as an abundant fishery. Thus, the first colony permanently settled with official approval and support in North America was Virginia in 1607. As regards our interest in the early history of identity registration, the government of Virginia provides an important first precedent which indicates that parish registration was, indeed, highly valued as a priority among the early modern English.

After its initial settlement from 1607, the Virginia Company's charter was revoked in 1624 and the colony transferred to royal authority as a Crown colony. Soon after, in 1632, in the context of a growing population, the Grand Assembly of Virginia required ministers from every parish to present themselves annually at court to provide a register of all burials, christenings and marriages (Shapiro 1950, 86). At this time the population of Virginia stood at just over 2,500, though it was to reach over 18,000 by 1650 and almost 60,000 by 1700 (42,170 white and 16,398 black inhabitants). It could be considered rather unsurprising, however, in a Crown colony, which was governed as a province (with its governor and his council appointed by the Crown and having right of veto and dissolution over the Assembly of representatives of the province's freeholders), that the Anglican parish registration system would be rapidly established. It might be argued that this does not necessarily provide evidence of the attitudes towards such systems of identity registration of the settlers themselves but rather of their governors – ultimately the Crown. This is why the comparative evidence provided by the early history of Massachusetts, the other most important and equally fast-growing early English settlement in North America, can be of considerable interest.[15]

[15] By 1650 the two principal New England settlements of Massachusetts Bay (including the counties of Maine) and Plymouth Bay between them had a population of just under 17,000. This almost equalled Virginia's total at that time of nearly 19,000 and between the two they constituted most of the 50,000 settlers in North America at that date (New York, Connecticut and Maryland comprised more or less all of the rest, each with just over 4,000 settlers). By the 1730s these two major settlements each contained about 120,000 inhabitants and were still at that date clearly the two most populous colonies in North America (though being fast caught up by Pennsylvania). On the eve of the American Revolution in 1770, of the 2.165 million people in the North American colonies, Virginia's population was greatest with 447,000 (about 40 per cent of whom were slaves). Massachusetts (still including Maine) had 267,000 and Pennsylvania followed with 240,000. Next most populous was Maryland with 203,000, then North Carolina with 197,000, Connecticut with 184,000, New York with 163,000, South Carolina with 124,000, and New Jersey with 117,000. All other states still had no more than half New Jersey's population in 1770. Source: Historical Statistics of the United States Millennial Edition Online, Eg1–59. With thanks to Dennis Hodgson for advice on these early American colonies' population totals.

New England was mainly populated by dissenters from the English established church and was settled independently of the English Crown. The New Plymouth colony of course was the first such to be settled in New England, with the arrival in 1620 of the 102 Separatist Dissenters, or 'Pilgrims', aboard the *Mayflower*. The subsequent Massachusetts Bay colony settlement dated from 1630 but was larger and was the first to be constituted by a self-governing charter. From 1691 it formally absorbed the Plymouth settlement and it also included from 1660 the counties of Maine (which only subsequently became a separate state in 1820).

Massachusetts was from the outset in 1630 a relatively independent political corporation, created by letters patent from the Crown, which gave the colonists control over the land and their own powers of legislative government (only in 1692 did Massachusetts reluctantly became a Provincial Colony by royal charter). The settlers formed a General Court immediately in 1630, as their legislative body, whose representatives were elected by all freemen of the colony, provided they were Christian. It is interesting for our purposes, therefore, that within just a further few years this more autonomous new colony had also passed its first registration laws, in 1639. It is furthermore extremely clear that the recording of property ownership for legal purposes was the main motive for the registration laws in the eyes of the twenty or so independent communities of colonists which by then comprised Massachusetts. Thus, the Massachusetts Bay colony's law convened by the General Court in Boston in 1639 stated: 'That there be records kept of all wills, administration, and inventories, as also of the days of every marriage, birth and death of every person within this jurisdiction' (Gutman 1958, 60).

At that time the population was mostly settled in twenty-two officially recognized, fairly widely-dispersed townships. According to Gutman,

> The records were to be kept by the recorder of each town, an appointed official whose job also included making records of the place of each man's house and lands, the judgements in every Court and a record of all purchases by the Indians and from the Indians.
>
> (Gutman 1958, 60)

It was also required that these records were certified once each year by the General Court itself, stipulating that without this certification they would have no legal status. Robert Gutman also notes, however, that 'The law did not specify who was to inform the recorder of these events, but whoever the person was, he was ordered to pay the recorder one penny for each event registered' (Gutman 1958, 60–61). Finally, any town failing to send its records annually for certification would be fined £2.

Gutman reports that two more laws were required in 1642 and 1644 to perfect this system (and then a third in 1657 because of rapid immigration and a further doubling in the number of townships and expansion in the area of the colony). The net effect of these additional laws was to place responsibility for collecting the information of births, deaths and marriages on each town's clerk of the writs, a legal officer of the colony's county courts, while the magistrates' court of each town was to replace the General Court as the authority granting legal certification to the record. From 1644 'all parents, masters of servants, executors and administrators' were charged to bring information of vital events to the clerk, with fines for neglect of this duty (Gutman 1958, 63). By 1645 the Plymouth Bay colony had also endowed itself with a General Court (it had initially been owned by an oligarchy), and the following year it passed its own registration law, which was very similar to the 1644 version of the Massachusetts law.

According to Gutman there was one further, final legislative change to the Massachusetts registration system in the pre-revolutionary period. This occurred after the English Crown revoked the truculently independent and self-governing colony's charter in 1684, replacing it, after protracted negotiations, with a new royal charter as the Province of Massachusetts Bay in 1692. However, this certainly did not result in the imposition of a parish registration system on the Anglican model in this religiously independent colony. Registration was now more entirely placed in the hands of the town clerks, to such an extent that they were no longer required to send copies of their records to the central certifying and archiving office of the General Court. Gutman argues that there was a logic to this because the town clerks were now appointed subject to the approval of the General Court and therefore they were in effect officials of the Court, such that their records acquired the same status as legal evidence as those of the Court itself. Gutman further explains that, given the widely dispersed nature of settlement in over eighty towns across the enlarged province of Massachusetts and the poor state of communications, this form of delegation, and local archiving of these legal documents, made good practical and administrative sense, 'Since the majority use of vital records during this period was as evidence in disputes in local courts', and hence there was also a new provision allowing the clerks themselves, rather than the central government, to issue certified copies of their records for use in courts of law (Gutman 1958, 71).

With no centralized administrative mechanism to check on the clerks' diligence, there was no system of penalties on the clerks for defective or missing entries. However, the question of how to ensure a full and accurate set of legal records, which as we have seen had always been a practical consideration of all English registration measures since Cromwell's original injunction of 1538, was not neglected. Instead it was to be achieved in a different way with a range of other incentives and controls. First, it was clearly stated in 1692 that the clerk 'is empowered and required to take an account of all persons that shall be born or die' (Gutman 1958, 70); second, the clerk was for the first time required to record the name and surname of parents of both the newborn and the deceased and to give the time of the event. To comply with this instruction would clearly require a relatively full and informed, firsthand interview with the relevant informant, and the stipulation to record all the collateral family detail was a well-judged device to guard against future falsification or attempts to tamper with the record, as was the insistence that the register book be made from high quality parchment. Third, the clerk was given a handsome incentive to ensure full compliance in his local population. It was the duty of *any* person 'related to or concerned for' a person born or dying to inform the clerk within thirty days (Gutman 1958, 70). The clerk was empowered to bring before the Justice of the Peace anybody in the county neglecting this duty, from whom the clerk would personally receive 5/- as forfeit if convicted. The clerk was also personally incentivized for routine registrations, for which he received a fee of 3 pence for each one; and also a fee of 6 pence for each subsequent copy supplied as a certificate for legal purposes (Gutman 1958, 70).

Thus, in the colony of Massachusetts, communities of independent Englishmen during the early seventeenth century, despite wishing to have nothing to do with the Crown and the established church, were nevertheless keen to endow themselves with a locally-devolved civil registration system which recorded their vital events and gave their record permanent legal validity, following practice in the mother country, primarily because they recognized the economic importance to themselves and their posterity of recording births, deaths and marriages, as of equivalent value to legal records of their property holdings and land purchases. It can also be seen that information on best practices regarding registration flowed in both directions across the Atlantic. This dissenting colony had devised solutions in the 1640s to a number of the practical problems which were to be faced and solved in similar ways in the following decade in the mother country during the Interregnum, when the Puritan regimes wished to redesign a registration system which dispensed with the services of the Anglican parish ministers. Fees had to be charged to pay for the work, and in the absence of diocesan discipline over parish ministers, the secular recording agent now had to be monitored and incentivized. In 1650s old England, as in 1640s New England, the mechanism of a fine was introduced to ensure regular transmission of copies of his register to the secular monitoring authority, for certification of legal validity and secure deposit (Tate 1969, 47).

To summarize, the colony of Massachusetts, despite its dissenting, independent and self-governing complexion, had also set up, in the course of the seventeenth century, a widely devolved, carefully incentivized and secure system of legal-civil registration inspired by, but quite distinct from, the Anglican registers of the mother country, aspects of which in turn appear to have been copied in England during its own temporary Puritan ascendancy.

The English overseas in the Caribbean in the seventeenth century

In the remainder of this chapter I will review the history of the forms of registration that were adopted by Englishmen forming settlements overseas elsewhere in the seventeenth century. Given space constraints, I will look only at the range of Caribbean settlements, which in fact constitute most of the cases of early English settlement and formation of self-governing communities before 1700.[16] My principal guide and source of information is volume III of the great work of reference created by the demographer Robert René Kuczynski (1876–1947), his uncompleted four-volume *Demographic Survey of the British Colonial Empire* (Kuczynski 1953).[17] As will be seen, a variety of practices were adopted in these varying circumstances but it was also almost always the case that the establishment of a legal identity registration system was viewed as a relatively high priority.

In the Caribbean, Barbados in 1661 appears to be the first colony to have legislated for the registration by the church of christenings, marriages and burials on the island, with the relevant clause of the Act proclaiming that this was explicitly modelled on the practices in the mother country for the advantage of 'Posterity', a reference to the legal inheritance functions of such records:

> Clause IV. And whereas it hath been and still is a laudable Constitution and Custom of our native County [*sic*], to have in every Parish a true and perfect Register kept of all Christenings, Marriages, and Burials . . . which hath been found, and is found to be of much advantage to Posterity: Be it therefore enacted . . . by the President, Council and Assembly . . . as a Duty incumbent on every Minister in his respective Parish within this Island, do keep a true and perfect Register of all and singular the Christenings, Marriages and Burials within the respective Parishes (the Churchwardens of every Parish to provide a large Book fit for the keeping the said Register) . . . [and to provide] a Certificate of the same into the Secretary's Office, in the month of March yearly, there to remain on Record [with penalty of 1,000 lbs 'Muscovadoe Sugar' for failing to make the annual return].
>
> (Kuczynski 1953, 82–84)

Barbados was settled very early, from 1627, and then grew fast (2,000 settlers by the end of 1628 had grown to a population of 20,000 whites by 1680), but in fact the first successful and lasting British colony in the Caribbean was established three years earlier in 1624 on St Christopher, often known as St Kitts and paired

[16] The early British presence in India in the seventeenth century took the form more of stations trading with the indigenous populations and their governments, rather than attempts at extensive settlement, ownership and occupation of land, as in the Caribbean, where the indigenous Arawak and other populations were typically pushed out or exterminated by the European incomers, who then created their own new forms of government.

[17] Page references are to the Harvester Press edition of 1977. Three of the projected four volumes were published between 1948 and 1953, covering the Americas and Africa. In a note on p. x of the posthumously published second volume, published in 1949, it is stated that the manuscripts of both Volume III, dealing with 'America, the Atlantic and Oceania', and Volume IV, dealing with Europe and Asia, were 'almost completed' before Kuczynski died, and that in 1948–1949 they were 'now being prepared for publication by Dr Brigitte Long' (his daughter and research assistant). However, only Volume III appeared (in 1953), lacking the projected 'Oceania' section. I have not so far been able to track down the possible whereabouts of Kuczynski's unpublished manuscripts.

with its sister island Nevis, which was also settled by the English from 1628.[18] From the 1640s St Kitts and Nevis developed to become a leading producer of sugar cane in the Caribbean, using imported African slave labour working for estate landowners.

The first known documentation relating to registration on either island is somewhat later than that on Barbados. On Nevis in 1681 there was passed 'An Act for Ministers' Dues, etc' which stipulated 'That the inhabitants of each Parish in this island shall pay . . . 2000 lbs of sugar [per year] to each Clerk who is to keep a Register of all Christenings and Burials in each Parish' (with any neglect by the clerk to be fined by 'the General and Council') (Kuczynski 1953, 305). This Act was upgraded in 1705 and 1724 with provisions 'That in every Parish Church there shall be kept three large Paper Books for the publick Service of the said Parish', one for Parish Accounts, one for the Vestry Acts, 'a third as a Register for Christenings, Marriages, and Funerals, the last of which to be kept by the Minister only' (Kuczynski 1953, 305). On St Kitts the first documentation of registration appears in 1711 when 'an Act for regulating the Vestries' stipulated 'That in every Parish Church shall be kept two large Paper Books for the publick service of the said Parish', one for the Parish Accounts to be kept by the churchwardens, and one 'as a Register for Christenings, Marriages, and Funerals, to be kept by the Minister only' (Kuczynski 1953, 305). An Act for Regulating Vestries in 1727 made more elaborate provisions: every minister was required to keep records in a bound book provided to them, with a fee of 1/6 for each christening, marriage and funeral; and a £5 fine for neglecting an entry was to be deducted from the salary of the minister by churchwardens and 'applied to the Use of the Poor of the same Parish' (Kuczynski 1953, 305).

Jamaica was another early prize possession of the English in the Caribbean, producing sugar cane and coffee with slave labour. Seized for England in 1655 during Cromwell's Protectorate, it had a population of 4,000–5,000 whites and 1,500 blacks in 1660 (which subsequently grew rapidly, reaching 15,000 whites, 40,0000 of mixed race, 5,000 free blacks, and 311,000 slaves at the date of emancipation, 1 August 1834). At a general session of the governor, council and assembly of Jamaica in 1664, an Act was passed that 'all marriages, births, and burials be recorded by the minister and sent to the secretary's office [of the Council]' (Kuczynski 1953, 240). This may have been stimulated to some extent by the arrival in 1662 of Lord Windsor, who brought with him a Royal Proclamation declaring that all children born of English subjects in Jamaica should be regarded as free citizens of England. However it was soon found that merely legislating for

[18] The indigenous inhabitants of St Kitts were massacred in the Kalinago genocide of 1626 and the island was then formally partitioned between the English and French, with the English gaining complete control from 1713 onwards after several decades of uneasy peace interspersed with conflict whenever the two powers were at war with each other, which was often.

such an institution without giving attention to administrative practicalities was insufficient. In 1670 the governor responded to a request from HM Commissioners about numbers of deaths of both blacks and whites over the previous seven years, that 'neither can any account be given of the dead, the settlements being so far asunder, and few brought to the parish-church to be buried, and many a parish having yet no church, nor wardens, nor other officers, so that no account could be kept thereof' (though it is known that in 1673 when Sir Henry Morgan became Lieutenant-Governor there were already 17,272 persons in Jamaica) (Kuczynski 1953, 240).

Consequently in 1683 compulsory registration of 'Births, Christenings, Marriages and Burials' was introduced for the rapidly growing colony of Jamaica by 'An Act for the Maintenance of Ministers, and the Poor, and Erecting and Repairing Churches'. This stated that, by the authority of the 'Governour, Councel and Assembly', 'the Church-Wardens of each respective Parish' were to buy 'one Fair, well-bound Book, wherein the Minister, and in case there be no Minister . . . the Respective Church Wardens, upon notices thereof given by the Masters of the several Families . . . under the Penalty of five Pounds, shall Register . . . by the Clerk of the Vestry of that Parish' all persons' births, christenings, marriages or burials 'within the said Parish, under the penalty of five Pounds for every such Default', and the clerk receive 'a fee for each Entry Fifteen Pence and no more'. A system of fines for attempts at falsification by any official or person, 'as the Laws of England provide against such as Steal, Raze or Imbezil, Records', was also instituted with one half (Moiety) of such 'Forefeitures or Penalties' going to 'the Poor of the Parish where the fault is committed, the other Moiety or half part to the Informer, to be recovered by Bill, Plaint or Information in any of his Majesties Courts of Record in this Island'. Finally, as to the essentially legal purpose of all this, it was stated that 'all such Entries duly made and kept as aforesaid at all times hereafter be Deemed, Judged and taken as an Authentique Record of all such Births, Christenings, Marriages, and Burials, and in all and every the Courts of Records in this Island' (Kuczynski 1953, 240).[19]

The Jamaican registration system of 1683 was, therefore, fairly closely modelled on the parish-based Anglican system, as re-established in Restoration England. Indeed the parish registration system is envisaged as an integral component in the more general aims of the Act, which are to establish practical and financial means for setting up and maintaining a system of parishes and their churches and ministers

[19] The 1683 Act was not thereafter superseded until the Acts of 1844, 1845, 1855 and 1858, which were all found to be ineffective because they replaced the elements of compulsion in the 1683 legislation with a merely voluntary principle, and so had to be replaced by two further Acts of 1877 and 1881, which re-established, under the office of Registrar-General for the island, compulsory registration of births and deaths and the keeping of 'Civil Status Registers and documents relating thereto' (i.e. 'all registers containing records or transcripts relating to births, baptisms, marriages, deaths and burials') (Kuczynski 1953, 241–242).

in Jamaica. As can be seen in the title of the Act, this is envisaged as requiring not only the means of 'Maintenance of Ministers' but also of maintaining 'the Poor' of the parish. Hence, it can be seen in this Jamaican legislation of the 1680s how it had become an ingrained model for Englishmen that to found a regime of sound self-government in a new territory, creation of a system of legal identity registration was almost as foundational as setting up the parish itself and devising some agreed means of maintaining the poor. Reflected in this legislation, these institutions are seen as the three essential building blocks which make a basic unit of English civic society, a functioning community, reflecting the design and influence of the Elizabethan system of 1598–1601, tying together the three institutions of parish, Poor Law and a legal membership registration list.

The integrated nature of the links between these three institutions is made even clearer in the legislation passed the following decade in Antigua in 1692, very similar in its provisions to the 1683 Jamaica Act. Antigua had been first settled in 1632 but it was only in 1692, by which time the island's population had grown to an estimated 5,000 (Edwards 1819, 475), that a law was passed requiring compulsory registration of christenings, burials and marriages, in 'An Act for dividing this island into Parishes and Maintenance of Ministers, the Poor and erecting and repairing churches' (Kuczynski 1953, 286). The Act's title thus makes it clear that it was only when it became necessary to divide the island's growing and prospering population into separate parishes (five were created in 1692) that it was deemed essential to require a record of who was obligated to contribute to the separate costs of supporting the three essential institutions of the minister, the church building and 'the Poor' in each parish. By this time the principle of having a 'settlement' in the parish of one's birth, conferring entitlements to relief and obligations to contribute to the Poor fund, had become thoroughly institutionalized in England and Wales (with the formalization of the rules in the 'Settlement Acts' of 1662) (Charlesworth 2010). Here we helpfully see spelled out more clearly in the legislation for Antigua what had been implied also in the Jamaican legislation of 1683. Once a newly-settled territory had grown to the point where it was agreed that it was necessary to divide itself up into multiple parishes, parish-based registration of births and marriages became important for fair allocation of entitlements and obligations among the parishes, particularly with respect to their assumed function of maintaining the poor. Serving its other primary purpose of property title registration, the 1692 Antigua law was also careful to specify that these new records, kept by the churchwardens on the authority of the island's Chief Governor, were to be deemed of legal status as 'authentick Record . . . in all and every the Courts of Record in this island', with punishment according to the law of England for any falsification' (Kuczynski 1953, 286–287).

One further crucial difference between these two colonial parish registration systems in Jamaica and Antigua and that prevailing in England and Wales at the time was the provision to charge for the recording of all events, with a hefty

15 pence fee for each entry, to be paid direct to the clerk of the vestry, and half of the enormous £5 fines for defaulters to be devoted to maintaining the poor. These arrangements reflect attempts in the colonies to overcome the practical difficulties of modelling their parish functions and registration systems on the established Anglican practices in England, while lacking in these newly-settled territories either endowed, salaried curates or a rate-funded Poor Law, which respectively provided the resources for the parish model of governance to work effectively in England. The colonies needed to attempt to pay for these two functions and raise funds accordingly in different ways.

This review of the history of registration in St Kitts and Nevis, Barbados, Jamaica and Antigua exhausts the set of earliest Caribbean English settlements which also passed their first registration laws during the seventeenth century, within 100 years of Elizabeth's formalization of the English system, *c.* 1598–1601. Most other subsequent English possessions in the region were late eighteenth-century or early nineteenth-century acquisitions of conquest from the French, such as St Vincent, Grenada and Dominica,[20] or from the Dutch, as with British Guiana.[21]

The history of registration in St Vincent, for instance, one of these latecomers to English rule, illustrates how registration legislation in British colonies in the Caribbean in the mid- and late eighteenth century was still strongly modelled on the Jamaica Act of 1683. In St Vincent in 1767 Clause XII of an 'Act for regulating the Vestries in this Island, empowering them to raise Taxes within their respective Parishes, and directing the application of the same' stipulated that churchwardens for each parish were to buy a 'fair and well-bound Book', wherein the minister, or in his absence churchwardens, would ensure that the Clerk of the Vestry of the Parish registered 'the Times of Christenings, Marriages and Burials' of all in the parish, with fines of 60 shillings for 'the Masters of the several Families', should they fail to inform, and fines of £20 for default of his duty by the clerk. The clerk was also positively incentivized by receipt of a fee of 3 shillings for every register entry, and receipt of the same fee for making a copy out of the Register Book to

[20] On St Vincent fierce Carib resistance prevented European settlement until the eighteenth century. French settlers began plantations with African slaves from 1719 but it was ceded to British rule in 1763 (though it was briefly back in French hands from 1779 to 1783). Grenada, which became a British possession in 1783 after the treaty of Versailles (part of the Peace of Paris), had not been successfully settled by the French before 1705. Dominica had been settled mainly by French missionaries since 1635 and was not permanently under British rule until after the 1783 Peace of Paris. Its subsequent constitutional history was unusual, in that for nearly three decades from 1838 until 1865 it became the only British Caribbean colony with a black-controlled legislature of smallholders, whose interests were opposed to those of the wealthy English planter elite.

[21] British Guiana was settled by the Dutch from 1616 onwards, with the British assuming control in the late eighteenth century and the Dutch formally ceding their three possessions (Essequibo, Berbice and Demerara) to the British in 1814. The many islands of the Bahamas, another subsequent British possession, had been principally a convenient location for pirate bands to base themselves, until declared a Crown colony in 1717 followed by a sustained campaign to expel the pirates.

be attested by the minister or churchwardens (Kuczynski 1953, 437). In 1810 a further 'Act to provide for the care of the Public Register of Marriages, Baptisms, and Burials and to make the same a Public Record' was passed, which attended to the concern to ensure permanence to these valuable legal records generated over the previous four decades. The Act stipulated that for the islands of St Vincent, Bequia and the Grenadines the records in these registers 'be deemed and considered to every intent and purpose a Public Record', and therefore all historic records that could be recovered were to be copied 'at the Public Expense' into two well-bound books of strong paper under the inspection of a Committee of the Legislature, with one of these books delivered to the Rector and the other retained in the Register's Office with all future records of marriages, christenings and burials entered into them (Kuczynski 1953, 437).

What happened when a colony did not establish a registration system during either the seventeenth or even the eighteenth century was spelled out at length as late as 1820 in the preamble to the relevant legislation in Tobago, when it finally passed 'An Act to supply the Defect of a Church Register, and to compel the due and orderly Keeping thereof in future' (Kuczynski 1953, 348).[22] The legislators explained that this Act was made,

> Whereas through the Want of a Church Register kept of the Baptisms, Marriages and Burials, performed according to the Rites of the Established Church, by means whereof the Legal Proof of such Baptisms, Marriages and Burials becomes often extremely difficult, and the same may in the course of a few Years become impracticable, unless some Provision be made for preserving the Evidence of such Baptisms, Marriages and Burials, without which great Injustice and Prejudice may accrue to Persons whose Right may hereafter depend on the Production of such Evidence.
>
> (Kuczynski 1953, 348)

Thus, this brief review indicates that the principal motives for the creation of a registration system – namely, the wish for a robust legal record of personal identities and kinship relations for property transmission purposes – which we have seen clearly expressed in the seventeenth- and early eighteenth-century legislation relating to English settlement in North America and the Caribbean, also remained a continuous dominant motive of English settlers overseas right through to the end of the eighteenth and into the early nineteenth century. There are no signs yet of the concern to use the registration information for matters of public health, or criminal surveillance, or as economic indices, which became much more frequent aims in the course of the nineteenth century in the British empire and elsewhere.

[22] Tobago was fought over as a colonial possession between the Dutch, Spanish, French, British and even US powers throughout the entire seventeenth and eighteenth centuries, with consequently little continuity of government or sustained agricultural development, until finally ceded permanently to Britain in 1815. Trinidad had been continuously under Spanish rule until ceded to Britain in 1802. The two islands were made a single colony in 1889.

Concluding discussion

In conclusion, I would offer a few reflections on the foregoing comparative account of the history of identity registration measures among the English and the English overseas in the early modern period: first, summary observations on the comparative account presented; second, a comment on the important issue, which has not been explicitly discussed so far, of practical efficacy of the various laws and ordinances in the American and Caribbean colonies; and finally, a brief suggestion of the wider historiographical significance of this story of the widespread proliferation of laws attempting to institute systems of universal identity registration for the free subjects of the English Crown in the early modern period from the sixteenth until the early nineteenth century.

First, the comparative evidence assembled on the English settlements and colonies seems to indicate that while Englishmen in the seventeenth and eighteenth centuries did not arrive in new territories with the immediate and pre-established intention of setting up legal-civic registration systems, in almost all cases, whether at the behest of Crown-appointed governors or of the independent settlers themselves, it always emerged as a priority, and quite often early in the settlement's history, within just two or three decades of its foundation and the growth in the settler population. When a settlement reached approximately 4,000 free inhabitants this seems to have often been a demographic point at which the formulation of registration laws and administrative systems seems to have come to be perceived as a priority, if it had not already been promulgated. Often this was in association with the settlement patterns having become sufficiently geographically dispersed that at this point it was recognized by the inhabitants that a single place of collective worship was no longer practical and that there needed to be multiple parishes formed, with separate incumbents. Recognizing the need for multiple parishes brought up the question of a register of membership, because of the financial obligations which were acknowledged to follow, relating to support for a minister, the church building and the poor of the parish, following the firmly-entrenched model of English parish local government established by the Elizabethan Poor Laws.

The legislation promulgated in all settlements also repeatedly reiterated the value of vital registration for the free settlers' posterity, meaning the importance of establishing a secure legal record of identity relations as a key to property ownership and capacity to transmit that ownership intergenerationally with safety. Here we see a fundamental institution for the global spread of commercial and capitalist relations being legislated into existence as a contemporaneously appreciated priority by the English as they diffused and settled.

Secondly, there is the practical question of the effectiveness, persistence and efficiency of all these different colonial registration systems that were created by the English during the early modern period. So far the impression has been given of much positive legislative activity and energy devoted to this prosaic business of government and the law. However, did these laws all work in the manner envisaged, and if not, why not? In England itself historical demographers have confirmed that in the many parishes with surviving registers we can have substantial confidence that the majority of the eligible populace's births and deaths, at least, were reliably captured in the parish registers until the closing decades of the eighteenth century (the uniformity of coverage of marriages through the Anglican registers is believed to have been rather more variable, at least until the intervention of Lord Hardwicke's Act in 1753 which mandated that henceforth all legally valid marriages had to be performed *in facie ecclesiae*) (Brown 1981, 135).

It seems that in most cases outside England and Wales, including even in Massachusetts, the colonial registration systems, whose originating acts of government have been discussed here, did not achieve in practice anything approaching universality of coverage, efficiency and persistence over the long run of the ensuing eighteenth century. Of course even the system in England became mired in inefficiency during the closing decades of the eighteenth century and opening decades of the nineteenth century, when its methods of operation were increasingly subject to urgent ecclesiastical and then government review, eventually leading to the complete overhaul of the system and the establishment of a civil registration system, administered and funded by the central state, by the two Marriage and Registration Acts of 1836. But it seems, from the poor and patchy survival of records consulted by demographic historians, that there were more fundamental practical problems which became more quickly manifest in many of the British settlements overseas, such that they may never have functioned as universal registration systems genuinely available and effective for the whole of the free population of the territory, as they apparently did in England and Wales.[23]

The irony here is that it was the monarchical, ecclesiastically-organized early modern system of the Old World which came closest to providing the national population of England and Wales with all the advantages of a modern civil registration system, rather than the more secular systems operated elsewhere in the English-speaking world, such as in Massachusetts. One reason for the greater longevity and effectiveness of the English system was undoubtedly the advantage of having a cost-less set of reasonably well-disciplined and disciplinable curates to keep and preserve the registers. As was shown during the Interregnum, when the English had to pay for their registrations the populace and the registering agents then became less compliant. But probably an equally important factor which

[23] This is the view expressed by Kuczynski regarding most of the Caribbean territories he surveyed. In relation to North America, the English-speaking colonies have left a patchwork of surviving records of varying quality which are reviewed in the various chapters of Vinovskis (1980); this is in contrast to the excellent and abundant registers maintained and preserved by the French colonists in seventeenth- and eighteenth-century Canada (Charbonneau *et al.* 2000, 102).

explains the success and persistence of the system in England must lie in the way in which it was functionally so closely integrated into the highly unusual and relatively well-resourced universalist Poor Law, through the laws of settlement entitlements. This accounts for compliance even among the great mass of the poor, who could not aspire to transmit real property to their heirs. The Poor Law's settlement rules gave the masses a different form of property or entitlement and with it a very tangible reason to want to have their infants start life with a clear birthright to their right of settlement publicly asserted and permanently recorded in the parish register. This would guarantee for the child an entitlement for the rest of their life to a sufficient share of their parish's collective wealth to be safe from destitution. In the American colonies, where many of the poor were immigrants not born in the territory and where there was an open frontier, such comprehensive Poor Law settlement rules and practices were apparently not adopted (Szreter 2013). It is also the case that any putative universality of such integrated systems of registration and social security provision was complicated in the North American and Caribbean contexts by the practice of perpetual bondage slavery, which developed widely during the latter half of the seventeenth century, creating an entirely different set of race-based relationships between the property-owning and the labouring classes in these societies. As Engerman shows, in Chapter 12 in this volume, paradoxically in the Caribbean colonies universal identity registration for black slaves only became an object of government at the point in the early nineteenth century when the authorities in London decided this would be an effective method for hastening the abolition of the institution.

Finally, let us consider the historiographical significance of this history of repeated early modern efforts by the English to create legal, civic registration systems for themselves in so many different circumstances. The account offered here may provide the basis for an interpretation with some significance, if it is the case that Englishmen, regardless of their religious denomination, came to use and consciously to value and actively defend or promote identity registration as a system of practical legal and civil rights during the course of the three early modern centuries, the sixteenth, seventeenth and eighteenth. If that can be shown to have been the case it would demonstrate how an officially-sanctioned national system, originally instituted by Thomas Cromwell to register the ceremonies of the established church marking individuals' reproductive rites of passage to fulfil a political aim to exclude from their property holdings those who would seek to defy the monarch by practising a distinct religious faith, was turned, over ensuing decades, into a virtually universal civil system of legal registration of identities and kinship relationships, in order to sustain around the globe the needs of a system of private capital accumulation and intergenerational transmission of wealth in a non-confessional commercial society. However, although this seems to reflect the primary intention of many of the legislative acts examined here, this comparative review would also seem to indicate that such a system only became fully effective and persisted in practice where it was integrated with a universalist social security system, as in the parishes of England and Wales. The substantial and continuous history there of these twinned institutions from 1598 would imply that the moral, literary and political theory of abstract human rights, invented in the late eighteenth and early nineteenth centuries (Hunt 2007), was in a sense a rationalization of a set of legal and administrative rules and practices with which Englishmen had become thoroughly familiar and which they had sought to promulgate in many different environments over the course of the previous two centuries. That in turn would suggest a re-evaluation of our understanding of the causal interplay and narrative between the history of ideas, government, laws, social practices and economic needs, in understanding the long-term history of the emergence of that which we have come to term 'human rights'.

References

Anderson, Benedict R. 1991. *Imagined Communities: Reflections on the Origin and Spread of Nationalism*. London: Verso.

Basten, S. 2006. 'From Rose's Bill to Rose's Act: A Reappraisal of the 1812 Parish Register Act.' *Local Population Studies* 76: 43–62.

Baxter, S. 2012. 'The Making of Domesday Book and the Languages of Lordship in Conquered England.' In *Conceptualizing Multilingualism in Medieval England c. 800–c. 1250*, ed. Elizabeth M. Tyler. Turnhout: Brepols, 271–308.

Bayly, C. A. 2004. *The Birth of the Modern World, 1780–1914: Global Connections and Comparisons*. Oxford: Wiley-Blackwell.

Bossy, J. 1985. *Christianity in the West, 1400–1700*. Oxford: Oxford University Press.

Brown, R. L. 1981. 'The Rise and Fall of the Fleet Marriages.' In *Marriage and Society: Studies in the Social History of Marriage*, ed. R. B. Outhwaite. London: Europa, 117–136.

Charbonneau, H., B. Desjardins, J. Légaré and H. Denis. 2000. 'The Population of the St. Lawrence Valley, 1608–1760.' In *A Population History of North America*, ed. M. R. Haines and R. H. Steckel (Cambridge: Cambridge University Press), 99–142.

Charlesworth, L. 2010. *Welfare's Forgotten Past: A Socio-Legal History of the Poor Law*. London: Routledge.

Cressy, D. 1980. *Literacy and the Social Order: Reading and Writing in Tudor and Stuart England*. Cambridge: Cambridge University Press.

Edge, P. G. 1928. 'Vital Registration in Europe: The Development of Official Statistics and Some Differences in Practice.' *Journal of the Royal Statistical Society* 91(3): 346–393.

Edwards, B. 1819. *The History, Civil and Commercial, of the West Indies: With a Continuation to the Present Time*, 5th edn. London: G. and W. B. Whittaker.

Elton, G. R. 1985. *Policy and Police: The Enforcement of the Reformation in the Age of Thomas Cromwell*. Cambridge: Cambridge University Press.

Foucault, M. 2007. *Security, Territory, Population: Lectures at the Collège de France, 1977–78*, trans. Graham Burchell. Basingstoke: Palgrave Macmillan.

García y García, A. 1997. *Synodicon hispanum*, vol. VII. Madrid: Biblioteca de Autores Cristianos.

Gutman, R. 1958. 'Birth and Death Registration in Massachusetts. I. The Colonial Background, 1639–1800.' *The Milbank Memorial Fund Quarterly* 36(1): 58–74.

Hacking, I. 1991. 'How Should We Do the History of Statistics.' In *The Foucault Effect: Studies in Governmentality*, ed. Graham Burchell, Colin Gordon and Peter Miller. Chicago: University of Chicago Press, 181–195.

Hindle, S. 2004. *On the Parish?: The Micro-Politics of Poor Relief in Rural England, c. 1550–1750*. New York: Oxford University Press.

Hunt, L. A. 2007. *Inventing Human Rights: A History*. New York: W.W. Norton & Company.

Hyams, P. 1987. '"No Register of Title": The Domesday Inquest and Land Adjudication.' *Anglo-Norman Studies* 9: 127–141.

Kuczynski, R. R. 1953. *Demographic Survey of the British Colonial Empire*, vol. III, *West Indian and American Territories*. London: Oxford University Press.

Shapiro, S. 1950. 'Development of Birth Registration and Birth Statistics in the United States.' *Population Studies* 4(1): 86–111.

Slack, P. 1988. *Poverty and Policy in Tudor and Stuart England*. London: Longman.

—— 1990. *The English Poor Law, 1531–1782*. Cambridge: Cambridge University Press.

Snell, K. D. M. 1987. *Annals of the Labouring Poor: Social Change and Agrarian England, 1660–1900*. Cambridge: Cambridge University Press.

Szreter, S. 2007. 'The Right of Registration: Development, Identity Registration, and Social Security – A Historical Perspective.' *World Development* 35(1): 67–86.

—— 2011. Children with a (Local) State: Identity Registration at Birth in English History since 1538. In *Children without a State: A Global Human Rights Challenge*, ed. J. Bhabha. Cambridge, MA: MIT Press, 331–351.

—— 2013. 'Why Were the English Parish Registers Created and How Did They Persist? A Case Study in the Use of the Comparative Method in History.' In *People, Papers, and Practices: Identification and Registration in Transnational Perspective, 1500–2010*, ed. Ilsen About, James Brown and Gayle Lonergan. Basingstoke: Palgrave Macmillan, ch. 9.

Tanner, N. P. 1990. *Decrees of the Ecumenical Councils: Nicaea I to Lateran V*. Washington, DC: Georgetown University Press.

Tate, W. E. 1969. *The Parish Chest: A Study of the Records of Parochial Administration in England*, 3rd edn. Cambridge: Cambridge University Press.

Taylor, J. S. 1989. *Poverty, Migration, and Settlement in the Industrial Revolution: Sojourners' Narratives*. Palo Alto, CA: Society for the Promotion of Science and Scholarship.

Vann, R. T. and D. Eversley. 1992. *Friends in Life and Death: British and Irish Quakers in the Demographic Transition*. Cambridge: Cambridge University Press.

Vinovskis, M. 1980. *Studies in American Historical Demography*. New York: Academic Press.

Wrigley, E. A. and R. S. Schofield. 1981. *The Population History of England, 1541–1871: A Reconstruction*. Cambridge: Cambridge University Press.

3

Too Much Information? Too Little Coordination? (Civil) Registration in Nineteenth-Century Germany

ANDREAS FAHRMEIR

Introduction

The history of population registration in nineteenth-century Germany involves a number of paradoxes. Any contemporary travel guide emphasized how obsessed German states' local officials were with registering travellers (John Murray 1854, xviii; Chambers 1839, 71). Yet, in arguably more important respects, German states' central government officials seemed remarkably lacking in curiosity. East of the Rhine, state registers of births, marriages and deaths were introduced in Prussia only in 1874 (Oesfeld 1874), and in the rest of the German empire two years later (*Deutsches Reichsgesetzblatt* 1875). Apparently, officials at various levels of the administration associated different types of registers with different aims they considered more or less useful. Localities placed particular emphasis on the control of movement, as this had implications for relief claims, as discussed below. Central governments, by contrast, remained content with formulating rules for registers kept by ecclesiastical authorities, and ensuring access to the data they contained, until late in the nineteenth century, when a combination of state–church conflict and increased demand for statistical information induced state governments to take over the registration of births, marriages and death directly.

The second paradox concerns the place of (civil) registration in German historiography. As the 1937 National Socialist *Personenstandsgesetz* and the 1939 census highlighted, documentation of racial status (as well as of hereditary illnesses, political opinions, so-called anti-social behaviour, criminal records, and so on) was crucial to the project of creating a 'racial state' (Burleigh and Wippermann 1991), first in Germany, then throughout German-occupied Europe. The 1939 census was the first data-gathering project designed to consolidate, in one central register, all the information the regime required on every resident, in a format which permitted the rapid sorting of data on individuals according to a variety of criteria. Its success depended in part on information also contained in registers of births, deaths and

Proceedings of the British Academy **182**, 93–112.

marriages, of criminals, 'deviants', patients, or inmates in mental institutions. The project of the 'racial state' was therefore shaped by what such registers did and did not contain.

For instance, the 'family books' introduced for all couples married from 1937 in order to increase their pride in their Aryan ancestry were to state 'citizenship, Reichsbürgerrecht[1] and racial classification' (*Deutsches Reichsgesetzblatt* 1937, § 14, 1147). Usually, however, racial classification had to be deduced from registers that contained information on religious affiliation – just like post-1937 birth registers (where racial status was not entered explicitly) were to do. The existence of official registers linking individual biographies to parents' religious views thus greatly facilitated the project of ascertaining 'race' defined as parents' or grandparents' religion. 'Race' thus became a 'fact' that could be established with few bureaucratic complications – simply by cross-referencing documents accessible to the bureaucracy. This left minimal scope for resistance against this classification through debates on classification criteria, obfuscation of results or corruption – and was thus very different from what basing race, for instance, on physical 'examinations' by 'specialists' would have produced: much more ambiguous outcomes and a far greater potential for manipulation which would have provided at least some form of escape route (Meyer 2003).

Though the information in registers thus became a matter of greater or fewer rights, and ultimately of life and death for millions of individuals, their evolution has rarely been studied. Even for National Socialist Germany, interest in how registers and census data fed into a system of racial classification has remained limited to Aly's pathbreaking book and Black's study of the technology employed – possibly because whether and how census data were used to draw up lists for deportations remains unclear (Aly 1984; Black 2001).

It is less surprising that the introduction of 'civil' registration during the late nineteenth-century *Kulturkampf* between liberal-Protestant state authorities and the Catholic church is treated as little more than a footnote to the more captivating stories of imprisoned bishops, deported priests, and Catholic mass mobilization (Borutta 2010; Blaschke 2009). Moreover, unlike in the case of civil marriages (Schubert 1987), German civil registration of births and deaths did not represent such an obvious break with tradition. The introduction of civil marriages removed the site of the legally binding wedding from churches to registry offices (*Standesämter*). It thus created an entirely new ceremony which had to be inserted

[1] The concept of a *Reichsbürgerrecht* was introduced in the 1935 Nuremberg laws. It was to distinguish politically reliable, Aryan citizens of the German empire from mere inhabitants. While it was clear that citizens classed as non-Aryans and Aryan citizens deprived of their civil rights by a court judgment were not *Reichsbürger*, the proposed *Reichsbürger*-register – which would surely have excluded individuals with known left-wing sympathies, for example – was never drawn up. See Gosewinkel (2001, 383–393).

into the traditional sequence of wedding rituals. Given the history of confrontation between the Catholic church and Protestant or secularizing states dating back to the Napoleonic era, it also represented a clear victory of the latter position over the former. By contrast, the registration of births and deaths alongside and in addition to that of baptisms and burials had a long tradition. More importantly, the act of registration could be (and usually was) delegated to professionals such as midwives, doctors or undertakers. The insertion of religious information into civil records of births and deaths was never seriously questioned, making German public registration decidedly less secular than its French counterpart. While Austrian censuses have recently attracted some interest in the context of comparative empire studies (Leonhard 2009, 53–78), German registers are mainly mined for demographic data and used by family historians, but rarely studied in their own right (see, for instance, Knodel 1988).

Accordingly, Germany's historical bibliography contains a grand total of twenty-two publications on 'Personenstandsbücher' (*Jahresberichte für deutsche Geschichte*, consulted 4 January 2010), mainly written to celebrate registry office anniversaries (Horn 2006) or to guide family historians in their perusal of the archives (Joergens and Reinicke 2006; Bauernfeind 2009). Characteristically, one title, on 'French' civil registers in Germany west of the Rhine, is a partial reprint of a guide for civil registrars and individuals researching their ancestry to document 'racial purity', originally published in Munich in 1942 (Schwan 2006). It is thus far from the typical *captatio benevolentiae* if I note that this chapter can only provide a very tentative outline of what is a new subject for historical research in Germany.

Given these limitations, I propose to attempt three things: to sketch the history and purpose of the official registration of births, marriages and deaths in German states; to discuss whether the official surveillance of movement produced competing types of registration; and to make a few remarks on the uses and abuses of lists and registers.

Births, marriages and deaths – from ecclesiastical to civil registration

In German states, as elsewhere in *ancien régime* Europe, the registration of births, marriages and deaths (or, more precisely, of births, baptisms, marriages, and burials) was originally a matter for ecclesiastical authorities. The precise origins and aims of German *Kirchenbücher* are difficult to reconstruct. Where they survive, they have been mined mainly for demographic information or edited for use in family research; the most comprehensive study of German medieval parish life to date focuses on the parish economy rather than the administration of parishioners (Pleiss 2004; Bauer 2008; Reitemeier 2005). The first registers appear to have been lists of baptisms – possibly in order to provide eternal documentation of an individual's acceptance into the community of the church. In spite of a canon law requirement to keep such registers, introduced in 1140, few are documented in Germany prior to the fifteenth century. Lists of baptisms, marriages, confirmations and deaths became mandatory in ecclesiastical law with the reformation and the Tridentine reforms. In theory, there was thus little distinction between Catholic, Lutheran and Calvinist regions; statements on practice are difficult to make, however, given the extent of record loss and destruction in the course of the Thirty Years' War (*Lexikon des Mittelalters* 1977). At present[2] there is nothing to suggest that the intended uses of these registers were anything other than ecclesiastical: to document parish membership, and to keep a record of sacraments received. Of course, proof of marriage could have implications outside the parish community, and in cases where the family relationships between brides and grooms were in doubt, research in parish registers could establish whether the couple were about to contravene regulations against the marriage of close relatives. However, their use as a more general point of reference is contradicted by the existence of alternative 'matriculation books', documenting, for instance, receptions into communities of burghers, guilds, students, craftsmen or respectable paupers, described in detail in Chapter 8 by Looijesteijn and van Leeuwen, all of which have their equivalents in German territories.

Ecclesiastical registers could occasionally acquire uses of significance to the purposes of the state even in the early modern period. For example, they could prove that individuals were entitled to emigrate as members of a minority faith under the terms of the 1555 Peace of Augsburg (Boden und Schmidt 2006, 57–59). However, state interest in ecclesiastical records only took off in the later eighteenth century, as 'enlightened' or 'reform' absolutism sought to rein in the power of clerical authorities and to regulate individuals' lives for the good of the state in ever greater detail. Prussia's *Allgemeines Landrecht* is a prime example of this trend. In one sense, it respected the division of powers between the state and the church: it recognized that valid marriages were concluded by priests without the aid of any state officials. It stated, moreover, that foreigners' marriages were subject only to the laws of the religious community (and not those of the territory) to which they belonged (*Allgemeines Landrecht für die preußischen Staaten* (henceforth *ALR*), Teil II, Titel 1, §§ 136ff.). But for Prussians, things looked very different, as 1,129 additional articles spelled out who was eligible to marry whom (and who might offer dispensation from some of these conditions), who could give or withhold consent, who had to be notified in what manner of couples' intent to marry, what promises to marry meant in law, and so on and so forth. In addition, while only a priest could wed, judges could divorce according to rules laid down in the *Allgemeines Landrecht* (*ALR* II, 1, §§ 1–1131).

[2] Regrettably, the new edition of the *Handwörterbuch zur deutschen Rechtsgeschichte* had not yet reached the letter 'K'.

It will therefore come as no surprise that the *Allgemeines Landrecht* also instructed priests on how to keep registers of births, baptisms, marriages and burials (*ALR* II, 11, §§ 481–503). Although priests were not instructed to register divorces, marriage entries had to state whether brides or grooms had been wed before, whether they were still under the tutelage of their parents or guardians, and how parents' or guardians' consent had been documented (§§ 483ff.). Entries of births had to include parents' 'estate' or rank (§ 485). When recording the births of children born out of wedlock, priests were required to determine whether the mother could provide for her child; if they did not think she could, they had to inform the secular authorities (§§ 487ff.). When recording burials, priests had to note the cause of death (as reported to them) and had to ascertain the corpse's identity from reliable witnesses (§§ 492–494).

In order to ensure that church registers embraced the entire population, ministers of tolerated religious communities were obliged to inform an established parish of any baptisms, marriages or burials they performed; these had to be included in this parish's register (§§ 498ff.). Anything that took place elsewhere, by contrast, did not have to be entered in parish registers, even if it concerned parish members.

Much of the information required was of more interest to the Prussian state than to the church. For instance, detailed information on married couples allowed secular authorities to monitor whether priests conformed to the prohibitions in the *Allgemeines Landrecht* against marriages without parental consent, between members of very different 'estates', between close blood relations, between adulterous couples, or by widowed women within nine months of their husband's death. Information on causes of death contained raw material for medical statistics, which could lead to an improved '*Medizinalpolizei*' or preventive health policy.

State interests did not merely require that data be recorded, but that state officials obtained access to it. For this reason, vergers or other parish assistants were to draw up a true copy of the registers, to have it verified by the priest in charge and to submit it to the local court of first instance once a year (§ 503).

The Prussian system thus placed the clergy of established churches (the so-called 'Augsburg confessions' of Catholicism, Lutheranism and reformed Protestantism) in charge of registering the population in ways which conformed to state interests. It had fairly close equivalents in most other German states, where similar rules had occasionally been introduced even earlier. For example, the principality of Jülich-Berg ordered copies of church registers to be submitted to secular officials in 1769, and the prince-bishopric of Cologne did so in 1779. Bavaria, by contrast, waited until 1803 (Boden and Schmidt 2006, 58; Oepen 2006, 79ff.). Regardless of such legislative details, it seems safe to assume that local and state officials could gain access to church records without much difficulty everywhere.

However, we know little about how well the system of registration functioned in practice. It is unclear whether dissenters' vital statistics had been registered at all in Prussia before 1794, or whether informal records or practices were simply rendered official by the *Allgemeines Landrecht*. It is unknown how closely parish priests adhered to orders to keep complete and comprehensive church records in a standard format. Public officials complained of sloppy and incomplete record-keeping; conversely, parishes claimed that they could not afford to pay for ink, paper and vergers' time to draw up duplicate registers (Günther and Schneider 2006, 92ff.). It is thus likely that some members of minority religious communities went unrecorded for reasons of information, time and parsimony (Boden and Schmidt 2006, 60).

We also lack information on how closely the 'estate' noted in ecclesiastical population registers conformed to individuals' formal membership in the nobility or the ranks of burghers. In some states, noble status had to be confirmed through entry in separate registers like the Bavarian 'Adelsmatrikel' (from 1808) or its Württemberg equivalent (from 1818) (Müller 1996; Renz 2004). In other states, recognition by an official 'Heroldsamt', like the Prussian one founded in 1855, was decisive (Kalm 1994). In an analogous manner, some towns compiled lists of newly accepted burghers (Fahrmeir 2005; Rittershausen *et al.* 1981), though such *Bürgerbücher* appear to have been replaced by individual certificates by the nineteenth century, some time before burgher status lost its legal significance.[3]

Analogous registers of villages' populations were exceptional, presumably because they were hardly required. In a local context, individuals' identities and formal and informal ranks were known to neighbours and officials alike. When Württemberg mandated the creation of *Familienbücher* (lists of resident families with information about their ancestry) in 1807 (Reyscher 1835), they were designed as copies of church registers sorted by family relationships rather than dates, and thus more practical to use in many contexts.

Outside Württemberg, *Ortssippenbücher* were apparently mainly propagated in the 1920s by *völkisch* circles interested in discovering the 'true' roots of the country's Germanic populace in immobile villages. Because they were in ideological fashion and provided convenient proof of collective Aryan descent for the Christian population, many *Ortssippenbücher* were compiled and published in the 1930s and 1940s – excluding, for obvious reasons, the non-Christian and the mobile population.[4]

[3] Burgher status (the German equivalent of the freedom of the city in England) provided individuals with residence rights in a town, the ability to set up shop as a craftsman or merchant, and the right to participate in a town's governance. It was generally acquired by descent or purchase. Reforms of municipal governance and the introduction of freedom of commerce and freedom of movement stripped burgher status of much of its practical relevance in German states from the 1840s. While the transition from the *Bürgergemeinde*, based on corporate membership, to the *Einwohnergemeinde*, based on duration of residence, was largely complete outside Bavaria by the 1860s, *Bürgerrecht* could still determine local voting rights around 1900.

[4] Some German family historians continue to use the term for local family reconstitution, though *Familienbücher* is the term more commonly employed these days (Imhof 1977, 23–27; a current list

In the second half of the nineteenth century, criticism of the patchwork registration system in Germany increased. The key reason was not that parish registers were unreliable indicators of rank or status, or that they removed individuals from the direct control of the state. Nor was this a result of liberal desire to emancipate citizens from clerical tutelage by removing registries from church control – which had shaped § 151 of the 1849 *Paulskirchenverfassung*.[5]

Rather, pressure originally came from bodies like the Association for Medical Statistics (*Deutscher Verein für medizinische Statistik*). It had petitioned the North German Confederation's *Reichstag* in 1870 to introduce a uniform system of civil registration and a central federal institute for medical statistics. The model the association looked to was Britain, considered the country most advanced in using data on the incidence of disease to improve the population's health. As deputy Dr Löwe explained in a debate characterized by cross-party harmony (with a little Catholic scepticism thrown in), the key problem with clerical control of registers was that they pre-sorted the data in ways unhelpful to anyone interested in public health questions. Civil registration was required because it would produce a statistic

> not of how many Catholic, Protestant and Jewish children are born and how many Protestants, Catholics and Jews die, but a statistic, how many are born in a particular room in a specific house, and how many died in this room, in this town, in this quarter &c.[6]

In the short term, the Franco-Prussian war and the foundation of the German empire focused attention elsewhere. When civil registration returned to the *Reichstag*'s agenda in 1872, the context had changed considerably. The controversial dogma of papal infallibility had placed the Catholic church under considerable internal strain, and tensions between ultramontane Catholics and *Altkatholiken* who parted company with the Pope spilled over into church–state relations – as they did throughout Europe (Clark and Kaiser 2003). Secular authorities were forced to decide how they should treat army chaplains or professors of theology jointly appointed by the church and the state who publicly disagreed with Rome, thus losing their licence to teach Catholic theology or to preach to the Catholic faithful. Liberals claimed that it was no longer possible for Catholics who questioned papal infallibility to wed in many parts of the empire, because these individuals were faced with the unbearable choice of leaving their church, taking leave of their reason or finding a dishonest compromise

of available publications can be found at http://wiki-de.genealogy.net/Kategorie:Deutsche_Ortssippenb%C3%BCcher_/_Reihe_A).

[5] 'Die Standesbücher werden von den bürgerlichen Behörden geführt', i.e. 'Estate books [civil registers] will be kept by the civil authorities'.

[6] 'Denn das [Civilstandsregister] ist keine Statistik, wie viele katholische, protestantische und israelitische Kinder geboren werden und wie viele Protestanten, Katholiken oder Juden sterben, sondern das ist die Statistik wie viele auf einem gewissen Raume in einem gewissen Hause geboren werden, und wie viele gestorben sind in dieser Lokalität, in dieser Stadt, in diesem Stadtviertel u.s.w.' (*Verhandlungen des Deutschen Reichstags* (1867/1870), vol. 11, 687–697, quotation at p. 693).

which allowed them to question papal infallibility without actually saying so. The introduction of civil marriages was an obvious solution, but made little sense without turning over the registration of births, marriages and deaths to civil authorities as well. On 16 June 1872, the *Reichstag* therefore approved a resolution calling for the introduction of civil weddings and civil registration, after a debate on anti-Jesuit legislation; the vote was 151 votes for and 100 against (*Verhandlungen des Deutschen Reichstags* (1872), vol. 2, 1150–1154).

In March 1873, the government announced that draft legislation on civil registration was all but prepared (*Verhandlungen des Deutschen Reichstags* (1873), vol. 1, 135ff.). National Liberals interpreted this as a sign of bureaucratic foot-dragging. Accordingly, the Bavarian deputy Joseph Völk (Vogt 1875), who had already sponsored the 1872 resolution, introduced proposals on civil marriage and civil registration in May 1873. The first debate was aborted on 4 June because not enough representatives attended. In 1874, the *Reichstag* approved a slightly amended bill based on what the Prussian government had introduced in the same year (*Verhandlungen des Deutschen Reichstags* (1873), vol. 2, 952–956; *Verhandlungen des Deutschen Reichstags* (1874), vol. 3, 204–208), and in 1875 an imperial law on civil registration passed both federal houses with governmental support.

During the general debates, the main point of contention was whether the *Reichstag* was the proper forum: whether registration was an area of state (*Staat*) competence. Removing the power over registration from the state was, however, precisely what Völk desired: everybody recognized that the law was intended to provide relief to Bavarian Catholics, but had no chance of success in the Bavarian parliament.

During the debates on details, practical questions proved to be controversial. Opponents of the law pointed out that it would not be easy to find competent registrars in rural areas, because the law excluded all clergymen (Protestants as well as Catholics) and some civil officials from the post. Moreover, the new Prussian law required registrars to collect less information than the *Allgemeines Landrecht* or other earlier regulations had done; yet, it turned out that the Prussian statistical office still desired to know whether children had been born out of wedlock, or what the precise causes of deaths were. However, as Catholic Centre Party deputy Windthorst pointed out, with a certain degree of *Schadenfreude*, questions which priests could ask legitimately became indecent when posed by state officials (*Verhandlungen des Deutschen Reichstags* (1874/1875), vol. 2, 987–1103, at 1005).

Apparently, secularizing the content of records entered no one's mind. Civil registers were to contain information on the 'religion' as well as on the 'occupation or rank' of parents, children, spouses and corpses as a matter of course.[7] Nor did the problems of dual record keeping disappear. Catholic criticisms of the compe-

[7] In Weimar, this was modified somewhat – henceforth, civil registrars could only demand to know about religion for statistical purposes, i.e. in most cases.

tence and reliability of local mayors or village headmen were shared by the imperial bureaucracy: judicial control of record-keeping was to remain in place, as was the practice of turning duplicate registers over to the courts of first instance (§ 14).

The purpose of civil registers was twofold. On the one hand, they provided annual snapshots of demographic data, passed on to central statistical offices by local registries on forms delivered to them free of charge, as the law stated in § 8. On the other hand, they could be consulted for information on family relationships (and religious affiliation), which could be relevant for inheritance claims, for example. However, the information they contained in this regard was not easily visible. Civil registers were not indexed (at least not routinely) and not centralized as in Britain's General Register Office, where they were stored, alphabetically indexed by surname, in Somerset House on the Thames in central London. It was therefore far from obvious where the entry on the birth of someone of an uncertain age who had died far from home could be found. Unlike in either Britain or France, where, as Gérard Noiriel has suggested, birth records became the central point of reference for determining identity (Noiriel 2001, 125; and see Chapter 5 in this volume), they were not particularly useful in German states. They offered no help in determining individuals' place of legal residence. The only German state that tied 'settlement' (*Heimat*)[8] to the place of birth was Saxony (and also Austria); the vast majority of others focused on the duration of (legal) residence, which did not emerge from civil registers (Müller 1841, 186, 205ff. and *passim*). Even for the purposes of census-construction, registers of births and deaths were not particularly helpful; the decisive number the Prussian statistical office was interested in for much of the nineteenth century was the so-called '*Zollvereins-Abrechnungsbevölkerung*', a combination of legally registered and resident population which determined the distribution of the German customs union's receipts among participating states (Schneider 2011). Recent research on nineteenth-century Germany also suggests that Prussia's bureaucracy was willing to rely quite strongly on citizens' good faith. Patrick Wagner's examination of rural bureaucracy documented that property records were often all but useless in practice, because they were not kept up to date (Wagner 2005). Andreas Thier points out that tax inspectors were expressly prohibited from enquiring intrusively into taxpayers' affairs (Thier 1999, 42, 48, 625). And, finally, neither ecclesiastical nor civil registers had to be consulted when individuals wished to obtain travel papers in German states, even though such travel papers in fact formed the basis of yet another type of register.

Explaining the profusion of extensive registers is difficult. It belies the Prussian state's reputation for parsimony in non-military matters. It served to delay administrative business. When they might have mattered, registers were either not used at all or turned out to be not comprehensive enough – even cradle-to-grave

[8] *Heimat*, sometimes also known as *Unterstützungswohnsitz*, was the place at which individuals were entitled to poor relief. See also below, 105.

registration of existence, civil status and place of residence (treated below) did not make house-to-house enquiries obsolete on census days.

One potential explanation could be the symbolic dimension of registration. After all, the design of population registers dated back to the early modern period, when, as Jürgen Schlumbohm argued, the purpose of the flood of preventive *Polizey* regulations which poured out of German territory's chancelleries was less to change subjects' behaviour than to project the image of an activist, ordering, competent and all-powerful ruler. Read in this way, registers may have been designed to do much more (but also much less) than to gather and store information for practical purposes. They documented that information should be available to the state judiciary, not just to local authorities or parishes. This suggested that the state was more efficient and professional than sloppy local (or ecclesiastical) authorities (Schlumbohm 1997). This reading of registers also explains why they were over-dimensioned. The desire to have information to hand for rare contingencies created an excess of information. All family relationships were registered; the alternative might have been to enquire about those which remained uncertain and gave rise to inheritance disputes, for example.

The proliferation of registers also indicates a lack of coordination between different branches of government. Family and inheritance, poor relief, public safety and political stability produced different registers, with overlapping, but not identical content.

Michael Schneider's recent *Habilitationsschrift* on the Prussian statistical office between 1860 and 1914 suggests that this process was also advanced by the additional layer of institutional competition in a state with a peculiar federal makeup. The head of Prussia's statistical office did not just argue that he needed more staff in order to supply data that his Belgian, French or British counterparts could provide easily, but he wished to be in a position to outspend his counterparts in other German states *and* the imperial statistical office. The late arrival of a federal state composed not of provinces or territories, but of relatively autonomous monarchies or free cities with individual traditions of registration and data-compilation thus provided a climate particularly conducive to intensive information-gathering.

Lists of travellers and registers of residents

Travel guides were right to insist on the relevance of 'papers'. Until the 1860s, travel within German states and across German states' borders required official permission, certified in a passport, *Wanderbuch*, *Heimatschein*, *Passkarte* or other document (for the period before 1870 see Fahrmeir 2000a, 2000b; for the period after 1870 see Reinecke 2010, which is the first overview of migration control in the German empire). The information contained in these 'papers' was copied frequently and comprised: name, age, occupation, physical description, and route and purpose of travel, though not religion (apart from passports issued for travel in post-1850s Austria (Burger 2000)). When the travel document was issued, it was entered on a list at the issuing office. When its bearer spent the night in an inn or in a private house, the details were noted on a register of guests and passed on to the police. When a traveller remained in one place for a few days, he had to turn his document over to the police, who made a different type of note. While passports for internal travel ceased to be mandatory after German unification, new arrivals still had to register with the authorities and present documentary proof of their identity. Some of the registers drawn up for the purpose of keeping track of movement (*Melderegister*) survive, and have been used to study the scale, range and purpose of migration, particularly in industrializing cities in western Germany (e.g. Hochstadt 1999).

In theory, therefore, the police forces of German states were in possession of a complete overview of residents' and visitors' movements, sorted in different ways for different purposes. Registers of passports issued were primarily intended to guarantee the authenticity of documents. In the early 1800s, some states' passports were drawn up as chirographs. Issuing offices kept a counterfoil of the passport with the same details, cut apart in a jagged line along a decorated border. By returning the passport to the issuing office, officials could verify whether it fitted where it had been torn off. In later decades, comparing the data on the passport and in the original register seemed sufficient. The decisive information was thus the passport's place of issue and serial number.

Visa registers kept at consulates or police stations were organized similarly, as were registers of visitors kept at inns or taverns. Looking for a particular name or a person matching a particular description was thus extremely cumbersome, and misidentifications were common (one particularly amusing example is documented by Siemann 1981). In this case, too, registers were better suited to tracking movements in statistical terms (though this was not, in fact, done at the time), than to following a particular person. Visa stamps on the backs of passports, by contrast, traced an individual's movements – but such documents remained with their bearers or were destroyed by the issuing office, which was supposed to cancel them at the end of the journey.

Registers of visitors were kept with a greater or lesser degree of precision. Whether travellers had to show passports depended on their class, and registers were apparently not usually read all that closely by the police (Mohl 1834; Muhs 1998, 83ff.; Fahrmeir 2000a, 118–122; 2008). Hotel-keepers' copies of travellers' registers were filed, kept for a while, and then discarded. Permits to remain in a town, or to travel along a certain route, were not necessarily copied into registers and sometimes not written down at all. Registers were therefore only useful to trace the fairly recent journey of someone who stood out in some way.

The main purpose of documentation and registration of movement was to control and direct travel (Noiriel 1998), not to study travel patterns or to reconstruct journeys. The laws and decrees regulating the use of passports in nineteenth-century German states contain a large number of motives: to prevent the overcrowding of job markets in particular places or occupations; to keep people who were politically suspect from entering politically sensitive areas such as capitals, or garrison or university towns; to reduce vagrancy, begging and the presence of 'Gypsies' (on the various meanings of the term, see Lucassen 1996); to prevent itinerant show-men or artistes from inducing a gullible population to spend money on futile entertainment; to prevent the importation of dangerous political ideas from France, Switzerland, Britain, or, in the 1850s, Bremen; or to prevent bandits and other people with sinister aims from roaming about the countryside (Vesque von Püttlingen 1842). As this rather jumbled list makes clear, very traditional concerns with a mobile and threatening underclass intermingled with quite modern desires to direct migration flows away from areas of low employment opportunities and a post-1793 fear of revolution and revolutionaries. Over time, however, the desire to turn travel into an innocuous activity by keeping thieves and revolutionaries from the roads by carefully checking the motives and credentials of all travellers came into conflict with the consequences of the transportation revolution; checking the documents of every person changing trains at major stations simply became impractical. After a relatively brief experiment with a sort of VIP-passport for well-to-do and trusted travellers (*Passkarten*), German states dispensed with systematic checks of travel documents (which had always taken place mainly at town gates and in taverns, not at border crossings) entirely from the 1860s. Instead, they moved to a system of retrospective regulation, deporting travellers who had turned out to be poor, unreliable or criminal – either to their native country, or to their domicile in a German state.

Even after German unification, the regulation of travel and residence remained a state affair; deportations or expulsions were generally from a state, not from the empire; *Reichsverweisungen*, which required a court order, were only rarely used (Reinecke 2010, 134–176).

Travel documents thus had the dual purpose of granting permission to travel and communicating information between police officials. Certifying travellers' identity beyond doubt, by contrast, was not their initial purpose. The key indication of this fact is that individual identity was not always specified; a passport could be issued to Mr Smith and his 'servants', and upper-class travellers did not have to bother with a personal description included in the passport. Until the 1850s, travellers could apply for passports where they happened to be; making them produce copies of birth or marriage certificates would therefore have been impractical. Having a local official or notable (mis)identify a person whose identity was in doubt seemed entirely sufficient – as in the case of Johannes Cato Kamerling, mentioned in Chapter 8. 'Lola Montez' or 'Essad Bey' are other examples of invented identities in the age of the 'documented citizen' (Spencer 1992, 19; Reiss 2005; Seymour 1996).

Registers of residents were kept with rather more care. In the nineteenth century, the duration of residence could be important for poor relief claims. Eighteenth-century German territories had no qualms about 'shoving'[9] paupers, criminals or dissidents across the nearest border. By the early nineteenth century, the drawbacks of such practices appeared to outweigh their fairly obvious benefits. Unregulated expulsions appeared to contribute to the formation of criminal gangs in woodlands located on the borders between states, like the notorious Spessart between Bavaria and Hesse-Darmstadt; and the risk that expelled paupers would fail to find any place of residence, and were thus condemned to die on the road, offended state officials' humanitarian sentiments. From the early 1800s, central government agencies prohibited localities from expelling people who had no place to go, thus obliging them to provide them with some form of poor relief. From the 1820s, legislation concerned with local governance (*Gemeindeordnungen*) assigned a domicile (*Heimat*) to every citizen of a German state. Finally, inter-state treaties determined how long non-citizens could be expelled from a state.

Rules on how *Heimat* was acquired and lost varied widely. All states agreed that emigration led to a loss of poor relief claims – but this could be prevented by obtaining a certificate of domicile (*Heimatschein*). While Saxony and Austria assigned domicile by the place of birth, Prussia emphasized the duration of residence (as little as one year from 1844). Many south German states tied *Heimat* to a combination of 'reception' into a locality, descent from a locality's members, written evidence of domicile, and the duration of residence (Bopp 1834; Doehl 1862; Fahrmeir 2000a, 170ff., 187–193). The process was conflict-ridden, as state governments imposed the rules according to which poor relief had to be dispensed, but placed the burden of funding it on local authorities, who could be quite creative in finding grounds for denying relief to recent and not so recent immigrants. In extreme cases, individuals could be shunted back and forth between localities for decades.

While evidence of domicile was thus the equivalent of a claim to poor relief, and therefore potentially valuable, the relationship of registration to rights was ambivalent. While registration could become the basis of poor relief claims – for example, by showing a sufficient length of residence in Prussia – it could also come back to haunt individuals by documenting that they had no claim to residence in a place in which they had lived most of their adult lives, leading to expulsion in old age. This was particularly likely in those states which made changing domicile very difficult. Moreover, towns could look through registers of residents and expel individuals seen as being at risk of poverty just before they became irremovable.

The introduction of freedom of movement in most of the German empire (Bavaria continued to have distinct rules) reduced the risk involved in registration

[9] The term was *Schub*, still found in *Abschiebung* for deportation today.

and increased the benefits. In addition to forming the basis of poor relief rights, registration also conferred voting rights on (most) adult males. However, as the case of the *Hauptmann von Köpenick* (Wilhelm Voigt) highlighted in 1906, the problem remained very real for convicted criminals, who were effectively tied to their official domicile. Wilhelm Voigt, a shoemaker with a long criminal record recently released from prison, dressed up as a Prussian army captain and commanded soldiers and gendarmes to aid him in 'requisitioning' over 3,000 Marks from the municipal treasury of the Berlin borough of Köpenick. Though it seems likely that Voigt was primarily interested in the millions of Marks supposedly stored in the strong-room there, when sentencing him the judges agreed that his inability to obtain residence papers for Berlin (his domicile was probably Tilsit) had contributed to his crime.

Residents' registers were thus important for claims on public funds as well as for political participation. They were usually indexed by names and places of residence. Their content was public, and thus subject to a degree of collective control. Arrivals were announced in newspapers (this type of content gave some of them their title, e.g. *Hamburger Fremdenblatt*, *Bayerischer Kurier – Münchener Fremdenblatt*; *Heidelberger Fremdenblatt*; *Mondorfer Kur- und Fremden-Blatt/Journal des bains de Mondorf. Liste des baigneurs*). Most towns printed address books that listed all longer-term residents by name, address and occupation (e.g. 'Berliner Adressbücher') – such sources were mined extensively in the course of the 1990s Frankfurt *Bürgertum*-project (Roth 1996; Mettele 1998). While earlier editions focused on prominent citizens, later versions became more and more comprehensive, until they were first complemented, then displaced, by telephone directories.

Summary: uses and abuses

In some ways, the registers of births, marriages and deaths on the one hand and of movement and residence on the other served complementary purposes. Both were used for the production of population statistics. Furthermore, German states drew up censuses using two methods: population counts and calculation from the previous totals, adding births and in-migration while subtracting deaths and out-migration.

One thing this exercise highlighted every time it was employed was that the bureaucratic system of travel registration did not work particularly well. Counts and calculations delivered very different results. In the state of Hesse-Kassel, for example, between 4,500 and 17,000 residents went missing between censuses – the higher figure was the equivalent of the population of the state's university town, Marburg (*Beiträge zur Statistik des vormaligen Kurfürstentums Hessen* 1866, vol. 1, 61ff.). In Württemberg, not even the internal controls added up: even with *Familienbücher*, the numbers of individuals registered as moving to another

Württemberg community were never the same as those moving to a Württemberg locality from within the state. Prussia had similar problems (*Württembergische Jahrbücher* 1823, particularly 1869, vol. I, 6 and 1871, vol. I, 378ff.; Markow 1889, 125–133). Part of the cause was 'illegal' emigration, but there was evidence of 'illegal' immigration as well.

What this demonstrated was that local authorities kept registers for purposes which were somewhat different from those of the central authorities. Whereas central state governments wanted to assign every citizen a place of residence, local officials were most interested in keeping the poor off their welfare rolls by preventing them from acquiring a legal residence (Küster 1995, 127–129). While the state wanted to prevent the emigration of potential soldiers, localities did not wish to place any obstacles in the way of poorer emigrants (Faltin 1987, 261–263). Thus, a comprehensive history of civil registration in nineteenth-century Germany would have to take much more account of regional variation as well as differences in the degree of professional commitment to the purposes of registration at different levels of the administration.

The censuses by calculation documented that different registers were indeed linked on occasion. Their purpose was to provide a comprehensive picture of the population while aiding officials (and members of the general public) who were in search of individuals' location or family relationships. What registers and documents did not do was to highlight differences in status prominently. Even though travel by Jews was subject to rules different from those for Christians in the early nineteenth century, passports did not automatically mention religion (Fahrmeir 2010). One explanation why information on religion was included in civil registers after 1876 could thus have been the assumption that it was not something that had to be kept from the state after it had ceased to be a cause for official discrimination after the completion of Jewish emancipation.

While foreign, particularly English, observers found the intrusiveness and near-divine status of German bureaucracy odd (Franzen 2001), the key complaints in Germany did not concern invasions of privacy but the effort it took to satisfy officials' demands for certification of obvious information. This indicated that, if it was intended as a tool for surveillance, the system of multiple registers did not work particularly well. Registers did not present the bureaucracy with a complete paper image of citizens' most salient characteristics, but citizens remained obliged to carry proof of their existence, residence rights or marital status from one official to the next. Germany was thus neither at the forefront of modern statistics – a fact much lamented in the first debates on civil registration – nor particularly prominent when it came to introducing modern techniques of recognizing individuals. Neither fingerprinting nor biometrical identification made particularly great inroads into registers kept in pre-1914 Germany (Cole 2001).

So what about continuities and discontinuities – uses and abuses? One discontinuity is the massive expansion of the system of registration and bureaucratic information. Contrary to appearances, registration and certification were not universal in pre-1914 Germany. They usually stopped at the upper classes. Whereas normal travellers had to obtain passports for every journey well into the 1860s, reliable frequent travellers could use annual *Passkarten* or rely on the fact that their good name would be recognized everywhere. Whereas passports issued to normal travellers contained their physical description (which made it necessary for them to appear at an issuing office), those issued to prominent individuals did not. And while the *Allgemeines Landrecht* had been concerned about the economic ability of 'normal' single mothers to care for their children, this did not, of course, apply to the well-to-do.

Such concerns with rank decreased (though they did not disappear completely) as a result of the First World War. For instance, all passports now included photographs – but members of the upper classes could still avoid going to passport offices in person (Krause 1925, 29). The number and type of registers increased immensely during the war – and their purposes changed. Nineteenth-century civil registers had first been called for as a tool to improve the observation of demographic developments with a view to identifying the causes of disease. This became markedly less important as Robert Koch's discovery of bacterial infections helped to shift the focus to medical migration control (Reinecke 2010, 34–54) and the search for vaccines. The novel registers of the unemployed, of Jewish soldiers (Rosenthal 2007), of foreign workers, or of individuals owning particular resources, drawn up after 1914, were designed to serve as a basis for authorities' decision-making in the short term and in ways which affected individuals. In this sense they were more similar to the documents produced in the course of the control of movement than to civil registers. They therefore provided a model for the experiments that followed in creating registration systems for social engineering, such as notably the National Socialist *Personenstandsgesetz*, in ways that the nineteenth-century registers of passports, travellers or residents in Germany never did. The ease of drawing up such registers and putting them to much more sinister uses was probably increased significantly, however, by the German population's long acquaintance with a tradition of being registered – often ineffectively so – by officials in many different contexts.

References

Allgemeines Landrecht für die preußischen Staaten. www.smixx.de/ra/Links_F-R/PrALR/pralr.html (accessed 17 July 2011).

—— www.koeblergerhard.de/Fontes/ALR1fuerdiepreussischenStaaten1794teil1.htm (accessed 17 July 2011).

Aly, Götz. 1984. *Die restlose Erfassung: Volkszählen, Identifizieren, Aussondern im Nationalsozialismus*. Berlin: Rotbuch Verlag.

Bauer, Martin. 2008. *Register zum Taufbuch der evangelischen Augustinergemeinde in Erfurt (1614–1655)*. Kleve: AMF Geschäftsstelle.

Bauernfeind, Walter. 2009. 'Die Personenstandsunterlagen des 19. und 20. Jahrhunderts im Stadtarchiv Nürnberg: Ein Bericht zur Überlieferung und Erschließung anlässlich der Übernahme der archivreifen Geburten-, Heirats- und Sterbebücher des Nürnberger Standesamts im Januar 2009.' *Archive in Bayern* 5: 15–34.

'Berliner Adressbücher.' http://adressbuch.zlb.de/ (accessed 17 July 2011).

Black, Edwin. 2001. *IBM und der Holocaust: die Verstrickung des Weltkonzerns in die Verbrechen der Nazis*. Berlin: Propyläen-Verl.

Blaschke, Olaf. 2009. 'Das Deutsche Kaiserreich im Zeitalter der Kulturkämpfe.' In *Das Deutsche Kaiserreich in der Kontroverse*, ed. Sven-Oliver Müller and Cornelius Torp. Göttingen: Vandenhoeck & Ruprecht, 186–202.

Boden, Ragna and Christoph Schmidt. 2006. 'Vom Kirchenbuch zum Personenstandsarchiv Detmold. Die Entwicklung des Personenstandswesens in Westfalen-Lippe.' In *Archive, Familienforschung und Geschichtswissenschaft: Annäherungen und Aufgaben*, vol. 7, *Veröffentlichungen des Landesarchivs Nordrhein-Westfalen*, ed. Bettina Joergens and Christian Reinicke. Düsseldorf: Landesarchiv Nordrhein-Westfalen, 56–73.

Bopp. 1834. 'Heimathsrecht (Indigenat).' In *Staats-Lexikon oder Encyclopädie der Staatswissenschaften*, vol. 7, ed. Carl von Rotteck and Carl Welcker. Altona: Johann Friedrich Hammerich, 665–672.

Borutta, Manuel. 2010. *Antikatholizismus: Deutschland und Italien im Zeitalter der europäischen Kulturkämpfe*. Göttingen: Vandenhoeck & Ruprecht.

Burger, Hannelore. 2000. 'Paßwesen und Staatsbürgerschaft.' In *Grenze und Staat: Passwesen, Staatsbürgerschaft, Heimatrecht und Fremdengesetzgebung in der österreichischen Monarchie 1750–1867*, ed. Waltraud Heindl and Edith Saurer. Wien: Böhlau, 3–172.

Burleigh, Michael and Wolfgang Wippermann. 1991. *The Racial State: Germany 1933–1945*. Cambridge: Cambridge University Press.

Chambers, William. 1839. *A Tour in Holland, the Countries on the Rhine, and Belgium: In the Autumn of 1838*. Edinburgh: William and Robert Chambers.

Clark, Christopher and Wolfram Kaiser, eds. 2003. *Culture Wars: Secular-Catholic Conflict in Nineteenth-Century Europe*. Cambridge: Cambridge University Press.

Cole, Simon. 2001. *Suspect Identities: A History of Fingerprinting and Criminal Identification*. Cambridge, MA: Harvard University Press.

Deutsches Reichsgesetzblatt. 1875. 'Gesetz über die Beurkundung des Personenstandes und die Eheschließung.' 23–40.

—— 1937. 'Personenstandsgesetz.' *Deutsches Reichsgesetzblatt*, 1146–1152.

Doehl, C. 1862. *Die Heimaths-Verhältnisse des Preussischen Staates: sowie dessen polizeiliche Beziehungen zum Auslande: nach amtlichen Quellen und authentischen Interpretationen*. Berlin: L. Gerschel.

Fahrmeir, Andreas. 2000a. *Citizens and Aliens: Foreigners and the Law in Britain and the German States, 1789–1870*. New York: Berghahn Books.

—— 2000b. 'Paßwesen und Staatsbildung im Deutschland des 19. Jahrhunderts.' *Historische Zeitschrift* 271: 57–91.

—— 2005. 'Bürgerbuch.' In *Enzyklopädie der Neuzeit*, vol. 2. Stuttgart: Metzler, 549f.

—— 2008. 'Klassen-Grenzen: Migrationskontrolle im 19. Jahrhundert.' *Rechtsgeschichte* 12: 125–138.

—— 2010. 'Ausweis und Passage: Reisende Juden in den deutschen Staaten des 19. Jahrhunderts.' *Simon Dubnow Institut Jahrbuch* 9: 119–138.

Faltin, Sigrid. 1987. *Die Auswanderung aus der Pfalz nach Nordamerika im 19. Jahrhundert: unter besonderer Beräcksichtigung des Landkommissariates Bergzabern*. Frankfurt am Main: P. Lang.

Franzen, Christoph. 2001. *Zivilisation und Konflikt: die Macdonald-Affäre und das britisch-preußische Verhältnis zur Zeit der Neuen Ära (1860–61)*. Siegburg: Schmitt.

Gosewinkel, Dieter. 2001. *Einbürgern und Ausschliessen: die Nationalisierung der Staatsangehörigkeit vom Deutschen Bund bis zur Bundesrepublik Deutschland*. Göttingen: Vandenhoeck & Ruprecht.

Günther, Wolfgang and Maja Schneider. 2006. 'Personenstandsüberlieferung in evangelischen Archiven unter besonderer Berücksichtigung von Westfalen und Lippe.' In *Archive, Familienforschung und Geschichtswissenschaft: Annäherungen und Aufgaben*, vol. 7, *Veröffentlichungen des Landesarchivs Nordrhein-Westfalen*, ed. Bettina Joergens and Christian Reinicke. Düsseldorf: Landesarchiv Nordrhein-Westfalen, 88–109.

Hochstadt, Steve. 1999. *Mobility and Modernity: Migration in Germany, 1820–1989*. Ann Arbor: University of Michigan Press.

Horn, Detlef. 2006. *100 Jahre Hemelinger Rathaus das Standesamt von Hemelingen*. Bremen: Sachbuch-Verlag.

Imhof, Arthur. 1977. *Einführung in die historische Demographie*. München: Beck.

Joergens, Bettina and Christian Reinicke. 2006. *Archive, Familienforschung und Geschichtswissenschaft: Annäherungen und Aufgaben*. Düsseldorf: Landesarchiv Nordrhein-Westfalen.

Jahresberichte für deutsche Geschichte – Ergebnisanzeige. http://jdgdb.bbaw.de/cgi-bin/jdg/cgi-bin/jdg (accessed 16 July 2011).

John Murray. 1854. *A hand-book for travellers on the Continent: being a guide through Holland, Belgium, Prussia and Northern Germany, and along the Rhine from Holland to Switzerland . . . With an index map*, 10th edn, etc. London: John Murray.

Kalm, Harald. 1994. *Das preussische Heroldsamt, 1855–1920: Adelsbehörde und Adelsrecht in der preussischen Verfassungsentwicklung*. Berlin: Duncker & Humblot.

Knodel, John. 1988. *Demographic Behavior in the Past: A Study of 14 German Village Populations in the Eighteenth and Nineteenth Centuries*. Cambridge: Cambridge University Press.

Krause, Johann. 1925. *Das deutsche Paßrecht: nach dem Stand vom 1. Januar 1925*. Berlin: Stilke.

Küster, Thomas. 1995. *Alte Armut und neues Bürgertum: öffentliche und private Fürsorge in Münster von der Ära Fürstenberg bis zum Ersten Weltkrieg (1756–1914)*. Münster: Aschendorff.

Leonhard, Jörn. 2009. *Empires und Nationalstaaten im 19. Jahrhundert*. Göttingen: Vandenhoeck & Ruprecht.

Lexikon des Mittelalters. 1977–1999. '"Matrikel, 1. Mittelalterliche Kirchenbücher."' In *Lexikon des Mittelalters*, vol. 6. Stuttgart: Metzler, 395.

Lucassen, Leo. 1996. *Zigeuner: die Geschichte eines polizeilichen Ordnungsbegriffes in Deutschland: 1700–1945*. Köln: Böhlau.

Markow, Alexis. 1889. *Das Wachstum der Bevölkerung und die Entwicklung der Aus- und Einwanderungen, Ab- und Zuzüge in Preussen und Preussens einzelnen Provinzen, Bezirken und Kreisgruppen von 1824 bis 1885*. Tübingen: Laupp.

Mettele, Gisela. 1998. *Bürgertum in Köln 1775–1870: Gemeinsinn und freie Association*. München: R. Oldenbourg.

Meyer, Beate. 2003. 'Hans Weinert, (Rasse)Anthropologe an der Universität Kiel von 1935 bis 1955.' In *Regionen im Nationalsozialismus*, vol. 10, *IZRG-Schriftenreihe*, ed. Michael Ruck and Karl Heinrich Pohl. Bielefeld: Verlag für Regionalgeschichte, 193–203.

Mohl, R[obert] von. 1834. 'Gensd'armerie.' In *Staats-Lexikon oder Encyclopädie der Staatswissenschaften*, vol. 6, ed. Carl von Rotteck and Carl Welcker. Altona: Johann Friedrich Hammerich, 514–518.

Muhs, Rudolf. 1998. 'Karl Blind: Ein Talent in der Wichtigmacherei.' In *Die Achtundvierziger: Lebensbilder aus der deutschen Revolution 1848–49*, ed. Sabine Freitag. München: C. H. Beck, 81–98, 312–315.

Müller, Alexander. 1841. *Die deutschen Auswanderungs-, Freizügigkeits- und Heimaths-Verhältnisse: Eine vergl. Darstellung der darüber in den Staaten des deutschen Bundes bes. in Oestreich, Preussen u. Sachsen*. Leipzig: Wienbrack.

Müller, Gerald. 1996. 'Das bayerische Reichsheroldenamt 1808–1825.' *Zeitschrift für bayerische Landesgeschichte* 59: 533–593.

Noiriel, Gérard. 1998. 'Surveiller les déplacements ou identifier les personnes? Contributions à l'histoire du passeport en France de la Ire à la IIIe république.' *Genèses: Sciences sociales et histoire* 30: 77–100.

—— 2001. 'Les pratiques policières d'identification des migrants et leurs enjeux pour l'histoire des relations de pouvoir. Contribution à une réflexion en longue durée.' In *Police et migrants*, ed. Caroline Douki, Marie-Claude Blanc-Chaléard, Nicole Dyonet and Vincent Milliot. Rennes: Presses universitaires de Rennes, 115–132.

Oepen, Joachim. 2006. 'Personenstandsüberlieferung in kirchlichen Archiven.' In *Archive, Familienforschung und Geschichtswissenschaft: Annäherungen und Aufgaben*, vol. 7, *Veröffentlichungen des Landesarchivs Nordrhein-Westfalen*, ed. Bettina Joergens and Joach Reinicke. Düsseldorf: Landesarchiv Nordrhein-Westfalen, 74–87.

Oesfeld, Max von. 1874. *Die Beurkundung des Personenstandes und die Form der Eheschliessung nach dem Preussischen Gesetz vom 9 März, 1874. Aus dem amtlichen Motiven und den Verhandlungen der beiden Häuser des Landtages ergänzt, erläutert, etc.* Breslau.

Pleiss, Detlev. 2004. 'Bevölkerungsschwund und Wiederbevölkerung des Henneberger Landes 1631–1660 im Spiegel der Kirchenbücher.' *Jahrbuch des Hennebergisch-Fränkischen Geschichtsvereins* 19: 155–217.

Reinecke, Christiane. 2010. *Grenzen der Freizügigkeit: Migrationskontrolle in Grossbritannien und Deutschland, 1880–1930*. München: R. Oldenbourg.

Reiss, Tom. 2005. *The Orientalist: Solving the Mystery of a Strange and a Dangerous Life*. New York: Random House.

Reitemeier, Arnd. 2005. *Pfarrkirchen in der Stadt des späten Mittelalters: Politik, Wirtschaft und Verwaltung*. Wiesbaden: F. Steiner Verlag.

Renz, Johannes. 2004. *Repertorien. Bestand E 157/1, Ministerium des Innern: Kommission für Adelsmatrikel (1442–) 1818–1924 (1931)*. Stuttgart: Hauptstaatsarchiv.

Reyscher, A. L., ed. 1835. 'General-Rescript, die Einführung neuer Kirche- und Familienbücher betr.' In *Vollständige, historische und kritisch bearbeitete Sammlung der württembergischen Gesetze*, vol. 9. Tübingen: Ludwig Friedrich Fues Kommission, 106–116.

Rittershausen, Konrad, Hans Jokisch and Hans-Jürgen Karp. 1981. *Das Bürgerbuch von Meseritz, 1731–1851*. Marburg/Lahn: J. G. Herder-Institut.

Rosenthal, Jacob. 2007. *Die Ehre des jüdischen Soldaten die Judenzählung im Ersten Weltkrieg und ihre Folgen*. Frankfurt am Main: Campus.

Roth, Ralf. 1996. *Stadt und Bürgertum in Frankfurt am Main: ein besonderer Weg von der standischen zur modernen Burgergesellschaft, 1790–1914*. München: Oldenbourg.

Schlumbohm, Jürgen. 1997. 'Gesetze, die nicht durchgesetzt werden – ein Strukturmerkmal des frühneuzeitlichen Staates?' *Geschichte und Gesellschaft* 23: 647–663.

Schneider, Michael C. 2011. 'Wissensproduktion im Staat: Das königlich preußische Statistische Bureau zwischen 1860 und 1914.' Habilitation, Goethe Universität, Frankfurt am Main.

Schubert, Werner. 1987. 'Preußen und die Zivilehe in der Nachmärzzeit.' *Zeitschrift der Savigny-Stiftung für Rechtsgeschichte, Germanistische Abteilung* 117: 216–246.

Schwan, Friedrich. 2006. *Die französischen Personenstandsurkunden im linksrheinischen Deutschland: ein Leitfaden für Standesbeamte und Ahnenforscher*, 2nd edn. Ludwigshafen: Pfälzisch-Rheinische Familienkunde.

Seymour, Bruce. 1996. *Lola Montez: A Life*. New Haven, CT: Yale University Press.

Siemann, Wolfram. 1981. 'Guiseppe Mazzini in Württemberg? Ein Fall staatspolizeilicher Fahndung im Reaktionssystem des Vormärz.' *Zeitschrift für Württembergische Landesgeschichte* 40: 547–560.

Spencer, Elaine. 1992. *Police and the Social Order in German Cities: The Düsseldorf District, 1848–1914*. DeKalb: Northern Illinois University Press.

Thier, Andreas. 1999. *Steuergesetzgebung und Verfassung in der konstitutionellen Monarchie: Staatssteuerreformen in Preussen, 1871–1893*. Frankfurt am Main: V. Klostermann.

Vesque von Püttlingen, Johann. 1842. *Die gesetzliche Behandlung der Auslaender in Oesterreich: nach d. daselbst gueltigen Civilrechts-, Straf-, Commerzial-, Militaer- u. Polizei-Normen, nebst e. einl. Abh. ueber d. oesterr.* Wien: Ueberreuter.

Vogt, Wilhelm. 1875. '"Völk, Joseph."' In *Allgemeine Deutsche Biographie*, vol. 40. Leipzig: Duncker & Humblot, 230–232. www.deutsche-biographie.de/sfz84016.html#azi (accessed 17 July 2011).

Wagner, Patrick. 2005. *Bauern, Junker und Beamte: lokale Herrschaft und Partizipation im Ostelbien des 19. Jahrhunderts*. Göttingen: Wallstein.

Württembergische Jahrbücher. 1823. *Württembergische Jahrbücher für vaterländische Geschichte, Geographie, Statistik und Topographie*. Stuttgart: Aue.

4

Japan's Civil Registration Systems Before and After the Meiji Restoration

OSAMU SAITO AND MASAHIRO SATO

Prologue

ON 8 FEBRUARY 1763, a 44-year-old poor peasant woman named Ken refused to affix her seal to that year's population register. Herman Ooms's intriguing account of Ken's lifelong struggle for justice begins with this unusual incident in Makibuse village of Shinano province (Ozaki 1985; Ooms 1996, ch. 1). The story involves a case of disinheritance and the subsequent murder of her disinherited brother, both of which had happened twenty-one years before the population register incident; in 1759 Ken had lodged a petition, which amounted to accusations directed at her uncle and village officials in relation to the murder case, but at the same time was seeking some sort of justice for that crime committed seventeen years earlier. The refusal to certify her household's entry in the register four years later, therefore, was a manifestation of her anger and resentment that such justice had not been done. Her misbehaved, gambling and drunken brother had been disowned by the mother, under 'the will of the lineage' and, presumably, under pressure from village officials as well, and it had been subsequent intra-lineage quarrels which had led to his violent death, beaten up by his uncle and fellow villagers. We learn from Ooms's expositions and interpretations of Tokugawa legal code and practice that one possible reason why the 'murder' was regarded as justifiable – and it was Ken who bore the brunt of the community's criticism – was the fact that he had been disowned by the parent, since, under Tokugawa law, those who were disowned became outlaws. We also learn that following her brother's death, her mother's eventual death, and her own third husband's disappearance, Ken lived alone in her house; she was the head of the household in 1763.

This brief account of a series of rather unusual events that took place in a small village some 250 years ago suggests something about how eighteenth-century Japan's civil registration system worked and how different it was from the one introduced after the Meiji Restoration of 1868. This chapter first traces the evolution of systems of household and land registration from Tokugawa times to the period of early Meiji reforms in the 1870s and 1880s, in an age in which markets in land and labour were expanding – slowly in the beginning, then accelerating towards the end of the period.[1] The tie between family and land was the building block of a society in which as many as 80 per cent of the population were classified as 'peasants'. Then a section on the new Meiji state's reform efforts turns to the issue of continuity and discontinuity, while the following section discusses if any progress was made by the Meiji reforms with respect to *civil identity* registration. The chapter ends with an account of another dispute which was brought before court some 120 years after Ken's dispute, in a different province. Though less eventful than in Ken's case, the Meiji dispute also involved a peasant woman and an attempted disinheritance. This 1880 story will, it is hoped, illustrate some of the key changes that took place in the significance of identity registration procedures at the village level across the Tokugawa-Meiji transition.

Tokugawa registration practices

When Japan introduced China's ancient state model in the seventh century CE, the package included a household registration system (see Chapter 1). However, this ancient experiment failed to take root and persist. It was not until the late sixteenth century that a renewed initiative in household registration was made. The period marked the end of a century-long era of warring states within Japan and, not surprisingly, the unifiers wanted to know more about the people and their land that came under their rule. Thus, the early modern concept of 'registration' started as a state project. Nevertheless, as we will see below, this should not be taken to imply that the early modern systems of registration worked only from above.

Land registration

Japan's early modern regime began with cadastral surveys. The series of surveys was undertaken from the 1580s onwards by the successive unifiers, Oda Nobunaga, Toyotomi Hideyoshi and Tokugawa Ieyasu. Their project of surveying was expected to serve as a means to separate samurai, professional warriors – who later became sedentary civil servants – from peasants, a class devoted, supposedly, entirely to agriculture. This was to facilitate the collection of taxes from the peasant class, and to tighten control over 300 *daimyō* (overlords) and the assignment of fiefs to them. In addition to these aims, the overlords themselves were interested in curbing geographical mobility of their own peasants; for them land and peasants were their

[1] For relationships between Tokugawa Japan's peasant household economy and factor markets, see Saito (2009).

power base, in both a fiscal and a military sense. Inevitably the whole process of surveying land and peasants was prolonged, but it is said to have been completed nearly everywhere by the end of the 1610s. Some overlords made second surveys later, trying to get hold of newly reclaimed areas of farmland.

With these surveys, the territorial boundaries of the village (*mura* – etymologically a 'cluster' of houses) were demarcated. The official status of the village community may be traced back to the seventh century when the Chinese system of government was introduced. However, it was not until the late sixteenth and early seventeenth centuries that the village's territory was authoritatively recorded and its status as an administrative unit was firmly established. The village was an autonomous organization with its own office created within the community. The office holders, restricted in many cases to the heads of prominent families, were selected by the village assembly, and it was they who managed village-level political affairs free from supervision from above (T. Sato 1990, 53–55; Smith 1959, 54–56). For the office and officers (we will have a closer look at how the village office worked in the next section) the cadastral compilations provided detailed information about the relationship between property-holding and identifiable persons. The villagers, who had to pay the land tax, were those whose names were recorded in the land register. However, the overlord's government did not levy the tax on an individual basis. Everywhere, it was the village community's responsibility to pay all the taxes levied collectively on the villagers' land; thus, the village had to pay the sum of all those taxes even when one or two failed to bring their shares in. As a result of this peculiar system of taxation (called *murauke*), while the overlord held the ultimate ownership of the entire territory, his government lost interest in the administration of individual-level landholdings, so that the individual peasants gained the right to use an individual plot of land in an exclusive manner and also the *de facto* right of disposal of that land, even though under Tokugawa law it is true that the 'perpetual sale' of cultivated land was prohibited.

In practice, however, sales did take place, often taking the form of 'a pledge irredeemable after ten years', although the number of years was in many cases a matter of mutual arrangement. On the other hand, the village community held a discretionary power in the land transaction process. Thus, every transaction involved both the seller's relatives, who countersealed the document, and the village officials, whose function was to 'affix an official seal and change the names in the land register' (Wigmore 1967–1986, pt 2: 11).[2] In fact, there existed more openly 'perpetual' sales of cultivated land. In such cases, the headman may not have affixed his official seal; yet, as a report of Mikawa province's Nukata district suggests, he was 'usually privy to it' (Wigmore 1967–1986, pt 2: 18). The land registers and other related documents were thus kept by village officials, never by samurai

[2] For the publication of this data collection, see note 5 below.

magistrates, suggesting that land registration during the Tokugawa period was administered almost exclusively by the village community.

In Ken's case, land registration did not play an important part (which was rather unusual since most disputes between Tokugawa villagers involved land). This is probably because Ken's family possessed only a minuscule amount of land. At the end of 1740 her family's holdings were only 0.19 *koku*; at the start of 1727 the figure had been 1.97 *koku*, even then an amount with which no family of four could make a living without extra earnings from non-farm by-employments (Ooms 1996, 50).[3] It was for this reason that Ken's brother got involved in horse trading, which was not regarded as a steady job in the Tokugawa agrarian world; it was this shady trade which eventually led him to a quarrel with his uncle, and hence to his violent death. However, as Ooms notes, their family had been a prominent, core member of the village; but over the period prior to the early eighteenth century, they had lost their properties one by one, presumably in the form of foreclosure of the mortgaged land. Thus landholdings did change hands and every change was registered at the village office. Indeed, it was the village community that kept lists of all plots of cultivated land, and the names of holders of the fields concerned and the titles thus certified, since any change in land ownership had tax implications. Owing to this, and also because of the absence of an independent institutional arrangement that could handle inter-village disputes, the village officials tried hard to keep market transactions in land within the village. In the administration of land registration, too, there was a tendency for the concepts of registration and entitlement not to extend beyond the village boundary.

Household registration

In addition to the village land registers, the Tokugawa regime launched a system of household registration later in the seventeenth century, as a religious survey (*shūmon aratame*). Following a decision to cut ties with the Jesuits, whose missionary activities were viewed as threatening, the Tokugawa shogunate government ordered all overlords in 1665 to take a religious census. In every village the officials drew up a new list of households and their members for inspection by the head of each household and the head priest of the respective temple; both affixed the seals to the compiled register, certifying that they were not believers in the prohibited cult of Christianity (Cornell and Hayami 1986; Hayami 2001, 26–37).

However, since this form of registration became annual from 1671 onwards, the compilation eventually gained an additional function, as keeping a register of households and population. Table 4.1 represents the format of a sample page from

[3] *Koku* is a capacity measure used for rice. Under Tokugawa rule every piece of land was assessed in terms of yields in rice-equivalents, and in those days it was widely recognized that a yield of one *koku* would be enough to feed an adult for a year.

a typical *shūmon* register in the year 1773. It lists the name and age of the principal householder at the head of the list, his religious affiliation and related information, the wife's age and religious information (if different), the children's names, sex and ages, and finally the totals for that household (for names only first names were given, which was a Tokugawa practice). Note that the term 'head of the household' (*koshu*) is not given, and that the name of the wife is omitted here. The latter cannot be taken to imply that women's position was weak in the peasant family, for, as the case of Ken of Makibuse indicates, peasant women sometimes behaved differently from that prescribed in samurai-adopted Confucian teachings (Walthall 1991, 60). On the other hand, the absence of a term for the head of household is probably a reflection of rural Tokugawa practice, since studies of Meiji family law have made it clear that the authority of male headship was strengthened during the Meiji period, implying that it had been weaker previously. In Tokugawa village customary practice, while the head was customarily a male, it did not mean that, as we will see below, women were legally excluded from the succession to headship, nor did it imply that the male head could act against interests of the corporate entity of the family (called '*ie*').

Every year in every village in the country, two registers were prepared: the original was filed in an office of the samurai magistrate in charge, while the duplicate remained with the village headman, implying that all the information contained in the register remained within the village. Moreover, once in every six years the aggregate results were reported to the shogunate government. In other words, a religious survey that had been started to stamp out Christianity now took on two

Table 4.1 A sample page from a *shūmon aratame* register

One household *NAME [Seal]*			
NAME	Age	Address and NAME of temple, denomination	[Seal]
Wife	Age	Address and NAME of temple, denomination	[Seal]
Daughter NAME	Age	Address and NAME of temple, denomination	[Seal]
Son NAME	Age	Address and NAME of temple, denomination	[Seal]
Daughter NAME	Age	Address and NAME of temple, denomination	[Seal]
Son NAME	Age	Address and NAME of temple, denomination	[Seal]
Total [ ] Of which Males [ ] Females [ ]			

Source: From the 1773 register, Kōmi village, Motosu-gun, Mino province.

Notes

1. The name and seal at the top of the page are those of the head of the list.
2. The name of the wife is not given.
3. The seal affixed at the end of each individual entry is that of a temple.

new functions: the government's undertaking of periodical censuses and local administrations' record-keeping.

It was the village office that administered all the registration procedures, kept the records and used them for any administrative purpose when necessary. There were all together more than 60,000 such villages in Tokugawa Japan, and each was administered by a group of about ten officials. They were capable of reading and drafting these as well as other formal documents in an almost identical style (called *oieryū*), which was accepted by both samurai and commoners across the country. Formal and informal schooling brought this style to children of many well-to-do peasants, so that one may say that 'there was no great difference, in terms of literacy, between peasant officialdom and samurai' (Moriya 1990).[4] Villagers, on the other hand, were entitled to make requests to the village office with respect to any matters of their members' civil status and registration. Some were not literate, as in Ken's case, but Ken apparently had no difficulty finding someone who was able to draft a formal request on her behalf (Ooms 1996, 40–41), suggesting that the general level of literacy among peasants was not low even in the mid-eighteenth century. Indeed, according to one estimate, 43 per cent of boys and 10 per cent of girls – the vast majority of whom were peasant children – acquired some form of basic literacy at school by the end of the Tokugawa period (Dore 1965, 317–322).

However, this should not be taken to imply that a *national* system of registration of demographic events came into existence. According to *Zenkoku minji kanrei ruishū*, compiled and published by the newly established Ministry of Justice in 1880, and translated into English later as *Law and Justice in Tokugawa Japan*,[5] the ways in which demographic events such as birth, marriage and death were registered varied from place to place. In the case of the registration of birth, for example, the 1880 *ruishū* reveals that, while in most cases the report was made to the village office, either orally or in writing, there were areas where it was given to the parish temple or neighbours, only. There were some other variations: for example, in the Abe and Udo districts of Suruga province, 'births are reported to the village office, but not registered. Those above ten years of age are annually entered in the official register, and only once in every seven years those below ten years of age are registered'; in the Moda district of Kazusa province, 'births must be reported immediately . . . but children below seven are usually excluded from the register' (Wigmore 1967–1986, pt 7: 15). There existed cases in which even conception was required to be reported to the village office, although as noted for Miyagi of Rikuzen province, 'the majority of people do not observe this rule because

[4] For the range of tasks the village officials did, see T. Sato (1990, 53–55, 61–62).

[5] The publication of John Henry Wigmore's translation of the *ruishū* started in 1892 as contributions to the *Transactions of the Asiatic Society of Japan*, but did not finish in his lifetime. The more comprehensive edition was published after the Second World War by the University of Tokyo Press (Wigmore 1967–1986).

of the trouble of writing'; and in a couple of districts of Chikuzen province, despite seemingly thorough supervision of 'births and nurture of infants' by 'special officers', 'the child presents himself at the religious survey' only at 7 years of age (Wigmore 1967–1986, pt 7: 17, 19, 20, 30).[6] It is likely that there were greater regional variations with respect to the registration of death, marriage and adoption. Indeed, although the 1880 volume simply notes that the procedures of registration were 'similar to those of births', it is recorded that in the district of Ise, 'Cases of death, marriage, adoption, etc. are not reported immediately, such changes of family members being all registered at the time of the religious survey [i.e. every six years]' (Wigmore 1967–1986, pt 7: 45, 108, 225).

All this suggests that the timing of registration varied considerably from place to place. On the other hand, there is no hint in the 1880 *ruishū* that Tokugawa Japan's identity registration was anything but compulsory. Everybody in the village entered the register; the only exception was small children who died early – in some exceptional cases, before the child reached 7 years of age, but in most cases, before the next year's annual household and population register was compiled. To put it differently, the Tokugawa system of civil registration was fairly universal; as for the commoners, the only problem lay in the area of vital registration.

In the early years of Tokugawa rule, after a series of famines and peasant disturbances in the 1630s and 1640s in particular, the shogunate government was preoccupied with the question of how to cope with village affairs. They produced a body of regulatory edicts and ordinances, according to which peasants were subjected to many restrictions on, for example, their own mobility. They were discouraged from leaving the village to work elsewhere, working land outside the village, and moving the household out of the village (Totman 1993, 111–113). This may be taken to suggest that the implementation of the religious (*shūmon*) registration system in the subsequent decades was in fact in order to take control of people's whereabouts across the country, and hence that it must have been effective in tying the peasants to the land. However, Ken's story indicates that both her father and brother were able to leave the village – to work in Edo (Tokyo) for two years in the father's case, and for five years in the brother's case. Temporal or seasonal migration was thus not uncommon, and in most cases out-migrants did not bother to notify their departure to the village office. Ken, too, tried to move her house formally out of the village in the later stage of her long battle with the village authorities. A cursory look at standard registration practice reveals that there existed a built-in procedure within the registration system:

> If a tradesman wishes to transfer to another province, a notification must be made to the local office, which issues a transfer certificate, and permits the applicant to leave

[6] Note that all ages were given in traditional Japanese *sai*, according to which a child was reckoned as 1 at birth.

> the place. Farmers, however, cannot leave unless they have appointed an heir, as they must pay land-taxes.
>
> (Wigmore 1967–1986, pt 7: 181)

The general rule, in other words, was that 'a person may remove and transfer his registration quite freely, if he notifies the local office and obtains the transfer certificate' (Wigmore 1967–1986, pt 7: 185, for the Katori district of Shimōsa province). This formal procedure enabled a non-heir son who established himself as an apprenticed tradesman or craftsman, or a branch household elsewhere, to move residence legally. On the other hand, the rule implies that the system allowed village authorities to regulate people's movement. It explains not only why actual procedures varied from district to district, but also the reason why peasants 'cannot leave unless they have appointed an heir'. Since the total amount of land taxes was fixed for a village, with the tax unit being the household, any change in the number of households in the village would affect everybody else's tax payment, as a result of which the village officials were far more concerned with the movement of a household than with that of an individual (Saito 2009, 185). All this meant that while the Tokugawa system of identity registration was universal in the sense that no one would be administratively invisible as long as he or she was a commoner, the village boundary mattered in relation to his or her own mobility.

However, there was an exception to these rules. As suggested above with respect to the disinheritance case of Ken's brother, the removal of one's name as a member of a particular household from the village's population register meant a loss of civil protection in Tokugawa society. Tokugawa civil code and practice allowed the head of the family to 'disown' a child:

> If a son or a younger brother misconducts himself and does not obey the admonition of the father or the elder brother, the latter may report the circumstances to the local office and he is reprimanded at the office. If he still does not reform, generally an application for disowning is made, and the authorities inquire into the circumstances, and if they decide that there is no probability of his reformation, they grant the application and remove his name from the register.[7]
>
> (Wigmore 1967–1986, pt 7: 211–212)

The act of disowning was called *kyūri* or *kandō*, the former meaning 'long separation' and the latter 'to consider the appropriate punishment' (Wigmore 1967–1986, pt 7: 211, n.7). This usage of words implies two things. One implication is that disowning a child was – to borrow the phrase from Ooms – a 'punishment' by the family and the community and also a 'protection against possible prosecution of his or her relatives and kumi [i.e. neighbourhood group] members for crimes he

[7] Strictly speaking, the right of the head of the family is different from the parental right. For example, the report from the Abe and Udo districts of Suruga province uses the former term, while that from Aki province's Aki district speaks of the latter (Wigmore 1967–1986, pt 7: 214, 220).

or she might commit' (Ooms 1996, 44). Also it is implied that, after being denied a place in the village community, the disowned could not obtain a certificate of transfer, either. Thus, the removal from the register (*chō-hazure*) meant that the disowned also lost all the kinds of 'protection' they could expect from the community. As the report from Izu province's Tagata district notes, the disowned became 'a vagrant' in most cases (Wigmore 1967–1986, pt 7: 215). Moreover, it is reported that in the Shiga district of Ōmi province, 'when a [registerless] person . . . returns without permission, the *hinin* watchman is ordered to drive him away' (Wigmore 1967–1986, pt 7: 216).[8] In other words, the disowned were outlaws.

It is probably because of this grave consequence that not just relatives but also village authorities were involved in the procedures of a disowning case, and, in fact, many authorities seem to have tried to avoid such a draconian outcome. Indeed, there were cases where the name of the disowned was not removed from the register but was just tagged or put in an appendix, or not removed unless he committed a crime twice (the former is found in Ōmi, Shimōsa, Hitachi and Sanuki provinces, while the latter is found in the Tōtōmi case; see Wigmore 1967–1986, pt 7: 214, 215, 216, 220–221). Moreover, the authorities were pleased to 'allow his name to be re-entered in the register' as soon as an application was made by the family on the grounds that he was 'reformed' (as in the Kii case; see Wigmore 1967–1986, pt 7: 220). On the other hand, the rules were such that there were always a sizeable number of the disowned.

They were joined by another type of registerless people. A chapter on absconding in the 1880 *ruishū* shows that when a person absconded, a two-stage search was made, with six months between the stages. 'After a lapse of a year [from the second search order], or sometimes three years, the absconder's name is removed from the register' (Wigmore 1967–1986, pt 7: 134). Seasonal and short-term out-migration without notification to the village office was tolerated on the assumption that they would eventually come home. In reality, however, there were a substantial number of people who failed to return to the village. Also, there were those who simply disappeared, such as those who failed to pay debts.

Obviously, not all local authorities removed the names of those people automatically. Some were apparently half-hearted in tracing missing villagers. In many cases, it seems that the names were not removed from the register unless 'it is feared that he may commit a crime while missing' (as in the case of Tajima province's Kinosaki district). One consequence of this practice is not surprising: as reported from the Miyazaki and Koyu districts of Hyuga province, 'very often a person calculated to be over a hundred years old is found' in the village population register

[8] The '*hinin* watchman' was an outcast person employed by the village community. There were many areas around Kyoto and Osaka where outcasts were involved in police work. Ōmi was one such area (Wigmore 1967–1986, pt 7: 7).

(Wigmore 1967–1986, pt 7: 149, 157–158). A majority of those 'centenarians' must have long since been dead elsewhere.

In other cases, however, the village authorities were more careful and meticulous. Those people were tagged or appended so that the village's *de facto* population could be reckoned separately from its *de jure* population (Cornell and Hayami 1986, 171–173; Hayami 2001, 28–31). A village of Mino province called Nishijo was one such case, where each household was appended with a section in which household members who had left the household to work elsewhere or to get married were recorded. Although the date of moving-out was not given, the section (called *sotogaki*, literally 'outside section') lists all those who moved out elsewhere and still stayed away (see Table 4.4 below; see also Saito and Hamano 2006, 164; Cornell and Hayami 1986, 171–172). Similar lists are said to have been compiled in many places and called differently; in Hitachi province's Ibaraki district, for example, it was called an 'appended register' (Wigmore 1967–1986, pt 7: 139, 126). In other cases, the village authorities compiled a separate register for those who were supposed to be in other provinces, listing not just 'absconders' but temporary out-migrants as well: for example, this is what village officials in Tōtōmi province's Sano district were doing (Wigmore 1967–1986, pt 7: 137).

All these examples may be taken to suggest that the village authorities tried to come to terms with the reality of out-migration. However, given the general custom quoted above, many must have become registerless eventually, and as contemporaries thought, most of the registerless drifted towards towns and cities. The historian Naotaro Sekiyama speculates, based on a remark by one overlord at the time of a famine in the late eighteenth century, that with both types of the registerless together they could have amounted to one million (Sekiyama 1958, 57, 155), though this is probably an overestimate.[9]

In principle, the outcasts were all registered, but separately from the commoners. The 1880 *ruishū* makes it clear that they were 'registered separately, and the temple register of each [category of the outcasts] is filed at the feudal office' (Wigmore 1967–1986, pt 7: 3). Sekiyama also notes that although in some provinces they may not have been included in population totals, individually they were all registered (1958, 90–92). However, while the ruling class of samurai are said to have been covered by religious surveys, their registers were apparently never compiled (Sekiyama 1958, 89–90), thus suggesting that Tokugawa Japan's civil registration was in practice implemented to cover the ruled, but not the ruling elite.

[9] The country's total population in this period is estimated to have been about 31 million.

The Meiji registration system

The Tokugawa regime collapsed in 1868. While the new regime took the form of a restoration of imperial rule, the pressing need for the 'Restoration' forces was perceived as being how to build a new nation state. Before the new government were competing models of state formation. One set of concerns was a debate over a centuries-old Chinese typology in government: central, bureaucratic rule (*gunken*) versus decentralized, feudal divisions (*hōken*). Since the Tokugawa regime was considered a typical example of the latter model, the new Meiji government opted for the former, which meant the increasing centralization of all systems. Another set of concerns was the balance to be achieved between an indigenous nationalism and Western influences in relation to the reforms the incoming government wanted to carry out. After the opening of the country in 1859, there was an influx of Western learning and ideas, giving rise to a period of 'civilization and enlightenment' (*bunmei kaika*). Many of the themes of the Japanese enlightenment were instrumental in institution-building, but at the same time the pro-Western arguments alarmed conservatives. Thus, the state had to make a delicate choice in many areas while attempting its institutional reforms. The registration of family and land was one such area.

Household registration

A new system of household registration was introduced in 1872. When promulgated, it was proudly proclaimed in the Preamble to this first Family Registration Law that:

> Any government's first and most important task is to clarify the count of households and the number of population. There is no need to be said that the protection of the people of the nation is the primary objective of this Sovereign State. Without a count of people to be protected, how could the protective duties be provided?[10]

The language used sounds Confucian: it was probably meant to appeal to the Confucian sentiment of benevolence, not to any version of modern welfare statism. It is therefore difficult to know what kind of 'protective duties' the government actually contemplated. On the other hand, there is evidence that the new government faced a 'law and order' problem in the capital city; as soon as the civil war with the Tokugawa and its allies was over, a large number of masterless samurai flowed into the metropolitan areas. Decrees and notices issued by a newly created Council prior to the promulgation of the Family Registration Law often mentioned the rampages of unregistered, penniless ex-samurai in Tokyo, relating this issue to the

[10] *Ordinance of the Grand Council of State*, no. 170, 1871.

urgency of tighter registration.[11] Whatever the ulterior motive of this literature, the Preamble to the 1872 law does suggest that the new government was committed to creating a *comprehensive* system of registration.

The abolition of the decentralized governance structure in the previous year paved the way to a centralized institution-building in the area of population accounting. An important departure from the Tokugawa past was made to bring all social classes (except the royal family) in every region of the country under a unified framework. Across the country, a standardized identity register was used. The entries in this 1872 register format were: address, ownership of the house, status distinction (aristocracy, ex-samurai, commoner, or new commoner), occupation, headship and the relation to the head, birth year, and age; for adopted or married-in members of the household, the address of the former residence, status, and the parents' names and status were also required to be entered – all registered with surnames. It was much more detailed than the Tokugawa register, although its entries were a little simplified later, as shown in Table 4.2.[12] It is important to realize that for the first time the ruling elite were treated equally with the ruled. Also, upon the Edict of Emancipation in 1871 the former outcasts were integrated into the commoner class, although in fact the added adjective 'new' in the 1872 register made their emancipation only nominal (discrimination against the former outcasts may well have increased rather than decreased).[13] It is believed that actual methods of recording and monitoring at the local level remained largely the same as in Tokugawa times. There was also a requirement to take a comprehensive survey of population and households once every six years, which had been another aspect of the Tokugawa-Meiji continuity (M. Sato 2002, 45–49).

Meiji Japan's civil code, which came into effect in 1898, is known for its unusually strong emphasis on the authority of the family head in its private law areas. Indeed, the adopted version was a product of a long, politicized discussion. An earlier draft in 1890, based largely on an individualist French model, was criticized by a group of conservative scholars as well as politicians, who argued that its adoption would destroy traditional family values as the draft did not make enough provisions for the head of the family. One spokesman for the group blasted it, saying that 'Loyalty and filial piety will perish with the enactment of the civil code.' It was a version revised substantially along this conservative line that was enacted eventually (see Frank *et al.* 2005, 3.1; Hirakawa 1989, 472–479).

The revision was most marked in the area of family law. Thus, according to the 1898 civil code, members of the family household or 'house' (*ie*) were subject to

[11] *Transmittals of the Executive Council*, nos. 261, 267, 323 and 358, 1869. The Gyōseikan (Executive Council) was replaced by the Dajōkan (Grand Council of State) in July 1869.

[12] A similar model register is tabulated in Winther (2008, 28). However, it is a form attached to an 1875 draft for the revision of family registration procedures, which did not materialize.

[13] The 1872 register was in use until post-war years. It was as late as 1968 that it was officially closed.

Table 4.2. Meiji household registration format

Date		
Address		
Status		
Former head NAME		
Date of succession of headship [Seal]		
	Head	NAME [Eldest] son of former head NAME Date of birth
Date of marriage-in [Second] daughter of NAME, status, address		
	Mother	NAME Wife of former head Date of birth
Date of marriage-in [Third] daughter of NAME, status, address		
	Wife	NAME Date of birth
	Eldest son	NAME Date of birth
	Eldest daughter	NAME Date of birth
	Second son	NAME Date of birth

Note: 1896 format adopted by the Home Ministry.

the authority of the head. Daughters-in-law and adopted children entered an *ie* and, hence, were registered as such only with the consent of its head (Article 750). The head could even determine a member's place of residence in so far as such an action was considered necessary for the family (Article 749). The primacy of the household head was firmly established by the 1898 civil code (de Becker 1921, 647–654; Frank *et al.* 2005, 283–285), although, as we will see below, it is important to realize that in areas other than family law, especially in property law, much of the individualist principle inherent in the earlier draft code of 1890 was in fact retained.

The Family Registration Law, revised at the time of the enactment of the 1898 civil code, did not alter the 1872 procedures greatly. However, its administration was transferred to the Ministry of Justice from the Home Ministry (to which the

Statistical Bureau belonged). With this change, a couple of small but important modifications were made. One was the exclusion of occupation from the entries in the registration form. Another was that the idea of census taking through registration data was abandoned, which became a separate agenda leading to the implementation by the Statistical Bureau of the first national census in 1920. Both may be taken to suggest that, under the 1898 regime, household registration was placed in the field of 'law and order', rather than that of 'population and statistics', making it clear that the central state was now fully prepared to deal with criminality on the one hand and local disputes over inheritance and privileges on the other (M. Sato 2002, 51, n.9).

Land registration

In 1872 another important change was made with respect to the registration question. A certificate of ownership (*chiken*) was issued to the holder of any parcel of land in the country, on which the name and address of the holder, the location, category and area of the parcel, and also its monetary value were indicated. Table 4.3 shows that the certificate was signed by the governor of a prefecture with his seal also affixed. The original was kept by the landholder himself and the copy filed at the prefectural office. With the issue of such certificates, the ownership of land property in the modern sense was formally established. In the next year the government announced a radical revision of taxation on land; the 1872 certificate was to be substituted by a new one in the course of the land tax reform, although it took several years to complete the whole process. When the owner sold a parcel of land to someone else, the transfer was endorsed at the local government office, where the name and address of the new owner were added on the back of the certificate. Clearly this ownership certificate, especially its copy kept by the prefectural office, served also as a register document, replacing the age-old framework based on cadastral surveys. This registration mode lasted until 1889 when a new type of land register was introduced, although the principal new features of the registration system established in 1872–1873 remained the same.

One crucial but probably unintended consequence of the whole reform was that the village community no longer mattered: the village administration lost its discretionary power to influence market transactions in land. Together with this new registration framework came a Western, centralized court system. The whole system enabled anyone to buy and sell a parcel of land across the administrative boundaries and, if the client failed to keep his promise, to take the case to court. The reason why the government underwent such a radical land reform was fiscal, to secure a stable source of tax revenue. In so doing, however, they brought in two important changes. First, the state formally granted the peasant landholder the title to that land. Second, the land tax was now to be paid in cash, not in kind. This monetization drive, together with the confirmation of absolute private ownership, enabled

Table 4.3. Certificate of land ownership

No. [ ]

CERTIFICATE

Location

Address
Owner NAME

Area

Monetary value

Issued upon inspection

NAME of Governor [Seal]

Date

NAME of Officer [Seal]

Source: An 1873 certificate issued by Akita prefecture. www.daito.ac.jp/~mnoguchi/tanto_kougi/kougi_fudosan/fudosan_chiken.htm.

transactions in land to take place more openly and frequently. The certificates thus functioned as marketable securities in the age of market expansion.

Given the significance of the land–family bond in the Tokugawa period, it is interesting to see if the primacy of the family head, identified in the registration of a household and its members, was also expressed in the above mode of land registration. Recently it has been argued that:

> Under the Meiji civil code that governed the household registers, wives, concubines, children, siblings, parents, extended or adopted family, and servants were enumerated as members of the head's household but, like livestock, land, and inanimate objects, they were bound to the head legally as his property.
>
> (Winther 2008, 27)

The statement is strong but metaphorical. Even so, what is suggested is that the head's authority extended to landed property, which is misleading. Indeed, a cursory look at the form of the certificate of ownership (see Table 4.3) reveals that there was no sign of familial information on any part of the document. It is also clear from the corresponding provisions of the 1898 civil code that an individual family member was allowed to own separate property in his or her own name (Article 748). In other words, on the death of the family head, the property right of the family land could be passed on separately from that of the headship. Given the weight of this legal evidence, therefore, it is wrong to conclude that both were centred on the corporate family household (*ie*): household registration was based on the *ie* concept, but land registration was not. As Joseph de Becker noted in 1921,

> the idea of property belonging to a house [*ie*] itself, and the head of the house being merely the manager thereof, is now obsolete from the legal point of view at least, although it must be conceded that many an old-fashioned and conscientious head of a house is still governed by that idea.
>
> (de Becker 1921, 637)

Legally speaking, the Tokugawa concept of family property and the idea of the head 'being merely the manager thereof' now gave way to a more individualist principle. Apparently, under the new Meiji regime, power relationships within the family changed. Headship was strengthened in both legal and economic-financial terms, enabling the family property to be more secure as long as the head remained risk-averse, but, paradoxically, much less so whenever he ventured to take a risk in a newly opened-up business world.

Tokugawa-Meiji comparisons

Having surveyed the evolution of registration systems in Japan from the seventeenth to the nineteenth century, one may ask whether or not progress in relation to *civil identity* registration was actually made in the Tokugawa-Meiji transition, and, if any, then what sort of progress it could be in terms of the liberal individualist and gender-egalitarian notions of 'modernity'?

Let us first examine the role of the family head in registration procedures. Here the yardstick cannot be the dichotomy of corporate versus individualist principle as in both Tokugawa and Meiji times the mode of registration was centred on the family household, not on the individual. A more realistic distinction is probably between management by face-to-face contacts and management by written documents. Although the degree to which written documentation played a role in Tokugawa village society should not be underestimated (Ooms 1996, 69–70), the early Meiji period did see a decisive shift taking place from the former to the latter mode of management.[14] In this respect, it is worth reiterating that in the Tokugawa register the headship was assumed, whereas under the Meiji civil code the head was a legally recognized status. In both Tokugawa and Meiji times, it is likely that people's perception of the family and their expectation about the role of the head remained virtually unchanged. Under traditional Japan's stem family system, one child stayed on in the household, who would inherit both headship and family property from the father. The child could be the eldest son, the youngest son, or even a daughter who would adopt a husband-in-law. When demographic events disrupted this procedure, a person with whom everybody in his or her kin group could agree would be chosen as a person suitable to look after the maintenance of family welfare and continuation. In almost all cases, probably, such tacit rules would present no problem (Nakane 1967, 2–4; Saito 2011b, 467–468).

However, there were always exceptional cases where one party's expectation differed sharply from the other party's in that kin group, which would lead to a family dispute or, as in Ken's story, even to litigation. If the family headship itself

[14] For the prevalence of tacit agreement in peasant transactions, see M. Sato (1985).

was at issue, things could be extremely difficult to solve – as far as Tokugawa society was concerned. Yet, in the Meiji world of management by written documents, the consequence could be different. The Meiji civil code was specific enough to appoint someone in the family as the head even when a prospective heir was absent (Frank *et al.* 2005, 316). Although the boundary and structure of the family might be difficult to define, its headship was thus rendered legally unmistakable.

Moreover, as emphasized above, the registration of landed property was carried out on an individualist principle even in the Meiji regime. This gap between the two registration principles could be another and independent source of complication, if the ownership of a piece of land was involved in a dispute. According to the Meiji legal framework, however, the name on the document was the owner of the real estate in question, whatever other kin people had said about his legitimacy as a genuine occupier of the land. To borrow the phrase used by a foreign commentator, the head was no longer a mere 'manager' of family property (de Becker 1921, 637). All this, it is believed, could, however, act against the interests of women in the family, since Meiji Japan's family law was patriarchal, reflecting much of Tokugawa-era samurai ideology – but somewhat different from the established practices of the peasant class. Thus, the early Meiji period saw male authority strengthened in the form of these headship functions. It is difficult to say, therefore, whether, in terms of gender equality through 'protection' by the state, much 'progress' was made between the two regimes.

The second area is that of vital registration. As we have seen, there was a tendency in Tokugawa times that babies were not immediately registered, as a result of which, those who died young may not have been recorded in the death register either. It is likely that such customs survived well into the early Meiji period. For example, even a doctor did not bother about writing a death certificate for those who died before 3 months of age. However, such under-enumerations are said to have declined substantially by 1890. In 1880 procedures for the notification of infectious diseases were formalized, and in 1884 a certificate of death by the medical practitioner became compulsory for burial, two developments which are believed to have been effective in reducing the numbers of unreported births and deaths (Takase 1991; Saito 2002, 115–117).

The third area to be examined is the question of disowning. As we have seen, the right of the head or the parents to disown a child could result – for the disowned – in a loss of any protection from the community in the Tokugawa past. However, this concept of disowning cannot be found in the provisions of the Meiji civil code. One may argue that the possibility of a prospective heir losing his right of inheritance (Article 891) and the head's aforementioned right to determine one's place of residence (Article 749) could be interpreted as legacies from Tokugawa practice. They do sound like conventional disinheritance. But in actuality, no one was allowed to ask the local office to remove his child's name from the register any longer: the right of the parent to do so was denied by the first Family

Registration Law of 1871. Although it was a reform in registration procedures, the traditional concept of disowning was apparently abandoned by Meiji law experts (Hiroi 1996). One implication of this decision was that the disinherited would no longer become registerless for that reason. However, there were still other factors that accounted for much registerlessness in the Tokugawa period, especially 'out-migration' (i.e. migration from the countryside to the town).

The fourth area is concerned with this question of how to register people who left the native village for a substantial period of time. After the Meiji reforms, their numbers were on the increase. A solution sought by the Meiji government was the introduction of a concept of 'staying temporarily' (*kiryū*). Under a new framework, a person who stayed in a place other than his or her *de jure* domicile (*honseki*) for more than ninety days was described as in *kiryū*.[15] Although one could move the *de jure* domicile, it was usually in the place where the *ie* – the family household he or she belonged to – was registered. According to regulations brought in with this concept, any persons who wanted to move their residence out of their *de jure* domicile were required to notify the village office for out-migration and also to notify the office of the place they were moving to. In the two offices, *kiryū* registers were compiled, one was an out-*kiryū* register and the other an in-*kiryū* register.

The term *kiryū* was new, but the idea was not. It can be traced back to appended registers of out-migrants that some Tokugawa villages devised. Table 4.4 is one such example, appended as an 'outside section' of one household's *shūmon* register. There are all together four people listed who had moved out from this household by the year of compilation – two were out working elsewhere and the other two married out. The latter are just for the administrative record, but the former could be crucially important, in the sense that if their names had been completely removed from the register, and if they had failed to register in their new places, they would

Table 4.4. An appended outside section (*sotogaki*) of a *shūmon aratame* register

Soto (Outside section)		
One person	Working in PLACE NAME	Daughter NAME, age
One person	Working for samurai household in PLACE NAME	Daughter NAME, age
One person	Married to NAME, address	Daughter NAME, age
One person	Married to NAME, address	Sister NAME, age

Source: Appended to a family household headed by a 65-year-old peasant, Nishijo village, Ampachi-gun, Mino province, 1804.

Note: No date of moving-out is recorded in this section of the register.

[15] This was defined in the *Kiryū* Act enacted in 1915. However, the earliest usage of the concept can be found in Dajōkan *fukoku*, no. 170, 1871.

have been registerless. The Meiji system incorporated this element, making it compulsory for the migrant to notify not only the village office but the town office as well and for both offices to keep the records. This incorporation was probably made for 'law and order' reasons, not as a protective measure. Whatever the reason, the consequence was that no one could in theory be administratively invisible.[16]

The system was far from perfect, however. Migration was increasing as industrialization and urbanization proceeded, and some of the migrants were extremely mobile. For anyone coming from the countryside to Tokyo in search of employment, it is likely that they filled in the form at both village and town offices, as an out-migrant in the village and as an in-migrant in a Tokyo ward. Probably they changed residence frequently within the metropolitan city until they finally settled down, where they would probably register again as an in-migrant in a new ward without submitting a notification of leave to the previous ward. This double-registration would not matter for the individual as long as they could find a job, but for population accounting, it caused a serious problem. Owing to such double counting of in-migrants, Tokyo's currently resident population in 1910 is said to have been in excess of 700,000, more than one-third of its total population of 2 million, reinforcing doubts about the validity of household registration information as population data and making the case for census taking even stronger (M. Sato 2002, 48–50).

Another problem was the whereabouts of those migrants who were stranded in an anonymous urban world. Being solitary in an urban environment was 'the principal cause of poverty', according to a 1923–1926 survey of the poor initiated by the city of Osaka – the city which pioneered the development of welfare administration in Japan. The problem was particularly serious for the elderly poor. Indeed, of those seeking welfare assistance in Osaka, 34 per cent were 60 years of age or older, as compared with 12 per cent for those under 15 years; and the proportion of solitary people increased from 59 per cent in the age group 15–59, to 80 per cent in the age group 60 plus (Tamai 2000, 107–109). We do not know how many of the solitary poor in Osaka were those who had eventually lost contact with their families in the native village, but it is likely that in a substantial number of cases their ties must have long since been cut. If those elderly people moved from one slum to another slum in the city, and if they lost interest in registering themselves in a new place, then they would easily become stranded and invisible administratively.

That said, it should be recognized that, compared with Tokugawa practice, in this respect the new Meiji system succeeded in reducing registerlessness drastically, which may have had significant implications for townward migrants. It must also

[16] After the Second World War this registration framework was abolished, giving way to a new residency registration arrangement. Under the post-war system almost all entitlements the citizen can claim are linked to the current residence, although duality with *de jure* registration is still maintained.

have been important in order to cope with the problem of child labour in an age in which industrialism was advancing while the state's provision for areas such as schooling was expanding.[17]

Epilogue

By way of concluding our account of the evolution of registration systems in eighteenth- and nineteenth-century Japan, we take a brief look at another village dispute that took place in 1880.[18] It was a court case initiated by a middle-aged peasant woman named Masata Hagiwara on 2 September that year. She demanded the return of a certificate of land ownership.

The centre stage was Kanai village of Kanagawa prefecture, some 20 km north of the Treaty port of Yokohama, and the lawsuit was against the village headman, accusing him of malpractice in administrative procedures. However, the real dispute was with her younger brother Rokuemon, who is said to have indulged in drinking and gambling. Masata was unmarried; she had been in service for about thirty years, but returned to the village when Rokuemon, who had already inherited both headship and ownership of the family land from his father, left for Yokohama. Since then she had looked after her retired father and helped him in working the land. In 1877, soon after Rokuemon left the house, she went to the office to report her brother's 'disappearance' (*shissō*), and she requested the headman to allow the Hagiwara family to disown Rokuemon and to remove his name from the register. Her argument was that she was entitled to do so on behalf of her father because it was she who was keeping the family economy going and looking after the ageing father, which, according to her understanding, meant that Rokuemon had abandoned the family household's business. As he was not living with the parent and other members of the household, he could no longer be a head of the Hagiwara family. The request was not accepted simply because there was no place for formal disowning procedures within the framework of Meiji family law.

Also in dispute was the family land. In 1878, soon after Rokuemon left Kanai village for Yokohama by filling in the *kiryū* form, he borrowed 400 yen, presumably as start-up capital for his business, on the security of the family's land in Kanai. Precisely speaking, he borrowed money by 'placing the land in pawn' (*shichiire*). Under this type of contract, the ownership was transferred to the lender but the occupier was allowed to till the land by paying the rent; in this particular case, the

[17] It is worth noting that there emerged a number of night classes, Sunday schools and childminders' classes for children sent away from home to work in towns and cities (Saito 2011a, 471–472), for which their registration must have been crucial.

[18] The following account draws on M. Sato (1985), which is based largely on the Kusanagi MSS in the Machida Archive, Tokyo. The village headman sued by Masata was from the Kusanagi family.

occupier was Masata, not Rokuemon. As a result of this, she came to know of her brother's financial venture. In order to keep the land in the family, she managed to raise the money and took back ownership of the land (and this was another reason for her to argue that her brother could not claim his family headship). During this period, the original certificate of ownership of the Hagiwaras' land, issued in 1872, had always been in Masata's hands. However, the land tax reform that started in 1873 required the 1872 certificate to be substituted for a new one; and as the complete substitution would take some time, the village administration was allowed to handle cases of change in ownership without the 1872 certificate being submitted. Rokuemon took advantage of this transitional measure; he sold the land off without letting his sister know about his transaction. She thus accused the headman of malpractice in the way in which he had handled the case of the land transaction.

Not surprisingly the decisions at the court in Yokohama and the Tokyo court of appeal were not in favour of Masata's claim. To quote the latter's decision, 'Rokuemon, in his capacity of the head of the household, liquidated his own property and made a transfer [of its ownership], an action in which another person cannot interfere'; by 'another person', of course, the judge meant the village headman, whom Masata accused in her lawsuit. If it had been in Tokugawa times, her arguments might have sounded somewhat more persuasive; any heir-son who was too unsettled to manage family business properly would not have been considered a head of the family.[19] Within the Meiji regime of law and practice, however, Masata's claim that she was the *de facto* head of the family became groundless under the new registration system. Moreover, both Rokuemon's sale of land and the headman's handling of the case were perfectly lawful and their documents flawless. The Meiji reforms acted against Masata's interests.

As for her brother, on the other hand, we do not know how he fared in the trading port of Yokohama. If he had been married and registered there, his children may have benefited from the Meiji reforms in identity registration. Provided that the children were also registered, they would have been entitled to receive state education in Yokohama, regardless of their father's business success or failure (although it is not unlikely that he failed in business and eventually became penniless), since Meiji Japan's education reform was thorough and universal. If Rokuemon had remained unmarried, however, the story might have been very different. Alienated from his family of origin and living in a large city like Yokohama, he would have – given the underdevelopment of Meiji Japan's welfare provisions – no recourse to social support if his business failed and, therefore, would only be 'discovered' as an anonymous dead body, just like some present-day

[19] In this respect, it is interesting to note that while Masata in her litigation document accused Rokuemon of having been 'prodigal' (*hōtō*) and 'unruly' (*burai*), two Kanai villagers described him with virtually the same words in their witness accounts.

centenarians who have been found long after they died, having lost contact with their family.[20]

References

de Becker, Joseph Ernest. 1921. *The Principles and Practice of the Civil Code of Japan*. London: Butterworth & Co.

Cornell, L. L. and Akira Hayami. 1986. 'The Shumon Aratame Cho: Japan's Population Registers.' *Journal of Family History* 11(4): 311–328.

Dore, Ronald Philip. 1965. *Education in Tokugawa, Japan*. Berkeley: University of California Press.

Frank, Ronald, Hans Peter Marutschke and Petra Schmidt. 2005. 'Civil Code.' In *History of Law in Japan since 1868*, ed. Wilhelm Röhl. Leiden: Brill, 166–329.

Hayami, Akira. 2001. *The Historical Demography of Pre-Modern Japan*. Tokyo: University of Tokyo Press.

Hirakawa, Sukehiro. 1989. 'Japan's Turn to the West.' In *The Cambridge History of Japan*, vol. 5: *The Nineteenth Century*, ed. Marius B. Jansen. Cambridge: Cambridge University Press, 432–498.

Hiroi, Tazuko. 1996. 'Oya no chōkai-ken no rekishi.' *Kyōikugaku kenkyū* 63(2): 119–128.

McCurry, Justin. 2010. 'Centenarians "Missing" Ahead of Japanese Day Honouring Elderly.' *The Guardian*, 12 August. www.guardian.co.uk/world/2010/aug/12/japan-missing-elderly-centenarians.

Moriya, Katsuhisa. 1990. 'Urban Networks and Information Networks.' In *Tokugawa Japan: The Social and Economic Antecedents of Modern Japan*, ed. Conrad D. Totman, Chie Nakane and Shinzaburō Ōishi. Tokyo: University of Tokyo Press, 97–123.

Nakane, Chie. 1967. *Kinship and Economic Organization in Rural Japan*. London: Athlone Press.

Ooms, Herman. 1996. *Tokugawa Village Practice: Class, Status, Power, Law*. Berkeley: University of California Press.

Ozaki, Yukiya. 1985. 'Shinshū Saku-gun Makibuse-mura Kenjo ikken: kinsei nōson joseishi-ron to shite.' *Rekishi hyōron* 149: 45–66.

Saito, Osamu. 2002. 'Meiji-ki no nyū-taiji shibō: Kita-Tama nōson no ichi jirei.' In *Kindai ikōki no jinkō to rekishi*, ed. A. Hayami. Kyoto: Mineruva Shobō, 99–118.

—— 2009. 'Land, Labour and Market Forces in Tokugawa Japan.' *Continuity and Change* 24(1): 169–196.

—— 2011a. 'Children's Work, Industrialism and the Family Economy in Japan, 1872–1926.' In *Child Labour's Global Past, 1650–2000*, ed. Elise Van Nederveen Meerkerk and Kristoffel Lieten. Bern: Peter Lang, 457–477.

—— 2011b. 'The Stem Family and Labour Markets: Reflections on Households and Firms in Japan's Economic Development.' *The History of the Family* 16(4): 466–480.

[20] The twenty-first-century fiasco about 'missing centenarians' is reported in *The Guardian*, 12 August 2010, summarized as: 'Authorities admit privacy laws and antiquated registration systems mean 200 elderly people are unaccounted for' (McCurry 2010).

Saito, Osamu and Kiyoshi Hamano. 2006. 'The Death of the Partner, Remarriage and Family Continuation in Tokugawa Japan: A Village Study.' *Revista de Demografía Histórica* 24(2): 155–178.

Sato, Masahiro. 1985. 'Meiji "kindai" hōsei no dōnyū to dentōteki kanshū-hō: kasan shoyū to kachō-ken no jirei kenkyū.' *Shakai keizaishigaku* 50(5): 585–604.

—— 2002. *Kokusei chōsa to Nihon kindai*. Tokyo: Iwanami Shoten.

Sato, Tsuneo. 1990. 'Tokugawa Villages and Agriculture.' In *Tokugawa Japan: The Social and Economic Antecedents of Modern Japan*, ed. Conrad D. Totman, Chie Nakane and Shinzaburō Ōishi. Tokyo: University of Tokyo Press, 37–80.

Sekiyama, Naotaro. 1958. *Kinsei Nihon no jinkō kōzō: Tokugawa jidai no jinkō chōsa to jinkō jōtai ni kansuru kenkyū.* Tokyo: Yoshikawa Kōbunkan.

Smith, Thomas C. 1959. *The Agrarian Origins of Modern Japan*. Stanford, CA: Stanford University Press.

Takase, Masato. 1991. '1890–1920 nen no waga kuni no Jinkō dōtai to jinkō seitai.' *Jinkōgaku Kenkyū* 14: 21–34.

Tamai, Kingo. 2000. 'Images of the Poor in an Official Survey of Osaka, 1923–1926.' *Continuity and Change* 15(1): 99–116.

Totman, Conrad D. 1993. *Early Modern Japan*. Berkeley: University of California Press.

Walthall, A. 1991. 'The Life Cycle of Farm Women in Tokugawa Japan.' In *Recreating Japanese Women, 1600–1945*, ed. Gail Lee Bernstein. Berkeley: University of California Press, 42–70.

Wigmore, John Henry, ed. 1967–1986. *Law and Justice in Tokugawa Japan: Materials for the History of Japanese Law and Justice under the Tokugawa Shogunate 1603–1867*, 16 vols. Tokyo: University of Tokyo Press.

Winther, Jennifer A. 2008. 'Household Enumeration in National Discourse: Three Moments in Modern Japanese History.' *Social Science History* 32(1): 19–46.

5

Civil Status and Identification in Nineteenth-Century France: A Matter of State Control?

PAUL-ANDRÉ ROSENTAL

IN FRANCE THE HISTORY OF IDENTIFICATION has become something of a research field in itself. Where the post-Revolutionary period is concerned, it has developed around two main axes: on the one hand the development of identity papers (Piazza 2004),[1] and, on the other, the techniques used by the state to identify individuals. From photographs and fingerprints in the late nineteenth century to today's biometrics, it reveals (and contests) the ever closer monitoring of individuals (Crettiez and Piazza 2006; About 2004).

In practice the choice of subject goes hand in hand with a choice of approach. Identity papers are regarded as one of the tools that allow the state to maintain its hold over civil society. Historians date the start of this process to the early days of the Third Republic and more precisely to the 1880s, a period when republican parliamentarians were gaining ground over the monarchists. Identity papers are thus seen as a supporting element in the nationalization of civil society, which a series of authors, who readily describe themselves as 'socio-historians', identify in other areas of public policy, notably in relation to immigration from abroad, a field closely linked to the development of identification policies. The background to all this is a more general movement challenging the idea of a golden age of French republicanism. This approach to identification adds weight to the critical side of the 'civil war of the pen' that, here as in other fields such as 'postcolonial' studies, has overturned the comfortable certainties of a historiography that tended to dwell on the virtues of the Republic.[2]

In relation to our subject here, these general orientations lead not only to a chronology, as has been noted, but also to a focus on a particular type of state intervention in the form of surveillance and notably policing, which is deliberately

[1] On passports see Torpey (2000), Noiriel (1998).
[2] In an extensive literature see for example Annie Stora-Lamarre (2005).

Proceedings of the British Academy **182**, 137–165. © The British Academy 2012.

emphasized to the exclusion of other possible functions of identification.[3] Historians have identified a recurring dialectic of identification that, from a civic perspective, calls for vigilance. Over the last 130 years, identification procedures have often been tested on populations described as 'dangerous', but who were in reality vulnerable, including vagrants, foreigners, Gypsies, prisoners and recidivists, colonials and, under the Vichy government, Jews. Yet these were systems typically extended also to the population of 'decent people' – an expression regularly used by supporters of identification procedures in order to reassure citizens of their positive purposes, in both the early twentieth century and now in 2012.[4] The identity card offers a paradigmatic example of this two-stage process: it was originally imposed on foreigners in 1917 and, following an attempt to make it compulsory under the Vichy government, became the subject of a decree of 1955 that extended its use across the French population as a whole.

There is also a second, anthropological dimension. This asserts that identity papers are the concrete materialization of a link between state power and the construction of the individual. Because identity in the administrative sense shapes identity in the sense of self-awareness, it is said to bind individuals to the state at a fundamental level. Pierre Piazza offers a pithy description of this process: 'it is also in claiming [the] [identity] card and handling it regularly that many French people have certainly felt the nation more keenly in their inner selves' (Piazza 2004, 17–18). Is this a postulate or an empirical observation? So far the systematicity, coherence and efficacy attributed to the state's stamp on individual minds seems to be an expression of belief rather than the conclusion of ethnographic investigations.

It is true that contemporary historians have also explored several related instances of the creation of identification systems, besides the process of entering information on cards for policing purposes, each of which can be subsumed under the recently-coined notion of 'encarding'. Gérard Noiriel has devoted a study to the links between the development of the social state and the gathering of information on forms: he has revealed the degree to which the procedures for tracking individuals arising out of the application of the law of 1910 on pensions for urban and agricultural workers generated distrust among working people, reinforcing their

[3] The historian Gérard Noiriel, pioneer of the field in France, has primarily considered identification from the point of view of policing, while also acknowledging that, in addition to the role it plays in securing market transactions, it is 'one of the fundamental means of social connection, for individuals can only form relationships if they are distinct from each other' (2007, 3–4).

[4] During the parliamentary debate underway in France on the development of biometrics, the conservative senator François Pillet continued a long terminological tradition by defending the creation of a file covering 'forty million decent people' (quotation from Borredon 2011, 8). Among other occurrences, this phrase (and reasoning) echo the reaction generated, under the Vichy regime, by the plan to create an identity document 'that will cause consternation among forgers and cause rejoicing among all decent people' (article from the magazine *Les Nouveaux Temps* cited by Piazza 2004).

suspicion that the introduction of the new system of allowances was motivated entirely by an ideology serving productivity and profit rather than the well-being of workers. Gilles Laferté has questioned the economic identification process required to obtain credit, relating it, as he says, to 'classic issues of encarding' (Laferté 2010, 2–5; for the USA, see also Hyman 2011).

Essentially, the focus of today's historians of the late modern period in France on one – important but not exclusive – aspect of identification, and their predilection for an evolutionist scenario vaguely transposed from Michel Foucault's *Discipline and Punish*,[5] contrasts with the broader, more complex and nuanced vision of historians of earlier periods (Moatti 2007, 27–55; Moatti and Kaiser 2007; Denis 2008). The slippery slope towards monitoring, surveillance and indeed repression is certainly an ever-present parameter within the state apparatus and its study has usefully helped challenge the overly apologetic – one might even say 'angelic' – vision that once dominated in studies of the institutions of the Republic. But its unilateral interpretation can be countered by critiques similar to those I have made in the related field of the history of citizenship (Rosental 2011). On the one hand, an exclusive focus on these particular identity papers takes no account of *other* documents that, strictly speaking, underpin the administrative identity of individuals, otherwise known as their 'civil status' registration documents (see next section). On the other hand, it reduces to unambiguous functionality a state approach that is, on the contrary, and in its very construction, multiple and often paradoxical. This tendency goes hand in hand with a hypostasis of the state. The intense desire for control and absolute efficacy attributed to the state has its equivalent only in the supposed irrationality of its 'submissive' citizens, hypnotized by the illusion of majesty generated by the manipulative techniques of the authorities. This naivety leads them to fall into the trap of an 'ever more pronounced administrative colonization of the world they live in': if citizens accept fetishes, in the form of identity papers, this is supposedly because these offer the bearers a form of 'gratification'.[6]

If, on the contrary, we accept the demands of a social history that seeks to understand reasons for action, the history of identification seems to me, *mutatis mutandis*, to raise similar questions to that of policies on migration. Often reduced to identification and control, in reality these policies constantly restage the difficulty for the state of reconciling the contradictory aims assigned to the ministries of which it is composed. The maintenance of social regulation, market adjustment,

[5] For a critique of this linear approach, see, on a related subject, Mary D. Lewis (2007), who pays more attention to the political and administrative contexts specific to different moments in history.

[6] 'How were the police able to obtain the submission of an ever growing number [of citizens] to this document when they were in no way constrained to hold it? [. . .] The document may have seemed gratifying to them as an assertion and valorisation of themselves, by consolidating for them, at a time when the affirmation of the modern state was playing a role in transforming society into an atomized collection of individuals, the sense that their singularity was being recognized' (the quotations in this paragraph are taken from Piazza 2004, 14, 17).

and integration into 'international society' are aims of equal importance but are often pushed into the background (Rosental 2011, 365; see also, in the same field, Spire 2005). I shall try to give an account of the diverse functions and administrative practices relating to the identification of individuals, and the way in which their limitations enable us to infer the aims of state action.

The limits of civil status: what does the state know?

In February 1914, a widower with the surname Thomas, first forename Louis and second forename Ernest, approached the authorities in his town with a view to wedding his second wife. He discovered, 'with amazement', that he was already married. The registry office was categorical: his birth certificate contained a note in the margin indicating that, on 11 March 1911, he had married 'a lady Mauboussin, of whom he had never heard until that moment'. Enquiries indicated that his identity had been stolen by a stranger named Louis (Bernard) Thomas. Louis (Ernest) complained to the police and Louis (Bernard) was arrested, but protested that he had acted in good faith and managed to have the charges against him dropped. The error was due, as the investigation proved, to the conditions in which the wedding of Louis Bernard Thomas and Elisabeth Mauboussin had taken place. In 1911, the lady had obtained a total dispensation from wedding fees via the St Vincent de Paul Society. The only document provided by Louis Bernard Thomas was the card showing him to be a voter in the 15th arrondissement in Paris, bearing only the name Louis Thomas. The confusion arose from a coincidence of circumstances: Louis (Ernest) was, like Louis (Bernard), born in Pontoise in the Paris region, the two men's ages were almost identical and the first marriage of Louis (Ernest) had not been noted on his birth certificate, making him an unexceptional candidate for marriage. Meanwhile Louis (Bernard), 'himself did not know he had any other given name and was not very sure of the precise date of his birth'.

This story, which was quite widely covered in the press of its day, is only one of countless anecdotes to be found in civil law treatises and theses that have considered the quality of civil status documentation since the nineteenth century (Boisseau 1914).[7] Although it is not an exception,[8] its value is clearly not linked to its representative nature; it is a 'case' providing material for legal debate[9] and indeed raises several questions that are central to our argument here. The first

[7] All the quotations shown are from this source.

[8] Raymond Lyon cites the case of a man who suffered a similar problem at more or less the same time but, seven years later, had still not obtained the resolution of a complaint he had made in 1909 of 'usurpation of [his] civil status by a stranger to contract a marriage' (Lyon 1921, 105–106).

[9] See the articles on this issue in Jean-Claude Passeron and Jacques Revel (2005), and also Yan Thomas (2007).

concerns the means and efficacy of the state's monitoring of individuals. In France, identification ultimately relies on civil status registration, and more specifically on the birth certificate, the only exclusive, universal document provided to all living persons born in the country.[10] Assuming that this document is drawn up correctly – which is not in dispute in this case – we still have to determine whether it permits the unambiguous identification of individuals in their everyday interactions.

Here the answer is in the negative. There is nothing unusual in the fact that the St Vincent de Paul Society settled for a voter's card to verify the identity of a person seeking its aid. Far into the twentieth century (and still today) many documents can be used as identification tools, as the law on occasion recognizes.[11] Many of them record a usual forename rather than the forenames officially declared on the birth certificate, which are comparatively stable and harder to change than the surname itself, any modification of which nevertheless requires 'a decree given in the Council of State and ratified by the court' (Boisseau 1914, 155). In the early twentieth century we can clearly see this difference between the foundational status of the birth certificate and its actual usage – reflected in the ignorance of the interested party himself, who was unaware of both the existence of his second forename and his precise date of birth.

The confusion of the two Thomases was also due to the failure of an administrative tool that historians have neglected to study: the 'notes in the margin' added to birth certificates to establish a link with the administrative and judicial events that punctuate the lives of individuals, and which had been duly added to Louis Ernest's birth certificate. I shall return to this later, but note here that, since 1897, the commune in which a couple are married has been required to contact their respective birth communes so that the latter will include a record of their marriage on their birth certificates. The importance of this is clear from this case: it is a way of both avoiding identity theft, of which examples abound, and preventing bigamy, a crime 'primarily committed in France by individuals whose first wedding had taken place in the French colonies' (Lenoël 1879, 13).

So, in addition to the issue of procedure, the Thomas case raises that of aims: what is the function of identification? Is it simple or multiple, and on the basis of

[10] The registration of civil status is in practice independent of both nationality and religion. In this it differs from parish registers which, through a series of orders beginning in 1539, were supposed systematically to record the baptisms, marriages and burials of Catholics, Jews being excluded and Protestants placed in a situation that varied according to period and local practices (Cabourdin and Dupâquier 1988, 11).

[11] The law of 27 October 1940 on identification explicitly mentions the widespread use of several means of identification: 'voter's card, driving licence, administrative commissions, passports, combatant's card, *livret de famille* [family record book], *livret militaire* [military record book], birth certificate, membership card for certain groups (société de la Légion d'honneur, Touring club de France), cards provided by local authorities and police stations' (Piazza 2004, 257). On the widespread use of the voter's card for identification from the mid-nineteenth century, see Michel Offerlé (1993).

what considerations does the state carry it out? I should like to return to these questions from a non-teleological point of view. My analysis will neither rely on the development of new identification tools in the twentieth century, nor on a chronology pre-determined by the succession of political regimes, nor on a strictly French perspective. My angle of approach is rather that of the long chronology of administrative action, of the constraints imposed on this action and of the description of these constraints by contemporaries in the different periods. When seen from a long-term perspective and compared to its European neighbours, France reveals a major particularity: it has no population books, the registers that, for different reasons in a variety of countries (Italy, Germany, the Netherlands, Belgium), have been listing households within each commune and noting their destination when they moved elsewhere since the mid-nineteenth century[12] and sometimes earlier (Sweden) (Gutmann and van de Walle 1978). So in France it is impossible to track individuals throughout their lives, a material difficulty for any social historian dealing with archives of names.

France is even more singular in deciding not to use the solution adopted in England and Wales in 1836 to compensate for this problem. Having no population registers either, the British created a two-tier system centralizing civil status documents at the local and national level, through the General Register Office (GRO) (Szreter 1991).[13]

> In France, conversely, it was not possible to do this. As no general list had been drawn up, it was necessary, in the absence of any information, to write to the mayor of every commune in France and to consult the decennial tables of every clerk of the civil courts of the urban arrondissements!
>
> (Mellanville 1915, 78)

So it is through the reverse of a 'Benthamite' vision that we must approach the issue of the history of identification in France: before considering its excesses, we must consider the reasons for its failings. The problem is not just the difficulty of tracing the familial, geographic or other origins of particular individuals, still more their later lives, through the French registration system. A question is posed by the mismatch between what can be called the 'monumental' value conferred on civil

[12] So the 'general register' project, referred to by Gérard Noiriel in his 'Introduction' cited above, should be understood by default. It may indeed constitute a monstrosity of administrative imagination. But more prosaically, had it been adopted, at the time this would have signified the transposition to France of a mode of recording that became commonplace elsewhere in continental Europe (though interestingly not in England – see next footnote). If we advance the hypothesis that historically the registration of individuals is closely linked to systems of social assistance and security, a hypothesis that I readily uphold and which finds some verification in Vincent Denis (2008), it cannot be ruled out that under-recording of populations in France is linked to the particularly scattered nature, until the late nineteenth century, of its welfare regime, as studied by Pierre Rosanvallon (1990, 139ff.).

[13] The practice was subsequently extended, under their own separate Registry Offices, to the populations of Scotland (1855) and Ireland (1864).

status by the law – as we shall see, its registration documents are deliberately constructed as permanent and unchangeable – and the gaps in the registration of individuals. The details of these were known and recognized by jurists and solutions to the problem suggested. To what extent has the French state sought to remedy these failings, given that civil status – rather than identity documents – provides the legal foundation of individual identity?

What state monitoring?

The historians of identification for policing purposes readily take the 'beginning of population movements' (i.e. mass migration within France) as a starting point for the encarding of individuals: this moment, opportunely located in the 1880s, is said to have involved 'the progressive crumbling of community-based sociability' (Piazza 2004, 21). But long-distance migration progressed far more slowly in France than in the rest of industrial Europe, and, as has been recently shown, its increased momentum was a continuous process throughout the nineteenth century.[14] To seize on the 1880s as a supposed moment of major change can have no rationale, other than to legitimate a starting point that coincides opportunely with the beginnings of the republican era.

In 1849 the magistrate Arnould Bonneville de Marsangy justified his plan to establish the *Casier judiciaire* – a police record making it possible to track the movements of individuals, and notably recidivists – by the need to respond to 'cosmopolitanism' and the increased mobility of populations linked to the development of the railways (Farcy 1990, 9). Thus, 'travelling habits that the writers of the Civil Code had not foreseen' (Lenoël 1879, 5) had already begun to spread by that time. The case of the *registres matricules* offers further proof of the arbitrary nature of taking the 1880s as the 'standard' for dating increased attention to monitoring migration. These were rolls maintained by the gendarmerie, tracking all men aged 20–45 who had not been declared unfit for military service. It is hard to find a document more precisely reflecting the motives commonly advanced to explain the development of identification in the 1880s, but this register was fully functional from the early 1870s, in other words a decade before the start of the republican period proper. This date is no more significant of a change in mobility. The key factor was institutional, with the establishment of universal conscription by the law of 27 July 1872, as a legislative reaction to the national disaster of defeat in the Franco-Prussian war.

In reality, far from being a determining factor in the supposedly sudden shift from identification through community acquaintance to monitoring from a distance, the

[14] See Paul-André Rosental (1999), which establishes the continuous nature of the rise of what we could call settlement migration.

growth of migration was a continuous process gathering pace throughout the nineteenth century, overlaid by the effects of administrative and juridical approaches that must also be reconstructed. Here too, the chronology offers no validation of the 'Third Republic' tropism. Once again, it was under the July monarchy that the failings of the system for registering individual identities were first recognized, and more ambitious plans formulated. In 1844, J. B. Hébert, doyen of Rouen notaries, proposed a general registration system based on birth certificates, which would make it possible to track the property of individuals throughout their lives (Hébert 1844).

Seventy years later Paul Boisseau de Mellanville provided a good summary of this bold plan, which went beyond merely centralizing data on the status of individuals, seeking to include their property as well.

> In the ten days [following] the birth, the mayor must send [. . .] a copy of the registration of birth of every individual to the mortgages registrar. The latter, having a special register for each canton, records the birth on this register. The record is numbered, and this number becomes the individual's registration number, remaining with him until death. The mortgages registrar informs the mayor of the number given to the record of the birth and the civil status registrar is required to note this number on a list of persons registered in the commune.
>
> (Mellanville 1915, 59–60)

This 1844 project, the first of a long tradition,[15] contains all the later terms of the debate on identification. In the first place, Hébert lays down the foundations of a system to coordinate different forms of registration, making it possible not only to reconstruct the former life-path of individuals but also – as the *registres matricules* later did – to track their later movements:

> the first place of registration is the place of birth; but that place is not immutable, and to change it one need only notify the Mortgages Registry and have one's account transferred to the record of the registrar with jurisdiction over the new commune in which one has chosen to reside.
>
> (Mellanville 1915, 59)

Hébert's plan was also innovatory in using civil status, the basis of individual identification, as the basis of a system of wider information. The proposal to link individuals to their property raises a fundamental issue neglected by historians of the late modern period. Historically, the establishment of systematic registration concerned property rather than people. The state first delegated this registration to notaries in the Middle Ages; it is often forgotten that, in theory, the edict of Villers-

[15] Henry-Léopold Legrand proposes the centralization, based in the birth commune of individuals, of all the documentation related to their birth (e.g. adoption, recognition or naturalization), marriage (e.g. divorce, reconciliation), parentage (e.g. legitimization, adoption) and other aspects (e.g. guardianship, bankruptcy judgments) (1900). Pierre Piazza mistakenly gives the date of the first plan to number identity as 1916 (2004, 28).

Cotterêts of 1539 made notaries co-signatories to the parish registers with priests (Cabourdin and Dupâquier 1988, 11–13). The *Ancien Régime* progressively built up a specific administrative service, the 'Control', for recording and taxing deeds (notary acts), as well as some private agreements and administrative and judicial decisions. In the nineteenth century this fiscal organization, which was then called the Registration Service (*Enregistrement*), was gradually supplemented by the Mortgages Registry (*Hypothèques*), with the aim of putting title deeds to property and information about any resulting liability to costs in the public domain (Postel-Vinay 1998).

These two services recorded data on both property and persons and they did so far more clearly than the Land Registry (*Cadastre*), and on a more ambitious scale, the Registration Service by *canton* and the Mortgages Registry by *arrondissement*. Like the decennial tables of civil status under the Revolution, in the early nineteenth century the Registration Service began using semi-alphabetical (by surname initial) 'tables' on which were recorded, for each canton and for periods that varied with the sub-population addressed (usually a few years), lists of vendors and buyers, landlords and deceased persons who had (or not) left an inheritance. The Mortgages Registry meanwhile ran a reference system involving several registers, making it possible to move from lists of surnames to individual forms on which each individual's property transactions were centrally collated and recorded.

It is particularly surprising that historians of identification should have neglected to consider these services, since their influence extended far beyond their intrinsic function. On the one hand, they have an obvious political importance throughout the period of tax-based suffrage, providing until 1848 a means of assessing personal wealth at a time when the rest of the fiscal system was focusing on 'actual taxing' (i.e. on an estimation of the value of economic assets).[16]

This is significant since, among other causes, the rejection of the government's attempt to use the evaluation of personal fortunes for fiscal purposes led to major tax revolts in 1841, to which I shall return. On the other hand, both the Mortgages Registry and the Registration Service served as models for projects to improve the identification of individuals, the first due to its systematic approach, the second through its efforts to centralize information on property at the national level. On 29 November 1865 an instruction from the Registration Service established a 'General Repertory' (*Répertoire Général*) that left the previous tabulating system behind and 'brought together, under the name of each taxpayer, the various events

[16] In French, 'actual taxing' (*fiscalité réelle*) is based on a given asset, without considering the owner's individual situation. For example, you will pay a given amount of tax for an apartment or a shop independently from your global wealth. By contrast, 'individual' or 'personal' taxing (*fiscalité personnelle*) depends on your global level of income or wealth. In nineteenth-century France, tax was mainly 'actual'. The 1841 project of reform aborted because it aimed at moving from actual to personal taxing. This is why the 'Registration Service' is so precious, providing insight on the global wealth of individuals.

of civil life affecting his person and property' (Lenoël 1879, 33); this was followed, in 1901, by a movement of the records from the cantonal to an integrated national archive. In terms of administrative technique, the General Repertory, established fifteen years after the *Casier judiciaire* (see above), represents one of the most successful combinations of the two identification systems in operation in the late nineteenth century. It used the old format of a register in chronological order, which, in this case, consisted of separate boxes listing transactions carried out by individuals, and the new solution of alphabetically classified forms, here termed 'mobile sheets', which, unlike tables, allowed new entries to be slotted in and the deceased to be removed and placed in the 'cemetery' without the need to cross them out.[17]

The link between civil status and the recording of property wealth selected by the notary Hébert in 1844 was not the only formula proposed. Jurists preferred a similar combination but involving the tracking of judicial records. The fact that this was generally referred to as a '*Casier civil*' or civil record[18] makes the template to which it referred explicit from the outset. As indicated in 1860 by one of its early promoters, Lionel d'Albiousse, a judge at the courts of Castellane and then Uzès, the model here is that of the *Casier judiciaire*, which had been established in 1850 in order to identify and sanction recidivists by centralizing records of all the arrests and judgments to which they had been subject (Farcy 1990).

Ambitions continued to grow over the following decades and each new formulation saw the development of ever more complete combinations of the civil status records and judicial history of individuals. In 1915, Paul Boisseau de Mellanville asserted the task of the *Casier civil* to be the recording of:

> the following registrations: birth, marriage and death, the births, marriages and deaths of all children, spouse's death certificate, legitimation, divorce, separation of spouses, division of property, conversion of separation of spouses into divorce, reconciliation. Civil Status Rectification: annulment of marriage, putative marriage, judgement on claim or dispute of status, judgement replacing a death certificate, adoption order, interdiction, *conseil judiciaire*, removal of paternal authority, criminal forfeiture, rehabilitation, absence, emancipation, withdrawal of emancipation, judicial mortgage, public employment involving legal mortgage, naturalization, change of name, marriage contract, recognition of natural child, guardianship, joint guardianship, unofficial guardianship, prohibition on the wife's incurring household expenses, status of trader, bankrupt, judicial liquidation, authorization of married woman to trade.
> (Mellanville 1915, 32)

Here we can begin to see the significance of expanding the current historiographic conception beyond that of merely identifying vulnerable populations by

[17] On the functioning of the registry, in addition to the lists of departmental archives in the 3Q series, see the treatises produced by the administration for its agents, such as Édouard Maguéro and Alfred Gautier (Maguéro and Gautier 1901, 204ff. on the General Repertory). A good account of what was at stake in the move from register to form is proposed by Sandrine Kott (1998).

[18] Of the series of books published after 1860, see notably Lionel d'Albiousse (1863).

means of identity records and anthropometry. We cannot understand the history of identification, and particularly the role played in it by the state, unless we recognize the diversity of its functions and of its agents' viewpoints. It was civil status, and not identity papers, on which all aspects of identification were based, as this alone determined, precisely, the 'status' of individuals. This alternative history of identity can also be told in terms of a desire to control. In practice it was accompanied by a much closer monitoring of individuals, using ever more substantial administrative techniques. The idea formulated by Hébert in 1844 of numbering all individuals according to their place of birth was not unique. In 1879 Albert Lenoël proposed to prevent confusion between individuals with the same name by obliging notaries and public officers to 'designate individuals not only by their name, but also by their place and date of birth', even on private deeds (Lenoël 1879, 36). In 1897 Édouard Levivier, who had a background as a notary, suggested that a number should be added to the margin of every individual's birth certificate (Levivier 1897).

This solution was finally adopted by the French national statistics service during the Second World War, and today serves as the universal identifier of residents in France. The question of whether this was a product or inevitable consequence of the importance of the registration of births is not crucial here.[19] More important is the question it poses concerning state functioning. If surveillance were the state's first impulse, it is hard to understand why it was not quicker to implement a system that had been formulated with great precision: aims, contents and procedures were set out in detail from the 1840s.

Once again, we are dealing with absence rather than presence. Presented by historiography as 'Benthamite', the creation of identity papers in the late nineteenth century was on a scale far more modest than that of projects proposed in the same period. At this time Édouard Levivier aspired to establish the far more ambitious '*livret individuel*', a personal record that would combine the functions of the *livret de famille* or family record, created in 1877, with those of the identity card and a *casier d'état civil* or civil status record. His plan was based on the mobility and availability of civil status data, expanded to include certain judicial actions, such as the legitimation of illegitimate children, and including the signature, description and photograph of the individual (Levivier 1897).

In addition to the non-establishment of a population register system as was common elsewhere in Europe from the eighteenth century, questions are raised by the previously mentioned refusal, in the 1830s, to import the British model, more

[19] The creator of this system, René Carmille, Armed Forces Comptroller, notes in passing, 'the idea of identifying all individuals by a number in figures referring to their place and date of birth was fairly widespread in France. The Demography Department has received numerous letters from a wide variety of people claiming to have invented the system. Some even believe they have a right to compensation for the wrong caused them by the state, that "took" their invention' (1942, 124, n.1).

in tune with the data collected in France. Such timidity cannot be reduced to a concern to keep down costs by an 'impoverished state' (Koselleck 2009). This is demonstrated, as we have seen, by the case of the *registres matricules*, which are ignored by historians of identification despite the fact that they imposed a far more systematic and authoritarian system on the great majority of the male population than that of identity papers. When the state saw that it was really in its interest, it spent the money necessary to track individuals (giving the gendarmerie another task), adopting a repressive system without hesitation. As the aim was to ensure complete, rapid military mobilization, the sanctions against men who omitted to inform the gendarmerie of their change of address involved harsh fines and indeed prison sentences. The result, according to recent historical studies, was that the administrative arrangements were acted upon and the tracking of individuals was highly reliable (Farcy and Faure 2002; Kesztenbaum 2006).[20] By contrast, although the proportion of unclaimed bodies was in decline at the time, a quarter of the corpses deposited in the Paris morgue in the late nineteenth century were not reclaimed, partly for lack of identification (Bertherat 2003, 28–29).

So we need to ask why the registration of individuals was not more systematic. The first reason, mentioned above, is the heterogeneity of state organization. The desire for surveillance attributed to the state as a whole by some historians was in reality confined only to some of its services. The second reason, to which I shall return later, is the place of civil society in a liberal regime. A fine connoisseur of projects for the centralization and usage of civil status for judicial and fiscal purposes, Paul Boisseau de Mellanville described registration systems in 1915 the better to denounce them. His liberal indignation at the 'real inquisition' that would be introduced by the application of Hébert's system is overlaid by more traditionalist recriminations directed at that of Levivier:

> The act of numbering every individual at birth, beyond the material difficulties of its application, is repugnant to our ideas. The name that acts to individualize every person was borne, almost always, by the parents; it preserves a quantity of memories and, by passing from one individual to the next, acts to mark lineage and preserve the family. A simple number, even when merely added to the name, in order to assist research or state services, has something brutal and impersonal about it, [something] too mathematical.
>
> (Mellanville 1915, 59, 67)

Should we then divide the state into a police-based element, said to have attained its goals and imposed authoritarian identification processes, and an opposing liberal

[20] Moreover, the existence and quality of the *registres matricules* poses a question to historians of identification that they have apparently failed to consider. The creation mentioned above of individual identification numbers is attributed to the desire of the Vichy regime to prepare for clandestine mobilization against the occupation as and when possible. But it is hard to understand why this was necessary, given that the desired information was already accessible.

element that did not perfect the systems for recording civil status or make them join them up with other areas, out of a concern for the reaction of civil society?[21] It is here that the over-hasty phenomenology of encarding poses a problem for a more open-ended approach to this history. From the point of view of people's daily lives, aside from the creation of identifying numbers under the Vichy government, civil status is almost certainly no more significantly obtrusive today than it was in the nineteenth century. But the fact that people have to clutch their birth certificates 'to their hearts' (Noiriel) on only very rare occasions does not signify that an administrative revolution has not discreetly taken place.

In 1886 France introduced the technique of the 'note in the margin'. Rather than constructing registers or an *ad hoc* administration, this consisted of noting later events affecting individuals in the margin of their birth certificate. In reality this cannot be described as an entirely new procedure: provision had been made for it from the outset by the Civil Code, but it was reserved for the reconciliation of civil status and, in particular, the recognition of illegitimate children, the importance of which I shall return to later. Although we are here in the famous decade of the 1880s, its reactivation was motivated not by 'the end of face-to-face relations' as communities dissolved, but, once again, by a legal change: in the form of the re-establishment of divorce, which revived fears of bigamy, leading to a search for an appropriate administrative solution to prevent it (Noiriel 1998, 42).[22]

This re-employment of an old but little-used technique was soon widely extended, since it was appreciated that it was an effective response to an acknowledged administrative weakness of the French system for identifying individuals. From 1897 people's marriages were noted on their birth certificates. In 1945 the measure was extended to noting deaths; and ever since, up to this point, a person's entire life has been covered by civil status recording. From 1922 this tracking was even reinforced by an intergenerational dimension, with the date and place of birth of the parents being noted on their child's birth certificate.

Divorce and simple adoption have been noted in the margin of the birth certificate since 1932 and 1955 respectively, while the reconciliation of separated spouses has been noted on their marriage certificates since 1938. The First World War brought new notes of those who had 'died for France' and orphans of the state (i.e. children whose fathers had been killed at war), while a law of 1985 did the same for those who died as deportees during the Second World War. Immigration appeared in 1958 as a result of concern with assimilation at the time: note of a change or gallicization of name appeared in the margin of the civil status records of the individual involved, their spouse and any children still minors.

[21] The importance of liberal opposition to the excessive state monitoring of identification is described by Gérard Noiriel (1998).

[22] The prevention of bigamy was also a central aim of the previously mentioned projects for centralizing civil status documents (cf. d'Albiousse 1866).

This is a default mechanism. Through it a system of cross-referencing between documents was being gradually established, at minimal cost, which, not without some complication, made it possible to track individual itineraries in an ever more exhaustive way. This evolution is the unexpected fruit of a 'path dependence', the roots of which can be seen, in the mid-nineteenth century, in the failure to adopt the continental system of the population register or the British system of the GRO. This was the initial orientation to which the administrative solution of notes in the margin, almost invisible to the French citizens but clearly visible to those knowledgeable clerks and lawyers, gradually provided a response. Analysis confirms the remarks I have made here thus far: while the monitoring of individuals did indeed increase, this was not due to a global plan on the part of the state. The list of data included in the system of cross-referenced notes in the margin, like the chronology of their inclusion (such as naturalization in 1958 and deportation in 1985), confirms that their addition was dictated by the contingent effects of successive administrative or political contexts. The same can be said of the list of data left out by this system: unlike the more ambitious projects of the jurists, the main judicial events in the lives of individuals were not, in fact, included in this system of cross-references.

Information at source

To borrow a founding notion of science studies, the history of state control has to be symmetrical. Rather than confining itself to commenting on (and criticizing) the growing technical refinement of this control, any analysis must also recognize what it deliberately leaves out. Such an approach forbids us to remain focused on the administration, as to do so would be to forget that, far from submitting to the history of their own identification, individuals and groups have been active participants in it. I shall start by considering this aspect from the perspective of 'civil status errors', a major category of juridical discussion in the nineteenth century.

The history of civil status in France confirms a dialectics often highlighted by historians of identification. In the nineteenth century, as in the twentieth, the Middle Ages and the modern period, the development of systems for registering identity never entirely replaced recognition by interpersonal familiarity. Declarations of civil status are still based on acquaintance, whether operating negatively to denounce the illegality of a marriage (publication of banns, announcements in official publications) or positively (the use of witnesses in registering civil status). The importance of the practice of publication to achieve verification, the limitations of which have always been inherent in its localized nature, has been further eroded by increased mobility and urbanization.[23] The failings of the formal, legal system

[23] Paul Boisseau de Mellanville presents all these means of publication (1915, 38–39). He criticizes both 'the overly limited geographical and social areas of distribution' of publications (the *Journal Officiel*

are moreover reflected in the development of a private market in information in the form of specialized directories for professionals. There are few available studies on this phenomenon, since the historiography of identification has focused so closely on the state, neglecting the market to the point of reducing it to a mysterious interplay of 'occult forces' (Noiriel 2007, 3).

Where the use of witnesses was concerned, treatises on civil status constantly reported and deplored the way that registration was carried out. One recurrent complaint concerns witnesses' low level of acquaintance with the person whose status they have come to authenticate. One jurist offers a picturesque sociography of this phenomenon:

> We know how things go in practice. Let us take the case of a birth. The father, filled with joy at the event, arrives at the *Mairie* with the two witnesses required by law and recruited as often as not in the street, professional witnesses, who have never seen the declarant before and who, for a modest recompense, present themselves at the registry office several times a day.

In the country, witnesses

> know the declarant, but how can they be required to provide particular information, such as the spelling of the father's name, when the father is often unsure of it himself? [. . .] Let us take the case of a death. The law requires it to be declared by two witnesses, the closest relatives or neighbours of the deceased. But usually the former remain at the deathbed and the latter, in the cities at least, do not know him. So the declaration is made by friends, and often also by employees of the undertaker. And there are so many errors! The death certificate, simplest of civil status documents, is the one that contains the greatest number of inaccuracies, the rectification of which is not always asked for, since the production of a death certificate is less frequent than that of a birth certificate. An individual who has left his legitimate wife for another woman with whom he lives as a spouse is declared, by witnesses of entirely good faith, to be her husband.[24]
>
> (Boisseau 1914, 164–165)

Another source of frequent errors was the absence of declarants and witnesses at the time when the documentation was drawn up. 'The registration is never written in two copies; the second register is signed blank and written up later, copying from

for absences, in other words the recording of deceased persons, the *Bulletin des Lois* for changes of name, and also department-based newspapers for bankruptcies and liquidations in their area). Where wedding banns were concerned, while considering that 'in the *Mairies*, it is true, the posters are well read, as the news they announce, particularly marriages, are a matter of general curiosity; moreover the *Mairie* is quintessentially a place that people pass through', he deplores the fact that 'in the large working class centres, however, all this news very often goes unnoticed as there is so much of it, and there is no paradox in maintaining that while notices are often read, it is because people have heard the news it contains from somewhere else and their curiosity has already been awakened'.

[24] Conversely, in the author's estimation, fewer errors are noted on marriage certificates, which are drawn up on the basis of documents rather than declarations.

the first. The information is simply noted down on a sheet and the signatures obtained; a few days later the secretary finishes his work, after which the mayor signs' (Crozes 1921, 21–22; see also Mersier 1873, 43; Lyon 1921, 42; Boisseau 1914, 164). These criticisms were not just the fantasies of lawyers. They were the product of the annual verification of the registers, which, by virtue of article 53 of the Civil Code and a later order of 26 November 1823, the public prosecutor was required to undertake (Crozes 1921, 19). On occasion unannounced checks produced even more damning results: during a surprise visit to the registry office of Corbeil on 21 February 1893, the deputy public prosecutor discovered, to his amazement,

> on opening the registers of the current year that no registration of birth had been written up since 1 January 1893. He opened the register of deaths and made the same observation [. . .]. So [they] appeared in the extraordinary form of signatures, spaced out on immaculate sheets, but of registrations not a trace. The latter, noted on a jotter, had not yet been written into the registers.
>
> (Boisseau 1914, 56–57)

Of all the errors in carrying out the procedures, the most numerous concerned the spelling of the surname (Boisseau 1914, 166). There were even – although these were extreme cases – children for whom the registration of birth does not provide them with a surname at all.[25] All these inaccuracies created an 'uncertainty in which one is often placed concerning the identities of the contracting parties themselves. It is hard to believe how frequently the entries show names that are misspelled, inaccurate or incomplete forenames and false descriptions' (Lenoël 1879, 35). These mistakes cannot be reduced to the status of anecdotes: behind their picturesque quality lies the whole issue of the legal and political significance of civil status. In practice it was juridically very difficult to rectify documentation, and the technical aspects of doing so are discussed in specific legal treatises. It came under the jurisdiction of the public prosecutor and, without exception, every case had to be judged in court.[26] The procedure was lengthy and also costly – indeed it went along with a specific form of assistance to paupers, in order that it should not stigmatize them excessively.[27] True, there were customary ways around it, notably

[25] This was the case of a child born in 1884 in the 12th arrondissement of Paris, whose father is not named. The secretary at the *mairie*, counter to jurisprudence, refused to give the child the surname of his mother, who had not recognized him. So his three forenames, Fernand-Jules-Raymond, became his surname ('along the lines of Geoffroy-Saint-Hilaire'), which became a problem in the eyes of the individual concerned and his two witnesses at the registration in 1912 of the birth of his own son, Fernand-François Fernand-Jules-Raymond (Boisseau 1914, 261–262).

[26] A notice from the Council of State of 30 March 1808 provides for 'an exception to the strict principle of rectification by the court' in cases where 'persons planning to marry produce documentation on the occasion of which rectification proves unavoidable', such as that of a misspelled surname on the birth certificate (Crozes 1921, 23).

[27] 'When the notice is on loose paper, there is reason to add, where the stamp usually goes, the words "Law of 10 December 1850" and not "marriage between paupers"'(Anon. 1920, 20).

when mayors rectified the records on their own initiative, 'as long as they had both copies of the registers to hand' (in other words before the prosecutor's verification during the calendar year, after which one of the two registers was sent to the office of the clerk of the court). But the elements that we have previously described make it clear that these unofficial rectifications could prove worse than the original mistake, adding their own blunders to the mix.[28]

One of the achievements of the history of identification is to have refuted oversimplified oppositions between societies based on writing and those based on oral accounts, between identification by acquaintance and identification by official document.[29] The problems in certifying civil status registration confirm the limitations of such facile evolutionism by emphasizing the importance of the degree to which individuals are known to the registrars themselves. The official may be in control of some sources of error 'thanks to the knowledge of the local area he may have if he has lived there a long time. But if he is transferred, the indications on the list will lose the major part of their value for his successor' (Lenoël 1879, 35).

Civil status policies

I began by evoking the political dimension of the apparently 'technical' difficulties of identification. Consideration of the problem of identical names, which can reach considerable proportions in some localities, enables us to go further. 'There are some villages, in Savoie for example, where all the inhabitants have the same patronymic surname and have been given the same forename, that of the village's patron saint' (Lenoël 1879, 35). Such a state of affairs was of course due in part to the particular structure of mountain regions: demographic historians and anthropologists have amply revealed the scale of endogamy in many valleys of the Pyrenees and Savoie (Fernet *et al.* 1975; Abelson 1978; Prost and Boëtsch 2005). But it would be illusory to reduce this confusion of surnames to a vaguely culturalist trait. To the relatively limited stock of surnames can be added the effect of deliberate strategies for blurring identities through the re-use of the same forenames for siblings in the same family. Laurence Fontaine has shown this effect in the valley of the Oisans, where it was a decoy strategy practised by generations of families dependent on peddling for their survival, and thus structurally in debt to creditors who provided them with the capital required for their activities. The redundancy of forenames, overlaying that of surnames, was a ruse in the game of cat and mouse

[28] According to Paul Crozes, 'this process is very dangerous because it opens the door to all kinds of arbitrary effects' (1921, 19ff.).

[29] Gérard Noiriel offers a highly contemporary example of the procedures for examining the dossiers of asylum seekers (see Noiriel 1991, 204ff.).

between (often international and indeed transcontinental) networks of peddlers and creditors (Fontaine 1984).

Before considering these issues we must ask whether families actually registered at their local registry office or, more precisely, whether they did so before the deadline. This question has long been neglected, as it seemed accepted that the registration of demographic movements was established early (under the *Ancien Régime*) and systematically. However, around fifteen years ago the demographic historian Noël Bonneuil advanced a more nuanced view (Bonneuil 1997). Going back to the statistical data of the Statistique Générale de la France, which kept accounts of population movements and numbers based on censuses and also, ultimately, civil status data, Bonneuil revealed an under-registration of births, probably due to the delay of fathers in registering births. The effect of this is not massive but it is significant enough to go some way to explaining the antecedence traditionally attributed to France in regard to fertility reduction. Most importantly, its very uneven regional distribution reveals a coherent structure: under-declaration was more frequent in the departments that, a priori, were the last to come under the control of the centralized state. While Bonneuil's thesis has not given rise to the historiographical discussion it deserves, it points to a direction of research which has been followed since by studies which also question the possible under-registration of children, notably girls, at birth and its possible repercussions on measurements of infant mortality (Gourdon and Rollet 2009; Brian and Jaisson 2007).

Above and beyond its demographic significance, this question raises a fundamental point for our concerns here by recalling the importance of acceptance (or what French historians tend to call 'consent', cf. in two fields, Prochasson 2008; Delalande 2011), in the development of administrative identification. Here again, there is reason to relativize the generally accepted view where the history of the recording of identity is concerned. Andrea Rusnock has recalled the extent to which, in the eighteenth century, the French and British elites were reticent when it came to the conduct of censuses, managing to delay their implementation for fifty years after they were established in Sweden (Rusnock 2009). As late as 1841 in France, as we have mentioned, there was a wave of revolts against the five-yearly census, due to confusion over its relationship to a planned fiscal reform (Caron 2002). There can thus be no finalism postulating a gradual evolution in the sensitivity of populations to the registration of their identities: Pierre Piazza discusses the failure of the attempt to make use of the 'Frenchman's identity card' – compulsory under the Vichy government – certainly in part for technical reasons (lack of paper combining with poor knowledge of the legal mechanisms on the part of some employees), but also due to distrust of the regime and the occupiers (on all these points see Piazza 2004, 247ff.). So all in all we should take seriously the studies carried out by some historians on what can be called consent to civil status: examples taken from socio-historical contexts other than contemporary France remind us that, even in this apparently trivial domain, the state has to construct a satisfactory political relationship in order to maintain its control.[30]

We are here at the opposite pole from the vision in which an overarching state exploits the passivity – not to say open naivety – of those it administers. Rather than 'explaining' the spread of identification techniques by alienation and a lack of rationality on the part of the registered populace, it is better to analyse reasons for action and conditions for acceptance. Why do individuals subscribe to identification? We know the answer today among partisans of registration for policing purposes, who present it as the inevitable consequence of identity theft, and ultimately not too bothersome to the category of 'decent people' whose durability I mentioned above.

But the study of texts produced in the nineteenth century (here by civil law specialists) reveals a different concern, centring on neither the relationship between individuals and the state, nor the negative vision of identity theft – two issues which are, of course, undeniably important. The issue then was rather one of creating stable relations between individuals, a concern shared by citizens themselves, who were the first to ask for identification. The jurist Paul Boisseau de Mellanville articulated their expectations by insisting on the 'advantages to be gained by third parties from widespread publicity given to civil status. It would give contracts and agreements a security unknown until now' (Mellanville 1915, 15). Taking this argument to its extremes, the author ultimately 'maintains that the status of persons, in modern societies, does not belong to them in any absolute way'. If this view from 1915 is worthy of interest, it is because it is orthogonal to the way the issue is approached today. For this author what matters is not the relationship between an individual, whose legal status must be preserved, and an overweening state, but the possibility of underpinning connections between individuals.

Even if it is not unique, or constant through time, the concern to stabilize links between individuals is one of those most frequently advanced in the nineteenth century in writings on identification. In concrete terms, it concerns first and foremost the issue of marriage. Without returning to bigamy here, this issue was fundamental to any commercial transaction because it affected a creditor's hope of recovering his costs in the case of default by the debtor. Let us imagine that 'a man whose civil status is unknown to me borrows a sum from me and that, as a guarantee of reimbursement, he offers me a mortgage on his property. I should like to know whether he is or has been married and whether, as a consequence, I should fear one or several legal mortgages that might take precedence over mine.' In practice, 'whatever the marriage settlement, the law gives the wife a legal mortgage on her husband's property. This is her guarantee against the risks of the administration of

[30] We can make a contrast with the example of Kosovo analysed by Morgane Labbé (2000, chs 3 and 4). In the 1980s the struggle against Serbian power took the form of a rejection of its administration and the collapse of civil status declarations.

marriage, the necessary corrective to her incapacity and dependence.' This protection covered all the rights of the wife: 'recovery or restoration of dowry, actions and indemnities of all kinds to be claimed on the dissolution of the marriage' (the quotations in this paragraph are taken from Lenoël 1879, 5, 17). Information on marital status thus became a precondition for the viability of economic transactions.

> How can one find it out? If I know where [the debtor] was born and precisely that he was married in the same commune, I will without difficulty find the documentation that will reveal his marriage to me and hence the legal mortgage that will take precedence over my own. But if his marriage was celebrated in a different commune, the registry office will tell me nothing useful, since I will be unable to discover the registration of marriage or, if I succeed, it will be because I am otherwise informed of the event it relates.

The place of gender in the construction of the civil law plays a fundamental role in this uncertainty, for the marriage settlement affected the wife's legal capacity to alienate or mortgage property she owned herself. She was subject to her husband's authorization under a settlement providing for commonality of property, but excluded in the case of a dowry-based settlement, where any mortgage or alienation of the wife's dowry property was null and void. It was thus vital for third parties to know the marriage settlement of the persons with whom they were contracting. Before the law of 10 July 1850, which established that the nature of the marriage contract must be made public, this information was often inaccessible to them, leading to 'abuses and fraud', the fear of which

> paralysed transactions or rendered them difficult. The only means by which spouses could reassure third parties was to show them their marriage contract; but when there had not really been one, [the latter] could not verify in any sure way that there were no matrimonial agreements. So prudence often caused them not to proceed.[31]

Of equal structural importance was the issue of inheritance, which carried risks of fraud through the concealment of heirs. How could one be sure that all the heirs of a deceased person had been informed and gathered together when 'to find his children's birth certificates one must first know where they were drawn up' (Lenoël 1879, 5)? The risk of omission did not only affect the heirs thus despoiled. It also extended to third parties, notably those who found themselves in possession of property passed on following a death: 'nothing guarantees them against action based on a petition of heredity, nor against action to reduce donation that may be

[31] Émile Mersier adds that the law of 10 July 1850 stipulates that the civil status officer must 'tell the future spouses, and the persons authorizing the marriage if they are present, to declare whether a marriage contract has been made and, if so, the date of this contract and the names and place of residence of the notary who received it'. The same article gives the public prosecutor the right 'to require the rectification of the documentation, in relation to the omission or error, without prejudice to the rights of the interested parties' (Mersier 1873, 376–377).

undertaken by a descendant omitted when the inheritance was apportioned and whose appearance changes the available portion' (Lenoël 1879, 10).

The importance of identification in the construction of civil society has been largely ignored by a historiography quick to reduce the state to its police functions, even though identification is crucial throughout the nineteenth century (see Chapter 15). The close parallels between this concern to minimize the ambiguity and risk surrounding any transaction and those revealed in Stanziani's studies of economic and juridical history are evident (Stanziani 2011). The state's strategy for reducing uncertainty in the markets is part of the creation of a 'liberal' society in every sense of the word, economic of course, but also political. To understand this we must return more precisely to what is meant by 'consent' in relation to identification.

Negotiating transparency

The difficulty mentioned above of rectifying errors on civil status documents results from a deliberate choice made long ago by the state. It can be seen under the *Ancien Régime*, in a royal declaration of 9 April 1736, soon registered by the Paris parliament, which submits 'deeds that come into the categories of baptisms, marriages, burials, investitures, noviciates and professions [to the] courts or other competent judges' (Crozes 1921, 7). A priori, this is a manifestation of the staging of state dominance commonly described by historiography. The reference to theatre is not metaphorical in relation to 'state actions', whether they concerned a claim ('establishing or protecting a person's status') or dispute ('depriving a person enjoying a status, claimed not to be his, of the advantages he draws from it'): 'to show clearly the full importance of such affairs, only a few years ago appeals on judgements of status had to be judged by the Court in official session, with counsellors sitting in red robes' (Boisseau 1914, 228).

This staging was in fact on a par with the importance of the object over which the state thus asserted its supremacy. During the Revolutionary period, Chabot de l'Allier gave the clearest expression of this before the legislative body: 'civil status registers are a sacred record, the slightest alteration of which is a violation. They are in the keeping of the courts and not at their discretion.' The near-irreversible nature of the documents contributes to this sacredness:[32]

[32] Reine Leroy's difficulty in recovering her surname in the early nineteenth century reflects the construction of the irreversibility of registration on civil status documentation. Born in Chablis in 1793, she had a surname and forename that soon had 'dangerously monarchical' connotations. Her father prudently adopted the pseudonym Brille at this time and it was under this surname that his death was registered in 1807. Sixteen years later, at her wedding on 13 January 1823, Reine Leroy 'found herself unable to produce Pierre Leroy's death certificate' and to have the registers rectified. She appears in the register as Reine Leroy, 'adult daughter of Pierre Leroy, known as Brille, deceased in this town and registered under the said name of Brille on 5 November 1807 [. . .]. The said Reine Leroy and the

> it would seem that once the written elements have been established and the signatures given, the document becomes forever untouchable on pain of sacrilege: it is born of a formalist ceremony that gives it force despite its imperfections. The very people who performed the rite cannot correct them.
>
> (Crozes 1921, 17)

But the definition of this sacredness and inviolability is more complex than it appears. In part, it is an extension of property rights. If civil status is sacred, this is because it belongs to citizens 'and this property, inviolable like all others, can be permitted only [by] the same rules and forms' (Boisseau 1914, 13). The law of 6 Fructidor year II moreover established that 'surnames constitute a property that cannot be taken away to the prejudice of those to whom they belong' (Mersier 1873, 445).

But does this mean the analogy is indisputable? In practice it soon reaches its limits with the inalienability of identity, which is not constructed as a tradable good. Whereas individuals can, in principle, dispose of all their property, 'where the status of persons is concerned, it is absolutely impossible to dispose of this status. Any convention is absolutely null and void in relation to the status of persons.' Like a child renouncing his paternity claim against his father, 'it is similarly also forbidden to renounce in advance a claim to one's status. As a result any transaction relating to the status of individuals is strictly prohibited' (Marquant 1977), and it is removed 'from the set of actions that creditors may pursue against their debtor' (Boisseau 1914, 229).

As a property right that is at once absolutely guaranteed by the state and limited in the possibility allowed its possessors to dispose of it, civil status is akin to *majorat*, a type of property theoretically prohibited by post-Revolutionary legislation. Following this reasoning enables us to introduce an actor I have not mentioned thus far: the 'family'. Obscured by today's historiography of identification in the late modern period, which, anachronistically, focuses exclusively on the issue of protecting the individual against the state, it is omnipresent in the writings of nineteenth-century jurists. The assertion of family rights is concomitant with the promulgation of the Civil Code: this is the meaning of a notice by the Council of State of 12 Nivôse, X (2 January 1802) concerning the apparently technical, but in reality fundamental, issue of rectifications of civil status.

In the early nineteenth century, based on the precedent of the obligatory rectifications of the civil status registers of the departments of western France following the civil war in Vendée (law of 2 Floréal year III, 21 April 1795), the

four witnesses present and hereafter named under oath stated that her father's real name was Leroy and that, if he was given the name Brille in the documents of 1807 and 1818, this was because he was known in Chablis only by this name, which he had adopted'. His case is known to jurists because, in December 1823, the mayor of Chablis, to whom the affair had been referred by Reine Leroy, asked the public prosecutor of Auxerre to tell him 'the procedure to follow to have the name Brille removed from the registers and replaced by that of "Leroy"' (Boisseau 1914, 17–18).

Ministries of Justice and the Interior sought to correct the civil status registers of the Ardèche, 'in which errors, omissions and falsifications have been committed'. The Council of State pronounced against this request.

> The principles on which the status of men rests counter any rectification of registers that is not the result of a judgement provoked by the parties interested in requesting or speaking against rectification; these principles have always been respected as the most solid guarantee of social order [. . .]; they cannot be departed from without disturbing families and prejudicing established rights.
>
> (Boisseau 1914, 11)

There is nothing gratuitous or rhetorical about the reference to the family here: it gives a nuance to received ideas, often originated by counter-revolutionary jurists, concerning the 'individualism' of the Civil Code. In reality, the place that law was to continue to preserve for the family after the fall of the *Ancien Régime* informed one of the great juridical debates of the Revolution and was simultaneously a matter of fierce negotiation (Goy 1988, 84–115). The issue was constantly raised throughout the nineteenth century. To understand it we must supplement the purely individual vision of the application of the Civil Code with considerations that, in contemporary terms, concern the 'honour' and 'pecuniary interests' of families (Boisseau 1914, 228). This shift of viewpoint can also be applied to identity theft, which far from remaining at the exclusively individual level, as would be the case today, often involved generations of families, even if this great theme of the early modern period was reduced in the nineteenth century to the category of the 'romantic'.[33]

The state's guarantee of stable identification also applied to the protection of qualities attached to individuals. Far from being confined to aspects that define civil status today, such as age, sex and marital status, these extended to indicators of social position, as reflected in the obligation to include principal decorations on civil status documents.[34] The issue of the nobility is most apparent here: there was reason to 'subject to close verification the desire of those who alter their names, add a particle or conceitedly enhance them with pompous noble qualifications' (Anon. 1920, 25). But it extended to apparently more trivial indicators, as in the case of the 'chambermaid' who, in 1913, felt the need, despite a profession which 'though not glorious, is entirely honourable' (Boisseau 1914, 204), to have her son's birth certificate rectified by the civil court of Versailles so that she would

[33] Christian Biet (2002) highlights the importance of the juridical construction of the family in the literature of the early modern period. For the nineteenth century, Crozes discusses the obstacles placed in the way of rectification of civil status deeds: 'in the name of ancient formulae, of a sacred respect for the registers, the necessity to go to court to obtain the correction of an inaccuracy was maintained. This procedure seemed legitimate in a period dominated by a fear of fraudulent changes to civil status. The talk was all of alteration of the registers, falsified documents and substitutions. The period has changed, these romantic fears are less likely to be realized' (Crozes 1921, 158).

[34] 'Mention of the *Légion d'honneur*, *Médaille militaire* and *Croix de guerre*, excluding of all other decorations, is compulsory for any person named in a civil status document' (Anon. 1920, 4).

henceforward be shown as 'without profession', hoping this would preserve his future interests.[35]

Arrangements relating to age were also used in strategies for active self-promotion. Perhaps the most spectacular case concerns Henriette T., born in 1866 in a small Brittany village, whose death in the same region in 1907 did not prevent her marrying two years later, in 1909, in the department of the Seine. The deception was the work of her aunt Marie-Josèphe, sixteen years her senior. 'To make herself look younger to her future husband', she took advantage of her move to the Paris region to obtain Henriette's birth certificate and produce it when her own marriage certificate was being drawn up in 1909 (Boisseau 1914, 263).

Once again this anecdote conceals a fundamental issue, central to all considerations of the publicity to be given to civil status documentation, which is the treatment that should be given to certain vulnerable populations, and first among them illegitimate children.

> For some individuals there would be a disadvantage to seeing their civil status published in this way. The law strives to favour as far as possible the raising of the social status of persons who have a juridical stain on their record: prisoners, bankrupts and so on. Only recently it modified article 57 of the Civil Code in order to preserve illegitimate children from indiscretions.[36]
>
> (Mellanville 1915, 15)

In theory, 'civil status documentation is public' and 'any person can have extracts from the registers delivered to them by the depositaries of these registers' (Mersier 1873, 36). But in practice many jurists believed that 'as far as the security of third parties allows, the private life of the individual should be preserved from disparagement' (Mellanville 1915, 15). So, in the domain of identification we find a dialectics that is not dissimilar to that described by Stanziani in relation to the circulation of economic information: maintaining the conditions necessary for market functioning could require the violation of principles of transparent information or an acceptance of its opacities. In the late nineteenth century this reasoning legitimated an acknowledgement of the constitutive asymmetry of relations between owners and employees and sellers and consumers (Stanziani 2011).

Where identification is concerned, evolution was not linear: as we have seen, the law of 1850 had increased public access to the registration of marriages. But

[35] Social history studies confirm the tendency to 'over-value' the declared profession whenever possible, notably for migrants who married with no possibility that the in-laws would meet (Rosental 1999, 128, n.9). Comparable observations can be found in Pierre Bourdieu (1980, 253, n.3). Note in Chapter 10 the similar naming tactics employed by non-Ganda immigrant parents to enhance their children's status in twentieth-century Uganda.

[36] Gérard Noiriel mentions comparable dynamics in adjacent fields. It was in the name of 'what one could call respect for private life [. . .] that measures were adopted prohibiting stigmatizing aspects of an individual's past from being made public. The law of 1832 abolishing the branding of criminals is an illustration of this new conception' (1998, 97).

in 1906, 'fearing that, out of simple curiosity or even a desire to do harm to some individual, proof of illegitimate descent might be sought in the civil status registers', the law circumscribed access to civil status documentation. 'Previously, all persons desiring to procure a [civil status] certificate were able to do so; they had only to write to the mayor who, in exchange for the fixed sum, delivered the document.' Now only interested parties, their ascendants or descendants, guardians or legal representatives, or the public prosecutor could do so: 'the others are reduced either to direct consultation or to extracts in the legal sense, in other words incomplete copies containing only the indispensable information' (this quotation and those that precede it are taken from Mellanville 1915, 40–41, 107). Subsequent legislation merely sharpened these distinctions. Not long before, in 1899, a comparable evolution had restricted public access to the *Casier judiciaire*. A victim of its own success with big business, it had ultimately prevented those with a criminal record from gaining access to the jobs market, locking them into the very life of recidivism that it had been intended to combat (Farcy 1990, 22).

Overall, the long nineteenth century became dominated by the idea that identification by civil status – the basis of the administrative definition of individuals to a far greater extent than identity papers – had to result from the balancing of several objectives. Some, of course, were truly linked to state control and regulation: thus age acquired a crucial importance with conscription (for men), the first laws protecting children from work and the introduction of compulsory schooling. But fundamentally, it was the establishment of relatively stable and transparent social and economic links that guided thinking on identification. This aim met with support from the population, concerned to minimize uncertainties in exchanges. Its implementation required the legislation to create the best balance it could in two areas. In the first place, robust civil status documentation, which supposed its near-irreversibility, had to be reconciled with the flexibility necessary for the rectification of aberrations: there is a real historicity to this decision, involving the consent of the population.[37] But secondly, and perhaps most importantly, the great problem faced by nineteenth-century law was to establish how to reconcile the need to maintain both public access to civil status documentation and the protection of individuals. If we absolutely must establish a parallel between the identification issues of times gone by and those of the present day, this quest for optimal transparency is an issue rendered central today by the circulation of information on the internet.

[37] For Crozes, for example, with the First World War and the proliferation of civil status errors, 'less importance was attached to the information included on the registers: their sacred nature was diminished. Administrative rectification was received without resistance and with satisfaction' (1921, 158).

References

Abelson, Andrew. 1978. 'Population Structure in the Western Pyrenees: Social Class, Migration and the Frequency of Consanguineous Marriage, 1850 to 1910.' *Annals of Human Biology* 5(2): 165–178.

About, Ilsen. 2004. 'Les fondations d'un système national d'identification policière en France (1893–1914).' *Genèses* 54(1): 28–52.

d'Albiousse, Lionel. 1863. *De l'établissement dans tous les greffes des tribunaux de première instance des casiers de l'état civil et des objets divers sur le modèle du casier judiciaire*. Paris: A. Marescq.

—— 1866. *De la suppression du crime de bigamie par l'établissement d'un casier de l'état civil sur le modèle du casier judiciaire*. Paris: A. Marescq.

Anon. 1920. *Formulaire général des actes de l'état-civil adopté par la commission de l'état civil instituée au ministère de la justice*. Elbeuf-sur-Seine: Impr. administrative Allain.

Bertherat, Bruno. 2003. 'Ces morts dont personne ne veut.' *L'Histoire* 282(12): 28–29.

Biet, Christian. 2002. *Droit et littérature sous l'Ancien Régime: le jeu de la valeur et de la loi*. Paris: H. Champion.

Boisseau, Robert. 1914. *Des jugements tendant à établir, reconstituer, rectifier ou annuler les actes de l'état civil*. Paris: Arthur Rousseau.

Boisseau de Mellanville, Paul. 1915. *La centralisation de l'état civil*. Troyes: Impr. Gustave Frémont.

Bonneuil, Noël. 1997. *Transformation of the French Demographic Landscape, 1806–1906*. Oxford: Clarendon Press.

Borredon, Laurent. 2011. 'Le projet de carte d'identité biométrique fait craindre un fichage généralisé.' *Le Monde*, 13 September.

Bourdieu, Pierre. 1980. *Le sens pratique*. Paris: Editions de Minuit.

Brian, Éric and Marie Jaisson. 2007. *Le sexisme de la première heure: hasard et sociologie*. Paris: Raisons d'agir éditions.

Cabourdin, Guy and Jacques Dupâquier. 1988. 'Les sources et les institutions.' In *Histoire de la population française*, ed. Jacques Dupâquier. Paris: Presses universitaires de France, 2: 9–50.

Carmille, René. 1942. *La mécanographie dans les administrations*. 2nd edn. Paris: Recueil Sirey.

Caron, Jean-Claude. 2002. *L'été rouge: chronique de la révolte populaire en France, 1841*. Paris: Aubier.

Crettiez, Xavier and Pierre Piazza. 2006. *Du papier à la biométrie: identifier les individus*. Paris: Presses de la fondation nationale des sciences politiques.

Crozes, Paul. 1921. *La rectification des actes de l'État civil (les lois du 18 avril 1918 et du 20 novembre 1919)*. Toulouse: Impr. Veuve Bonnet.

Delalande, Nicolas. 2011. *Les batailles de l'impôt: consentement et résistances de 1789 à nos jours*. Paris: Seuil.

Denis, Vincent. 2008. *Une histoire de l'identité: France, 1715–1815*. Paris: Champ Vallon.

Farcy, Jean-Claude. 1990. 'Le casier judiciaire au XIXe siècle.' *Bulletin du Centre d'Histoire de la France Contemporaine* 11: 5–30.

Farcy, Jean-Claude and Alain Faure. 2002. *Une génération de Français à l'épreuve de la mobilité. Vers et dans Paris: recherche sur la mobilité des individus à la fin du XIXe siècle*. Paris: Éds de l'INED.

Fernet, Pierre, Albert Jacquard and Lucienne Jakobi. 1975. 'Mariages et filiations dans la vallée pyrénéenne de l'Ouzom depuis 1744.' *Population* 30: 187–196.

Fontaine, Laurence. 1984. *Le voyage et la mémoire: colporteurs de l'Oisans au XIXe siècle*. Lyon: Presses universitaires de Lyon.

Gourdon, Vincent and Catherine Rollet. 2009. 'Les mort-nés à Paris au XIXe siècle: enjeux sociaux, juridiques et médicaux d'une catégorie statistique.' *Population* 64(4): 687–722.

Goy, Joseph. 1988. 'La Révolution française et la famille.' In *Histoire de la population française*, ed. Jacques Dupâquier. Paris: Presses universitaires de France, 3: 84–115.

Gutmann, Myron P. and Etienne van de Walle. 1978. 'New Sources for Social and Demographic History: The Belgian Population Registers.' *Social Science History* 2(2): 121–143.

Hébert, Jean-Baptiste. 1844. *De l'utilité d'un système général d'immatriculation des hommes, des immeubles et des titres, et de quelques points se rattachant au notariat*. Rouen: Impr. D. Brière.

Hyman, Louis. 2011. *Debtor Nation: The History of America in Red Ink*. Princeton, NJ: Princeton University Press.

Kesztenbaum, Lionel. 2006. 'Une histoire d'espace et de patrimoine. Familles et migration dans la France de la Troisième République, 1870–1940.' Ph.D. dissertation, Institut d'Études Politiques de Paris.

Koselleck, Reinhart. 2009. 'La désagrégation de la "maison" comme entité de domination. Quelques remarques sur l'évolution du droit réglementant maison, famille et domesticité en Prusse entre la Révolution française et 1848.' In *Historicités*, ed. Christian Delacroix, François Dosse and Patrick Garcia. Paris: La Découverte, 85–104.

Kott, Sandrine. 1998. 'La "mise en fiches" de la société allemande. Les individus, l'état et la législation à la fin du XIXe siècle.' In *L'État contre la politique. Les expressions historiques de l'étatisation*, ed. Martine Kaluszynski and Sophie Wahnich. Paris: L'Harmattan, 105–123.

Labbé, Morgane. 2000. *La population à l'échelle des frontières: une démographie politique de l'Europe contemporaine*. Paris: Éditions de l'École des hautes études en sciences sociales.

Laferté, Gilles. 2010. 'L'identification économique.' *Genèses* 79(2): 2–5.

Legrand, Henry-Léopold. 1900. *De la publicité concernant l'état et la capacité des personnes (le casier civil)*. Paris: A. Rousseau.

Lenoël, Albert. 1879. *Projet d'établissement d'un casier d'état-civil et d'un casier fiscal*. Paris: Impr. A. Chaix.

Levivier, Édouard. 1897. *Étude des moyens les plus propres à assurer la sécurité des transactions et notamment des transactions immobilières*. Paris: A. Rousseau.

Lewis, Mary Dewhurst. 2007. *The Boundaries of the Republic: Migrant Rights and the Limits of Universalism in France, 1918–1940*. Stanford, CA: Stanford University Press.

Lyon, Raymond. 1921. *Jugements et ordonnances de rectification d'actes de l'état-civil: examen de quelques difficultés*. Paris: Jouve.

Maguéro, Édouard André and Alfred Gautier. 1901. *Répertoire de manutention et de comptabilité de l'Enregistrement, des domaines et du timbre*. Paris: Administration de la Revue de l'Enregistrement.

Marquant, Robert. 1977. *L'état civil et l'état des personnes*. Paris: Masson.

Mersier, Émile. 1873. *Traité théorique et pratique des actes de l'état civil*. . . Paris: Librairie Paul Dupont & A. Marescq.

Moatti, Claudia. 2007. 'Reconnaissance et identification des personnes dans la Rome antique.' In *L'identification: genèse d'un travail d'État*, ed. Gérard Noiriel and Ilsen About. Paris: Belin, 27–55.

Moatti, Claudia and Wolfgang Kaiser. 2007. *Gens de passage en Méditerranée de l'Antiquité à l'époque moderne: procédures de contrôle et d'identification*. Paris: Maisonneuve & Larose.

Noiriel, Gérard. 1991. *La tyrannie du national: le droit d'asile en Europe, 1793–1993*. Paris: Calmann-Lévy.

—— 1998. 'Surveiller les déplacements ou identifier les personnes? Contribution à l'histoire du passeport en France de la Ie à la IIIe République.' *Genèses* 30(1): 77–100.

—— 2007. 'Introduction.' In *L'identification: genèse d'un travail d'État*, ed. Gérard Noiriel and Ilsen About. Paris: Belin, 3–26.

Offerlé, Michel. 1993. 'L'électeur et ses papiers. Enquête sur les cartes et les listes électorales (1848–1939).' *Genèses* 13(1): 29–53.

Passeron, Jean-Claude and Jacques Revel, eds. 2005. *Penser par cas*. Paris: Éditions de l'EHESS.

Piazza, Pierre. 2004. *Histoire de la carte nationale d'identité*. Paris: Odile Jacob.

Postel-Vinay, Gilles. 1998. *La terre et l'argent: l'agriculture et le crédit en France du XVIIIe au début du XXe siècle*. Paris: Albin Michel.

Prochasson, Christophe. 2008. *1914–1918: retours d'expériences*. Paris: Tallandier.

Prost, Michel and Gilles Boëtsch. 2005. 'Biodémographie et migrations matrimoniales dans l'ecosystème alpin. Les populations montagnardes des Massifs du Dauphiné du 16e au 19e siècle.' *Antropo* 10: 1–18.

Rosanvallon, Pierre. 1990. *L'État en France de 1789 à nos jours*. Paris: Éds du Seuil.

Rosental, Paul-André. 1999. *Les sentiers invisibles. Espace, familles et migrations dans la France du XIXe siècle*. Paris: Éditions de l'EHESS.

—— 2011. 'Migrations, souveraineté, droits sociaux protéger et expulser les étrangers en Europe du XIXe siècle à nos jours.' *Annales. Histoire, Sciences sociales* 66(2): 335–373.

Rusnock, Andrea A. 2009. *Vital Accounts: Quantifying Health and Population in Eighteenth-Century England and France*. Cambridge: Cambridge University Press.

Spire, Alexis. 2005. *Etrangers à la carte: l'administration de l'immigration en France, 1945–1975*. Paris: Grasset.

Stanziani, Alessandro. 2011. *French Capitalism in Comparative Perspective, XVIIIth–XXth Century*. Cambridge: Cambridge University Press.

Stora-Lamarre, Annie. 2005. *La République des faibles: les origines intellectuelles du droit républicain, 1870–1914*. Paris: Armand Colin.

Szreter, Simon. 1991. 'The General Register Office and the Public Health Movement in Britain, 1837–1914: A Comparative Perspective.' *Social History of Medicine* 4(3): 435–463.

Thomas, Yan. 2007. 'L'enfant à naître et l'"héritier sien". Sujet de pouvoir et sujet de vie en droit romain.' *Annales. Histoire, Sciences Sociales* 62(1): 29–68.

Torpey, John C. 2000. *The Invention of the Passport: Surveillance, Citizenship, and the State*. Cambridge: Cambridge University Press.

Part II

REGISTRATION AS NEGOTIATED RECOGNITION

6

Identity Registration in the Classical Mediterranean World

REBECCA FLEMMING

THE SECOND CHAPTER OF LUKE'S GOSPEL famously opens with the statement:

> Now it happened in those days that a decree went out from Ceasar Augustus that all the world should be registered (*apographesthai*). This registration (*apographê*) first occurred when Quirinus was governor of Syria. And all went to be registered, each to his own city.
>
> (Luke 2: 1–3)

Other sources confirm that, around AD 6, Judaea (up until then a 'client kingdom' of Rome, under the rule of Herod the Great and his, rather less great, successors) became a prefecture under the overall control of the Roman governor of Syria, an annexe of that province, and, as part of this provincial reorganization a census was conducted, by Quirinus and his officials.[1]

A provincial census, an overall assessment of the wealth and human resources of conquered territory, was a standard part of the empire-building process under Augustus. Victor in the final episodes of the civil wars which eventually pulled Rome's republican system apart (most decisively victorious in the battle of Actium in 31 BC), Augustus had to work hard to re-establish a stable political system in Rome and her empire, a regime now centred around himself as the 'foremost/first man' (*princeps*) of the Roman state, and which he would pass on to his selected successors on his death in AD 14. Extensive overseas conquests, and the consolidation of those gains, while developing more integrated structures of imperial rule across all of Rome's vast domains, were a key part of this project. A provincial census of the Gauls in 27 BC was followed by similar surveys of people and their assets, not just in Syria, but also, for example, in Lusitania, and probably

[1] Josephus, *Jewish Antiquities* 17.355, 18.2 and 26; *Inscriptiones Latinae Selectae* 2683. This, of course, is rather chronologically problematic for Luke; and, indeed, there are other difficulties with his account, too, over which much ink has been spilt.

Proceedings of the British Academy **182**, 169–190.

Egypt.[2] That the purpose of these registers was essentially exploitative – mainly to calculate the amount of tribute that would be paid by a province, by its various cities and districts, in taxation to Rome, on occasion also to enable the levying of troops to serve in Rome's armies – is clear, and the first census might be met by local resistance, even revolt, before the system settled down.[3]

In some provinces, however, the local population was already familiar with a system of registration for the purposes of exploitation. Under its previous rulers – the Macedonian Ptolemies – Egypt had developed a complex and encompassing fiscal and registrative package.[4] They, too, were building on past, Pharaonic (and probably also Persian), practice, with catalogues of cattle dating back to the Old Kingdom (*c.* 2400 BC) and of people (and animals) back to the early New Kingdom (*c.* 1450 BC). These latter catalogues were especially concerned to list occupations since the regime relied heavily on corvée labour for a range of particular royal projects, and for the general maintenance of the irrigation system on which Egyptian agriculture depended. Under the Ptolemies the collection of information about the population became focused on taxation – on the extraction of tax revenues, monetary revenues, centred on the (almost) universal 'salt tax' (*halikê*) – and the process became more literate, with written documents – household declarations, tax-registers, and receipts – proliferating.[5] An already substantial bureaucracy was adapted to the new demands, the changing shape and operation, of Macedonian rule.

Still, though the slippage involved in the Authorized Version's translation of Luke, in which Augustus decreed that 'all the world should be *taxed*', is perhaps acceptable in an imperial context, it is misleading in many others. 'Registration' had quite different valences and purposes in other polities in the classical Mediterranean world, including, for example, democratic Athens in the fifth and fourth centuries BC, and, indeed, within the citizen census of the Roman Republic, on which later provincial practice was partly based. This latter will be the main focus of this essay, as the most richly attested of ancient registration cultures, and the one which best displays the complexities involved; but it is also worth saying a bit more about Athens, both as a valuable counterpoint to Republican Rome in

[2] And probably others, though dated evidence is scarce: see Brunt (1990, 345–346), for a collection of the relevant material. Augustus' successors continued this practice. For the difficult case of Egypt see Rathbone (1993).

[3] The Romans, of course, extracted payment from their provinces before Augustus, under the Republic, usually in the form of reparations and through tax farming; Augustus regularized the system, but diversity persisted in various ways.

[4] Ptolemy I, a leading general of Alexander the Great (Alexander III of Macedon), established his rule of Egypt as Alexander's vast empire was broken up into successor kingdoms following his death in 323 BC. The last of the dynasty was Cleopatra VII, defeated (with Marc Antony) by Augustus at Actium in 31 BC; Egypt was then annexed by Rome. On registration and enumeration in Ptolemaic Egypt, and their precedents, see the magisterial study of Clarysse and Thompson (2006).

[5] The precise relationship between the Ptolemaic '*halikê*' and the salt after which it is named is unclear, for it basically functioned as a capitation tax: see Clarysse and Thompson (2006, vol. 2: 36–44).

particular, and as further illustration of the variety of ways in which ancient states explicitly recognized their people, and recorded that recognition.

For, while by no means identical kinds of states, democratic Athens (*c.* 503–338 BC) and Republican Rome (*c.* 509–31 BC) shared certain key features which contrast, to some extent, with the monarchic and imperial formations discussed so far. Both were, at least in their origins, autonomous city-states, constructed around concepts of shared community membership – citizenship – and collective self-governance. Interactions between the state and the people were, in this context, self-encounters, rather than crossing any real divide, a point emphasized by the lack of any developed state apparatus in either case. Similarly, the armies of both democratic Athens and Republican Rome were, essentially, citizen militia, the citizenry under arms, and military service was as much a privilege as an obligation of belonging to the community, heavily valorized in Greek and Roman culture. Moreover, the two were resistant to imposing any form of regular direct taxation on their citizens, an ideological opposition that found practical support in the resources of empire in both cases, and also for Athens, the silver mines at nearby Laureion. The intrusion of empire, again, into this narrative serves, of course, to emphasize that the entitlements of membership may come at the expense of others: there are always exclusions, the subordination and subjection of non-citizens. Their arrangement of these latter elements is part of what differs between Athens and Rome, and is reflected in their divergent approaches to civil registration, but this divergence extends well beyond such variation, too, responding to a whole range of factors, in interesting, and perhaps even unpredictable, ways.

Democratic Athens

Democratic Athens was not much interested in the enumeration of its people, but it did systematically register sections of the population, albeit in quite a distinctive way. Two groups went on the most official lists – that is adult male citizens, on the one hand, and adult male and some adult female metics (*metoikoi*, 'resident aliens') and manumitted slaves, on the other – groups which occupied quite different positions in Athenian society, one politically pre-eminent, the other marginal; and which were recorded for contrasting reasons.[6] Citizen registration publicly recognized

[6] It is unclear to what extent foreign residents (that is, citizens of other cities who migrated to Athens) and freed slaves were placed in the same category as 'metics'; the status and situation of these two, free(-ish) non-citizen resident groups certainly had much in common, but distinctions are also made, and have been recently emphasized in Zelnick-Abramovitz (2005, esp. 4–5, 99–107, 308–315). Even if manumission did not automatically make someone a metic, however, there does seem to have been a drift in that direction, and it should be remembered that the descendants of freed slaves in Athens inherited that status in some way – they did not become citizens unless an explicit grant was made – so a loose, encompassing grouping will have resulted, and it seems to have taken the 'metic' title.

that a man had now become a fully participating member of the democracy; it affirmed that pre-eminence, within a specific institutional framework, and while the registration of foreign residents and freed slaves partook of that same framework, it functioned to establish a relation of subordination within the workings of the *polis*, to confirm that marginality. There were other lists around – relating to aspects of military service, for instance, and (probably) various indirect taxes – but they lack even the somewhat fragile significance of the citizen and metic registers.

An aspect of this fragility, the distinctive character of Athenian civic registration, was its local organization. This had its origins in the reforms of Cleisthenes in 508/507 BC, which divided the city and its surrounding territory into 'demes' and made them the basis of the new political system which developed: that is, democracy.[7] The matrix through which citizenship was now to be recognized and organized was this network of demes, geographically defined political entities which were carefully grouped into ten tribes (*phylai*), to provide the basic political infrastructure for democratic Athens. Exactly how many demes Cleisthenes established is unclear, but the figure is unlikely to be very different from the 139 of the classical *polis*; a city-state encompassing a territory of around 2,500 square kilometres, and a citizen population in the region of 100,000 (men, women and children).[8] As constituent wards of the city, and towns, villages and hamlets of the surrounding territory of Attica, the demes varied in size (though the numbers they contained were balanced out at the tribal level), but none would have been that large, as they were designed to comprise units of communal knowledge and control. Each had a leading official – a '*demarch*' – and an assembly, among other organizational features, and these were the main players in the processes of registration for both citizens and metics. While institutions of the *polis* itself, the council and courts, had some oversight of, and engagement with, these activities, there is scant evidence for any central compilation of deme lists: there was no universal register of citizens, and perhaps no central register of anyone else either.

Composed around the middle of the fourth century BC, the Aristotelian work on the 'constitution' (*politeia*) of the Athenians describes the then-current process of citizen registration in some detail:

> Men born of citizen (*astoi*) parentage on both sides belong to the political/citizen-body (*politeia*), they are registered (*engraphesthai*) among the demesmen when they have reached the age of eighteen. When they are being enrolled, the demesmen decide, by vote under oath, first, whether they appear to have reached the age which the law

[7] Whitehead (1986) is the classic study of the deme system.

[8] Athenian indifference to enumeration makes population estimates tricky, but most come in the 20,000–35,000 range for adult male citizens, probably peaking in the fifth century BC, and declining into the fourth. For a recent summary of the debate, with bibliography, see, for example, Oliver (2007, 78–87) and Akrigg (2011).

> prescribes – and, if they do not so appear, they return to being 'boys' once again – and secondly, whether [each one] is free and born in accordance with the laws. Then, if they should vote against him as being not free, he appeals to the jury-court (*dikastêrion*), and the demesmen choose five of their number as accusers; if it is decided [by the court] that he has no right to be registered, the *polis* sells him [into slavery], but if he wins the demesmen are obliged to register him. After this the council (*boulê*) scrutinises those who have been registered, and if it is decided that someone is younger than eighteen, the demesmen who registered him are fined.[9]

There is some debate about the accuracy of this account, even for the fourth century: in particular, the strict division of jurisdiction in respect to decisions about age, and about parentage, seems unlikely in practice; but the basic picture is clear enough. On reaching the age of 18, a young man born of parents who are both citizens (*astoi*: belong to the city, the *astu*) is registered in the deme, that is, he is written into the list of demesmen – the *lexiarchikon grammateion* – which appears elsewhere in the historical record. This registration occurs in a deme assembly, and all the demesmen present vote (under oath, as always) on whether those before them have reached the required age, and are the free and legitimate sons of citizen parents, that is, were born in accordance with Pericles' citizenship law of 451/450 BC, which required a citizen mother as well as a citizen father.[10] This vote is appealable in the city's law-courts, though the stakes are high, and the council of the city also scrutinizes those newly registered. The same deme assembly, probably held near the beginning of the administrative year, would also vote to enrol adoptive rather than natural sons of demesmen, and any newly enfranchised aliens who had selected, or been allotted to, that deme.[11] Since the requirements for adoption were the same as for citizenship, that is to say only legitimate children of two *astoi* could be adopted, and the actual enfranchisement of foreigners was effected by a vote of the assembly of the whole city, in all these cases therefore the deme registers those who are already citizens, by birth, adoption, or decree. This process of registration does not make citizens, but officially recognizes them, and records that recognition, within the public political setting of the deme.

The sense in which registration is a matter of ritual and record but not definition is emphasized in a range of contexts: most obviously in legal disputes about citizenship involving the deme-lists themselves. A general scrutiny of all the local registers ordered in 346/345 BC, for instance, led to some men being struck off and

[9] Aristotle, *Ath. Pol.* 42.1–2. This passage reflects the ambiguities of 'citizenship' in Greek states, which were usually, of course, not democratic. Belonging to a city was generally a status acquired through descent, and always brought with it a share in the state's '*hiera kai hosia*', cult and civic practices, for both men and women, but not necessarily political participation. It entailed rights of property and inheritance, as well as of involvement in the exchange between the human community and the gods according to ancestral tradition, but perhaps no more than that. Aristotle discusses these problems of definition at the beginning of Book 3 of the *Politics* (1274b–1278b).

[10] See Blok (2009) for a recent and full discussion of the law.

[11] Whitehead (1986, 103).

then fighting for reinstatement in the courts.[12] Allegations of personal enmity, manipulation of the deme assembly, and false accusations are combined in such cases with positive claims of status based on a network of living witnesses to key communal events which speak to the individual's legitimate citizen parentage, and broader civic participation.[13] All this is more important than being on a list or not, and there is little evidence that the *lexiarchika grammateia* were ever used to check eligibility for the various entitlements that being 'of the *politeia*' brought with it in democratic Athens: that is, participation in the assembly, council, and law-courts, and the holding of public office. Moreover, though Pericles' citizenship law brought women's status as *astoi* (or not) into sharper relief, they never appeared on any register.[14] The absence of any reference to the deme-lists in connection with eligibility for public office is particularly striking, since there was a process of scrutiny for each candidate, in which use of deme registers would certainly have been very practical, but in which personal testimony is systematically preferred.

Beyond citizens themselves, metics and freed-persons were also registered in their demes of residence: when their stay became long enough to require it, following manumission, or, presumably, on attaining adulthood, or just moving house, within these categories. They also had to register a '*prostates*', an Athenian citizen who acted as some kind of legal sponsor or representative, who provided a point of reference for them in the Athenian legal and civic system.[15] On registering they also became liable for military service and direct taxation. The '*metoikion*', the metic-tax, which was, in many ways, the most important marker of their subordinate status, was a kind of taxation that no Athenian citizen was burdened with, levied at the rate of twelve drachmae a year for a man and six drachmae for a woman (that is, an independent woman who had neither a husband nor a son to pay for her); the relationship of manumitted slaves to this tax is unclear, but they do seem to have had to make some payments.[16] The *metoikion* was farmed out by the board of officials who organized state contracts (the *poletai*) to tax collectors on an annual basis. How this all operated in practice is uncertain, however, and though farming out a fixed tax suggests that the central authorities, the *poletai* and

[12] The reasons for Demophilus' decree ordering this universal scrutiny are unclear; for discussion of the resulting law cases see Whitehead (1986, 104–109) and Kapparis (2005).

[13] On the priority of living witnesses in these matters, see especially Scafuro (1994).

[14] On female citizenship in general see Patterson (1986) and Osborne (1997).

[15] The precise role of the *prostates*, who had to be the former master for a freed slave in Athens, is unclear. Unlike in some other Greek cities, they did not actually have to act for the metic in court, but perhaps functioned as the witness of their status and identity, and vouched for their standing in some way. See Whitehead (1977, 91) and Zelnick-Abramovitz (2005, 248–262).

[16] Thus, one later Greek lexicographer defines a metic as 'one who pays the *metoikion*' (Pollux 3.55); see also Whitehead (1977, 75–77). Given that a skilled worker in Athens might earn around a drachma a day, the tax is not heavy, but the contrast with the (at least directly) un-taxed citizens is emphasized by the practice of state payment for a range of civic activities, from jury- to military-service. On freed slaves, whose military liabilities are also debatable, see Zelnick-Abramovitz (2005, 308–315).

the council under whose auspices they worked, knew how many metics there were, information which would have been most easily acquired through regular collation of deme registers, there is no evidence that this process in fact occurred.[17] Even the figure of 10,000 metics produced in the population count organized by Demetrius of Phalerum, after he took control of Athens on behalf of their Macedonian overlords in 317 BC, looks more like an estimate of the kind that might be used for such tax purposes than a careful calculation based on information from the demes.[18] It does provide a sense of the rough size of this (substantial) group, however, or, at least of its adult, tax-paying portion.

In many ways, however, it was the non-citizens who paid the price for this rather casual attitude to registration, and, indeed, for the non-authoritative nature of Athenian registers in general. Both resident aliens and freed slaves were permanently at risk of being charged with not having a *prostates*, and not paying their taxes, and if convicted the penalty was enslavement. The precise nature of the action brought against them is debated, and this seems to be an area in which the foreign resident and former slave diverge significantly, but such cases have certainly made their mark on the historical record in various ways, testifying to the vulnerable position of non-citizens in Athens.[19] A good defence, or indeed deterrent, would have been provided by a more robust public registration system. If official lists of metics, their *prostatai*, and tax payments had been accessible and authoritative, then the sorts of events described, for example, in a Demosthenic law-court speech from the fourth century BC would have been avoided.[20] The case is against Aristogeiton, for state debt, and as part of the customary demolition of character it is alleged that he seized his metic mistress Zobia (who had done nothing but help him) and dragged her off to the office of the tax collectors, where, if it had not happened that her *metoikion* had been paid, she would have been sold. The Greek is unclear about the means by which it is established that she was not in arrears, whether this was a matter of written record or not; but certainly, in order to support these accusations against Aristogeiton, Zobia's *prostates* is called as a witness, and the tax collectors: no documents are adduced, or referred to.[21]

[17] Whitehead (1977, 77) suggests that there was a central register kept by the office of the *poletai*, or the *polemarch*, the official with judicial responsibility for metics, but he admits this is speculative.

[18] The Macedonian hegemony of Greece was established by Philip II (Alexander the Great's father) in 338 BC, and brought Athenian democracy, at least as an autonomous entity, to an end (after Macedonian domination comes Roman rule). Wealth restrictions on political participation followed, and Demetrius' population count (reported at Athenaeus 7.272b–c) is part of this reform process.

[19] Vulnerability much emphasized in recent scholarship: Patterson (2000) and Meyer (2010, esp. 28–47). Charges against a metic could be brought by anyone who wished to, and the incentive in such cases was that a successful prosecutor was entitled to a share of the proceeds: i.e. the sale of the metic and their property.

[20] Demosthenes 25.5.

[21] That tax receipts, rather than registers, might be available to be consulted is, however, suggested in another law case: Demosthenes 57.33–4.

Registration in democratic Athens was, therefore, distinctive in many ways, particularly in its local organization, and its performative character. Registration was a ritual, a social event, rather than a process which generated an authoritative document, a 'register' in any very strong sense of the term. Adult male citizens fully participated in that ritual, both had their status validated and validated the status of others; while metics' involvement was more partial, their agency compromised by their registration with a *prostates*, and their concomitant inability to witness others' status: the ritual was one of subordinated integration. This fitted in with, enacted, the key values, and organizational principles, of the democracy, which was based on public participation, personal and family networks, and an exclusive sense of community.

Republican Rome

In contrast to the rather patchy registration practices of classical Greek city-states, such as that outlined for democratic Athens, and their lack of interest in enumeration, Rome adopted a systematic approach to both. The Roman 'census', and the word is theirs, combined record, ordering, moral scrutiny, and counting of their citizen population, and involved interaction with the divine. It began, so the stories go, back in the time when the city was ruled by kings and was in the process of formation as community and polity; it continued into the Republic, traditionally founded in 509 BC, when elected magistrates replaced the expelled King Tarqin, and the informal royal council and popular assembly started to move towards creating the powerful political partnership of 'senate and people of Rome'; and it managed the transition from central Italian city-state to global empire over the centuries to come. There were changes along the way, most significant perhaps in the aftermath of the Social War (91–89 BC), when Rome granted citizenship to all the communities in Italy south of the Po, and became a quite different kind of state than previously – though not a very stable one, as the Republic would last only about half a century longer and Roman governance would once again take a more monarchic form under Augustus, after 31 BC.

It was not only Roman power and territory, but also people, the Roman citizenry – *cives Romani* – that increased over this period (with some losses along the way), and not just in lock-step with the other two. The most decisive episode of enlargement was the enfranchisement of Italy during and after the Social War (fought against some of Rome's Italian allies, that is her '*socii*'); and Roman notions of citizenship were always more inclusive than the Greek. The citizen-body, the '*civitas*', was steadily augmented in the Republic by the manumission of slaves, immigration to the metropolis (and some Roman colonies), and a range of grants to individuals and groups; as well as some early territorial incorporations, and later colonial foundations. It is particularly worth noting that in Rome the freed slave became a citizen, a slightly hampered citizen in the first instance, but with all legal impediments removed in a generation, in contrast to the Greek tradition, already described for Athens, in which manumitted slaves joined the ranks of the free non-citizens; but this is part of a more generally open approach of the Romans to *civitas*. Not that the borders of the category were unguarded, or that status did not matter. Roman citizenship brought with it a rich set of entitlements and obligations, political and military, legal and religious, social, economic, and ideological, with women being excluded from the first two domains, but certainly not the rest – the wider patterns of communal membership and participation; though the expansion of citizenship shifted the balance between these elements, and would eventually diffuse its importance.[22]

The figures recorded in the annals of Roman history give a sense of this expanding citizen body, despite the many problems that attend on them. So, a census and '*lustrum*' – the latter being the complex sacrifice and communal ritual which completed the assessment process – are reported to have been conducted in 508 BC, in Rome's first year as a Republic, with the number of assessed citizens announced as 130,000.[23] In the *lustrum* of 234/233 BC, during the decades of Rome's Italian hegemony prior to Hannibal's invasion of the peninsula, and when, according to Peter Brunt in his magisterial study *Italian Manpower: 225* BC–AD *14* ([1971]1987), accounts begin to be more reliable, the declaration was 270,713 assessed citizens, a number which had risen to 900,000 in the *lustrum* of 70/69 BC, not long after the Social War.[24] This was the final, full census of the Republic, when the system was already unravelling; but a return to traditional practice in this area was a key part of Augustus' programme of political and cultural restoration after the civil wars. As he himself proclaims: 'I conducted a census of the people with Marcus Agrippa as my colleague. I performed the *lustrum* 42 years after the last one [i.e. in 28 BC]; in that *lustrum* the assessed heads of Roman citizens were 4,063,000' (*Res Gestae* 8.2).

Debate currently rages about the accuracy of these figures and what they represent.[25] Are these the numbers of adult male citizens, as in Athens, for example; or all citizens – men, women and children – as were certainly recorded later in Roman Egypt, for instance; or was the calculation according to some other principle? Was the procedure for the census stable across the centuries, but perhaps more or less rigorously carried out, or did the methods change, in particular to achieve the massive Augustan figure in 28 BC? These are all important questions, which have

[22] The classic study of the Roman citizenship and its expansion is Sherwin-White ([1939] 1973); see also Gardner (1993).

[23] Dionysius of Halicarnassus, *Roman Antiquities* 5.20.

[24] Livy, *Periochae* 20 and 98. A table of recorded figures for all Republican and Augustan *lustra* can be found in Brunt ([1971]1987), 13; the discussion about the reliability of the figures is on pp. 26–43.

[25] See, for example, Scheidel (2008), Hin (2008), and Launaro (2011, 25–50), for recent discussion.

a dramatic impact on how the demography of Roman Italy is understood, with wider ramifications for the history of the Roman Republic; but the focus here is on the process and socio-cultural significance of registration not the statistical results of enumeration, hitherto a rather overlooked part of the whole business, but itself crucial in many respects. Still, a rough sense of the scale of the undertaking is vital, as also a feel for the level of Roman self-consciousness about their population practices. That censuses and *lustra* were a standard feature of Roman historical narratives and formed part of Rome's communal record demonstrates their contemporary significance, a point which Augustus' actions in this respect emphasize further.[26] One highly influential Roman historian, Livy, writing in the Augustan period, even goes so far as to assert that Rome's rise from insignificant central Italian city to world superpower was predicated, in no small part, on its regular assessment of the citizen-body: the census was, for him, one of the most fundamental, and beneficial, institutions of the Roman state.[27] Not, it should be said, because it produced useful data, but because it engendered and sustained good order and effective organization in war and peace; indeed, the number with which Livy concludes his account of the first ever census and *lustrum* in Rome comes as something of a surprise, as counting the citizens had not been mentioned in the discussion up till then, even though it would become integral to the process.[28]

In terms of regularity, Republican censuses occurred on a roughly quinquennial schedule, with various gaps, crises, and procedural developments along the way.[29] From 443 BC, two 'censors' were elected to see each assessment cycle through, which was expected to take around eighteen months, as well as carrying out a growing number of other tasks and responsibilities, which might take longer. The office was one of great prestige and some power, which usually came towards the end of an individual's sequence of magistracies, and so was held by senior and distinguished figures from the Roman elite. Once the censors opened the census, it was the duty of Roman citizens to present themselves before the competent authorities, and to provide the information required under the *formula censoria*, under oath. They had to declare, orally, their full name, their father's name (or their patron's name if a freedman; that is, the name of the former master who had manumitted them), their tribe, their age, and their property, giving both a summary description and a valuation. They may also have had to supply the names and ages of their children, and perhaps the name of their wife also; certainly they were often

[26] They went into the annual records kept by the *pontifices* (one of the priestly colleges in Rome) – the *annales maximi* – and from there, and through each other, into a range of annalistic and historical writings.

[27] Livy 1.42.4–5.

[28] Livy 1.44.2.

[29] For discussion of the Republican census as process, see Suolahti (1963, 32–47); Brunt ([1971] 1987, 15–25); Nicolet (1980, 48–88); and Northwood (2008, 257–265).

asked about their marital and generative situation.[30] Further undertakings about their conduct might also be demanded, as the censors saw fit. The declaration of information – *professio* – was recorded in writing, by scribes, and a complete account for each census was compiled, which could be consulted in certain circumstances, as will be discussed later.

The censors had extensive powers of enforcement and judgement. A fundamental aspect of the census was the ordering of the people into six 'classes', subdivided into centuries, on a scale of property qualifications, and their distribution into the thirty-five Roman 'tribes', with both allocations essentially under the control of the censors. The level of the property qualifications had already been established, and, though originally geographical entities, tribes were now hereditary, so the situation should have been made clear in the declaration, the rough accuracy of which was generally assured by its nature as a public, oral oath, subject to censorial scrutiny. However, the censors could change the rules, counting possessions they disapproved of as valued differently from land, for example, or moving politically problematic groups – such as freedmen – between tribes, more or less as they wished.[31] Other, more individual, punitive options were also available to them, and might be deployed as punishment for a range of misdemeanours, from evasion of military service to neglect of agricultural land and mocking the censorial process itself; but might also result from simple personal animosity.[32]

Alongside its ideological significance through enactment of general Roman principles of hierarchy and order, this ranking and placement mattered practically in a number of ways. Initially focused on military organization – on mustering, structuring, and paying for the army – at least as the stories go, as the Roman Republican state developed it was the political ramifications of the census which became most crucial. Still, until the reforms of Marius in 106 BC, those in the lowest class were excluded from serving in the legions, though they might (and did) serve in the navy; and both tribe and century played some role in the organization of the military levy (*dilectus*).[33] Similarly, until Roman victories in the wealthy Hellenistic

[30] Only Dionysius mentions declaring wives and children: *Roman Antiquities* 4.15.6 and 5.73.3 (including children's ages); while Cicero makes a rather different kind of reference to the censors' interest in assessing offspring (and ages): *Laws* 3.7. Questions about marital status, cast as standard, appear at Aulus Gellius 4.20.1 and 4.3.2 (also 17.21.44).

[31] Censorial control over valuation: e.g. Livy 39.44.2–3 (censorship of Cato); tribal movement of freedmen: e.g. Livy 45.15.1–6.

[32] There was a punitive grouping – the *aerarii* – in which persons could be placed. Its exact nature is unclear, but being listed as such certainly entailed ignominy and perhaps financial penalty, too; the votes of those classified as *aerarii* were cast in a special (non-)century, and so barely counted: the best discussion is Grieve (1983). On the various causes of punishment see Astin (1988).

[33] How any lists of individuals, rather than their classification into the relevant groups, played a role in this process is less clear, at least once Rome reached a significant size in the Republican period. There are reports for early Rome of a literal 'roll-call' (e.g. Livy 3.10.1), but by the time of the Hannibalic War it seems that going through the lists of *iuniores* (those aged between 17 and 45 and liable for regular

East in 167 BC, liability for *tributum* – the closest Rome came to directly taxing its citizens – was determined by class: the wealthier contributed most to the cost of any campaign, and the sixth class, the poorest, were again pretty much exempt.[34] But it was in terms of power that the real pay-back for registering and being assessed occurred, at least for those with plenty of property to declare. In the Republican political system, popular assemblies, organized by both century and tribe, were the locus of annual elections for the various magistracies and of voting on legislative proposals, war and peace, and other matters of state. Because of the particular form of group voting which characterized these assemblies – in which all groups counted equally, regardless of size, and votes were cast in a certain order – being in the top centuries gave an individual's vote far greater weight. There were eighty ordinary centuries in the *prima classis*, the 'first class', together with a further eighteen special centuries of cavalrymen (*equites*), in comparison to twenty or thirty for the next four (alongside a few extra), and just one at the bottom. Also, being in one of the thirty-one smaller, more exclusive, 'rural' tribes (and not in one of the four huge and sprawling 'urban' ones) increased the value of an individual's vote. Indeed, with 193 centuries in total, many elections and issues were decided entirely within the top ranks. In addition, only those in the *prima classis* were eligible to stand for election.

What the censors could not do, however, was expel anyone from the system as a whole. C. Claudius Pulcher, censor in 169 BC, states that: 'to take away citizenship (*civitas*) and freedom (*libertas*); not simply to determine where a person will be assessed (*censere*), but to exclude them from the census entirely', is outside his powers (Livy 45.15.1–6). Nor could they, or anyone else, compel participation in the census. It is reported that Servius Tullius, the early king credited with invention of the Roman census system, instituted severe penalties for non-registration: the threat of death or imprisonment, according to Livy (1.44.1), or the forfeit of property, being whipped and sold into slavery, according to another author of the Augustan period.[35] However, this does not seem to have been a Republican reality, though deceitful, ill-intentioned, avoidance of the census may have been actionable and punishable (by flogging and sale of property).[36] No such cases, or penalties,

military call-up) was not usual practice, since the censors of 214 BC do it only because they have time on their hands and some particular concerns (Livy 24.18.7). On the *dilectus* generally, see Brunt ([1971] 1987, 625–634).

[34] On *tributum* see Nicolet (1976).

[35] This time writing his history of Rome in Greek, that is Dionysius of Halicarnassus (4.15.6)

[36] This is the position set out in the Oscan law partially preserved on a fragmentary bronze tablet from Bantia in southern Italy, and perhaps dating to the early first century BC (Crawford 1996). The text briefly describes the local census (IV.9–10), but it is likely to be as indebted to Roman practice here as elsewhere, perhaps even adapting procedures from the nearby Latin colony of Venusia. This would certainly be a practical approach, reserving the possibility of prosecution and punishment, if necessary: see Moatti (2009).

in relation to *incensi* – those who have not given an account of themselves and their property to the authorities – are recorded, despite the occasional loose evocation of such possibilities, and plenty of general reportage around the census, including punishments for other things. Indeed, instances of failure, or inability, to appear before the censors proliferate over the course of the Republic. Troops serving overseas at the relevant time were not generally included, for example: Livy mentions that, in 204 BC, the *lustrum* was unusually delayed because the censors had sent out across the provinces to discover how many Roman citizens were stationed in the various armies around the empire (29.37.6). A more individual case is described by Cicero, the great statesman and orator of the late Republic: L. Annius was able to avoid the strictures of the *lex Voconia* – a law preventing those in the *prima classis* from instituting female heirs – because, though certainly wealthy enough to be affected, he was *incensus*, and so had not been assessed; and Cicero does not condemn him for that state, nor does he suggest that anyone else would either.[37]

The point is, as all the versions of the Servian penalties underline (just as they emphasize the intrinsically coercive nature of a royal state), that citizenship did not depend on the census and *lustrum*. It was generated elsewhere, by birth and law, just as in Athens. Communal membership and all that entailed had a separate existence, which the census could record, but did not engender, or even prove. This is explicitly stated by Cicero in a famous law case of 62 BC: 'The census does not establish citizenship (*ius civitatis*)', he unequivocally asserts (*Pro Archia* 11). And though he is defending a man – Archias – whose citizen status has been challenged, and who had not been included in any Roman census, and so is hardly going to argue the reverse, this fits so well with all the other evidence that there is little reason to doubt him. Everybody knows, says Cicero, that his client was away from Rome, on campaign with the general Lucullus, at the times of the last two censuses. Moreover, Cicero can offer a mixture of personal testimony and written record to demonstrate that Archias (originally a Greek from Antioch) followed proper procedure in becoming a Roman citizen, and that he lived in Rome as a citizen, doing all the things good Roman citizens do, such as making wills and receiving legacies under Roman law, and participating in various patterns of public reward and recognition. As in classical Athens, the emphasis is on living, respectable and reliable, witnesses to the various stages of the process of acquiring *civitas*; but where official documents – *publicae tabulae* – are available, Cicero certainly refers to them – they do have some weight.[38]

[37] Cicero, *Verrines* 2.1.104–107.

[38] The stark contrast drawn by Meyer (2004, esp. 12–43) between an Athenian legal system based entirely on personal testimony, and a Roman system where the document was king, is, therefore, much exaggerated; though there is more of a place for documents in Rome, and their role was to become greater under the empire. For a more nuanced view see Gardner (1986).

The sense in which documentation, its absence and presence, was part of the legal debate, on both sides, is significant, however, despite its lack of decisiveness.[39] It is clear that the products of various kinds of registration could be referred to, in a meaningful way, and it has been suggested – mostly by those with enumerative interests in the census as a reasonably complete account – that being *census*, being on the record, was of practical use to those at the bottom, as well as the top, of Roman society; that registration was generally beneficial to all individual citizens as well as the state, with its organizational and ideological concerns. Thus, Brunt argues that being on the register would have helped even the lowest down the social order assert the legal privileges and voting rights of the *civis Romanus*.[40] These claims are hard to support, however, since, though Roman voting procedure did allow for individual scrutiny of each voter, there is no evidence that, at least in the tribal assemblies, this was done on anything other than a very informal level (if at all); and what went on in the centuriate assembly, where the top centuries were small enough to be self-regulating, was irrelevant to the majority.[41] Moreover, as Archias demonstrates, access to the Roman legal system was not particularly assisted by being in the census. However, his case did not involve perhaps the most paradigmatic of Roman citizen rights, that of *provocatio* – the (theoretical) guarantee against execution without trial, and, by the middle of the Republic, also against flogging – which Brunt certainly draws attention to in this context.[42] However, in most of the recorded examples where *provocatio* is invoked, status is not at issue; these cases are all about the proper and improper exercise of power more broadly. The one exception to this rule – though rather later (and, again, biblical) – is the apostle Paul, but at no point is his oral declaration of Roman citizenship questioned, no one ever checks on his status.[43]

Still, it is surely not irrelevant that the main term used to refer to the sixth, lowest, 'class' is '*capite censi*', literally those 'assessed by head' (though '*caput*/head' really signifies the legal concept of a person), not by property (on account of its insufficiency).[44] This suggests that they did register: that the ideological significance of the census was as strong for them as anyone else, even if the practical ramifications were negligible; that they too were defined by their assessment by the state. There is also an interesting exception to the rule that citizenship is

[39] In the absence of the prosecution speech, of course, whether Archias' absence from the census had been explicitly raised, and in what way, is unknown; so Cicero might simply have been covering the bases rather than responding to a specific accusation. The result of the case is also unknown, though the indications are, since Archias stays in Rome, that he (and Cicero) prevailed.

[40] Brunt ([1971] 1987, 34).

[41] See Mouritsen (2001, 113).

[42] Brunt ([1971] 1987, 34); and on *provocatio* in general, see Lintott (1972).

[43] *Acts* 22: 25–29.

[44] The other term is '*proletarii*', apparently on account of the offspring ('*proles*') they contributed to the state: Cicero, *Republic* 2.40; cf. Aulus Gellius 16.10.

generated outside the confines of the census, which adds a further dimension to the possible benefits of individual engagement with the process, even (or especially) at a distance from its upper echelons. This is in respect to one of the three standard modes of manumission, at least in the Republic, which are, as later jurists such as Gaius consistently list them, 'by *vindicta* (a ritualized legal fiction), by census, or by will' (*Institutes* 1.17, 35). If a slave rightfully owned by a Roman citizen makes a declaration for the census, with the agreement of his master, he becomes a Roman citizen; though it is a nice point, explains Cicero, whether his freedom commences at the moment his declaration is recorded, or at the moment of the *lustrum*, which completes – perhaps actualizes – the census (*Orator* 1.183). Either way, however, citizenship for these individuals is constituted through the census (*censu*); and it may be that a similar outcome is hoped for by another group of new citizens, or at least aspirants to that status, who also illustrate that registration, being on lists, could be of individual importance, as well as a key corporate enterprise.

Livy records a couple of occasions in the early second century BC when embassies from Latin colonies and Italian allies complained to the Roman senate that large numbers of their *cives* had migrated to Rome, and been registered (*censa*) there. In 187 BC, for example, a magistrate was charged with discovering these persons, and, if anyone, or their parents, was proved to have been registered in another Italian community reasonably recently (since the census of 202 BC), they would be sent back to their own, or their parental, community (Livy 39.3.4–6). Consequently, 12,000 were returned. The actual law in this area is vague, and debated, and it would be interesting to know what the content of the declarations these migrants made to the censors had been; there is no suggestion they were forsworn, that they had in any way lied under oath (or they would have been in real trouble).[45] Still it seems clear that the incomers considered that registration would help establish, if not constitute, their change of citizenship – make them Roman; and, though the census turned out not to be constitutive, or, at least, that their transmutation was reversible, they were not completely wrong. The same action prior to 202 BC would have had a different result, and if they could not be found on another list, they stayed Roman.

As these events also show, registration of their own citizens was a reasonably common feature of Italian communities outside Rome at this time.[46] This is hardly surprising, both in terms of the broader patterns of Mediterranean practice and the particularities of their relations with Rome. Most Italian states were obliged to provide troops for Rome, by the terms of the various uneven treaties imposed in the course of the Roman conquest of the peninsula, or, in the case of the Latin colonies Rome had herself founded to support her domination of Italy, by the terms

[45] The best discussion of the law on migration to Rome is Broadhead (2001).

[46] A prevalence already indicated by the law from Bantia, a small city with no particular political significance in its region.

of their foundation. Whenever she needed armies, Rome ordered a levy of her own citizens and that the Latins and allies supply soldiery according to the *formula togatorum*, the means by which Rome determined the number each city or people was to produce. Much is unclear about the *formula*, but it seems that, having decided the overall figure required, this was then divided amongst the relevant states in rough proportion to their manpower, or at least Rome's understanding of their young manpower, their number of *iuniores*.[47] The Latins and allies then organized their own drafts, on a local basis, and making use of their own censuses, in the case of Latin colonies where institutions were modelled on those of the mother city, or looser registers, such as the cumulative lists of citizens kept by the Greek cities of southern Italy, such as Heraclea, before the Social War.[48] The specific difficulties created by migration to Rome in this situation, implicit in the episode of 187 BC, are made explicit, rhetorically exaggerated even, in repeat complaints made to the Roman senate by Latin and Italian embassies just a decade later. In 177 BC they reported that 4,000 families had moved from amongst the Paeligni and Samnites (federated tribal states in central Italy) to the Latin colony of Fregellae, though no reduction had been made to their military levies (Livy 41.8.5–12), while resource problems were also again being caused by their citizens moving to, and registering in, Rome: so that, they alleged, with a flourish, 'in just a few *lustra*, their now deserted towns and fields would not be able to furnish a single soldier'. The senate agreed measures to stop and even to attempt to reverse these processes (Livy 42.10.2).

It is interesting to note that, though these were, in some senses, Roman resources, there was no central effort to keep track of them. It was the Italian communities themselves who had to bring change, crisis even, to the attention of Rome, which otherwise assumed a steady state. Indeed, the response to this movement was attempted reversal, to stay with the formula. The point is further emphasized, with a twist, by the particular case of the twelve Latin colonies which, in 209 BC, after eight years of war with Hannibal, claimed total exhaustion and refused to provide Rome with any more men or money. Once Roman fortunes were restored, and the Carthaginians were on the retreat, in 204 BC, the colonies were punished with double levies, an annual tax, and a census to be conducted according to the formula issued by the censors in Rome, which would be sworn by the colonial censors, and brought to Rome (Livy 29.15.9–10). This the twelve colonies duly did, and the Roman censors received these local censuses directly after they had completed the *lustrum*; something which 'had never happened before', according to Livy, but was to ensure

[47] Baronowski (1984).

[48] Cicero reports (*Pro Archia* 6 and 8) that Archias 'was written into' (*ascriptus*) the citizen-lists of various Italian cities, most importantly Heraclea, on his way to becoming a Roman citizen. This kind of register is rather different from the Roman census, however, lacking its more communal cyclical and ritual aspect, and the key feature of assessment.

that their military and financial resources were now a matter of permanent public record. Rome's treatment of the twelve recusant colonies, the penal use of the census, imposing its terms and centralizing its report, with the shift in ownership of the relevant information that results, can be seen as foreshadowing a more systematic imperial practice from the time of Augustus onwards: the use of provincial censuses to assess the resources now available for exploitation by the Roman rulers.

The key event before that was the settlement following the Social War, and the grant of Roman citizenship to all Italian communities south of the Po. It was Julius Caesar, as dictator in 45 BC, who seems to have been the first to adopt a systematic approach to the new administrative landscape of Italy, but he was building on various aspects of previous practice, perhaps including various *ad hoc* recent developments. There were also some points of departure at least implicit in the structure which was now established. Basically, as the bronze inscription of the Table of Heraclea sets out, within sixty days of learning that a census was being conducted in Rome, the highest local magistrate had to conduct a census of the members of his community (who were now, as members, Roman citizens).[49] He was to receive from all of them, under oath, their name, their father's or patron's name, their tribe, their age, and an account of their property, 'according to the formula of the census which has been published at Rome by whoever is then about to conduct the census of the people'; and he was to ensure that all this was reported in the public records (*tabulae publicae*) of his municipality (lines 146–149). Following their compilation, these books were then to be sent to Rome, carried by officially selected envoys, who must present them to those conducting the census at Rome at least sixty days before the close of the census of the people. The magistrates at Rome, censors or otherwise, had five days to ensure that the contents of these books were honestly and accurately copied into their public records, and were stored in the same place as all the rest of the *tabulae*, 'in which the census of the people is written out' (line 156). The law also provided for those with multiple domiciles, and who had already registered at Rome, not to have to repeat the process locally.

There is no suggestion here, as there is in some accounts of the earlier censuses in the city of Rome itself, that fathers might declare their children, and husbands their wives. Declarations were to be received from all citizens, and, by the early imperial period, certainly, women seem to be registered in exactly the same way as men.[50] This is, explicitly, an individualized, and apparently standardized, kind of registration. In addition, the system represented by the inscription from Heraclea

[49] The Table of Heraclea (named after its place of discovery) contains a range of regulatory provisions from the last years of the Republic: see Crawford (1996) for text, translation and discussion.

[50] Unfortunately this evidence is preserved in a list of the long-lived compiled by Phlegon of Tralles (*Fragments of the Greek Historians* 235 Fr. 37), so whether children were also included remains obscure.

seems to have lost the moral dimension, the *regimen morum*, so crucial to the Roman census up till then. What is being transmitted to Rome, accurately transmitted, is information, not judgement; information that includes an assessment of property, according to Roman rules, but nothing more. One of the issues at stake in registering at Rome was, in some sense, inviting full censorial scrutiny, which would become increasingly limited to the real elite, while legislation of wider scope took on other aspects of the censors' role. It is hard to think how it could, practically, have been otherwise, in this world of wide-spread citizenship, when Rome had to give up even the pretence of being a city-state; but the significance of the shifts involved should not be underestimated, shifts which were then deepened and solidified under Augustus.

These were not, however, moves towards a more utilitarian, statistical, census practice in relation to Roman citizens, at least as events turned out. What Julius Caesar's plans were remain obscure, since his assassination in 44 BC brought his programme of administrative reform to an abrupt halt, and though his great-nephew, and adopted son and heir, Augustus, picked up some of the pieces after 31 BC, whether the way he put Roman citizen, provincial subject and imperial state together, his evolving fiscal, military and political settlement, bears much relationship to that previously envisioned is uncertain. Three key Augustan developments are most significant in this respect: the falling away of political participation except amongst the elite, as elections were re-structured (and eventually, almost immediately after Augustus' death, passed to the senate: Tacitus, *Annals* 1.15); the 'professionalization' of the Roman army, so that military service became, by and large, a career choice not an obligation; and the placing of the burden of direct taxation on the provinces – *tributum* was now paid by those outside Italy.[51] So, in his emphatic revival of the citizen census and *lustrum*, now more thorough in its registration of *cives Romani* in Italy and beyond, Augustus was not looking to create the fullest lists of those liable for military and monetary levies. That kind of resource management was more a matter for the emerging provincial censuses – such as that of Quirinus in Syria – which catalogued non-citizens, their wealth, property, and other features, by city or other administrative unit.

Not that citizen status was now entirely disassociated from the military and fiscal organization of the state: Roman citizens enrolled in the legions (or the elite praetorian guards), which had more advantageous terms of service than the non-citizen auxiliary units, and enjoyed some tax exemptions on Italian property, as well as broader legal privileges. But Augustus' interests were focused (as was

[51] This is, of course, to simplify more complex patterns: citizen conscription was not entirely over, for instance; Augustus instituted a (rather restricted) inheritance tax on Roman citizens in Italy; and the popular element never entirely disappeared from Roman politics, transferring to the more informal setting of the circus and arena. On Augustus' military, fiscal and political moves, see Crook (1996), Keppie (1996), and Rathbone (1996).

traditional) on the upper echelons of the citizen census, on the centrally produced hierarchy it generated, and the overall magnitude of the citizen-body. The new *princeps* differentiated the top class further, and more strongly, than before, and utilized the basic structure of the census in building a joined-up social order right across the empire.[52] The figures he proclaimed rose over the course of his principate: in Augustus' third and final *lustrum*, conducted with his adopted son and heir, Tiberius, in the last year of his life, AD 14, the number of Roman citizens assessed was declared to be 4,937,000 (*Res Gestae* 8.4).

Thus, distinctions both between Roman citizens and others, and within these categories, were ideologically meaningful, and practically significant, for the maintenance and functioning of the empire, for its ruler, its ruling elite, and its wider populations. Taxation and other forms of resource extraction, and management, were part of this significance, but that was never going to be all that was at stake in these shifting encounters between people and state. Registrations of privilege as well as of exploitation would persist and interweave over the centuries; one of the markers of Roman statehood would continue to be the articulation of the two, the arbitration of different categories of belonging.

Conclusion

Despite the various differences in form and content, the registration systems of democratic Athens and Republican Rome share some key features. Neither is definitive of status. Identity is basically determined elsewhere, and is then meant to be recorded on deme registers and census rolls. For Rome this is a record of full members only, while for Athens, both the fullest and the most partial of participants in the state (taking slaves to be totally excluded) are listed. Both processes are public affairs. In Rome the *professio* takes centre stage – the individual declaration to authority – and the audience of (rough) peers, those who are there to make their professions, too, provide a generic form of validation by their presence: that they hear what is said, what is claimed. In Athens, on the other hand, the action is more collective: there is no individual declaration and no audience. Claims emerge from the social and political structure of the city: seventeen years after the ritual introduction of any newborn boys to their family and the larger social grouping of their father's phatry ('brotherhood'), the survivors will be considered in the deme assemblies. The deme debates and the deme decides, with some central oversight. The demesmen make themselves witnesses to citizenship, to the entry into full *politeia*, in a far more important way than going on a list does. While for the Romans not only personal testimony but also being listed count; they see strengths and

[52] On Augustus and the census, see Nicolet (1984).

weaknesses in both as forms of proof. However, Athens and Rome converge again in their positive presumption that, if someone appears at the relevant deme meeting, if they present themselves at the census, that is part of behaving like a citizen, which needs to be disproved, rather than the reverse. Indeed, in these communities more broadly, appropriate behaviour does a lot of work in the formation and recognition of identity anyway.

The commonalities and divergences in their registrative projects and practices can in many ways be correlated to larger-scale similarities and differences between Athens and Rome in terms of state formation and political structure, and historical and social development. They can also, in the context of this volume, be located within much broader patterns of convergence and variety between polities and communities across time and space. This is a pattern, moreover, which clearly and importantly reaches back far beyond modernity in both East and West, and many places in between. Civil registration is a key feature of many ancient states, democratic, oligarchic, and monarchic; large and small; city-states and empires; not in exactly the same way, taking the same form, of course, but always about membership and privilege as well as subordination and exploitation.

References

Akrigg, B. 2011. 'Demogaphy and Classical Athens.' In *Demography and the Graeco-Roman World: New Insights and Approaches*, ed. C. Holleran and A. Pudsey. Cambridge: Cambridge University Press, 37–59.

Astin, A. E. 1988. '*Regimen Morum*.' *Journal for Roman Studies* 78: 14–34.

Baronowski, D. W. 1984. 'The *Formula Togatorum*.' *Historia* 33: 248–252.

Blok, J. 2009. 'Perikles' Citizenship Law: A New Perspective.' *Historia* 58: 141–170.

Broadhead, W. 2001. 'Rome's Migration Policy and the So-Called *Ius Migrandi*.' *Cahiers Glotz* 12: 69–89.

Brunt, P. 1987. *Italian Manpower: 225 BC–AD 14*, rev. edn. Oxford: Oxford University Press.

—— 1990. 'The Revenues of Rome.' In *Roman Imperial Themes*. Oxford: Oxford University Press.

Clarysse, W. and D. Thompson. 2006. *Counting the People in Hellenistic Egypt*, 2 vols. Cambridge: Cambridge University Press.

Crawford, M. H. 1996. *Roman Statutes*, 2 vols. London: Institute of Classical Studies.

Crook, J. A. 1996. 'Political History, 30 BC to AD 14.' In *The Cambridge Ancient History: The Augustan Empire, 43 BC–AD 69*, 2nd edn, ed. A. K. Bowman, E. Champlin and A. Lintott. Cambridge: Cambridge University Press, 70–112.

Gardner, J. 1986. 'Proofs of Status in the Roman World.' *Bulletin of the Institute of Classical Studies* 33: 1–14.

—— 1993. *Being a Roman Citizen*. London: Routledge.

Grieve, L. 1983. '*Tabulae Caeritum*.' In *Studies in Latin Literature and Roman History III*, ed. C. Deroux . Brussels: Éditions Latomus, 26–43.

Hin, S. 2008. 'Counting Romans.' In *People, Land, and Politics: Demographic Developments and the Transformation of Roman Italy, 300 BC–AD 14*, ed. L. de Ligt and S. Northwood. Leiden: Brill, 187–238.

Kapparis, K. 2005. 'Immigration and Citizenship Procedures in Athenian Law.' *Revue Internationale des Droits de'Antiquité* 52: 71–113.

Keppie, L. 1996. 'The Army and the Navy.' In *The Cambridge Ancient History: The Augustan Empire, 43 BC–AD 69*, 2nd edn, ed. A. K. Bowman, E. Champlin and A. Lintott. Cambridge: Cambridge University Press, 371–395.

Launaro, A. 2011. *Peasants and Slaves: The Rural Population of Roman Italy (200 BC to AD 100)*. Cambridge: Cambridge University Press.

Lintott, A. 1972. '*Provocatio* from the Struggle of the Orders to the Principate.' *Aufstieg und Niedergang der römischen Welt* 1.2. Berlin: Walter de Gruyter, 226–267.

Meyer, E. A. 2004. *Legitimacy and Law in the Roman World: Tabulae in Roman Belief and Practice*. Cambridge: Cambridge University Press.

—— 2010. *Metics and the Athenian Phialai-Inscriptions: A Study in Athenian Epigraphy and Law*. Wiesbaden: Franz Steiner Verlag.

Moatti, C. 2009. 'Le traitement des absents à Rome à l'époque républicaine et au début de l'empire: quelques considérations.' In *Le monde de l'itinérance en Méditerranée de l'antiquité à l'époque moderne: procédures de contrôle et d'identification*, ed. C. Moatti, W. Kaiser and C. Pébarthe. Paris: Diffusion de Boccard, 321–349.

Mouritsen, M. 2001. *Plebs and Politics in the Late Roman Republic*. Cambridge: Cambridge University Press.

Nicolet, C. 1976. *Tributum. Recherches sur la fiscalité directe sous la République Romaine.* Bonn: Habelt.

—— 1980. *The World of the Citizen in Republican Rome*, trans. P. S. Falla. London: Batsford.

—— 1984. 'Augustus, Government and the Propertied Class.' In *Caesar Augustus: Seven Aspects*, ed. F. Millar and E. Segal. Oxford: Oxford University Press, 89–128.

Northwood, S. 2008. 'Census and Tributum.' In *People, Land, and Politics: Demographic Developments and the Transformation of Roman Italy, 300 BC–AD 14*, ed. L. de Ligt and S. Northwood. Leiden: Brill, 257–270.

Oliver, G. J. 2007. *War, Food, and Politics in Early Hellenistic Athens*. Oxford: Oxford University Press.

Osborne, R. 1997. 'Law, the Democratic Citizen and the Representation of Women in Classical Athens.' *Past and Present* 135: 3–33.

Patterson, C. 1986. '*Hai Attikai*: The Other Athenians.' *Helios* 13: 49–67.

—— 2000. 'The Hospitality of Athenian Justice: The Metic in Court.' In *Law and Social Status in Classical Athens*, ed. V. Hunter and J. Edmondson. Oxford: Oxford University Press, 93–112.

Rathbone, D. W. 1993. 'Egypt, Augustus and Roman Taxation.' *Cahiers Glotz* 4: 81–112.

—— 1996. 'The Imperial Finances.' In *The Cambridge Ancient History: The Augustan Empire, 43 BC–AD 69*, 2nd edn, ed. A. K. Bowman, E. Champlin and A. Lintott. Cambridge: Cambridge University Press, 309–323.

Scafuro, A. C. 1994. 'Witnessing and False Witnessing: Proving Citizenship and Kin Identity in Fourth-Century Athens.' In *Athenian Identity and Civic Ideology*, ed. A. L. Boegehold and A. C. Scafuro. Baltimore, MD: Johns Hopkins University Press, 156–198.

Scheidel, W. 2008. 'Roman Population Size: The Logic of the Debate.' In *People, Land, and Politics: Demographic Developments and the Transformation of Roman Italy, 300 BC–AD 14*, ed. L. de Ligt and S. Northwood. Leiden: Brill, 17–70.

Sherwin-White, A. N. 1973. *The Roman Citizenship*, 2nd edn. Oxford: Oxford University Press.

Suolahti, J. 1963. *The Roman Censors: A Study on Social Structure*. Helsinki Suomalainen Tiedakatemia.

Whitehead, D. 1977. *The Ideology of the Athenian Metic*. Cambridge: Cambridge Philological Society.

—— 1986. *The Demes of Attica, 508/7–c.250 BC: A Political and Social Study*. Princeton, NJ: Princeton University Press.

Zelnick-Abramovitz, R. 2005. *Not Wholly Free: The Concept of Manumission and the Status of Manumitted Slaves in the Ancient Greek World*. Leiden: Brill.

7

Naming, Identifying and Authorizing Movement in Early Modern Spain and Spanish America

TAMAR HERZOG

IN THE FOLLOWING PAGES, I will examine two issues that correspond to present-day preoccupations, namely, controlling movement and identifying people in early modern Spain and Spanish America. Whether they led to the proliferation of registries, and what the status of these was, are other questions. As I will argue in the conclusion, in both Spain and Spanish America (as elsewhere in Europe) the early modern age was a period of administrative expansion, both enabled by and legitimizing the transfer of oral knowledge to written form. For many, the appearance of lists that named individuals and classified them in certain ways demonstrated both the administrative push for 'legibility' as well as its relative 'success'. Nonetheless, if we are to historicize record-keeping, we also need to examine under what circumstances legibility was required (or at least preferred) and the extent to which early modern registries were able to operate the transformation from oral to written, by questioning, not only their specific competence, but also their inherent capability to determine who was who, and who had the right to which treatment.

Authorizing movement in peninsular Spain

Spanish early modern political structures were based on the premise that individuals were free to emigrate from one place to another. Whether this principle was adopted because of the particular conditions of the medieval re-conquest (*reconquista*) that promoted immigration mainly from northern Spain to the south; whether it was inspired by Roman law which portrayed human communities as voluntary associations and defended the right of individuals to become their members (Kirshner 1973; Ullmann 1988);[1] whether it expressed royal struggle against noble privilege;

[1] On the reception of Ius Comune in Spain see Font Rius (1967) and Clavero Salvador (1976).

Proceedings of the British Academy **182**, 191–209.

whether it was possible because of the absence, as some have suggested, of 'true' feudalism in Spain; or, perhaps, all of the above – we will quite probably never know. However, what we do know is that it was constantly reaffirmed in different pieces of legislation which instructed that 'any person who lives and resides in any city, town or village of our kingdoms . . . that wishes to live in another . . . can do so', and insisted that prohibiting such a movement would be 'against justice and reason and against their liberty, which is notorious to all'.[2] Such behaviour would 'silently introduce servitude in men who are free, inhibiting them from living and residing where they wanted and detaining them against their will where they do not want to live; if this happened it would be unjust and against all Law and reason'.[3] These legal enactments were not a dead letter. During the early modern period, the principle of freedom of immigration was constantly appealed to and

[2] *Recopilación de Castilla*, law 1, title 9, book 7, and *Novísima Recopilación*, laws 1–3 and 6, title 26. The original version reads: 'Qualesquier personas que viven y moran en qualesquier ciudades, villas y lugares destsos nuestros reinos y señoríos, así de realengo como de abadengo, órdenes y señorío y behetrías, que se quisieren pasar a vivir de ellos a otros lugares y partes con sus bienes y hacienda, lo puedan hacer y avecindarse en ellos y sacar sus ganados, pan y vino y otros mantenimientos y todos los otros sus bienes muebles.' The term liberty was specifically mentioned in a provision given by King Fernando on 5 July 1477, which stated, 'some of the said my vassals, using their liberty, move to live and reside in the said town and its territory [and prohibiting it] is against justice and reason and against their liberty, which – as is known to all –, would be a bad example' ('algunos de los tales sus vasallos, usando de su libertad, se pasan a vivir y morar a la dicha villa y a su tierra [y prohibirlo es] contra justicia y razón y contra su libertad, la cual como a todos es notorio, es cosa de mal ejemplo') (reproduced in Cayetano Martín 1992, 111–114).

[3] A *Pragmática* of 1480 ordered: 'Some of our subjects and natives informed us that having been citizens and residents in some of the said cities, towns and villages, aware that it may suit them and good to move to live and reside to another or other places and settle in them, they go and pass with their wives and children to these other places, which they prefer and that as a result the councils, officials and honourable citizens of the places where they were citizens before and their proprietors impede and disturb them . . . Because of this behaviour and orders, we say, they silently introduce a type of servitude among free men so that they cannot live or reside where they want and against their wish they are detained to live in the places where their proprietors or councils want, where they do not want to live, to which we say that if this was to happen it would be very unjust and against all law and reason . . . we order that in the future you would allow any men or women, citizens and inhabitants of any of these said cities, town and villages, to leave and move and reside in another or any other one.' ('por parte de algunos nuestros súbitos y naturales nos es hecha relación que ellos siendo vecinos y moradores en algunas de las dichas ciudades, villas y lugares, conociendo que les viene bien y que es cumplidero a ellos pasarse a vivir y morar a otro u otros lugares y avecindar en ellos, se van y pasan con sus mujeres e hijos a los otros lugares que más les place y que por esta causa los concejos, oficiales y hombres buenos de los lugares donde primeramente eran vecinos y los dueños de ellos les impiden y perturban . . . por las cuales cosas y mandamientos diz que calladamente se induce especie de servidumbre a los hombres libres para que no puedan vivir ni morar donde quisieren y contra su voluntad hayan de ser detenidos de morada en los lugares que los dueños de ellos o sus concejos quisieran, donde ellos no quieren vivir, lo cual diz que, si así pasase, sería muy injusto y contra todo derecho y razón . . . mandamos que de aquí delante dejedes a cualquier hombres y mujeres, vecinos y moradores de cualquier de estas dichas ciudades, villas y lugares, irse y pasarse a vivir y morar a otra u otras cualesquiera.') This *Pragmática* was reproduced in the *Cédula* of 17 October 1544 (Konetzke 1953, vol. 1, no. 149).

applied by litigants, jurists, judges and local and royal administrators. Litigants invoked it in courts, insisting that a 'natural law' authorized their movement, which no community or lord could prohibit because 'the passage from one place to another was a free act according to royal law'.[4] This freedom became so central to political debates that in the sixteenth century Francisco Vitoria transformed it into a method to justify Spanish presence in the New World, which according to him was unjustified otherwise. Not only did the freedom of immigration justify colonialism (colonialism consisting of the free movement of Spaniards to the Americas), but, for it to justify colonialism, Vitoria had to argue that it was not a particular Spanish arrangement but instead a central element of natural law. It therefore could be applied not only in Spain but all over the globe. Among other things, it obliged Indians even if they did not know or care about it (Vitoria 1991, 277–284).

The freedom of immigration, so cherished in contemporary sources, had one clear exception: although it allowed individuals to move from one community to another, it prohibited them from remaining on their own.[5] The lack of insertion in a community, any community, was equalled to a complete personal liberty, which could not be tolerated because individuals living outside the confines of a known community also lived outside the social and religious norms.[6] Free movement, therefore, was accompanied by rules that required all individuals to integrate and insert themselves – usually by becoming citizens (*vecinos*) – in a community, and that penalized those who did not. It was also accompanied by legislation that enforced settlement on people who lived on their own or who constantly moved from one place to the other. Already at the end of the fifteenth century this reasoning was applied to Gypsies, accused not only of anti-social and anti-Christian behaviour, but also identified as permanent vagrants whose 'redemption' required that they establish a permanent place of residence.[7] By the late seventeenth, and more clearly

[4] Opinion of Luis Verdugo, dated 10 February 1702, in Archivo Villa de Madrid (hereafter AVM), Secretaría 2-348-23. The original version reads: 'according to the liberty that according to natural law we have, each one can renounce the citizenship he has in one place and live and become citizens of another, which he choses' ('conforme a la libertad que conforme a derecho natural tenemos, cada uno puede renunciar la vecindad que tuviese en un lugar y vivir y avecindarse en otro el que eligiese'). Petition of Germán Salcedo, dated 20 July 1788, in Archivo de la Chancillería de Valladolid (hereafter ACV), Pleitos Civiles–Pérez Alonso (Fenecidos) 3522-1. The original version reads: 'cannot deny it [citizenship) as it is a free act according to the laws to move from one citizenship to another' ('no tiene arbitrio para dejar de concederla [la vecindad] por ser acto libre según leyes el pasarse de una vecindad a otra').

[5] These issues and others are explored in greater length in Herzog (2003, 28–29), and Herzog (2007a).

[6] AVM, Secretaría 2-348-23. Pedro Fernández Navarrete argued that these people were dangerous because they did not serve the republic, marry or pay taxes. The original version reads: 'Como son vagantes y sin domicilio seguro, ni sirven la república, ni contraen matrimonio, ni pagan pechos ni tributos, siendo solo carga y gravamen de los pueblos' (1982, 87).

[7] These issues are treated at greater length in Herzog (2003, 128–133) and Herzog (2008). The literature on anti-Gypsies legislation in Spain is abundant. Some of the most important titles are: Sánchez Ortega (1976, 1977); Leblon (1985); Peñafiel (1985). Much of the anti-Gypsy legislation can be found in ACV,

in the eighteenth century, it was also applied to day labourers and other salaried persons, many of whom were now stigmatized as vagrants and were persecuted as such (Herzog 2002, 2007a, 520–522). It was generally claimed that as people whose association with the community depended solely on having been contracted to do certain things, such persons were inherently and constitutionally foreign. After all, they would go elsewhere if offered better terms, and their relationship with the community would expire after their work-related tasks ceased. Rather than being marginalized because they were poor (which was often the case), these people were theoretically rejected because they were potentially mobile; indeed, too mobile for a community that – although permitting immigration – also thought of itself as an all-encompassing human association that featured bonds of *longue durée* trust and dependency.

People were thus free to immigrate, but this freedom did not always guarantee that in practice they would be allowed to leave their communities or that they would be happily received in their destination. As I have argued elsewhere, movement was often accompanied by struggle, motivated by competition for resources, animosity or prejudice.[8] Small communities could reject the establishment of people so rich that their economic activities could upset the local balance or encroach on local resources. Others resented the presence of foreign poor, whom they needed to support. At times, conflict emerged between surgeons competing for the same clientele, or old rivals who were now in a position to influence the way their enemies would be received (or rejected). Some communities, arguing that their members were all petty nobles (*hidalgos*) or pure-of-blood (*pureza de sangre*) – that is, with no memory of having had ancestors of Jewish or Muslim origin or condemned for heretic practices – struggled against the presence of immigrants who, according to them, did not fulfil these requirements.

Regardless, the massive presence of immigrants and the basic assumption that movement was allowed did mean that until the nineteenth century most measures developed in Spain were meant to ensure *not* that individuals and families would not move, but that their movement would culminate in their insertion in new communities. By the eighteenth century, with the growing stigmatization and persecution of vagrants, this implied a growing control over those moving and a greater wish to distinguish those who were moving for 'good reasons' from those who were not. During this period, Gypsies were ordered to present themselves periodically to the local authorities, to register their names and places of residence, as well as to give information about their families, occupations, and properties.

SA, Ced/Prg. C.10–88; C.10–139; C.12–18; C.12–18; and C.12–53, and in Archivo General de Simancas (hereafter AGS), Gracia y Justicia (hereafter GJ), 1004. AGS, GJ 1005 and 1006 also include additional information about the prosecution of Gypsies. The content of many of these measures is summarized in the *Novísima Recopilación*, title 16, book 12.

8 These issues are treated at greater length in Herzog (2003).

Although the authorities were charged with ensuring that they complied with these orders, records make it clear that their arrival in Castilian municipalities was often noted by the inhabitants, who immediately reported on them.[9]

Contemporary to this was also the proliferation of passports, that is, of documents that ensured the authorities that those on the move were 'good people' and that their movement was justified.[10] A typical eighteenth-century passport attested the name of its bearer, the name of his or her parents, place of origin (native of . . .), occupation, age and, at times, a physical description ('short', 'tall', 'dark', 'curly hair', and so forth). It explained the reasons for the move and qualified it as valid (normally using the term *justo motivo*). Passports were signed by local authorities, royal authorities, or military commanders. They were given to individuals or to family groups, including service personnel. What began in the Middle Ages as a measure to protect travellers and ensure freedom of movement, especially when it required crossing different jurisdictions (a *laissez-passer*), also became, in mid-eighteenth-century Spain, a means of control. It now recommended the person bearing the document but also guaranteed that his movement from one place to the other, both inside and outside Spain, was authorized. Inside Spain, passport bearers had to formally present themselves to the local authorities in the community of passage or destination.[11] By the early nineteenth century, both royal and local authorities were instructed *not* to give passports or licences of transit to individuals whom they did not know personally, or whose behaviour was less than desirable. By 1820, movement both inside and outside Spain without such a passport or licence became prohibited, and those who travelled without these documents could be incarcerated for doing so. By 1824, all those inhabiting a settlement had to register their names in local police rolls and they were prohibited from allowing visitors to stay in their houses, or rent lodging, without these visitors previously registering with the local police.

Authorizing movement to the Americas

Despite Vitoria's belief that the Spanish presence in the New World was authorized by the freedom of immigration that existed in natural law, soon after the discovery of the Americas, the Spanish monarchs passed a series of laws that regulated

[9] These control measures are described in the *Pragmática* of 12 June 1695, in ACV, SA, Ced/Prg. C.8–88. On the way people reacted to the arrival of Gypsies in town, see Martínez Martínez (1998, 102–104).

[10] The historiography regarding passports in Spain is very limited and mainly refers to the nineteenth century (Galende Díaz and García Ruipérez 2004a, 113–114, 2004b; Castells Arteche 1974).

[11] See, for example, the case of Joseph de San Juan, described in Archivo Municipal de Valladolid, Gobierno Municipal XVIII, caja 63, 2, fols. 32–33. See also López García (1998, 469). On these transformations in other parts of Europe, see Groebner (2007, 151–181, 227–238).

movement between the Old and the New World. Instituting a legal monopoly, they restricted trade and immigration to the Americas, only allowing individuals who were 'natives of the kingdoms of Spain' and who were 'pure of blood' to engage in these activities.[12] As a result of this monopoly, individuals who wanted to travel to the New World had to receive a licence from the Council of the Indies (which sat in Madrid) and the House of Trade (*Casa de Contratación*), which sat in Seville, the main port of communication and trade with Spanish America.[13] Declaring their names, the reasons for which they wanted to travel, and attesting that they were both natives and pure-of-blood, candidates were also under the obligation to supply proof. Proof of status usually consisted of a baptismal record (which, unless contested, was assumed to prove also that they were natives of Spain) and the records of an investigation conducted in their birthplace regarding their purity of blood. Licences were usually collective: rather than including a single name they were granted to individuals and their household, both family members and servants. Those included in these licences were identified by name, age, special corporal signs, and their relationship to the petitioner. Because licensing procedures were long and costly, many attempted to avoid them by immigrating to the Americas illegally or using false papers. Or, at least, this was the impression of the authorities and merchants on both sides of the ocean, who constantly complained about lax implementation and corrupt practices.

Proceedings authorizing travel, immigration and trade to the Americas were closely watched by the merchant guild (*consulado*) established in Seville in 1543.[14] Representing all merchants legally trading in that city and meant to serve primarily as a court for commercial litigation, by the seventeenth century and more clearly in the next century, the guild also defended certain practices and lobbied for legislation that would protect and favour its members (Herzog 2003, 97–105). Since under theories of mercantilist thought it was generally believed that the less competition the better, in their position as privileged individuals who could engage in commerce with the New World, members of the merchant guild attempted to ensure that as many people as possible would be excluded from the transatlantic trade. In order to achieve this goal, the guild or its individual members frequently

[12] *Recopilación de Indias*, law 28, title 27, book 9, refers to 'natives of our kingdoms of Castile, León, Aragón, Valencia, Catalonia, Navarra, Mallorca and Menorca'. Nevertheless, administrative and judicial records identify this group as including 'natives of the kingdoms of Spain'. It is unclear whether previous to this declaration, natives of the crown of Aragón were permitted to immigrate and to trade in the New World (Veitia Linaje 1945, 328–329; Ramos Pérez 1976; Morales Álvárez 1980, 22–24).

[13] The House of Trade was the royal court charged with controlling and directing all communication and trade with the Indies (Gildas 1955; Crespo Solana 1996; Cerrera Pery 1997). Licensing proceedings have been studied by Jacobs (1991, 1995) and Salinero (2007, 2009). See also *Recopilación de Indias*, titles 27 and 46, book 9.

[14] The guild was studied by Smith (1940), Real Díaz (1968) and Heredia Herrera (1970). See also *Recopilación de Indias*, title 46, book 9.

intervened in licensing processes. In 1633 this intervention became official, after the Crown recognized the guild as an 'interested party' in all decisions concerning the 'nativeness of people in order to trade in the Indies' (Domínguez Ortiz 1959, 233). As an interested party, the guild was asked to give its opinion on the nativeness or foreignness of candidates for travel and immigration. On most occasions, merchants collaborated eagerly with this newly acquired function. Whenever the classification of people was debated, individual merchants or the guild acting for them, personified in the courts, wrote allegations, presented petitions, and acted in all possible ways to ensure that nativeness would be acknowledged only in individuals who met with their approval.

Complaints about the presence (despite these prohibitions) of many foreigners in the Americas usually brought about campaigns, in which local authorities attempted to locate illegal immigrants and expel them from the continent.[15] During these campaigns, it often became clear that the category of 'native of the kingdoms of Spain' was not self-evident, and that many individuals classified as foreigners were in fact natives (and vice versa).[16] Having secured a licence to travel to the New World was considered insufficient proof because it was often evident that people managed to get licences without good reason or by falsifying their names and the information regarding their origin and descent. Those caught in expulsion campaigns conducted in the Americas who wanted to remain in the New World were required to prove again, from scratch, that they were natives and pure-of-blood.[17] For many, this requirement was an incredible hardship as having to collect proof on the other side of the ocean was both costly and time-consuming. As a result, many appealed instead to their public reputation and presented witnesses who either knew them and their families in Spain or who could attest that by public voice and fame (*voz pública y fama*) they were indeed natives.[18] Yet, success often depended not on the facts of the matter but on the question of whether individuals

[15] Archivo General de la Nación, Lima (hereafter AGN/L), Real Tribunal del Consulado (hereafter RTC), contencioso 252, cuaderno 61, 51–52; document of 1 March 1760 in Archivo General de Indias (hereafter AGI), consulados 892A; and the guild's letter of 1 March 1759 in AGI, consulados 794. See also decision of 23 February 1764 in AGN/L, RTC, contencioso 252, cuaderno 77, 10–11. In his memoirs, viceroy Manuel de Amat y Juniet recognized the guild's contribution to the expulsion campaigns (Rodríguez Casado and Pérez Embid 1947, 225–226).

[16] Examples of lists of foreigners compiled by Lima's merchant guild are found in AGN/L, RTC, contencioso 252, cuaderno 61. See also the representation of the merchant guild of Cádiz, dated 1789, in AGI, consulados 62, 6 bis, and AGI, consulados 92, no. 3.

[17] AGN/L, RTC, contencioso 252, cuaderno 61.

[18] AGN/L, RTC, contencioso 252, cuaderno 77, 1–9. On occasions, other authorities operating under different circumstances were nevertheless willing to accept licences of passage as proofs. This happened, for example, in 1678 in Buenos Aires, when the city council (*cabildo*) refused to proceed against several 'Greek merchants' because the licences they carried certified that they were Spaniards: *Acuerdos del extinguido cabildo de Buenos Aires*. Buenos Aires: Archivo General de la Nación, 1907–1934, v. 15, book X, 216–217.

on expulsion rolls had local rivals who were willing to invest time, energy and money to be rid of them. It depended on how insistent these rivals were and whether candidates for expulsion and their rivals could reach a compromise – for example, the promise to avoid certain commercial activities if they were allowed to remain. Legally, it was unclear whether these hearings, in which royal judges ruled whether a person was or was not a native of Spain (and thus, whether he should be expelled), were administrative or judicial. Because the nature of the proceedings was debatable, it was unclear who carried the burden of proof, and whether individuals involved in them had the right to a due process.[19]

Control over travel between Spain and the Americas also worked inversely. Individuals born in or resident in the New World had to request a licence to go to Spain and another one in order to return. Applied both to individuals of Spanish and those of indigenous descent, this requirement was mainly explained by the need to control the population of the colonies and ensure that it did not diminish. Implicitly, however, it meant that those born or living in the Americas had no automatic right to go to Spain, nor had they a right to be in the Americas.

Authorizing movement inside the Americas

Having secured a licence to immigrate to the Americas, hypothetically, in the New World Spaniards were free to move from one settlement to another as they would be in Spain. However, this was not the case with the native population. In theory, in their condition as vassals and subjects, Indians were also free to travel and immigrate. The authorities were constantly instructed not to prohibit such movement because the Indians, too, 'had the liberty to settle where it was best for them'. Indeed, as in Spain, the only insistence was that they settled – that they did not live on their own or constantly change residence.[20] In practice, however, it was

[19] These questions are treated at great length by Herzog (2003), 116.

[20] A royal order dated 1544 decreed, 'and now we were informed that some of you, our said justices, have impeded or are impeding, that the Indians and citizens and inhabitants of these parts move from one village to other, or move their houses, and because our wish is that the natives of those parts [America] would be treated as the subjects and vassals of these parts [Spain] and would enjoy Spanish law . . . it was decided that we must order . . . that seeing the sanction law that is included, you would obey and comply with it in all and for all . . . with all the Indians and citizens and inhabitants of those parts . . .' ('y ahora nos somos informados que algunas de vos las dichas nuestras justicias habéis impedido e impedís, que los indios vecinos y moradores de esas partes no pasen a vivir de unos pueblos a otros ni muevan sus casas, y porque nuestra voluntad es que los naturales de esas partes sean tratados como los súbditos y vasallos de estos reinos y que gocen de las leyes de ellos . . . fue acordado que debíamos mandar . . . que veáis la dicha ley pragmática sanción que de suso va incorporada y la guardéis y cumpláis en todo y por todo . . . con todos los indios vecinos y moradores naturales de estas partes . . .'). *Cédula* of 17 October 1544 (in Konetzke 1953). It refers to the *Pragmática* of 1480 mentioned in note 3. Similarly, in 1570 it was once again attested that 'each one has . . . liberty to settle in the

generally assumed – although not always clearly specified in the laws – that this freedom could be exercised only after natives had completed their religious and civic conversion.[21] Until then, in their condition as minors, they were required to remain under the guidance and tutelage of civil and ecclesiastical authorities in special settlements devised for that end (Mörner 1963, 64; Simpson 1934, 31–32). Those who escaped from these settlements could be forced to return and others could be punished for attempting to flee. Regardless of these rules, we do know that Indians who should have been allowed to move from one settlement to the other inside the Americas were often obliged to stay, while others, prohibited from immigrating internally, managed to circulate, and in great numbers. Because of the scale of this process of native dislocation, by the seventeenth and more clearly in the next century, native communities were no longer conceived as agglomerates defined by family or ethnic ties. On the contrary, they became centres in which many people of different origins coincided. As a result, over time, practices allowing Indians to change their communal inscription evolved. Although not legalizing movement *per se*, they made it acceptable by allowing those moving to integrate into the community of reception, where they could become right- and obligation-bearing individuals.[22]

Who was who? Naming and identifying

In order to authorize (or control) movement, it was of vital importance to identify who was who. This involved two separate actions: to acknowledge individuals by name and to ensure that they were who they claimed to be. Naming practices in early modern Spain and Spanish America are difficult to follow. For many years historians assumed that there were absolutely no rules indicating who would be called what, or guaranteeing that a person would use the same name throughout

place where he chooses best' ('cada uno tiene . . . libertad de avecindarse en la población que mejor le cuadrare'), but that this could be done 'under the condition that they would choose one and, after they do, they would be compelled to be there, and would not continue to change (their places of residence), which should not be permitted, because, in this way, they would never have a settlement' ('con tal que escogen de una vez, y después escogido sean compelidos a que acudan allí y no anden variando, ni se les debe dar lugar a ello, porque nunca acabarían de tener asiento' . . . 'Parecer cerca de la necesidad que hay de juntar los indios de la provincia de Tlaxcala que están derramados . . .' (in Sullivan 1999, 38–39)). Similar ideas were expressed in the letter written by Juan Vázquez de Acuña, *corregidor* of Quito, on 4 April 1636, AGI, Quito, 32, no. 33.

[21] Native freedom of immigration was authorized 'except where, because of native re-settlement, it was ordered to the contrary' ('excepto donde por las reducciones, que por nuestro mandado estuvieren hechas, se haya dispuesto lo contrario'). *Recopilación de Indias*, law 12, title I, book VI.

[22] The literature on forastero Indians deals with these developments. These subjects are described at greater length in Herzog (2003, 61, 62, 2006).

his or her life.[23] These historians pointed out that the same people could be called differently in different documents or moments, thus assuming that variations were both legally allowed and socially acceptable. They therefore explained that although names and surnames became a common phenomenon in Spain in the Middle Ages, and although they generalized in the fifteenth century and by the seventeenth century in some urban milieux in Spain and Spanish America as many as nine in ten persons used surnames, names were not truly helpful in identifying people (Ansón Calvo 1979, 339).[24] Among other things, some pointed out that under early modern conditions your name mattered only on very few occasions. Immigration (mainly to the Americas) required that you identify yourself. So did property holding (which in the Middle Ages was often attributed to family groups, not individuals) and inheritance (which in Spain and Spanish America was equally distributed among all descendants, both male and female) (Pastor 1993, 23–37). Naming as a way to trace family genealogy was also important in purity-of-blood proceedings because they sought to establish whether certain individuals were descended of heretics (up to a third generation) or of Jewish or Muslim ancestors (a permanent stain). These proceedings, instituted by different corporations, orders and towns from the mid-fifteenth century, became extremely powerful in the early modern period, and they were also implemented across the Atlantic. Having initially maintained their original design there, in the New World they suffered mutations that, among other things, stigmatized people of African descent as 'impure' (Martínez 2008).

The church may also have played a role in attributing and fixing names and surnames because, in the fifteenth century, preoccupied with the violation of the canon-law prohibition of marriage among close relatives, Cardinal Cisneros (1436–1517), primate of Castile, ordered parochial registries to be instituted in the kingdom. The Council of Trent (1563), concerned about the same questions, issued similar orders, mainly focused on the need to register birth and marriage, and applying them to the entire Catholic world (Bermejo Castrillo 1997, 117–118). Although these registries only included the gender of the newborn, his or her given name and the names and surnames of parents and godparents, without identifying the surname of the newborn, it was generally believed that he or she would take on the surnames belonging to his or her parents and, in their absence, those of the godparents. Because of the non-existence in Spain (and eventually Spanish America) of other registries of birth and affiliation, parochial registries became the main (and often the only) proof of identity. Since most individuals used them throughout their life to demonstrate their place of baptism (often considered also

[23] For a detailed description of this literature, as well as the issue of naming, see Herzog (2007b). In the most recent publication on this subject, most (although not all) authors specifically referring to Spain and Spanish America maintained this line, insisting that naming had no rules, that immigrants took advantage of this laxity to change their names, and so forth (see Salinero and Testón Núñez 2010).

[24] A somewhat similar situation can be seen in Mexico City, as described by Cope (1994, 58–67).

proof of their place of birth) and affiliation, baptismal records often coined the name and surnames that they would use throughout their lives. Most people, however, rarely needed formally to certify their identity, because it was never called for. Avoiding incest or allowing property-holding and inheritance-receiving may have required knowing who was who, but as long as people resided in the same community or region, and as long as there was no question regarding their affiliation, there was no need to depend on registries.

Although formal occasions for making your identity known were few and most were linked to either immigration (the move to a community in which you were unknown, or the loss of memory of an individual by their community of origin) or conflict, it is clear that in both Spain and Spanish America contemporaries believed that names were telling. Most assumed that those called similarly were related, that a son bore his father's name and that names indicated origin, and they bitterly protested when such was not the case.[25] On occasions, protest gave rise to a formal civil action. This mainly happened when someone, somewhere, felt offended or compromised by the name another person had used. It was generally argued that this use was not innocent but instead was meant to convey a false impression, for example, the impression that the person using the name was a relative of a certain family, or the son of a certain man.[26] By the same token, those who used their name and surname to brand their products could appeal against the actions of others who were using the same name to sell theirs.[27] In all these cases, at stake was not so much the name itself, but why it was adopted and what kind of information it conveyed. In short, how individuals called themselves was nobody else's business, early modern litigants argued; but it became somebody else's business if it injured them.[28]

Judges reviewing these cases confirmed these allegations. In both Spain and Spanish America they referred litigants to Roman Law doctrines which, from as early as the fourteenth century, pointed out that names could be chosen at liberty as long as they were not meant to propagate false images. Because it was generally believed that under normal circumstances individuals would never wilfully change their names, the legal assumption was that those who did so had something to hide (Cavallar *et al.* 1994, 52–53, 61–64, 145–147). Following these beliefs, many Italian city-states adopted procedures authorizing an official change of name. These

[25] Letter of the viceroy of Peru, dated 11 September 1681, AGI, Lima, 81, cuaderno 4, no. 20. Similar concerns were expressed by Lima's merchant guild on 16 December 1761, AGN/L, RTC, Secretaría General, varios 4, cuaderno 122.

[26] Bearing the same surname helped children to establish affiliation with their parents. See, for example, Expediente de 29.1.1738, Archivo Nacional/Quito, Hijos Naturales y Expósitos, caja 1.

[27] ACV, PC, Pérez Alonso (Fenecidos) 3017.002, and ACV, PC, Masas (Olvidados) 1045.009.

[28] RCV, PC, Pérez Alonso (Fenecidos) 2900.002, and 'Autos sobre los bienes de Bartolomé García, también llamado Bartolomé García de la Gasca, difunto abintestato que murió en Potosí (1633)', AGI, contratación 934, no. 7-1, fol. 1R and no. 7-5, fol. 1V.

procedures guaranteed that those changing their name had nothing to hide, that this change did not injure third parties, and it made name changing public. Spanish law (also applied in Spanish America) followed these procedures. The Castilian thirteenth-century law code (*Siete Partidas*) punished those who maliciously changed their names or who took on the name of another, arguing that they were forgers and their action constituted falsification.[29] Spanish legal doctrine followed suit, affirming that this rule implied that name changing should be prohibited, because changing your name always potentially injured or confused someone (Gómez y Azevedo, cited by García-Gallo 1950; Valera 1878, 293–295, 224–225). Fearing opposition, in both Spain and Spanish America, individuals who wanted to change their name requested a licence from the courts.[30] However, in most cases, the name they wanted to adopt was already theirs. According to their allegations, it belonged to them *de facto*; what they now wanted to do was to adopt it also *de jure*.[31]

If courts were one method by which to guarantee the legitimate use of names, recourse to experts was another. As early as the fifteenth century, naming experts appeared in Castile. Called 'kings of arms' (*reyes de armas*), these individuals were charged with verifying affiliation as well as the use of surnames and coats of arms (Cascante 1956, 106–109; Valera 1878, n.42, 236; Ceballos-Escalera y Gila 1993). Because the aim was to avoid confusion, from the sixteenth century, kings of arms were granted a monopoly over these issues. Accordingly, only they could certify the right to use certain names and only they could inspect (and censure when needed) the usage of names and arms. Although kings of arms only cared about the use of a restricted list of names and arms, mostly associated with the nobility, their existence gave rise to a new science concerned with genealogy. Kings of arms usually owned archives, in which they collected baptismal, marriage and death records, as well as testaments and other documents that could shed light on affiliation, names and arms. They authored books with information on surnames

[29] The original version reads: 'hace falsedad aquel que cambia maliciosamente el nombre que ha tomado o tomando nombre de otro o diciendo que es hijo de rey o de otra persona honrada sabiendo que no lo era'. Siete Partidas, Partida 7, title VII, law 2.

[30] In 1781, for example, Bernardo Pablo de Killi Kelly requested to add 'Linch' as his first surname, explaining that it was the surname of his paternal grandmother. He also wanted to use the arms associated with the surname: petition of 1 February 1781, Archivo Histórico Nacional, Consejos 11.136. Agustín Andrés, resident of Buenos Aires, requested in 1784 to correct his second surname from Lascano to Erezcano: Archivo General de la Nación/Buenos Aires, sección IX, 35-2-3, 1784. Somewhat similar was the case of Eustaquio Lino Antonio Muñoz, vecino of Burgos, who requested in 1807 to add to his surnames that of Goyeneche in order to prove that he originated in the province of Vizcaya and thus was worthy of recognition as hidalgo (Gandía 1930, 161, n.23).

[31] Most common was the case of children born out of wedlock. In 1787, Juana Mañueco y Marcos supplied proof of her affiliation arguing that her father, who had her outside wedlock, allowed her to use his surname: decreto of the Cámara de Castilla dated 1 August 1787, AGS, GJ, 872. Somewhat similar was the case of Félix e Isidoro Bonet whose father called him by his surname: decreto of 14 November 1787, AGS, GJ 873.

and corresponded with colleagues in other parts of Europe.[32] The value of their opinion was such that in 1761 their certificates were equated with those of royal notaries, enjoying the status of public documents that by law could not be questioned or contradicted. Extremely important in Madrid and present in provincial capitals too, kings of arms were conspicuously absent from Spanish America.

Although similar rules regarding naming operated in Spain and the Americas, it is possible that in the New World they were implemented with a greater zeal. After all, in the Americas there was a greater possibility of confusion on the one hand, and greater control over immigration and movement on the other. Proving your identity, as we have already seen, was needed in order to travel legally to the New World and to defend yourself if your name was included on expulsion rolls. These factors guaranteed that many Spaniards obtained papers (mostly certified copies of their baptism record) for the first time in their lives when attempting to cross the Atlantic. The necessity to identify oneself, however, proved permanent in the Americas. Not only were you always a possible candidate for expulsion – especially when not a native Castilian-speaker (many Spaniards were suspected of foreignness because of their limited use of Castilian; many of them spoke Basque, Catalan, Galician and so forth) – but also constant immigration inside the American continent made the need for identification (and re-identification) stronger. Since early modern Spaniards assumed that as long as you remained in your jurisdiction of origin there was no necessity to identify yourself because you were personally known, they also concluded that identity papers were required when you immigrated. As an eighteenth-century witness explained, because he was in 'lands not his' (i.e. the Americas), he needed, and indeed carried with him always, a copy of his baptismal record.[33] Thus, although many took advantage of movement and immigration in order to refashion themselves anew, also changing their names, it is more than probable that most did not.[34] Furthermore, in the American setting baptismal records had another very important function which they lacked in Spain. In addition to certifying your name and place of baptism (theoretically your place of birth) – as they did elsewhere – by the seventeenth century, with the appearance of separate registries for 'Spaniards', 'Indians' and 'mestizos' in the New World, baptismal records also served to prove your ethnicity. A matter of pride and social reputation, this classification also carried with it a practical weight. For example, some taxes were only paid by Indians; only Indians could enjoy the free services of a legal defender; only Indians could reside in certain communities, and so forth.

[32] Biblioteca Nacional/Madrid, Mss. 11.468, 11.469 and 11.826; Ceballos-Escalera y Gila (1993, 112, n.63, 152).

[33] The original version reads: 'por andar en tierras ajenas'. See the case of Juan de Horta (Minchom 1994, 158, n.45). Research supports such claims: Béatrice Fraenkel argues that immigration required identification, while remaining in your original community did not (Fraenkel 2007, 284).

[34] The possible link between immigration and name changing was recently reaffirmed in Testón Núñez and Sánchez Rubio (2010).

Also particular to the New World was a royal and ecclesiastical policy of forcing the native population to adopt Spanish names and to use them consistently throughout their lives. Here, too, church regulations may have been important. The third Council of Lima (1583), for example, ordered that all Indians immediately cease using their 'gentile and idolatrous' names and instead only identify themselves with names that were 'common among Christians' (Abercrombie 1998, n.53). In 1646, the Royal Provincial Court (*audiencia*) of Guatemala followed suit, indicating that natives should have a 'patronymic and Castilian surname'. The aim, it declared, was twofold. On the one hand, the use of gentile names reminded Indians of their previous, pre-Christian and pre-Spanish existence. On the other, the use of Spanish names guaranteed legibility. It allowed the authorities to know better who was who, and who had to pay which taxes.[35] Although these efforts were generally successful, it is nevertheless clear that native names, or at least some native names in some places, did survive, enabling indigenous communities and individuals to remember who they were and what they (once) stood for (Ramírez 2010).

Conclusions

Spanish and Spanish American early modern rules and mechanisms regarding movement were both similar to and different from the ones we currently have. Historians of Spain and Spanish America have often insisted on chaos. They describe a naming system that had no sensible rules, and a constant movement that was not controlled or willed. However, archival research testifies that there were many rules in place. Some favoured movement, others discouraged it. On occasions, individuals were allowed to do as they wished; on others they were constrained by obedience to the authorities' wishes. One way or the other, even if past practices were not organized in the way they are supposed to be in bureaucratic democracies today, it is nevertheless clear that early modern authorities and individuals were engaged with many of the same issues that face us now. They asked themselves if movement was good or bad, which movement should be encouraged, and how to develop mechanisms to ensure the desired results were obtained.

[35] The original version reads: 'because the names, middle-names and surnames exist only to identify the individual and subject that wishes to be known by them, for that end the patronymic and surnames of Castille can be used, so that they [the Indians] would be identified and differentiate more surely and clearly . . . as the council of Lima mandated, exiling the names they used during their gentility' ('pues los nombres, cognombres y apellidos solamente son para significar el individuo y sujeto del hombre que se quiere conocer, para ello se puede usar los patronímicos y apellidos de Castilla con que vendrán a señalarse en más cierta y clara diferencia y conocimiento más individual de unos a otros, como lo mandó un concilio de Lima desterrando los nombres de su gentilidad') (Carrasco 1970, 218, n.54).

Although record-keeping systems evolved during the early modern period, with *laissez-passer*, passports, local registries and other documents, and although from the fifteenth century births were registered and so were names, it is nevertheless clear that during this period in both Spain and Spanish America most interactions within the region were still oral. On most occasions, identity documents and registries were conceived as means to replace personal knowledge, when such could not be attested because of distance (immigration) or size (in large communities). In all other contexts, they were not needed, or produced. This was a world in which registries sometimes existed, but in which they were never considered conclusive (Herzog 2003, 17–118). Rather than constituting the person as the bearer of certain rights and duties, they indicated he may be thus. Rather than operating a transformation (making someone worthy of a certain treatment by the act of registering him or her), they recognized the validity of a change in status that had transpired beforehand, in fact sanctioning what oral negotiations had already consecrated. More often than not, rather than representing a 'reality', registries gave proof of attempts by authorities, local or royal, to control reality, attempts that were habitually rejected by both social members and the courts.

In short, while outside the boundaries of the community registration documents could act as proof, inside it they could and often were either completely ignored or even rejected. Reproducing some elements of these dynamics, scribes and notaries (*escribanos* and *notarios*), who in theory were the official guarantors of the faithfulness, even justness, of registries, ended up implicitly confessing their inferior, indeed secondary, status. Obeying the rules of their profession and the formulas they habitually reproduced, they declared who they were and why the documents they had authored were trustworthy.[36] They were usually followed by a second scribe who guaranteed that they were indeed scribes and had the authority to authenticate this information. A third, normally higher-ranking, scribe then intervened to identify the first two and protest their truthfulness. By the end of this process, rather than affirming veracity, this succession of 'guarantors of truth' only attested to the socially, even if not legally, doubtful status of both scribes and their registers.

Writing was meant to facilitate some things. It could be used to make certain claims, but in early modern Spain and Spanish America, at least, it did not replace orality unless orality (in the form of reputation and performance) had already failed in this particular context. Perhaps at stake was the difficult transition from a system that trusted people to a system that trusted documents (Clanchy 1993, 295–299). Perhaps it represented a struggle over who had the ultimate monopoly over what constituted 'truth'. But one way or the other, during the early modern age (and perhaps beyond), written registries always coexisted with an oral knowledge that

[36] This was the habitual practice among Spanish and Spanish American notaries (both *escribanos* and *notaries*). On these professions and their work in a colonial context, see Herzog (1996).

either opposed or converged with them. How these two different registers coexisted (and perhaps coexist today) is a story we still need to explore.

References

Abercrombie, Thomas Alan. 1998. *Pathways of Memory and Power: Ethnography and History among an Andean People*. Madison: University of Wisconsin Press.

Ansón Calvo, María del Carmen. 1979. 'Institucionalización de los apellidos como método de identificación individual en la sociedad española del siglo XVII.' *Revista de historia Jerónimo Zurita* 35–36: 339–358.

Bermejo Castrillo, Manuel. 1997. *Parentesco, matrimonio, propiedad y herencia en la Castilla Altomedieval*. Madrid: Universidad Carlos III de Madrid: Boletín Oficial del Estado.

Carrasco, Pedro. 1970. 'La introducción de apellidos castellanos entre los mayas alteños.' In *Historia y sociedad en el mundo de habla española: Homenaje a José Miranda*, ed. Bernardo García Martínez, Victoria Lerner, Andrés Lira, Guillermo Palacios and Irene Vázquez. México: El Colegio de México.

Cascante, Ignacio Vicente. 1956. *Heráldica general y fuentes de las armas de España*. Barcelona: Salvat.

Castells Arteche, José Manuel. 1974. *El derecho de libre desplazamiento y el pasaporte en España*. Madrid: Seminarios y Ediciones.

Cavallar, Osvaldo, Susanne Degenring and Julius Kirshner, eds. 1994. *A Grammar of Signs: Bartolo Da Sassoferrato's Tract on Insignia and Coats of Arms*. Berkeley: Robbins Collection, University of California at Berkeley.

Cayetano Martín, María del Carmen, ed. 1992. *Documentos del Archivo de Villa: Reyes Católicos I (1475–1479)*. Ayuntamiento de Madrid, Area de Cultura, Educación, Juventud y Deportes, Archivo de Villa.

Ceballos-Escalera y Gila, Alfonso. 1993. *Heraldos y reyes de armas en la corte de España*. Madrid: Prensa y Ediciones Iberoamericanas S.A.

Cerrera Pery, José. 1997. *La Casa de Contratación y el Consejo de Indias: las razones de un superministerio*. Madrid: Ministerio de Defensa.

Clanchy, M. T. 1993. *From Memory to Written Record, England 1066–1307*. Oxford: Blackwell.

Clavero Salvador, Bartolomé. 1976. 'Notas sobre el derecho territorial castellano, 1367–1445.' *Historia, instituciones, documentos* 3: 141–166.

Cope, Douglas R. 1994. *The Limits of Racial Domination: Plebeian Society in Colonial Mexico City, 1660–1720*. Madison: University of Wisconsin Press.

Crespo Solana, Ana. 1996. *La Casa de Contratación y la Intendencia General de la Marina en Cádiz, 1717–1730*. Cádiz: Universidad de Cádiz.

Domínguez Ortiz, Antonio. 1959. 'La Concesión de "naturaleza para comerciar en Indias" durante el siglo XVII.' *Revista de Indias* 19(76): 227–239.

Fernández Navarrete, Pedro. 1982. *Conservacion de monarquías y discursos políticos: sobre la gran consulta que el consejo hizo al señor Rey don Felipe Tercero*, ed. Michael D. Gordon. Madrid: Instituto de Estudios Fiscales.

Font Rius, José María. 1967. 'La recepción del derecho romano en la peninsula ibérica durante la edad media.' *Recueil de Mémoires et Travaux* 6: 85–104.

Fraenkel, Béatrice. 2007. 'Preuves et éprueves de l'identification.' In *Gens de passage en Méditerranée de l'Antiquité à l'époque moderne: procédures de contrôle et d'identification*, ed. Claude Moatti and Wolfgang Kaiser. Paris: Maisonneuve & Larose, 279–291.

Galende Díaz, Juan Carlos and Mariano García Ruipérez. 2004a. 'Los pasaportes, pases y otros documentos de control e identidad personal en España durante la primera mitad del siglo XIX: estudio archivístico y diplomático.' *Hidalguía: la revista de genealogía, nobleza y armas* 302: 113–144.

—— 2004b. 'Los pasaportes, pases y otros documentos de control e identidad personal en España durante la primera mitad del siglo XIX.' *Hidalguía: la revista de genealogía, nobleza y armas* 303: 169–208.

Gandía, Enrique de. 1930. *Del origen de los nombres y apellidos y de la ciencia genealógica*. Buenos Aires: Librería y editorial 'La Facultad'.

García-Gallo, Alfonso. 1950. *Curso de historia del derecho español*, vol. 2(1). Madrid: Artes Gráficas y Ediciones.

Gildas, Bernard. 1955. 'La Casa de la Contratación de Sevilla, luego de Cádiz en el siglo XVIII.' *Anuario de Estudios Americanos* 12: 253–286.

Groebner, Valentin. 2007. *Who Are You? Identification, Deception, and Surveillance in Early Modern Europe*, trans. Mark Kyburz and John Peck. New York: Zone Books.

Heredia Herrera, Antonia. 1970. '"Apuntes para la historia del Consulado de la Universidad de Cargadores a Indias en Sevilla y Cádiz."' *Anuario de Estudios Americanos* 27: 219–274.

Herzog, Tamar. 1996. *Mediación, archivos y ejercicio: los escribanos de Quito (siglo XVII–XVIII)*. Frankfurt: Vittorio Klostermann.

—— 2002. 'Vecindad y oficio en Castilla: la libertad económica y la exclusión política en el siglo XVIII.' In *Furor et rabies: violencia, conflicto y marginación en la Edad Moderna*, ed. José Ignacio Fortea, Juan E. Gelabert and Tomás A. Mantecón. Cantabria: Ed. Universidad de Cantabria, 239–252.

—— 2003. *Defining Nations: Immigrants and Citizens in Early Modern Spain and Spanish America*. New Haven, CT: Yale University Press.

—— 2006. 'Indiani e cowboys: il ruolo dell'indigeno nel diritto e nell'immaginario ispano-coloniale.' In *Oltremare: diritto e istituzioni dal colonialismo all'età postcoloniale*, ed. Aldo Mazzacane. Naples: CUEN, 9–44.

—— 2007a. 'Terres et déserts, société et sauvagerie.' *Annales. Histoire, Sciences Sociales* 62(3): 507–538.

—— 2007b. 'Nombres y apellidos: ¿Cómo se llamaban las personas en Castilla e Hispanoamérica durante la época moderna?' *Jahrbuch für Geschichtevon Staat, Wirtschaft und Gesellschaft Lateinamerikas* 44: 1–36.

—— 2008. 'Penser l'exclusion: les discours espagnols et hispano-américains sur l'"Autre" (autours de 1740–1811).' In *Pour une histoire souterraine des Amériques: Jeux de mémoires – Enjeux d'identités, mélanges offerts à Nathan Wachtel*, ed. Anath Ariel de Vidas. Paris: L'Harmattan, 173–196.

Jacobs, Auke P. 1991. 'Legal and Illegal Emigration from Seville, 1550–1650.' In *'To Make America': European Emigration in the Early Modern Period*, ed. Ida Altman and James P. P. Horn. Berkeley: University of California Press.

—— 1995. *Los movimientos migratorios entre Castilla e Hispanoamérica durante el reinado de Felipe III, 1598–1621*. Amsterdam: Rodopi.

Kirshner, Julius. 1973. 'Civitas Sibi Faciat Civem: Bartolus of Sassoferrato's Doctrine on the Making of a Citizen.' *Speculum* 48(4): 694–713.

Konetzke, R. 1953. *Colección de documentos para la historia de la formación social de Hispanoamérica, 1493–1810*, vol. 1. Madrid: Consejo superior de investigaciones cientificas.

Leblon, Bernard. 1985. *Les gitans d'Espagne: le prix de la différence*. Paris: Presses universitaires de France.

López García, José Miguel. 1998. *El impacto de la corte en Castilla: Madrid y su territorio en la época moderna*. Madrid: Siglo XXI de España Editores.

Martínez, María Elena. 2008. *Genealogical Fictions: Limpieza de Sangre, Religion, and Gender in Colonial Mexico*. Stanford, CA: Stanford University Press.

Martínez Martínez, Manuel. 1998. *La minoría gitana de la Provincia de Almería durante la crisis del antiguo régimen (1750–1811)*. Almeria: Instituto de Estudios Almerienses.

Minchom, Martin. 1994. *The People of Quito, 1690–1810: Change and Unrest in the Underclass*. Boulder, CO: Westview Press.

Morales Alvárez, Juan M. 1980. *Los extranjeros con carta de naturaleza de las Indias, durante la segunda mitad del siglo XVIII*. Caracas: Academia Nacional de la Historia.

Mörner, M. 1963. 'Las comunidades de indígenas y legislación segregacionista en el Nuevo Reino de Granada.' *Anuario Colombiano de Historia Social y de la Cultura* 1(1): 63–84.

Pastor, Reina. 1993. *Resistencias y luchas campesinas en la época del crecimiento y consolidación de la formación feudal Castilla y León, siglos X–XIII*. Madrid: Siglo XXI. Editores.

Peñafiel, Ramón Antonio. 1985. 'Gitanos en Murcia en la primera mitad del siglo XVIII. Integración o extinción.' *Anales de historia contemporánea* 4: 7–34.

Ramírez, Susan Elizabeth. 2010. 'Bajo el nombre de los antepasados: la memoria viva en los Andes, siglos XVI–XVII.' In *Un juego de engaños: movilidad, nombres y apellidos en los siglos XV a XVIII*, ed. Gregorio Salinero and Isabel Testón Núñez. Madrid: Casa de Velázquez., 163–186.

Ramos Pérez, Demetrio. 1976. 'La aparente exclusión de los aragoneses de las Indias: una medida de alta política de don Fernando el Católico.' *Estudios*, 7–40.

Real Díaz, José Joaquín. 1968. 'El Consulado de cargadores a Indias: su documento fundacional.' *Archivo hispalense: revista histórica, literaria y artística* 48(147): 279–291.

Rodríguez Casado, Vincente and Florentino Pérez Embid, eds. 1947. *Manuel de Amat y Juniet – virrey del Perú 1761–1776. Memoria de gobierno*. Seville: Escuela de Estudios Hispanoamericanos.

Salinero, Gregorio. 2007. 'Sous le régime des licences. L'identificacion des migrants vers les Indes espagnoles, XVI, XVII siècles.' In *Gens de passage en Méditerranée de l'Antiquité à l'époque moderne: procédures de contrôle et d'identification*, ed. Claude Moatti and Wolfgang Kaiser. Paris: Maisonneuve & Larose, 345–367.

—— 2009. 'Aux Indes! Les conditions faites à l'émigration aux Indes depuis la péninsule Ibérique aux XVIe et XVIIe siècles.' In *Le monde de l'itinérance en Méditerranée de l'Antiquité à l'époque moderne: procédures de contrôle et d'identification*, ed. Claude Moatti, Christophe Pébarthe and Wolfgang Kaiser. Bordeaux: Ausonius, 408–428.

Salinero, Gregorio and Isabel Testón Núñez, eds. 2010. *Un juego de engaños: movilidad, nombres y apellidos en los siglos XV a XVIII*. Madrid: Casa de Velázquez.

Sánchez Ortega, María Helena. 1976. *Documentación selecta sobre la situación de los gitanos españoles en el siglo XVIII*. Madrid: Editora Nacional.

—— 1977. *Los gitanos españoles: el periodo borbónico*. Madrid: Castellote.

Simpson, Lesley Byrd. 1934. 'Studies in the Administration of the Indians in New Spain.' *Ibero Americana* 7: 31–129.

Smith, Robert Sidney. 1940. *The Spanish Guild Merchant: A History of the Consulado, 1250–1700*. Durham, NC: Duke University Press.

Sullivan, J. 1999. 'Un dialogo sobre la congregacion en Tlaxcala.' *Colonial Latin American Review* 8(1): 35–59.

Testón Núñez, Isabel and Rocío Sánchez Rubio. 2010. 'Identidad fingida y migraciones atlánticas (siglos XVI–XVIII).' In *Un juego de engaños: movilidad, nombres y apellidos en los siglos XV a XVIII*, ed. Gregorio Salinero and Isabel Testón Núñez. Madrid: Casa de Velázquez, 87–101.

Ullmann, Walter. 1988. 'Personality and Territoriality in the "Defensor Pacis": The Problem of Political Humanism.' In *Law and Jurisdiction in the Middle Ages*, ed. George Garnett. London: Variorum Reprints.

Valera, Mosen Diego. 1878. *Epístolas enviadas en diversos tiempos e a diversas personas*. Madrid: Imprenta de Miguel Ginesta.

Veitía Linaje, Joseph de. 1945. *Norte de la contratación de las Indias occidentales*. Buenos Aires: Comisión argentina de fomento interamericano.

Vitoria, Francisco de. 1991. *Political Writings*, ed. Anthony Pagden and Jeremy Lawrance. Cambridge: Cambridge University Press.

8

Establishing and Registering Identity in the Dutch Republic[1]

HENK LOOIJESTEIJN AND MARCO H. D. VAN LEEUWEN

Introduction

IN 1764 A STRANGER CHOSE TO SETTLE in the small Dutch town of Brouwershaven in the province of Zeeland. Upon his arrival on 24 February 1764, he sought out, without making himself known, the eldest minister of the local Dutch Reformed church, claiming to represent a godly physician who wished to settle in a 'quiet place, such as this' and desired some information. The minister asked him where the mysterious physician had obtained his diploma, whether he was of the Reformed faith, and whether he was a confirmed member of that church. The stranger replied that the physician had studied in Duisburg, where he had obtained his diploma, and was indeed a member of the Reformed church. The minister referred him to the town secretary. There, the stranger had to undergo much the same procedure. He told the secretary that the physician lived in Rheinberg and wished to settle in Brouwershaven. The secretary first enquired whether the physician was of the Reformed faith. Having been satisfied in this regard, he enquired as to why a physician would want to settle in Brouwershaven, which had little opportunity for a medical practice. The stranger replied that the physician was looking for a place to worship freely, which, as a Protestant, he could not do in Catholic Rheinberg. The secretary then mentioned a further obstacle, emphasizing that Brouwershaven was already well served by two excellent surgeons. The stranger replied that the physician would establish a pharmacy, and that, anyway, he was already well endowed with material goods and not in need of a large practice.

[1] This chapter was first presented as a paper at the International Conference on the Comparative History of Civil Registration, St John's College, Cambridge, 7–10 September 2010. We would like to thank Keith Breckenridge, Edward Higgs, Simon Szreter, and the other conference participants, as well as Lex Heerma van Voss, Clé Lesger, Piet Lourens, Jan Lucassen, Elise van Nederveen Meerkerk and Henk van Nierop for their comments on the original paper, and Chris Gordon for editing the text.

The secretary then referred him to the burgomaster, while inviting him to return to his house in the evening.

That evening, the stranger was subjected to yet another round of questioning, this time by the secretary and the minister jointly. Only then did the stranger reveal that he himself was the physician, going by the name of Johannes Cato Kamerling. The secretary then took closer note of his appearance: on the face of it, Kamerling did indeed seem to be both religious and wealthy. The two town dignitaries enquired further about the doctor's personal background, and every question was met with a convincing response.

Well satisfied with their evening conversation, the secretary set in motion the next step in the process of admitting Kamerling as a burgher of Brouwershaven: he was accepted, provided he submitted his diploma and attestation of good conduct and bought citizenship. Accordingly, Kamerling travelled back to Rheinberg to obtain an attestation from the Reformed church, which he submitted on his return to the minister, complete with the seal of the consistory of Rheinberg. According to Kamerling, it also served as an attestation from Rheinberg's civic authorities, and the Brouwershaven council accepted his claim without requiring a separate civic attestation. Much to its satisfaction, Kamerling also submitted to the town council his university diploma, with two barely recognizable seals attached to it from the university and the city of Duisburg. Accordingly, Johannes Cato Kamerling was admitted in Brouwershaven as burgher and physician (Viergever 1766, 1: 8–24, 28–29, 40–49).

Within a few months, Kamerling proposed to the burgomaster's daughter. Her father was pleased with the prospective match, but required more evidence that Kamerling was who he claimed to be. Given that engagements in the Dutch Republic often lasted several years, the burgomaster might well be excused for imposing this delay. Kamerling obtained further proof of his identity in the form of a declaration from the secretary of Rheinberg concerning his family, and a copy of the will of his wealthy cousin, from whom he stood to inherit a considerable sum. The secretary, the minister, and the burgomaster were suitably impressed, and Kamerling and his bride were duly wed on 31 July 1764 – less than six months after he had arrived in Brouwershaven (Viergever 1766, 1: 78, 103–118, 154; Haks 1982, 111).

This case illustrates the ways in which an early modern Dutchman could establish whether a stranger whom he encountered was indeed the person whom he claimed to be. It shows that in the initial contact, the appearance and behaviour of the stranger were considered important, and he would be expected to provide certain documents – an attestation of good conduct from the church council and magistrate of his place of origin, and, in this case, also a university degree. For good measure, the newcomer was questioned also by the town's senior minister and secretary during an ostensibly social occasion whose purpose was to allow them to become better acquainted with him. On presentation of the required documents the newcomer was accepted as a new burgher, though being accepted as a member, by marriage, of the town's elite required additional evidence. From this particular case involving a small town, it also emerges that church officials and the magistrate cooperated in obtaining the required evidence, which was supplied by their counterparts from the applicant's place of origin. This 'system' of establishing identity was operational throughout the Dutch Republic. It was especially important as the Republic was a country of immigration for much of its existence.

Hundreds of thousands of migrants settled permanently in the Netherlands, while more or less equal numbers sojourned in the Republic on their way to other destinations, and still other migrants worked as seasonal labourers in the herring fishery, shipping, peat digging, infrastructural projects such as land reclamation, canal construction, urban expansion, haymaking, harvesting, and the processing of commercial crops. In terms of numbers, the proportion of migrants in the coastal areas of the Netherlands was around half the entire male working population (J. Lucassen 1994, 181). Not all migrants stayed and worked throughout the year, but in terms of the number of years worked the proportion of migrants in the economy was just 10 per cent of the Republic's population as a whole, while in the province of Holland it was twice that (de Vries and van der Woude 1997, 72–73). Though the Republic was a country of immigration, internal migration was also an important feature. The economic development of the Netherlands had created a significant urban proletariat early on, and, as a consequence of developments in the agrarian sector, a growing number of impoverished smallholders emerged determined to seek their fortunes in the cities (Prak 1998).

In an era in which the difference between migrants and vagrants was often difficult to discern, and even smart dress on a stranger often proved to be a ruse – especially in the Dutch Republic where there were no sumptuary laws – universal distrust was the common fate of all who happened to come to a community where they were unknown and unconnected. In the Dutch Republic there existed a whole set of ways to establish an individual's identity, and a rudimentary 'system' of identity registration, essentially established at the local levels of town and parish. In this chapter, this rudimentary 'system' will be discussed, chiefly on the basis of secondary sources.

Identity registration has not been a prime concern of Dutch historians,[2] so this chapter may be regarded as providing a first description of the ways in which the Dutch established an individual's identity. Given the exploratory nature of our contribution, we abstain from placing the Dutch case in an international context, trusting that the other contributions to this volume will supply some of that context. The ways in which the early modern Dutch established and registered identity were many and diverse, as we will see, and one can confidently assume that some less

[2] Studies such as those by Groebner (2004) and Higgs (2004) do not exist for the Netherlands.

familiar ways of identification have been missed here, while others can be mentioned only in passing. Furthermore, partly by accident and partly by design, it is the methods used to establish identity in Amsterdam that will feature prominently in this chapter. That city has been better studied than other cities in the Dutch Republic, and it is blessed with an interesting source for the history of identity registration, the *Amsterdamsche Secretary*, a register and 'example book' containing all sorts of types of certificate drawn up by the secretaries of the city and its magistrates.[3]

Because of its size and importance it may safely be assumed that no other town in the Dutch Republic had a bureaucracy that was so well developed. Taking Amsterdam as the primary focus of this chapter, but not ignoring the rest of the Republic, we hope to be able to review the most important ways in which ordinary Dutch citizens would most likely be required to identify themselves at some stage of their life.

Identity registration by the church: baptisms, burials and marriages

At the Council of Trent, which ended in 1563, the Catholic church resolved that henceforth parish priests were to keep records of baptisms and marriages. The parish priest was required to perform every marriage ceremony in the presence of two or more witnesses, in order to end the practice of clandestine marriages. Baptisms also had to be registered, with the date of the baptism, the names of the parents, and the names of the godparents being recorded. The Council of Trent remained silent about burials, but in any case its reforms came too late to be implemented in the northern Netherlands, which was by then being ripped apart by the wars of religion which eventually led to the emergence of the Dutch Republic. Only in royalist and Catholic Amsterdam were baptisms registered from as early as 1564, and marriages from 1565 – before the city grudgingly joined the Revolt in 1578 (Hagoort 2010, 2).[4] In general, however, baptism registers were not introduced until the 1570s and 1580s, with the Reformation. Baptism registration was usually introduced by the Dutch Reformed church, which in 1574 made it a rule that every congregation should keep registers of baptisms, confirmations, marriages, and burials (Hagoort 2010, 1).[5] Accordingly, the Dutch Reformed church took over the duty of registering baptisms,

[3] It can occasionally be found in public collections such as the Amsterdam City Archives (SAA), and the Special Collections of the Netherlands Economic History Archives (NEHA), housed at the International Institute of Social History. We have consulted the latter copy.

[4] Gouda's parish church of Sint Jan might have registered baptisms and marriages prior to the Reformation, but none of those records have survived (Abels *et al.* 2002, 43).

[5] Baptism was not actually an indispensable sacrament in the eyes of the Dutch Reformed Church.

marriages and burials from the Catholic church after the Reformation and regarded it as a general Christian service provided not just to the Dutch Reformed but to all Christians. Not surprisingly, then, a great number of baptized children were not actually of Dutch Reformed parentage. Gradually, however, other denominations started to baptize their children themselves, and to keep separate registers of those baptisms. This development can be traced in Amsterdam, Dordrecht and The Hague for example (Frijhoff *et al.* 1998, 277; 2004, 396; Wijsenbeek 2005, 208).[6]

Baptismal registers usually contained the names of the child, the parents, and the witnesses, and the date of the baptism. The date of birth was rarely noted, as baptisms usually followed soon after birth. The sextons, who kept the register, did not always follow the prescriptions laid down by the church: sometimes they omitted the names of the mother and the witnesses. In Amsterdam it was not until 1611 that the church council decided to check the registers to see whether they were being kept properly, an exercise repeated in 1622, and later on as well. In 1695 Amsterdam's Walloon church started registering dates of birth also. As a rule, Catholics always baptized their children the day they were born, making a note in the register when that was not the case (Hagoort 2010, 2).

The magistrate encouraged non-Reformed churches to keep registers of births or baptisms. In the case of the Amsterdam Mennonites, the absence of a register of newborns led to problems because the magistrates required a baptism certificate from those who wanted to become burghers, as those certificates could be used to prove the identity of the father. From 1714 onwards the Mennonites were required to keep registers of births; the Sephardic Jews and the Ashkenazi Jews followed later, in 1735 and 1739 respectively.[7]

A development similar to that in Amsterdam and Dordrecht took place elsewhere in the Dutch Republic. In Nijmegen too, from 1591 onwards everyone was in principle obliged to have their children baptized in the Dutch Reformed church. The church baptism registers have been preserved from 1608 onwards. Eventually there, too, dissenters resolved to draw up their own registers: the Walloon baptism register first came into effect in 1644, and the Lutheran in 1674; the Catholic baptism registers must be regarded as being complete from 1672 onwards. In Utrecht Mennonites kept registers from 1653, and Lutherans from 1670 (Bots and Kuys 2005, 305; Rommes 1998, 57).

It seems that the magistracy increasingly grew to appreciate the importance of well-kept baptism registers. In Amsterdam it required churches not only to keep registers, but, from 1785 onwards, also to submit a copy to the town hall every six months. From then on until the Napoleonic registration law of 1811, every six months

[6] For a complete overview of surviving baptism, marriage, and burial registers in the Netherlands see Wijnaendts van Resandt and Booma (1998).

[7] Jews also kept circumcision registers; those were not of interest to magistrates, however, and were kept by the mohels themselves (Hagoort 2010, 2, 6).

the sextons and other church dignitaries collected the registers from the town hall to have them updated, returning them afterwards. From 1792 onwards the States of Holland required the exact date and place of birth to be recorded as well. The council of Amsterdam's Dutch Reformed church decided in 1807 to add the gender of the newborn. Gradually, the registers thus gave more and more information, and the magistrate imposed increasingly detailed requirements in relation to the registration of births and baptisms. That might have reflected the fact that extracts from the registers were regularly required, as evidence, for example, of the place where one was born, or where one's parents were born (Hagoort 2010, 2).[8]

A similar form of registration, but one originally characteristic only of the Dutch Reformed church, concerned confirmed members of the church. For Calvinists, only those who had been confirmed could take part in the Lord's Supper or apply for church poor relief. All congregations had to keep these confirmation registers. Those for Utrecht, for example, have been preserved from as early as 1579. All newcomers who had been a member of a Dutch Reformed church elsewhere were required to supply an attestation from their home congregation, irrespective of whether they were settling in Utrecht permanently or living there temporarily. The same applied to other Protestant churches, though sometimes not until much later. Utrecht's Lutheran church, for example, did not adopt the habit of requesting attestations from immigrants until the eighteenth century (Rommes 1998, 56). Ordinarily those attestations would be accepted only from trusted and known congregations, but there were exceptions: from 1615 onwards the council of Nijmegen's Dutch Reformed church accepted new members who had fled from the wars in Germany on the basis of attestations of doubtful origin, often wondering about the 'Christian zeal' of those refugees (Schimmel 1966, 23). The confirmation registers served to inform church officials about whether someone was a member, and entitled to receive an attestation if he or she were to move elsewhere. The attestation itself usually named the migrant in question, certified that he or she was a church member, and of good conduct, and was signed by a minister of the elders of the original congregation. Without an attestation, one could not expect to partake fully in the religious life of one's new congregation.

Registration of burials was another form of church registration which the magistracy concerned itself with, but only to a limited extent. Few regulations were drawn up. Sextons of every church, or, in Amsterdam at least, gravediggers appointed by the magistrate, maintained registers of those who were buried in their churches or graveyards, and they kept separate registers of those who owned a grave in the church. Those records served primarily a financial purpose: burials were a source of income for church and magistrate (Frijhoff *et al*. 2004, 396).[9]

[8] Unfortunately, because of the lack of research we know little about the issuing of these extracts, and the purposes they served.

[9] Later on, the sexton and gravedigger were often the same person (Hagoort 2010, 5).

The magistracy seems to have taken an interest in the registration of burials only when it was of direct concern, such as when a tax on burials was imposed in the province of Holland on 26 October 1695. In Amsterdam, this tax was supposed to be collected by the gravediggers, but already by 3 December 1695 it was decided that the town secretary would collect the tax; from then on he kept a tax register which in fact served as a burial register (Hagoort 2010, 5). Other cities seem to have followed Amsterdam's innovation: in Gouda, for example, from 1697 onwards all burials were registered in the burial tax register. Also in Gouda, from 1730 onwards deaths of children at birth had to be reported by the midwives to the burgomasters as part of an effort to exercise greater control over the midwives (Abels *et al.* 2002, 298, 301). Apart for taxation purposes, registering deaths was important in other ways, as will be seen below. On remarrying, for example, widows and widowers were required to provide evidence of the death of their previous spouse, and the sextons of Amsterdam were required to report to the orphan masters the deaths of the parents of any underage children.

The only form of population registration the magistrate supervised closely was marriage registration. Marriage was important to the magistrate given its implications for property transfer: it was essential that marriages be universally recognized, so that no one could doubt the legitimacy of the couple's offspring and their entitlement to inherit property held by their parents. Registration of marriages was necessary to prevent clandestine marriages, bigamous marriages, and marriages between individuals who were too closely related – all events which were likely to lead to conflict and disputed inheritances. The province of Holland introduced a uniform marriage law on 1 April 1580 which gave the option to marry before a magistrate or before a minister of the Dutch Reformed church. For three consecutive weeks banns were read out at the town hall or in church, allowing an opportunity for any impediment to the marriage to be made known. This measure was intended to end the practice of clandestine marriage. Minors wishing to marry had to show written proof of consent from their parents. If, in the case of sailors or soldiers, parental consent could not be obtained due to distance, the consent of the captain or an officer would suffice.

A number of cities had their own marriage regulations. For example, in Amsterdam until 1604 it was also possible to marry before a notary (Haks 1982, 114–115; van der Heijden 1998, 45–46, 50–53, 68). As a direct consequence of the Reformation, in 1578 Amsterdam's magistracy appointed a committee for matrimonial affairs to register non-Dutch Reformed marriages. Every couple had to appear with their parents or guardians to answer questions about their age, whether their parents had consented to the marriage, whether they were related in any way, and at what address they lived. After their wedding date had been announced on three consecutive Sundays, Dutch Reformed couples married in church, while dissenters could marry before a notary or, from 1604 onwards, in the presence of two aldermen. Ordinarily their names, places of birth, and those of their witnesses were noted. Exceptionally, it was customary in Amsterdam to note the age, as well as, until about 1715, the occupation of the bridegroom, and after 1755 the religion of the betrothed (Frijhoff *et al.* 2004, 292, 396). After the wedding, the secretaries could issue a testimony confirming that a couple had indeed been married in the jurisdiction of Amsterdam (N.N. 1726, 314–316). From 1581 onwards, the committee for matrimonial affairs kept two betrothal registers, one for the church, and one for the marriages at the town hall before the aldermen (if one of the partners was Dutch Reformed, the intended marriage would be listed in both registers).[10]

In Amsterdam, church sextons were also clerks serving the committee for matrimonial affairs, and they kept both church and town hall registers. Prospective marriage partners were obliged to marry within a month of the banns having been read out for the third and final time. Committee members checked whether the couple actually did so. In Rotterdam the Dutch Reformed church kept a marriage register from 1573 onwards. Three years later the magistracy resolved that all couples wishing to marry should appear first before a magistrate. It thus also became possible to marry before the aldermen instead of in church. In Gouda, it was possible to marry before a magistrate from as early as 1581, when the civil marriage register took effect (Abels *et al.* 2002, 298–299; Hagoort 2010, 4).

Though the magistracy had great influence in determining how marriages were concluded and registered, the Dutch Reformed church occasionally exercised additional control. Thus, from 1574 onwards, it required widows and widowers to prove that their first spouse had died (van der Heijden 1998, 72, 75).[11] The church also tried to influence the marriage policy of the magistracy. In Nijmegen in 1592 magistrates made it possible for couples to opt to be married before them. Hitherto, some of the city's Catholic inhabitants had left the city rather than be married before a minister of the Dutch Reformed church. The Calvinist church council urged magistrates not to marry couples whose banns had not been announced on three consecutive weekends, and also urged that those from outside the city be required to submit attestations certifying they were not engaged to someone else. It also requested magistrates to ensure that those whose banns had been announced did actually marry; apparently, many couples did not (Schimmel 1966, 10–11).

It was only at the end of the seventeenth century that the magistracy, at least in the province of Holland, started systematically to register all marriages for tax purposes. From then on a tax register at the Amsterdam town hall served as a duplicate marriage register. This development also took place in other cities

[10] From 1578 to 1636 a separate register was kept in which the betrothals of couples where one of the couple lived outside Amsterdam were recorded. The oldest register also noted how long the couple had lived in Amsterdam. If one of the prospective spouses had been living in Amsterdam for less than three years, the banns also had to be announced in their place of origin (Hagoort 2010, 3).

[11] Unfortunately, nothing is said of the sort of evidence they had to present.

(Hagoort 2010, 5).[12] The magistrate also registered cases when marriages broke up. In Gouda, separations – forty-two in the seventeenth century and 243 in the eighteenth century – were registered in the *publicatieboeken* ('publication books'). In Amsterdam, separations were listed in the *huwelijkskrakeelregisters* (or 'matrimonial disputes registers') (Abels *et al.* 2002, 300).[13]

It appears that usually magistrates intervened in the registration of births, marriages and deaths only for the purpose of safeguarding property (marriage) or the payment of taxation (marriage, burial). It also seems that during the course of the eighteenth century their interest increased. The magistracy gradually intervened more and more in the actual registration, and either persuaded or ordered all churches to follow the example of the Dutch Reformed church. It thus began to encroach on terrain it had originally been content to leave to the churches. This development seemed to foreshadow the events of 1811, when the registration of births, marriages and deaths became a matter for the state alone.[14]

Identity registration by the magistrate: citizenship registers

In the early years of the Dutch Republic, local magistrates had generally not been particularly interested in keeping records of changes in population, one reason being that the system of taxation largely comprised levies on goods rather than on the income or wealth of individuals. Magistrates therefore seldom expressed an interest in the number of inhabitants. Population censuses were extremely rare and almost always for taxation purposes; therefore, they often extended only to those who had something to contribute and ignored those who did not. Moreover, such censuses were never national: usually local, occasionally provincial, and typically a one-time occurrence only.[15] The only major census the province of Holland undertook dates from 1622, when every inhabitant of Holland had to pay one guilder towards the war effort, and it was never repeated. This reluctance may have emanated from a political concern and a religious one. Politically, the census of

[12] In Gouda, for example, after 1696 all marriages were additionally registered in the marriage tax register (Abels *et al.* 2002, 298–299), while in Dordrecht marriage registration had been transferred from the church to the city government as early as 1691 (Frijhoff *et al* 1998, 69).

[13] The Amsterdam registers have been preserved for the period 1592 to 1810 (Hagoort 2010, 14).

[14] For some time after 1811 the new administration did not function fully, and did not cover all births, as is shown from comparisons between the new civil registers and the church registers – which of course are still kept even today (Kok 1991, 34–36).

[15] They could also be very specific in nature: thus in 1749 the sheriff of Wanneperveen drew up a register of the migrant peat-cutters working temporarily in his jurisdiction, listing, among other things, their names, the names of their employers, and their place and province of origin. This register too was related to several taxation-related surveys in that year. Such registers of migrant labourers were very rare however. (Personal communication from Piet Lourens and Jan Lucassen.)

1622 served as a highly evident statement of the relative importance of the individual cities of Holland, and subsequent generations of Holland's regents preferred to maintain the division of influence manifested in that census – with cities such as Dordrecht and Haarlem retaining a considerable influence even though Rotterdam became larger and Leiden wealthier. The Republic's local magistrates were thus reluctant to conduct population censuses, so that no one would know how many people actually lived in their jurisdictions (Frijhoff *et al.* 1998, 76). Some voices within the Dutch Reformed church were opposed to censuses. Had not the Lord punished King David for holding a census among the Israelites by inflicting a devastating epidemic on them? In an era in which plague regularly ravaged the Dutch Republic, church ministers were unlikely to forget David's punishment. The first nationwide census was not in fact held until 1795, after the fall of the Dutch Republic.

The magistrates of Dutch cities, towns and villages did register their poorer, middling and upper classes. Indeed, the registration of those in need of poor relief was of great concern to all magistrates, as virtually all local authorities strove to minimize the number of people dependent on poor relief in their jurisdictions. Throughout the early modern age, magistrates devoted considerable energy, as we will see, to limiting the number of dependent poor. Much less in need of regulation, partly because it had been established for much longer, was the registration of burghers, that is inhabitants of urban communities who enjoyed full citizenship rights in their community as well as certain other rights – such as freedom from tolls and eligibility for guild membership.

Citizenship registers were already in use in the Middle Ages, providing information on the new burghers of a city. Some from that era have survived: Gouda, for example, kept registers of new burghers from at least 1390, when the first surviving register begins, but the registers are complete only from 1501 onwards (Abels *et al.* 2002, 45, 305, graph). Not all citizenship registers are alike. Amsterdam's registers contain information on the name of the applicant, their sponsors – often a father, father-in-law, or employer – their occupation, their sponsor's occupation, the name of the applicant's wife if she herself was a burgher, the date on which the applicant had sworn the requisite oath of obedience, and whether the appropriate fee had been paid. Amsterdam's citizenship registers have survived intact from 1655.[16] In some cities the registers have not survived at all, but no city would have gone without them.[17]

Becoming a burgher did not simply mean being registered as a burgher; it also entailed the possibility of identifying oneself as such. Prospective burghers had

[16] For the period prior to 1655, only one register of burghers who had obtained citizenship through marriage (from 1647 to 1655) and two registers of burghers who had purchased citizenship (1584–1605 and 1636–1652) have survived.

[17] Other cities where these registers have been preserved include 's-Hertogenbosch, Zwolle, and Rotterdam (Vos and Bosmans 1997, 56; Hove 2005, 364; Schoor 1999, 329).

to swear an oath of obedience and pay a fee, after which they would be given a *burgerceel* ('certificate of citizenship'), on which their name, the text of the oath, and confirmation that the fee had been paid were written, thus enabling them to prove that they were a burgher. In Amsterdam the document was also available in French and English, no doubt for the benefit of the large English and Walloon communities. Indigenous burghers could also request a written statement confirming their status, as could burghers who had become citizens by marriage to an Amsterdam burgher (N.N. 1726, 297–299). Prospective burghers born in Amsterdam might have had to supply evidence that they had indeed been born in Amsterdam. Nijmegen had a similar requirement: from 30 July 1641 it required new burghers to provide evidence that their ancestors had been burghers by supplying the letters of citizenship those ancestors had obtained. Prior to that the magistrate had relied on applicants to speak the truth; henceforth, written evidence was required. Failure to supply that evidence meant one had to pay the full fee (Schimmel 1966, 40). This particular form of identity registration does seem to have been revenue-based.

In Amsterdam, aside from the standard documents of citizenship, there were also separate citizenship documents for Mennonites, who gave a promise instead of swearing an oath, and Jews. Inhabitants could also swear their loyalty and be recognized as residents (*inwoonders* or *ingezetenen*) if they wished merely to set up a shop or trade in a sector not subject to guild regulations; they would then obtain a similar document. If one lost one's *burgerceel*, one could request a replacement extract from the citizenship registers (N.N. 1726, 301–303).

For those who could afford the fee, it was fairly easy to become a burgher of Amsterdam and other towns in the west of the Republic. Towns in the east often required more evidence of one's identity.[18] In Utrecht, for example, applicants for citizenship had to present an attestation of good conduct from their place of origin. From 1654 this attestation had to specify the religion of the applicant: this seems to have been a prelude to the decision in subsequent years no longer to accept Catholics as burghers.[19] In Nijmegen too, from 1593 onwards new burghers had to submit a sealed written attestation of their good conduct.[20] Amsterdam, more accommodating when it came to newcomers, did not require such statements.

Only a minority of Amsterdam's inhabitants had acquired citizenship. This implied that most Amsterdammers had no means of identifying themselves as such. Amsterdam had thousands of visitors, temporary immigrants, and many others who

[18] See Lourens and Lucassen (2000), 11, 43, for the distinction between the more liberal cities in the west and the stricter cities in the east.

[19] In fact magistrates reserved the right to make exceptions, and they frequently did (Rommes 1998, 41).

[20] In the case of religious refugees who desired to become citizens of Nijmegen, the magistrate sometimes accepted an attestation of good conduct from other parties, such as, in one case in 1615, an attestation from the deposed Protestant magistrate of Aix-la-Chapelle (Schimmel 1966, 22).

lived there permanently without being registered (Kuijpers 2005, 123, 127–128). This was part of a more or less conscious policy by Amsterdam, which as late as 1668 was greatly concerned with expanding its urban population and tried to make the city as attractive as possible to migrants.

Occasionally, registers of non-burghers were kept: between 1670 and 1747, for example, Amsterdam kept registers of *ingezetenen*, or residents. *Ingezetenen* were non-burghers registered as residents, which allowed them certain minor privileges, such as eligibility for membership of some – though not all – guilds; indeed, guilds gradually restricted the recruitment of new members to burghers, so that the *ingezetenschap* eventually disappeared (Schimmel 1966, 134–135; Kuijpers 2005, 122–123).[21] With its register of residents, Amsterdam was an exception. The magistrate did sometimes, as a temporary measure, register non-burghers resident in its jurisdiction during wartime. Similarly, in times of trouble, in 1505 and 1565 for example, Utrecht ordered its innkeepers to register their guests, and to show the registers to the magistrate, but these rules were apparently temporary. Utrecht sometimes required strangers who had not become burghers to swear an oath of loyalty to the city.[22] In Nijmegen, in 1592, just after the city had been seized by the Dutch, the magistrates concluded that there were many new inhabitants whose names and origins were unknown to the city authorities. They ordered those who had entered the city within the past seven years to present themselves at the town hall, though it is uncertain whether they actually did so. As a rule, throughout the early modern period the magistrates registered only burghers. Occasionally, other groups were registered in response to exceptional circumstances; once those circumstances had abated, the magistracy lost any interest in keeping records of these other groups (Schimmel 1966, 13, 15). There were exceptions to this rule, some of which will be discussed below. First, however, we will discuss the types of personal identification that urban magistrates could offer their citizens, before going on to discuss the widespread practice of 'outsourcing' identity registration by urban magistrates.

Other forms of identity registration by the magistrate: passports, letters of recommendation, *attestaties de vita*

The diversity of certificates that citizens could request from the magistrate can be demonstrated using a rare Amsterdam source, the *Amsterdamsche Secretary*. An Amsterdam magistrate could supply burghers having to leave their jurisdiction

[21] These registers can be found in SAA 5033: Archief van Burgemeesters; Poorterboeken.

[22] In 1542, 1552 and 1565, for example. Name, place of origin, and often occupation and age, and sometimes other details were registered. In 1565 the same measure was taken in Nijmegen (Rommes 1998, 50, 63–64).

with passports and letters of recommendation to be shown to foreign rulers or other magistrates within the Dutch Republic. We give an extensive overview here to show the considerable array of means of identification available to a Dutch burgher.

Passports did not, in fact, have entirely the same function as they do today; they were temporary identity documents issued for specific purposes. In the seventeenth century, passports were issued within the Dutch Republic in times of war, notably if a burgher wished to trade in a frontier area where war was being waged (N.N. 1726, 282). In 1593, for example, Nijmegen's magistracy decreed that those who had left Nijmegen to live in other places controlled by the king of Spain must obtain a passport from a magistrate if they wished to return to the city.[23] Likewise, the magistrate could issue a passport for a sutler – a merchant selling provisions to the army in the field – wishing to travel to Dutch positions, requesting any magistrate in the territories *en route* to allow free passage. Travellers abroad could also be granted a passport, which specified their city of origin, and where they wished to travel to, and requested foreign jurisdictions to allow the traveller to pass without let or hindrance (N.N. 1726, 283–288).

Letters of recommendation served to facilitate access to foreign rulers and other Dutch magistrates, and were written in the name of the burgomasters and addressed to named sovereigns. Burghers could request such letters from the burgomasters, for example if they wished to travel to the Court of Holland in The Hague, or wished to trade somewhere. The magistrate could also issue a testimonial vouching for the person requesting it: for example, an *acte van legaliteit* ('act of legality') could be given to a notary, so that the latter could prove he was bona fide (N.N. 1726, 310–311). He could produce this to show to his clients. Similar testimonials existed for messengers of merchants, appointed by the city, 'so that everywhere he may be recognized as such, assisted, and trusted'.[24] These testimonials needed the consent of the burgomasters or secretaries before they could be issued. Though not identity papers as such, they could be used as a means of identification, as the magistrate would issue them only to burghers or inhabitants of the city.

The same applies to a number of other documents issued by the magistrate, those documents predominantly serving the economic interests of the inhabitants of the city. Amsterdam's burghers were exempt from tolls while travelling within the County of Holland, provided they carried a *tolbrief* ('letter of toll') issued by the magistrate, which confirmed they had lived for at least a year and a day in Amsterdam. The letter would also include the specific mark the burgher used to brand his merchandise, so that the toll collectors could recognize his goods. Skippers travelling outside the Netherlands could request a *zeebrief* ('certificate of registry'),

[23] The city could demand that these passports – which could also be issued to its inhabitants – be returned (Schimmel 1966, 14).

[24] 'Op dat hy over al voor zodanig zoude warden erkent, geholpen en vertrouwt' (N.N. 1726, 311–312).

in which Amsterdam declared that the skipper had sworn that his ship was a Dutch ship, asking all magistrates to assist him if necessary. Those skippers sailing for Italian harbours could request a *gezondbrief* ('bill of health'), in which the magistrate declared their ship and crew to be free from the plague and other contagious diseases. Otherwise, Italian port authorities could detain them and submit them to quarantine (N.N. 1726, 289–295). A skipper could also obtain a declaration, or 'affirmation', from the burgomasters that his ship was based in Amsterdam; even though 'according to the general rule no one may testify on his own behalf, this rule is not so rigid and sometimes exceptions are made to it', meaning that it was sufficient for skippers to swear an oath and that they did not require witnesses.[25] Similarly, merchants could request a declaration to the effect that certain goods belonged to them; such a declaration could subsequently be presented to foreign authorities (N.N. 1726, 320–321).

Equally important were the documents necessary in civil court cases, though they were different in that their purpose was to establish not the identity of the burgher who requested them, but that of witnesses who could not be present in person before Amsterdam's aldermen. Such a document was termed a *lettere requisitoriaal*, a generic name for any written request from one magistrate to another. It could, for example, be a request to supply witness testimony in a civil lawsuit: 'to obtain testimony of the truth from a stranger'.[26] If one of the parties needed testimony from a witness living in a distant jurisdiction, a request would be sent to the appropriate magistrate, who would normally comply by sending copies of the testimony given in his presence (N.N. 1726, 208–210).

The magistrate could also establish the reliability of documents drawn up by citizens. Amsterdammers could draw up attestations and declarations on behalf of one another before burgomasters, aldermen, secretaries, or notaries and witnesses. The declarations made before burgomasters were called *certificaties*, or certifications. They certified attestations made by Amsterdam's inhabitants, drawn up before notaries and now verified by means of an oath sworn before the magistrate (N.N. 1726, 326–327). This procedure was necessary because Dutch notaries were not permitted to administer oaths.

Especially important in establishing identity were *attestaties de vita* (or life certificates), which could be issued by the secretaries, but also, if they required an oath, by the burgomasters. In the *attestaties de vita* two witnesses were required to appear before the burgomasters to certify that a third person, A, X years old and born in C, was still alive and residing in D, and that this person was, for example, entitled to the income from a certain annuity. Such declarations, confirmed on oath, were required for instance by the States of Friesland if anyone wanted to collect

[25] 'Volgens den gemeenen Regel, niemand in zyn eigen zaak getuigen mag, zo is echter deze Regel zo vast niet, of ze lyd somtyds wel eenige exceptie' (N.N. 1726, 318–319).
[26] 'Om Getuygenis der waarheit te hebben van een Vreemdeling' (N.N. 1726, 69).

the interest on the annuities issued by that province. These attestations were preprinted forms. They were available in Dutch but also in French, for the benefit of foreign powers, such as the king of Denmark or the city of Paris, both of which issued annuities to Dutch citizens (N.N. 1726, 327–328, 330–333). Since Dutch notaries were not allowed to administer oaths, *attestaties de vita* needed to be validated by the client, who would request a copy of the certificate from the notary and have it validated first by presenting it to the city's secretaries and then to the burgomasters, and lastly by confirming it on oath. The witnesses were required to be present when the secretary read the *attestatie de vita* and they also had to swear an oath before the burgomasters.[27]

The validity of passports, letters of recommendation, *attestaties de vita*, and suchlike was time-bound, though it might be possible to renew them annually. Moreover, they were often limited in effect. They could thus be used to establish one's identity only for a limited time, in a certain specified area – for example for one journey back and forth only. Once their validity had expired, they were of no value to the individual.[28]

'Outsourcing' middle-class registration: guilds and the Orphan Chamber (*weeskamer*)

The preceding paragraphs illustrate how important citizenship was in an urban environment, and that cities spent a great deal of effort to register burghers and supply them with means of identification outside the city walls. The modest bureaucracy of Dutch cities was unable, however, to provide burghers with all the forms of identity registration required. The solution was to 'outsource' many of these. Apart from entrusting the registration of baptisms, marriages and burials to the churches, the magistrate entrusted semi-public bodies with other forms of identity registration.

Guilds needed to keep track of their members. In 1617 in the city of Nijmegen, for example, the magistrate decreed that before settling as an artisan, a newcomer had to either provide evidence he had made a 'masterpiece' or do so under the auspices of the Nijmegen guilds. This measure purported to preserve the quality of artisanal production, while, at the same time, serving to regulate entry to the labour market. From 1642 onwards, all newcomers to a Nijmegen guild also had to present to the guild authorities a written attestation from the city's secretary that they had paid the fee for citizenship and sworn the required oath. This measure

[27] Mennonites and Jews were not required to swear an oath (N.N. 1726, 334–338).

[28] It is not clear how one could be sure if a document had ceased to be valid: presumably there were indication marks on the document itself, such as the date of issue; that might also explain why no registers were kept.

was introduced after several new burghers had obtained citizenship and then attempted to join the guilds without actually paying the citizenship fee.

Registration of the middle classes by the guilds was not a marginal phenomenon in the Dutch Republic. In small cities the various trades were often exercised by a relatively small group of individuals, and formal registration was not always necessary. In a city such as Amsterdam, however, the number of guild members was much higher, and it was necessary to register them. Of Amsterdam's male labour force, a quarter consisted of guild masters and 60 per cent of journeymen, leaving a mere 15 per cent beyond the control of the guilds (Lourens and Lucassen 1998, 123, 127–128).

Guilds kept registers of their prime active members, the masters,[29] and some registered the names of apprentices and journeymen too. They might also keep records of whether bakers or silversmiths had produced a masterpiece, for instance, or of the marks used by their members. Occasionally, a register of deceased guild members was kept. Guilds sometimes even registered non-members: between 1684 and 1694 the surgeons' guild, for example, registered cases of barber-surgeon activities by non-members. This was one way to control a closely related part of the labour market, and often those non-members had to pay for, as it were, not being incorporated by the guild.

From as early as the mid-sixteenth century, rather formal arrangements existed in the form of insurance provided by the Dutch guilds. Artisans and journeymen paid a small amount per week for this insurance, which they themselves administrated. In 1811 the proportion of the male labour force with some type of formal mutual insurance may have been as high as 42 per cent in Utrecht, 55 per cent in Leiden, and at least 22 per cent in Amsterdam. Guild insurance primarily meant assistance in the event of burial, followed in importance by insurance compensating for lost income in the event of illness, and insurance to cover the costs of medication and the physician's or surgeon's fee. A few guilds offered members old age or widow's pensions. Insurance necessarily involves establishing the claims of individuals, and this in turn led to rules and regulations and to the registration of the commencement of the insurance and of certain characteristics of the insured, such as name, age, gender, place of residence, and health status (Bos 1998; van Leeuwen 2011).

Another example of a semi-public organization entrusted with middle-class identity registration was the Orphan Chamber. Often founded to care for burgher orphans and half-orphans, orphan chambers were run by unsalaried members –

[29] In Amsterdam, registers have survived for the guilds of the carpenters; painters; tinsmiths; booksellers, printers, and bookbinders; surgeons; compass makers and sail makers; goldsmiths and silversmiths; skippers; saw-millers; leatherworkers; tailors; pastry-bakers; corn carriers; corn skippers; corn measurers; corn millers; brokers; basket-makers; bricklayers; shipwrights; blacksmiths; peat-carriers; weighing-house carriers; and wine-merchants (van Eeghen 1951, *passim*).

often magistrates or their relatives – on a fairly independent basis. If a married burgher with children died in Amsterdam, the remaining parent had to provide proof, by means of documents drawn up and registered by the orphan masters, of the property their children stood to inherit on attaining the age of majority. If the surviving parent wished to remarry, he or she had to obtain a letter of consent from the orphan masters to be presented to the secretary of the city and the committee for matrimonial affairs before the banns could be announced (N.N. 1726, 350–353). In Amsterdam, the sextons of every church and churchyard were obliged to report to the Orphan Chamber each week the names of those buried who had left minors as heirs. The orphan masters recorded their names in death registers, a different one for each church and cemetery. Surviving pauper parents, who were unable to give their half-orphaned children anything, were listed as such in the death registers.[30] The registers for Amsterdam have been preserved. They contain less information than the burial registers, as they record only those leaving minors as heirs. In some cases they predate the burial registers, the earliest register dating from 1563 (Kretzschmar 2010, 1–2). The orphan masters could also designate a guardian, if none had been appointed in the deceased's will, and issue a certificate of guardianship to that guardian, whose name was then registered in the *Voogdyboek* (the 'Book of Guardianship'). Further, the guardians had to request approval from the orphan masters for all other acts of administration (N.N. 1726, 356–359, 362–363).

'Outsourcing' lower-class registration: registering and identifying the poor

While the orphans of burghers were registered by the Orphan Chamber, other semi-public organs took care of those receiving assistance lower down the social scale. During the Reformation a multiplicity of religious denominations had emerged, each of which established its own charity.[31] Each religious denomination of any significance wanted its own patronage and protection, while municipal poor relief existed for those whom the churches failed to help. In Amsterdam, for example, almost all religious denominations maintained an ecclesiastical poor relief agency to provide for the 'ordinary' poor, while many also ran almshouses for elderly parishioners and orphanages for the boys and girls of their co-religionists. There

[30] However, if the deceased died outside the city or at sea, they were registered in the so-called *Kalisboek* (literally the 'Book of Poor Fellows'). In both cases the surviving parent, supported by a witness from the deceased's side of the family, had to declare their inability to give their children anything from the deceased's estate (N.N. 1726, 354–355).

[31] The precise development over time and the degree of success in centralizing poor relief varied from city to city (van Nederveen Meerkerk and Vermeesch 2010, 135–154).

existed two municipal poor relief agencies, each covering one half of the town, and a burgher as well as an ordinary orphanage. Finally, like many other cities, Amsterdam had a number of almshouses. The poor relief system was thus fragmented across religious and secular lines, with a further distinction according to social status and religious denomination (Prak 1998; van Leeuwen 2000b; van Nederveen Meerkerk and Vermeesch 2010).[32]

At any one time, a sizeable proportion of the Dutch population was being assisted by a poor relief organization. In times of hardship, this figure could rise substantially, and during the period of extreme poverty experienced in Amsterdam at the end of the eighteenth century about half the city's population were in receipt of a modest, *ad hoc* allowance. Given that assistance could be provided during most stages of the life cycle – to a child in a pauper family, to single mothers and underemployed families with many children, and to the elderly – it is conceivable that, even disregarding one-off donations, a large proportion, and perhaps even the majority, of the urban population were assisted during at least part of their life.

This largesse was a result of several factors, including the modernity of the Dutch economy, with many migrants – either from villages in the Dutch Republic or from abroad – moving to the cities of this heavily urbanized country. This footloose population contributed to the welfare of the Republic, but it also needed assistance during times of hardship. It was not just kindness that dictated they should be helped. It was also wise to do so, since the wealthy and the middle classes in the cities were surrounded, literally, by those who might be tempted to take in desperation that which was not given to them in benevolence.

A myriad of relief agencies existed, dispensing relief from their endowments, from the coins given by churchgoers, from the liberal bequests made in wills, and from grants from the city authorities. Having funds to dispense was one thing; having appropriate registration systems was another. The fact that relief was broken down by place and church helped the authorities keep track of recipients, but the many poor relief administrators still needed to keep documentary records of who received what. They used pauper books for the purpose. Many of these have been lost, but some have survived. Just as they form a valuable window on a substantial proportion of the Dutch urban population for social historians of the early modern era, they also formed a valuable registration resource for early modern poor relief administrators.

What did the pauper books register? Those for Amsterdam's Catholic Charity in the late eighteenth century noted the first name and the surname of the applicant – usually a woman – their marital status and the name of their spouse (or former spouse), if any, age, address, number of minor children, the name of their confessor, and, of course, the amounts given in winter and in summer (Faber and van Leeuwen

[32] The following is described in more detail in van Leeuwen (2012).

1987, 15, 1991). This was more than sufficient information to enable the Catholic administrators to keep track of the poor. Other relief agencies in Amsterdam and in cities such as Zwolle, Delft and Groningen had similar registration systems.[33]

Measures of control were in place, such as those at the Amsterdam Municipal Charity, where an application for support began with a visit to the district warden. From the seventeenth century onwards Amsterdam was divided into districts, each headed by a warden, who issued the certificates of poverty which applicants for relief had to submit to the Municipal Charity, and who distributed vouchers for free education in charity schools. Before issuing the requisite certificate the warden was expected to visit the pauper applicants, who were then required to report to the offices of the Municipal Charity, armed with their declarations from the warden and one or more extracts from the baptismal or birth registers, or from the marriage banns or marriage registers. The regents would then decide whether or not to register them for assistance. Applicants who were sick were also required to produce a certificate from a municipal doctor, surgeon, or midwife. Witnesses would sometimes be brought along to add force to an application.

Registration took place at the beginning of summer and the beginning of winter, when the regents, sitting at their desks, would hear applications. If all the conditions had been satisfied, district welfare officers would register an applicant and enter the following personal details in the registration book: first name and surname, age, marital status, place of birth, any illnesses or disabilities, and names and ages of spouses and of any surviving children. These particulars were passed on to the district welfare officers or the *consentvrouwen* ('licence women'). The licence women were concerned only with the 'licence holders' – applicants registered as holding an official licence to be paid their relief money at home. These applicants tended to be the sick, the elderly, and families with a large number of children, who found it difficult to attend the relief office each week, and so the licence women visited them at home to hand over relief money in person.

[33] In Zwolle in the second half of the seventeenth century, the Municipal Charity also registered occupation and other information it found of interest, such as the earnings of the children (and whether they should work more), place of birth in the case of immigrants, religion, health, value and nature of their possessions, such as clothing, and whether items had been pawned (Wijngaarden 2000, ch. 4). Similar information was registered for Delft in the seventeenth century. See van der Vlis (2001, ch. 4), and for the city of Groningen in the seventeenth and eighteenth centuries see Buursma (2009, 95–98, *et passim*). From at least the end of the seventeenth century the Leeuwarden municipal agency collected similar information (Spaans 1997, 258–262). A small family reconstitution study of Amsterdam Catholic paupers has systematically linked data from the pauper books to data in the registers of baptism, marriage, and burials. This gives us a clue as to the completeness and reliability of both types of registration source. Both types of source were found generally to accord with one another in terms of the number and age of the children and the parents. It is clear, however, that the spelling of surnames had not yet taken on a fixed form, as the following examples illustrate. One surname was spelled variously as Celi(e), Se(e)li(e), and Ze(e)lie; another as Bre(e)mon(d) and Brymon(t); and a third as Spigthold, Spegtholt, Spighof(f), and Spegthoff (Faber and Van Leeuwen 1991).

The regents of the Amsterdam Municipal Charity would on occasion ask for supplementary evidence from applicants, should doubts arise during their registration or as a result of subsequent enquiries. They would try to discover whether the applicant was indeed out of work and, if so, why. Former employers would be approached, and if the applicant's willingness to seek work was in doubt he had to provide proof that he was looking for work. If there were doubts about whether the applicant had actually lived in Amsterdam for the requisite number of years, the police could be asked to investigate whether he was, in fact, a newcomer to the city. Poor relief institutions used elaborate registration procedures. An application for relief had to be supported with documents and declarations by witnesses. At irregular intervals, various officials would check on the accuracy of the information supplied. Every resident of Amsterdam applying for relief was visited by an inspector, and even after registration inspectors would visit the homes of applicants at least once a year to check on their current circumstances.[34]

Delft's poor relief administrators strove to obtain as much information on their poor as possible in order 'to know them completely' ('volcomelijc te leeren kennen'; van der Vlis 2001, ch. 4, esp. 102).[35] A veritable network of informers existed in this town, as well as in other towns, who, often voluntarily, supplied the relief agency with information on paupers (see also Buursma 2009, 118–124). It is interesting to note that in the city of Leeuwarden, magistrates recruited wardens from the lower ranks of society, who were then required to provide information to the municipal relief agency on the paupers amongst whom they lived and about whom they were therefore well informed (Spaans 1997, 216).[36]

For the migrant poor there was a special system of registration, at least in some Dutch cities.[37] Since the end of the seventeenth century some Dutch towns – though not Amsterdam – had used letters of surety (*acte van indemniteit, acte van cautie*) to stem the influx of the poor. A letter of surety was a promise by a person or an

[34] The administrators of the Catholic Charity in Amsterdam required written proof from the warden that the applicant had lived in Amsterdam for a number of years, as well as written proof from a priest that the applicant had attended Mass at Easter. Naturally, a copy of their baptism entry also had to be provided (Faber and van Leeuwen 1991, 21; Buursma 2009, 118–124). Lutherans who applied for charity had to present two witnesses to testify that the applicant had been attending Holy Communion for several years (Kuijpers 2005, 349). On registration, control, and fraud by Lutheran poor in Amsterdam in the seventeenth and eighteenth centuries, see Kuijpers (2005), 313–315.

[35] The city's procedures for registration and for monitoring fraud were similar to those described for Amsterdam; they included an investigation by the warden, an interview with the administrators, often in the presence of witnesses, and, if necessary, a further investigation by the deputy bailiff, who might make enquiries with the applicant's neighbours.

[36] This had the disadvantage, however, that the wardens were not always up to the task. Some were semi-illiterate and had to be replaced.

[37] This is described in more detail in van Leeuwen (2012). This article explains how Dutch poor relief agencies were able to continuously cope with the influx of migrants claiming relief, in part by means of the letters of surety.

organization to pay for the relief of named individuals if they required assistance within a specified number of years. Normally the letter took the form of a certificate, or surety, issued by a town council, or a poor relief organization run by the town, to a resident on leaving that town. From 1682 to 1785, for example, Leiden issued letters of surety for emigrants which were valid for periods of two to three years, and also required immigrants to present their own letters of surety (C. Davids 1978, esp. 174). Only Leiden's own citizens had the right of admission to, or the right to settle freely in, the city. Citizenship was obtained by birth as the child of a citizen, or through purchase. Migrants wishing to purchase citizenship had to present a letter of surety. Leiden was divided into 130 districts, and district wardens ensured that nobody offered accommodation to migrants without a letter of citizenship or surety. A similar system governing residence was in operation in other parts of the Netherlands, including the city of Rotterdam and the province of Drenthe (Gras 1989; van Voorst van Beest 1955).

Letters of surety issued to Leiden immigrants contained the name of the institution issuing the document, the name of the immigrant, the date of issue, the place of origin, and the date of burghership, if any. In two-thirds of cases the letter was actually drawn up before a Leiden notary. In that case, it usually also stated the occupation of the immigrant, and the names and occupations of those who stood surety and the duration of that surety. If issued outside Leiden, a letter of surety sometimes also contained details of the immigrant's family and their ages. Leiden's outgoing letters of surety included the name of the Leiden relief agency, the date of issue, the name of the emigrant, the place of destination, and the composition and ages of the emigrant's family.[38]

Similarly, from the end of the seventeenth century, Rotterdam's wardens closely monitored those who lived in their district. They checked whether non-Rotterdammers had a certificate of admission (*acte van admissie*). The newcomers who did not were referred to the Admissions Commissioners, or their names were given to the constabulary, who would have illegal migrants evicted from the city. Admission was granted if applicants could provide for themselves and had the necessary papers, which included either a letter of surety to the value of 300 guilders from their place of origin or a letter of surety signed by family members, friends, fellow countrymen, or employers. Only those immigrants with the right of admission and who had lived in Rotterdam for more than two years without having had recourse to assistance were eligible for relief (Van Voorst van Beest 1955, 10–22).

From 1649 onwards Haarlem's magistrates used the wardens of the various neighbourhoods as controllers and registrars of population movements in their

[38] The letters of surety collected by Leiden's poor relief body that have been preserved cover a large proportion of the Republic's territory, including the towns and rural areas of South and North Holland, and parts of Gelderland, North Brabant, and Overijssel (C. Davids 1978, 151).

districts.[39] From then on, Haarlem residents were required to report to the warden if they were renting out accommodation to strangers. The warden kept a register of everyone living in his neighbourhood, registering co-residents and their occupation or trade. In that way he became more of a public servant than the neighbourhood representative he had been before (Dorren 2001, 65, 81). The magistrate was especially concerned to keep out poor strangers, in order not to further burden the city's system of poor relief. In Haarlem, only those who received a certificate of admission in four consecutive years became eligible for municipal poor relief. Despite these strict rules, the wardens often failed to observe them, and permitted strangers without certificates of admission to stay (Dorren 1998, 73–74; 2001, 86).

The letters of surety system developed at the end of the seventeenth century in response to local rules governing domicile. In 1682 the States of Holland declared that 'all such persons who have moved from any place to the towns or to the countryside shall, after a period of one year, be deemed no longer to belong to the place from which they have moved' (quoted in C. Davids 1978, 187, n.16). When an indigent individual migrated to a town in Holland, that town could recover the costs of support from his or her town of origin for a maximum of only one year. Other provinces followed this example and introduced similar rules.[40] At that time, towns were faced with a growing influx of poor migrants whom they had to support from the start. It appears that towns started to demand letters of surety to put a stop to this. Leiden, for instance, required the wardens to keep out 'poor people from outside the town, beggars, wheedlers, vagrants, vagabonds, idlers, and other undesirables' whom the town would otherwise have to support (quoted in C. Davids 1978, 147).

From the end of the seventeenth century the poor were thus increasingly subject to a system of identity registration to prevent them from becoming a burden on the poor relief agencies of the cities in which they were strangers. However, Amsterdam was in permanent need of new blood and absorbed large numbers of poor Dutchmen and – beyond the Republic – foreigners, whom the city could channel towards its colonial endeavours. The Dutch East India Company, or *Vereenigde Oost-Indische Compagnie* (VOC), was especially desperate for men to fill its lower ranks and to serve as sailors or soldiers. It is to the registering of those occupational groups that we will now turn.

[39] There were 108 districts in the eighteenth century. These neighbourhoods played an important role in the years 1580–1650, due to the massive influx of immigrants, but their importance swiftly declined after 1700 (Dorren 1998, 77–78).

[40] The states of Utrecht in 1687, Zeeland in 1705, Overijssel in 1767, and the Estates General acting for Limburg and Brabant in 1792 (Luttenberg 1837, 13–15, 41–42, 49–53).

Registering sailors and soldiers

As we have seen, the Dutch city authorities 'outsourced' the registration of guild members, orphans, and the urban poor, preferring to concentrate on registering burghers. Occasionally magistrates did register the identity of non-burghers as part of a wider urban policy to promote the local economy and out of a concern for public order.

Maritime Dutch cities – and Amsterdam more than any other – often experienced public disturbances on the waterfront, where sailors met to enjoy the delights of life ashore after a long uncomfortable voyage. Carousing led to arguments and brawls. In the seventeenth century, Amsterdam – but also Rotterdam, then a fairly small but growing port – appointed a port sheriff, or *waterschout*, to deal with all forms of disturbance and crime on the waterfront.[41] These included the tendency of sailors to abscond with an advance from the skipper who had hired them, or to show up too late for the work agreed, or else to take up a job on another ship, to the inconvenience of merchants and their skippers. One of the port sheriff's duties was to keep the muster-roll of departing ships' crews, which he was to read aloud after it had been completed. He was also present when the ship returned, when the crew would receive their salary. On the muster-roll the sheriff noted each sailor's surname, first name, place of residence, and the agreed pay. A skipper could use the muster-roll to force a contracted sailor to show up – and if he did not appear the port sheriff could prosecute the sailor for breach of contract. The sheriff would also check to see whether the sailor was still bound by any previous contracts and whether he was still formally engaged elsewhere (van Vooren 1916, 98, 100, 105–106; van Zijverden 1998, 140).

By the eighteenth century muster-rolls had become pre-printed forms on which the port sheriff filled in each sailor's name, rank, age, place of origin, monthly salary, and sometimes the name of the person who had recruited them. All sailors had to sign the muster-roll. On the roll, the port sheriff noted the name of the captain, the ship, its destination, and the date on which the roll had been drawn up.[42] The muster-rolls were kept in the custody of the sheriff, with the skipper being provided a copy.[43]

It was not easy to enforce sailors' compliance with their contracts. In Rotterdam in 1726 the port sheriff became obliged to keep a register of deserters, making it possible to trace recidivists, who were punished more severely than first-time offenders (van Vooren 1916, 106). His position was clearly an important one in

[41] Amsterdam appointed its first port sheriff in 1641; Rotterdam appointed a similar functionary in 1645, who later also became known as the port sheriff (van Zijverden 1998, 137–155; van Vooren 1916, 98–117). The office of port sheriff continued to exist until it was abolished in 1989. By then, its responsibilities were largely restricted to monitoring merchant seamen (van Zijverden 1998, 139–140).

[42] In the nineteenth century the sailors engaged had to produce some means of identification, sign with their names, and appoint a person to stand surety for them (van Zijverden 1998, 143–144).

[43] In Amsterdam muster-rolls have been preserved for the period 1747–1852 (van Zijverden 1998, 147).

the harbours of maritime cities, and illustrates the importance those ports attached to a well-ordered maritime labour market. Indeed, the port sheriff's muster-roll registration was deemed so important that it became an exception to the common pattern of urban magistrates devolving identity registration to third parties as much as possible.

The muster-roll thus played an important role in the recruitment of sailors. It was similarly important when it came to registering soldiers and sailors recruited for the Dutch army and the Dutch East India and West India companies. Clearly, such registration did not take place at the city level, but instead at the level of 'national' organizations. It was also very important to the Dutch Republic as a whole: the Dutch East India Company and the Dutch West India Company (WIC) played a dominant role in establishing and continuing the pattern of Dutch colonial expansion, and given that the Dutch Republic was at war for 105 of the 207 years of its existence, the army was obviously a key feature of the Republic's state apparatus. The muster-rolls were central to registering those who were to fight in wars. Both the VOC and the WIC hired sailors on an impressive scale, but neither utilized the services of the port sheriff, using instead their own mustering administration (van Zijverden 1998, 147). Not much is known about the WIC's administration since most of the relevant records have disappeared, but one presumes it was similar to that of the VOC, on which the WIC was modelled. Much more is known about the VOC's administration and the records it kept.

Registration of sailors by the VOC started at the point of recruitment, when they were superficially examined by a committee of directors and maritime officers. No identification was required. Specialists were examined more strictly. In the case of an engineer, for example, a testimonial concerning his skills could be required. If the applicant was approved, the clerk noted his name, place of birth, rank, and salary. Clerks wrote these data, primarily for salary registration purposes, on muster-rolls, one for each ship. Each voyage thus resulted in a single muster-roll. That roll comprised the principal record relating to the sailors – who were hired for one voyage only.

Sailing with the VOC was a high-risk affair, and many sailors and soldiers failed to survive. Even so, the VOC did not register to whom the salary of a deceased employee should be paid. A sailor or soldier wishing to make sure that any wages owed to him would be paid to his next of kin in the event of his death had to supply them with information on which VOC ship he was sailing with, in what capacity, and under which skipper, and preferably also the date of departure and the expected date of arrival at the ship's destination (van Gelder 1997, 143–144, 147).

In the Dutch army, too, the muster-roll was the central document listing and registering soldiers. Whereas in other states war led to increasing central registration of the soldiers serving in those wars, in the Dutch Republic financial responsibility for the army was and remained divided among its provinces, with each paying a proportion of the costs. In theory, each province had its own *stadholder* responsible for military affairs. In practice, there were at most only two stadholders at any one time. They cooperated closely in military matters, in collaboration with a number of central bodies such as the Council of State. The Republic's army did not centralize the mustering of armies. In fact, the army consisted of companies led by an officer who was responsible for hiring his own soldiers. Sometimes entire regiments and their officers were raised that way. The Estates General or the Council of State drew up contracts with company commanders and paid them a specified sum intended to cover their pay and the costs of recruiting soldiers (Nimwegen 2010, 30–33). The commanders listed the names of their men on muster-rolls. Once everyone had been accounted for, the commissary would seal the muster-rolls and send them to the Council of State, which was responsible for actually paying the soldiers (Nimwegen 2010, 47).[44]

Apparently the central authorities did not see any reason to preserve these lists – more or less complete lists of soldiers have survived only for 1780–1781. By then, these lists had become printed documents on which the company commander noted a soldier's name, the date he was hired, for how long he had been hired, his height, age, place of birth, religion, previous occupation, whether and for how long he had served before, and whether he had a wife and children to look after. This level of information density was unusual, and it is unclear why the central commander wanted to know all this. One surmises that it was connected to attempts by the last two stadholders, William IV and his son William V, to obtain a clearer picture of the state of the military.[45]

From 1749 onwards commanders formally had to report regularly on the conduct of their officers, though there is no trace in the records that they actually did so. It was not until 1772 that William V issued detailed ordinances setting out how officers and their conduct should be registered. These conduct lists were also pre-printed. It was possible to include first names and surnames, current age, place of birth, religion, whether the officer was married and had children, how long he had served in the regiment and in what rank, whether he had previously served in another Dutch or foreign regiment, and for how long, which languages he spoke, whether he was diligent, what skills he had, whether he was of good character, how accomplished he was in military drill, and whether he should be promoted. In the period 1773–1795 such lists were indeed compiled, though not for the entire army, and not for every year. Many of them have been preserved. Their primary purpose seems to have been to allow the stadholder to fill vacancies in such a way that he could advance the careers of diligent officers and pass over those of lesser ability (Zwitzer 1991, 107–108, 208).

[44] Those rolls also noted whether someone was sick, wounded, or on guard, and where they were, so that the muster commissary could inspect and count all the soldiers. He noted particulars for each soldier, such as weaponry, where he came from, and how long he had been with the company.

[45] Zwitzer gives no explanation of why all this information was included (Zwitzer 1991, 46, 179).

The conduct registers of the officers – and perhaps also the detailed lists of common soldiers compiled in the late eighteenth century – were thus late additions to early modern Dutch identity registration. Perhaps in practice they became effective only during the last stadholdership. For most of the Dutch Republic's existence there was only limited registration of army personnel owing to the devolved organizational structure of the army, a peculiarity which reflected that of the Republic as a whole.

Establishing the identities of the criminal underclass

Important as sailors and soldiers were to the Dutch Republic, they enjoyed a bad reputation. Dutch authorities were very distrustful of this vast reservoir of drifting men in the Republic's fleets and armies, and not entirely without reason. Especially in times of war, the difference between a soldier and a criminal was more one of degree than kind – at least in the eyes of the magistrates. This leads us back to the urban magistrates and the way they tried to keep a grip on the criminal underclass of the Dutch Republic.

As we have noted, local magistrates in the Dutch Republic, and, to some extent, the provincial authorities, spent considerable effort in monitoring the lower strata of society. The lowest stratum was regarded as exceptionally prone to criminal activity and could be controlled only with great difficulty, as its members were often itinerant and registered nowhere. A criminal career in the Dutch Republic often involved much travelling. This created problems of prevention and punishment in a society where the judiciary was primarily based locally. Magistrates had to cooperate, with varying degrees of success, to punish wrongdoers drifting from one jurisdiction to another, exacerbated by the age-old practice of punishment by exile. As part of their punishment, criminals were often declared dishonourable. This meant they lost all hope of being granted credit, and of a decent livelihood, in the jurisdiction in which they had been punished. They were usually exiled – imprisonment was rarer – and that more or less forced them to take up a criminal career elsewhere.

Up to, and during, the sixteenth century, punishment sometimes took the form of either corporeal mutilation or branding – depending on the seriousness of the crime. Amputating his ear made it possible for a man best avoided to be easily recognized. It became impossible for him to earn a decent living anywhere. Increasingly, during the sixteenth century, such punishments were thought undesirable, by humanists among others. Corporeal mutilation gradually fell out of use: the last case of a criminal having an ear amputated in Amsterdam was in 1650. A punishment which endured longer involved a cut to the cheek, but it too was not without its opponents: in 1668 some aldermen opposed it on the grounds that one should never deform the face of the culprit. Branding the face had fallen into disuse by the sixteenth century. Another visible mutilation, cutting off a thumb, was recorded in Amsterdam for the last time in 1748, although eighteen years later the sheriff was still requesting its imposition (Spierenburg 1978, 114–115). After 1650, mutilation seems increasingly to have been confined to less visible parts of the body, making it more difficult to recognize a convicted criminal.

Flogging and branding did not fall into disuse, though. The purpose of flogging was not to identify a criminal as such, though the telltale scars on his back certainly required him to keep it covered in later life.[46] Branding was a means of visibly registering a convicted criminal. In the Middle Ages branding had usually been applied to part of the face, to the cheek, or the forehead. By the mid-sixteenth century, shoulder branding became more common. This change from more to less visible branding seems to attest to a growing revulsion against the practice: henceforth, convicts could conceal the brand mark under their clothing. For this reason, prisoners suspected of a certain crime were often physically examined to see if they had been marked earlier. The brand mark could easily be identified as each criminal court had its own branding iron for the purpose. Amsterdam's brand mark consisted of the three St Andrew's crosses that also appeared on the city's coat of arms. A special variant was formed by pressing both sides of a red-hot sword onto the back of the convict, creating an X-shaped scar. Flogging and branding were usually combined, with the flogging preceding the branding. Occasionally, convicts tried to have the brand mark erased: one had his mark 'skinned out' by a physician, another used quicklime. As a result, the judicial authorities distrusted all forms of shoulder scar (Thuijs 2008, 220; Spierenburg 1978, 76–77; Egmond 1993, 27).

The enduring practice of branding enabled magistrates to establish whether a prisoner had been engaged in criminal activities or not. As recidivism was regarded as aggravating the seriousness of an offence, increasing the likelihood of the death penalty being imposed – even for non-capital offences – branding remained important for purposes of identification.

The magistrate was often confronted with suspects from the margins of society, such as gypsies and other vagrants of whom little was known. Interrogation served to establish their name, place of birth, age, sex, place of domicile, marital status, occupation, and, sometimes, also whether they had family (Egmond 1993, 24). Magistrates often recorded the information obtained on the criminal underworld in their files for later use.[47] In the case of grave crimes, the magistrate might conduct a more extensive inquiry and contact other courts, sometimes discovering that this procedure only complicated matters, because several vagrants used the same nickname,[48] a common practice to create identity confusion (Egmond 1993, 26).[49]

[46] Flogging was always done on the bare back (Spierenburg 1978, 75).

[47] See Thuijs (2008, 71), for one particular case.

[48] As was the case with a certain 'Glory of Holland', of which there were two or three around 1718 (Egmond 1993, 25–26).

[49] See also Thuijs (2008, 20–21). It was not uncommon to have a whole set of false names (Thuijs 2008, 22, 31–32, 91).

As a group, gypsies caused magistrates less difficulty when it came to ethnic identity – if only because Dutch early modern authorities routinely combined different groups of travelling people under the catch-all phrase ‘heathens’ or ‘Egyptians’ (L. Lucassen 1990, 13–14, 21). They were characterized by their dress, language, and names. Individually, however, they appear to have been more difficult to identify, due to their habit of adopting names that did not accord with Dutch practice, so creating confusion. Moreover, gypsies in detention seem to have adopted a tactic of identifying themselves and their place of birth, age, relatives, and occupations in different ways the longer they were detained, creating a ‘proliferation of identities’, much to the annoyance and exasperation of Dutch courts. Suspects often changed their names. Jewish naming practices also led to many difficulties, as Jewish vagrants usually had only a first name, using their father’s name as a patronymic – like many Dutch, but in practice they resorted to a much more restricted pool of names. As these were extremely common, it was often hard to distinguish between first names, surnames, nicknames, and aliases (Egmond 1993, 87–90, 112–113).[50]

Having said that, magistrates seem not always to have been overly concerned about the precise identity of a prisoner. At least one historian has claimed that the average court was not interested in actually establishing the identity of the defendant as it was not particularly relevant for determining the sentence (Thuijs 2008, 19). Furthermore, during the Dutch Republic the authorities did in fact maintain a system of centrally registering convicts in the best way available to them: using the branded bodies of convicts as a register.[51]

Other ways to establish identity

Early modern Dutchmen could rely on the ecclesiastical and civil authorities to register and establish their identity. The most important means of doing so have already been discussed, but there were other ways of establishing identity too.

To prevent a single mother and her children falling into poverty, the magistrate, church, and family were keen to establish the identity of the father. Sometimes, the father would acknowledge his paternity in a written statement to that effect, but often this required testimony that the mother and father had had intercourse with one another. In one recorded case, the father was identified because the child had the same hereditary deformity, but such evidence was rare. In normal cases, judges could ask the contending parties to swear an oath. Oaths made by men were considered of greater value than those made by women, but women had another

[50] The problem of identifying gypsies more or less ceased because they had been driven out of the Republic by 1750 (L. Lucassen 1990, 27, 34).

[51] For skin marks as a means of identification see also Groebner (2004, 68–84).

weapon (Haks 1982, 90). When an unmarried woman was in labour, the midwife – almost always appointed by the local authorities and oath-bound[52] – was to ask her who the father was. If she refused to say, the midwife was not permitted to continue to help her. After naming the father, the woman had to swear an oath to the midwife with witnesses present. The declaration by the midwife, confirmed by a notary, carried great weight in the event of a trial. It was not uncommon for fathers to try to persuade the midwife not to ask for the name of the father, or to 'forget' it. More often, however, they tried to persuade the mother not to name, or even to misname, the father, lured by the promise of financial assistance. If the mother did name the father, she was often believed by the judges. In Leiden, for example, in 65 per cent of cases between 1671 and 1795 the mother was proven right, and the father ordered to pay for the upkeep of the child (Haks 1982, 85–86, 90–91; van der Heijden 1998, 123). This practice of swearing on oath the name of the father was abolished by the Code Civil of 1811, though it continued for a time.[53]

The web of sworn midwives could not catch all single mothers. Throughout the early modern age, desperate mothers – or perhaps fathers – left their offspring at the door of the local orphanage. The notes they left with the foundlings may be regarded as a peculiar form of identity registration. Sometimes orphanages maintained books in which the notes found on the foundlings were kept. These notes – often giving names, age, and religion – were pasted onto a page. Sometimes a playing card cut in half had been tied to the note by the person leaving it, so that he or she could reclaim the child at some point using the other half. If they did not, the half playing card remained attached to the foundling register for ever (van Leeuwen 2000a, 64).[54]

Factors shaping identity registration in the Dutch Republic

So far, we have discussed each method of identity registration, its origin and nature, in the early modern Dutch Republic separately. This has allowed us to present a variety of such methods in some detail. We do not want to argue that all these measures originated from a single common source. Nor do we want to claim that they were so closely connected as to have constituted a single system. At the same time, we feel it is fair to conclude that, taken together, the various registration methods discussed above covered almost the entire population of the Dutch Republic at some stage in their life, regardless of whether they were rich, middle-class, or poor; migrant or sedentary; and regardless of their religion. To a large extent,

[52] If she was not, her declaration was taken less seriously (Haks 1982, 91).

[53] A form of 'paternity act' was reintroduced in 1909 (Kok 1991, 37).

[54] See also Wagenaar (2009, 56–59), for examples from the nineteenth century.

the methods of identity registration employed in the Golden Age predated the Reformation, or in some cases – citizenship registers, for example – originated as early as the late Middle Ages. This was the case for the registration of baptisms, marriages and burials, and for the way in which guilds registered the urban male labour force. These registration methods evolved in the early modern era in specific ways relating to the following general factors: the Reformation, the decentralized political structure of the Dutch Republic, growing literacy, and the flowering of a modern economy.

The Reformation had the enduring double effect in the Netherlands of both a separation of secular authority, as exercised by the magistrate, and ecclesiastical authority, as exercised by the church, and a proliferation of ecclesiastical authorities. Henceforth, there could not be a single poor relief agency; there would be many agencies caring for the poorer members of their particular congregation; and the magistrate would need to assume a measure of control and provide care for those poor who for some reason or other the church declined to help. There could no longer be one, Catholic, method of registering life-course changes; instead, we find various registers for Catholics, Calvinists, Lutherans, Jews, and Mennonites. Though this proliferation of registration created problems of uniformity, comprehensiveness, and coordination, that registration was also devolved to smaller units, which were able to monitor more easily what was happening and which usually had a strong interest in vigilance: after all, the well-being – if not the souls – of their fellow believers was at stake.

Lacking a strong central state apparatus, Dutch administration was decentralized in a corporatist fashion.[55] Corporatism is a political system in which government – in the case of the Dutch Republic, mostly urban government – devolves some of its powers to civic associations. Towns had transferred a number of key responsibilities to corporations, the most important of which were the guilds. Those corporations had a considerable degree of autonomy, with their own members, self-government, their own statutes, capital, and income. Their activities were monitored by local government. Guilds, too, were bodies governed by public law and ultimately subject to the authority of the town government, which sometimes also approved their annual accounts. In the event of a dispute with his guild, a guildsman could always appeal to the town government. If rumours of fraud or maladministration were serious enough, the town government would launch an inquiry. This decentralization created problems, notably with regard to migrants, but it also made registration easier in the sense that it took place within the corporation of stakeholders itself – thus saving on state bureaucracy – and with more legitimacy than if left to the state.

[55] Histories of the Dutch Republic include those by Israel (1995), Prak (2005), K. Davids and Lucassen (1995), and de Vries and van der Woude (1997). On corporatism see Prak (1999) and van Nierop (1997).

The modern Dutch economy of the Golden Age created problems with regard to identity registration. A sizeable proportion of the population were highly mobile: though not all came from outside the Dutch Republic, many were at least born in a place other than that in which they lived. To deal with the problems that migration gave rise to, churches requested documents proving confirmation, guilds would require proof of apprenticeship or mastership, and relief agencies and the city authorities would demand letters of surety. The fact that Amsterdam was a key centre in the global network of trade, financial services, and information meant further proof of identity would be required from merchants, skippers, buyers and sellers of bonds and annuities, and the like. The modern economy thus not only needed such documents, it also provided the urban infrastructure to produce them.

It seems a paradox that, equipped with a weak central state and a small bureaucracy, the Dutch Republic succeeded fairly well in supplying its inhabitants with the forms of identity registration they needed, and succeeded fairly well in knowing, when it needed to, who they were. One answer to this apparent paradox might be that in this densely populated, modern, urban economy it was both possible to devolve much of the responsibility for registration to local associations of citizens, and wise to do so.[56] It relieved some of the burden on the administration and the treasury, and it was effective, as citizens took an interest in registration control and were in many cases in the best position to monitor it and uncover fraud. Of course, the lack of a centralized state and a numerically powerful bureaucracy created a myriad of ways in which identity was locally registered and monitored.

Some problems went beyond the level of the community though, notably in the case of the travelling poor, absconding sojourning sailors, and migrating military men. These could have created havoc in key areas of the Dutch national and imperial economy. It is interesting to note that in these cases the usual practice of outsourcing registration to local groups of citizens was supplemented or replaced by supra-local measures and bodies. Perhaps one has to grant the rather diffuse political structure of the Dutch Republic a certain amount of credit for its flexibility.

Epilogue: limits to early modern identity registration

The fact that registration existed does not mean it was either comprehensive or effective, and it is to these points that we will now turn. Of course the mere existence of a register does not imply it was properly kept. Since the late fourteenth century, in the city of Utrecht, for example, those who became burghers had to be registered in the so-called *stedelijk publicatieboek* or *buurspraakboek* ('town publication

[56] There is a nice contrast to be pointed up here between the efficiency of the Dutch devolved system and the ineffectiveness of the German centralized system, according to Fahrmeir (2000).

book' or 'neighbour book'). From 1611 onwards, new burghers first had to pay a fee to the treasurer before being entered in the register. However, though they were registered in the treasury accounts, their names were not always subsequently inscribed in the burgher register, which increasingly became incomplete.[57]

It was not just the magistracy registers that had lacunae; church registers suffered the same fate. In Dordrecht, for example, post-Reformation baptism registration was far from faultless due to the 'growing pains' experienced by the new church: it was not until 1578 that those problems had been adequately resolved. Even afterwards, lacunae remained, due for instance to ministers in some cases delaying and then forgetting to register – thus the baptism of arguably the most famous Dutch statesman, Johan de Witt (1625–1672), went unrecorded.[58]

As registration systems were local, they often differed in content and presentation. In Amsterdam and Leiden, registers were kept of the publication of marriage banns, with names, birthplace, place of residence, and often occupation being recorded. Amsterdam recorded the couple's ages as well. In Utrecht, however, registration was haphazard, at least initially: the marriage registers of the Dutch Reformed church have been preserved only for the years 1590–1595 and again from 1600. Few details were registered: usually only the names of the couple, and sometimes their place of origin. Especially in the case of brides and bridegrooms from the elite, the register often mentions only their name – even the customary designation of whether the bride and bridegroom were widowed was often omitted. Nor was the place of origin usually noted for the many soldiers in Utrecht (Rommes 1998, 53–54).

Other forms of registration showed similar problems. Nijmegen often had problems with river skippers who bought citizenship in order to obtain letters of toll from the city granting them exemption from excises on the River Waal but who did not settle in Nijmegen. From 8 November 1592 those skippers were required to present a *wettelijcke attestatie*, a 'lawful attestation', confirming that they had renounced the citizenship of their place of origin; they were also required to rent and live in a house in Nijmegen. They were to renew their oath and letter of citizenship annually; nevertheless, despite further tightening of the rules,

[57] This may have caused occasional problems for the city's secretaries, but they were presumably aware of the necessity of consulting the treasury accounts. In 1700 a new register was introduced. It was more reliable than the previous one, but names that appeared in the treasury accounts were still sometimes omitted from the new register (Rommes 1998, 45).

[58] It was only from 1635 onwards that baptized children were properly registered. The same applies to Dordrecht's burial registers: they were kept regularly only from the end of the seventeenth century; before that date they were very incomplete. The earliest burial registers from Dordrecht churches date from 1632 and 1636, but in plague years for example only half of deaths were recorded in them (Frijhoff *et al.* 1998, 86–87, 96–98). Something similar happened in Leiden, where during the epidemic of 1669–1670 officials temporarily suspended recording burials due to the overwhelming number of people dying (van Maanen 2005, 45).

problems with skippers evading the requirements were to recur from time to time (Schimmel 1966, 13, 58–60). Another problem in Nijmegen concerned citizenship. Since 1623 one had to be a member of the Dutch Reformed church – or at least not a Catholic or a Jew – in order to obtain burghership rights. Some 'lapsed' Catholics returned to their original faith after acquiring citizenship. For a while, those burghers whose deceit became apparent were subsequently stripped of their citizenship. Eventually, however, the magistracy lost interest in the problem, although the practice seems to have continued (Schimmel 1966, 45–48).[59]

Registration systems also had limits in other respects. Some individuals were economical with the truth. The early modern Dutch authorities relied much on personal oaths.[60] If people were brazen enough to commit perjury, there was often little early modern society could do immediately. For example, despite all the precautions inherent in the system of marriage banns, it proved possible for two Leiden women, Cornelia Gerritsdr van Breugel and Elisabeth Boleyn, who had already lived together for a time, to marry one another. Boleyn moved temporarily to Amsterdam, followed soon afterwards by van Breugel dressed in men's clothes. In 1685 they were married as man and wife in Amsterdam's New Church, where Cornelia used the name Cornelis. They returned to Leiden as husband and wife, but after two and a half years Cornelis decided to revert to being Cornelia and dressed in women's clothes. It was only then that the couple were found out. In 1688 they were exiled from Leiden and forbidden to live together again (Dekker and van de Pol 1989, 83).[61] There were similar cases concerning transvestite women. In one celebrated case a couple lived together for three years without the wife discovering her husband's true sex. All that time, the husband had refused to have sex with his wife. The discovery of her husband's true sex apparently came as a great shock to her (Dekker and van de Pol 1989, 89–90).[62]

In certain walks of life, during the early modern period, men – and women – had ample opportunity to disguise their gender, especially in the army and the fleet, where the Dutch tended not to be too particular about who enlisted. In the Dutch Republic, uneducated young men from the lower classes had few options; the same could be said of young women from those classes. Women sometimes managed to hide their identity – as a person and as a woman – for years on end.

[59] Between 1721 and 1743 this ban ceased to be enforced, and Jews too could henceforth become burghers of Nijmegen. By 1789, it had been effectively abolished (Schimmel 1966, 68, 74, 102). Other eastern Dutch cities too tried to close their gates to anyone who was not Dutch Reformed (Lourens and Lucassen 2000).

[60] Nijmegen is one example. In 1619 all citizens were ordered to personally renew their oath before the burgomasters (Schimmel 1966, 30).

[61] It is not known how this couple managed to fool the authorities. Did they forge the necessary documents? Perhaps those documents were not always actually required.

[62] One such woman, Barbara Adriaens, twice married another woman, once in Amsterdam in 1632 and subsequently in Groningen (Dekker and van de Pol 1989, 84–85).

How often this occurred is impossible to tell,[63] but that it was perhaps not infrequent is attested to by an offhand remark made by the Amsterdam burgomaster and national politician, Nicolaas Cornelisz Witsen, who wrote to a friend: 'but how many examples could I not give of women, who did manly service on our ships, and conducted themselves extraordinarily bravely';[64] he remarked how 'I myself have discovered women dressed as soldiers in our army, and made them change clothes'.[65] The occurrence of women posing as men was certainly common enough for notaries' manuals to treat the question of the validity of instruments drawn up before male witnesses who turned out to be women. Some offenders were so successful in hiding their sex that it was only on the scaffold or on their deathbed that their true sex was discovered. If a man was suspected of being a woman, an array of 'tricks' was available to the authorities to ascertain 'his' true sex: one involved placing a spinning-wheel close to the person: a woman would show an interest, a man would not; another was to throw a ball – in trying to catch it, a woman would spread her legs as if she were wearing a skirt; a third was to scatter peas on the floor – supposedly a man would keep his balance, a woman would not. That women could successfully pose as men may have been partly related to the lack of centralized bureaucracy in the early modern age. When, in the nineteenth century, the Dutch state became ever more bureaucratized, erecting barriers in the form of central registration of all births, marriages, and deaths, military conscription and medical examinations, the phenomenon of transvestite women successfully assuming a male identity disappeared completely (Dekker and van de Pol 1989, 36–37, 65, 127, 130).

When it came to enlisting in the fleet or the army, it was not just women who made use of proxies. Men did too. The rather superficial registration of the identity of sailors and soldiers offered ample opportunity for fraud: one could enlist under a false name, or claim a false place of birth. There were many cases of sailors, esteemed by recruiters for their considerable ability, enlisting under another name, after which a sailor of lesser ability actually showed up to do the work (van Gelder 1997, 49, 145–146; 2003, 177). This problem was apparently sometimes solved, or at least addressed, by the Dutch East India Company, which occasionally registered not just name, place of origin, age, and occupation, but also physical traits, such as the colour of eyes and hair, making it possible to check more closely those who showed up for work.[66] This might have gone some way to solving the

63 Rudolf Dekker and Lotte van de Pol investigated the occurrence of women posing as men in the early modern Dutch Republic and identified 120 individual cases, almost all from the seventeenth and eighteenth centuries (Dekker and van de Pol 1989, 13, 25).

64 '[. . .] maar wat zoude ik al voorbeelden van vrouwen kunnen verhalen, die op onze schepen mannendienst hebben gedaan, en zich bijzonder dapper gedroegen' (Dekker and van de Pol 1989, 12).

65 '[. . .] ikzelve in onze legers vrouwen in soldatenklederen hebbe ontdekt, en van kleding doen veranderen' (Dekker and van de Pol 1989, 12).

66 Personal communication from Matthias van Rossum.

problem of enlistment by proxy, but it certainly did not stop women dressed as men from enlisting. It appears, however, that throughout its existence the VOC never tried to turn this more detailed registration into permanent company policy; name and place of birth remained the only categories of personal information the muster clerks normally registered, though nationality and age were sometimes also asked.[67] The permanent need for VOC hands meant that the company placed as few obstacles as possible in the way of the many hopefuls who applied for the lowly jobs of company sailor and soldier. Having said that, once aboard ship it was often quickly discovered that a sailor was not as experienced as he had claimed to be, and the VOC officers usually punished them by making them work harder. Another danger was that of the proxy issuing at registration a *maandbrief*, a 'monthly letter' to a relative, who stayed in the Republic and collected his salary on his behalf. On his return, the VOC employee being proxied for might discover that his identity fraud had not paid off because the proxy himself had been fraudulent. One could expect little sympathy from the VOC in such cases. Perhaps this is why the problem, though widespread, was never adequately dealt with. A similar problem occurred with company soldiers – able-bodied men with a smattering of superficial military skills proxied for invalids and old men (van Gelder 1997, 145–146, 149; 2003, 177–178).

As with VOC sailors and soldiers, identity fraud was an option for soldiers in the Dutch army. Army contractors often lured away existing soldiers, providing companies with battle-ready soldiers and allowing them to swiftly raise a full-strength unit. The soldiers were then listed on the muster-roll under a false name. This was a problem, as the nominal strength of the army no longer corresponded to its actual strength, and the commanders of the companies from which the frauds had absconded incurred financial loss. To counter this, in 1588 the Estates General decreed that all mustering should take place in the same place on the same day and at the same hour, in order to prevent commanders 'borrowing' each other's soldiers in an attempt to make their companies complete. In 1599 they were also forbidden to mix 'any burghers, peasants, sutlers, freebooters, soldiers from other companies' among their soldiers during the inspection by the muster commissary. During campaigns, the muster commissary ensured that a tally of any losses was made by means of musters, in order to prevent having to pay out more than was necessary for the men actually surviving. In response, company commanders routinely included many more soldiers on the muster-roll than they actually employed, so that they minimized their financial losses. This fraud was extensive, and according to contemporaries the Dutch army was one-third weaker than the payrolls suggested. Though this was not all due to fraud, the stadholder and his staff usually took into account a difference between paper and effective strength of about 25 to 30 per

[67] The procedure *c.* 1669 also involved asking about nationality (van Gelder 1997, 144; Ketting 2002, 66); the procedure *c.* 1752 also involved asking about age (van Gelder 2003, 179). It appears, however, that these extra categories were not listed in the VOC salary records (van Gelder 2003, 491).

cent. The stadholder knew how to respond to the problem. Regardless of all the fraud, in the 1630s and 1640s the Dutch army was three-quarters the size of the French army (60,000 compared with 80,000 men). 'The war effort of the Dutch Republic was impressive indeed' (Nimwegen 2010, 30, 45–48).

Then there was the problem of forged documents. One way or another, documents could be falsified. During the first three decades of the eighteenth century a family gang travelled throughout the Dutch Republic on the pretext of collecting money for a worthy cause. Collectors were required to have a magistrate's permit in order to collect. The family fabricated such permits by turning passports, issued to them under some pretext or other, into fake permits, a strategy made easier by the fact that permits and passports were of similar size. The text, identifying the bearer and signed by an authority, was usually accompanied by some sad story about the misfortune that had befallen certain buildings and places, and a register, in which all those who gave and the amounts they had given could be listed.[68] In 1724, a member of the gang was caught. His passport, issued by a notary in the name of the States of Holland, stated his name and gave the name and signature of the notary. The falsifier had managed to remove the word 'passport' and replace it with the word 'permit'. A tragic story had been written on the back, and several seals attached. With such a false passport bearing the name of a trusted authority, it was easier to persuade victims to give to an apparently worthy cause. Brazenly, the gang went round The Hague and Rotterdam, using their false permits, collecting money at the homes of state dignitaries and local regents, some of whom made considerable donations. Their names, and the amounts given in the register of donators, induced others to give as liberally.[69]

Despite the wide scope for falsifying documents, the registration systems in place in the Dutch Republic could have the desired effect. After all, we know about the collection racket because it repeatedly failed. And even if a person had successfully cleared the hurdles set up by the systems, he was not safe if his antecedents gave rise to suspicion, as will be illustrated, finally, by the case of Dr Kamerling, mentioned in the introduction.

For a while, Kamerling lived the life of a respected burgher, fathering a son with his wife, and taking part in his father-in-law's business. Gradually, however, suspicions emerged about his background. Despite, so he claimed, engaging in a lively correspondence with his 'Rheinberg sister', there was always a reason she could not visit. Furthermore, he became increasingly suspect owing to dubious

[68] See also Chapter 9.

[69] The pseudo-collectors were found out, however, and tried by the same councillors of the Court of Holland at whose door they had collected earlier. Earlier, in 1714, the gang had been caught because the minister of the church in Winschoten, having become mistrustful, had written to Hanau in Hessen to enquire whether the village for which the collection had been held had indeed burned down, and discovered it had not (Thuijs 2008, 89, 91, 185–186).

business dealings. Kamerling always knew how to allay the burgomaster's suspicions, but eventually only his father-in-law and wife still trusted him. Others in the Brouwershaven administration did not. Although they had previously relied on the documents he had submitted, they now secretly enquired about him in Rheinberg and Duisburg. The letters they received in response confirmed their suspicions: Johannes Cato Kamerling was known neither in Rheinberg nor in Duisburg, and the same counted for his sister. He had forged his credentials. Kamerling was subpoenaed and interrogated, but denied lying about his identity, even after the bailiff had shown him the letters from Germany. He was placed under arrest. A committee was sent to Rheinberg and Duisburg. Upon their return the committee confirmed that Kamerling was not known in those cities. It took a few further rounds of interrogation before Kamerling admitted not only to forging his identity but also to previously having tricked various other people out of money. Two surgeons then examined him and discovered he had once been branded. Kamerling then confessed to having been branded in Rotterdam for forging letters of exchange, and revealed his true identity: Abraham Maggaris, born in Middelburg. He was a recidivist, so the punishment was severe, although it could have been worse. On 15 November 1765 he was flogged, branded with the double sword, and condemned to life imprisonment in Middelburg (Viergever 1767, 2: 5–46, 53–54, 57–79, 83–138, 142–144).[70] Despite attempts to escape, Abraham Maggaris, alias Johannes Cato Kamerling, ended his days in prison in Middelburg in 1803. By then the Dutch Republic had predeceased him by eight years.[71]

Kamerling's case serves to illustrate the considerable potential effectiveness of the early modern Dutch 'system' of establishing and registering identity. If the Brouwershaven authorities had been more suspicious of the seals on Kamerling's identity documents, he might have been found out much earlier. The authorities in Rheinberg and Duisburg would have informed Brouwershaven that he was not the person he claimed to be. The Brouwershaven elite may well have realized this – why else would they have consented to the town secretary publishing their version of the whole affair? While their motives in agreeing to publication are not clear, the apologetic tone suggests they were the laughing stock of their peers elsewhere in the Republic.

[70] This recalls the celebrated case of Martin Guerre in sixteenth-century France (Davis 1983). Our story also illustrates Tamar Herzog's central point in Chapter 7 about 'performativity' and registration.
[71] For an impression of the new regulations and the growing means available to register identity in the new era see Welten (2007). The French revolutionary predilection for registration makes it much easier for historians to follow individual lives. For the increasing bureaucratic paperwork required to marry, sometimes leading to people not marrying because they were unable to submit the required papers, see Kok (1991, 54). See also van Eijl and Lucassen (2007) and L. Lucassen (2001, 2002, 2003).

References

Abels, P. H. A. M., K. Goudriaan, N. D. B. Habermehl and J. H. Kompagnie, eds. 2002. *Duizend jaar Gouda: Een stadsgeschiedenis*. Hilversum: Uitgeverij Verloren.

Bos, Sandra Beatrice. 1998. *'Uyt liefde tot malcander': Onderlinge hulpverlening binnen de Noord-Nederlandse gilden in internationaal perspectief (1570–1820)*. Amsterdam: Stichting beheer IISG.

Bots, Hans and Jan Kuys, eds. 2005. *Nijmegen. Geschiedenis van de oudste stad van Nederland. Deel II. Middeleeuwen en Nieuwe Tijd*. Wormer: Inmerc.

Buursma, A. 2009. *'Dese bekommerlijke tijden': armenzorg, armen en armoede in de stad Groningen 1594–1795*. Assen: Van Gorcum.

Davids, C. 1978. 'Migratie te Leiden in de achttiende eeuw. Een onderzoek op grond van de acten van cautie.' In *Een stad in achteruitgang: sociaal-historische studies over Leiden in de achttiende eeuw*, ed. Herman A. Diederiks, D. J. Noordam and C. A. Davids. Leiden: Rijksuniversiteit, 146–192.

Davids, Karel and Jan Lucassen, eds. 1995. *A Miracle Mirrored: The Dutch Republic in European Perspective*. Cambridge: Cambridge University Press.

Davis, Natalie Zemon. 1983. *The Return of Martin Guerre*. Cambridge, MA: Harvard University Press.

Dekker, Rudolf and Lotte van de Pol, eds. 1989. *Vrouwen in mannenkleren: de geschiedenis van een tegendraadse traditie Europa, 1500–1800*. Amsterdam: Wereldbibliotheek.

Dorren, Gabrielle. 1998. *Het soet vergaren: Haarlems buurtleven in de zeventiende eeuw*. Haarlem: Arcadia.

—— 2001. *Eenheid en verscheidenheid: de burgers van Haarlem in de Gouden Eeuw*. Amsterdam: Prometheus/Bert Bakker.

van Eeghen, I. H. 1951. *Archief van de Gilden en het brouwerscollege*. Amsterdam: Stadsarchief.

Egmond, Florike. 1993. *Underworlds: Organized Crime in the Netherlands 1650–1800*. Cambridge: Polity Press.

van Eijl, Corrie and Leo Lucassen. 2007. 'Holland Beyond the Borders: Emigration and the Dutch State, 1850–1940.' In *Citizenship and Those Who Leave: The Politics of Emigration and Expatriation*, ed. Nancy L. Green and François Weil. Urbana: University of Illinois Press, 156–175.

Faber, J. A. and Marco H. D. van Leeuwen. 1987. *Amsterdamse katholieke bedeelden, 1750–1850: een gezinsreconstructie*. Amsterdam: Historisch Seminarium van de Universiteit van Amsterdam.

—— 1991. 'Les assistés catholiques d'Amsterdam, 1750–1850: un exemple d'application particulière de la méthode de reconstitution des familles', trans. J. P. Bardet. *Annales de démographie historique* 23: 239–253.

Fahrmeir, Andreas. 2000. *Citizens and Aliens: Foreigners and the Law in Britain and the German States, 1789–1870*. New York: Berghahn Books.

Frijhoff, Willem, Hubert P. H. Nusteling and Marijke Spies, eds. 1998. *Geschiedenis van Dordrecht van 1572 tot 1813: Deel II*. Hilversum: Uitgeverij Verloren.

Frijhoff, Willem, Maarten Roy Prak and Marijke Carasso-Kok, eds. 2004. *Geschiedenis van Amsterdam: Centrum van de wereld 1578–1650*. Amsterdam: SUN.

van Gelder, Roelof. 1997. *Het Oost-Indisch avontuur: Duitsers in dienst van de VOC (1600–1800)*. Amsterdam: SUN.

—— 2003. *Naporra's omweg: het leven van een VOC-matroos (1731–1793)*. Amsterdam: Atlas.

Gras, H. 1989. *Op de grens van het bestaan: armen en armenzorg in Drenthe 1700–1800*. Zuidwolde: Stichting Het Drentse Boek.

Groebner, Valentin. 2004. *Der Schein der Person: Steckbrief, Ausweis und Kontrolle im Europa des Mittelalters*. Munich: C. H. Beck.

Hagoort, L. 2010. 'Inleiding op de collectie doop-, trouw- en begraafboeken te Amsterdam.' In *Archiefinventaris Archief van de Burgerlijke Stand; Doop-, trouw- en begraafboeken van Amsterdam*. Amsterdam: Stadsarchief, 1–15.

Haks, Donald. 1982. *Huwelijk en gezin in Holland in de 17de en 18de eeuw: processtukken en moralisten over aspecten van het laat 17de- en 18de-eeuwse Gezinsleven*. Assen: Van Gorcum.

van der Heijden, Manon. 1998. *Huwelijk in Holland: stedelijke rechtspraak en kerkelijke tucht, 1550–1700*. Amsterdam: Bert Bakker.

Higgs, E. 2004. *Information State in England: The Central Collection of Information on Citizens, 1500–2000*. Basingstoke: Palgrave Macmillan.

ten Hove, J. 2005. *Geschiedenis van Zwolle*. Zwolle: Historisch Centrum Overijssel: Waanders.

Israel, Jonathan Irvine. 1995. *The Dutch Republic: Its Rise, Greatness, and Fall, 1477–1806*. Oxford: Oxford University Press.

Ketting, Herman. 2002. *Leven, werk en rebellie aan boord van Oost-Indiëvaarders (1595–±1650)*. Amsterdam: Aksant.

Kok, Jan. 1991. *Langs verboden wegen: de achtergronden van buitenechtelijke geboorten in Noord-Holland, 1812–1914*. Hilversum: Uitgeverij Verloren.

Kretzschmar, L. P. E. 2010. *Archiefinventaris 5004. Archief van de Weeskamer; Begraafregisters*. Amsterdam: Stadsarchief.

Kuijpers, Erika. 2005. *Migrantenstad: immigratie en sociale verhoudingen in 17e-eeuws Amsterdam*. Hilversum: Uitgeverij Verloren.

van Leeuwen, Marco H. D. 2000a. *De rijke Republiek. Gilden, assuradeurs en armenzorg 1500-1800*. In Jacques van Gerwen and Marco H. D. van Leeuwen, *Zoeken naar zekerheid. Risico's, preventie, verzekeringen en andere zekerheidsregelingen in Nederland 1500-2000*. Amsterdam/The Hague, vol. I.

—— 2000b. *The Logic of Charity: Amsterdam, 1800–50*. New York: Palgrave Macmillan.

—— 2011. 'Guilds and Middle-Class Welfare, 1550–1800: Provisions for Burial, Sickness, Old Age, and Widowhood.' *Economic History Review*. http://onlinelibrary.wiley.com/doi/10.1111/j.1468-0289.2011.00602.x/abstract.

—— 2012. 'Overrun by Hungry Hordes? Migrants' Entitlements to Poor Relief in the Netherlands, 16th–20th Centuries.' In *Migration, Settlement and Belonging in Europe, 1500–2000: Comparative Perspective*, ed. S. Hindle and A. Winter. New York: Berghahn.

Lourens, Piet and Jan Lucassen. 1998. 'Ambachtsgilden binnen een handelskapitalistische stad: aanzetten voor een analyse van Amsterdam ca. 1700.' *NEHA-Jaarboek voor economische, bedrijfs- en techniekgeschiedenis* 61: 121–162.

—— 2000. 'Zunftlandschaften in den Niederlanden und im benachbarten Deutschland.' In *Zunftlandschaften in Deutschland und den Niederlanden im Vergleich: Kolloquium der*

Historischen Kommission für Westfalen am 6. und 7. November 1997 auf Haus Welbergen, ed. Wilfried Reininghaus. Münster: Aschendorff, 11–43.

Lucassen, Jan. 1994. 'The Netherlands, the Dutch and Long-Distance Migration, in the Late Sixteenth to Early Nineteenth Centuries.' In *Europeans on the Move: Studies on European Migration, 1500–1800*, ed. Nicholas P. Canny. Oxford: Clarendon Press, 153–191.

Lucassen, Leo. 1990. *En men noemde hen zigeuners: de geschiedenis van Kaldarasch, Ursari, Lowara en Sinti in Nederland, 1750–1944*. Amsterdam: Stichting beheer IISG.

—— 2001. 'A Many Headed Monster: The Evolution of the Passport System in the Netherlands and Germany in the Long Nineteenth Century.' In *Documenting Individual Identity: The Development of State Practices in the Modern World*, ed. Jane Caplan and John C. Torpey. Princeton, NJ: Princeton University Press, 235–255.

—— 2002. 'Administrative into Social Control: The Aliens Police and Foreign Female Servants in the Netherlands, 1918–1940.' *Social History* 27: 327–342.

—— 2003. 'Revolutionaries into Beggars: Alien Policies in the Netherlands 1814–1914.' In *Migration Control in the North Atlantic World: The Evolution of State Practices in Europe and the United States from the French Revolution to the Inter-War Period*, ed. Andreas Fahrmeir, Olivier Faron and Patrick Weil. New York: Berghahn Books, 178–191.

Luttenberg, G. 1837. *Vervolg op het Groot Plakkaatboek of verzameling van wetten betrekkelijk het openbaar bestuur in de Nederlanden. Armwezen*. Zwolle: n.p.

van Maanen, R. C. J. 2005. *Leiden: De geschiedenis van een Hollandse stad. Deel II. 1574–1795*. Leiden: Stichting Geschiedschrijving Leiden.

N.N. 1726. *Amsterdamsche Secretary, bestaande in formulieren van schepenen-kennissen, Quytscheldingen, Schat-brieven, en andere, die gewoonlijk daar gebruikt worden*. Amsterdam: n.p.

van Nederveen Meerkerk, Elise and Griet Vermeesch. 2010. 'Reforming Outdoor Relief: Changes in Urban Provisions for the Poor in the Northern and Southern Low Countries (c. 1500–1800).' In *Serving the Urban Community: The Rise of Public Facilities in the Low Countries*, ed. Manon van der Heijden, Elise van Nederveen Meerkerk, Griet Vermeesch and Martijn van der Burg. Amsterdam: Askant, 135–154.

van Nierop, Henk. 1997. 'Popular Participation in Politics in the Dutch Republic.' In *Resistance, Representation, and Community*, ed. Peter Blickle. Oxford: European Science Foundation, Clarendon Press, 272–290.

Nimwegen, Olaf van. 2010. *The Dutch Army and the Military Revolutions, 1588–1688*. Woodbridge: Boydell & Brewer.

Prak, M. 1998. 'Armenzorg 1500–1800.' In *Studies over zekerheidsarrangementen: risico's, risicobestrijding en verzekeringen in Nederland vanaf de Middeleeuwen*, ed. J. L. J. M. van Gerwen and Marco H. D. van Leeuwen. The Hague: Verbond van Verzekeraars/NEHA, 49–90.

—— 1999. *Republikeinse veelheid, democratisch enkelvoud: sociale verandering in het Revolutietijdvak, 's-Hertogenbosch 1770–1820*. Nijmegen: SUN.

—— 2005. *The Dutch Republic in the Seventeenth Century: The Golden Age*. Cambridge: Cambridge University Press.

Rommes, Ronald Nicolaas Johannes. 1998. *Oost, west, Utrecht best?: driehonderd jaar migratie en migranten in de stad Utrecht (begin 16e–begin 19e eeuw)*. Amsterdam: Stichting Amsterdamse Historische Reeks.

Schimmel, Johannes Andreas. 1966. *Burgerrecht te Nijmegen, 1592–1810: geschiedenis van de verlening en burgerlijst*. Tilburg: Stichting Zuidelijk Historisch Contact.

Schoor, Arie van der. 1999. *Stad in aanwas: geschiedenis van Rotterdam tot 1813*. Zwolle: Waanders.

Spaans, Joke. 1997. *Armenzorg in Friesland 1500–1800: publieke zorg en particuliere liefdadigheid in zes Friese steden Leeuwarden, Bolsward, Franeker, Sneek, Dokkum en Harlingen*. Hilversum: Uitgeverij Verloren.

Spierenburg, Pieter. 1978. 'Judicial Violence in the Dutch Republic: Corporal Punishment, Executions and Torture in Amsterdam 1650–1750.' Ph.D. dissertation, Amsterdam University.

Thuijs, Franciscus. 2008. *De ware Jaco: Jacob Frederik Muller, alias Jaco (1690–1718), zijn criminele wereld, zijn berechting en zijn leven na de dood*. Hilversum: Verloren.

Viergever, Daniel. 1766. *De schyndeugd op het tweede schavot of Waaragtig verhaal hoe zeeker geschavotteerden deugniet en rasphuis-boef zich uitgevende onder de verdichte naam van Johan Cato Kamerling voor een doctor in de geneeskunde . . . het zoverre gebragt heeft, . . .*, vol. 1. Zierikzee.

—— 1767. *De schyndeugd op het tweede schavot of Waaragtig verhaal hoe zeeker geschavotteerden deugniet en rasphuis-boef zich uitgevende onder de verdichte naam van Johan Cato Kamerling voor een doctor in de geneeskunde . . . het zoverre gebragt heeft, . . .*, vol. 2. Zierikzee.

van der Vlis, Ingrid. 2001. *Leven in armoede: Delftse bedeelden in de zeventiende eeuw*. Amsterdam: Prometheus/Bert Bakker.

van Vooren, P. 1916. 'De Rotterdamsche waterschout.' *Rotterdams Jaarboekje 1916*, 98–117.

van Voorst van Beest, C. W. 1955. *De katholieke armenzorg te Rotterdam in de 17e en de 18e eeuw*. The Hague: Excelsior.

Vos, A. and J. Bosmans. 1997. *'s-Hertogenbosch: de geschiedenis van een Brabantse stad 1629–1990*. Zwolle: Waanders.

de Vries, Jan and A. M. van der Woude. 1997. *The First Modern Economy: Success, Failure, and Perseverance of the Dutch Economy, 1500–1815*. Cambridge: Cambridge University Press.

Wagenaar, Lodewijk. 2009. *In het Weeshuis: de zorg voor de Burgerwezen van Amsterdam 1580–1960*. Bussum: Uitgeverij, Thoth.

Welten, J. 2007. *In dienst voor Napoleons Europese droom: de verstoring van de plattelandssamenleving in Weert*. Leuven: Davidsfonds.

Wijnaendts van Resandt, Willem and Jan Gerard Jakob Booma. 1998. *Repertorium DTB: Globaal overzicht van de nederlandse doop-, trouw- en begraafregisters e.d. van voor de invoering van de burgerlijke Stand*. The Hague: Centraal Bureau voor Genealogie.

van Wijngaarden, Hilde. 2000. *Zorg voor de kost: armenzorg, arbeid en onderlinge hulp in Zwolle, 1650–1700*. Amsterdam: Prometheus/Bert Bakker.

Wijsenbeek, Thera, ed. 2005. *Den Haag: geschiedenis van de stad*, vol. 2. Zwolle: Waanders.

van Zijverden, Jan. 1998. 'Het bevolkingsregister voor de scheepsbewoners: de waterschout van Amsterdam en de monsterrol.' *Jaarboek Centraal Bureau voor Genealogie* 52: 137–155.

Zwitzer, H. L. 1991. *'De militie van den staat': het leger van de Republiek der Verenigde Nederlanden*. Amsterdam: Van Soeren.

9

The Identity Thieves of the Indian Ocean: Forgery, Fraud and the Origins of South African Immigration Control, 1890s–1920s

ANDREW MACDONALD

> They are quite rude and great fools in the Colony but they consider the man as their friend who wishes them bribes. Now the man landed himself in the colony by giving bribes is enjoying before your bloody eyes, but you bloody fool cannot do anything else to him.
>
> Anonymous note found in Durban Immigration Offices, 1910

> The answering of questions and the putting them down in writing are two different things.
>
> Abdul Cadir, 1914

> Is there any use in keeping a register at all then? The government has spent thousands of pounds in compiling the registers. Why not burn them along with the Registers of Birth and Deaths and the Mining Commissioners and the Deeds Office Registers?
>
> Montfort Chamney, 1914

Introduction

IN MID-1948, WHILE MOST SOUTH AFRICANS were digesting news of the National Party's election triumph, the Union capital witnessed seven short exchanges of gunfire (Chief Inspector, South African Police, 1948). Spread out over six months, they happened variously at a football field, at a Marabastad house, at the Coronation Café and near the old Barracks. Involved was an off-duty bureaucrat named P. J. L. Otto in a borrowed Studebaker. Also involved were a shop assistant called Nkosi, the driver Singh, the gangster Bonny Rocker, the silk-merchant Akoob, and a teenager called Naidoo. These now barely remembered confrontations were score-settling fights over the betrayal of a touting syndicate that linked the Immigration Office at Pretoria with Indian migrants in Mozambique and India. What follows traces the story of subversive networks working within the department – networks that took root a half-century earlier.

Proceedings of the British Academy **182**, 253–276.

This chapter is also about the conjuring of a documentary system for the exclusion of 'undesirable' migrants in the early twentieth century. Although South Africa's most numerous long-distance migrants were 'tropical Africans' (Crush *et al.* 1991), Indian travellers became the most direct object of exclusion. Yet, prior to around 1900 policy makers had nothing quite fit for purpose. Such documentary systems as did exist had functioned to import, immobilize or channel African, Asian and even British labour within certain districts (Bull 1991; Breckenridge 2008). Something more restrictive had to actively and urgently be brought into being. Policy makers in each of the colonies settled on compulsory registration for resident 'Asiatics' – those who did not or could not register were deemed prohibited immigrants (Huttenback 1976; Bradlow 1978; Bhana and Brain 1990; Klaaren 2004; Peberdy 2008). Whilst these residence permits were administered separately across the colonies, they worked in a similar fashion: any Asian wishing to temporarily depart from South Africa required a permit if he hoped to return at a later date. This was a means to paralyse and limit the circular migration common among members of South Asian diasporas. The requirements for this permit were stringent: several years' residence, with established business and/or property interests. Such permits were 'routinely denied' (Dhupelia-Mesthrie 2009b, 4). Yet if this is now well-trodden ground since Huttenback's first study, this chapter explores how this formidable system of exclusion could be deflected and even appropriated by semi-official touts, while keeping one eye on the onerous, repressive and ultimately dangerous features of an exclusionary border regime.

As will be demonstrated here, there was little that was straightforward about this process. Thinking of conjuring in its alternative sense, registry files could also be made to disappear and reappear. A documentation regime that was both onerous and inadequately supervised attracted profit-seeking touts – the latter flourished in colonial contexts which lacked the organic, long-standing and pastoral forms of local government described in some other chapters. Through an expansive economy of false permits in the two decades after 1900, official identity in the southwestern Indian Ocean was imposed, appropriated, bought, stolen and lost. Annually, cases of known official impostors averaged in the mid-hundreds, perhaps occasionally reaching a thousand. But the precise number is less important than the panic that touting provoked amongst officials and migrant leaders.

The system discussed here thus contrasts rather than corresponds with those described in many of the other contributions in this volume. It emerged out of South Africa's exceptional demographic circumstances: designed by and for the protection of a numerically insecure white settler population against an ethnically alien population with sophisticated networks of regional migration. Yet Indian migrants were still a relatively small, confined and easily identifiable group, and officials were not faced with the challenges of registering a large internal citizenry. Administrators freely admitted their desire to limit claims on entry. Simply put, getting a certificate as proof of registration was to be made as *difficult* as possible.

With such narrow aims, there were thus no pretensions to creating a registry for the expanded purposes of welfare provision, incorporation into wider religious, legal or political orders, or even for military conscription or labour stimulation. On the surface, then, this registry generated very little social appeal for those who were subject to it. While this chapter explores how bureaucratic violence could be deflected, it is not an attempt to identify redemptive features or to cast it as something other than repressive and dangerous.

Nevertheless, what follows highlights three key processes in the making of South African international borders. The first is that human agents have a habit of marching out of tune with even the most rigorous, repressive registration regimes. A kind of value attached to the residence permits (sometimes termed 'certificates of domicile' or 'certificates of identity') because this document secured cross-border movement and facilitated trade, property accumulation, employment and inheritance, even if it did not offer any formal political citizenship. I take inspiration from Sadiq's notion of 'documentary citizenship', where unwanted immigrants devise novel pathways to a functional form of citizenship through an eclectic variety of paper forms, regardless of their legality (Sadiq 2010). The second related process concerns the forces of fraud and manipulation inherent in all registration systems. I give some historical depth to Ross Anderson's work which illustrates human elements and insider subversion within secure systems. 'Implementation blunders and ramshackle administration' afford great opportunity to sophisticated criminal networks, which are drawn to valuable record sets (Anderson 1993, 215–277). This qualifies Sadiq's position: reliance on profit-turning criminal syndicates for fake documents brings its own set of problems and may not be as liberating as Sadiq hopes. Finally, the phenomenon of touting discussed here shows that an 'informal economy' worked even *within* bureaucratic spaces – usually considered the quintessence of formality. As has been shown elsewhere, gatekeeping officials in the colonial world worked less to restrict traffic than to profit from it – the bureaucracy rent by rivalry, patronage and fragility as a consequence (Cooper 2002, 156–190; Bayart 1999, 32–48).

Migration in the southwest Indian Ocean to 1897

Transoceanic, independent merchant migration off the eastern coast of southern Africa was largely the preserve of South Asians. By the early twentieth century there were around 250,000 such individuals involved in trade and finance operating globally (Markowitz 2008, 220–249). Of these around 40,000 were active in the southwest Indian Ocean, which may be defined as an economic sphere encompassing Mauritius, Reunion, Madagascar, Kenya, Tanganyika, the Rhodesias, Nyasaland, Portuguese East Africa, Zanzibar and South Africa (where 12,000 had interests by 1921). Overwhelmingly male, traders and their employees tended to come from the Patidar, Lohana, Bhatia, Memon and Khoja (Ismaili and Itn'ashari) castes of the Kutch, Kathiawar and Surat coasts of Gujarat. A minority were Chettiars from Tamil Nadu, Konkanis from coastal Maharashtra, and Bhaibands from landlocked Hyderabad. For a variety of debated reasons – trade liberalization, ecological stress on the subcontinent, new-found mercantile energy abroad, colonial neglect or, conversely, encouragement – this migration had accelerated rapidly in the second half of the nineteenth century.

Until the late nineteenth century, Asian migrants travelling to the southwestern Indian Ocean did so through their insertion into diasporic family trading units (Morrell and Padayachee 1991; Vahed 2005; JESHO 2007). In response to hostile European imperial monopolies and competitive local rivalries, these 'families' engaged in a defensive extension of kinship, entered into strategic partnerships and recruited a wide range of commercial, domestic and spiritual staff from trusted pools. In this context, long-distance migration entailed relations of personal dependence, patronage and marriage, as well as access to credit, information and religious sanction provided by the 'big men' of the transnational firms. Even those who moved within the more formal structures of empire, such as indenture or the civil service, did so through *sirdar*, kin-based networks of information, recruitment and remittance (Carter 1995). This decentralized, patrimonial system of managing mobility came under threat in the late nineteenth century.

In southern Africa of the 1880s, Asians had become well represented, whether as plantation workers, 'colonial-born' free Indians, 'passenger' merchants, or something in between (Dhupelia-Mesthrie 2009a). Settler associations took great issue with urban Asian settlement (Huttenback 1976; Martens 2006; Lake and Reynolds 2008). The associations pathologized Asian settlers and argued that they undercut white trade and reduced domestic 'standards of civilization' in European homes. This argument, familiar across the Anglosphere, was taken up by the colonial intelligentsia who used the press to push law-makers to target Asian commercial, political and residential interests. These pressures reached critical mass in Natal, in 1897, when the region's first Immigration Restriction Act was passed. The major technology of exclusion was a European language 'dictation test' to sidestep an imperial veto on 'class legislation'. This was followed by similar enactments in the Cape, Orange Free State and the Transvaal over the next decade, which extended immigration restriction to poor, diseased or criminal Europeans.

These were consolidated in the 1913 Aliens Act after the colonies unified into an independent political entity of South Africa (Peberdy 2008). That year, all Asians and 'coloured persons' (excepting African labourers) were made inadmissible on account of their ethnicity. They had to face a uniformed officer, and an interrogation in an unfamiliar language, and offer their finger impressions, on pain of arrest, detention or deportation. Perhaps the most significant development over this decade was the growth of massive archives in which all Asian immigrants were catalogued. In theory, each ever-fattening, numbered file became a repository of photographs, fingerprints, physical descriptions – a raft of biographical data and supporting documentation (Dhupelia-Mesthrie 2011). This infrastructure was managed through regional immigration departments, headed by a Principal Immigration Officer in each province. The South African example – on the surface of things a quintessential example of a state project to achieve legibility, surveillance and the repressive immobilization of migrants (Scott 1998; Caplan and Torpey 2001) – provided the inspiration for similar developments in the Rhodesias and Portuguese East Africa.

Making heuristic use of Ann Stoler's recent discussion of 'epistemic anxieties' within colonial governmentality, and using a wider range of sources than Dhupelia-Mesthrie's important studies on the Indian immigration archive at the Cape, what follows demonstrates how this immigration bureaucracy was, in fact, profoundly unstable from within (Stoler 2009). Taking the anti-Indian immigration administration as a starting- rather than an end-point, I consider the material consequences and opportunities for accumulation that such a bottle-necked, sometimes disintegrating registration system presented to colonial subjects, be they Asians or the generally underpaid white staffers on the lower rungs of the bureaucracy. Thus what follows is less about the politics underpinning exclusion and more about the praxis of an embattled bureaucracy.

Permits, permit markets, and reform, 1897–1906

Archival troubles first developed in Natal during 1897–1899. Widespread support for total restriction encountered, almost immediately, major difficulties. The 'literacy test' led to the proliferation of 'certificates of ability'. International commerce had to be accommodated by a variety of 'embarkation permits' for short-term visitors. Visiting and 'transit' passes were urgently produced in an attempt to regulate the refugee crisis during the war. The lack of detention and deportation infrastructure meant 'temporary permits' were awarded to prohibited arrivals and numerous 'deserving cases'. Certificates of exemption were given to priests, teachers, bookmakers, and those 'well-known' to Europeans. Entry also became possible through various letters of permission signed by colonial civil servants. Most importantly, successful legal challenges for the rights of resident Indians led to a 'Certificate of Domicile' (MacDonald 2007: 129–145).

After the war, officials across the South African colonies continued to see these kinds of permits as the best way of resolving multiple pressures. Increased migration intensified settler calls for restriction in the Transvaal and the Cape, whilst Indians continued to contest prohibition orders through politically and legally articulate leadership. In Transvaal, where the tension was most acute, policy makers established a full-time Permit Office, issuing 'registration certificates' to pre-war residents only, interviewing applicants on a case-by-case basis. Residence certificates became part of the Cape's new 1902 law and, in Natal, were ratified in a 1903 amendment. Besides their sheer variation, the problem with these early permits was that they were issued as stand-alone documents, were not recorded in any formal index, and identification information was scant. The system was widely decentralized and individual magistrates had very uneven interest in, and resources for, enquiries into claims; letters of reference became notoriously untrustworthy (Natal Principal Immigration Officer (hereafter N-PIO) 1897, 1902a, 1902b, 6, 1903a, 1903b; Cape Principal Immigration Officer (hereafter C-PIO) 1904, 17–18, 1905, 6; Transvaal Principal Immigration Officer (hereafter T-PIO) 1905a, 1905b, 1905c).

In the epistemic void created by state incapacity, an extensive economy in residence certificates evolved, linking the ports of the Indian Ocean. Transactions took place principally in Lourenço Marques, Beira, Zanzibar, Mombasa, Mauritius, Bombay, Madras and Calcutta. The main drivers of this were the Indian family merchant houses. That this was so was a function of the relative familiarity with paper regimes, colonial and otherwise. Indian merchants had long been entangled with structures of colonial power in the western Indian Ocean, often taking on commercial and political risk on the imperial frontier on behalf of European powers (Oishi 2007). Through this they had become adept at negotiating with gatekeepers, appropriating tokens of citizenship, operating with licensing and banking systems to secure their vested interests. The residence certificate in South Africa was simply one amongst many paper forms necessary for business. And as Chapters 11 and 13 in this volume demonstrate, registration was an important component of political and economic cultures both in the Indian subcontinent and in Muslim Africa through which the Indian merchant houses moved. Registering accounts, taxes, rents, and court cases had been essential for decades, even centuries, prior to the colonial state's elaboration of extensive systems of permits, registers and identification for vital events (Singha 2000; and see Chapters 11 and 13 in this volume). The merchant houses were more than competent in understanding the workings and significance of the South African migration regime.

There were essentially two ways for documents to enter the market (N-PIO 1902c, 1902d, 1902e, 1903a, 18, 1903b, 1904, 1905a, 1905b, 11, 1906a, 1906b, 1910, 1912; Governor-General 1906). The most common required a legitimately resident Indian to apply in South Africa for his papers. This could be done multiple times with different magistrates. Once obtained, the documents were then posted, smuggled or simply carried out of South Africa by accomplices. These documents might get sent direct to 'clients' who were personally known to the sender, but as the market became more complex, they were sent to 'clearing houses'. These were often in stores, hotels, cafés and brothels in the aforementioned ports. Skilled brokers facilitated this collection and distribution of residence certificates. Sub-agents actively solicited business by making door-to-door visits in Indian villages and calling on individuals who were known to be considering a move. Once a residence certificate was sold, the buyer would then travel to South Africa and simply impersonate the registered holder since there was little on the document itself to conclusively prove identity.

The certificates gradually gained in monetary value. These brokerage houses became more sophisticated – where once they might merely have acted as exchange marketplaces, they diversified into the altering and endorsement of certificates (the going rate was about £5 per document). With a certificate came some rudimentary coaching in what to expect from South African immigration officials, the kind of questions one might be expected to answer, and some basic topographical and social knowledge of the destination. Some migrants arrived with multiple certificates as a form of insurance against theft; in some extreme cases impersonation required self-mutilation so that bodily scars might tally.

The second tactic was slightly more complex and required more coordination. This involved the intending migrant applying for his own domicile certificate (as opposed to buying one), but by purchasing false reference letters, testimonials, affidavits, oaths and signatures to accompany the application. These testimonials secured and proved fictitious family relationships; friends and colleagues were entered as sons or fathers (and less commonly, as wives or daughters). Other testimonials confirmed that Indian migrants were Cape Malays or Mauritian, both of whom enjoyed, at this stage, exemption from anti-Indian laws. Some testimonials simply confirmed long-term residency but stated that original certificates were lost or stolen. Permit officers had no way of proving otherwise. Testimonials to one's identity from magistrates in India were popular. It was 'extremely easy' for men to make up family relationships as local magistrates had no way of knowing when the traveller had come 'from hundreds of miles up-country' (Governor-General 1906). Those offering such testimonial services to migrants were up to date on the laws and legal situation of Indians. They coordinated paid witnesses – elite Indian merchants and interpreters and white traders or lawyers were most valued. With increased professionalism came more painstaking attention to detail. Sellers of testimonials were careful to equip themselves with the right kind of paper and were fluent in the particular phraseology of the bureaucracy.

The extent of fraudulent documentation was hard to quantify. Department officials relied on rumour and hearsay, learning of ringmasters and syndicates through tip-offs. These came from several sources: from within the competitive permit underworld; from legitimate Indians fearing the repercussions of criminality; from political and commercial rivalries amongst Indian traders, who used the immigration department to thwart one another's ambitions. Yet what officials did know was enough to alarm them. In post-war Durban, with the PIO feeling 'outwitted all the time' and that the system was 'evaded over and over again in many directions', officials confiscated just under a thousand fraudulent certificates after 1903 (N-PIO 1902b, 6, 1905b). Given that each certificate could have been put to use multiple times, that figure gave only an indication of the actual number of illegal border crossings. In 1904, the Cape PIO felt the residence certificates were so unreliable that the office stopped using them as a primary means of identification. The Johannesburg office noted that false documents were 'very common' and 'a large number of Asiatics are coming in, or attempting to come in, on the faith of the permits bought, stolen or loaned'. Records for the first six months in 1906 showed that almost 300 official impostors were *known* to have entered the Transvaal (Governor-General 1906, annex 5). By 1906, an operator in South African certificates working between Bombay and Durban had over 500 clients on his waiting list (Governor-General 1906). A fuller investigation in Durban found sixteen traders in identity, turning an average annual profit of £400 each. On the other side of the ocean, police believed that 'there cannot be a suspicion of doubt that a [residence] permit market thrives' in Bombay (Governor-General 1906). Although not every migrant leaving India had false documentation, these quantifications were enough to send administrators into acute panic.

By 1906 the crisis had reached higher offices of state. The key thinker on the issue was Lionel Curtis, then Assistant Colonial Secretary and at the beginning of an influential career in late imperial politics. He met with senior administrators and police authorities and reflected on matters in a definitive thirty-page statement (Curtis 1906). Curtis began with a theoretical justification of restrictive border controls and tried to reconcile his 'odious duty' with imperial liberalism and colonial developmentalism. Strictly limiting Indians' rights of movement to only pre-war residents would, he argued, protect white jobs in the 'higher duties' of industry, commerce and government. This would, indirectly, protect the 'aboriginal races' who remained in the government's paternal custody. Completing this harmony, the border system would protect the prosperity of South Africa in the wider imperial economy. Despite the existing problems of the residence certificate system, he retained an abiding faith in its utility to give teeth to his philosophy and, however unpleasant, secure a *just* arrangement. What mattered was that a far more rigorous system of identification should prevail than the willy-nilly efforts thus far. The post-war residence certificate regime in the South African colonies had floundered because no serious thought had been given to keeping adequate track of the identity of applicants and holders of documents; the key was proper record-keeping. It is to the technical and managerial aspects that we turn here, leaving to one side the implications of Asian restriction with respect to organized politics (which oscillated between moments of accommodation and radicalization within South African Indian communities) and struggles within the home (for these, see Swan 1987; Freund 1995; Vahed 1997; Desai and Vahed 2007).

Curtis gave life to his archival fantasy. The major component of this was fingerprinting. Since its arrival in South Africa via Edward Henry from the Bengal police, it had been put to effective use with the 64,000 indentured Chinese miners on the Rand (Richardson 1982; Breckenridge 2001). For six months prior to his systematic intervention, Curtis already had police in a few Transvaal towns collecting impressions from departing Indians and those found with false documents.

Curtis's aim was to extend, centralize and standardize this across the South African colonies. The first step was to demand immediate registration, and re-registration where necessary, of all Indians already arrived or arriving at the Transvaal border. The second was to take the residence certificates out of the hands of magistrates and committees and into specialized administrative offices. In these record rooms would be collected files on every individual Indian – resident or prohibited – who came into contact with officials. They were to contain a full set of impressions (rather than just a thumb), all official known biographical data, affidavits and legal correspondence. All application forms and declarations were put into a standard form. Each file was numbered and indexed. Every Indian was therefore connected to a single name, a number, a set of finger impressions and a biographical file. Smelling out ineligible intruders was made simple by detecting inconsistencies between these. Curtis's third step was to bring uniformity to all the immigration offices in Johannesburg, Pretoria, Durban and Cape Town, and a branch at Lourenço Marques. The same system was to be set up in these centres, so that records were to be, in theory, integrated, systematized and cross-referenced. This provided the core of the Asiatic Registration and amended Immigration Acts promulgated across South Africa between 1906 and 1908. An archive was established that would amount to 40,000–50,000 individual case files by the early 1920s.

Curtis's documentary straitjacket for Asian migrants had international parallels, particularly in California (McKeown 2008, 268–291). In very similar ways, Chinese immigrants there were processed by a week-long detention and extensive interviews to establish biographical histories. The interviews were held in predictable spaces, with predictable words and predictable hierarchies. Thereafter they were similarly inserted into sophisticated cross-referenced filing systems whose contents served as proof of official identity in all subsequent administrative decision-making (Dhupelia-Mesthrie 2009b). Yet against this it must be said there were several pertinent differences in South Africa: a weaker colonial state, a much less predictable set of encounters spread over a vast geographic area, the deployment of a simpler form of identity verification (the thumbprint), and the widespread infiltration of criminal and touting syndicates *within* the immigration department. The story here thus suggests a globally modest but regionally significant qualification of McKeown's thesis.

Disintegration, agents and clerks, 1906–1915

Curtis's utopian dreams proved to be ill-founded. There was little by way of existing infrastructure or institutional memory for the specific tasks of exclusion. Existing migration bureaucracies were widely scattered and had been designed to encourage, stimulate, discipline and confine labour forces *within* a given region. Kruger's Transvaal Republic had apparently made some administrative attempts to register arriving Indians, but Curtis believes whatever records had been created had been destroyed prior to the war and were, in any case, in Dutch (Curtis 1906, 13).

Staff with requisite experience were hard to come by. Even senior staff had obscure qualifications. Untrained in any formal way, they learned through on-the-job, trial-and-error experience. Best equipped was the Transvaal which vested authority in the multilingual Montfort Chamney, a tea planter from Assam. In Durban the first PIO, Harry Smith, had been an administrator of labour-contracts at the harbour. His deputy and later successor, Godfrey Dick, came from the Natal Fisheries Department. At Cape Town, the Madagascan-born Wilfred Cousins came to the immigration department in 1906 after a career that included an unfinished degree in history at Oxford, a stint as a Cape Town prisons inspector, and a clerkship in the Health Department. This group all struggled with the volume and complexities of numerous applications in a multilingual working environment. They battled with unsuitable accommodation, uncoordinated communications, low pay scales, and low morale, leading to a 'chaotic state' and 'extreme weakness' of the record-keeping systems. Files and finances were in arrears by years, fingerprints had not been fully classified and catalogued in any uniform way, and junior clerks were not insisting on any hard-and-fast rules, in order to avoid an outcry (N-PIO 1908, 2, 1912, 1919; Reports of the Select Committee on the Cape Immigration Department 1907, 1908, 1909, 87–113; Burley 1913; Public Services Commissioner 1919a). Chamney, driven to distraction in 1914, rhetorically suggested the registers be burned, so unreliable had they become (Chamney 1914a). An inspection from the Transvaal three years later reported on the 'comparative uselessness' of the Cape collection and could only 'express astonishment at the state of affairs' still prevailing there (Secretary for Interior 1917). The differences in organization between the three principal centres essentially made the registration regimes unintelligible to one another.

Given the manifest pressures which clerks were under, they had come to rely on a number of informal Indian agents to help capture and record migrants' identities. From the official perspective, agents were most useful for their linguistic abilities, but they also helped achieve some organizational efficiency: putting migrants' petitions and claims into intelligible and predictable order for rule-bound officials, by transferring fees and vetting references. As Gandhi implored his constituency to refuse registration, clerks and agents worked to achieve the opposite. Migrants appreciated the agents' work for just the same reasons, actively enabling successful outcomes. Demand for their services also came from established merchants, who wished to import Indian men as shop assistants and servants.

Agents at the immigration offices generally fell into two categories: predominantly South Indian, upwardly mobile mission-educated men who had earned their stripes representing the grievances of indentured workers or government clerks or teachers (Badassy 2003, 41–76). The majority of agents at the new immigration departments were, however, mostly Muslim men with connections in the merchant trading houses. They had gained familiarity with South Africa by extended residence, but also travelled back and forth across the Indian Ocean as they recruited employees. They generally began their careers in the immigration department as occasional, informal interpreters. The longer they stayed, the deeper the symbiosis with officials and the more opportunities to accumulate political and financial power.

In addition to their familiarity with the workings of the South African immigration departments, these men, aided by a network of sub-agents, worked around the shipping offices, wharves and villages in the likely locations in Asia and Africa noted above. They were familiar with the laws, latest amendments to rules, loopholes and, of course, all the required documentation. They continued the transactions established during the war, buying and selling documents, connecting 'families' and, occasionally, providing the accoutrements for a fake priest. As important were testimonials, which were sourced, self-penned, bought and copied. Curtis's reforms merely ensured the agents developed more sophisticated techniques. A coherent narrative of these techniques can be constructed from the multiple witness statements during enquiries in 1909 and, importantly, in 1915 (Report of the Select Committee on the Immigration Department 1909; Enquiry into Administration of Immigration Depot, Cape Town, 1915 (hereafter Enquiry, CT); Enquiry into Administration of Immigration Depot, Pretoria, 1915 (hereafter Enquiry, PTA)). Dhupelia-Mesthrie has touched on these 'cat and mouse' games but these newly uncovered archival materials allow for a fuller story to be reconstructed, linking the syndicates to Pretoria, Durban and Cape Town.

In Cape Town, where mere photographs were accepted as proof of identity until 1911, agents organized portraits to be taken of their clients in India. They took care that the final print did not reveal details that suggested the photograph was not taken in Cape Town – for example, clients were told not to clothe themselves in garb only seen in India. The picture was then sent to a paid impostor in South Africa, who duly applied for a residence certificate. Once issued, this residence certificate was then posted back or delivered by hand by yet another agent.

Fingerprinting provided more of a challenge. To get around the problem, the agents procured blank forms from the departmental offices. These forms were then sent to a client in India to complete for himself and to approach a sub-agent with the requisite paraphernalia for taking official-looking thumb impressions. If this were not possible, the client was instructed to set off anyway for South Africa with the incomplete form. On arrival, the client would be met on board by an agent and spirited away to the agent's house or office (which was sometimes in the immigration department building) and his fingerprints quickly applied to the forms. This could still be a problem when shipping companies would not issue a ticket in India without the passenger having complete immigration documentation. In these cases the agent would simply apply his own thumb impressions to a client's form, and post it on (knowing shipping lines would not actually check the accuracy of

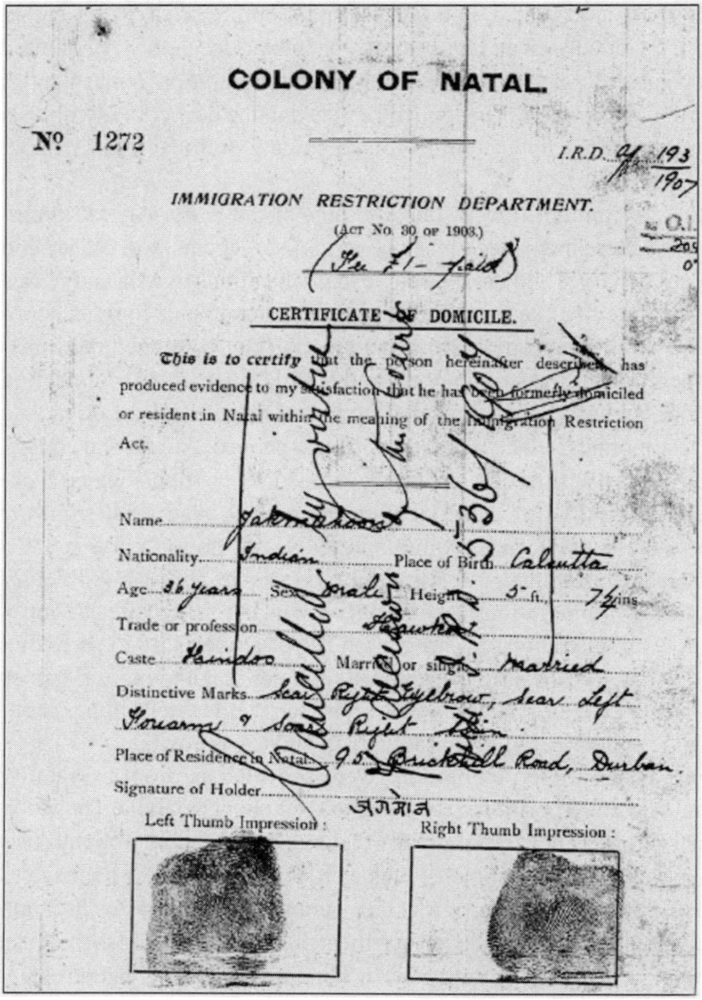

COLONY OF NATAL.

Nº 1272

I.R.D. 193/1907

IMMIGRATION RESTRICTION DEPARTMENT.

(Act No. 30 of 1903.)

(Fee £1- paid)

CERTIFICATE OF DOMICILE.

This is to certify that the person hereinafter described has produced evidence to my satisfaction that he has been formerly domiciled or resident in Natal within the meaning of the Immigration Restriction Act.

Name

Nationality Indian Place of Birth Calcutta

Age 36 years Sex male Height 5 ft. 7¼ ins

Trade or profession Hawker

Caste Hindoo Married or single Married

Distinctive Marks Scar Right Eyebrow, Scar Left Forearm & Scar Right Chin.

Place of Residence in Natal 95 Brickhill Road, Durban.

Signature of Holder

Left Thumb Impression: Right Thumb Impression:

Figure 9.1. Fraudulent certificate of domicile, Natal 1907

the finger impressions). The ruse was unlikely to be detected even by the immigration clerks, for the simple reason that some of them were in on the game.

Alert readers will have noted that the schemes required some clandestine assistance from the immigration department itself. Some senior clerks – beneath the noses of the PIOs – sold and marketed their assistance, apparently beginning around 1906–7 when new general rules made it harder for migrants to get the necessary paperwork. Clerks touted in application offices, on the docks and in detention depots. They provided the crucial link in the fraud in any of three ways: first, by selling blank forms to agents and then receiving them fully aware of the false details; second, by taking smudged impressions of fingers so that a fraudulent file was hard to detect and harder still to prove in a court of law. Finally, they gave keys to the record rooms and cabinets to agents, so that the latter might borrow, alter and destroy information as required on behalf of clients. Far from being a sudden pretext which officials cooked up to justify tightening controls, these schemes had been under way for several years, since at least 1904 (Dhupelia-Mesthrie 2009b, 16), and had indeed been reported at several junctures thereafter, to no avail.

Suspicion fell, in Cape Town, on William van Reede van Oudtshoorn, with the possible connivance of two of his relatives working as junior clerks. In Pretoria, the fingerprint expert Henry Burley provided the key. That Burley should be involved in the schemes was especially problematic, since he had been recruited from the Foreign Labour Department, having been a leading light in registering Chinese labourers. In Durban, official reports on corrupt water police who doled out blank certificates appeared more intermittently but subversion appeared equally wholesale and persistent (Criminal Investigation Department (Durban) 1908; *The Mercury* 1908, 1910; N-PIO 1917, 16).

Depending on the layers of deception required, the cost to a migrant started at £5 but averaged between £20 and £50 (rising as high as £175 in some cases). Some offered payment-by-result. Migrants could pay in gold, silver or coin and received no receipts. When the cost was prohibitive, employers in South Africa advanced the fee, with the migrant expected to repay his sponsor through wage-deductions or a period of free labour. Agents might also weigh up a client's means and status before quoting a price. Some might increase fees in the middle of an operation, effectively extorting additional monies with the threat of exposure. As this economy grew more complex, so did the potential for profit.

The over-worked departmental clerks sought only to deal with agents who could bring in informal fees. Allegiances and loyalties produced an atmosphere of rank favouritism. For Indians without an agent, clerks refused to meet them, placed obstructions in their way, scrutinized their applications with undue severity, made unpredictable decisions, arbitrarily raised official fees, and threatened detention and deportation. The point of this was, always, to push migrants into the hands of the money-generating agents, whose clients breezed through the encounter. Agents, for their part, obscured the true state of affairs from clients, who sometimes were none the wiser. Yet if any Indian moved to expose the scheme or make a fuss, he was threatened with having his own files 'crooked'.

Migrant associations, attempted murder and forgers

This atmosphere of conspiracy, favouritism and extortion drew attention. Several reformist associations within the Indian trading elite began to campaign sporadically on the issue (Vartak 1915). This was part of a more general mobilization in the wake of Gandhi's calls for *satyagraha*, but these deputations represented different interests and did not necessarily act in concert (Swan 1987). They were driven by a variety of instrumental and altruistic concerns. First, they sought to make political capital as they manoeuvred for Indians' support and state legitimacy. Reputable lawyers and merchants (of which the leaderships were chiefly comprised) saw a threat to their status from increasingly powerful big men of the migrant political-economy. Agents were diverting clients from established law firms and were much more successful at countering the laws. Most important, however, was a genuine concern for the welfare of swindled, indebted migrants who, in some cases, had become embroiled in violence. For those *satyagrahi* reformers, what, after all, could be more abhorrent to personal honour, moral discipline and autonomy than rank fraud, blackmail and extortion? As well as the colonial state, *satyagrahis* – indeed Gandhi himself – often had to struggle against interests within the Indian merchant community. The power of the touts doubtless contributed to Gandhi's disillusionment with the judicial promise of fingerprinting, for which he initially had some enthusiasm as a token of progressive administration (Gandhi 1927, ch. 86; McKeown 2008; Breckenridge 2011).

Despite the pleas to investigate evidence of bribery on a large scale, authorities did not act. The PIO in Cape Town was on sick leave in 1907; in 1908 evidence could not be located in time for a full investigation; in 1909 it was 'not deemed expedient to inquire too minutely into matters' (Reports of the Select Committee on the Cape Immigration Department 1907, 1908, 1909, i, iii, v). In 1913 complaints to Pretoria were ignored owing to a lack of any definite evidence, even though the police *were* aware of serious problems. That year, however, events showed how unsustainable this situation had become.

Mohamed Ebrahim, a Konkani villager and shop assistant, travelled to South Africa on papers procured via a network of agents in Bombay and Cape Town (Enquiry, CT, 160–185). Ebrahim was collected by a tout and a conspiring clerk in a car at Cape Town's dock, then spirited away to be deceptively inserted into the records. Before leaving he had been quoted £12, but as he sat in the Cape Town office, further monies were extorted by the agents so that his debt rose to £40. After initially paying up (with the help of his employer in South Africa), Ebrahim thought he had been overcharged by the department. Aggrieved and unaware of the game, he returned to the immigration offices where he mistakenly believed his fees had been lodged. He received no sympathy from the clerks and the PIO, Wilfred Cousins, who professed ignorance of the entire matter. Ebrahim, confused, desperate and overcome by what he described as a 'sort of madness', attacked the staff and made an attempt on the life of Cousins, who received a serious injury. In the trial that followed, Ebrahim received four years. But the agents at the centre of the fiasco were able to manipulate testimonies and ensure that the trial remained narrowly focused on the assault and not on the bluffs that underpinned it.

This scandal was merely one of many animating Indian debates in South Africa during 1913–1914. The issue of fraud was subsumed, if not sidelined, in the 1914 Indian Inquiry Commission into the anti-tax strikes and Indian marriage, but it hardly fell from the agenda. Galvanized by the more conciliatory stance of the government, a more concerted effort was made by the associations to reform the immigration department (Vartak 1915). In 1915, they finally succeeded in winning an internal inquiry into operations at Cape Town and Pretoria. With the government eager to establish trust with Indian migrants more generally, witnesses were given amnesty if they came forward with evidence. Unlike the sporadic nature of earlier complaints, several hundred Indians came forward, bravely, to volunteer evidence.

The 1915 inquiries revealed widespread collusion. In Cape Town, the official count found 'at least' 200 confirmed cases of fraud in files under the watch of senior clerk van Reede van Oudtshoorn. After 380 typed pages were spent on just the first fourteen cases, the commissioner had seen enough to pronounce the long-term accusations against van Oudtshoorn fully justified and found him guilty of collusion (Hewitt 1915). Estimates from Indian spokesmen were in fact much higher than the official count (Enquiry, CT, 152–159, 197–200, 202–219). Pillay, part-time interpreter and schoolmaster, estimated that 80–90 per cent of files were fraudulent. Advisers from the Konkani Muslim League said that one agent alone had brought in 200 at a profit of £1,500; another believed 'not one quarter of the fraud had come to light'. As noted, political or commercial rivalries gave the accusers plenty of reason to libel the agents since the latter were themselves well-established, prosperous dealers. Of the handful of agents on whom van Oudtshoorn relied, the most successful were Abdullah 'Fatty' Dawood (a 'person of some position') and Abdul Cadir, one-time cigar-maker in Mauritius and general importer in South Africa. They presided over a chain of patrons in Cape Town who helped circulate money, information and people, especially through the provision of false testimonials. These included European and Indian merchants, as well as the often unheralded South Asian proletariat of Cape Town: fruit-sellers, boot-makers, butchers, hawkers and office clerks (Enquiry, CT, 8, 101–102, 123–125; see also Dhupelia-Mesthrie 2009a).

The Cape commissioner could only grope his way towards the truth, since the very records created to establish identity and life history had been tampered with. And with such a large cast of protagonists and antagonists, the scope for bluffs, betrayals and protection was wide. Rumours swirled that even during the sittings agents were entering the record rooms and manipulating files (Hewitt 1915). In his long, case-by-case testimony, Cousins seemed genuinely bamboozled by events and had clearly lost control over his staff (Enquiry, CT, 275–379). Van Oudtshoorn was sent for trial in 1916 to face charges of fraud dating back to 1911. He was shrewd enough to exploit the confused atmosphere; casting doubt on the documentary evidence (even though he had himself created it), he blamed a vendetta by Cousins and suggested he had been framed by the agents. The judge was forced to admit too much 'reasonable doubt'. But in closing the case he found the Cape office 'very unsatisfactory [and] deplorable' and said he had never witnessed, in a long career, a government department where there had been such 'an absence altogether of any system' or records (*Cape Times* 1916). But full responsibility would have to lie with van Oudtshoorn's superiors for allowing such a lax state of affairs to persist.

The Pretoria commission found similar disorder (Clarence 1915). Confining the investigation to files generated during only the previous six months, investigators found 1,000 cases of forgery, with individual agents responsible for forty to sixty at a time. After taking over 900 pages of complaints from more than 200 Transvaal Indians, the commissioner concluded the latter were 'fully justified' to believe that the Pretoria office had been 'entirely abandoned to the most ingenious and vicious frauds by perjury and deceit'. Principal agents included Ali Mohamed Khamissa, a general dealer who had first raised Gandhi's ire in 1907 for secretly issuing certificates from his Pretoria store in the middle of the night (Gandhi 1907). Henry L. Burley was the clerk singularly implicated. The circumstantial evidence in Clarence's report was damning: most fraud took place during the PIO's absence, when Burley deputized. Burley's record cabinets were consistently found unlocked and insecure. Initial visits by the commissioner found Burley in 'an excitable and agitated state of mind'. Acting on lawyers' advice, Burley refused to give evidence and immediately resigned his post. Coincidentally, the forgeries came to an abrupt halt with the appointment of a successor. The commissioner entertained the possibility of Burley being 'unqualified for the intricate work of [his] office', but Burley had been employed as 'Fingerprint Expert' for the Foreign Labour Department for five years and had been the author of several authoritative, measured reports on that office's successes and refinements. The commissioner urged a warrant of arrest.

As in the van Oudtshoorn case, however, there was a difficulty. The nature of the forgery – deliberately 'slovenly', smudged fingerprints – covered up tracks brilliantly by manipulating the state's own record of identity. A legal defence of mere incompetence or negligence would be enough to avoid a conviction. The commissioner was in no doubt of Burley's guilt but in the end legal advisers did not think a prosecution would be successful.

Montfort Chamney was also accused by the British Indian Association of accepting £400 in bribes, remitted to a London account. There was again no 'direct evidence' but Chamney won few accolades in the final report for his inexplicable toleration of Burley's known eccentricities. Choosing his words carefully, the commissioner judged Chamney 'not strictly consistent in the performance of his duties' and 'not free from blame' for allowing his department to become 'beset by fraud on every side'. That Khamissa was, during proceedings, openly boasting that he had £10,000 available to suppress evidence and that clients and sub-agents had been paid to leave the country under threat of punishment served only to confirm the commissioner's misgivings. Despite the lack of legal action, the commissioner reported to the minister that 'a very vast field of crime has only been slightly exposed'. The department suffered from 'deeply hidden corruption' and had been under the 'mysterious control' of agents.

Durban escaped a formal investigation, for reasons that are unclear. Even still, by 1912, 1,080 fraudulent certificates and another 1,665 old certificates still in use had been confiscated (N-PIO 1912, 4). A year after the van Oudtshoorn and Burley revelations, the Natal PIO wrote to the minister that the 'malignant evil' of extortion by agents using the department's name was 'rampant', and begged 'the more responsible members of the Indian community' to come forward and help him detect the weak points (N-PIO 1917, 6).

With the removal of van Oudtshoorn and Burley's resignation 'under a cloud', the opportunities for migrants dwindled in the registration offices in the principal urban centres. Yet the effect of this was merely to displace, rather than smother, subversion. If migrants could not insert themselves into the registries, they could instead equip themselves with fake documents before reaching the Union and then avoid a full examination by professional gatekeepers. This was in practice quite easy, although it did require giving the Transvaal Asiatic Office a wide berth.

The main factor was the lack of infrastructure at entry points along the Union's eastern and northern land-borders, making a rail journey from Lourenço Marques and Beira an attractive proposition for those with rigged papers. This had been a long-term problem for officials, an inadvertent side-effect of investment in rail links to stimulate labour, trade and even tourist traffic between the British and Portuguese colonies (Katzenellenbogen 1982). A small Komatipoort office, under the Transvaal PIO, was staffed by a constantly shifting corps of frontier police ill-trained in the arts of immigration control (Komatipoort Immigration Office Reports 1913–1919; MacDonald 2011). Notoriously hot and unhealthy to colonial bodies and minds, the department found it exceptionally hard to recruit the right calibre of men to the border town. Attempts were made to circulate officials between offices, but as one senior staffer put it, experience with border officers over the 1910s had been 'a continual record of sickness, dissatisfaction and grievance' (Long 1924). Komatipoort officers were limited to examining immigrants on the train: they complained examination was impossible when the scheduled stop was a mere nine minutes, of the lack of light to see residence certificates, and even of the ubiquitous sweat which smudged documents. When occasional attempts were made to detrain and detain Indians, travelling *satyagrahis* organized to protest loudly against maltreatment, forcing frontier officers to become increasingly chary of insult. Thus while the Indian press publicized the 'Black Hole of Komatipoort', officials privately worried the post had become a black hole for record-keeping.

The northern border posts – in and around the rail junctions of Mafikeng and Kimberley – were worse (Immigration Station Inspections 1912–1918). Similar lack of training was compounded by the failure to circulate official instructions and to appoint responsible men. When Chamney surveyed the situation at the border towns in 1914, he found 'the system is intrinsically at fault' (Chamney 1914b). By 1917 officials felt that the situation remained 'very severe' and the number of unrecorded migrants 'not in scores but hundreds' (N-PIO 1917, 37). In 1921 the Natal PIO visited Komatipoort and still found the weaknesses 'considerable if not alarming' (N-PIO 1921).

In the meanwhile, prohibited immigrants were diverting to Lourenço Marques and Beira from where busy rail routes ran to the Union. In the Portuguese East African towns, South African immigration departments had some presence to intercept the traffic, but were hamstrung by jurisdictional limits. The Portuguese had instituted their own restrictive immigration laws, but the system worked through monetary deposits that were no real match for wealthy abetters. South African fraud syndicates flourished (Chamney 1915; Dick 1913, 1915; Cousins 1915, 1–10; see also numerous case reports in BNS 1/1/323 24/74. Vols 1–15). They worked in hotels, in stores, and from homes; on ships and in trains. Indian traders, 'clever and enterprising Greeks', 'Cape Boys', 'Eurasians' and 'white residents' all became involved in the 'systematic sale' of 'excellent imitation certificates' to Indian and Chinese travellers, some providing a sophisticated back-up of witnesses and supplementary proofs.

In Bombay in the early 1920s it remained quite possible to obtain a South African certificate (Parthek 1921; N-PIO 1922; *Times of India* 1925, 1926). When ships departing South Africa arrived back in Bombay, they were boarded by Parsi agents who solicited and paid for any residence certificates belonging to returning South Asians (or even their deceased relatives). These documents were then taken to a private office where the thumbprints were erased with particular chemicals. Sub-agents spread out through the Bombay countryside would then sound out those who desired to go to South Africa. If a bargain was struck, agents produced between 100 and 200 certificates and a search was made for the one that was the closest match in description and detail. New fingerprints were applied. In this way, groups of ten to twelve people per ship of the British India Company Line travelled to Lourenço Marques, with certain pursers in on the deal.

Conclusions

Exposures continued to be supplied by Indian tip-offs. Grateful South African immigration departments embarked on their most rigorous efforts yet toward record-keeping efficiency from 1915, although reforms were cumulative and unevenly applied over time and space (Secretary for Interior 1915; C-PIO 1915; Conference of Immigration Officials 1917; Public Services Commissioner 1919b; T-PIO 1923; Long 1926). Agents were banned from offices. Staff salaries were improved and better training in fingerprinting and detection was inaugurated. Rules governing all aspects of business were standardized across the departments. Officials secured record collections and circulated statistical information across all regional offices. At the frontiers, where it took longer to establish bureaucratic competency, high-level pressure was exerted to ensure cooperation with the railways. Official points of entry were identified, doing away with many of the smaller stations. Regular tours of inspection and revolving staff were inaugurated to prevent officers 'getting into a groove'. Stations were provided with modern technologies of communication and lighting.

These reforms certainly helped crush the syndicates, an effort that was aided by Indian controls *on exit* and the fact that it was simply becoming harder, with time, for young men to claim pre-1900 residence. Yet this did not mean the problem had ceased. During the 1920s and 1930s Indians were avoiding the bureaucracy altogether, using motor cars and corrupt train conductors to enter the Union through Swaziland, where an elaborate system of touts, forwarding forms, safe houses and Swazi guides was developed to smuggle Indian, Chinese and Madeiran men (MacDonald 2011).

Insider subversion would return to the immigration department in the 1940s. Migration agents now enjoyed access to records as informers to immigration detectives (Chief Inspector, SAP 1948). Amongst these were the Akoob brothers, who ran the Enza Silk Bazaar in Pretoria. They arranged with a Bombay sarang, sub-agents at Lourenço Marques' dock and immigration officers at Komatipoort and Pretoria to help prohibited immigrants. Officers P. H. L. Otto and B. P. Wilson agreed to burn incriminating records on the outskirts of Pretoria; around 500 files went up in smoke in 1948. In return they received cash, tailored suits and even a motor car. One Salee Bhamjee, who himself had 'a most improper' role as a money-lender to clerks, betrayed the syndicate following a professional rivalry (whose exact contours are somewhat murky). The fallout drew two urban gangs 'of the Al-Capone type' into a violent conflict. Scores were settled in the seven shoot-outs across Pretoria where this chapter began. Otto (who had narrowly missed a bullet in the head) was rapidly transferred to Bloemfontein. As the guns went silent and the National Party surveyed its bureaucratic inheritance, many in the immigration department agreed that Otto would never be able to regain the confidence and trust of those with whom he worked.

This chapter has illustrated how patrimonial structures of managing migration collided, and then became entangled, with rigid, centrally legislated forms of restrictive control based on the registration of migrants. I have traced the emergence of residence permits, tokens of the system, and shown how these were transacted along the networks established by long-established Indian merchant houses. This proliferating economy provoked important reforms in record-keeping, notably a centralized system of fingerprint registration, through the key figure of Lionel Curtis in 1906–1907. Yet despite Curtis's blueprint and elaborate efforts to realize it, record-keeping at many of South Africa's immigration offices remained in great disarray for another fifteen years. The epistemic gap was filled by shrewd touting syndicates who ensured the permit economy would persist and indeed flourish. More stringent record-keeping was finally in place by the 1920s, due, in part, to revelations by and support from migrant associations, although as the events of the 1940s suggest, semi-official touting never entirely disappeared. A century later, the issues remain a challenge for the beleaguered Department of Home Affairs who must constantly negotiate with 'immigration practitioners', much as their colonial predecessors did a century earlier (*The Star* 2010; *Pretoria News* 2010; *Daily News* 2010). Such touting economies are an important part of the landscape of colonial, and post-colonial, registration regimes.

Once a state creates a registration system linked to valued benefits there will always be issues of contest and negotiation elicited from among those the scheme is intended to exclude, as they seek to subvert, evade or confound its operation to pursue their own interests. Thus, an integral part of the longer-term project which this volume seeks to promote – the recovery of a comparative history of identity registration in all its dimensions – will ultimately involve recovering also the performative histories of illicit and semi-licit challenge that accompany such regimes, as shown here in the case of South Africa's Asian border controls.

References

Neither the primary nor the secondary sources cited here are exhaustive. For a further guide to the literature, readers are directed to my own dissertation (2012), listed below, from which this chapter has been drawn.

Primary sources

Burley, H. 1913. Correspondence with T-PIO, 24 December. SAB/BNS 1/1/342 68/74.
Cape Principal Immigration Officer. 1904. Annual Report.
—— 1905. Annual Report.
—— 1915. Correspondence with Secretary for Interior, 19 August. SAB/BNS 1/2/5 A145.
Cape Times. 1916. 'Van Oudtshoorn Acquitted', 12 February.
Chamney, M. 1914a. Appeal No. 36. Purboo Valabh. 20 April. SAB/BNS 1/1/311.
—— 1914b. Correspondence with Sec. of the Interior, 30 April. SAB/BNS1/1/354 111/74. Vol. 2.
—— 1915. Confidential Memorandum on Illicit Immigration of Asiatics to the Transvaal.
Chief Inspector, South African Police. 1948. Correspondence with Deputy Commissioner. 17 December. SAB/BNS 1/1/323 27/74. Vol. 12.
Clarence, B. 1915. Report to Sec. of Interior, 3 August. SAB/BNS 1/2/6 A146(a).
Conference of Immigration Officials. 1917. Report. SAB/BAL 27 A4403.
Cousins, W. 1915. Report to Sec. for the Interior, 23 November. SAB/BNS 27/74 1/1/323 27/74.

Criminal Investigation Department (Durban). 1908. Correspondence re: Certain Indians Alleged to be illegally in the Union. NAB/IRD 95/239/1908.

Curtis, L. 1906. Position of Asiatics in the Transvaal. TAB/LTG 97/3. 1 May.

Daily News. 2010. 'Immigration Practitioners', 11 August.

Dick, G. 1913. Correspondence with Secretary for Interior, 28 October. SAB/BNS 1/1/367 162/74. Vol. 1.

—— 1915. Memorandum on Illicit Immigration of Asiatics, 23 November. SAB/BNS 1/1/367 162/74. Vol. 1.

Enquiry into Administration of Immigration Depot, Pretoria, 1915. SAB/BNS 1/2/5 A146 (A).

Enquiry into Administration of Immigration Depot, Cape Town, 1915. SAB/BNS 1/2/5 A145.

Gandhi, M. K. 1907. 'New Law – Ghastly Betrayal.' *Indian Opinion*, 3 August.

—— 1927. *An Autobiography, or the Story of My Experiments with Truth*, trans. Mahadev Desai. Ahmadabad: Navajivan Publishing House.

Governor-General. 1906. Reports on Illicit Immigration of Indians (Bombay, Delagoa Bay, Transvaal). GG 201/967/06.

Hewitt, B. 1915. Correspondence with Shaw, 25 May. SAB/ BNS 1/2/5 A145.

Immigration Station Inspections. 1912–1918. Northern Cape, 26 November 1912; Mafikeng, 12 March 1913; Natal and Orange Free State, 27 May 1913; Northern Cape, 12 May 1918; Transvaal , 9 October 1918. SAB/BNS 1/1/320 27/74

Komatipoort Immigration Office Reports. 1913–1919. SAB/BNS 1/1/354 111/74. Vols 1–3.

Long, A. T. 1924. Correspondence with Owen-Smith, 27 March. SAB/BAL 31/A7974.

—— 1926. Report on Immigration and Habit Forming Drugs, 19 November. SAB/BNS 1/1/354 111/74. Vol. 3.

The Mercury. 1908. 'Asiatic Immigration', 7 February.

—— 1910. 'Alleged Forgeries', 31 August.

Natal Principal Immigration Officer. 1897. Correspondence re: Record Books in Connection with Immigration Restriction Act, 1897. NAB/IRD 1/71/1897.

—— 1902a. Correspondence. Certificates of Domicile produced by Indians. NAB/IRD 7/129/1902.

—— 1902b. NAB/Annual Report, 1902.

—— 1902c. Anonymous correspondence re: false passes. NAB/IRD 7/58/1902.

—— 1902d. Correspondence re: Certificate of Domicile produced by Indians. NAB/IRD 7/129/1902.

—— 1902e. Correspondence re: Allegations made by Indian Storekeepers. NAB/IRD 7/682/1902.

—— 1903a. NAB/Annual Report, 1903.

—— 1903b. Memorandum on Visiting and Embarkation Pass System. NAB/IRD 38/694/1903.

—— 1904. Correspondence re: improper issue of permits. NAB/IRD 31/994/1904.

—— 1905a. Correspondence re: claims for Certificates of Domicile. NAB/IRD 35/142/1905.

—— 1905b. Annual Report.

—— 1906a. Correspondence re: selling of affidavits and Natal Certificates of Domicile at Bombay. IRD 56/1045/1906.

—— 1906b. Correspondence re: Preparation of Affidavits for Certificates of Domicile under the Immigration Restriction Act. IRD 58/1353/1906.

—— 1908. Annual Report.
—— 1910. Anonymous notes. IRD 81/258/1910.
—— 1911. Correspondence with Sec. of Interior, 1 July. IRD 92/1904/1911.
—— 1912. Anonymous notes. IRD 94/125/1912.
—— 1917. Annual Report. SAB/BNS 1/1/597 2/129.
—— 1919. Memorandum, 29 March. SAB/BNS 1/1/320 27/74.
—— 1921. Memorandum: 'Illicit Immigration of Asiatics', 4 March. SAB/BNS 1/1/323 27/74. Vol. 7.
—— 1922. Correspondence with Secretary for the Interior, 9 March. SAB/BNS 27/74 1/1/323 27/74. Vol. 8
Parthek, V. 1921. 'Illicit Traffic of Indians from Bombay by Messrs Ismail Vahed and Cassim Fancy of Bombay', 7 September. SAB/BNS 27/74 1/1/323 27/74. Vol. 8.
Pretoria News. 2010. 'Massive ID Fraud Bungle', 20 July.
Public Services Commissioner. 1919a. Report on the Immigration Department (Cape), 1 March. SAB/BNS 1/1/363 138/74.
—— 1919b. Acting Sec. to Department of the Interior re: Union Immigration Offices, 31 March. SAB/BNS 1/1/320 27/74.
Reports of the Select Committee on the Cape Immigration Department. 1907, 1908 and 1909. Cape Colonial Publications.
Secretary for Interior. 1915. Correspondence with Principal Immigration Officer, 5 July. SAB/CIAA 40/M149.
—— 1917. Correspondence with Under Sec. for the Interior, 30 April. SAB/BNS 1/1/320 27/74.
The Star. 2010. 'Bogus Home Affairs Operators Arrested', 4 August.
Times of India. 1925. 'Passengers Duped. Alleged Forgery of Passports', 13 November.
—— 1926. 'Emigrants Duped. A Clever Trick', 26 January.
Transvaal Principal Immigration Officer. 1905a. Correspondence re: Examination of Permits & Instructions to Police. SAB/CIAA 26/ M2. Vol. 1.
—— 1905b. Correspondence re: Establishment of Advisory Boards 1905–6. SAB/CIAA 27/M4.
—— 1905c. Correspondence re: Inspection of Permits, 1905–6. SAB/CIAA 27/M5. Vol. 6.
—— 1923. Correspondence with Secretary for the Interior, 28 December. SAB/BNS 1/1/320 24/74. Vol. 2.
Vartak, V. R. 1915. Memorandum, 18 May. SAB/BNS 1/2/5 A145.

Secondary sources

Anderson, R. 1993. 'Why Cryptosystems Fail.' *Proceedings of the 1st ACM Conference on Computer and Communications Security*, 215–227.
Badassy, P. 2003. '"A Diabolical Conspiracy": The Life of and World of Henry Louis Paul (1862–1935).' *Journal of Natal and Zulu History* 21: 41–76.
Bayart, J.-F. 1999. 'The "Social Capital" of the Felonious State, or the Ruses of Political Intelligence.' In *The Criminalization of the State in Africa*, ed. J. F. Bayart, S. Ellis and B. Hibou. Oxford: James Curry, 32–48.
Bhana, S. and J. Brain. 1990. *Setting Down Roots: Indian Migrants in South Africa, 1860–1911*. Johannesburg: University Press.

Bradlow, E. 1978. 'Immigration into the Union 1910–1948: Policies and Attitudes.' Ph.D. dissertation, University of Cape Town.

Breckenridge, K. 2001. 'Flesh Made Words: Fingerprinting and the Archival Imperative in the Union of South Africa, 1900–1930.' Paper presented at History and African Studies Seminar, University of KwaZulu-Natal, 2 October.

—— 2008. 'Power without Knowledge: Three Nineteenth Century Colonialisms in South Africa.' *Journal of Natal and Zulu History* 26: 3–30.

—— 2011. 'Gandhi's Progressive Disillusionment: Thumbs, Fingers, and the Rejection of Scientific Modernism in Hind Swaraj.' *Public Culture* 23(2): 331–348.

Bull, E. 1991. *Aided Immigration from Britain to South Africa, 1857–1867*. Pretoria: Human Sciences Research Council Press.

Caplan, J. and J. Torpey, eds. 2001. *Documenting Individual Identity: The Development of State Practices in the Modern World*. Princeton, NJ: Princeton University Press.

Carter, M. 1995. *Servants, Sirdars and Settlers: Indians in Mauritius, 1834–1874*. Oxford: Oxford University Press.

Cooper, F. 2002. *Africa since 1940: The Past of the Present*. Cambridge: Cambridge University Press.

Crush, J., A. Jeeves and D. Yudelman. 1991. *South Africa's Labour Empire: A History of Black Migrancy to the Gold Mines*. Boulder, CO: Westview Press.

Desai, A. and G. Vahed. 2007. *Inside Indenture: A South African Story, 1860–1914*. Durban: Madiba Press.

Dhupelia-Mesthrie, U. 2009a. 'The Passenger Indian as Worker: Indian Immigrants in Cape Town in the Early Twentieth Century.' *African Studies* 68(1): 111–134.

—— 2009b. 'Cat and Mouse Games: The State, Indians in the Cape and the Permit System, 1906–1920s.' Paper presented at conference, 'Identifying the Person: Past, Present and Future', St Anthony's College, University of Oxford, 26–27 September.

—— 2011. 'The Form, the Permit and the Photograph: An Archive of Mobility between South Africa and India.' *Journal of Asian and African Studies* 46(6): 650–662.

Freund, B. 1995. *Insiders and Outsiders: The Indian Working Class of Durban, 1910–1990*. Portsmouth: Heinemann.

Huttenback, R. 1976. *Racism and Empire: White Settlers and Coloured Immigrants in the British Self-Governing Colonies, 1830–1910*. Ithaca, NY: Cornell University Press.

JESHO (*Journal of the Economic and Social History of the Orient*). 2007. Special issue on 'Spatial and Temporal Continuities of Merchant Networks in South Asia and the Indian Ocean.' 50(3).

Katzenellenbogen, S. E. 1982. *South Africa and Southern Mozambique: Labour, Railways, and Trade in the Making of a Relationship*. Manchester: Manchester University Press.

Klaaren, J. 2004. 'Migrating to Citizenship: Mobility, Law, and Nationality in South Africa, 1897–1937.' Ph.D. dissertation, Yale University.

Lake, M. and H. Reynolds. 2008. *Drawing the Global Colour Line: White Men's Countries and the International Challenge of Racial Equality*. Cambridge: Cambridge University Press.

MacDonald, A. 2007. 'Strangers in a Strange Land: Undesirables and Border Controls in Colonial Durban 1897–1910.' MA dissertation, University of KwaZulu-Natal.

—— 2012. 'Colonial Trespassers in the Making of South Africa's International Borders, c. 1900–1950.' Ph.D. dissertation, University of Cambridge.

Markowitz, C. 2008. *Merchants, Traders and Entrepreneurs: Indian Business in the Colonial Era.* Basingstoke: Palgrave Macmillan.

Martens, J. 2006. 'A Transnational History of Immigration Restriction: Natal and New South Wales, 1896–97.' *Journal of Commonwealth and Imperial History* 34(3): 323–344.

McKeown, A. 2008. *Melancholy Order: Asian Migration and the Globalization of Borders.* New York: Columbia University Press.

Morrell, R. and V. Padayachee. 1991. 'Indian Merchants and Dukawallahs in the Natal Economy.' *Journal of Southern African Studies* 17(1): 71–102.

Oishi, T. 2007. 'Indian Muslim Merchants in Mozambique and South Africa: Intra-Regional Networks in Strategic Association with State Institutions, 1870s–1930s.' *Journal of Economic and Social History of the Orient* 50(3): 287–324.

Peberdy, S. 2008. *Selecting Immigrants: National Identity and South Africa's Immigration Policies, 1910–2008.* Johannesburg: Witwatersrand University Press.

Richardson, P. 1982. *Chinese Mine Labour in the Transvaal.* London: Macmillan.

Sadiq, K. 2010. *Paper Citizens: How Illegal Immigrants Acquire Citizenship in Developing Countries.* Oxford: Oxford University Press.

Scott, J. C. 1998. *Seeing Like a State: How Certain Schemes to Improve the Human Condition Have Failed.* New Haven, CT: Yale University Press.

Singha, R. 2000. 'Settle, Mobilize, Verify: Identification Practices in Colonial India.' *Studies in History* 16: 151–198.

Stoler, A. L. 2009. *Along the Archival Grain: Epistemic Anxieties and Colonial Common Sense.* Princeton, NJ: Princeton University Press.

Swan, M. 1987. 'Ideology in Organised Indian Politics, 1891–1948.' In *The Politics of Race, Class and Nationalism in Twentieth Century South Africa*, ed. S. Marks and S. Trapido. Harlow: Longman, 182–253.

Vahed, Goolam. 1997. 'The Making of Indianness: Indian Politics in South Africa during the 1930s and 1940s.' *Journal of Natal and Zulu History* 17: 1–36.

—— 2005. 'Passengers, Partnerships, and Promissory Notes: Gujarati Traders in Colonial Natal, 1870–1920.' *International Journal of African Historical Studies* 38(3): 449–479.

10

Parish Baptism Registers, Vital Registration and Fixing Identities in Uganda[1]

SHANE DOYLE

Introduction

VITAL REGISTRATION HAS A DUAL FUNCTION. It can serve equally as a foundation for poverty alleviation and social justice, and as a means of state control through the better monitoring of citizens and exclusion of non-citizens. These twin, opposing, aims can be seen with unusual clarity in Uganda today. The National Resistance Movement government of President Yoweri Museveni, in power since 1986, has introduced civil registration using humanitarian rhetoric adopted from Western liberal donors, but employing mechanisms which suggest that the regime is as much concerned with reducing its own vulnerability as that of widows, orphans and other marginalized groups. The responsibility for administering biometric registration has been given not to the social welfare arm of the state but to the security services.

This is not the first time that Uganda has created a system of civil registration. In the early colonial period one of the most comprehensive systems of population recording in twentieth-century Africa was introduced, achieving levels of compliance far in excess of anything reached by the current Ugandan government, despite the latter's technological advantages. In part, the relative success of colonial-era vital registration was an indication of the bureaucratic effectiveness of local government in Uganda during the period of British over-rule (*c.* 1900–1962). It is remarkable how dense the state was in Ugandan societies such as Buganda, where in 1921 one in every thirty men was a chief (Uganda Protectorate 1922, 58). But what ensured that most people did register births and deaths was a broad range of incentives, from direct penalties for non-registration to indirect benefits such as enhanced inheritance rights.[2] The colonial state in Uganda was surprisingly

[1] Research for this paper has been funded by the AHRC, the British Academy and the ESRC. Thanks are due to Keith Breckenridge, Charles Otim, Gerald Lubega, Simon Szreter and Sarah Walters.

[2] For the story of marriage registration in Uganda, see Doyle (2012).

successful in terms of the number of vital events that were recorded, but less so at ensuring that the names that were recorded were a unique, permanent and accurate method of identifying and tracking individuals over their life course. The focus of this chapter is on the mutability and multiplicity of names in East Africa, and on the difficulties that this creates for the state. The adoption of biometrics by post-colonial governments is in large part designed to bypass the complexities of naming in Africa (Doyle 2009).

But what was a problem for the central state in the past was an opportunity for the marginalized. Immigrants' ability to pass themselves and their children off as indigenes by adopting names typical of the host ethnic group helps explain how Ugandan societies absorbed huge numbers of incomers from neighbouring territories with relative ease during the colonial period. The complicity of local elites in this process of ethnic re-identification is a significant example of how the flexibility of name-based registration helped local government to achieve economic growth and social integration. It is uncertain whether civil registration could be used to secure these same goals in contemporary Uganda, as the local agents of the state today have less autonomy from central control, and seem less constrained by rural networks of clientage.

Previous attempts at civil registration in Uganda

Civil registration in twentieth-century Uganda was a contentious and imperfect means of identifying individuals. Nonetheless, Uganda's system of vital registration was one of the most comprehensive in colonial Africa. In the area where registration worked best, the kingdom of Buganda, it seems that a clear majority of births and deaths were registered during the colonial period. If the recent investment in civil registration in a number of African countries is to achieve its goal of fixing a unique and unchanging identity on each of their citizens, then the lessons of Uganda's experiment would be worth learning.[3]

The requirement that all births and deaths had to be registered at the local sub-county headquarters was first trialled in the kingdom of Buganda, then extended to the rest of southern Uganda in 1911–1912, and subsequently rolled out across the rest of the Protectorate over the following ten to fifteen years.[4] The recording of vital events was never thought to be entirely comprehensive or fully accurate during the colonial period. To some degree omissions and errors reflected the uneven enthusiasm of local bureaucrats for filling in forms, but in addition the region's many unmarried mothers, recently-arrived immigrants and people living

[3] Countries which have invested significantly in registration in recent years include Ghana, Nigeria, Rwanda, Senegal and Zambia.
[4] Uganda Protectorate, Annual Medical Reports 1908–38, National Archives (NA), CO/685/1-23.

alone were less likely to have their births and deaths reported than citizens who were more integrated into local social networks. Past experience in East Africa suggests that it was people on the margins of society who tended to escape the notice of the state. It is likely, too, that across this region female children, no matter how well integrated the family, would have been less likely to appear in the registers than their brothers, because of their lower status. Vital rates were not broken down by sex in Uganda, but in the neighbouring Bukoba district of Tanganyika, for instance, 18 per cent more male than female children were recorded in the birth register, and 13 per cent more boys than girls appeared in the death register, even though contemporary surveys found that the local population had an even sex ratio at birth and higher rates of female than male child mortality.[5]

One of the enduring weaknesses of the colonial vital registration data was the credulity of many European officials, a tendency that was especially noticeable when the figures reinforced widely held preconceptions. Bunyoro, for example, was a district thought to suffer the highest rates of syphilis in colonial Uganda. Some observers believed that almost all adults were infected with the disease at some point in their lives. When the first vital statistics were provided by Bunyoro's chiefs in 1911 the principal medical officer suggested that some infant deaths might have been misrecorded as stillbirths. Yet, in the decade that followed no other medical officer questioned chiefs' statistics which consistently showed that more than a third of all births were stillborn, a proportion that was so unbelievably high that chiefs must have been misrecording some miscarriages or neonatal deaths. Only when metropolitan sexually transmitted disease specialists warned that Ugandan methods of syphilis diagnosis were unsound, and that nowhere else in the world did syphilis account for all stillbirths, did colonial doctors stop using the stillbirth data as proof of near universal syphilitic infection.[6]

In the 1920s the level of European supervision of chiefly data collection was reduced and new, more time-consuming registration forms were employed. Unsurprisingly the number of vital events recorded by chiefs declined. Mortality fell much faster than fertility, but this may have partly reflected the distorting effect of local regulations. In Buganda the fine for failing to register a birth was twenty times greater than that for the non-registration of a death, while pro-natalist legislation exempted men who registered five or more live births from paying tax

[5] A. Richards and P. Reining, 'Report on Fertility Surveys in Buganda and Buhaya, 1952' (University of Dar es Salaam Library (UDSML), EAF Cory 373); Bukoba District Annual Report (BDAR) 1925, Tanzania National Archives (TNA) 1733/3:46 (AB40); BDAR 1926, TNA 215/77/A; BDAR 1927, TNA 215/77/A; BDAR 1928, TNA 215/77/B; BDAR 1929, TNA 215/77/C; BDAR 1930, TNA 215/77/D; BDAR 1934, TNA 215/1136; BDAR 1938, TNA 215/1548; A. Culwick, 'The Population Problem in the Bukoba District' (Bukoba, 1938, UDSML, EAF Cory 239), 20–24.

[6] Medical report, 20 June 1911, National Archives (NA), CO/536/42; Alison Neilans, 'Some Notes on the Memorandum Issued by the Colonial Office Concerning Anti-Venereal Measures in Uganda, 1922', NCVD Uganda 1908–54, Women's Library, 3AMS/D/49.

and providing labour service. Nonetheless, this trend was regarded by local medical opinion as clear evidence of the success of recent health initiatives rather than reason to check the accuracy of data collection. It is hard to believe, for example, that the opening of a few dispensaries and ante-natal centres in Bunyoro was credited with causing infant mortality there to decline from 535 per 1,000 in 1926 to 62 in 1938, overall death rates to halve, and stillbirths to fall from a third to a twelfth of all births (Anon. 1947; Kuczynski 1949, 113).

Only in the late 1940s and early 1950s was the declining reliability of vital registration fully recognized, due to the holding of a comprehensive census in 1948, the growing popularity of hospital maternity services, and the comparison of registration data with the results of local population surveys. What these showed was that the success of registration depended on the conscientiousness of the individual chiefs. Detailed investigation also revealed widespread confusion over the distinction between miscarriages, stillbirths and neonatal deaths. Vital registration continued but its results were not published in annual medical reports after 1949. It is likely that this withdrawal of official recognition would have reduced the quality of the data recorded still further. The entire system collapsed in Uganda in the 1960s with the post-colonial abolition of the indigenous kingdoms and the Uganda People's Congress's takeover of local government. Like many of Idi Amin's presidential decrees, his demand in 1973 that registration must again become compulsory across the entire country came to nothing as his regime sank into chaos (Uganda Protectorate 1949, 1950, 1953).

By the 1980s Uganda's achievements in civil registration had been largely forgotten. Only in hospitals were births and deaths routinely registered, and most people had to rely on the church registers of baptism archived in local parish offices if they needed some form of official proof of their birth and citizenship.[7] Yet the recording of around 100,000 vital events per annum in the early colonial period was a remarkable demonstration of administrative capacity by indigenous rural chiefs. It should also be recognized that the failings of the colonial-era system were experienced much more strongly in some areas of Uganda than in others. In Buganda the internal consistency of the data was far superior to that of any other district in colonial Uganda. Infant mortality and stillbirth rates were never as wildly high as in districts such as Bunyoro, and declined much more gradually than elsewhere. Buganda's birth and death rates fluctuated far less over time than those recorded in societies such as Ankole, where in the 1930s both rates nearly halved

[7] It seems surprising that church registers of baptism and burial, which have been used as a proxy for state registration in many societies in the past, were ignored by Uganda's colonial government. In part the reason for this neglect of a potentially valuable resource may have been an exaggerated belief in the accuracy of civil registration by chiefs. More significant though was the realization that even in Uganda, one of the most Christianized countries in colonial Africa, the parish registers captured only a minority of the population until the later colonial period.

within a few years. As the graph in Figure 10.1 shows, the numbers of births and deaths per 1,000 in Buganda was impressively consistent over time.

The major weakness of the vital rates in Buganda was not the recording of vital events but the estimation of the total population, the denominator in the calculations of birth and death rates. So many immigrants came into Buganda during the colonial period that the census of 1959 found that they almost outnumbered the indigenous Ganda. The difficulty, though, of tracking immigrants' movements meant that their increase between each census was grossly underestimated. Moreover, as many of these immigrants were largely hidden from the Ganda state, the degree to which they complied with the registration laws is uncertain.

Only in 1948 was it possible for the colonial state to evaluate the comprehensiveness of vital registration in Buganda. The census of that year for the first time gathered data on fertility and mortality which showed that in Buganda the crude birth and death rates were 30 and 24 per 1,000 respectively. These results indicated that the vital registration system in that year had failed to record 35 per cent of births and 44 per cent of deaths. Clearly civil registration in Buganda was far from perfect by 1948, but it is very likely that it would have been more accurate a generation earlier, when immigrants constituted a much smaller proportion of the population, and before the colonial state simultaneously complicated the process

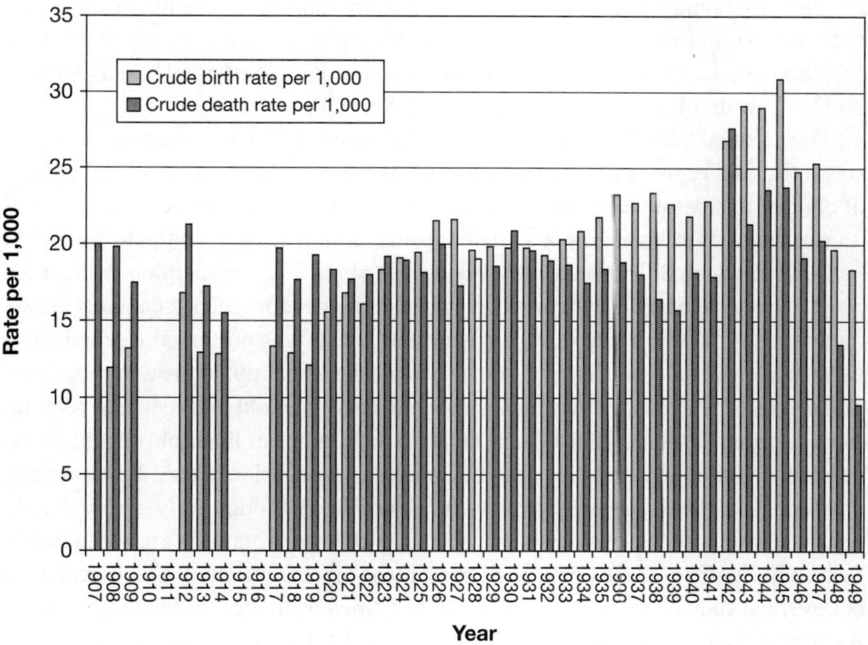

Figure 10.1. Crude birth rate and crude death rate per 1,000 in Buganda, 1907–1949, from vital registration records

of registration and reduced its supervision of chiefly record-keeping. It should be noted that Buganda's system, even in decline, was still far superior to the methods of population recording instituted by the post-war French empire, as described in Chapter 15 in this volume, and indeed to almost any other system in tropical Africa (East African Statistical Department 1950, 1961).

Buganda's achievement then needs to be explained. Several factors seem significant. First, although no system of vital registration existed in pre-colonial Buganda, in this exceptionally centralized and militarily expansionist state, chiefs were expected to keep a tally of active adult males within their jurisdictions for the purposes of tax and war, during the nineteenth century at least (Reid 2002). Second, Buganda's distinctiveness increased further in the late nineteenth century when it became one of the few areas in Africa where mass conversion to Christianity preceded the colonial takeover. By the 1890s, literacy, achieved through conversion to one of the world religions, had become a basic requirement for chiefly appointment, ensuring that Buganda possessed an indigenous administration capable of regularized record-keeping far in advance of the tropical African norm. Religion provided the stimulus as well as the capacity for keeping accounts. Political competition, as European influence grew in the late 1880s and 1890s, increasingly required the counting of the members of the several religio-political parties in order to assert the right to an appropriate number of chiefships. In this new politics of numbers Buganda's crusading chiefs found ready support among their missionary mentors, who already kept track of their adherents through the registration of catechumens, baptism, marriage, attendance at the major feasts, and burial (Médard 2007a; Low and Pratt 1960; Twaddle 1988, 81–92).

The colonial takeover formed the third influence on the development of enthusiasm for vital registration. European officials remodelled the hierarchical system of chiefship, creating a pyramidal bureaucracy that lent itself to the collection and transmission of information, and ensuring that administrative competence would be the primary qualification for promotion. Buganda's self-perception as the most progressive of Britain's African possessions further encouraged acceptance of the mundane task of birth and death registration, which was presented to chiefs as a marker of civilized, modern government. More significantly, white administrators also created one of the few systems of individualized freehold land tenure in colonial Africa, primarily to cement Ganda loyalty to the empire. Freehold reconfigured politics in Buganda, ensuring that questions of succession would be unusually prominent in the kingdom's courts and councils. Although only a few Ganda received freehold estates initially, their rapid fragmentation, and Buganda's extremely inclusive rules of inheritance, meant that very many Ganda came to believe that they or their children might be named as an heir to landed property. As Simon Szreter argues in Chapter 2, the need for proof of consanguinity can provide an essential stimulus for the masses to register their offspring. Fines and tax-breaks provided further encouragement (Mukwaya 1953).

The most powerful motivation for the development of this enormous programme of state monitoring, however, was the belief that the population of Buganda, and indeed of southern Uganda more widely, was in terminal decline. Civil war, violent conquest, recurrent famine and successive epidemics had accompanied the region's absorption into empire and seemed to promise the decimation of what was formerly one of the most densely populated parts of Africa. In 1908 East Africa's leading physician claimed that three-quarters of Ganda babies were miscarried, stillborn or died in the first week after delivery. Other commentators made even more cataclysmic claims based on even weaker evidence, creating a sense of crisis which prompted Uganda's colonial administration to seek accurate demographic data relating to the entire population under its protection. Buganda's chiefly council, convinced that demographic decline was the result of moral collapse and growing female autonomy, had already passed legislation aiming to ensure that all marriages were recorded as early as 1896, and so agreed readily to the suggestion in 1908 that all births and deaths should be registered as well (Kuczynski 1949, 119–120; Cunningham 1905, 159–161).[8] A generalized sense of demographic crisis seems to have been the crucial factor which motivated so many chiefs to ensure compliance with this intrusive and inconvenient process.

Fixing identities

Many of the needs of the state, such as the monitoring of populations or the planning of public health interventions, require that vital registration be both comprehensive and accurate. As we have seen, the system of recording vital events in colonial Uganda was impressive in its scope, given the mobility of its population, but it was far from universal. Moreover, it is likely that it also failed in the task of identifying correctly who belonged to Uganda's citizenry, and then fixing on each individual a unique identifier that would guarantee specific rights and obligations, and enable the state to follow the life course of an individual, from birth to marriage to death. This process is rarely entirely straightforward in any society. A common complication in many societies is the potential confusion associated with women's assumption of their husband's name at marriage. In practice, though, problems of subsequent misidentification have typically been avoided by recording both the bride's father's and husband's names during the registration of marriage. But in societies to the west of Lake Victoria individuals have changed their names for a range of reasons at various points in their lives without formalizing their new

[8] Walker to Baylis, 1 December 1907, Birmingham, CMS archives, G3/A7/0/1907/190; Evidence supplied by A. Cook in Lambkin, Mission to the Uganda Protectorate on the Prevalence of Venereal Diseases. Summary of Evidence, December 1907, NA, CO/536/15; Buganda Lukiiko Archives, 1894–1918, 28 January 1896.

identities with the state. Naming traditions in this region encouraged this tendency towards self-reidentification. Many societies in Uganda had an individualizing system of naming, where children typically were given a name that was created uniquely for them, and that would not automatically be passed on to the next generation. In the past, babies were often given names at birth which reflected the context in which their near relatives found themselves. In the early colonial period, a time of demographic crisis and sharp social conflict, such names often carried deeply negative connotations.

Analysis of the names registered at baptism in one Catholic parish in the western Ugandan kingdom of Bunyoro, for example, showed that almost 40 per cent of names given in the first quarter of the twentieth century referred to death. Over the entire colonial period one in twelve children were given names which demonstrated awareness of neighbours' or family members' concealed antagonism. There is an impressively large repertoire of Nyoro names which refer to hidden enemies, such as Beyeza (the bad pretend to be good). The naming of a child was an opportunity for redressing wrongs publicly while avoiding open confrontation. In the past, rejecting an unattractive birth-name was seen as a sign of disrespect for parental intent. In 1996 I interviewed two brothers both in their eighties who were named Mburamukoro (a waste of energy) and Tinkamanyire (I don't know). They admitted that such names were uncomfortable but they had retained them out of regard for their parents' sadness at losing so many newborn children. After the deaths of more than a dozen babies Mburamukoro's birth was greeted with natural cynicism, while his survival allowed his parents to give their next child a name that reflected their retreat from total pessimism – 'I don't know [if he will survive]'.

As time passed, however, it became common for an unpleasantly-named child on reaching adolescence to take on a more positive self-identification. The older generation regarded such renaming as yet another sign of the shameless individualism of the modern era, but for the young adopting a new name was an attempt to improve their life chances, given that education and employment increasingly took people away from the local community where the context of a descriptive name was understood. Many Nyoro names would have brought the bearer recurrent embarrassment. As Nyoro conceived of Death as a character with a malicious personality, parents often attempted to encourage it to move on, by pretending indifference to the newborn. Thus some babies were called after unattractive or unimportant objects, such as rats, goats, insects or monkeys, while names like Kizaireki (what a bad child we have produced!) were relatively common. Other names which were likely to be rejected were those such as Miteto, which questioned a person's paternity, or Byababi (people are bad), which expressed a particularly gloomy outlook on life (Doyle 2008, 361–382; cf. Hensley and Spencer 1985, 723–729; Seraydarian and Busse 1981, 253–257; O'Sullivan *et al.* 1988).

This practice of acquiring a new name in response to a change in a person's circumstances was also seen in the neighbouring kingdom of Buganda. In the early colonial period, chiefs and colonial administrators attempted to counter women's growing independence by passing a series of laws, some of which imposed heavy penalties on female adulterers and made divorce for women who had married in church almost impossible. In response many women expressed their dissatisfaction with becoming 'prisoners' within Christian marriage by giving themselves names such as Sirinagyendida (I will have nowhere to return) and Bwakwegayirira (marriage is a struggle of begging) (Musisi 2001, 176; 1991, 175–177, 181). The frequency with which Ugandans in the past possessed multiple names, and then utilized different names at different times when dealing with officialdom, is one of the most problematic aspects of family reconstitution in this region. My research into the region's demographic history drew me to Catholic parish registers of baptism, marriage and death, because these are the richest source of information still available on family relations during the colonial period.

One of the parishes selected for this study was Kisubi, which lies midway between Kampala and Entebbe in Buganda. In order to calculate changes in average birth intervals, marriage ages and family sizes over time in Buganda, more than 30,000 life events from the Kisubi parish registers were entered into a database so that family ties could be reconstructed. When the baptism database was sorted by the mothers' and fathers' names so that couples could be matched to the various children they christened over the years, time and again individuals appeared who seemed to have used alternative names.[9] Sometimes people simply modified their original names, perhaps abbreviating a clausal name, or abandoning a diminutive prefix as they got older. Men who acquired political office often used their official title as a personal name, while other men acquired supplementary descriptive names as adults which they came to prefer to the clan name they had been given at birth. Thus one man baptized his first two children calling himself Alan Kisomose, a name of the lungfish clan. For the baptism of his third child he gave his name as Alan Kisomose Jjuuko. Evidently delighted with his new name, which means 'that which reverberates', he was recorded only as Alan Jjuuko when he brought his last six children to be baptized. The most common cause of multiple naming was the ritually dangerous act of giving birth to twins. This not only caused the twins' parents to acquire new honorific titles, Ssalongo and Nnalongo, but also required that each twin and the six children who followed the twin birth would have pre-determined names in addition to their own personal names. So the child born after a twin birth would have a clan name or a situational name but would also always be called Kiiza. The problem for the historical demographer – and for the state – is that sometimes individuals would use their supplementary names, and sometimes

[9] In Buganda, unlike most neighbouring societies, most personal names were inherited from clan ancestors, though not usually the father, rather than referring to the circumstances of the birth.

Table 10.1. Twins and multiple naming

Baptism date	*Date of birth*	*Father's Christian name*	*Father's second name*	*Mother's Christian name*	*Mother's second name*	*Village*
09/12/1943	03/12/1943	Deusdedit	Mukasa	Maria	Nambirige	Kisubi
26/09/1946	19/09/1946	Deusdedit	Mukasa	Maria	Nnambirige	Kisubi
09/09/1948	08/07/1948	Deusdedit	Mukasa	Malia	Nambirige	Kisubi
14/02/1951	13/02/1951	Deusdedit	Mukasa	Maria	Nambirige	Kisubi
30/04/1953	30/04/1952	Deus	Ssalongo Mukasa	Malya	Nalongo Nambirige	Kisubi
30/04/1953	30/04/1952	Deus	Ssalongo Mukasa	Maria	Nalongo Nambirige	Kisubi
27/05/1955	26/05/1955	Deusdedit	Ssalongo Mukasa	Maria	Nnalongo Nnambirige	Kisubi
24/06/1956	24/06/1956	Deusdedit	Mukasa	Malia	Nambirije	Kisubi

their own personal names. Table 10.1 gives a sense of the difficulty in tracking individuals following the birth of twins.[10]

The examples given above demonstrate the potential which existed for the state to lose sight of individuals who used different names in successive encounters with officialdom. Of course many individuals would have altered which name they utilized during dealings with bureaucracy with no intent to deceive, but it seems likely that others would have considered there was little to be gained from consistency in self-identification, which would leave them exposed to tax, labour service and other unpleasant demands of the state.

Much more significant, though, was the deliberate use of naming to redesignate individuals' ethnicity. Uganda's censuses, perhaps the most thorough in colonial Africa, consistently showed that the numbers of Ganda (the principal and most powerful, Luganda-speaking people in the region centred on Kampala) in Buganda grew far faster than they should have according to the rate of natural increase calculated from vital registration data. As we have seen, the recording of vital events was imperfect but, because it tended to encourage the reporting of births more than deaths, the civil registration system would have overestimated rather than underestimated natural increase. It seems clear that the Ganda ethnic group expanded during the colonial period in large part because of the absorption of non-Ganda.

[10] Only where an individual had the same Christian name, the same spouse and lived in the same village was it assumed that the different last name did not indicate simply that this was a different person. Personal names have been altered to ensure individuals' anonymity.

This was not an entirely new phenomenon. The history of the pre-colonial kingdom of Buganda was shaped by rapid expansion, raiding and economic prosperity. Conquered areas were subjugated and then gradually Gandaized. Large numbers of slaves were acquired from neighbouring areas and allocated to private individuals and state officials, while Buganda's wealth drew in free immigrants with specialist skills such as herders and smelters. Ethnic assimilation seems to have been exceptionally easy in Buganda, primarily because of the nature of the kingdom's clans. Notionally clanship was based on common descent but in practice marital exogamy and totem avoidance rather than genealogical relationship defined clan identity. As clans in this region were highly dispersed, and often very large, and because different clans in different ethnic groups often shared the same totem, it was relatively easy for immigrants, on arriving as a stranger in a community, to claim membership of a clan, and thus full citizenship within Ganda society. The abundance of land and above all chiefs' eagerness to acquire new clients in this highly competitive kingdom also facilitated the absorption of outsiders. Runaway slaves, for example, who could conceal their foreignness, were able to achieve integration into a local community by attaching themselves to a patron in need of followers (Médard 2007b, 1–30; Hanson 2003).

These mechanisms of incorporation survived the colonial takeover intact, for European rule imposed few restrictions on the relatively malleable nature of identity in this region. The doctrine of indirect rule in practice prioritized geographical over ethnic identities, while the compulsion towards administrative efficiency saw a succession of minor ethnic groups disappear from census schedules, swallowed up by their larger neighbours. Universal labour shortages meant that immigrants from other colonies were accepted enthusiastically, despite their reputation as bearers of a range of communicable diseases, from sleeping sickness to tuberculosis. The comings and goings at key border crossings were recorded assiduously, but the ability of migrants to evade the monitoring of the state was openly acknowledged (Uganda Protectorate 1932; Richards 1973; see also Chapter 9 for other examples).

Buganda was rewarded for its alliance with the agents of the British empire in the 1890s by being allowed to double in size at the expense of its neighbours. The scale and rapidity of this expansion caused the Ganda royal government to construct a policy of ethnic assimilation that was remarkable for its comprehensiveness. The mechanisms by which incorporated peoples on the periphery of the kingdom were deliberately re-identified as Ganda are best evidenced on the northern borderland. The indigenous Nyoro population there were forbidden from using their own language, dancing their own dances, or expressing loyalty to their former king across the district border. The primary technique which forced Nyoro to accept a Ganda identity was the imposition of Ganda names on Nyoro when they came into contact with any of the institutions associated with the Ganda royal government. So if Nyoro had their births registered, went to school or to the clinic, were summoned to court, or wished to purchase land, they were required to accept a new name which defined them as Ganda. Such individuals then had two names, and two ethnic identities (Doyle 2009, 284–302).

This redefinition of all indigenes as Ganda was resented by the Nyoro but was approved, it seems, by all Ganda. Ganda opinion was much more divided by the endeavours of immigrants to pass themselves, or more commonly their children, off as members of the host ethnic group. There was much to gain by becoming Ganda. Buganda was the wealthiest society in East Africa during the colonial period, and enjoyed the best educational and medical facilities in the region, and unparalleled constitutional autonomy under British over-rule. The city of Kampala, its sugar and tea plantations, and above all its tens of thousands of coffee and cotton farms, drew in labour migrants from as far away as Kenya, Burundi and western Tanganyika. By 1959 immigrants officially made up 45 per cent of Buganda's total population. In reality their numbers were almost certainly underestimated for many migrants decided not just to stay in Buganda but to try to become Ganda by acquiring a new name (East African Statistical Department 1961).

In the early 1950s the eminent British anthropologist Audrey Richards was invited by the colonial state to lead an investigation into the relationship between economic migrants and the host population. Her field notebooks are full of recorded conversations where Ganda discussed the possibility of complete assimilation. The consensus was that immigrants could resemble Ganda after a number of years of imitating Ganda habits, customs and accent. 'If an immigrant adopted Baganda dress and washed himself and his clothes, and got money, and married a Muganda woman, then he might be *like* a Muganda in three years. Otherwise it took a very long time.' But being like a Ganda, and being taken for a Ganda, were different things. Another of Richards's informants claimed: 'You always know a man is a Munyaruanda. However long he has lived in the place.'[11] What the Ganda did acknowledge, however, was that the children of immigrants could grow up as Ganda.[12] Not all incomers were admirers of their Ganda hosts, but the largest immigrant group, the Rwanda, regarded Buganda as a haven from the extreme poverty and oppression of their homeland. As one stated, 'I think that Ganda customs are better. I shall never go back to my home. I don't like the government in my country. I want to work here and when I have children I shall give them Ganda names and get a plot for them' (Gutkind 1954, 63).[13]

Initially it seems that all Ganda welcomed labour migrants from poorer parts of East Africa. Householders' prestige grew as they were freed from manual work

[11] A. Richards papers, London School of Economics Archives (LSE), 7/18, Mutuba II, Busiro, 26 January 1951; 7/16, Banyaruanda, July 1950.

[12] Richards papers, LSE, 7/19, Conversation at Mut. V. Gomb., Kyagwe, 27 February 1951.

[13] Richards papers, LSE, 7/18, Mutuba II, Busiro, 26 January 1951; 7/19, Bulamesi, 15 June 1951; 7/16, Sabagabo of Busiro, 17 November 1950; 7/18, Busiro, Musisi (Musigiri Semeoni Kayanda), 17 November 1950.

and assumed the role of patron to their seasonal clients. But, as migrants began to settle in such numbers that they outnumbered the indigenes in much of Buganda, a division on class lines emerged in Ganda communities. Larger landlords' readiness to welcome immigrants as rent-paying tenants outraged the Ganda peasantry who found it increasingly difficult to recruit migrant labour on acceptable terms. Chiefs' willingness to allow foreigners to open up wasteland for cultivation was viewed by ordinary Ganda as another example of the elite's greed for rent and clients, especially when the cleared forests and reclaimed swamps proved to be more fertile than the Ganda's long-established gardens. The anxieties of Ganda farmers stemmed from the perception that immigrants not only worked harder than they did, but also they were more fertile. Fearing that they would soon be swamped by incomers, rural Ganda demanded, unsuccessfully, that laws should be imposed to deprive outsiders of tenancy rights and force them back onto the labour market. It is striking that in colonial Buganda the self-interest of chiefs, the agents of the state, would have encouraged the use of the vital registration system as a mechanism of inclusion, permitting immigrants who had attempted to integrate themselves into the local community to claim citizenship by identifying themselves as Ganda (Hanson 2003, 176, 194).[14]

Assimilation was so rapid in colonial Buganda not only because of the openness of the clan system and chiefs' need to attract clients – factors which had endured the transition to European over-rule. Also the urban intimacy and detachment from the extended family experienced in Kampala fostered intermarriage, while the existence of freehold removed the need for immigrants to secure the approval of an entire community in order to obtain land. Most significantly, the almost universal provision of education accelerated immigrants' children's absorption of the host society's culture. However, negative factors also played a role. Richards learned in the 1950s that the Rwanda tried so hard to shed their identity in large part because they were 'so despised' by the Ganda. The Ganda's chauvinistic emphasis on the inferiority of other ethnic groups, combined with the provision of numerous routes to re-identification, motivated the mass adoption of new identities.[15]

A sense of the scale of the reinvention of identity in colonial Africa can be obtained from further analysis of the naming patterns contained in the Kisubi parish register of baptism. It is almost impossible to trace individual immigrants who changed their own names, but it is possible to observe how frequent it was for parents to attempt to alter both the ethnicity and the nationality of their children. The beginning of this process of rebranding was the giving of names which were specific to the Ganda ethnic group. As most Ganda names are unique to Buganda

[14] Richards papers, LSE, 7/19, G. Mut. 7, Kyagwe, M. Musaale, 1951; 7/19, Bulamesi, 15 June 1951; 7/18, Notes on meeting at Sabawali's private home and Sabadu's Lukiko, Mumyuka's gombolola, Busiro saza, 20 January 1951; 7/16, Banyaruanda, 14 November 1950; 7/19, Mutuba VIII, Mulyanti.
[15] Richards papers, LSE, 7/19, Tea estate, 2 November 1950.

it was possible to identify the great majority of the parents and children within this register as Ganda or non-Ganda. Given that names in this region should typically follow the cultural traditions of the father, situations where the name of a child was typically Ganda but that of the father was not were defined as examples of re-identification. The Kisubi baptism register shows that over the course of the colonial period 27 per cent of male immigrants, around 500 individuals, gave a Ganda name to their children. This was more likely to happen where the immigrants were in a relationship with a Ganda woman but the practice was still extremely common where both partners were non-Ganda. One of the best examples of this practice appeared in the register in August 1947. A couple whose names indicate they were probably from Burundi baptized two children, one aged 3, the other 9 months, on the same day. They had called their first child Omwanabuganda – little one of the Ganda – which, if it was supposed to be an integrative strategy, would certainly have failed, as such names were a clear mark of the outsider. By the time their second child was born they had worked out how assimilation operated in Buganda, through adoption into, or more likely an asserted claim to belong to, a Ganda clan. Accordingly they called their second child Nasozi, a female name indicating membership of Buganda's Njovu clan.

Parents' attempts to Gandaize their children formed a prominent part of the immigrant experience from the start of colonial rule, as the graph in Figure 10.2 shows. The variation over time in the frequency with which Ganda names were given to foreign babies is interesting but not easy to explain. It seems likely that fluctuations were linked to changes in the security of tenure offered to foreign tenants by landowners, as well as to the ebb and flow of Ganda ethnic nationalism, but oral informants willing to discuss the motivations behind their re-identification were understandably difficult to locate.[16]

Conclusion and epilogue

A number of lessons can be learned from Uganda's experiments with vital registration during the colonial period. The relatively high level of popular compliance with the laws of population recording was the result not only of direct incentives in the form of penalties and tax-breaks, but also of a broader range of benefits, of which rights to inheritance that depended on formal identification were most important. The declining reliability of the colonial system after the 1920s demon-

[16] A large number of interviews relating to ethnic identity were conducted in Buganda. In those areas which had formerly belonged to the neighbouring kingdom of Bunyoro, Nyoro informants were generally willing to discuss the strategies employed by the Buganda state which were aimed to ensure their cultural as well as physical incorporation. In the heartland of Buganda, however, long-resident immigrants proved evasive when questioned about processes of assimilation.

Figure 10.2. Percentage of children in the Kisubi baptism register born to non-Ganda fathers who had Ganda names

strated the importance of bureaucratic simplicity and supervision. Most importantly, the frequency with which individuals changed their names, or had their names changed for them, explains to a large extent the current enthusiasm of African governments for biometric systems of population registration. Systems of nominal registration in Uganda made it difficult for the state to monitor its population, but possessed a flexibility which served three important social purposes. They helped maintain the interest of local elites in the operation of the state, they facilitated the integration of a community which was becoming rapidly more diverse, and they enabled individuals to adopt a new identity. Advocates of vital registration typically focus on the right to possess a permanent, recognized identity, but in the past the right to change a name has also protected the vulnerable.[17]

Individuals' rejection of a fixed personal or ethnic identity is more than an essentially technical difficulty obstructing the development of a system of full vital registration in East Africa. It is a symptom of the contentiousness of identity politics. The national project in Uganda, which requires that the state determine who is entitled to citizenship and the benefits that this carries, and who is not, raises difficult questions. Uganda's borders are largely arbitrary lines on a map, almost impossible to police, and typically bear no relation to the region's rather fuzzy ethnic boundaries. A large proportion of the current population are descendants of immigrants from other territories. Indeed one of the slurs commonly used to undermine the

[17] The right to an identity has been endorsed by all signatories to the United Nations' Convention on the Rights of the Child.

current president is the unfounded accusation that his father was from Rwanda. It is a matter of debate on what date Ugandans first existed, as a nationality. On one level, the politics of identity are the politics of boundaries, physical, temporal and conceptual.

However, liberal advocates of civil registration argue that its most fundamental purpose is not to serve as a mechanism of inclusion and exclusion, but to guarantee the most basic of all human rights, the right to an identity, the right to a name (cf. UNICEF 2011). From the possession of a confirmed identity flows a series of secondary rights, such as access to the services of a state or protection of rights to legitimate inheritance. The desire to protect widows, orphans and other vulnerable groups resulted in Plan International and UNICEF providing the Ugandan government with substantial funding in the early 1990s to re-establish the universal recording of vital events. The state's responsibility to record all births, deaths and marriages moreover was reaffirmed in a 1994 law and then enshrined in the 1995 constitution. Yet by 2003 only around 4 per cent of all births were being registered, due, it was claimed, to staff shortages. The problems of under-resourcing have been partially solved through further donor support, but still only around 26 per cent of children's births are registered, a far weaker performance than that achieved under colonial rule. Under-reporting of vital events is thought to continue partly because staffing levels are adequate in only 60 per cent of districts, but also because the cost of obtaining a certificate is unaffordable for the poor. The basic fees are relatively high in themselves, and in addition it is popularly believed that bureaucrats sometimes demand additional payment to dispense evidence of an individual's citizenship or identity, on the basis that such documentation is regarded as a route to significant material benefits, such as a passport, government bursary, or inheritance. Nonetheless, growing pressure to ensure that only citizens benefit from state provision of education and health care has forced large numbers of people in Uganda to apply retrospectively for birth certificates, at significant formal and informal cost (Plan International 2010; Anon. 2002).[18]

The revival of interest in vital registration in the last decade or so in Uganda can be seen as another example of President Museveni's willingness to go along with a Western liberal agenda in order to maintain a steady flow of aid. Museveni's regime has guaranteed a high level of female representation at every level of government; the Ugandan economy is one of the most liberalized in Africa; it has stabilized its national debt; its HIV prevention programme is exceptionally effective; and it has arguably done more to reduce poverty than any other African government. The unending flow of reforming legislation in Uganda is often tokenistic or strategically self-interested, but enough has been delivered to ensure that over the past twenty-five years few countries in the world have received more

[18] See Chapter 19 for further discussion of the inequities of paper-based registration, and the potential superiority, in welfare terms, of a biometric system detached from the local state.

aid per capita from donors than Uganda. Until recently half of Uganda's national income was donor-sourced (Adam and Gunning 2002, 2045–2056).

This official enthusiasm for liberal reform is far from popular within some sections of Ugandan society. The premise, on which calls for full vital registration are based, that all members of a society share equal basic rights, is not generally recognized within rural communities in Great Lakes Africa. Pan-Africanist philosophers of the twentieth century may have claimed that concepts like *ubuntu* (shared humanity) and *ujamaa* (familyhood) demonstrated African moral superiority over the atomized West, but politics in modern Africa have rarely demonstrated a deep commitment to universal as opposed to collective rights (Tutu 2009; Nyerere 1973). In interviews male elders emphasized that rights were accrued and that the stability of both family and society depended on patriarchal restriction on female autonomy. Informants concluded that the rise in divorce was ultimately due to the new demanding nature of their wives, which they blamed on 'whites and their human rights'. 'People got so taken up with equality. Women changed and they tended to think that they were equal to men, that they could behave like a man. So in the end husband and wife couldn't be together.' The sexual precocity of the young and their refusal to settle down and marry were again blamed on Western influence.

> When this issue of women's and children's rights came in, it spoilt everything in marriage and childhood. That's the reason why many schools have been burnt. You the teacher cannot say anything to a child who misbehaves. Should you try to, you will end up in the hands of the police. We parents no longer have authority. I used to cane my children whenever they were in the wrong, but now if you beat them, they tell you that you don't have the authority to do so . . . Long ago the dress a girl wore would go down beyond the knees. But today her dress stops at her buttocks and if you try to advise her, she would say 'it's my right.'[19]

Human rights are held responsible by elderly informants for a range of social ills, serving as a convenient shorthand for the advancement of the individual under a largely gender-neutral legal system, religions that have stressed personal salvation, an educational system that gave some encouragement to freedom of thought, and a market economy that provided women with a new sense of value and the young with a means of acquiring wealth independently of their parents. The humanitarian benefits that it is hoped vital registration will deliver are not likely to win universal approval in this region.

Yet Museveni's growing enthusiasm for vital registration in part reflects his awareness that local attitudes towards the rights of the weak, and especially of children, are shifting rapidly. While rural elders may complain about children's rights, the recent furore over homosexuality and child sacrifice shows that popular anxiety about the vulnerability of children is at a level that would have been

[19] Male Focus Group Discussion (FGD), Bukoto, 24 August 2004; Male FGD, Kitala, 1 September 2004; Int. LLS, Bukunda, Masaka, 21 August 2004.

unimaginable a generation ago. Ideas about the family in some sectors of Ugandan society appear to have changed significantly in recent years (Epprecht 2010, 768–779; Caplan 2010, 4–7).

Vital registration can enhance social justice, but it also provides the state with new powers of social control. Uganda has been so popular with international donors not only because of its strategic adoption of a series of liberal reforms, but also because of its enthusiastic participation in the global war on terror. Uganda has sent troops into Somalia to combat Islamists on behalf of the African Union; it has supported southern Sudanese secession; it has reportedly allowed the US to detain and interrogate suspected terrorists within its territory; and it has labelled some of its own opposition movements as fundamentalist-inspired. The international war on terror has enabled the Ugandan government to limit journalistic coverage of anti-government protest and has allowed suspects to be detained without legal representation for prolonged periods (Whitaker 2010, 639–662). It was not at all surprising to learn that the first use of biometrics in Uganda was within the Ugandan army, regarded as perhaps the greatest danger to Museveni's hold on power. Nor was it a shock to learn that the bulk of the money invested in 2010 in biometric identity recording was directed to the security services rather than the immigration department, the Electoral Commission or the office of the Registrar-General. In the same year international observers criticized Uganda's Electoral Commission's initial plan to introduce biometric voter registration only in urban areas, which tend to vote for the opposition. Such concerns are not without foundation. Following the 2006 general election Uganda's Supreme Court ruled that Electoral Commission officials in some constituencies had removed individuals believed to be opposition supporters from the voting register. Opposition politicians are now claiming that facial recognition software and the development of biometric membership cards for the ruling party will make it easier to disenfranchise opponents of the government (Independent Team 2010; Habati 2010; Matsiko 2010). It may be that biometrics will lead to a new way of defining who should be excluded from the benefits of community membership.[20]

References

Adam, Christopher S. and Jan Willem Gunning. 2002. 'Redesigning the Aid Contract: Donors' Use of Performance Indicators in Uganda.' *World Development* 30(12): 2045–2056.

Anon. 1947. 'The Buganda Births and Deaths Registration Law, 31 May 1923.' In *The Native Laws of Buganda*. Kampala: Government Printer.

[20] It is equally possible that the Ugandan government, like those of Ghana and Nigeria, will find the expense of electronic identification for the entire population unsupportable. Cf. Breckenridge (2010, 648).

Anon. 2002. 'Birth Certificate Now Vital for University Admission.' *New Vision*, 2 December.

Breckenridge, Keith. 2010. 'The World's First Biometric Money: Ghana's e-Zwich and the Contemporary Influence of South African Biometrics.' *Africa: The Journal of the International African Institute* 80(4): 642–662.

Caplan, Pat. 2010. '"Child Sacrifice" in Uganda? The BBC, "Witch Doctors" and Anthropologists.' *Anthropology Today* 26(2): 4–7.

Cunningham, James Frederick. 1905. *Uganda and Its Peoples: Notes on the Protectorate of Uganda, Especially the Anthropology and Ethnology of Its Indigenous Races*. London: Hutchinson & Co.

Doyle, Shane. 2008. '"The Child of Death": Personal Names and Parental Attitudes towards Mortality in Bunyoro, Western Uganda, 1900–2005.' *Journal of African History* 49(3): 361–382.

—— 2009. 'Immigrants and Indigenes: The Lost Counties Dispute and the Evolution of Ethnic Identity in Colonial Buganda.' *Journal of Eastern African Studies* 3(2): 284–302.

—— 2012. *Before HIV: Sexuality, Fertility and Mortality in East Africa, 1900–1980*. Oxford: Oxford University Press.

East African Statistical Department. 1950. *African Population of the Uganda Protectorate 1948: Geographical and Tribal Studies*. Nairobi: Government Printer.

—— 1961. *Uganda Census 1959*. Nairobi: Government Printer.

Epprecht, Mark. 2010. 'The Making of "African Sexuality": Early Sources, Current Debates.' *History Compass* 8(8): 768–779.

Gutkind, Peter Claus Wolfgang. 1954. *A Preliminary Report of Mulago, Kampala, Uganda, 1954*. Cambridge: TS, African Studies Centre Library.

Habati, Mubatsi. 2010. 'Uganda: Are Missing Voters Names Deliberate?' *The Independent (Kampala)*, 6 April. http://allafrica.com/stories/201004070714.html.

Hanson, Holly Elisabeth. 2003. *Landed Obligation: The Practice of Power in Buganda*. Portsmouth: Heinemann.

Hensley, Wayne E. and Barbara A. Spencer. 1985. 'The Effect of First Names on Perceptions of Female Attractiveness.' *Sex Roles* 12(7–8): 723–729.

Independent Team. 2010. 'Uganda: German, U.S., UK Envoys Fight over EC Tender.' *The Independent (Kampala)*, 18 May. http://allafrica.com/stories/201005190739.html?page=2.

Kuczynski, Robert René. 1949. *Demographic Survey of the British Colonial Empire*, vol. II. Oxford: Oxford University Press.

Low, Donald Anthony and Robert Cranford Pratt. 1960. *Buganda and British Overrule, 1900–1955: Two Studies*. Oxford: Oxford University Press.

Matsiko, Haggai. 2010. 'Independent (Kampala).' *The Independent (Kampala)*, 10 August. http://allafrica.com/stories/201008110816.html.

Médard, Henri. 2007a. *Le royaume du Buganda au XIXe siècle: mutations politiques et religieuses d'un ancien État d'Afrique de l'Est*. Paris: Karthala.

—— 2007b. 'Introduction.' In *Slavery in the Great Lakes Region of East Africa*, ed. Henri Médard and Shane Declan Doyle. Oxford: James Currey, 1–30.

Mukwaya, Augustine. 1953. *Land Tenure in Buganda, Present Day Tendencies*. Kampala: East African Institute of Social Research.

Musisi, Nakanyike. 1991. 'Transformations of Baganda Women: From the Earliest Times to the Demise of the Kingdom in 1966.' Ph.D. dissertation, University of Toronto.

—— 2001. 'Gender and the Cultural Construction of "Bad Women" in the Development of Kampala-Kibuga, 1900–1962.' In *'Wicked' Women and the Reconfiguration of Gender in Africa*, ed. Dorothy L. Hodgson and Sheryl A. McCurdy. Portsmouth: Heinemann, 171–187.

Nyerere, Julius K. 1973. *Ujamaa: Essays on Socialism*. Oxford: Oxford University Press.

O'Sullivan, Chris S., Audrey Chen, Simani Mohapatra, Lee Sigelman and Erik Lewis. 1988. 'Voting in Ignorance: The Politics of Smooth-Sounding Names.' *Journal of Applied Social Psychology* 18(13): 1094–1106.

Plan International. 2010. 'Impact of the Universal Birth Registration Campaign.' *Plan International*. http://plan-international.org/birthregistration/resources/country-case-studies/uganda.

Reid, Richard. 2002. *Political Power in Pre-Colonial Buganda: Economy, Society and Warfare in the Nineteenth Century*. Oxford: James Currey.

Richards, Audrey. 1973. *Economic Development and Tribal Change: A Study of Immigrant Labour in Buganda*. Oxford: Oxford University Press.

Seraydarian, Louisa and Thomas Busse. 1981. 'First-Name Stereotypes and Essay Grading.' *Journal of Psychology: Interdisciplinary and Applied* 108: 253–257.

Tutu, Desmond. 2009. *No Future without Forgiveness*. New York: Doubleday.

Twaddle, Michael. 1988. 'The Emergence of Politico-Religious Groupings in Late Nineteenth-Century Buganda.' *Journal of African History* 29(1): 81–92.

Uganda Protectorate. 1922. *1921 Census*. Entebbe: Government Printer.

—— 1932. *1931 Census*. Entebbe: Government Printer.

—— 1949. *Annual Medical Report 1948*. Entebbe: Government Printer.

—— 1950. *Annual Medical Report 1949*. Entebbe: Government Printer.

—— 1953. *Annual Medical Report 1952*. Entebbe: Government Printer.

UNICEF. 2011. 'Child Protection from Violence, Exploitation and Abuse: Registration.' www.unicef.org/protection/index_birthregistration.html.

Whitaker, Beth Elise. 2010. 'Compliance among Weak States: Africa and the Counter-Terrorism Regime.' *Review of International Studies* 36(3): 639–662.

Part III

EMPIRES AND REGISTRATION

11

Identity Registration in India During and After the Raj

RAVINDRAN GOPINATH

THE KEY QUESTION that this chapter attempts to answer is the apparent contradiction between the colonial Indian state's encyclopaedic attempts at statistical recording and the absence of individual identity registration. The colonial government while counting and recording virtually everything from people to property to natural resources somehow did not feel the need to register individual identity. For the Indian population social aggregates such as caste, despite official misgivings, continued throughout the colonial period to be a proxy for individual identity.

Understanding the absence of individual identity registration in a regime obsessed with counting and recording requires an investigation of the long-run neglect of individual identity registration from the pre-colonial period to the end of colonialism. The ascription of identity and its registration, ubiquitous objectives of modern state policy, has had a long though historically and geographically varied trajectory. A variety of states in their attempts to maximize surplus extraction have tried to control and therefore attempted to fix their actual and potential resources, human or inanimate, both spatially and socially. However, such strategies of enumeration exhibit a great deal of variation across cultures, polities and political economies. In the context of India, registration of identities has played a crucial, though not exclusive, role in the construction/reconstruction and development of social identities.

This chapter is a broad survey of practices of registration in colonial India. Though the main part of this chapter deals with the colonial period in Indian history, we begin our discussion with the pre-colonial period as a baseline to highlight the changes that occurred in enumerative practices with British conquest and subsequently under the colonial administration. Similarly, the last section of the chapter looks at identity registration in the post-colonial period, culminating with the currently ongoing project to enumerate the entire population of India using biometric technologies of registration.

Registration is merely the act of listing someone or something by an institution that commands authority or legitimacy. States and non-state institutions such as

Proceedings of the British Academy **182**, 299–322. © The British Academy 2012.

religious bodies and communitarian groups often registered individual constituents as well as properties and larger social aggregates. For instance, the Ain-i-Akbari, the administrative gazetteer and manual produced during Akbar's reign in the sixteenth century, required the accountant 'to record the name of each peasant, together with that of his ancestor' with the assessment details (Habib 1999, 271). A similar directive is found in the last major Mughal emperor Aurangazeb's reign, where village assessment is fixed after individual assessment (Habib 1999, 271). According to Irfan Habib, this individual assessment and recording was often fictitious (Habib 1999, 273). Similarly, Susan Bayly remarks that the basis of later colonial caste demarcations began as exercises of caste enumeration for 'popularizing older guru networks and holy places', which were later institutionalized as fixed categories in the enumerative statistics of the colonial census (Bayly 1999, 140). She thus suggests that initial objectives of the aggregation of people into castes clearly diverged from the later colonial categories of statistical enumeration and grouping. Emphasizing the modern character of caste associations, Rudolph and Rudolph have commented that they acted as modern collective organizations with their head office, publications, list of members and organizational chart (Leonard 1978; Wallerstein 1966, 140; Rudolph and Rudolph 1966). The extent and completeness of such registration of castes, especially in the case of state-sponsored listings, exhibited a long-term secular increase, but does this suggest more thorough enumeration or did the impetus to such change derive, rather, from the accumulation of a succession of qualitatively different notions of people and of the distribution of resources held by different systems of government?

On the basis of the Kautilya's Arthashastra, a classical treatise on government and economics written some time between the fourth and second centuries BCE, it has been asserted that early Indians conducted censuses and kept detailed registers of individuals right down to the level of villages. Village accountants, or Gopas, each responsible for five to ten villages, acted as census takers. They recorded the adult population, and household income and expenditure and details of merchants and artisans (Shamasastry 1915). Though the record-keeping and registration prescribed in the Arthashastra is of an extremely high level, given the vastness of the Mauryan empire of that period, it appears that this manual was likely to have been largely prescriptive in nature. The minuteness and detail of record-keeping described and recommended in the Arthashastra cannot even be achieved by the twenty-first-century Indian state. Further, in the absence of any surviving evidence for such enumeration and registration, it appears that this may have been only a prescriptive manual of best practices. However, similar practices have been suggested for Zhou China, another iron age empire, where there is stronger surviving evidence (see von Glahn's description of Shang Yang's reforms and enumerations 361–338 BCE in Chapter 1 in this volume).

In the Indian case, the first documented evidence that technologies of registration were not only well known but also practised occurs in the sixteenth century. At this point there was, however, apparently a very limited registration of Indians as individuals, despite the fact that enumeration exercises in the post-colonial period represent a continuity with an already-established practice in the pre-colonial period under a constantly expanding and powerful bureaucratic apparatus at that time. A related issue which therefore demands attention is whether caste and other communal groupings may have been perceived in both pre-colonial and colonial periods as providing a convenient and satisfactory proxy for individual registration, resulting in very limited attempts at listing individuals.

Identities are always manifold, compound, historically contingent and continuously re-constructed. The identity ascribed by the colonial state always coexisted in tension with multiple other identities, traditional or forged in opposition to the colonial state. Investigation of a theme as large and complex as identity in India is beyond the scope of this chapter, which will therefore limit itself to discussing the registration of identities and rights that the state considered to be true and legitimate.

This chapter will argue, on the basis of evidence from registration related to population, demography, anthropological investigations and landed property, that the overwhelming concerns of the state and the practical limits to governance imposed by geography, demography and the absence of popular traditions of individual identity registration defined the trajectory and the very partial nature of registering individuals in India while simultaneously developing an elaborate arithmetic of social aggregates.

From populousness to population

Populations, or at least the numbers of some groups of people, were counted by governments long before the development of modern states. Despite this apparent continuity in practice of counting people, Foucault makes the important point that 'Population is undoubtedly an idea and a reality that is absolutely modern in relation to the functioning of political power, but also in relation to knowledge and political theory, prior to the eighteenth century' (Foucault *et al.* 2007). Drawing upon Bruce Curtis's article on Foucault's concepts of governmentality, I argue that, though enumerative practices had pre-colonial antecedents, the important distinction to make is that a shift occurred from the earlier concept of 'populousness' to the modern concept of 'population' (Curtis 2002). Whereas population is dependent on the establishment of practical equivalences among subjects and one common abstract essence, the logic of populousness centres on the hierarchical differentiation of essences. If this distinction between populousness and population is accepted in the apparently absolute form proposed by Foucault then a direct descent from one to the other cannot be made. In fact, the 'discovery' of population constitutes a rupture rather than a continuity from earlier modes of enumeration.

Recent historical writing on India has argued that enumeration in colonial India was not an alien imposition but that it was built upon earlier practices of counting both peoples and things (see Peabody 2001; S. Guha 2003). In India there has been a close association between enumeration and registration. The registration of individuals, i.e. individuals as constituents of population, though rare and infrequent, was preceded in India by the enumeration of territorial or caste populations. It is indeed true that enumeration was not unknown in India even before British rule. The Mughals regularly maintained identity registers of nobles and soldiers. Miniature portraits were maintained of nobles while the paymaster of the army verified the identity of troopers by distinguishing bodily marks (Zaidi 1982). Emperors and rulers sporadically ordered larger-scale enumerations of houses, looms, ploughs and even heads of households, with some of these survey findings being categorized in terms of important castes.

Notable examples of such enumerations from northern and western India include Abul Fazl's *Ain-i-Akbari or The Institutes of Akbar* (*c.* 1595), Munhata Nainsi's *Marwar ra Pargana ri Vigat* (*c.* 1666) and Ali Muhammad Khan's estimates for Gujarat in 1761 in *Mirat-i-Ahmadi*. Just about everything, including gods, fruits, revenue, agriculture, wages, prices, ornaments and metrology, is discussed. What is notably absent is any figure for the population size of the territory or region being discussed. For example, the quantitative information on the province or *subah* of Allahabad reads as follows:

> This *Súbah* contains ten *Sarkárs*, and 177 *Parganahs*. Revenue 21 *krors*, 24 *lakhs* and 27,819 *dáms* (Rs. 53,10,695-7-9) and 12 *lakhs* of betel leaves. Of these *Parganahs* 131 pay revenue from crops charged at special rates. Measured land 39,68,018 *bighas*, 3 *biswas*, yielding a revenue of 20 *krors*, 29 *lakhs* 71,224 *dáms* (Rs. 50,74,280-9). The remaining 46 *Parganahs* pay the general *bigah* rate. They are rated at 94 *lakhs*, 56,595 *dáms* (Rs. 2,36,424-14). Of this, 1 *kror*, 11 *lakhs*, 65,417 *dáms* (Rs. 279,135-6-6) are *Suyúrghál*. The province furnishes 11,375 Cavalry, 237,870 Infantry and 323 elephants.
>
> (Abul Fazl Allami 1891, 160)

There is no evidence whatsoever in the *Ain* that the Mughals at the height of their power were interested in counting the population of their realm.

Turning to the other much discussed enumeration carried out by Nainsi for Marwar, we once again find the mention of caste and listing of houses and inventories of tools and implements, but this should not be mistaken to be a proto-census attempting to count people (Bhadani 1979; Peabody 2001). In our enthusiasm to find continuities between the pre-colonial and the colonial such enumerative exercises that were carried out for ascertaining the productive and revenue-paying capacity of the land should not be confused with the logic of the colonial census. From what we know of the Mughal state and its semi-autonomous dependencies, it is indeed difficult to argue for an organic and internal connection between their enumerative practices and that of the colonial state in India.

Different groups of people, defined by occupation and caste, became important for these states only insofar as their activities and numbers had a bearing on military recruitment, mobilizing capabilities and the payment of revenue (Perlin 1993, 36–58). Though individual identity registration was not practised or even mentioned as an objective of government, systematic enumeration of entire town populations, as opposed to the recording and counting of soldiers and nobles, had become more frequent in the pre-colonial period. While the early colonial state, too, initially began tentative enumerations that shared much in common with pre-colonial enumerations, what was significantly new was a count of population divided by sex and age and into different religious, ritual and occupational classes. This was unprecedented in the enumerative history of India. Thus the early colonial censuses mark a definite break from the sporadic head counts and *khanashoomaries* (literally, house lists) of the earlier regimes. As the British East India Company expanded its territorial control over the Indian subcontinent, annexing kingdoms and indirectly controlling vanquished kings and princes, it simultaneously embarked on a massive project of first gathering information and then ordering it.

The map and the census were two important technologies of registration introduced and developed by the colonial state in India. The significance of these innovations lay in their scalability. From the small-scale map which showed subcontinental and regional geographical, economic and social patterns, one could zoom right into the village with large-scale, sixteen-inch cadastral maps. The map, in parallel with the all-India census, allowed the state to aggregate and disaggregate with ease at desired administrative levels, geographical spaces and social aggregates.

Within just ten years of the British East India Company's first major victory at the Battle of Plassey in Bengal in 1757, James Rennell was appointed the first Surveyor-General (Rennell 1781, 1792). As early as 1817 the Great Trignometrical Survey of India was established and even before its formal establishment the triangulation of southern India had been started by William Lambton, who was to become the first Surveyor-General of India. Apart from cartographically registering the newly acquired territories of the East India Company in India, the Survey, inspired by scientific curiosity, measured a section of the Great Arc. Early colonial cartography not only mapped territory but also played an important role in enabling the possibility of registering private property and revenue liabilities of Indian peasants and landlords.

The registration of property

The Permanent Settlement of land revenue in Bengal in 1793 marks the first crucial and significant break from earlier forms of Mughal revenue administration undertaken by the East India Company. The Permanent Settlement, inspired by ideologies and theories ranging from mercantilism to physiocracy and *laissez-faire*, broke with earlier practices of revenue collection and land rights by formally declaring private property in land and fixing land revenue in perpetuity. It was hoped that the Permanent Settlement would foster rapid economic growth by transforming the Bengal zamindar, now invested with private property rights and shorn of all extra-economic powers, into a class akin to the English improving farmer. This class, it was believed, would also become staunch supporters of British rule, once the benefits of these changes became evident (R. Guha 1982, esp. ch. 1).

However, subsequent history clearly showed that the Bengal zamindar remained a *rentier* rather than being transformed into a capitalist farmer. The agrarian economy of Bengal declined, without either the state or the actual cultivator benefiting in any way. This state of affairs prompted the government to jettison the Permanent Settlement for a variety of temporary settlements in the rest of the country. What is significant is that as the colonial state began to extend its reach from the top of the Indian class hierarchy into the villages, it attempted to directly extract land revenue from the cultivator (the Ryotwari settlement) or the dominant village coparcenaries (the village or Mahalwari settlements) (Baden-Powell 1892).

This shift was accompanied by the development of Utilitarianism into the dominant ideology of the new colonial state by the third decade of the nineteenth century. Based on the Ricardian theory of rent, the state attempted to scientifically estimate the land revenue with the actual cultivator. This entailed a massive survey of agricultural landholdings, estimating the output and fertility of soils, and registering the revenue-paying cultivators of the country, most importantly in cultivator-based or Ryotwari tenurial systems. The Ryotwari settlement was most prevalent in the Presidencies of Madras and Bombay and in Assam.

The British, after abandoning the initial Permanent Settlement model of land revenue, began paying attention to cadastral detail first in the Salem district of Madras Presidency in 1793–1798. In 1904, cadastral surveys were transferred to the provinces, resulting in two broad methods of survey which were based on (i) the village map system, and (ii) the field measurement book (FMB). The former was prevalent in northern India where the Mahalwari and zamindari systems were important, whereas the southern Madras province and Bombay adopted the FMB system (Kumar 2005, 242).

Under this system a cadastral survey was carried out and this was to be updated through revising re-surveys. After the cadastral survey a title register detailing the name of the holder or holders, the field's identification number and the tax liabilities was produced. The survey department maintained cadastral records in the form of field measurement books or FMBs and village maps along with lists of revenue particulars of each survey field and village sub-division. The revenue department maintained the register of rights, which was known by different regional terms, where ownership and possession were recorded. The registration department kept a record of land transactions through sale, purchase and gifting in the form of notarized deeds.

In the village-based settlements of the North-Western Provinces and the Punjab, village bodies were responsible for the payment of revenue. When the village was largely under the control of one big landlord the settlement resembled the zamindari settlement, whereas when there were many smaller farmers, the revenue collection arrangements were closer to the Ryotwari pattern. In permanently settled zamindari tracts, where the government revenue was fixed in perpetuity, not much attention was paid to land records. Even in temporarily settled areas, very often the title deed was executed with the larger landed magnates and not the actual cultivator. The coverage of land registration focused on agricultural lands to the exclusion of marginal lands and forests. While the latter did support people, for generations the users of these lands were denied any legal ownership title.

The details of the village map and the FMB along with the register of rights and the registration of land deeds would suggest that there was indeed a highly developed system of registration where the individual and his private property in land were being recorded on a substantial scale.[1] Revenue records mentioning individual names and tax obligations also existed in Mughal India. Despite the existence of these records it would be erroneous to mistake them for individual identity registers. The centralized Mughal state in medieval India as well as the colonial government under the British were primarily interested in such record-keeping for purposes of revenue collection and revenue maximization. Large sections of the population that did not have direct relationship to revenue-paying agricultural production were not covered by these tax registers and cadastral maps. Smith (2004, 169) comments that 'the culture of mapping did not extend to a heuristic use of field maps, for instance the use of the pattern of holdings as evidence of right'.

Further, as David Washbrook pointed out of the Anglo-Indian legal system, because it was located against the

> background of a state-dominated economy and an agrarian society in which the possession of land was a function of the political system, the Anglo-Indian law begins to take on a different set of meanings. Its main purpose, so far from protecting the private rights of subjects, may be better seen as providing a range of secondary services for the Company, both as 'state' and as 'shield' for European business interests, which helped to translate political power into money.
>
> (Washbrook 1981, 668)

The contradiction between public law designed to further individual freedoms and unfettered private property, on the one hand, and the social constraints of personal law, on the other, continued throughout British rule. Thus, the revenue and land records of both the Mughals and the British colonial state were essentially registers of the claims of the state over the social surplus, and only much later were some of these records used as evidence of private property.

[1] There are references to cadastral surveys in Indian history going back to ancient history. The southern Indian Chola king, Raja Raja, is supposed to have carried out such an exercise about 1,000 years ago. In the medieval period, Sher Shah Suri classified land by fertility and the crop grown to devise land tax schedules. This was further refined in the reign of Akbar, by Todar Mal. Detailed methods were worked out to estimate the crop output and to commute the state's share into money rates (Habib 1999).

The registration of revenue obligations and tenurial terms of a section of the population did not provide an alternative register of individual identity. This is evidenced by the fact that neither the colonial state nor the independent government of India turned to the revenue registers to ascertain population and individual identities.

Counting and classifying Indians: census and vital registration

Early population enumerations commenced as the East India Company began to expand and administer their newly conquered lands in India. Though these enumerations were limited to towns and specific localities, the important fact is that population as a whole was first estimated and then counted. No longer was enumeration restricted to land controllers, military chiefs and economically important occupations. In the early nineteenth century, Francis Buchanan made rudimentary but important surveys in southern India and Gangetic eastern India (Hamilton 1925). In 1824 Lieutenants Ward and Conner were entrusted with the survey of the recently acquired territory of Malabar. In Malabar a subsequent series of quinquennial censuses was preceded by population enumerations in 1821 and 1827 (Ward 1828a, 1828b). The first relatively comprehensive set of population estimates was presented to the House of Commons in 1857. This was entitled 'A Return on the Area and Population of Each Division of Each Presidency of India, from the Latest Inquiries'. The population counted here amounted to about 43–44 per cent of the population estimated between 1881 and 1901. This data is supposed to have been collected with the help of revenue officials in the early 1850s but the methods of collection remain unknown (Visaria and Visaria 1983, 467).

Probably the first census in India to classify the enumerated population by sex, age, caste and dwelling units was Henry Walter's 1830 census of Dacca city (Srivastava 1983). This however did not record individual identity and was not an identity register. Though a number of provincial and local enumerations were carried out in different parts of the country in the second half of the century before 1871, the census of the North-Western Provinces taken on the night of 31 December 1852, with a reference date of 1 January 1853, was the first census conducted on modern lines (Natarajan 1971, 1). In 1849 the government of India directed provincial governments to conduct quinquennial population enumerations on the lines of those that were to be carried out in the North-Western Provinces by revenue officials. The Board of Revenue in a circular to all Collectors asked them to follow the North-Western Provinces' pattern, with due attention to local specificities, while conducting the proposed quinquennial censuses (Board of Revenue 1850). As Madras was the only Presidency to implement this directive in full, regular five-yearly censuses were peculiar to the Madras Presidency.

Before the beginning of the quinquennial censuses, apart from population enumerations of smaller areas, two province-wide censuses were conducted in

1821–1822 and 1836–1838. All these censuses were plagued by marked under-registration of females and severe undercounting. The first Madras census held in 1822 counted the population at just under 13.5 million (13,476,923).

Madras, in contrast to other Presidencies, had an early-established history of population enumeration. Here the Board of Revenue required each district head to make quinquennial returns of the population of his district. The methods employed in the enumerations of 1821–1822 and 1836–1837 are not known (Census Report 1872). In 1849, the government of India decided to conduct five-yearly population counts employing revenue officials. This resulted in quinquennial censuses in Madras between 1851–1852 and 1866–1867. The fifth quinquennial census, of 1871–1872, was merged with the first imperial census. Village magistrates and accountants who had conducted the earlier censuses were deputed as enumerators for the first all-India census.

Population enumeration which had started sporadically and in geographically limited areas, spurred by immediate revenue needs and a desire to cartographically define acquired territories, had thus developed by the last two decades of the nineteenth century into a definite and regular enumerative institution. The decennial all-India census, especially from 1881, was fairly reliable in terms of total population coverage and did include reasonably comparable serial data on occupations, marital status, caste, language, migration and diseases, in addition to the standard demographic data on age, sex and population. However birth and death data were not collected by the decennial census, and, importantly, individual details cannot be found in the decennial censuses.

Births and deaths

Unlike the population enumeration, the first instance of recording births and deaths comes from Delhi, in 1833 – *Selected Statistics relating to the population of Delhi, outside the Royal Palace, 1833*. This gives an age–sex distribution of the population and vital rates for males and females. The frequent epidemics, scarcities and famines and the consequent high death rate provided the context for the recording of first deaths and then births. Concerned with the high mortality of its European troops, the army played an important role in developing and commenting on the methods of recording births and deaths.

The history of vital registration can be dated in India from the middle of the nineteenth century. Village-level revenue officials – and in some provinces the police – were entrusted with the work of recording deaths and later births. Sanitary Commissioners of the different provinces of India collated their monthly returns into annual reports which were then sent to the Sanitary Commissioner for the government of India at the centre. However, the varied forms in which the statistics were collected and the severe under-enumeration of deaths led the government of India to order a more standardized collection of mortality figures that would immediately show the relative mortality of different geographical and regional units.[2]

The system of civil death registration that was in practice was criticized by the army Sanitary Commissioner who advocated that the British practice of registration should be introduced in India (Gopinath 2010). This was resisted on the grounds that Indians were still not ready for such registration and that this would have to wait for the enactment of legislation requiring compulsory registration of deaths. While the government of India was still concerned only with the counting of deaths, the province of Berar pioneered the registration of births in 1866.

The Bengal Births and Deaths Registration Act was passed in 1873 and this was subsequently adopted by the contiguous states of Orissa and Bihar. Military cantonments made the registration of deaths and births within twenty-four hours of occurrence mandatory. By 1875 the provincial governments of Bengal, North-Western Provinces and Punjab had selected areas for strictly supervised registration of deaths. In Bombay and Madras death and birth registration was carried out in the municipal towns. Concerned with the problem of severe under-registration, the government, while still not making birth and death registration compulsory, asked provincial governments to take steps to make registration more efficient. In 1878 the government directed local authorities to conduct spot checks in areas of unusually high or low birth and death rates. Consequently, in the 1880s and 1890s, Punjab, the Central Provinces, Bengal and Madras took legislative and executive measures to strengthen birth and death registration (Natarajan 1971, 6).

The last quarter of the nineteenth century witnessed India being ravaged by unprecedented famine deaths. The colossal toll of human life claimed by these not entirely natural calamities forced the government to set up the Indian Famine Commission. The Indian Famine Commission of 1878–1880 published draft codes for administrative action to prevent and mitigate famines. These draft codes which were circulated to the provinces as model codes did not find general acceptance, prompting the Revenue and Agricultural Department of the government of India to issue a 'provisional' code. The final Famine Codes were a combination of the 'draft' and 'provisional' codes (Natarajan 1971, 5–6).

The registration of vital statistics was emphasized by the Famine Commission as an early warning system for impending famines. The Commission recommended:

- That the registration of births and deaths should be made legally obligatory in villages as well as towns;
- That regular monthly publication of the main vital statistics should be enforced;

[2] 'For sanitary purposes it is indispensible to know the relative mortality in small and, as far as possible, well defined tracts, to ascertain the death-rates in each of these communities; to see how far this arises from preventable causes, and to apply the remedies. It is only in this way that we can hope to acquire accurate knowledge of the circumstances under which the disease arises and to make vital statistics the stepping-stone to sanitary reforms' (Natarajan 1971).

- That in each unit of registration, the Registrar should be able to read and write, so that this recollection might be supported by a record made at the time the event occurred;
- That the officer-in-charge of the registration of each group of villages should be supplied with the census population of each village, and also with the numbers showing what in the opinion of the Sanitary Commissioner would be the average numbers of births and deaths in such population, and that any excess or deficiency should be made the subject of a special report;
- That the Health Officer of the district should at once bring to the notice of the Collector and the Sanitary Commissioner any serious indication presented by these reports, and that in all the cases the Collector of the district should see the monthly vital statistics as soon as they are compiled; and
- That it should be the special duty of the Sanitary Commissioner to warn the Government of any unusual rise in the death-rate, in order that the cause of such rise might be enquired into.

(Natarajan 1971, 5–6)

Despite the importance attached to vital statistics recording, the government was of the opinion that the time had not yet come to make the registration of births and deaths obligatory. Vital registration was most efficient in the Central Provinces and the Punjab, where there were instances of penal action against defaulters in municipal towns. In Bengal the task of registration was transferred from the police to municipal agencies, resulting in deterioration in recording. Finally, on 1 October 1888 the Births, Deaths and Marriages Registration Act came into force for the whole of British India, providing for voluntary registration of births, deaths and marriages. However, this had little impact on the level of registration as most Indians neither felt the need for such registration nor understood the practice. In the last decade of the nineteenth century provincial governments made renewed attempts to improve registration. Punjab appointed special officers; Bengal reverted to the practice of using the police to collect statistics; and the Civil Surgeon was entrusted with the task of compiling vital statistics in the Central Provinces. By 1897, registration, at least putatively, covered the bulk of the population of British India (see Table 11.1).

The figures in Table 11.1 should not be mistaken for the actual level of registration, conveying only the population where registration was possible. By 1903, nominally, 79.9 per cent of the population of British India was officially covered by vital registration. In 1911, on comparing the increase in population between 1901 and 1911 as returned by the census with the excess of registered births over deaths, it was found that excess births accounted for only 78 per cent of the population increase. Even this figure suggests an exaggerated level of birth registration when set out against estimates of under-registration at the provincial and district levels, which ranged from 20 per cent to 60 per cent for completeness of death registration in the districts of Madras from 1881 to 1911 (estimated from Natarajan 1971, 7).

Table 11.1. Percentage of population covered by registration (1897)

Province	*Registration coverage (%)*
Bengal	99.6
Assam	91.7
North-Western Provinces and Oudh	100.0
Punjab	98.5
Central Provinces	88.1
Berar	98.5
Madras	91.5
Bombay	99.9
Coorg	100.0

Source: Natarajan 1971, 7.

Recording health in early twentieth-century India

After late nineteenth-century colonial anxieties focused on Indian famine and disease, in the early twentieth century, Indian economists began to address population – specifically in terms of birth and death rates – within a broader rubric of trying to understand Indian poverty and its role as an obstacle to national modernity. During the 1920s and 1930s especially, the nature of the relationship between poverty and population underwent intense scrutiny and contest.

In the first two decades of the twentieth century a general shift took place in the administration of public health and vital registration. Health and vital statistics were transferred to the provincial level of government under the Montague-Chelmsford Constitutional Reforms of 1919; and in 1920–1921 Municipality and Local Board Acts were passed to facilitate the extension of public health according to the requirements of the different provinces (Mushtaq 2009). It was recognized that the existing collecting agencies could not possibly be expected to file plausible returns of the cause of death. In an attempt to provide better cause-of-death statistics, the governments of Bengal, United Provinces and Madras instituted enquiries and decided to introduce supplementary forms to disaggregate and register the previously generic term of 'fevers' in more specific disease categories. Similarly, a detailed classification of infant deaths by age was also introduced.

Voluntary registration was still the rule in India, however. In 1930 only Bengal insisted on compulsory rural and urban registration. In the other provinces only in the larger villages and municipal towns was registration mandatory. However, making registration compulsory did not automatically lead to better coverage and reporting. Ironically in the case of Madras Presidency non-compulsory areas reported more complete birth and death rates than areas where registration was compulsory. This was because the local revenue official stopped detailed investigation once registration was made legally compulsory and the people at large did not bother to register.

Thus, a variety of official commissions both before and after independence continued to emphasize the crucial need for improved collection of vital statistics. These included the Royal Commission on Agriculture (1924), the Royal Commission on Labour (1928), the Central Advisory Board on Health (1939), the Health Survey and Development Committee (1946), the Vital Statistics Committee (1949) and the Committee on the Pattern of Statistical Units for Health Departments (1960). In view of the variations in the quality and coverage of vital registration, the Bhore Committee also recommended a number of steps to improve the gathering of statistics on vital events in India (Health Survey and Development Committee 1946).

The absence of attention to individual identity

The above discussion clearly suggests that the colonial state wanted to accumulate social information in increasingly standardized and numerical formats that would be amenable to easy comparison across the widely varied imperial possessions. A Government Order of the Madras government in 1871 commented:

> His Excellency in Council observes that excessive costliness is not the only unfortunate effect of the want of organization which left each Local Government to invent a scheme of its own, irrespective of what is being done in other Provinces. There was, in fact, no unity of plan or central supervision, and the results did not contain the materials required for the comparative statistics of the Empire.
>
> (Dirks 2001, 198)

It was in this context of unsatisfactory comparative statistics and information that W. W. Hunter, the author of the *Annals of Rural Bengal*, was tasked in 1869 with preparing a plan for an imperial gazetteer (Hunter 1970). In 1877 Hunter was designated the director of gazetteers, and the all-India census, which began in 1871–1872, formed the basic foundation of the gazetteers project. The gazetteers attempted to provide a compendium of social, economic, historical, geographical and climatic information on the province or district concerned. Information for the administrative unit's social topography and demography, mortality and fertility was based on census data.

While the work of the editor or compiler of the gazetteer was relatively straightforward and simple, having only to compile information from other existing sources, the census commissioners had to imagine and operationalize categories for mapping the varied and complex social topography of the subcontinent. Caste and religion provided the two main markers of social difference. W. R. Cornish, the Superintendent of Census Operations for Madras in 1871, remarked, 'A Census Report is scarcely the place for a dissertation on the religious persuasions of the people; but the questions will probably be asked, what are these distinctive sects?' (Dirks 2001, 201).

While enumerating religious differences was relatively easy, enumerating and ordering castes was an exercise that was fraught with conceptual ambiguities and practical difficulties. At the time of the first two all-India censuses of 1871–1872 and 1881 the ascriptive Hindu notion of *varna*, derived from the Brahmanical scriptures, was employed to classify castes. Waterfield, of the Statistics and Commerce Division of the India Office, was of the view that *varna* should be replaced by a listing of castes that were important in each region (Dirks 2001, 201). The Madras Census Commissioner, Lewis McIver, disagreed with the use of *varna* or any single organizing principle for the classification of castes and argued for the use of occupational criteria, especially for the sudra castes.

The exasperation of the census taker when faced with the task of enumerating and classifying the castes of India is clearly evident in the comment made by India's first census commissioner, W. C. Plowden, in the introduction to the census of the North-Western Provinces:

> The whole question of caste is so confused, and the difficulty of securing correct returns on this subject is so great, that I hope on another occasion no attempt will be made to obtain information as to the castes and tribes of the population.

Finally in 1891 the census gave up *varna* as the basis of caste classification, in favour of enumeration based on occupations (Dirks 2001, 211). However, despite such comments, caste not only continued to be enumerated by the colonial census takers up to 1931, but the number of castes proliferated and campaigns for inclusion and upward mobility in their classification became more vigorous.

By the early nineteenth century, phrenology, which first developed in France after its Viennese creator, Dr Franz Joseph Gall, moved there, rose in popularity in Britain and America (McLaren 1981). This nineteenth-century science, despite its many detractors, was soon embraced by the colonial bureaucracy, both as a classificatory tool and as a forensic procedure. Phrenology and anthropometric statistics collected by the colonial administration suggest the race-caste identification in the colonial constructions of caste and identity in India.

The following paragraph, based on Clare Anderson's important study, clearly brings out how European colonial powers, even when pursuing a supposed line of scientific enquiry, used different yardsticks in identifying colonial and European crania. The Phrenological Society of Edinburgh, one of the many Phrenological Societies of the period in Europe, meticulously examined, described and recorded new skulls, and then preserved them in the 'National Skulls Cabinet'. Skulls were listed by their provenance and if possible by the character of the individual. In general terms, European crania were viewed as superior to all others.

European skulls were always seen as having belonged to an individual, who was named and described. The so-called 'National Skulls', in contrast, were usually represented collectively. We know very few of the micro-histories attributable to these individuals. In 1822 Ram Mohan Roy sent a selection of twelve 'Hindoo crania' to be examined by Dr George Paterson, a member of the Edinburgh Society, whose findings, published in the Society's journal, pointed to the conspicuous development of 'acquisitiveness and secretiveness' in the Hindu. Nothing was known of the skulls donated by Roy, for instance, except the 'general qualities' they revealed about 'the Hindus' (Anderson 2004, 18–84).

In 1866 the government of India authorized the collection of skulls for 'scientific purposes' (Anderson 2004, 186). While phrenology *per se* never became a major scientific project of the colonial Indian state, anthropometric investigations, such as the monumental collection of statistical data on Indians categorized by caste and region, received official sanction. The entire second volume of Risley's *The Tribes and Castes of Bengal* is devoted to such statistics (Risley 1891). Subsequently a similar exercise was undertaken for the Todas of southwestern India in 1909 (Thurston and Rangachari 1975). Before Thurston we find Marshall conducting a phrenological survey of the Todas in the early 1870s (Marshall and Pope 1873).

Thus what repeatedly emerges from the enumerative strategies of the colonial state in India was that it counted only social aggregates, namely populations divided by religion, race and caste. These putative identities defined variously at different points in time were invested with certain traits which supposedly held good for each of its members. Racial and caste traits included courage, diligence, craftiness, slothfulness and frailty. Caste, race and religion, once established and enumerated, were believed to provide a good guide to individual characteristics. Was this flawed conceptualization born of colonial ignorance and the arrogance of the imperial ruler, or was it a shortcut forced upon the state by the complexities and vastness of its empire coupled with the parsimonious nature of the colonial governance?

Why the individual was never counted and registered in India, in stark contrast to other Asian cultures, such as China or Japan (see Chapters 1 and 4), would necessitate conjecture. Speculating historically, it may be argued that unlike Britain or China and Japan, India never had a religious or secular tradition of registering individuals. Historical evidence for such early forms of individual registration in India was limited to the military. Another possible reason for the absence of individual identity registration may have been the large size of political units. However, this argument is weak as even small kingdoms evidenced no such enumerative practices. A more plausible explanation may have been the ideological consensus that the units such as the village and kin groups constituted units of society, rather than the individual. In colonial India, too, while the village was taxed and revenue villages were created for purposes of taxation, individuals in the village were never registered. Cadastral maps were prepared, but while individual claims to cultivation were recognized, individuals were not enumerated. This was possibly connected to the frequent divorce between individual land rights and the actual cultivator (Bagchi 2009). While the Indian village was definitely not unchanging, socially equal and self-reliant, the village was largely a source of surplus and later of labour, while being relatively small and socially close-knit. Though inequalities and differences existed within the village, the inhabitants were known to each other without the need for an identity register. In pre-colonial India, especially Mughal north India, the actual collection of state revenues from the village was the responsibility of the zamindar. The tax-paying cultivators of the village community usually belonged to the caste of the zamindar. The state largely impinged on this rural scene to collect taxes, recruit soldiers and more infrequently to provide tax holidays in times of acute distress. Inter-village and village–town trade existed in Mughal times and this grew substantially with the colonial commercialization of agriculture. However, given the assumed dominance of group identities on the one hand, and the absence of a welfarist state on the other, state intervention at the level of the village, where most Indians resided, was minimal. In such circumstances social and occupational aggregations worked fairly well as proxies for individual identity. Caste and kin groupings, which often overlapped substantially with occupational and class distinctions, worked satisfactorily (for a state whose interests were largely limited to the extraction of surplus) in regions where social change was slow to develop.

The developmental need to count

After independence, in response to the Bhore Committee's recommendations, the government created the Office of the Registrar General of India in 1951. The work of collecting and compiling vital statistics was once again transferred from the Director of Health Services to the newly created Office of the Registrar General in 1960. In 1969, the Registration of Births and Deaths Act was enacted to standardize and coordinate the registration of vital events across the country. These statistics were then compiled and published annually as the Vital Statistics of India by the Registrar General.

It has been claimed that, '[t]he machinery engaged in registration received the rudest shock during World War II when it went completely out of gear and the work was neglected in favour of all-out war efforts. The registration system has been on the downgrade ever since' (Registrar General 1971). The uncorrected crude birth and death rates registered a fall of 47 and 57 per cent respectively in the period from 1939 to 1945 in Madras. Thus, after levels of vital registration in India had improved in the 1920s and 1930s, the level and coverage of vital registration continued to deteriorate after independence. Though the population in non-compulsory areas constituted only 1.5 per cent of the total population, non-inclusion of data from defaulting registration units reduced the coverage to 70 per cent (Bhat *et al.* 1984). When compared to estimates of births and deaths derived from the dual-record Sample Registration System (see next section), the vital statistics showed under-registration of between 40 and 50 per cent (India, Registrar General 1964, 213–228); and such estimates of under-registration for the period 1941–1950 were lower than those for the 1960s and 1970s (Bhat *et al.* 1984, 28). This worsening of registration has been explained by the increased load placed on the fragile registration agency by the sharp and continued post-war growth of population. Provinces with rapid population growth were marked by sharp declines in registration coverage and levels (Ghosh 1956, 53–68). The territorial reorganization of states in the 1950s also led to some disruption in the registration of vital events, with the transfer of various districts and villages to newly created states. The Registrar General responded to this unfortunate state of the nation's vital registration by inaugurating the dual-record Sample Registration System.

The Sample Registration System

The dual-record Sample Registration System (SRS) was started in 1964 as a pilot in a few states, and the system was in place nationally by 1969. It consisted of continuous enumeration of births and deaths by an enumerator, and an independent survey every six months by an outside supervisor in a stratified sample of locations designed to be representative of each Indian state. The local enumerator was usually a school teacher who made a listing of houses in the sample area and kept a record of residents present, residents who had left and visitors. He was helped by the village midwife and the village revenue officer in keeping track of the movement of people, pregnancies and deaths. Every January and July an outside supervisor came and counted these vital events. Non-matching or partially matching events were investigated by another official or by both the enumerator and supervisor. However, despite being far superior, in terms of statistical accuracy, to the unknown uncertainties of the fragmented Civil Registration Data, the SRS gives figures only for entire states. Due to the sampling-frame design, reliable data cannot be published separately for sub-state units such as divisions, districts and villages, since the collected data are based on a simple stratified random sample rather than exhaustive collection for all individuals.

In spite of its shortcomings the Civil Registration Data continues to be produced at the state level, with its quality varying widely between states, as can be demonstrated by comparison of its results with the more accurate SRS estimates (see Table 11.2).

What Table 11.2 suggests is that richer states and/or those with better development indices have shown a much better record of implementation of a complete civil registration system in recent times. Without good-quality civil registration data, development planning and the delivery of welfare services at the micro-level become difficult. The absence of development in turn impedes civil registration by a lack of public demand to be counted and allowing the local-level bureaucracy to remain complacent and negligent.

Table 11.2. Level of birth registration as a percentage of SRS, 1985–1995

India/state	*1985*	*1995*
India	**39.0**	**55.0**
Andhra Pradesh	26.9	34.4
Bihar	20	18.7
Gujarat	62.1	96.3
Haryana	60.8	73.4
Karnataka	40.4	86.5
Kerala	94.8	101.7
Madhya Pradesh	46.3	50.8
Maharashtra	64.7	80.3
Orissa	47.6	58.6
Punjab	74.2	92.4
Rajasthan	16.4	23.7
Tamil Nadu	67.7	90.3
Uttar Pradesh	13.6	40.6
West Bengal	13.5	64.3

Source: www.unescap.org/stat/meet/esgs2/esgs2_india.pdf.

Note: The level of registration exceeds 100 per cent in Kerala in 1995 because people from the neighbouring states/Union Territories came to Kerala to avail themselves of its better medical facilities and due to the *de facto* method of registration of all births registered in these states/Union Territories. In the more accurate SRS, such births are accounted at the place of usual residence of the mother.

State disengagement, the imperative to enumerate, and the popular need to be counted

It was in 1951, within just six years of India gaining freedom and experiencing communal violence on an unprecedented scale, that India had its first democratic general election based on universal franchise. This required the generation of a nationwide record of adult Indians who would constitute the electorate. Within two years of independence an Election Commission was established and the Representation of People Act was passed by parliament. Sukumar Sen, the first Election Commissioner of independent India, accomplished the mammoth task of registering the names of 176 million adult voters, of whom about 85 per cent were illiterate (R. Guha 2008, 133). These electoral rolls constitute India's first identity register.

Whereas civil registration had been dismissed in the early twentieth century as the 'idle curiosity of an eccentric Sircar' by the village enumerator, in today's India state-certified identity is at a premium – whether in the form of a ration card or a voter's photo identity card (Guilmoto 1988). While this is the case at the level of the individual, the so-called 'backward classes' are clamouring to be counted and are demanding in many places a socially lower, constitutional reserved classification because that entitles them to increasingly scarce state welfare services and opportunities. With a resurgence of identity politics based on religion, language, region, caste and access to state resources, there is also a countervailing increasing anxiety, especially amongst some of the urban poor (often migrants), to have their citizenship certified. This has led to a great demand on all sides, and for various reasons, for identity certificates, including among the urban poor, many of whom are migrants from the poorest states of India (Rupambara 2007; Agarwal and Taneja 2005).

The Indian state today, in pursuing a path of neo-liberal growth, seeks to disengage itself from the commitments of the earlier *dirigiste* Nehruvian model. The state or public sector is being rapidly dismantled to allow the entry of private corporations into basic areas such as health, education, public utilities, etc. The public distribution system, which had previously provided basic food items such as grain, oil and sugar at lower than market prices to the population at large, is now available only for targeted distribution. In the latest Economic Survey, the government hopes to bring about inclusive growth by supporting the very poor by food coupons rather than through subsidies (India. Office of the Economic Adviser, 2011–2012). In this context it hopes that the Unique ID (UID) programme will help reduce leakages and facilitate efficient transfers to the very poor. However, how the UID, which does not ask questions about economic or social status, will help in identifying the rightful recipient of state aid, remains unclear. Thus, the Unique Identity Authority of India, set up by the Planning Commission and headed by Nandan Nilekani, an important software entrepreneur, is the latest in the historic series of enumerative experiments reviewed here that have been carried out in India. It seems paradoxical that when the state is looking to the working of the free market to bring about inclusive growth, advances in technology are being harnessed to create a biometric database of all the residents of the country, with the stated objective of bringing about better governance and lowering inequities. The state continues to count but the question remains as to who is being counted and registered and to what end?

Conclusion

This essay is essentially the history of an absence – the absence of individual identity registration in pre-colonial and colonial India. The pre-colonial state counted its actual and potential taxable resources and its dispersed military assets and possible threats. The population as a whole was not counted, and caste, when recorded, was always within the above logic. While individual responsibility was recognized in theory, and as best practice as far as tax obligations were concerned, in practice, the village as a whole and the zamindars became the minimal primary social units recognized by the state for its various interventions.

The early colonial state, concerned primarily with maximizing revenue, continued with enumerating assets, both actual and potential, but significantly added population to the list of such valued objects of account. Gradually and haltingly, the localized enumerations of people were systematized, resulting by the late nineteenth century in the colonial all-India census. The census played an important role in the development of the caste system in India, as it experimented with caste classifications based on ascriptive Brahmanical Hindu scriptures and occupational criteria. With the census attempting a social ranking of caste and its enumeration, caste proliferation soon reached unprecedented levels. The census and its methods of counting in many ways popularized the statistical technology of counting, stimulating subsequent identity registration by caste associations in colonial and, one may add, independent India.

As opposed to the fairly complete and regular all-India decennial census, the registration of deaths and then births was much more incomplete and variable in quality across the different provinces of India. The counting of deaths and births received a new impetus when the colonial state, faced with the huge toll of famine deaths, felt the acute necessity of recording the annual and monthly movements in deaths. Similarly, in the early twentieth century, welfarist and developmental concerns, as well as various Royal Commissions to enquire into industrial labour and agriculture, echoed the Famine Commission's earlier call for a better and more detailed registration of vital events. Public health measures remained extremely limited for the Indian population, however, and so continuous registration made little sense to both the enumerator and the enumerated when they found that this had little impact on their daily lives.

The colonial state, and, one may add, the medieval Mughal Indian state, were primarily interested in the extraction of surplus. While elaborate procedures of land revenue collection were prescribed by each, there was ambivalence in practice concerning individual agency. While individual responsibilities were repeatedly highlighted and appropriate procedures were developed, in actual practice we find that collective aggregates such as putative village communities and communities of cultivators often became the operational units of revenue realization. Neither state nor temples (which like the church in medieval Europe were important land controllers) counted and registered their individual subjects.

This raises the question of why the individual was not counted and registered in either medieval or colonial India. The tentative answer may lie in the favourable land-to-labour ratio in medieval India, coupled with the huge geographical size of the centralized empire and its large population. The favourable land-to-labour ratio appears to have ensured the relative insignificance of private property rights in land and made usufructuary rights more relevant. Putative communities of caste and village worked as convenient and economical proxies for political control and revenue collection.

The colonial state, despite having more advanced technologies of governance, never attempted individual identity registration, except partially for cadastral purposes, relying on group categories, based on beliefs about caste, race and religion as sufficient identifying attributes.

After independence the Indian state greatly increased expenditure on public welfare but only in a few states did state welfare services reach the intended population. Civil registration, which had seen some improvement in the 1930s, had become abysmal during the 1940s and 1950s, forcing the Registrar General to come up with the alternative of the Sample Registration System, which was not a real substitute for continuous individual registration. However, states with a better record of attention to human development were marked by superior civil registration data.

It was only after freeing itself from colonial rule and with its belief in democracy based on universal suffrage that the independent Indian state undertook the unprecedented mammoth task of registering its adult population in electoral rolls immediately after attaining independence. However, this did not translate into a sustained effort to maintain a vital registration system across India.

From the 1990s the state began to abdicate its social responsibilities to market forces. This is also the period when identity politics and more recently the threats of terrorism and armed insurgency have gained ground. The state has been forced to count caste groups once again after this was consciously stopped in 1931. Similarly the latest technology is being harnessed to provide identity registration for those Indians who can establish their identity and want to be so registered. Whether this exercise will include the entire population of India or be limited to the so-called 'middle class' remains to be seen. This high-tech UID project will possibly ensure greater security surveillance and an amelioration of the problem of leakages in targeted governmental support schemes, but it cannot provide a socially and politically neutral technological fix for unequal India's poverty and associated contradictions.

References

Abul Fazl Allami. 1891. *Ain-I-Akbari*, trans. Colonel S. Jarrett, vol. II. Calcutta: Baptist Mission Press.

ADB/UNESCAP Concluding Workshop on Enhancing Social and Gender Statistics, Bangkok. 2003. 'Development of Demographic Database for Micro (District) Level Planning in India: Exploration of Alternative Data Sources.' www.unescap.org/stat/meet/esgs2/esgs2_india.pdf.

Agarwal, Siddharth and Shivani Taneja. 2005. 'All Slums Are Not Equal: Child Health Conditions among the Urban Poor.' http://openmed.nic.in/26/01/AllSlumsareNotEqual.pdf.

Anderson, Clare. 2004. *Legible Bodies: Race, Criminality, and Colonialism in South Asia*. Oxford: Berg.

Baden-Powell, B. H. 1892. *The Land-Systems of British India*. Oxford: Clarendon Press.

Bagchi, Amiya Kumar. 2009. *Colonialism and Indian Economy*. New Delhi: Oxford University Press.

Bayly, Susan. 1999. *Caste, Society and Politics in India from the Eighteenth Century to the Modern Age*. New York: Cambridge University Press.

Bhadani, L. 1979. 'Population of Marwar in the Middle of the Seventeenth Century.' *Indian Economic and Social History Review* 16: 415–427.

Bhat, P. N. Mari, Samuel H. Preston and Tim Dyson. 1984. *Vital Rates in India, 1961–81*. Washington, DC: National Academy Press.

Board of Revenue. 1850. Circular to all Collectors, dated 17 February 1850, No. 298.

Census Report. 1872. Vols. I– II, I.D.C. Micro Edition India Office Library and Records. 1964 Census of India, 1872–1951 [microform] IDC, [Zug, Switzerland]: vols I–II 1872.

Curtis, Bruce. 2002. 'Foucault on Governmentality and Population: The Impossible Discovery.' *Canadian Journal of Sociology* 27: 505–533.

Dirks, Nicholas B. 2001. *Castes of Mind: Colonialism and the Making of Modern India*. Princeton, NJ: Princeton University Press.

Foucault, Michel, Michel Senellart, François Ewald and Alessandro Fontana. 2007. *Security, Territory, Population: Lectures at the Collège de France, 1977–78*. Basingstoke: Palgrave Macmillan.

Ghosh, D. 1956. 'The Trend of the Birth Rate in India, 1911–50.' *Population Studies* 10(1): 53–68.

Gopinath, R. 2010. *Historical Demography and Agrarian Regimes*. New Delhi: Orient Blackswan.

Guha, Ranajit. 1982. *A Rule of Property for Bengal: An Essay on the Idea of Permanent Settlement*, 2nd edn. New Delhi: Orient Longman.

Guha, Ramachandra. 2008. *India after Gandhi: The History of the World's Largest Democracy*. Delhi: Picador.

Guha, Sumit. 2003. 'The Politics of Identity and Enumeration in India c.1600–1990.' *Comparative Studies in Society and History* 45: 148–167.

Guilmoto, Christophe Z. 1988. 'The Sircar's Idle Curiosity: Critical Evaluation of Tamil Nadu's Demographic Sources, 1871–1981.' Madras Institute of Development Studies.

Habib, Irfan. 1999. *The Agrarian System of Mughal India, 1556–1707*. New Delhi: Oxford University Press.

Hamilton, Francis. 1925. *Journal of Francis Buchanan (afterwards Hamilton) kept during the survey of the districts of Patna and Gaya in 1811–1812*. Patna: Superintendent, Govt. Print., Bihar and Orissa.

Health Survey and Development Committee. 1946. *Report of the Health Survey and Development Committee*. Delhi: Manager of Publications.

Hunter, William Wilson. 1970. *Annals of Rural Bengal*. New York: Johnson Reprint Corp.

India, Census of. Vital Registration. http://censusindia.gov.in/Vital_Statistics/SRS/Sample_Registration_System.aspx.

India. Commercial Intelligence Dept., India. Dept. of Commercial Intelligence and Statistics, and India. Office of the Economic Adviser. 1923. Statistical abstract for British India with statistics, where available, relating to certain Indian states. Superintendent Government Printing, India.

India. Office of the Economic Adviser, and India. Central Statistical Organisation. Statistical abstract, India. Manager of Publications.

India, Registrar General. 1964. *Vital Statistics of India for 1961*. New Delhi: Manager of Publications.

Kumar, S. Suresh. 2005. 'Do We Need a Digital Cadastre?' In *Computerisation of Land Records*, ed. W. Habibullah and M. Ahuja. New Delhi: Sage Publications, 241–255.

Leonard, Karen Isaksen. 1978. *Social History of an Indian Caste: The Kayasths of Hyderabad*. Berkeley: University of California Press.

Madras (Presidency) Economic Adviser. [from old catalog]. 1949. *A statistical atlas of the Madras Province. Rev. and brought up to the end of fasli 1350 (1940–41)*. Madras: Economic Adviser to the Govt.

Marshall, William E. and G. U. Pope. 1873. *A phrenologist amongst the Todas, or, The study of a primitive tribe in south India: history, character, customs, religion, infanticide, polyandry, language*. London: Longmans, Green.

McLaren, Angus. 1981. 'A Prehistory of the Social Sciences: Phrenology in France.' *Comparative Studies in Society and History* 23: 3–22.

Mushtaq, M. U. 2009. 'Public Health in British India: A Brief Account of the History of Medical Services and Disease Prevention in Colonial India.' www.ijcm.org.in/article.asp?issn=0970-0218;year=2009.

Natarajan, D. 1971. *Civil Registration System in India: A Perspective*. New Delhi: Office of the Registrar General.

Peabody, Norbert. 2001. 'Cents, Sense and Census: Human Inventories in Late Precolonial India.' *Comparative Studies in Society and History* 43: 819–850.

Perlin, Frank. 1993. *The Invisible City: Monetary, Administrative and Popular Infrastructure in Asia and Europe 1500–1900*. Aldershot: Variorum Reprints.

Registrar General. 1971. *India Paper*. New Delhi: Office of the Registrar General.

Rennell, James. 1781. *A Bengal atlas: containing maps of the theatre of war and commerce on that side of Hindostan*. [London].

—— 1792. *Memoir of a map of Hindoostan; or, The Mogul empire: with an introduction, illustrative of the geography and present division of that country: and a map of the countries situated between the heads of the Indian rivers, and the Caspian Sea*. London: Printed by W. Bulmer and Co. for the author.

Risley, H. H. 1891. *The Tribes and Castes of Bengal*. Calcutta: The Bengal Secretariat Press.

Rudolph, L. I. and S. Hoeber Rudolph. 1966. 'The Political Role of India's Caste Associations.' In *Social Change: The Colonial Situation*, ed. Immanuel Wallerstein. New York: J. Wiley.

Rupambara. 2007. 'Financial Inclusion of the Urban Poor: Issues and Options.' *CAB Calling*. cab.org.in/...%20The%20Indian%20Experience%20(Special%20Issue).

Shamasastry, R. 1915. 'Arthashastra', Book II, Chapter 35. www.bharatadesam.com/literature/kautilya_arthashastra/arthashastra_2.php.

Smith, Richard Saumarez. 2004. 'Mapping Landed Property: A Necessary Technology of Imperial Rule?' In *Constituting Modernity: Private Property in the East and West*, ed. H. Islamoğlu. New York: I. B. Tauris.

Srivastava, S. C. 1983. *Indian Census in Perspective*. Delhi: Offices of the Registrar General.

Thurston, Edgar and K. Rangachari. 1975. *Castes and Tribes of Southern India*. Delhi: Cosmo.

Visaria, Leela and Praveen Visaria. 1983. 'Population.' In *Cambridge Economic History of India*, vol. II, ed. Dharma Kumar and Meghnad Desai. New Delhi: Orient Longman.

Wallerstein, Immanuel Maurice. 1966. *Social Change: The Colonial Situation*. New York: Wiley.

Ward, B. S. 1828a. *Memoirs, Triangles and Statistics of Malabar*. New Delhi.

—— 1828b. *A Canashoomaree or Statistical Table of the Province of Malabar*. New Delhi.

Washbrook, D. A. 1981. 'Law, State and Agrarian Society in Colonial India.' *Modern Asian Studies* 15: 649–721.

Zaidi, S. Inayet Ali. 1982. 'Rozinadar Troopers under Sawai Jai Singh of Jaipur.' *Indian Historical Review* 10.

12

Monitoring the Abolition of the International Slave Trade: Slave Registration in the British Caribbean

STANLEY L. ENGERMAN

I

THIS CHAPTER WILL DEAL with an unusual form of population registration, one that is well-ordered and detailed, but undertaken for a quite different purpose than the others discussed in this volume. This is the registration of slaves in the British West Indies and other British slave colonies between 1813 and 1834 – the legal ending of slavery in the British colonies. The purpose of this registration, advocated by James Stephen in the British Colonial Office, was to close what he perceived to be a loophole in the British ending of the transatlantic slave trade in 1808.[1] Stephen argued, based on his interpretation of estimates of the Trinidad slave population from the colony's recent poll-tax information, that there was extensive smuggling of slaves into Trinidad (and elsewhere) from the British colonies and the colonies of foreign nations, since the British navy was not large enough to halt this trade. Unless this smuggling was stopped, the closing of the slave trade would be ineffective and meaningless. The proposed solution was a detailed listing of every slave in each of the colonies in some base year and then a subsequent updating every few years to account for increases and decreases in the slave population, linking movements from one plantation to another when they occurred. In that way any smuggled slave would become apparent.

Stephen had argued in 1814 that there had been smuggling of some 4,500 slaves into Trinidad in the year before registration. This estimate was based on a comparison of the 1811 tax counts and the then available 1813 slave registers, and also a comparison of the ratio of plantation (rural) to personal slaves in Trinidad and elsewhere. A recent calculation of the structure of the time pattern of registration by A. Meredith John suggests that, 'There is no convincing evidence to support

[1] See, in particular, the volumes by James Stephen (1814a, 1814b, 1816a, 1816b). Discussions of this registration can be found in, among other sources, Brereton (1982), Higman (1984) and Klingberg (1926).

Proceedings of the British Academy **182**, 323–333.

the contention that slaves were smuggled into Trinidad and registered as *plantation* slaves' (John 1988). A further source of doubt comes from the unnamed author of the 1839 edition of Clarkson's *History of the Abolition of the Slave Trade*, which, while playing up the role of Clarkson and limiting those of William Wilberforce and Stephen, suggests that it was only Stephen who had believed in widespread smuggling (Clarkson 1839; see also Colonist 1816 and Jordan 1816). Stephen, however, argued that even if there had been no evidence of smuggling before, it was always a distinct possibility in the future.

Slaves could be legally imported from the British and French islands with licences from governors and custom houses, with a quota of about 3 per cent of the extant slave population, the exact amount to be set by the then rate of growth of the population on the island. There were periodic changes in these laws, but movements were never halted.

Stephen argued, also, that such a form of registration might help to ultimately end slavery by providing a reliable set of estimates of population levels and rates of natural increase or decrease. By demonstrating the declining slave populations in the colonies, slave-owners could be made aware that better care and treatment of the slaves was necessary, and it was hoped that these improvements would bring about the ending of slavery, after some uncertain time period. The general pattern of natural decrease in the West Indies was long known from the over fifty-five censuses in the British Caribbean colonies between 1623 and 1775. These, however, were counts of people and lacked the precision of the regulations and the naming of specific individuals that Stephen advocated (Wells 1975).

The politics of introducing registration gave rise to disputes between the abolitionist supporters and the owners of slaves in the colonies, reflecting, in part, disagreements about the status of slavery and the general issues of metropolitan-colonial relations (Schuyler 1929). A central issue was whether metropolitan legislation imposed the same system on all colonies or a looser arrangement that permitted each colony to separately introduce legislation. Attempts to introduce uniform legislation were unsuccessful, which meant that each colony could create its own system as long as it followed the Colonial Office's wishes to have a registration system. It was decided to take the second route, first introducing registration in the Crown colonies (such as Trinidad, as well as St Lucia and Mauritius), with the other colonies then introducing their own schemes. By 1819, all colonies had some system, and it was generally accepted that adjustments were to be made every three years. Thus, while some data was collected for all islands, they did differ in the amount of information collected, and the specific years for which collections were made (see Higman 1984, 8, 12–13). Enforcement was achieved by the threat of loss of title to unregistered slaves, and difficulties in obtaining funds from British lenders with which to purchase slaves in the absence of a recorded title.

Arguing that registration was not a novel method, Stephen noted that Grenada had established a scheme for listings of free coloureds after 1786, providing, among other things, information on: name, residence, age, colour, sex, occupation, and means to freedom, with the intent to 'prevent further sudden increase of free negroes'. He could also have mentioned the registration in Ceylon between 1806 and 1808, which was required as proof of title (see Benians *et al.* 1929, 520–521). Stephen did discuss the long-time listing of ships, the registration of which was part of the control of shipping imposed as part of the Navigation Acts, to establish precedence for his policies. Ship listing had started in the middle of the seventeenth century, although central listing of all British ships did not start until 1786.

The arguments against regulation were rather familiar and described by Stephen as an opposition that was similar to that against the abolition of the slave trade. First, it was, for example, alleged that this was mainly a method to introduce controls and regulations to bring about the ending of slavery – a stepping stone to achieve that broader end, or at least to achieve the amelioration of slavery. Second, it was argued that registration was not needed since it was denied that any smuggling had occurred or would occur in the future. Finally, there was the issue of what was permissible, under colonial policy, in terms of British government interference in the internal affairs of the colonies. The metropolis was responsible for trade regulations and the colonies for tax policy. The costs of registration were to be paid by the slave-owners, and, it was argued, this tax was a violation of colonial rights (Schuyler 1929). Stephen, in response, argued that the implicit tax due to registration was less than the magnitude of the property tax paid in England. These arguments of the slave-owners were ultimately unsuccessful and registration was introduced, if not to the full satisfaction of abolitionists, at least more to their wishes than to those of slave-owners in the slave colonies. After the end of slavery, most colonies introduced a detailed census, patterned after the British model, in the 1840s and every ten years thereafter – a form of data collection that some thought, at first, was an attempt to reintroduce slavery since ex-slaves could be recorded by name, making it possible to trace their past status (Roberts 1957).

Other variants of registration and recording of slaves were also related to the desire to reduce the smuggling of slaves after the legal ending of the transatlantic slave trade. The British pressured the Dutch to end an illegal slave trade into Surinam after 1823 by a system of annual reporting of the number of slaves owned and the changes over time (Emmer 1998; Everaert 2011). The US Population Census counted slaves only by numbers between 1790 and 1810, and by age and sex from 1820 to 1840. In 1850 and 1860 they added a listing of slave-owners by name, but did not include information on slaves, other than number, age, sex, and colour (Wright 1900). After 1808, the United States, which officially ended the transatlantic slave trade in the same year as Britain, sought to control coastal shipping of slaves to prevent the introduction of international imports. Each slave shipped was to be listed by age, name, gender, height, and colour, as well as ports of arrival and departure, date of certification by collector of customs, captain's name, name of vessel, dates when loaded and unloaded from the vessel (if over

40 tons), as well as the name and place of residence of the owner or shipper (see Appendix B; Wesley 1942; Steckel 1979). Slave-owners in the United States felt that such a policy would ultimately lead to emancipation, but the certificates do not seem to have played a role in the abolition debates.

II

The description here of the collection and analysis of the West Indian slave registration data will centre on Trinidad, since Trinidad was the first to introduce registration, and, as a Crown colony, had its form imposed by the Colonial Office. It was held as a model for others, had the more complete information, and has usefully been analysed by others. Trinidad produced mainly sugar but also coffee, cocoa and cotton, and played a major role in the discussion of the ending of slavery. It was captured from Spain in 1797 and, like Guiana (acquired from the Dutch), had an abundance of land relative to the present labour force of slaves. Many thought that if unlimited slave imports were permitted, the ending of the slave system would be very distant, on economic grounds – Wilberforce (and Pitt) estimated the time scale at over 200 years, even if migration to the new areas were restricted.[2] Thus, limits were imposed on the inter-island trade, which were intended to contain slavery's expansion. In 1813 Trinidad's slave population was 17,087 plantation slaves and 8,630 personal slaves (urban), representing two-thirds of the island's total population.

The information collected in 1813 for each slave in Trinidad was as follows (John 1988):

- Name[3]
- Surname
- Colour
- Age
- Gender
- Occupation
- Height[4]

[2] See the discussion of Wilberforce, in Engerman (2008).

[3] There is some controversy about who chose the names recorded, and whether it was the slaves or the slave-owners who determined the name, since the information was provided to the registrar by the slave-owners. Given that some of the listed names were rather satiric or insulting, clearly not all names represented slave choices. Similar naming issues are discussed for other forms of registration by Herzog (Chapter 7) and by Doyle (Chapter 10), but in these cases the choices are presumably made by those registering.

[4] The concern with the information on height was presumably for purposes of identifying slaves, and there is no indication that it was meant to be used as an index of health and well-being. No registrations included data on slave prices.

- Family relations
- Presence of country marks
- Creole or African
- Place of birth, in Africa or the West Indies.

The slaves were listed by plantation, and data included owner's name, principal crop, size of unit (number of slaves), and parish located (see Appendix A).

Higman provides a checklist of information collected on other islands as well as dates of collection. In addition, he provides a detailed breakdown of various demographic measures based on these registration forms. Other breakdowns were presented by John and by Friedman who, with Higman, demonstrate the richness of this particular data collection.

For Trinidad updated information was collected for 1815 and 1816. As a help to scholarly analysis, the information for 1815 and 1816 (and other years) was presented in the same volume as the 1813 data (John 1988). Then, for Trinidad, there are separate books for 1816 and every three years thereafter until 1834. The other islands sometimes used different years, but with similar spacing. For those slaves with any changes in status, the updates recorded the nature of such changes under the following headings:

Additions:	Birth	Subtractions:	Death
	Purchases		Sales
	Imports		Manumissions
	Inheritance		Exports
	Gifts		Runaway
			Bequest
			Gift

III

The procedures for data collection and preparation were:

- Each slave-owner was to provide a list of slaves
- This list was to be entered in a book by a clerk in the Registrar's Office
- A duplicate set was sent to London to ensure that records survived
- A fee was charged to slave-owners of 10s. per return to registrar, plus 1s. per slave listed.

The registrations seemed to go rather smoothly after their initiation, and there were apparently no major complaints thereafter. In part, this was due to the next step in the abolitionist attack on slavery: the introduction of an amelioration policy in 1823 after parliamentary debate. Amelioration measures were deemed necessary since neither the ending of the slave trade nor the registration system had succeeded in providing the changes in slavery hoped for. Based upon a series of Orders in

Council – some parts accepted by some colonies, others reacted against – there were changes in slave treatment, but no move to emancipation. By this time slave registration continued but was not a source of political disagreement.

In this period, except for the presentation of total population figures, and only rather specific overall totals, little use was made of these registrations. Recently, with the advent of computer technology and its capacity to handle individual-level data, there have been detailed studies, primarily for Trinidad, using the information on heights, mortality, fertility, and patterns of family relations, among other categories, to examine changes in patterns of health and family formation. These studies focus on the years 1813, 1815 and 1816, since no one yet has undertaken the more complex task of linking into subsequent years (Fogel 1989, 125–126, 142–143, 148–151, 218; Fogel *et al.* 1992, 119–140, 286–291).

Thus, this chapter has documented how very diverse were the histories and disputed purposes of identity registration systems, even within a single colonial empire – the British – at a single point in time and in the same region of the world – the Caribbean. At a time when parish registration systems for free settlers, established in earlier centuries on several of these islands (discussed in Chapter 2), were typically failing to be sustained efficiently, new and efficient identity registration systems for slaves were nevertheless being brought into existence. However, these were not, as one might suppose, to provide an efficient inventory of slavers' chattels, but for the express purpose of bringing about a relatively speedy end to a system now declared immoral by the metropolitan elite, both by halting illegal imports and by influencing the treatment of slaves. Furthermore, though resisted in part, some of these registers were kept sufficiently assiduously that they have proved to be of value to quantitative historians two centuries later.

Appendix A: Schedule for the return of slaves in Trinidad in 1813

Name	*Surname*	*Colour*	*Employment*	*Age*	*Height*	*Country*	*Marks*	*Relations [?]*
LIST OF FAMILIES OF SLAVES on the Plantation *A.B.* (or of the said *E.F.*)								
Anthony	Williamson	Negro	Driver	41	5 feet 10 inches	Creole of this island	A scar on the right cheek	Husband of Sarah, and father of John/Jake and Samuel Williamson
Sarah	Williamson	Negro	Seamstress	38	5 feet	Same	Has lost the fourth toe of the left foot	Wife of Anthony and mother of John/Jake and Samuel Williamson
John/Jake	Williamson	Negro	Labourer	20		Same	No marks	Son of Anthony and Sarah Williamson
Samuel	Williamson	Negro	In the little grass gang	10	4 feet 3 inches	Same	A drop, in the left shoulder, from a vessel	Son of Anthony and Sarah Williamson, and brother of John/Jake Williamson
GENERAL LIST OF MALE SLAVES on the said Plantation, (or of the said *E.F.*)								
Jack	Thomas	Negro	Boiler	35	5 feet 9 inches	Creole of St. Kitts	Lame in the right leg	
Ned	Smith	Mulatto	Cooper	40	5 feet 10 inches	Creole of St. Vincents	No marks	
Sampson	Strong	Negro	Labourer	23	5 feet 8 inches	African, from the Westland coast	Country marks, two scars on each cheek	
George	Ward	Negro	Labourer	20	5 feet 7 inches	African, from the Gold Coast	Has lost the first joint of the middle toe, left foot	

Name	*Surname*	*Colour*	*Employment*	*Age*	*Height*	*Country*	*Marks*	*Relations [?]*
			GENERAL LIST OF FEMALE SLAVES on the said Plantation, (or of the said *E.F.*)					
Phillis	Johnson	Negro	Labourer	42	5 feet 1 inch	African, from Congo	No Marks	
Susan	Savage	Negro	Labourer	39	4 feet 11 inches	African, from Gold Coast	Country scars on the arms	
Betty	Edwards	Negro	Washer	39	4 feet 10 inches	Creole of this island	No marks	
Sally	Baker	Mulatto	In the little weeding gang	11	4 feet 3 inches	Same	Cyst in the eye	

The whole number of Slaves on the said Plantation *C.D.* (or of the said *E.F.*) is twelve,

A true Return

A.B. January 1st, 1813

Source: C.O. 295/28, f. 264: Order in Council for the Registration of Slaves in Trinidad, 26 March 1812. Reproduced by courtesy of the Public Record Office, London.

Appendix B: Slave manifests of coastwise vessels filed at New Orleans, Louisiana, 1807–1860

Shields, Ashburn & Co.—Printers.

MANIFEST of NEGROES, MULATTOES, and PERSONS OF COLOUR, taken on board the *Schooner Ceres* of *Norfolk* whereof *Samuel W Brown* is Master, burthen *98 47/95* tons, to be transported to the Port of *New Orleans* for the purpose of being sold or disposed of as Slaves, or to be held to service or labor.

NUMBER OF ENTRIES.	NAMES.	SEX.	AGE. yrs	HEIGHT. Feet.	HEIGHT. Inches.	Whether Negro, Mulatto, or Person of Colour.	Owners' or Shippers' Names, and places of residence.
1	Jupiter	male	22	5	8	Black	Joseph Granier, Merchant, of the Borough of Norfolk
2	Ned	do	19	5	3	do	
3	John	do	10	4	11	do	
4	Abraham	do	9	3	10	do	
5	Savage	do	10	4	½	do	
6	Charles	do	9	4	—	do	
7	George	do	15	4	11	do	
8	Baba	do	12	4	4½	mulatto	
9	Judy	female	19	5	½	Black	
10	Sarah	do	23	5	6	do	
11	Louisa	do	16	5	3	do	
12	Letty	do	14	4	8¾	do	
13	Celia	do	15	4	11½	do	
14	Cloe	do	14	5	—	do	
15	Minny	do	11	4	7½	do	
16	Maria	do	10	4	4½	do	
17	Ann	do	11	4	4½	do	
18	Viney	do	10	4	3¾	do	
19	Julia	do	11	4	3½	do	
20	Maria	do	9	3	11	do	

I *Joseph Granier* do solemnly, sincerely, and truly swear, to the best of my knowledge and belief, that the persons above specified, were not imported or brought into the United States since the first day of January, eighteen hundred and eight, and that under the Laws of the State of Virginia, they are held to serve or labor as Slaves.—So HELP ME GOD.

Jos. Granier

Collector's Office, Norfolk,
December 4th 1822

Sworn to before me,

Js. Johnson COLLECTOR

Source: NARA Customs Service, Record Group 36, National Archives, Washington, DC. Roll 02.

References

Benians, E. A., J. Holland Rose and A. P. Newton. eds. 1929. *Cambridge History of the British Empire*, vol. 2. Cambridge: Cambridge University Press.

Brereton, Bridget. 1982. *History of Modern Trinidad 1783–1962*. Kingston: Heinemann.

Clarkson, Thomas. 1839. *The History of the Rise, Progress and Accomplishment of the Abolition of the African Slave-Trade, by the British Parliament*. London: John W. Parker.

Colonist. 1816. *The Edinburgh review and the West Indies: with observations on the pamphlets of Messrs. Stephen, Macaulay, &c. and remarks on the slave registry bill*. Glasgow: Printed for John Smith and Son.

Emmer, P. C. 1998. *The Dutch in the Atlantic Economy, 1580–1880: Trade, Slavery and Emancipation*. Aldershot: Ashgate.

Engerman, Stanley L. 2008. 'Emancipation Schemes: Different Ways of Ending Slavery.' In *Slave Systems: Ancient and Modern*, ed. Enrico Dal Lago and Constantina Katsari. Cambridge: Cambridge University Press, 265–282.

Everaert, Huub. 2011. 'The Unknown Father in Suriname, 1838 to 1873.' Unpublished.

Fogel, Robert William. 1989. *Without Consent or Contract: The Rise and Fall of American Slavery*. New York: Norton.

Fogel, Robert William, Ralph A. Galantine and Richard L. Manning. 1992. *Without Consent or Contract: The Rise and Fall of American Slavery: Evidence and Methods*. New York: Norton.

Higman, B. W. 1984. *Slave Populations of the British Caribbean, 1807–1834*. Baltimore, MD: Johns Hopkins University Press.

John, A. Meredith. 1988. *The Plantation Slaves of Trinidad, 1783–1816: A Mathematical and Demographic Enquiry*. Cambridge: Cambridge University Press.

Jordan, Gibbes Walker. 1816. *An Examination of the Principles of the Slave Registry Bill and of the Means of Emancipation Proposed by the Authors of the Bill*. London: Printed for T. Cadell and W. Davies.

Klingberg, Frank. 1926. *The Anti-Slavery Movement in England; a Study in English Humanitarianism*. New Haven, CT: Yale University Press.

Roberts, George W. 1957. *The Population of Jamaica*. Cambridge: Cambridge University Press.

Schuyler, Robert Livingston. 1929. *Parliament and the British Empire: Some Constitutional Controversies Concerning Imperial Legislative Jurisdiction*. New York: Columbia University Press.

Steckel, Richard H. 1979. 'Slave Height Profiles from Coastwise Manifests.' *Explorations in Economic History* 16(4): 363–380.

Stephen, James. 1814a. *Reasons for establishing a registry of slaves in the British colonies: being a report of a committee of the African Institution (Short Version)*. London: Ellerton and Henderson.

—— 1814b. *Reasons for establishing a registry of slaves in the British colonies: being a report of a committee of the African Institution*. London: Ellerton and Henderson.

——. 1816a. *A Defence of the Bill for Registration of Slaves, in Letters to William Wilberforce. Letter the First*. London: Printed for J. Butterworth.

—— 1816b. *A Defence of the Bill for the Registration of Slaves: In Letters to William Wilberforce Esq. MP: Letter the Second*. London: Printed for J. Butterworth and Son, Fleet-Street; and J. Hatchard, Piccadilly.

Wells, Robert V. 1975. *The Population of the British Colonies in America Before 1776: A Survey of Census Data*. Princeton, NJ: Princeton University Press.

Wesley, Charles H. 1942. 'Manifests of Slave Shipments along the Waterways, 1800–1864.' *Journal of Negro History* 17: 155–176.

Wright, Carroll Davidson. 1900. The history and growth of the United States census: prep. for the Senate Committee on the census. Washington, DC: Government Printing Office.

13

Birth of the 'Secular' Individual: Medical and Legal Methods of Identification in Nineteenth-Century Egypt

KHALED FAHMY

THIS CHAPTER DELINEATES THE WAYS in which ambitiously independent governors in the nineteenth-century Egyptian province of the Ottoman empire pushed through a sustained series of medico-administrative and legal changes over the course of several decades which were primarily designed to enhance the military and internal security of their control over the province. In so doing, these medico-administrative and legal changes created, within an Islamic jurisdiction, entirely novel administrative definitions and legal processes of identity verification, which carried profound implications for a novel, much more individualized conception of identity. In this case it can be clearly historically documented how it was that bureaucratic forms of identity registration found necessary and expedient to the purposes of state of the governor in Egypt gave rise to a novel legal practice and ultimately to a concept of the individual, rather than any clear prior concept of the individual and their rights having called forth a registration procedure.

In the course of the first half of the nineteenth century the state in Egypt moved towards new forms of individualized identification and registration prompted by military reform, especially the recruitment needs of a domestically conscripted army. These administrative measures, drawn from the new large conscript armies of post-Napoleonic Europe, served as the motor of individualization, ironically bolstering the very personalized forms of power that were deployed by Egypt's governors, most notably Mehmed Ali and his family. Similarly, a wide-ranging programme of public health, with its roots in the need to keep soldiers well enough to fight, spread through Egypt after the 1820s, producing a statistically-driven state-power that was directed at the conditions of health in the cities, and amongst child-bearing women in particular. Mehmed Ali also deliberately extended the logic of individualization into Egyptian law, requiring new forms of named and written identification in place of the reputational and oral witnesses that were common in sharīʻa. The chapter concludes with a discussion of the official certificates of identification and movement control that were used to control peasants in particular.

Proceedings of the British Academy **182**, 335–355.

Ottoman Egypt: sovereign power and the logic of exaction

Throughout the first three centuries of Ottoman rule in Egypt we cannot discern any awareness by the authorities of what Foucault would call the 'problem of population'. As is shown below, there was indeed a concern about the 'populousness' of Egypt, i.e. the overall well-being and tranquillity of the residents of this wealthy province of the empire. However, it was primarily as an index of the wealth of his empire that the Ottoman sultan was interested in the residents of Egypt. The sultan, his viziers and his governors were also concerned about Egypt's ability to feed the empire and also to provide enough food for the poor and needy pilgrims during the annual Hajj.

Remarkably absent from the Ottoman administrative mind was any effective means to deal with the repeated plague epidemics that were known since the middle of the fourteenth century to hit the country every nine years (see Chapter 11; Dols 1979, 167–168; quoted in Mikhail 2011, 214–230). Indeed, Nāsir Ibrāhīm, who has studied Egyptian social and economic crises during the seventeenth century, remarks that it was very rare for Ottoman governors or for Mamluk emirs to pay any attention to matters of public hygiene. 'It is absolutely impossible to notice any significant presence of an overall administrative policy in light of the near total absence of specialized bodies [that provided] . . . health services' (Ibrāhīm 1998, 184).

It is not that the Ottoman authorities were unconcerned about health matters in Egypt or that, more specifically, they did not worry about the devastating impact of plague on such an important province. Egypt was considered the bread basket of the Ottoman empire, and the Ottomans had set up a complex administrative and economic system that guaranteed that food grains from Egypt were regularly sent to the capital, as well as to Hijaz to support the annual Hajj. Any disruption of this vital supply of food was taken very seriously. Furthermore, both contemporary chroniclers and the orders sent from Istanbul to its governors in Cairo show that another concern foremost in the mind of the Ottoman authorities was the usual breakdown of law and order following a low Nile, famines and plague epidemics.[1] Following the 1695 drought, for example, an angry mob stormed the Citadel of Cairo asking the authorities to provide food rations. When the governor failed to contain these disturbances, Istanbul summarily dismissed him and appointed a new governor in his place (al-Damurdāshī Katkhudā 'Azabān 1989, 29). Related to this security concern was the fear that the lack of order in Egypt following plagues

1 As Alan Mikhail (2011, 227) shows, there was a causal link between these three phenomena: low Niles usually led to famines, which in turn affected the health of the population. The weakened natural immunity made people susceptible to an outbreak of plague, and helped in turning a small outbreak into an epidemic. It was the close link between these three phenomena that led many people to believe that plague was endemic to Egypt.

and famines would make it easier for fugitives from the central authorities to seek refuge there. 'Indeed in very strong language, Ottoman authorities ordered those [Ottoman] leaders still present in Egypt to prevent any fugitives from the state from entering the province to hide' (Mikhail 2011, 223).

But it was the concern about revenue from one of its wealthiest provinces that informed the Ottoman administration's immediate reaction to news of an outbreak of plague in Egypt. For example, al-Damurdāshī (d. 1755) says that in the wake of the 1695–1696 plague, the Ottoman governor was quick to collect the administrative tax paid on title deeds, the *hulwān*, from peasants who were keen to get hold of lands made vacant after their owners had died. He used parts of these funds to celebrate the circumcision of his sons and also that of 200 boys from among Egypt's poor (al-Damurdāshī Katkhudā 'Azabān 1989, 31–33; al-Jabartī 1994, 1: 163). Following the devastating plague epidemic of 1791 an imperial *firman* was sent to the governor in Cairo ordering him to provide information on which Ottoman officials had fled the country so that the state could seize their property and moneys (al-Jabartī 1994, 3: 295).[2]

At the same time, various Ottoman governors were aware that a balance needed to be struck between this 'exaction logic' and the need to preserve the peace following a plague epidemic. Thus we see Maksūd Pasha, the Ottoman governor in 1643, ordering the officials of *bayt al-māl* – a government body responsible for, among other things, registering the legacies of the deceased – to desist from going about their business during the plague. The contemporary chronicler al-Bakrī (d. 1650) says that in issuing this order the governor wanted to lift the financial burden from the plague victims' survivors. He adds that the delayed burials that such registration entailed prompted the governor to cancel the required registration of the dead, and that 'survivors should bury their dead without registration'.[3] Thus although the Ottomans were very aware of the significance of Egypt and its productive capacities for the wealth and well-being of their empire, they never developed a policy that could be interpreted as signalling an understanding of the 'problem of population'. They were indeed concerned to maintain the productivity of Egypt but there were no specific measures put in place to account for, or to increase the productivity of, its population. The Ottoman sultans and their governors in Egypt ruled according to what Foucault would call 'the reason of state', which although it involved a concern with 'numbering the people' (Glass 1973) – taking stock of the population as it is an index of the wealth of the realm – did not express an interest in the 'population' as an abstraction.

[2] Başbakanlık Osmanlı Arşivi (Prime Ministry's Ottoman Archives, Istanbul), Hattı Hümayun, 1412/57500 (29 Z 1205/29 August 1791); quoted in Mikhail 2011, 224.

[3] Muhammad ibn Abī al-Surūr al-Bakrī, 'al-Kawākib al-Sā'ira fi Akhbār Misr al-Qāhira', fol. 80, quoted in Ibrāhīm 1998, 187.

Quarantines and their 'refined declension'

On 24 March 1799, placards were put up throughout Cairo with regulations printed by the French military authorities which had established themselves in Egypt the previous year. The regulations read as follows:

> An address to the people of Cairo, Bulaq, Old Cairo and vicinity. You shall obey, uphold and observe, without opposition, the orders. Anybody opposing them will encounter abundant vengeance, painful punishment and severe retribution. They are precautions against the disease of the plague. In the case of anybody whom you know certainly, or believe imagine, or suspect to be suffering from this illness in any place, house, caravansary or building, it is your duty and obligation to establish a quarantine, and the place must be closed off. The elder of the quarter or street in which this occurs must immediately inform the French officer who is the district supervisor. He, in turn, will report it to the shaykh al-balad, the commandant of Cairo and its districts. This must be done promptly. The same holds true for every community of Egypt, her provinces, and districts. If any physicians examine and verify an incident of this disease, each of them must go to the local commandant and report it to him, so that the latter can give appropriate orders to protect and safeguard from this illness. Any of the chiefs of sections, elders of quarters, and police of districts who has information concerning this disease and does not record it will be punished as the commandant sees fit. Neighbourhood elders will be punished with 100 lashes for failure to report. It is also decreed that anyone who is infected, or in whose house a case occurred among his family or relatives, and who moves from his house to somewhere else, shall suffer capital punishment.
>
> (al-Jabartī 1994, 3: 81–82)

As indicated above, there was nothing in the health measures devised by the Ottoman administration in Egypt that remotely resembled this quarantine regulation. The logic that lay behind quarantines and the associated military-style regulation of population would take several decades to develop in Egypt and one can see it eventually culminating in the late 1840s with the undertaking of the first nationwide census. It is therefore necessary to follow this logic step by step in order to highlight not only its genealogical development but also its archaeological ruptures.

Following the departure of the French in 1801 and the accession of Mehmed Ali Pasha as Ottoman governor of Egypt, quarantines were repeatedly imposed at the outbreak of the plague and other epidemics, most notably cholera. Thus, when plague spread to different parts of Lower Egypt in 1813, the Pasha ordered a quarantine on Giza where he intended to reside. 'The chiefs of police were instructed to order the people and shop owners to keep their places constantly swept, sprinkled and clean and to air their clothes' (al-Jabartī 1994, 4: 244). During his long reign Mehmed Ali repeatedly expressed his firm belief in the efficacy of quarantines and he ordered their imposition during numerous plague and cholera epidemics. In 1828, for example, he ordered his son-in-law, Müharrem Bey, who was governor of Alexandria, to consult with foreign consuls in the city to draft quarantine regulations and to enforce them in the rapidly expanding port city (Sāmī 1928, 2: 228). Besides Alexandria, quarantines were imposed on the ports of Damietta in 1829 and Rosetta in 1831. Eventually, and facing the alarming outbreak of the cholera pandemic of 1831–1832, an international quarantine board was established in Alexandria composed of the different European consuls in the city, the first such attempt at international disease control (Kuhnke 1990, 94).

Between the early quarantine of 1813 and the ones imposed in the 1830s and later a significant difference can be detected. For one, whereas the 1813 quarantine imposed on Giza was ordered primarily 'thanks to the desire [of the Pasha and his entourage] for the life of this world and their fear of the plague', as al-Jabartī disparagingly remarks (1994, 4: 244), the later quarantines did not aim at protecting a particular set of people, however haughty their status might have been, but at safeguarding the population as such. The difference between the 1813 quarantine and the later ones is indicative of what Foucault would call the transformation of the concept of population from sovereignty to governmentality. In other words, between the 1813 quarantine and the quarantines of the 1820s and 1830s the 'problem of population' had emerged for those governing Egypt.

Conscription and the emergence of the population problem

To understand this transformation in the concept of population in Egypt in the first half of the nineteenth century, it is necessary to place these transformations in their military context. Thus, it is important to keep in mind that initially Mehmed Ali's sole source of legitimacy as governor of Egypt was the *firman* that arrived from Istanbul bestowing on him this coveted governorship. However, the sultan only issued this *firman* with reluctance after his previous attempts to assign other governors had failed. Unlike previous governors of Egypt, who would typically have come from within the establishment in Istanbul, who would have been known within the leading households there, and for whom the governorship of Egypt would have been but a step in their advancement within the empire's bureaucracy, Mehmed Ali was a complete unknown quantity to the ruling factions of the capital. Besides all this, Egypt was too important a province to be entrusted to an outsider, and it was only a matter of time before Istanbul would try to remove him from this coveted position. These questions about how he was regarded in Istanbul must have caused deep anxiety for Mehmed Ali – an anxiety that was heightened by the fact that the investiture *firmans* were valid only for one year, and had to be renewed from year to year – making him wonder how long his tenure as governor of Egypt might last.

After failing in his attempts to build an army from foreign sources (Fahmy 1997, 85–111), Mehmed Ali took a fateful decision in February 1822 to turn to the population of Egypt to create the disciplined army that he felt was desperately needed to protect his realm and shore up his nascent household government. In letters to his provincial governors in Upper Egypt he ordered the gathering of 4,000 peasants to be sent to specially created training camps in Aswan. Initially it was decided that these peasants would be conscripted for a period of only three years, after which time they were to be given a stamped certificate proving that they had served in the army, and also a lifelong exemption from the land tax. In practice, however, these conscripts were often pressed into the army for life.

The decision to conscript Egyptians marks a decisive turning point in Mehmed Ali's administration and one can safely say that what Foucault would call the 'problem of population' made itself manifestly obvious as a direct result of difficulties encountered in pressing Egyptian peasants into the new army and in finding ways to keep them from deserting or from falling prey to disease. In what follows, we trace the different measures put in place to deal with these problems.

In its early days conscription followed the same 'logic of exaction' that characterized sovereign power. A conscription gang would descend on any given village and proceed to gather as many men as they could, sometimes with the assistance of the village shaykh, sometimes not, 'without any order, arrangement, inscription or lot-drawing' (Bowring 1840). These men would then be tied together with ropes around their necks in groups of six or eight (Planat 1830, 76–77). They would be marched off to the training camps escorted by the conscription gang, leaving behind 'a heart-stricken, sorrowful group [of wives, mothers and children], some absorbed in sullen grief, others weeping bitterly' (St. John 1834, 2: 277).

It did not take much time for the authorities to discover the serious drawbacks of this logic of exaction. For one thing, this crude system of conscription triggered a serious backlash of resistance, and for two years the government was busy quelling two huge revolts, one in the Delta and the other in Upper Egypt. For another, it was soon discovered that many people were gathered from their villages and thus removed from the productive agricultural sector only to be found too old or infirm to serve in the army. Most seriously, the authorities suffered from the critical lack of any reliable information on the population. As early as 1825 when Mehmed Ali was informed that 7,494 men had been gathered for the army during the previous year, he wrote back to the director of the newly established War Department enquiring what this figure really meant: 'We have to know in the first place the number of men demanded from each province and the number actually gathered so that we know the number still remaining.'[4] In an earlier order the Pasha wrote to the same official telling him to prepare a register giving the names of those soldiers who had been pressed into the army so far, with the information broken down to the province, department, district and village from which they had been gathered.[5] Similarly, in order to replace those soldiers who had died or deserted,

[4] Egyptian National Archives (hereafter ENA), Ma'iyya Saniyya, Reg. no. S/1/48/2, letter no. 102, 9 Muharram 1241/25 August 1825.

[5] ENA, Ma'iyya Saniyya, Reg. no. S/1/48/1, letter no. 192, 25 Jumād Thānī 1239/27 February 1824.

detailed registers had to be drafted, stating, name by name, the provinces from which they had been conscripted.[6]

Desertion and absconding were the most serious problems that continued to irk the military authorities in their constant attempts to keep the army from falling apart completely. Even well into the 1830s desertion reached epidemic proportions: an investigation carried out in 1837 put the number of deserters in the army at 60,000, in addition to 20,000 deserters from the navy. Given that the size of the army at that time could not have exceeded 130,000, this meant that for every two conscripts, one soldier had managed to escape.

In the early years of the army the authorities attempted to curb desertion by branding the bodies of conscripts so that they could easily identify them and return them to their military units.[7] Gradually, an alternative method was used, namely the compilation of specific registers giving the name, physical description, village and province of the deserter so that orders could be sent to the village shaykh to arrest the said deserter.[8] By the 1830s, to stamp out the widespread phenomenon of desertion and absconding, it was decreed that every villager should carry a stamped certificate or passport (*tadhkara*) which should state his name, his father's name, his physical description, and his village. If found roaming around the countryside without this certificate, he would be immediately sent back to his village of origin. Even village shaykhs were ordered to carry these *tadhkaras* on entering Cairo.[9] Ultimately a special government department, the Department of Catching Absconders, *ma'mūriyyat dhabt al-missahhabīn*, was established in the mid-1830s (Najm 1989).

The birth of the medical and public hygiene establishment

We thus see the gradual abandonment in Egypt of ways of thinking of the population that were characteristic of sovereign power, and the steady adoption of new policing techniques that attempted to detect, account for and fix individual members of the population. A key turning point of the emergence of the 'problem of population' was the founding in 1827 of a new medical school which was aimed initially at producing doctors needed for the army. The director of this new impressive institution was a French doctor from Marseilles named Antoine-Barthélemy Clot who had been hired two years earlier, in February 1825, by Mehmed Ali as chief medical officer of the newly founded army. Over a number

[6] ENA, Ma'iyya Saniyya, Reg. no. S/1/48/1, letter no. 101, 21 Rabi' Thānī 1239/26 December 1823.

[7] ENA, Ma'iyya Saniyya, Reg. no. S/1/48/2, letter 360, 22 Sha'bān 1241/7 October 1825. This seems to have been applied mostly to naval soldiers. The tattoo was a sign of a ship and/or an anchor.

[8] ENA, Ma'iyya Saniyya, Reg. no. S/1/48/1, letter 364, 23 Jumad Awwal 1239/21 July 1824.

[9] ENA, Ma'iyya Saniyya, Reg. no. S/1/48/4, letter 226, 5 Rabī' Awwal 1249/23 July 1833.

of meetings with the Pasha the Frenchman argued that experience had shown that the ravages of disease had a more disastrous effect on the soldiers than wounds suffered on the battlefield, and that the best way to protect the new army was to found a medical corps to train doctors locally. Dr Clot added that towards that end he proposed to teach a nucleus of 150 students in a newly constructed medical school that would eventually supply the army with doctors, surgeons and pharmacists. A few years later, a British traveller visited that medical establishment (located at Abū-Za'bal to the northeast of Cairo) and wrote a very favourable account of it (St. John 1834, 2: 401–402). In 1837 – ten years after its foundation – Dr Clot persuaded the Pasha that the school-hospital was too far from Cairo; that patients incurred considerable costs to go there and that it had to be moved nearer to the city. After some hesitation, Mehmed Ali gave his orders for the school to be moved to Qasr al-'Ainī, in Cairo's western environs, and from that time till the present day the medical complex came to be known as the Qasr al-'Ainī medical school and hospital.

In a few years Qasr al-'Ainī managed to teach around 420 doctors for the Pasha's army and navy (Sandwith 1901, 11); moreover, it soon became a centre of a far-flung medical establishment that reached well beyond the confines of the military.

The School of Midwives

Another key institution that played a decisive role in the 'production of population' was the School of Midwives, founded in 1832. The origins of the school lay in the realization that, in addition to plague and cholera, Egypt was suffering from a high rate of smallpox infection among its infant population. It has been estimated that, by the early 1820s, 50,000–60,000 children were falling prey to smallpox annually, making it responsible, alone, for increasing the infant mortality rate by forty or fifty per thousand, increasing, in turn, the overall annual death rate by something between three and four per thousand (Panzac 1987, 18). In response, as early as 1819 the Pasha ordered his deputy to institute a programme of vaccination against smallpox throughout the country (Sāmī 1928, 2: 278, letter dated 5 Ca 1234/2 March 1819). Five years later, in 1824, the Pasha requested M. Drovetti, the French Consul-General, to secure a number of doctors from France who could administer a wide vaccination programme in the countryside. Three such doctors arrived in Egypt and started to vaccinate the fellahin against smallpox in various provinces in Lower Egypt, then moving to Middle Egypt the following year. After Dr Clot's arrival in 1825 and his taking over the entire health establishment, he persuaded the Pasha that any effective control of smallpox and other diseases necessitated checking the health and hygiene of women and children, who had hitherto not been the target of public policy. Women, Dr Clot reasoned, 'must be trained to help safeguard the health of Egypt's women and children' (Kuhnke 1990, 123). Concerned about the size of the population and the heavy burdens of his various conscription and corvée orders, the Pasha finally accepted the counsel of his chief medical adviser and in 1832 approved the establishment of a school for midwives.

The Shura al-Atibba: the far-flung public hygiene establishment

By the late 1830s and early 1840s the hundreds of doctors who graduated from Qasr al-'Ainī were no longer tied to the army; they had been appointed to serve in public clinics that had been opened in urban centres. These young doctors were also sent to the factories, schools, dockyards and government establishments that had been erected throughout Egypt. Most importantly, the young graduates of Qasr al-'Ainī and the female graduates of the School of Midwives were appointed to the police stations in urban centres and in provincial headquarters in rural areas.

Placed under the jurisdiction of the General Health Board in Alexandria (Majlis Umūm al-Siḥḥa), these numerous male and female physicians, nurses and pharmacists were entrusted with wide-ranging duties (see Kuhnke 1990, 167–177, appendices 1 and 2). Besides conducting preliminary check-ups on urgent cases and issuing *tadhkaras* permitting patients to be admitted to hospitals, these health officials were also responsible for conducting a nationwide vaccination programme against smallpox for all children (a programme that seems to have been quite successful), for overseeing the intricate operation of imposing strict quarantine regulations during epidemics (especially cholera and plague), and for supervising an elaborate system of forensic medicine to decide on suspected homicides and various other suspicious cases. In addition to being posted at police stations, these new graduates of Qasr al-'Ainī were also posted in the newly founded health clinics of Cairo, the *makātib al-siḥḥa*. These were public clinics offering medical services to the urban population free of charge. Reportedly, 21,468 outpatients were treated between 1845 (when the first six such clinics were established) and 1848, when their number was raised to eight: six for Cairo's eight quarters (*tumn*s), one for Būlāq, and one for Old Cairo. These clinics treated common ailments such as ophthalmia, scabies, syphilis, and dislocated or broken limbs. In addition, they were to offer 'free consultation for all the city's inhabitants; emergency aid to victims of drowning or asphyxiation; dressing injuries; free vaccination; dispatching hakimas [i.e. the women graduates of the School of Midwives] to confinement cases, [and] verifying and certifying causes of death' (see Kuhnke 1990, 142, which is all derived from *al-Waqā'i' al-Misriyya*, Mehmed Ali's gazette).

Besides treating prostitutes who constituted a grave danger to the health of the fighting force, the graduates of the School of Midwives were eventually appointed in police stations to work as forensic doctors (mostly checking female corpses and establishing the cause of death). They were also deployed as important government officials to administer the traditional midwives who numbered in the thousands and who had the necessary information about newborn babies. These young women (their number was very small: not exceeding sixty at any one time) therefore were more than simple midwives: they were female doctors entrusted with many crucial duties in the rapidly expanding public health administration. While still far short of a national system of birth registration, the vital information gathered from the traditional midwives by these young female doctors played a crucial role in expanding the reach of the public health establishment to the female half of the population (Fahmy 1998).

The 1848 census and the triumph of governmentality

As we have seen, Mehmed Ali and his military authorities were keen to have as accurate a picture as possible of the population of Egypt from as early as the 1820s. The different attempts to count the rural population were based on house counts and it was on the basis of these house counts that estimates of population were produced. Starting from the early 1840s, however, one can detect a shift from population estimates to counting the population – that is, genuine census-taking. That shift was made possible as a result of the far-flung public hygiene establishment described above. The public clinics in urban centres and the provincial headquarters, the nationwide system of registering newborn babies as well as accounting for all cases of death, and the incorporation within that public health establishment of the thousands of traditional midwives and rural barber-surgeons – all of these factors made it possible to launch a census based on counting individuals and not just houses.

In their study of the 1848 census, Cuno and Reimer assert that,

> while there was census activity throughout the mid to late 1840s, the only thorough enumeration of the population of Egypt in those years was begun in either late 1263/1847 or early 1264/1848. Unlike a modern census it was not carried out in a single day . . . but neither were its data compiled over a two- to three-year period . . . Rather, it appears that the 1848 census was completed over a period of several months. In Cairo it was carried out from late January to late July 1848, while in the provinces it may have begun somewhat earlier. Further archival research may result in precise dates for the entire census of 1848, but at any rate it appears to have been completed in less than a year.
>
> (Cuno and Reimer 1997, 200)

The registers of this impressive census (which number more than 7,000 registers, all preserved in the Egyptian National Archives) give a breakdown of the population by location, ethnicity and sex, with a comprehensive listing of the ages and occupations of the males, while the females were listed as either adults or juveniles. Foreigners and migrants are also listed.

The 1848 census marks a crucial turning point in the story of the emergence of the problem of population in nineteenth-century Egypt. From as early as 1827 Mehmed Ali had remarked that 'the welfare of the people depends on a good census',[10] and twenty years later he seemed to have managed to produce exactly that: a good census. This census was a product of over two decades of experimenting with different ways to control, monitor and police the population. From the early days in which men were rounded up with ropes around their necks or were tattooed so that they might be detectable after desertion from the army, to the time they were forced to carry passports on moving from one village to another, the administration had come a long way with its ability to enlist the village shaykhs to produce the vital information needed to compile the census. With this tool at hand the government could now produce 'demographic estimates, the calculation of the pyramid of ages, different life expectancies and levels of mortality, studies of the reciprocal relations of growth of wealth and growth of population, various measures of incitement to marriage and procreation . . .' (Foucault 1980, 171).

As an example of what now became possible in an Egypt of censuses we can turn to the detailed statistical report written in 1874 by Cairo's Chief Health Inspector and presented to the Privy Council to be submitted ultimately to the Khedive (as Egypt's governors came to be known, starting from 1867), and see the degree of confidence in the public hygiene administration with which it was written. The report not only had an estimate of the overall population of Cairo (450,000), but it also had precise figures of the mortality of each quarter and their progression over time. The Egyptian public health officials therefore could compile these figures and use them to read the city, so to speak – map them out to detect which neighbourhoods were more salubrious than others and then deduce conclusions and make specific policy proposals.

Equally important was the ease with which Cairo's Chief Health Inspector could compare the public hygiene situation of his city with that of major European cities.[11] Despite enumerating many factors that he deemed harmful to Cairo's air (the *khalīj*, i.e. the waterway that bisected the city from south to north, sewers, cesspools, cemeteries and slaughterhouses) – factors that might have been peculiar to Cairo – he nevertheless reached the conclusion that, in the final analysis, there was nothing fundamentally different that marked Cairo off from other major cities. It was overcrowdedness, as measured by the number of inhabitants per house, rather than any cultural, religious or climatic factors that most affected the salubriousness of the city; and with reliable figures about this particular factor at his fingertips, he could then compare Cairo's mortality figures with those of European cities.

With their origins lying ultimately in Mehmed Ali's founding of a modern army in order to make his position in Egypt secure and to alter the relationship between Cairo and Istanbul, the medical and public health administrations grew rapidly through the 1820s and 1840s, managing to produce an impressively precise national

[10] ENA, Ma'iyya Saniyya, Reg. no. S/1/48/3, letter 107, 2 Sha'bān 1242/1 March 1827.

[11] ENA, Majlis al-Khusūsī, Reg. no. S/11/8/22, doc. no. 10, pp. 12–14, 17 Shawwāl 1291/27 November 1874.

census at the end of that period. With that census as a database and with periodic updating based on revising natality and mortality figures supplied by midwives and undertakers, respectively, the authorities had at their disposal a tool that made it possible to think of and deal with the inhabitants of Egypt in terms of 'population', i.e. as capable of being aggregated in terms of age, gender and ethnicity, and analysed in terms of their locality and professions, and subjected to government policy in the areas of employment and internal migration.

The role of law in Mehmed Ali's project

If we shift our analysis from the fields of medicine and public hygiene to those of law and public order we can see how the appearance of the problem of population also entailed an 'individuating logic' of far-reaching consequences. The records of various legal bodies established in the nineteenth century show us how this individuating logic was deployed not only by the state and its agencies but also by members of the population as well. As early as the late 1820s Mehmed Ali had hit upon the importance of following earlier Ottoman practices in adapting the law to be a tool to consolidate his rule in Egypt and to tighten his grip over this Ottoman province. During the decades to follow and up to the early 1880s a complex legal system was created in Egypt that effectively set Egypt off as a realm independent from the Ottoman empire. This emerging legal system was predicated on supplementing the sharī'a courts, which had been operational in Egypt for centuries, with what was referred to as *siyāsa* – discretionary powers exercised by Mehmed Ali and his descendants to adjudicate criminal cases in novel legal institutions called *majālis siyāsiyya*: *siyāsa* councils. While elucidating the nature of this complex legal system is beyond the bounds of this study, what is of concern here is to show how the new administrative tools of identifying people, which were the product of the medical and public hygiene establishments, were employed by the *siyāsa* councils, and how the notion of individuality that these tools gave rise to was fundamentally different from that which had traditionally informed the sharī'a courts.

Soon after arriving in Egypt, Mehmed Ali turned to members of his immediate family to help him run his newly-won province. However, having hit upon the idea of establishing a loyal household as the best strategy with which to ensconce himself in Egypt, the problem that now confronted the Pasha was how to control the members of this household and to keep them in check. Fatherly words of advice sometimes worked; at other times, firm punishments had to be meted out. But Mehmed Ali knew that these were only palliative measures and his political instincts told him that a more lasting solution had to be found.

It was here that law proved to be invaluable, for there is ample evidence to show the Pasha was intimately aware of how previous dynasts, especially the

Ottomans, attempted to use law as a tool for consolidating their rule. Of particular importance was how the Ottomans – that is, in the narrow sense of the word, 'the house of Osman' – attempted to rein in their elite members, the *'askari* class, so as to prevent them from encroaching on the rights of their subjects, the *re'aya* (Arabic: *ra'iyya*). Here the Ottoman sultans relied on the classical Islamic concept of *siyāsa shar'iyya* which allowed the ruler to pass legislation that was seen as complementary to Islamic law, the sharī'a. The Ottomans called the resulting legal codes '*qānūn*s', and the increasingly sophisticated legal system that ensued from such acts of legislation was known as '*siyaset*' (Arabic: *siyāsa*). They thereby supplemented sharī'a, which is most vocal in private law matters, with *siyaset*, which is strongest in matters pertaining to public law (see Peters 2005, 69–102; and Imber 1997, 24–62).

Of particular value to Mehmed Ali were the *qanunnameh*s, or legal codes, that the Ottoman sultans had been repeatedly passing to prevent their elite members from abusing the privileges granted to them and from encroaching on the rights of the commoners. From the late 1820s the Pasha started to pass many such legal codes in Egypt to organize various aspects of his relationship with both his elites and his subjects. Called *qānūn*s, they had no precedent within Ottoman Egypt as never before had there been an Ottoman governor who had given himself such legislative rights. These codes attempted to control the members of the household elite by criminalizing some of their acts (bribery, laziness, negligence, feigning ignorance of orders and regulations, etc.) and by stipulating corresponding punishments (mostly fines and imprisonment, physical punishment being reserved for the commoners). At the same time, these legal codes defined the crimes committed by the commoners and set fixed penalties for their perpetrators.

More significantly, and in parallel with the traditional sharī'a courts, numerous *siyāsa* councils were established and were staffed by provincial and/or bureaucratic administrators to implement the *qānūn*s that the Pasha had passed. Again what concerns us here is not so much the overall contrast between sharī'a and *siyāsa* with regard to notions of justice, or the procedural and substantial differences between the respective means of adjudicating legal cases. Rather, what is of interest is how these two different branches of the legal system went about establishing the identity of litigants appearing in front of their respective institutions: the sharī'a court and the *siyāsa* council.

The sharī'a has elaborate rules to establish personal identity. Like other pre-modern legal systems (see Chapters 6 and 7), sharī'a identifies individuals by locating them carefully in their social setting and by taking note of their embodied relations. In his court, the *qādī* (i.e. judge) would do this by relying on upright individuals who had a good reputation in their community and who would be able to vouch for those people living in a given area who used the court to settle their disputes. Indeed, the jurists agreed that the *qādī* could not accept the testimony of witnesses unknown to him until their probity had been ascertained by reputable individuals.[12] Those reputable individuals, known as *shuhūd al-ḥāl* or *al-shuhūd al-'udūl*, were an essential part of the court and 'the entire weight in the identification of witnesses rested on the human links of interpersonal knowledge' that they provided (Messick 2002, 256). Accordingly, they were often considered part of the regular personnel of the court, and the sharī'a court records often mentioned the *qādī*'s order appointing them to his court. Most crucially, *al-shuhūd al-'udūl* played a fundamental role in identifying the litigants. The following 1865 entry from the sharī'a court of Mansūra in the Delta is a good example of how the *al-shuhūd al-'udūl* helped the judge establish the identity of those individuals who appeared in his court:

> Al-'Adawī Tāhā al-Maghallāwī of Mansūra the son of the late Hajj Tāhā al-Saqqa [the water-carrier] arrived in the sharī'a court of Manusūra, and after he had been identified by the testimony (*ba'da thubūt ma'rifatihi bi-shahādat*) of both the honorable [*al-mukarram*] 'Abd al-Mit'āl Shāhīn al-Hāyik, the son of the late al-Mitwallī Shahīn, and Sayyid Ahmad al-Maghallāwī, the son of the late 'Alī Sayyid Ahmad, both from Mansūra, confessed and testified (*aqarra wa i'tarafa*) that . . .[13]

As can be seen from this typical entry, the litigant's name is not enough to identify him/her. Neither is it enough to mention the town of residence, or the father's profession. This information had to be corroborated by two *'udūl* witnesses, whose patronymic names and the names of their fathers are also recorded. These two *shuhūd al-'udūl*, 'Abd al-Mit'āl Shāhīn al-Hāyik and Sayyid Ahmad al-Maghallāwī, were denizens of the same city, Mansūra, and one has to assume that they knew the litigant in person, helping the *qādī* in the crucial task of establishing the identity of the litigants. In other words, the very initial stage of a legal case (and the entire legal system of the sharī'a) depends on closely embedding people in a communal context to fix their identity. The individual as an autonomous, isolated person, conceived of as existing outside locally-specific social relations, was an unknown category as far as the pre-modern legal system was concerned.

Siyāsa's methods of identification

By contrast, the *siyāsa* system knew none of these complex mechanisms of identifying litigants and witnesses. Instead, it appears that one's name, one's father's name and one's domicile were often enough for the *siyāsa* authorities to establish juridical identity. Occasionally one's profession was also stated. It was therefore typical for a record of a criminal case to start by simply stating such information, as follows:

[12] See, for example, Ibn Qudāmah (1970, vol. 10, 57).

[13] ENA, Mudīriyyat al-Daqahliyya, Mahkāmat al-Mansūra al-Shar'iyya, Reg. no. 2 (old no. 14), case no. 190, p. 20, 28 Rajab 1282/17 December 1865. For the role of the *shuhūd al-ḥāl* in identifying litigants, see Messick 2002, 255ff.; Faraḥāt 1988, 77.

> an individual (*shaks*) named Khalīl Sāba, the Greek grocer who lives in Tanta [in the Delta], filed a complaint with the deputy [governor] of the city (*mu'āwin al-bandar*) that two people had come to his drinking hole (*khammāra*), one named As'ad Dāghir and the second named 'Abdallah Tanūs al-Dayrūtī, and they were soon joined by Ibrahīm 'Abdallah al-Bayrūtī . . . Khalīl al-Dīb and Milḥim al-Sammāsh, all from Syria (*min al-diyār al-shāmiyya*) . . .[14]

Sometimes one's father's name was not even mentioned, as in the case of 'the woman (*al-ḥurma*) named Alfiyya who lives on Hārat Bahlawān in the Sayyida Zaynab district (*khutt*)' and who presented a petition to Dīwān Kethuda (Arabic: Katkhuda) accusing a certain Hajj Khidr of killing her son, Hassan.[15]

However, and as can be expected, in the absence of *'udūl* witnesses who could help in identifying litigants and witnesses, there was room within the *siyāsa* for people to lie about their true identity and to assume different names. Sometimes this was done for innocent reasons, as was the case with a woman who claimed her name was Khadra, the daughter of the late Muhammad al-Kharrāt originally from al-Munsūriyya, Gīza. When she was caught stealing in Cairo, she was sent back to her village, only for the Governorate of Gīza to write back saying that her true name was Sayyida, the daughter of Khadra. Asked why she had lied about her name, she answered that she went about by that name, Khadra, which, if truth be told, was in fact her mother's name, not hers.[16] In another instance, a man named Maḥmūd Mustafā from the town of Damanhūr in the Delta was caught red-handed stealing cloth in Cairo. In the police station he confessed that his real name was Khalīl Abū Tūr, that he was indeed from Damanhūr, but that earlier he had been convicted of theft, imprisoned, and had escaped from prison, and was currently on the run. Knowing that prior records were crucial in determining punishment, Khalīl was probably hoping to evade his prior record and thus receive a lighter punishment.[17]

[14] ENA, Majlis al-Ahkām, Reg. no. 7/10/31 (old no. 635), case no. 26, pp. 15–17, 8 Jumādā Awwal 1282/29 September 1865.

[15] ENA, Dhabtiyyat Misr, Reg. no. L/2/67/4, case no. 33, pp. 11–13, 8 Rabī' Thānī 1270/8 January 1854. Dīwān Kethuda, also known as Dīwān Khidīwī, was concerned with domestic, non-military affairs, and was presided over by the pasha's deputy, his *kethuda*, hence its name. Most of its responsibilities were taken over by Diwan al-Dākhiliyya, or the Department of the Interior, when this latter was established during Ismā'īl's reign.

[16] ENA, Dhabtiyya Misr, Reg. no. L/2/6/3 (old no. 2030), case no. 115, pp. 87–89, 3 Safar 1295/6 February 1878. She was still found guilty of theft and it was explicitly stated that her changing her name made her even more suspicious. See also the case where a slave was caught who had been using three names: ENA, Muhāfazat Misr, Reg. no. L/1/2/1, letter no. 4, from the Muhāfazat to the Dhabtiyya, p. 14, 8 Rabī' Awwal 1271/29 November 1854; and L/2/6/1 (old no. 2027), case 48, pp. 89–91, 16 Sha'bān 1294/26 August 1877, concerning a woman called Imbarka daughter of Mustafa al-Sabbākh who claimed that her name was Fatma daughter of 'Alī Muḥammad, when she was caught stealing some brass kitchen utensils.

[17] ENA, Dhabtiyyat Misr, Reg. no. L/2/6/2 (old no. 2028), case no. 113, pp. 23, 26, 8 Shawwāl 1294/5 October 1878.

To get around the frequent problem of people hiding their true identity by changing their names, it was common to add domiciles and professions as further markers to help with identification. For example, when the Governorate of Cairo (Muhāfazat Misr) wrote to the Cairo police headquarters (Dhabtiyyat Misr) to fetch a certain Muhammad Badawī for some legal dispute,[18] the Dhabtiyya wrote back saying that, 'without specifying this person's profession and his domicile it is impossible to locate him, as there are many people who carry this name'.[19] Eventually, it was only after receiving information saying that the man in question was a carriage driver (*sāyis*) who worked on the estate of the late Ibrāhīm Pasha Yeğen, that it proved possible to identify and arraign him.[20]

It was also common for people to assume different names, not as a means of evading a prior record but to assume the identity of their betters. And in a society which was highly hierarchical and whose legal system was not based on the principle of equality before the law, this was a very serious offence. A decree passed in 1845 stipulated that

> anyone who uses a false name or a false title in order to appear dignified and respected (*fī mazhar al-i'tibār wa'l-waqār*) or who puts on airs of being a feared person . . . will be sent to prison for a period not less than a year and not exceeding five years in addition to paying a fine ranging from 200 piastres to 12,000 piastres.[21]

Not having at its disposal an identity-establishing institution like sharī'a's *shuhūd al-'udūl*, and lacking such modern documents as picture IDs, fingerprinting, DNA tests, etc. (Caplan and Torpey 2001), the *siyāsa* authorities were extremely anxious about these drifting identities. This anxiety was most acute in the case of people who had no domicile and who roamed around the city with no clear residence and/or profession. As far as the authorities were concerned, these people could only mean trouble, and both police records and contemporary laws are replete with expressions of this anxiety (Ener 2003, 30–37). A man called Ibrāhīm Muḥammad, for example, was accused of petty theft, and the fact that 'he is [originally] from Cairo but has no known domicile, no relatives, works as a labourer in the morning and sleeps in the streets and in empty places [at night]' was enough to convict him. When Muhammad Darwīsh seduced a military cadet into dropping out of school and going with him to Alexandria to spend a good time together, and when his military school

[18] ENA, Dhabtiyyat Misr, Reg. no. L/2/40/9 (old no. 529), Wārid 'Ardhālāt, incoming letter from Muhāfazat Misr no. 1117, p. 48, 8 Rabī' Awwal 1279/3 September 1862.

[19] ENA, Dhabtiyyat Misr, Reg. no. L/2/11/12 (old no. 565), Sādir 'Ardhālāt, outgoing letter to Muhāfazat Misr no. 9, p. 7, 18 Rabī' Awwal 1279/13 September 1862.

[20] ENA, Dhabtiyyat Misr, Reg. no. L/2/11/12 (old no. 565), Sādir 'Ardhālāt, outgoing letter to Muhāfazat Misr no. 214, p. 85, 18 Rabī' Awwal 1279/13 September 1862.

[21] ENA, Majlis al-Ahkām, Daftar Majmū' Umūr Jinā'iyya, p. 47, law no. 4, 1261/1845. This is a unique and highly important register compiled during Ismā'īl's reign in an attempt to compile a list of previous criminal legislation. This register has recently been published in a highly informative edition (Helal 2011), where the relevant law appears on p. 275.

sent out a circular with his physical description, both young men were caught. Darwīsh was interrogated, and after it was found out that he was unemployed (*min dūn sinā'a*) and had no home (*lā maḥall yatawattan fīhi*), he was sentenced to one year in prison. Prison records would specify if a certain prisoner was 'with no domicile' (*lam yakun lahu ma'wā*).[22]

This anxiety about drifters and people with no known domicile is also easily detectable in laws. Mehmed Ali's first criminal legislation (1829) had a section about 'gypsies who are wandering around unemployed in Cairo . . . [others] who are harmful to the people and inhabitants of Cairo and the villages . . . people from Hejaz and Sudan and . . . slaves, fortunes-tellers, magicians and treasure-hunters . . .'. The law went on to say that those among these people just mentioned 'who are healthy are to be removed and sent to the ironworks, those of them who are young to the troops, and those of them who are very unfit to remote regions, i.e. places like Esna [in Upper Egypt]'(quoted in Peters 1999, 189). In 1863, soon after he became governor of Egypt, Ismā'īl Pasha wrote to Majlis al-Aḥkām, ordering that 'those unemployed who roamed around as they pleased' were to be sent to the War Ministry (*Dīwān al-Jihādiyya*) to be put to work by officers in a special platoon of convicts (*firqat al-mudhnibīn*). In 1880 a general circular was issued stating that,

> given that it has been known that there are [people] in the cities and ports who are homeless and unemployed and who roam around as they please and since these drifters have no purpose except to harm people, it was decided to arrest them, press them into the army, or send them to serve in eastern Sudan to get rid of their evil deeds (*wiqāyatan min shurūrihim*).
>
> (Jallād 1899, 3: 153)

Finally, in 1891 a special order was issued giving a precise legal definition to vagabondage and imprisoning people thus defined (*al-mutasharridīn*) for a period ranging from fifteen to forty-five days, with the possibility of exile (Āsāf 1895, 23–29).

As indicated above, one way to curb this problem of drifting identities was to order certain people to carry on them stamped certificates or 'passports', called *tadhkara*s. As early as the 1820s the authorities were issuing these *tadhkara*s, stating the first name, the patronymic name, the physical description, and the village of its bearer. On being caught without such a certificate a peasant would be immediately arrested and repatriated to his village (Fahmy 1997, 106). When it was found out that a black market had developed in these documents and that civilians were selling their passports to soldiers and sailors, Mehmed Ali issued an order to use alternative stamps for the different passports. Precise orders were issued to the

[22] ENA, Dīwān al-Tarsāna, Reg. no. M/14/4 (old no. 955), titled 'Qayd asmā' al-madhnūbīn bi-līmān tarsānat Iskandariyya', p. 23, 8 Jumād Awwal 1283/18 September 1866, entry of Muhammad Hassanien who also called himself Muhammad 'Azzūz.

Cairo police commissioner to arrest village shaykhs who arrived in Cairo with no *tadhkaras*.

Concerned about the growing number of Europeans arriving in Egypt in 1850, the authorities established a 'passport authority' (*qalam al-basabūrtū*) in Alexandria, and whenever a new ship called in port this new department would compile a register with the names, physical descriptions and characteristics (*asmā wa awsāf wa shamāyil*) of those on board who disembarked and proceeded to Cairo. This register was to be sent to the Cairo police.[23] A similar department was established in Suez.[24]

It is true that these bureaucratic innovations, i.e. using patronymic names, requiring a domicile, and issuing *tadhkara*s, were not innovations specific to the legal system. Nevertheless, they had very significant legal implications. For it was these bureaucratic devices that the *siyāsa* repeatedly relied on to identify litigants. Given the meticulous bureaucracy that the military and medical establishments had created (which were briefly sketched above), people had at their disposal a multiplicity of bureaucratic devices that they produced when approaching a police station in order to establish their identity. In addition to the *tadhkara*, the records show that people occasionally produced a vaccination certificate or a conscription certificate to prove that they were who they claimed to be.

Contrasted with the role played by the *'udūl* witnesses in a *qādī* court, which effectively embedded individual identity in its communal and local setting, the *siyāsa* relied on a complex and efficient bureaucracy to help ascertain the identity of litigants it dealt with. These new devices that the bureaucracy produced gave rise to a new notion of the individual that was independent of the social and communal setting. These scraps of paper with government stamps and seals on them allowed the state to deal with the individual as such, as an independent entity detached from his or her social milieu and isolated from his or her communal setting. This bureaucratization of identity gave rise to what can be called a '*siyāsa* subject' and had far-reaching implications for how the legal system came to be conceived of and how such basic notions as law, justice, and the individual came to be thought of.

[23] ENA, Diwān Khidīwī, Reg. no. S/2/18/1 (old no. 654), letter without no., pp. 138–140, 24 Dhū al-Hijja 1266/1 October 1850. When the Passport Department was late in compiling these registers, causing a backlog, the Alexandria Governorate wrote a reprimand letter: Muhāfazat Iskandariyya, Reg. no. L/3/1/33 (old no. 52), letter no. 24, p. 35, 28 Dhū al-Qa'da 1268/14 September 1852.

[24] ENA, Majlis Khusūsī, Reg. no. S/11/8/6 (old no. 68), doc. no. 63, pp. 99–100, 12 Dhū al-Qa'da 1280/19 April 1864.

Conclusion

The material presented in this chapter suggests that a transformation in the very notion of the individual had been effected in nineteenth-century Egypt. The first part of the chapter attempted to verify how precisely what Foucault called the 'problem of population' came to be defined in the first half of the nineteenth century in Egypt. By stressing the military and dynastic contexts in which different attempts to count the population took place, the first half of the chapter stressed the medical and public hygiene policies that made it possible by mid-century for the authorities to make a count of the population of Egypt.

The second half, by contrast, traced how a concurrent process of individuating people can also be traced within the field of law. This part of the chapter stressed the differences between the ways in which the two prongs of the legal system, sharī'ā and *siyāsa*, identified litigants. Lacking the meticulous social means of establishing identity which were deployed in the *qādī* courts and which had been theorized by the Muslim jurists and perfected in practice over the centuries, the *siyāsa* councils had to resort to alternative mechanisms to ensure that the litigants whom they dealt with were who they claimed to be. Instead of the *'udūl* witnesses, effectively the linchpin between the *qādī* and the community and who could establish not only the identity of litigants and witnesses but also their reputation, the *siyāsa* relied for the same purpose on the textual and documentary devices mentioned above: the census record, the passport, the vaccination certificate, proof of domicile and simple patronymic names.

The introduction of these novel devices of counting and identifying people had far-reaching implications. For these new textual devices not only enabled the *siyāsa* councils to rely on the government bureaucracy in order to ascertain identity; they also led to the appearance of a completely new concept of identity. In contrast to the *qādī* court practice of embedding individual identity in a communal setting and of relying on the community (the tribe, the extended family, the neighbourhood, the village, etc.) to establish the probity and reputation of individuals, the *siyāsa*, by relying instead on the documentary devices of the modern state, could appear to dispense with the communal context altogether as it found alternative means to establish identity, ascertain probity and check reputation.

It was this newly forged, free-floating individual and their bureaucratically-created identity that made the idea of equality thinkable. As is well known, before passing his judgments, the *qādī* has to consider such factors as the gender, the religion and the freedom status (in addition to sanity and age) of the litigants and witnesses appearing in his court. The amount of blood-money, the number of witnesses to be heard, the amount of inheritance a relict is to receive – all these and other questions cannot be addressed except after the *qādī* has paid close attention to whether his litigant is a man or a woman, a Muslim or a non-Muslim, a slave or a free person. By contrast, because it has at its disposal the new bureaucratic devices mentioned above, the *siyāsa* council can deal with individuals irrespective of gender or religion. It is not that the *siyāsa* archive has no mention of religion, gender or other personal qualifications – rather, these factors do not have a bearing on how a case is viewed, nor are they central in how a person presents himself/herself in front of the police or how he/she articulates his/her case.

The idea of equality before the law, therefore, so central in most accounts of secularization, was born not out of any deep belief in the Enlightenment ideals of the value of each and every individual. Nor was it the result of the pressure applied by European diplomats on leading intellectuals in Istanbul or Cairo to accept the principle of treating their Muslim and non-Muslim subjects equally. The equivalence that was established between members of the same polity was made possible, furthermore, not because of some successful pedagogical exercise that managed to conquer 'prejudice' and 'bigotry'. Rather, legal equality was born as a result of *siyāsa*'s successful attempt to uphold and maintain sharī'a while, at the same time, embracing modern medical and bureaucratic devices. In other words, sharī'a became secularized in nineteenth-century Egypt as a result not of limiting it to the realm of personal status, as is commonly believed, but because of the success of the *siyāsa*, its partner in crime, in embracing the individuating techniques of the modernizing, centralizing state.

References

Āsāf, Yūsuf. 1895. *al-Ta'dīlāt al-Qānūniyya allatī udkhilat 'alā al-qānūn al-ahlī al-Misrī*. Cairo: al-Matba'a al-'Umūmiyya.

Bowring, John. 1840. *Report on Egypt and Candia*. Foreign Office, Great Britain. London: Clowes.

Caplan, Jane and John C. Torpey. 2001. *Documenting Individual Identity: The Development of State Practices in the Modern World*. Princeton, NJ: Princeton University Press.

Cuno, Kenneth M. and Michael J. Reimer. 1997. 'The Census Registers of Nineteenth-Century Egypt: A New Source for Social Historians.' *British Journal of Middle Eastern Studies* 24(2): 193–216.

al-Damurdāshī Katkhudā 'Azabān, Aḥmad. 1989. *Kitāb al-Durra al-Muṣāna fī Akhbār al-Kināna*, ed. 'Abd al-Raḥīm 'Abd al-Raḥman 'Abd al-Raḥīm. Cairo: Institut Français d'Archéologie Orientale du Caire.

Ener, Mine. 2003. *Managing Egypt's Poor and the Politics of Benevolence, 1800–1952*. Princeton, NJ: Princeton University Press.

Fahmy, Khaled. 1997. *All the Pasha's Men: Mehmed Ali, His Army, and the Making of Modern Egypt*. Cairo: American University in Cairo Press.

—— 1998. 'Women, Medicine, and Power in Nineteenth-Century Egypt.' In *Remaking Women: Feminism and Modernity in the Middle East*, ed. Lila Abu-Lughod. Princeton, NJ: Princeton University Press, 35–72.

Faraḥāt, Muḥammad Nūr. 1988. *al-Qadā' al-Shar'ī fī Misr ī al-'Asr al-'Uthmānī*. Cairo: al-Hay'a al- 'Āmma lil-Kitāb.

Foucault, Michel. 1980. *Power/Knowledge: Selected Interviews and Other Writings, 1972–1977*, ed. Colin Gordon. New York: Pantheon.

Glass, D. V. 1973. *Numbering the People: The Eighteenth-Century Population Controversy and the Development of Census and Vital Statistics in Britain*. Farnborough: D. C. Heath.

Helal, Emad. 2011. *Wathā'iq al-Tashrī' al-Jinā'ī al-Misrī: Sijill 'Majmū' Umūr Jinā'iyya'*. Cairo: Dār al-Kutub.

Ibn Qudāmah. 1970. *al-Mughnī*. Cairo: Maktabat al-Qāhira.

Ibrāhīm, Nāṣir Aḥmad. 1998. *Al-Azmāt al-Ijtimā'iyya fī Misr fī al-Qarn al-Sābi' 'Ashr*. Cairo: Dār al-Āfāq al-'Arabiyya.

Imber, Colin. 1997. *Ebu's-su'ud: The Islamic Legal Tradition*. Stanford, CA: Stanford University Press.

al-Jabartī, 'Abd al-Raḥmān. 1994. 4 vols. *'Ajā'ib al-āthār fī 'l-tarājim wa'l-akhbār*, ed. Thomas Philipp and Moshe Perlmann. Stuttgart: Franz Steiner.

Jallād, Filīb. 1899. *Qāmūs al-Idāra wa'l-Qadā'*, vol. 3. Alexandria: Lāghūdākī.

Kuhnke, LaVerne. 1990. *Lives at Risk: Public Health in Nineteenth-Century Egypt*. Comparative Studies of Health Systems and Medical Care. Berkeley: University of California Press.

Messick, Brinkley. 2002. 'Evidence: From Memory to Archive.' *Islamic Law and Society* 9(2): 231–270.

Mikhail, Alan. 2011. *Nature and Empire in Ottoman Egypt: An Environmental History*. Cambridge: Cambridge University Press.

Najm, Zayn al-'Ābidīn S. 1989. 'Tasaḥḥub al-fallaḥin fi'asr Muḥammad Ali: Asbābuhu wa natā'ijuhu.' *The Egyptian Historical Review* 36: 259–316.

Panzac, Daniel. 1987. 'The Population of Egypt in the Nineteenth Century.' *Asian and African Studies* 21(1): 11–32.

Peters, Rudolph. 1999. '"For His Correction and as a Deterrent Example to Others": Mehmed Ali's First Criminal Legislation (1829–1830).' *Islamic Law and Society* 6: 164–193.

—— 2005. *Crime and Punishment in Islamic law: Theory and Practice from the Sixteenth to the Twenty-First Century*. Cambridge: Cambridge University Press.

Planat, Jules. 1830. *Histoire de la regeneration de l'Egypte*. Paris.

St. John, James Augustus. 1834. *Egypt and Mohammed Ali: Or, Travels in the Valley of the Nile*, vol. 2. London: Longman, Rees, Orme, Brown, Green & Longman.

Sāmī, Amīn. 1928. *Taqwīm Al-Nīl*, 2nd edn, vol. 2, ed. Aḥmad Zakarīyā al-Shilliq and Ṣalāḥ Faḍl. Cairo: Dār al-Ma'ārif.

Sandwith, F. M. 1901. 'The History of Kasr-el-Ainy.' *Records of the Egyptian Government School of Medicine* 1.

14

No Will to Know: The Rise and Fall of African Civil Registration in Twentieth-Century South Africa

KEITH BRECKENRIDGE

THIS CHAPTER FOLLOWS THE DEVELOPMENT and dismantling of civil registration for rural black people in South Africa in the first half of the twentieth century. The story is intriguing and important in several ways. The South African state was not poor, and, unlike its northern neighbours, it was not bereft of administrative capacity. Perhaps the best indicator of this wealth and bureaucratic capacity was the extension after 1944 of means-tested old-age pensions to black South Africans. By 1950 the state was spending over a million pounds a year on 200,000 African pensioners (Rycroft n.d.; Sagner 2000, 540). Dozens of different registration systems were also developed by the state during this period. To name only the largest of these: by the 1930s the Native Affairs Department (NAD) had in place a centralized system of tax registration that, in theory, recorded a name, identity number, and address for every African man in the country over the age of 18 (F. R. for Secretary for Native Affairs 1949). More provocative is the fact that the system of civil registration was actually working well in the Eastern Cape and in Natal in the early years of the twentieth century. It was deliberately foreclosed and then abruptly abandoned in 1922. But perhaps the most intriguing problem derives from that fact that historians of the South African state, and society, have characterized it as knowledge-driven. Why, then, did it choose not to gather the most basic kind of administrative information?

Uncertainty about population in Africa

Profound and intractable disagreements about the size, distribution and identity of national populations are endemic across the African continent (Adepoju 1981; Kwankye 1999). In South Africa the debate has centred around two issues that are critical to the prospects of the new democratic state: the first concerns the size, character and cost of the immigrant population, and the second deals with the

Proceedings of the British Academy **182**, 357–383. © The British Academy 2012.

demographic effects of the AIDS epidemic. In 2009, a half-century after the introduction of universal old-age pensions, nearly a decade after the introduction of a welfare system that delivers social grants to more than a quarter of the population, and after uncounted billions had been spent on epidemiology in South Africa, the different arms of the state disagreed publicly and vociferously about the reliability of the figures for mortality being used as the basis of state policies on HIV. This official squabble over mortality statistics prompted Rian Malan, a famously ill-tempered writer, to berate South African health scientists for not interrogating the 30 per cent increase in national mortality claimed by the Department of Home Affairs in 2008, which, if true, suggested that 'the Aids equivalent of an atom bomb has detonated among our people' (Mbanjwa 2009).

This uncertainty about population in Africa is a product of the faulty, indeed often non-existent, institutions of civil registration – the bureaucratic recording of individual births, marriages and deaths – that characterize states across the continent. 'In the African colony,' Cooper has observed, 'the state could not track the individual body or understand the dynamics of the social body' (Cooper 1996, 335; Kwankye 1999). Different forms of parish birth registration were common in many of the Christian areas on the continent (Doyle 2008; Zeitlyn 2005; Malherbe 2005, 2006, 2007), but, outside of Uganda (see Chapter 10), these have never formed part of an integrated national system of birth reporting. On the face of it, the absence of civil registration seems simply to reflect the incapacity of the twenty-first-century African state – in Ghana and Nigeria, for example, recent efforts to build civil registration systems have collapsed as administrative tenacity and the funds for temporary registrars both dwindled a year in to the projects. Yet the causality might actually run in the other direction. The failure of the colonial (and the pre-colonial) state to deliver systems of civil registration may provide a better account of the development of what Freund and Cooper have called the gatekeeper state than the economic explanations that have been offered to date. (See Chapter 15 for a very similar account of the collapse of the *état-civil* in Francophone Africa. On the gatekeeper state see Freund 1998; Cooper 1996, 465; 2002.)

The histories of these failures in Africa are important because civil registration, combined with some, even very austere, measure of social security, may be a prerequisite for the kinds of economic growth that we associate with the development of modern capitalism. Drawing out the implications of the national system of birth, death and marriage registration imposed by Henry VIII's Vicar-General in 1538, Szreter has suggested that 'a detailed continuous inventory of identities' may be a crucial part of the explanation for the puzzling manner in which the agricultural economy of England began to overhaul both the Netherlands and China from *c*. 1660 onwards (Szreter 2007, 72). Whether this strictly individualized welfarism should be viewed as a political quid pro quo in the long, cultural ascendancy of property rights that Corrigan and Sayer (1985) have described, or whether it was a special variant of the new sciences of population-obsessed government that

Foucault, and others, have tracked in the development of sixteenth-century European political institutions, the significance of this nexus of civil registration and welfare seems clear (Foucault 1991; Groebner 2007). Civil registration systems should be included in the shortlist of institutions that Acemoglu, Johnson and Robinson have suggested were the determinants of long-term economic growth (Acemoglu *et al.* 2001; this extremely influential study of sixty-four former colonies found that 'differences in institutions [land-holding, courts, parliamentary representation, bureaucracy] account for three-quarters of the differences in 1995 per-capita incomes'; see Feinstein 2005, 98).

The beneficial result of the recording of personal names has been obscured by the fact that, aside from private property and welfare (which even in the English case were famously bad-tempered between 1834 and 1948), identity registration was typically an instrument of nasty exactions – of taxes, rents, conscription and confession. Over most of the continent Africans were subjected to these demands under colonialism through the institutions of indirect rule. Demands for taxes or labour in many parts of Africa fell uniformly across all families, without regard to their capacity to support them (Iliffe 1988, 154). In South Africa taxes were levied differentially in the nineteenth century on the number of huts in each household within a chief's jurisdiction. But in the early part of the twentieth century, as wage labour replaced peasant farming as the main source of tax revenue, the burden of tax fell predominantly on the movement of adult men. One result was that, aside from special cases like the MaSarwa in Botswana, the poor were not easily identifiable, individually or as a group. Another, much more significant, consequence was that the mortality and morbidity of women and children became administratively invisible.

By the start of the twentieth century the blunt and blind administrative instrument of communal land tenure controlled by chiefs or headmen had become for colonial officials, and for many Africans, the preferred mechanism for a welfare net (Ntsebeza 2006, 74–75; Sagner 2000, 560). The conventional explanation that historians have offered for the prevalence of this system of 'hegemony on a shoestring' has been the systematic parsimony of the colonial state (Berry 1992). A reluctance to spend money on Africans in the countryside certainly contributed to the decline of civil registration, but there were other, more important, intellectual motivations. In this essay I want to show that the key administrative inadequacy of indirect rule in South Africa followed from the contested and constrained character of progressive ideas about the state in the decades after 1910. In short, a profound disagreement between those who sought to use scientific forms of policing – and particularly fingerprinting directed at adults – confronted the advocates of scientific public health informed by voluntary reporting. The primary result of this conflict was administrative inertia.

A modernist state?

There is an anomaly at work in this history, prompted by the dominant theoretical accounts of the South African state. Most of the important scholars of apartheid have stressed the way in which the bloated bureaucracy presented the work of government as intrinsically scientific. Posel in particular has drawn attention to the demented statistical obsessions of the Department of Bantu Administration in the 1960s (Posel 2000; Giliomee 2003 stresses Verwoerd's doctrinaire scientific personality in the developments of the late 1950s and early 1960s; on the place of science in the new bureaucracy, see also Evans 1997). It is true that in 1952, under Verwoerd's tenure, civil registration for Africans was restored and reinvigorated, but it was coercively arranged, intensely patriarchal, and funded much more stingily than the earlier system. This new effort was dramatically less successful than the early twentieth-century project; it was rapidly bogged down by the resistance and chaos generated by the social engineering effort in the late 1950s, and undone completely by the decision to impose independence on the bantustans in the 1960s (Secretary for Native Affairs 1955).

It would also be a mistake to draw too sharp a line between the scientific government of the apartheid state and the *ad hoc* paternalism of the segregationist period. By the 1920s the most important arguments in favour of racial segregation in South Africa were all framed in concert with transatlantic social science (Rich 1990). South African science, as Dubow has shown, reached its apogee under Smuts's patronage between 1929 and 1945, with the appointment to key positions of internationally respected scholars like Malherbe, van der Bijl and Schonland (Dubow 2006, 210–241). Similarly, the enumerative preoccupations, and capacity, of the South African state date from decades before apartheid, indeed from before the establishment of the Office of the Census and Statistics, in 1917 – something that was nicely demonstrated by the comprehensive time series published in *Union Statistics for 50 Years* in 1960 (South Africa 1960).

There is undeniably a close connection between the technologies of segregation and the broader project of bureaucratic rationality in the twentieth century. It is easy to see (as the film *District 9* shows) why historians might see South African society as an especially horrible instance of the iron cage of modernity (Weber 1905, 181). But I think that the power of this argument may have led us to misunderstand some key features of the colonial state. Under the influence of Weber's work on the remorseless development of bureaucratic rationality and Foucault's study of the sciences of government, scholars of this region have argued that the state had 'an insatiable appetite for information about the population it managed'(Crais 2002, 9). Scott's argument about the simplifications and categorizations that inhere in the operations of legibility – of the details that are lost in order to produce standardized ways of comprehending societies – has been particularly important here. Crais's study of the politics of the colonial state in the

Eastern Cape provides a very direct statement of this argument. 'A will to know,' he suggests, 'to identify, to categorize Africa according to the precepts of Western rationality formed an ineluctable part of both the politics and the practice of conquest' (Crais 2002, 96).

I am sceptical about this idea for many reasons, not the least of which is that bureaucratic rationality, and a more general popular enthusiasm for the 'will to know', are less than self-evident in contemporary South Africa. The politics of legibility has much deeper, and more influential, historical roots in Europe and Asia than Foucault allows in his writings on the growth of the disciplines after the Enlightenment (see Editors' Introduction to this volume). As Groebner's recent work shows, the documentary surveillance of the church and the municipalities in Europe was intense and ubiquitous, especially from the sixteenth century, but dating back almost the entire millennium to the book of the damned in the second half of the thirteenth century (Groebner 2007, 70). There is also a telling contrast between the long-term forms of state power that have developed in Africa and the 'book-based omniscience' of the mandarin bureaucracies (Woodside 2006, 82). And this tradition of textual administration has important echoes in the present. Consider the 1987 recommendation by Hu Yaobang, the Communist Party Secretary General, that cadres prepare themselves for government by reading books amounting to 200 million words, an accomplishment which the president of the Chinese academy of sciences assured worried youth, 'could actually be done in twenty years' (Woodside 2006, 81). In Egypt and in India the English colonial state in the nineteenth century battened on to already existing written systems of land and identity registration, for revenues and recruitment, while simultaneously complaining bitterly of the inadequacies and corruption of indigenous systems of government (see Chapter 11; Fahmy 1997; and, on registration particularly, Chapter 13; Milner 1894; Cohn 1997; Bayly 1999). In southern Africa there was no similar administrative bounty, and the colonial state sought, famously, to mobilize other forms of local authority in the defence of its power. This regional history of the colonial state suggests that, as Stoler has recently shown, an overarching imperial 'homage to reason was neither pervasive nor persuasive' (Stoler 2008, 58).

The failure of civil registration in South Africa followed from a particular political arrangement. Administrative concern for the registration of births and deaths was, as Foucault might expect, repeatedly fostered by the advocates of a system of public health, from 1900 through to the end of the 1940s. These progressive reformers were opposed, especially in Natal, by full-blooded opponents of bureaucratic intervention – key amongst them the wealthiest owners of the sugar plantations who also controlled the government after 1893. Later civil registration was also opposed by some of the state-appointed chiefs, and by the most pessimistic liberal magistrates defending personalized government.

But the weakness of the system of birth registration in South Africa stemmed from the fact that it faced a competing scheme for identity registration. From the early years of the twentieth century another group of progressive administrators – advocates of control from the mining industry, the police and the Pass Offices of the NAD – proposed compulsory universal fingerprinting of all African men as an alternative to universal civil registration. This obsession with fingerprinting as an instrument of central government control is one of the distinguishing features of the modern South African state. Its public history began in earnest when Mohandas K. Gandhi fought Lionel Curtis and Jan Smuts's efforts to register the Indian population of the Transvaal (Breckenridge 2011). In the generation after Smuts's struggle with Gandhi the advocates of universal biometric registration faced determined liberal scepticism in the state, and it was only in the 1940s, under apartheid, that the state enforced the early twentieth-century plans for compulsory fingerprint registration (Breckenridge 2005a, 2005b, 2008, 2011). But, as this chapter shows, in the same inter-war period the advocates of biometric registration succeeded in maligning the value of the information that was produced by delegated civil registration, and they provided the rationale for the system's dissolution. It was this unwieldy conflict between the policing and the public health branches of progressive government, combined with the absence of meaningful political representation, that, in the end, meant that the state consciously chose not to gather the most basic information about its African subjects.

A progressive deviation

The gathering of birth and death information from black people in South Africa began falteringly in Natal in the last years of the nineteenth century. Much earlier, in 1858, the colonial legislative council had proposed a census and registration of the African population, as part of the effort to coerce labour from Shepstone's tribal reserves. That proposal was rejected by the Lieutenant Governor as 'unnecessary interference'.[1] A new registration law was passed in 1896, aimed at the *Amakholwa* – the thousands of Africans married according to Christian rites and thus lying between the 5,000 in Natal who were legally exempted from the operations of customary law and the 350,000 who lived under chiefly government. Possession of an official Letter of Exemption essentially conferred on Africans some of the key rights of British citizenship. It entitled women to register (and bequeath) freehold property, and to access British courts; for men it allowed the vote. But the law demanded that an application for exemption could only be made by Africans who had passed through all of the requirements of mission life (monogamy, literacy, good character) and it was always fiercely policed in Natal. Importantly, children

[1] In 1869 the colony required that every African marriage had to be registered (and recorded centrally) at a cost to the applicants of £5. There is little evidence that the scheme ever worked in practice (Kline 1988, 58; Etherington 1989, 174; Lambert 1995, 46).

inherited their parents' status only if they were born prior to the issuing of the Letter of Exemption (Brookes 1924, 197–198). It was for his reason that the 1896 Act required Christian parents to register the birth, and death, of their children within thirty days, or face a £5 penalty. The Act specifically placed the burden of the registration – of both birth and death – on the parent, which suggests that it was concerned solely to limit the population that might claim exemption from customary law (Secretary for Native Affairs 1898). This measure also allowed the members of the new Responsible Government, who had previously been critics of the imperial government's adoption of Theophilus Shepstone's system of benign neglect, to do something, without actually stirring up change or, critically, incurring any expense.

Between 1846 and 1877 Shepstone had been almost solely responsible for the government of the African population of Natal, developing an *ad hoc* paternalism that had powerful effects on the form of the African colonial state. During this period he moulded a distinctive form of administration which relied on appointed chiefs as the agents of an undocumented system of government, and a crudely effective hut tax as the main source of colonial revenues. In return Shepstone worked hard, and effectively, to resist the settlers' claims to African land and labour. Under his system, the chiefs were supervised by a handful of appointed magistrates, each responsible for very large districts, several chiefs and thousands of homesteads. The title magistrate may be misleading. In the nineteenth century the individuals who were appointed as Native magistrates rarely had anything resembling legal training. In the following century the posts were typically filled, in Natal as in the rest of South Africa, by individuals who had distinguished themselves as officials in the NAD – in both centuries a mission background was much more important than legal experience (Dubow 1989, 99–101). The magistrate's work consisted, very largely, of gentle supervision of the chiefs in whose hands the daily routine of government rested unmolested. Shepstone's system of 'native agency' became synonymous, especially after 1900, with resisting cultural and economic change. (It was Welsh who first argued that it was Shepstone's method of indirect rule – which he extended to the Transvaal after 1877 – that provided the administrative and intellectual seedbed of apartheid, and, more recently, Mamdani who suggested that it provided the basis of colonial rule across the continent (Etherington 1989; Welsh 1971; Delius 1983; Mamdani 1996).)

By the turn of the century almost all of the local settler leaders had become enthusiasts for the doctrine (now habitually attributed to Shepstone) that the state should interfere as little as possible with African society (Welsh 1971, 229–231; Brookes 1924, in contrast, sees the Shepstone system as a model of energetic segregationism). The prime minister, Sir Hercules Robinson, a fierce critic of post-Shepstonian 'drift' before 1893, discovered the special virtues of ignorance after he took responsibility for government. The colony, he explained in the legislature, 'is to be congratulated that there is so little occasion to give information regarding native affairs, because it shows that the Native population is generally contented and that they give the Government very little reason for consideration or reflection' (Welsh 1971, 229).

Natal's enthusiasm for administrative drift lapsed momentarily during Milner's progressive remaking of the Boer Republics. In a flurry of legislative energy the colony passed a string of new capitation laws aimed at tightening the colonial state's grip on its individual African and Indian subjects. First amongst these was a new Pass Law, Act 49 of 1901 for the 'Identification of Native Servants', which adopted the passport, name registration and labour distribution elements from a very important pass law drafted by Jan Smuts in the Transvaal in 1899, but without the revenues that were raised there from employers. Following in the same vein as the earlier law that required converts to register births, in 1903 the colony extended the requirement that contract-expired indentured Indian migrants pay an annual £3 tax, to include their teenage children. Two years later, as the colony struggled to replace the custom revenues lost in the recession that followed the withdrawal of British troops, the Treasury pushed for a change in the organization of the taxes levied on Africans, moving from Shepstone's carefully designed hut assessment to a poll tax levied on all adult men in the colony, black and white. Although the new law exempted homestead heads who were already paying the hut tax, it struck at the heart of the old homestead political economy and pushed some of the Natal chiefs into rebellion (Marks 1970, 131–143; Guy 2005, 23–24; Lambert 1995, 167; Carton 2000, 118; Duminy 1989).

Hidden beneath these taxes was a capitation law of a different kind. In 1901, Natal passed a Public Health Act that required, amongst other progressive measures, the appointment of a colonial Health Officer and the establishment of the infrastructure of a basic health service. As Marcia Wright has shown, this fledgling health system was designed by a member of the Indian Medical Service who was brought to Natal in 1899 to act as Special Plague Adviser, bringing with him the experience of the IMS's effort to impose compulsory birth registration in the 1890s (see Chapter 11; and Wright 2007; the Durban municipality had, for decades, tried, without much success, to use sanitation laws against Indian landowners; Swanson (1983) called this the 'sanitation syndrome'). From the outset this service faced fierce and determined opposition from the leading figures of the settler government. Chief amongst these was Sir Liege Hulett, one of the most important planters, who, as Wright observes, 'growled that the Health Department was too expensive, not worth its cost'. It was Hulett – an outstanding Methodist, liberal patron of John Dube, and founder of Kearsney College – who led the ongoing effort to limit the costs and retrench the services that were planned in 1901 (Wright 2007, 161).

The first goal of the newly appointed Health Officer was to extend the comprehensive system of birth and death registration that was maintained for the indentured migrants to the wider population of Africans and Indians. 'The basis of all work for the improvement of the Public Health is Vital Statistics', he explained, and 'without strictness of registration no reliable statistics can be obtained' (Wright 2007, 159). This effort to establish a unitary system of civil registration in Natal failed in the face of determined opposition from the planters and from local doctors, but the fleeting enthusiasm for a public health system had one significant legislative effect: Act 25 of 1902 required the registration of all African births and deaths in the old colony of Natal, excluding the territory of Zululand.

The scheme for civil registration in Natal had some typically Shepstonian features. Under the law, responsibility for the notification of births and deaths fell on the male 'kraal head'. He was required, within three days, to report the event to the district Official Witness. These unsalaried positions had been created under the Natal Native Code of 1891 to sanction customary marriages, and they were rewarded through an increased allowance for *ukulobola*. The Official Witness was required to report all such events to the local magistrate within thirty days. For every recorded event – births and deaths – Official Witnesses were paid one shilling by the magistrate. This was a substantial fee at the time, amounting to the better part of a day's wage, and clearly the reason for the scheme's relatively rapid introduction. The legislation specifically prohibited the registration of stillbirths, but required that, 'in the case of children dying shortly after birth, both the birth and death must be registered'. Parents were permitted to report the names of children who died unnamed at a subsequent date, 'for insertion in to the register and the completion of the record' (Magistrate, Kranskop 1902; on the role of the Official Witnesses, see McClendon 1995). The new system did not cover all Africans. Couples married under Christian marriage rites remained outside of this system, and, along with the exempted, their births and deaths were incorporated in the register maintained by the colonial (and later provincial) registrar.

The convulsive expansion of administrative interventions, taxes, and registration, combined with the collapse of the war boom, the enduring effects of the Rinderpest epidemic of 1897, and a dramatic increase in population, made life very difficult for Africans in Natal. Discontent culminated, in the last days of the summer of 1906, in widespread protests and refusal to pay the new poll tax, and isolated acts of violence and ritual killing. After the rebellion had been brutally suppressed by colonial irregulars who took the opportunity to show off the skills in scorched-earth warfare they had learned against the Boers, the colony launched a grand commission, in July 1907, to consider the grievances of its African subjects (Guy 2005; Brookes 1924, 77). The committee, which included Native experts like Hulett, Maurice Evans and James Stuart, heard evidence from over 5,000 African witnesses; the report of these sittings is eloquent testimony to the discontent and distress of the household patriarchs, and their chiefs, in the face of the unworkable combination of the newly rationalizing state and Shepstone's reliance on 'Native agency'.

The senior men who came to address the commission protested bitterly about the new instruments of tax and surveillance; they worried about the moral effects of young men paying their own tax (and retaining their own tax receipts), complained about the increase in the hut tax to 14 shillings, of the dog tax and the stringent methods being used to control the movement and dipping of African-owned cattle. They fumed about the ways in which the old Shepstonian order was being deformed by white officials' expectations that they all be treated as chiefs, about the collapse of the careful practice of consultations and the ongoing decline in the prestige of the chiefs. And they protested at a host of new dangers: lawyers' fees, sex between whites and blacks, inadequate wages, the fencing off of private lands, and usurious money-lending.

Amidst this litany of protest the vital registration requirement was an insignificant source of grievance, but four men, amongst the hundreds who gave testimony and the thousands who attended the hearings, grumbled about the new law. The first to introduce the issue was Nduku from the Klip River Division in northern Natal. He complained that he had recently 'experienced much trouble in regard to the registration of births and death' and that he 'was punished if he did not register his child within the proper time'. He particularly objected to the requirement to provide a name hastily (Natal. Native Affairs Commission 1907, 736). Mzungulu, from Krantzkop, also complained of the requirement to name the child 'forthwith', and he asked, 'Why should a man for not reporting a death, be suspected of having committed a criminal offence?' (Natal. Native Affairs Commission 1907, 856). Faku, an iNkhosi from Ixopo, observed amidst a list of wider complaints that he was 'surprised' by the registration requirement (Natal. Native Affairs Commission 1907, 782). This small stream of evidence was hardly damning, but one witness, chief Sibewu of the Lower Umzimkulu Division, near Port Shepstone, made a much stronger point. His only comment was on civil registration, which he said was unnecessary, and he warned the committee that the people worried 'what the intention of the Government was when the children grow up' and that 'they felt it would get hold of them, and send them off to some other place' (Natal. Native Affairs Commission 1907, 808).

The report that was produced from the 1907 commission generally addressed the spirit and not the letter of the new laws regulating rural African families. It argued, for example, for more respectful treatment of homestead heads by the magistrates and their police, and for a more paternalistic approach to the attestation of the promissory notes that were the source of entangling debts. But, providing a classic example of the ways in which the segregationists sought out the idiom of African reaction as the justification of their own plans, the only specific legislative recommendation made by the committee was for the repeal of Act 25 of 1902, 'having regard to Native feeling thereon, the incompleteness of records, the exclusion of Zululand from its operation, and the cost of such registration' (Brookes 1924, 85). The legal requirement for civil registration was not withdrawn in 1907, but the commission's recommendation that it be abandoned hung like a Damoclean sword over the scheme for the remainder of its life.

Advance or retreat

Immediately after the formation of the Union in 1910 the new central government in Pretoria began to consider the question of how to move forward on the project of civil registration for Africans (Colonial Secretary 1910, 1911). In the Cape, compulsory civil registration had been introduced in the Transkeian Territories in 1899, but without the two critical elements that made the Natal scheme work: payment for local registrars and punishment for delinquents. In 1911 the national Department of the Interior (DOI) complained about the desultory character of the data from the Transkei. The annual number of registrations, which at no time represented anything like the actual number of births and deaths, had declined steadily, reaching a nadir of 4,000 in 1910. Smuts's officials in Pretoria worried – with their hands already busy with a registration struggle with Gandhi (Breckenridge 2011) – that the attitude of parents in the Transkei was 'either utterly apathetic or one of passive resistance'. And they wanted the issue laid before the Bunga so that 'the free discussion in all its bearings might result in the enlistment of the active cooperation of the Native Members of the Council' (Acting Under-Secretary for the Interior 1911). There was, at this stage, no question of abandoning the scheme. Instead, Stanford, the Chief Magistrate, announced the start of prosecutions for failing to register births and deaths (S. H. Stanford, Chief Magistrate, Transkeian Territories 1911).

The problem in the Cape was that registration, and prosecutions, were both the responsibility of poorly paid headmen, or *Izibonda* (for the special place of the headman, magistrate and the Bunga in the Transkei, see Beinart and Bundy 1987). 'The person to whom Government looks to see that the law is observed', Brownlee commented after prosecutions had begun, 'is the same person who is criminally liable for its observance and if he fails in his duty it can only be by accident that his omission in individual cases is discovered.' After the complaints from the DOI in 1911, the Transkei magistrates began to look for alternative ways of handling registration, and, after some debate, resolved that the most promising candidates for the position of local registrar were the teachers in government-funded schools. They then turned to Smuts's old department for the funds that would be required to reward teachers for taking on the processing of birth and registration forms – the suggested rate of payment had now fallen dramatically to between three and sixpence per event. In what must count as one of the world's finest examples of the old adage, penny wise and pound foolish, the DOI refused to accept responsibility for the £800 budget that would be required to make civil registration work in the Transkei, arguing that the matter was being held in 'abeyance until a uniform law is passed when all parts of the Union can be dealt with on the same basis' (Secretary for Interior 1913).

Accustomed as they were to administering a state without access to the funds they raised in taxes, the Cape magistrates changed their strategy, abandoning the idea that registrars should be paid for their work, and arguing instead for a change in the law in order to teach the moral lessons of registration. They argued, after 1913, that the regulations should be changed to place the burden of registration on to 'the owner [of the household where the vital event occurred] or person in charge for the time being'. This formulation, unlike the Natal system and the later requirements of civil registration under apartheid, left open the possibility that women would be legally responsible for the registration of their own children or grandchildren. Under this arrangement, headmen would be confined to their familiar role as policemen, ensuring that heads of households did their duty.

The idea was submitted to the provincial registrar for comment, and he produced an assessment of civil registration in the Transkei that was, in the long run, to have very powerful effects. He mocked the magistrates' request for relief for the overburdened and underpaid headmen, as 'with very few exceptions, the Headmen have not allowed the duty to weigh heavily upon them'. Working through the most conservative and undeveloped territories of Pondoland he pointed out that huge districts, like Bizana and Flagstaff, had not managed to register a single birth or death in the course of the previous year. Where registration was taking place in a more regular fashion it was typically 'made by relatives and friends and not by the Headmen'. Yet he held out very little hope that anyone else would be able to do the job any better. The headman, he pointed out, 'is constantly in touch with the Magistrate and has periodically to present himself at the Magistrate's office to draw his pay', whereas the ordinary head of household had hardly any contact with white officials. The registrar was also utterly sceptical about the magistrates' optimistic view that unpaid storekeepers would 'assist the natives, their customers, by completing information forms for them'. But he was mildly enthusiastic about the broader project of presenting a moral lesson. As the new arrangement, placing legal responsibility on the homestead head, 'would at least serve the useful purpose of introducing to the Natives the idea of individual responsibility for reporting births and deaths, which it is intended to enforce later, I think the experiment should be tried'. The Cape law was duly altered in September 1914, but no additional funding was allocated to registration, and the dismissive assessment of the quality of the data was what remained in the record.

A similar problem shaped the development of the system in Natal. Here the problem was not the infrequency or irregularity of returns (a problem that was manifestly solved by the one shilling payment to Official Witnesses), it was the fact that the entire territory north of the Thukela river was not covered by the scheme. After 1902 the old kingdom of Zululand had been reduced to a rump, covering less than half of its original territory, which was similar in extent to the colony of Natal. With much of its population living on land now purchased by whites, it was still home to about 200,000 people – approximately a third of the African population in the old colony (MacKinnon 1999, 101; Lambert 1989, 386). It was the exclusion of this recently annexed population that now threatened the workings of civil registration in Natal.

When Edward Dower, the former Cape Secretary of Native Affairs, began to act as the head of the new national Department of Native Affairs, he asked Arthur Shepstone – Theophilus's son and the Chief Native Commissioner of Natal – for advice about civil registration. Shepstone provided an enthusiastic assessment of the Natal system, concluding that, aside from problems of communication in the far northern districts of Ubombo, Ingwavuma and Hlabisa, he could 'see no reason why the births and deaths of all Natives should not be registered in Zululand; all that is required is that Act No 25 of 1902 be extended to that Territory and provisions made for the appointment of Official Witnesses' (Arthur Shepstone (Actg. Under Secretary for Native Affairs, Province of Natal) 1911). Much hinged on the mild word 'provisions', but Shepstone's suggestion was denied by an even more banal impediment. When Dower mentioned the idea of extending civil registration into Zululand to the DOI he received a sharp rebuke from Smuts, reminding him that the NAD was not responsible for 'vital statistics in the Union' and demanding that 'any correspondence on the subject' should be transferred to his department. Having established which department owned this process, the Secretary for the Interior added that nothing was going to be done for the foreseeable future (Arthur Shepstone (Actg. Under Secretary for Native Affairs, Province of Natal) 1911; Acting Secretary for Interior 1911; Edward Dower, [Acting?] Secretary for Native Affairs 1911; Secretary for Interior, Pretoria 1913). In his report on the matter, Dower consoled his minister by reminding him that the 1907 commission had recommended that civil registration should be abandoned in Natal.

The most deadly blow to the system of civil registration in Natal was not administered by the Transvaaler Smuts, nor by one of the Cape magistrates; it came from within the provincial bureaucracy. W. J. Clarke was the Chief Commissioner of Police in Natal from the end of the nineteenth century. He was an ardent administrative progressive, and dogged champion of a plan for universal fingerprint registration (W. J. Clarke, Chief Commissioner, Natal Police 1907; Pinto-Leite 1907). In February 1913 he wrote to his national superior condemning the quality of the registration data being gathered in Natal. Clarke cited two cases of fraud in the Weenen district where Official Witnesses had been convicted of falsely recording births and deaths; in one of them 'as many as 60 or 70 false entries' had been recorded. 'It seems to me the system is open to fraud', he reported, 'and that the returns, as published, are very unreliable' (W. J. Clarke, Chief Commissioner, Natal Police 1913). Much later, after the system had been abandoned, the Natal magistrates would protest the injustice of Clarke's accusations, but his charges were received by R. H. Addison, one of the Zululand magistrates who had no experience or sympathy for the workings of the Official Witnesses. Addison all but admitted that fraud was rife, proposed that heads of households should travel with the Witnesses to confirm registrations, and then reminded the permanent secretary that the 1907 commission had, in any case, suggested that the whole scheme should be abandoned (R. H. Addison, Acting Chief Native Commissioner, Natal 1913). But even this unfriendly assessment was not sufficient to end registration; for a decade the Natal scheme carried on.

Retrenchment

The early 1920s were difficult times in South Africa, as all over the world, with the economy battered by inflation, fiscal retrenchment and working-class protests. It was amidst the very grim fiscal and political atmosphere of 1922 that the NAD found itself the target of an efficiency evaluation by the independent committee of the Public Service Commission. The Public Service Commission took a scalpel to the administrative establishment that had been built up in the NAD after 1900, gutting, in particular, the regulators in the Johannesburg Government Native Labour Bureau and making the case that the whole of the department should be run along the lines of the skeletal administration in the rural districts of the Transvaal and Zululand (Dubow 1989, 81–87; Dubow 1986 shows that this downsizing was not permanent, and by 1928, under the rich diet produced by the 1927 Native Administration Act, the NAD was back to its earlier weight. Falwasser, H. G., Acting Director of Native Labour 1926).

By October 1922 a special cabinet-level audit – appropriately named after the Geddes Axe Committee that had slashed government spending in Britain – had discovered the £2,000 that was being used to pay Official Witnesses in Natal. The new Chief Native Commissioner in Natal, C. A. Wheelwright, had himself come from the remote and backward Zoutpansberg district, and he looked askance at the civil registration scheme. When Wheelwright asked the Natal magistrates for their views on the abolition of the payments for Official Witnesses none of them agreed that it would be a good idea. All but one reported that it would be 'a source of great hardship' and mean the end of the system of civil registration (Chief Native Commissioner, Pietermaritzburg 1922). It was Wheelwright who argued, on the basis of Clarke's 1913 police report, that the system was 'unreliable and not worth the expense involved' and, worse, that it encouraged fraud by offering a 'pecuniary inducement' (Secretary for Native Affairs, Pretoria 1922). Within weeks the payments had been suspended and the registration of African births and deaths immediately collapsed in Natal. The following year a new Births and Deaths Registration Act was published. The new Act, No. 17 of 1923, made registration of 'births, still-births and deaths of natives' compulsory only in urban areas, and left open the possibility that the DOI might declare registration compulsory in a specific rural district by regulation.

The public health challenge

Over the next two decades the advocates of a state-supported public health system lobbied continuously for the restoration of registration in the countryside. These efforts peaked in the early 1930s when Natal and Zululand faced an unusually severe malaria epidemic. An official effort to re-introduce registration by Official Witnesses was announced in July 1932, exactly a year after the International Conference on African Children that had been convened in Geneva by Eglantine Jebb's Save the Children International Union (see Chapter 17). The South African participation in the Geneva conference had been conspicuous, with three leading figures of the liberal establishment playing important parts: Alice Duncan, wife of the Governor-General, J. D. Rheinallt-Jones, the founder of the recently established Race Relations Institute, and Henri Junod, a Swiss missionary and author of one of the first great South African ethnographic monographs (Rich 1984, 22–32; Junod 1962). Junod's study covered the most remote areas of Zululand, but the links between the Geneva conference and the effort to restore vital registration were indirect at best. In Johannesburg the social reformers, and officials, like Rheinallt-Jones and Duncan, were much more concerned with regulating informal marriages than with the scientific benefits of birth and death registration (Britten 1930; Phillips 1938, 96–97; Posel 1995, 228–231). Yet the malaria epidemic drew the attention of important metropolitan researchers, including Professor N. H. Swellengrebel from the League of Nations, and the discontent about colonial registration that Marshall (in Chapter 17) traces in that organization may thus have found its way to Natal (MacKinnon 2001, 84).

The champions of registration during this period were two local officials: Dr George Park Ross, at the time district health officer in the national Department of Health, and Harry Lugg, then the Native Magistrate for Verulam, a picturesque sugar milling town on the Natal north coast that was surrounded by malarial cane fields and impoverished native reserves. Both men had long experience of the skeletal government of indirect rule, an interest in the use of Shepstonian 'native agency' as a remedy, and, importantly, they would go on to take up the most senior provincial posts in their respective departments. Their combined efforts to restore the payment to Official Witnesses began in June 1932, when Lugg appealed to the permanent secretary of the NAD to restore the old system of registration, without which the severity of the malaria epidemic 'will never be known'. After reminding the permanent secretary that 'the last census did not include the enumeration of Natives' he urged the department to invoke the terms of the 1923 Act to require the 'registration of births and deaths of all natives' (Harry Lugg, Native Commissioner, Verulam 1932).

A month later the most senior officials of the NAD and the newly formed Department of Health met in Durban to discuss a combined response to the malaria crisis. The main resolution of this meeting, reflecting the groundwork that Lugg and Park Ross had already completed, was that 'registration of births and deaths in Native Reserves should take place' (E. H. Cluver, Asst Health Officer 1932). While there were some signs of opposition, the principle, as the minutes show, was 'generally conceded' and the NAD accepted responsibility for the reintroduction of registration. Predictably, however, nothing happened. A month later, as the epidemic gathered steam, Park Ross wrote angrily to his departmental boss that 'nearly every District in Natal is now affected with malaria, and until reliable information in the shape of an official registration of deaths is provided, it is impossible to deal effectively with outbreaks of the disease'. As the NAD magistrates attempted to estimate the number of deaths in the countryside from the epidemic, Park Ross railed against a policy that effectively made the large-scale deaths of black people in the countryside officially invisible. 'We have here an official disease,' he protested, 'which, according to the returns has wiped out one-tenth of our population, and it apparently is to go unregistered' (Chief Native Commissioner, Pietermaritzburg 1932).

Faced with the inertia of the NAD, the Health Secretary tried to goad his peers at the Interior to remedy their glaring statistical shortcomings. This scientific reprimand pushed the Secretary of the Interior, after a delay of several months, to express his opposition to African registration directly. The registration of 'native births and deaths proved very unsatisfactory, both in Natal and in the Transkeian territories', he claimed, because 'Headmen appeared to have little interest in the duty'. The resulting registration of Africans was of 'small economic value', and the wisest policy (as far as the Department of the Interior was concerned) was to suspend registration in the countryside until some future when 'the native may be sufficiently advanced in the scale of civilization to realize the advantages of registration'. The NAD, he concluded, was welcome to come up with a scheme for implementing registration, but it would not be acceptable to the statisticians (and accountants) at the Interior unless it could be 'conclusively shewn that such a scheme would be of economic value and of real interest from a health point of view' (de Wet, Secretary for Interior, Pretoria 1933).

This cold rejection of the social value of African registration enraged Park Ross. He reminded his permanent secretary that 'an effective system of registering increase and deaths of cattle is in force in Native areas' and asked why it was 'impossible to evolve a similar system for human beings'. Park Ross acknowledged that there would be errors in the information provided by a system of registration in the Native Reserves, but, contradicting the bleak view that the statistics of African births and deaths would be economically worthless, he insisted that the returns would be 'of the utmost value' because they would help to protect the public health and 'save numbers of lives' (Senior Assistant Health Officer 1933). Park Ross promised to turn back to the NAD to try to get registration restarted. But the opposition of the Department of the Interior was sufficient to encourage J. M. Young, the Chief Native Commissioner (CNC) in Natal, to reject the idea. He declared that registration was worthless unless it could be implemented nationally, that the terrain and absence of roads in the reserves would make registration just another petty and unfulfillable burden, and that Africans generally, and chiefs and Official Witnesses in particular, were 'generally imbued with the same spirit of conservatism and distrust' that would undermine public participation. Shortly after Young had issued this rejection, he retired and was replaced as CNC by Harry Lugg.

Almost immediately Lugg tried to reopen the discussion about a special NAD registration effort. Drawing on his own long years as a magistrate he insisted that the claims that had been framed by the police and the officials at the DOI about widespread fraud were false. 'I have had considerable experience, extending over a period of twenty-one years, with the working of the Natal Act', he declared, and 'found no difficulty whatever in enforcing its provisions'. Against the official consensus that the individuals charged with responsibility for registration had generally neglected the work, he insisted that 'Native Official Witnesses carried out their duties faithfully and well.' And he contradicted the claim – circulating since the 1907 Native Affairs Commission – that Africans were generally suspicious of registration. 'The Natives regard the formal registration of a birth', he explained, 'as conferring added status to a child.' Finally, Lugg reminded his superior that the abolition of registration in 1923 was 'universally regretted by the Magistrates of this Province, for it left them with no means – except the Native Census (when held) – of ascertaining the increase of our Native population'. He now proposed a simpler and cheaper version of the original scheme, shifting responsibility for the one shilling payment for the registration of a birth on to the parents, but leaving the state responsibility for the fee for deaths. But Lugg's experience of the workings of the original system, and his insistence on its utility, could not soften his superior's concern about the financial difficulties the department faced in 1933 (Harry Lugg, Chief Native Commissioner, Natal 1933).

Park Ross and Lugg did not give up. They persisted throughout the 1930s in the effort to bring registration back to life. They were both very senior officials in their respective departments. But they faced entrenched inertia, skilled bureaucratic evasion and, most importantly, the unfounded but implacable view that African registrars would commit fraud to secure the payments for registration. By the middle of that decade, as the South African fiscal crisis dissolved away under the benign influence of an inflated gold price, the most senior figures in the NAD were using this argument – derived solely from Clarke's 1913 report in the official record – to overturn Park Ross's claims about the public health value of registration. Here they invoked Clarke's claim that registration events would be invented for gain which would mean that 'our vital statistics, about which the doctors are making such a fuss, will all go wrong' (D. L. Smit, Secretary for Native Affairs, Cape Town 1935).

As this last comment suggests, the effort to restore registration in South Africa was not the isolated obsession of Lugg and Park Ross. Throughout this period groups of doctors kept pushing for compulsory vital registration in the countryside.

In their efforts to rationalize the missing data, the leading officials in both the NAD and the Interior presented explanations that would have amused Franz Kafka. In 1942, for example, while the Allied armies were still on the defensive around the world, the hearings of the Beveridge Commission in Britain prompted the South African government to plan seriously for a national health service that would include the African population in the countryside (Marks 1997, 452–455). The division of the South African Medical Association (SAMA) for the Transkei, based as they were in the middle of the largest Native Reserve, made a public call for the restoration of civil registration to strengthen the political case for a nationalized health service. They wrote to the Secretary of Native Affairs, reminding him that their organization was 'wholeheartedly in favour of a State Medical Service for Natives' and asking the NAD to implement civil registration. Here again the doctors drew out the embarrassing comparison between the state's expectations for livestock and the requirements for people: 'if it is found necessary to register the Births and Deaths of cattle, it would appear that the registration of the Births and Deaths of the people should be even more necessary'. They cited the data from a single hospital in the Transkei to show the horrible effects of tuberculosis in the countryside – over 20 per cent of total deaths were derived from this single cause. 'Reliable statistics', they argued in a statement that echoes through to the recent HIV crisis, 'would make the need for a [national health] service abundantly clear' (Arnold H. Tonkin, Hon. Sec., South African Medical Association, Border Branch, Transkei Division 1942).

The NAD's response to this request highlights the ignominious deferment that had by this time became habitual in the department's responses to this question. 'What would be the use of statistics when the causes of death are inaccurate?' The official responsible for registration replied that, 'the state med[ical] service must come first, so that all Natives can have med[ical] attention. After that we can get accurate statistics' (see marginalia on Arnold H. Tonkin, Hon. Sec., South African Medical Association, Border Branch, Transkei Division 1942). The champion of the South African national health service, Henry Gluckman, was appointed Secretary of Health in 1945, but that was not enough to deliver his proposals. After 1943, as the Allies' global position improved, the bureaucracy's enthusiasm for social interventions declined rapidly, replaced by an increasingly feverish anti-communism and a determination to use force to stifle dissent among the black population (Moodie 1988). In the debates that followed, the extent and effects of disease in the countryside remained largely invisible, a statistical situation that has only begun to change very recently (Coovadia *et al*. 2009).

In the years immediately after the Second World War, organizations like SAMA, the National Child Welfare Association, the Anti-Tuberculosis Association and the African representatives in the Ciskeian General Council placed almost continuous pressure on the state to act (Secretary for Native Affairs 1947). In 1946 the NAD, 'being pressed on all sides to secure the introduction of a system of registration at the earliest possible date', attempted, again without any success, to persuade the Department of the Interior to take up the task (Mears, Secretary for Native Affairs 1946). Over the next few years they began to plan, fitfully, for a return to the system of Official Witnesses that had been working before 1922. Finding resources for registration remained a problem, even as the pensions for Africans were being paid out. In the new registration plan the fee to be paid to African registrars had been whittled down to three pence – in real terms a tiny fraction of the one-shilling payment that Official Witnesses had earned half a century earlier. The total that the NAD planned to spend on national registration – an additional amount of £5,000 per annum – was never a very large sum and it was certainly well within the state's reach throughout this period (Smuts 1949). But even these desultory efforts were swept away by the National Party's plans for Native Affairs after 1948. As the department turned to building elaborate and compulsory labour bureaus for African workers in the cities, and then, after 1952, to the even more ambitious and costly system of reference books for all black adults, urban and rural, the prospects of a national project of civil registration dimmed (Hindson 1981, 184–212).

By the end of the 1940s, the arguments about the virtues and prospects of civil registration had come full circle. Almost half a century earlier W. J. Clarke had suggested that registration, in the absence of fingerprinting, was 'open to fraud' and unreliable. For decades that flimsy (and fiercely contested) characterization of African registrars as frauds had been used as a pretext by those who sought to resist the continuous calls for a reliable system of civil registration. As the apartheid state began to take form, with a very large and renewed interest in fingerprinting as a remedy to the limits of the official documents of identification (Breckenridge 2005a), the most senior officials in the NAD, including those who had earlier been part of the Lugg–Park Ross campaign to restore registration, began to argue that only biometric registration could reliably establish the identity of Africans in the countryside. 'In view of the vast illiterate population, many of whom have no address or fixed abode, the Department is of opinion that the only practicable means of registration', Frank Rodseth, the departmental Under-Secretary, wrote, 'is by a system of finger prints' (F. R. for Secretary for Native Affairs 1949).

Conclusions

On the face of it the story of the failure of civil registration in South Africa is a familiar one of colonial state-building on the cheap (Rodney 1982, 200–230; Cooper 1996, 465–466, 2002, 5–6; Young 1994, 120; Berry 1992). The officials charged with making registration work simply lacked the funds to do it. It is certainly the case that the Native Affairs Department – without a constituency that was represented in parliament and often despised by the most influential African leaders – was always on the defensive about its budgets. Yet the amounts involved in building a large system of registration were actually very small. Even more importantly the advocates for registration typically came up with innovative ways to make registration pay for itself, and they often preferred to use existing instruments of indirect rule (such as headmen and dipping inspectors) to achieve it. Neither argument succeeded in overcoming the scepticism or vacillation of the bureaucracy. This history suggests that the South African state had the resources and the ambition to expand from its position as gatekeeper; the fact that it did not do so was – as many critics observed as it was happening – a product of its very limited ability to gather information about people in the countryside. In this sense the South African gatekeeper state – concerned to police and administer Africans only when they were in the cities – was a result, and not the cause, of the failure of universal registration. Nor was this lack of interest in the details of the lives of rural black people pre-ordained by the system of indirect rule; the reverse might easily have been true.

This brings me to the second straightforward explanation for the failure of registration: racism and racist views. Some of this is certainly correct. It was clearly the case that racist contempt informed the idea that all African registrars would act as frauds. The persistent failure of any real urgency on the part of the officials (especially at the DOI) charged with making government work in the tribal areas clearly followed from the absence of any meaningful sympathy with the black people who lived there. In this respect registration in South Africa follows a pattern of racialized government that is familiar elsewhere in Africa and in the United States (see Chapters 15 and 17; Skocpol 1992, 533; Shapiro 1950, 98–99). Nor can there be much doubt that the absence of reliable statistics on the appalling health conditions amongst black people in the countryside helped to strengthen the policy of official neglect. But racism cannot sufficiently account for the complete and prolonged failure of civil registration, not least because the most successful period of registration coincided with the era of the fiercest white supremacy (see especially Cell 1982; Lake and Reynolds 2008).

A more convincing explanation emerges from the forms of legal and political representation in South Africa (and elsewhere on the continent). Repeatedly a well-worked-out scientific argument about the costs and benefits of civil registration was allowed to die in the disagreements between departments, or amidst the more urgent fiscal demands of the Depression or the Second World War. It was the absence of a political constituency arguing for registration that allowed this inertia. Here the contrast with the many different forms of registration described by the others in this volume is striking, because both elites and the poor – who, in other contexts, sought registration for many different ends – were silenced by the workings of customary law. Indirect rule in rural South Africa, as in most of Africa, placed administrative processes in the hands of chiefs who were charged to substitute for a developing public sphere and political economy of literacy that was occurring in the towns (see Ntsebeza 2006 for an excellent account of how this worked in South

Africa). Customary law ensured that the legal arrangements for property typically avoided registration in the countryside (Berry 1993). Even more importantly, literate religious elites, which played very important roles in Europe, the Americas, China and Japan, were denied authority over people and property (as Doyle notes in Chapter 10). In the absence of either a popular or an elite constituency advocating for registration it was always an easy option for the bureaucracy to delay.

But there is another intriguing irony at work in this story. From the early 1950s the South African state undertook a massive project of fingerprint registration. It was chaotic and expensive and famously resisted by individuals and organizations. Yet, by the time of the establishment of full democracy and the beginnings of a universal system of social benefits, the entire adult population of South Africa had been registered biometrically (Breckenridge 2005a, 2005b; Edwards and Hecht 2010). And it was this centralized biometric population register which made possible the rapid and very wide delivery of the cash payments for child support that Lund and Ferguson describe below (Chapters 18 and 19). And it is this extremely efficient and highly scalable technology which underpins the current interest in a global system of cash grants for the poor (Hanlon *et al.* 2010, 38–39; Hanlon 2004, 199). It is especially paradoxical, in light of the fraught administrative history of South Africa, that the possibility for the worldwide unconditional social assistance regime that Ferguson describes in the concluding chapter of this volume has emerged from the South African state's preoccupation with fingerprinting as an alternative to local civil registration.

References

Acemoglu, Daron, Simon Johnson and James A. Robinson. 2001. 'The Colonial Origins of Comparative Development: An Empirical Investigation.' *American Economic Review* 91(5): 1369–1401.

Acting Secretary for Interior, Letter to Secretary for Native Affairs, Pretoria. 1911. 6 July. SAB NTS 9363 4/382 Natal and Zululand: Registration of births and deaths, 1911–1960.

Acting Under-Secretary for the Interior, Letter to Dower, Under Secretary for Native Affairs. 1911. 3 March. SAB NTS 9363 3/382 Transkeian territories: Registration of births and deaths, 1911–1960.

Addison, R. H., Acting Chief Native Commissioner, Natal, Letter to Secretary for Native Affairs, Pretoria. 1913. System of reporting Births and Deaths, Natal Natives. 24 February. SAB NTS 9363 4/382 Natal and Zululand: Registration of births and deaths, 1911–1960.

Adepoju, Aderanti. 1981. 'Military Rule and Population Issues in Nigeria.' *African Affairs* 80(318): 29–47.

Bayly, C. A. 1999. *Empire and Information: Intelligence Gathering and Social Communication in India, 1780–1870*. Cambridge: Cambridge University Press.

Beinart, William and Colin Bundy. 1987. 'A Voice in the Big House: The Career of Headman Enoch Mamba.' In *Hidden Struggles in Rural South Africa: Politics and Popular Movements in the Transkei and Eastern Cape, 1890–1930*. Cape Town: James Currey.

Berry, Sara. 1992. 'Hegemony on a Shoestring: Indirect Rule and Access to Agricultural Land.' *Africa: Journal of the International African Institute* 62(3): 327–355.

—— 1993. *No Condition is Permanent: The Social Dynamics of Agrarian Change in Sub-Saharan Africa*. Madison: University of Wisconsin Press.

Breckenridge, Keith. 2005a. 'Verwoerd's Bureau of Proof: Total Information in the Making of Apartheid.' *History Workshop Journal* 59: 83–109.

—— 2005b. 'The Biometric State: The Promise and Peril of Digital Government in the New South Africa.' *Journal of Southern African Studies* 31(2): 267–282.

—— 2008. 'The Elusive Panopticon: The HANIS Project and the Politics of Standards in South Africa.' In *Playing the ID Card: Surveillance, Security and Identity in Global Perspective*, ed. Colin Bennett and David Lyon. London: Routledge, 39–56.

—— 2011. 'Gandhi's Progressive Disillusionment: Thumbs, Fingers, and the Rejection of Scientific Modernism in Hind Swaraj.' *Public Culture* 23(2): 331–348.

Britten, H. 1930. 'The Need for the Registration of Customary Unions.' *Bantu Studies* 4(1): 269–277.

Brookes, Edgar. 1924. *The History of Native Policy in South Africa from 1830 to the Present Day*. Cape Town: Nasionale Pers.

Carton, Benedict. 2000. *Blood from your Children: The Colonial Origins of Generational Conflict in South Africa*. Pietermartizburg: University of Natal Press.

Cell, John W. 1982. *The Highest Stage of White Supremacy: The Origins of Segregation in South Africa and the American South*. Cambridge: Cambridge University Press.

Chief Native Commissioner, Pietermaritzburg, Letter to Secretary for Native Affairs, Pretoria. 1922. Registration of Native Births and Deaths. 22 December. SAB NTS 9363 4/382 Natal and Zululand: Registration of births and deaths, 1911–1960.

Chief Native Commissioner, Pietermaritzburg, Letter to Secretary for Native Affairs, Pretoria. 1932. 17 September. SAB NTS 9363 4/382 Natal and Zululand: Registration of births and deaths, 1911–1960.

Clarke, W. J., Chief Commissioner, Natal Police. 1907. *Evidence to Natal Native Affairs Commission, 1906–7*. Pietermaritzburg: Government Printer.

—— Letter to Secretary, South African Police. 1913. 12 February. SAB NTS 9363 4/382 Natal and Zululand: Registration of births and deaths, 1911–1960.

Cluver, E. H., Asst Health Officer. 1932. Malaria Conference held at Durban, Town Hall, on 1st July 1932. 4 July. SAB NTS 9363 4/382 Natal and Zululand: Registration of births and deaths, 1911–1960.

Cohn, Bernard S. 1997. *Colonialism and Its Forms of Knowledge: The British in India*. Delhi: Oxford University Press.

Colonial Secretary. 1910. NAB CSO 1893, 1910/4799 Secretary for Interior Pretoria Asks for Memorandum Shewing System Prevailing in Natal for Registration of Births and Deaths, Particularly Natives. Pietermaritzburg.

—— 1911. NAB CSO 1902, 1911/1482 Secretary for the Interior Pretoria: Asks to Be Furnished with a Memorandum Under Which the System of Registration of Births, Marriages and Deaths Is Administered.

Cooper, Frederick. 1996. *Decolonization and African Society: The Labor Question in French and British Africa*. Cambridge: Cambridge University Press.

—— 2002. *Africa Since 1940: The Past of the Present*. Cambridge: Cambridge University Press.

Coovadia, Hoosen, Rachel Jewkes, Peter Barron, David Sanders and Diane McIntyre. 2009. 'The Health and Health System of South Africa: Historical Roots of Current Public Health Challenges.' *The Lancet* 374 (9692): 817–834.

Corrigan, Philip Richard D. and Derek Sayer. 1985. *The Great Arch: English State Formation as Cultural Revolution*. Oxford: Blackwell.

Crais, Clifton. 2002. *The Politics of Evil: Magic, State Power, and the Political Imagination in South Africa*. Cambridge: Cambridge University Press.

Delius, Peter. 1983. *Land Belongs to Us: The Pedi Polity, the Boers and the British in the Nineteenth Century Transvaal*. Johannesburg: Ravan Press.

Dower, Edward, [Acting?] Secretary for Native Affairs, Letter to Burton, Minister for Native Affairs. 1911. Registration of Births and Deaths of Natives in Zululand. 18 July. SAB NTS 9363 4/382 Natal and Zululand: Registration of births and deaths, 1911–1960.

Doyle, Shane. 2008. '"The Child of Death": Personal Names and Parental Attitudes towards Mortality in Bunyoro, Western Uganda, 1900–2005.' *Journal of African History* 49(3): 361–382.

Dubow, Saul. 1986. 'Holding "a Just Balance between White and Black": The Native Affairs Department in South Africa c.1920–33.' *Journal of Southern African Studies* 12(2): 217–239.

—— 1989. *Racial Segregation and the Origins of Apartheid in South Africa, 1919–36*. Oxford: Macmillan in association with St Antony's College.

—— 2006. *A Commonwealth of Knowledge: Science, Sensibility, and White South Africa, 1820–2000*. Oxford: Oxford University Press. www.loc.gov/catdir/toc/ecip0616/200602 1303.html.

Duminy, Andrew. 1989. 'Towards Union, 1900–10.' In *Natal and Zululand from Earliest Times to 1910: A New History*, ed. Andrew Duminy and Bill Guest. Pietermaritzburg: University of Natal Press, 402–423.

Edwards, Paul N. and Gabrielle Hecht. 2010. 'History and the Technopolitics of Identity: The Case of Apartheid South Africa.' *Journal of Southern African Studies* 36(3): 619–639.

Etherington, Norman. 1989. The "Shepstone System" in the Colony of Natal and Beyond the Borders. In *Natal and Zululand from Earliest Times to 1910: A New History*, ed. Andrew Duminy and Bill Guest. Pietermaritzburg: University of Natal Press, 170–192.

Evans, Ivan. 1997. *Bureaucracy and Race: Native Administration in South Africa*. Berkeley: University of California Press.

Fahmy, Khaled. 1997. *All the Pasha's Men: Mehmed Ali, His Army, and the Making of Modern Egypt*. Cairo: American University in Cairo Press.

Falwasser, H. G., Acting Director of Native Labour. 1926. *Report of the Director of Native Labour*. Transvaal Administration, 1 November. TAD GNLB 380 11/11 Native Affairs Department General, 1921–1935.

Feinstein, C. H. 2005. *An Economic History of South Africa: Conquest, Discrimination, and Development*. The Ellen McArthur Lectures. Cambridge: Cambridge University Press.

Foucault, Michel. 1991. 'Governmentality.' In *The Foucault Effect: Studies in Governmentality with Two Lectures by and an Interview with Michel Foucault*, ed. Peter Burchell, Colin Gordon and Peter Miller. London: Harvester Wheatsheaf, 87–104.

Freund, Bill. 1998. *The Making of Contemporary Africa: The Development of African Society since 1800*. Boulder, CO: Lynn Riener.

F. R. for Secretary for Native Affairs, Letter to Director of Census and Statistics, Pretoria. 1949. National Register of Population. 12 October. SAB NTS 9360 2/382 Part 2 Registration of Births and Deaths (natives) in the Union (general File). 1947 to 1952.

Giliomee, Hermann. 2003. *The Afrikaners: Biography of a People*. Cape Town: Tafelberg.

Groebner, Valentin. 2007. *Who Are You? Identification, Deception, and Surveillance in Early Modern Europe*. New York: Zone Books.

Guy, Jeff. 2005. *The Maphumulo Uprising: War, Law and Ritual in the Zulu Rebellion*. Pietermaritzburg: University of KwaZulu-Natal Press.

Hanlon, J. 2004. 'It Is Possible to Just Give Money to the Poor.' In Jan P. Pronk *et al.*, *Catalysing Development? A Debate on Aid.* Development and Change Series. Oxford: Blackwell, 181–200.

Hanlon, J., D. Hulme and A. Barrientos. 2010. *Just Give Money to the Poor: The Development Revolution from the Global South*. Sterling, VA: Kumarian Press.

Hindson, Douglas. 1981. 'Pass Offices and Labour Bureaux: An Analysis of the Development of a National System of Pass Controls in South Africa.' Ph.D. dissertation, University of Sussex.

Iliffe, John. 1988. *The African Poor: A History*. Cambridge: Cambridge University Press.

Junod, Henri. 1962. *Life of a South African Tribe*, vols 1 and 2. New York: University Books.

Kline, Benjamin. 1988. *Genesis of Apartheid: British African Policy in the Colony of Natal, 1845–1893*. Lanham, MD: University Press of America.

Kwankye, S. O. 1999. 'The Vital Registration System in Ghana: A Relegated Option for Demographic Data Collection.' In *The African Population in the 21st Century*. Durban: Popline, 429–443.

Lake, M. and H. Reynolds. 2008. *Drawing the Global Colour Line: White Men's Countries and the International Challenge of Racial Equality*. Cambridge: Cambridge University Press.

Lambert, John. 1989. 'From Independence to Rebellion: African Society in Crisis, 1880–1910.' In *Natal and Zululand from Earliest Times to 1910: A New History*, ed. Andrew Duminy and Bill Guest. Pietermaritzburg: University of Natal, 373–401.

—— 1995. *Betrayed Trust: Africans and the State in Colonial Natal*. Pietermaritzburg: University of Natal Press.

Lugg, Harry, Chief Native Commissioner, Natal, Letter to Secretary for Native Affairs, Pretoria. 1933. Registration of Births and Deaths amongst Natives. 1 July. SAB NTS 9363 4/382 Natal and Zululand: Registration of births and deaths, 1911–1960.

Lugg, Harry, Native Commissioner, Verulam, Letter to Secretary for Native Affairs, Pretoria. 1932. Registration of Births and Deaths amongst Natives. 7 June. SAB NTS 9363 4/382 Natal and Zululand: Registration of births and deaths, 1911–1960.

MacKinnon, Aran S. 1999. 'The Persistence of the Cattle Economy in Zululand, South Africa, 1900–50.' *Canadian Journal of African Studies/Revue Canadienne des Études Africaines* 33(1): 98–135.

—— 2001. 'Of Oxford Bags and Twirling Canes: The State, Popular Responses, and Zulu Antimalaria Assistants in the Early-Twentieth-Century Zululand Malaria Campaigns.' *Radical History Review* 80: 76–100.

Magistrate, Kranskop. 1902. 1/KRK 3/1/4, KK931A/1902 Government Notice No. 799, 1902: Rules Re Registration of Births and Deaths of Natives. NAB.

Malherbe, V. C. 2005. 'In Onegt Verwekt: Law, Custom and Illegitimacy in Cape Town, 1800–1840.' *Journal of Southern African Studies* 31(1): 153–185.

—— 2006. 'Paternity and Illegitimacy: A Problem for Church and State at Cape Town, to the Mid 1800s.' *South African Historical Journal* 55: 66–87.

—— 2007. 'Born into Bastardy: The Out-of-Wedlock Child in Early Victorian Cape Town.' *Journal of Family History* 32(1): 21–44.

Mamdani, Mahmood. 1996. *Citizen and Subject: Contemporary Africa and the Legacy of Late Colonialism*. Cape Town: James Currey.

Marks, Shula. 1970. *Reluctant Rebellion: The 1906–8 Disturbances in Natal*. Oxford: Clarendon Press.

—— 1997. 'South Africa's Early Experiment in Social Medicine: Its Pioneers and Politics.' *American Journal of Public Health* 87(3): 452–459.

Mbanjwa, Xolani. 2009. 'So How Many People Are Dead, Exactly?' *The Star*, 17 November. www.iol.co.za/index.php?set_id=1&click_id=13&art_id=vn20091117040616655C294479.

McClendon, Thomas V. 1995. 'Tradition and Domestic Struggle in the Courtroom: Customary Law and the Control of Women in Segregation-Era Natal.' *International Journal of African Historical Studies* 28(3): 527–561.

Mears, Secretary for Native Affairs, Letter to Secretary for the Interior, Pretoria. 1946. Registration of Births and Deaths in Rural Native Areas. 10 May. SAB NTS 9360 2/382 Part 2 Registration of Births and Deaths (natives) in the Union (general File). 1947 to 1952.

Milner, Alfred. 1894. *England in Egypt*. London: Edward Arnold.

Moodie, T. Dunbar. 1988. 'The South African State and Industrial Conflict in the 1940s.' *International Journal of African Historical Studies* 21(1): 21–61.

Natal. Native Affairs Commission. 1907. *Evidence [of the] Native Affairs Commission, 1906–7*. Pietermaritzburg: P. Davis.

Ntsebeza, Lungisile. 2006. *Democracy Compromised: Chiefs and the Politics of Land in South Africa*. Cape Town: HSRC Press.

Phillips, Ray. 1938. *The Bantu in the City: A Study of Cultural Adjustment on the Witwatersrand*. Alice: Lovedale Press.

Pinto-Leite, N. P. 1907. 'The Finger-Prints.' *The Nonqai*, 31–33.

Posel, Deborah. 1995. 'State, Power, and Gender: Conflict over the Registration of African Customary Marriage in South Africa, 1910–1970.' *Journal of Historical Sociology* 8(3): 223–256.

—— 2000. 'A Mania for Measurement: Statistics and Statecraft in the Transition to Apartheid.' In *Science and Society in Southern Africa*, ed. Saul Dubow. Manchester: Manchester University Press, 116–142.

Rich, Paul B. 1984. *White Power and the Liberal Conscience: Racial Segregation and South African Liberalism, 1921*. Manchester: Manchester University Press.

—— 1990. 'Race, Science, and the Legitimization of White Supremacy in South Africa, 1902–1940.' *International Journal of African Historical Studies* 23(4): 665–687.

Rodney, Walter. 1982. *How Europe Underdeveloped Africa*. Washington, DC: Howard University Press.

Rycroft, Alan. n.d. 'Social Pensions and Poor Relief: An Exercise in Social Control.' Unpublished paper.

Sagner, Andreas. 2000. 'Ageing and Social Policy in South Africa: Historical Perspectives with Particular Reference to the Eastern Cape.' *Journal of Southern African Studies* 26(3): 523–553.

Secretary for Interior, Letter to Secretary for Native Affairs, Pretoria. 1913. 15 October. SAB NTS 9363 3/382 Transkeian territories: Registration of births and deaths, 1911–1960.

Secretary for Interior, Pretoria, Letter to Secretary for Native Affairs, Pretoria. 1913. 10 March. SAB NTS 9363 4/382 Natal and Zululand: Registration of births and deaths, 1911–1960.

Secretary for Native Affairs. 1898. *Circular: Registration of Birth.* Vol. 3/1/2. 1/KRK.

—— 1947. SAB NTS 9360 2/382 Part 2 Registration of Births and Deaths (natives) in the Union (general File). 1947 to 1952. Central Archives, Pretoria. www.national.archsrch.gov.za/sm300cv/smws/sm30ddf0?200806302009567CA78806&DN=00000002.

—— 1955. SAB NTS 9362 2/382 Part 4 Registration of Births and Deaths (natives) in the Union (general File). 1952 to 1955. Central Archives, Pretoria.

Secretary for Native Affairs, Pretoria. 1922. Memorandum: Geddes Axe Committee: Registration of Native Births and Deaths in Natal. 31 October. SAB NTS 9363 4/382 Natal and Zululand: Registration of births and deaths, 1911–1960.

Senior Assistant Health Officer, Letter to Secretary for Public Health. 1933. 13 March. SAB NTS 9363 4/382 Natal and Zululand: Registration of births and deaths, 1911–1960.

Shapiro, S. 1950. 'Development of Birth Registration and Birth Statistics in the United States.' *Population Studies* 4(1): 86–111.

Shepstone, Arthur (Actg. Under Secretary for Native Affairs, Province of Natal), Letter to Acting Secretary for Native Affairs, Pretoria. 1911. Registration of Births and Deaths (Natives in Zululand). 29 May. SAB NTS 9363 4/382 Natal and Zululand: Registration of births and deaths, 1911–1960.

Skocpol, Theda. 1992. *Protecting Soldiers and Mothers: The Political Origins of Social Policy in the United States*. Cambridge, MA: Harvard University Press.

Smit, D. L., Secretary for Native Affairs, Cape Town, Letter to Harry Lugg, Chief Native Commissioner, Natal. 1935. Registration of Births and Deaths of Natives. 26 February. SAB NTS 9363 4/382 Natal and Zululand: Registration of births and deaths, 1911–1960.

Smuts, H. H. L., Letter to Secretary for Native Affairs. 1949. Memo. 10 March. SAB NTS 9360 2/382 Part 2 Registration of Births and Deaths (natives) in the Union (general File). 1947 to 1952.

South Africa. 1960. *Union Statistics for Fifty Years – Uniestatistieke Oor Vyftig Jaar, 1910–1960: Jubilee Issue*. Pretoria: Government Printer.

Stanford, S. H., Chief Magistrate, Transkeian Territories, Letter to Dower, Secretary for Native Affairs. 1911. 3 March. SAB NTS 9363 3/382 Transkeian territories: Registration of births and deaths, 1911–1960.

Stoler, Ann Laura. 2008. *Along the Archival Grain: Epistemic Anxieties and Colonial Common Sense*. Princeton, NJ: Princeton University Press.

Swanson, Maynard W. 1983. '"The Asiatic Menace": Creating Segregation in Durban, 1870–1900.' *International Journal of African Historical Studies* 16(3): 401–421.

Szreter, Simon. 2007. 'The Right of Registration: Development, Identity Registration, and Social Security: A Historical Perspective.' *World Development* 35(1): 67–86.

Tonkin, Arnold H., Hon. Sec., South African Medical Association, Border Branch, Transkei Division, Letter to H. Lawrence, Minister of Interior. 1942. Registration of Births and

Deaths in Rural Native Areas. 28 April. SAB NTS 9360 2/382 Part 2 Registration of Births and Deaths (natives) in the Union (general File). 1947 to 1952.

Weber, Max. 1905. *The Protestant Ethic and the Spirit of Capitalism*. New York: Scribner and Sons.

Welsh, David John. 1971. *The Roots of Segregation: Native Policy in Natal (1845–1910)*. Cape Town: Oxford University Press.

de Wet, H. J., Secretary for Interior, Pretoria. 1933. Letter to E. N. Thornton, Secretary for Public Health, 9 February, SAB NTS 9363 4/382 Natal and Zululand: Registration of births and deaths, 1911–1960.

Woodside, Alexander. 2006. *Lost Modernities: China, Vietnam, Korea, and the Hazards of World History*. Cambridge, MA: Harvard University Press.

Wright, Marcia. 2007. 'Public Health among the Lineaments of the Colonial State in Natal, 1901–1910.' *Journal of Natal and Zulu History* 24: 134–153.

Young, M. Crawford. 1994. *The African Colonial State in Comparative Perspective*. New Haven, CT: Yale University Press.

Zeitlyn, David. 2005. 'The Documentary Impulse: Archives in the Bush.' *History in Africa* 32: 415–434.

15

Voting, Welfare and Registration: The Strange Fate of the État-Civil in French Africa, 1945–1960

FREDERICK COOPER*

IN 1946, THE FRENCH GOVERNMENT suddenly realized that it needed to know who its African subjects were. Such a realization not only came late, but was acted upon only partially and with many misgivings. This chapter focuses on a transformation in thinking about the relationship of colonized people to the state and the limits of that transformation.

Up to that point the French government had been concerned with identifying only a small minority of the people in its overseas territories – people from the metropole, the tiny number of Africans who had acquired French citizenship rights, former soldiers who were entitled to (minuscule) pensions, some categories of government workers, migrants to the metropole, and people whose economic roles resembled those of French nationals from Europe. For the mass of Africans, the state had little interest in a relationship to the individual subject. Africans were part of collectivities and the state connected to them through the vertical channels typical of empires, through a hierarchy of chiefs supervised by a *commandant de cercle*.[1] Taxes were collected by household, and it was the chiefly hierarchy that was supposed to figure out who belonged where, as well as whom to conscript when military service or compulsory labour was to be employed. The government made occasional noises about the need for a census, but before the war relied on officials' unsystematic estimates of the populations under their jurisdiction.[2]

* I am grateful to Keith Breckenridge, Paul-André Rosental, Tony Chafer and Alexander Keese for their comments on an earlier version of this chapter.

[1] For a related argument about South Africa – which one might think had even more incentive and resources for civil registration – see Chapter 14.

[2] For the somewhat different history of efforts during the first half of the twentieth century – largely ineffective – to count individuals and their life events in some territories in British colonial Africa, see Chapters 10 and 17. Some French officials clearly saw the need to get serious about keeping track of population, of individuals and of overall trends, both for practical purposes and to mark French sovereignty. But doing something about it, other than making data collection part of the duties of the local administrator, was another story. See Gervais and Mandé (2007).

Proceedings of the British Academy **182**, 385–412. © The British Academy 2012.

That some people under French rule should be counted and identified and others not was linked to the distinction between citizen – a rights-bearing individual – and subject, considered to be a French national but not a French citizen. This distinction was in turn justified by a difference in status: people whose origins lay in metropolitan France or who had been naturalized French possessed the *statut civil de droit commun* and their life-course events (marriage, inheritance, etc.) came under the French civil code. Indigenous peoples in conquered territories were considered to come under the personal status regime of their community – Islamic law in some cases, 'customary law' in others; they had a *statut personnel*. If, at first glance, the distinction seemed to respect the plurality of legal regimes in French colonies, it was the basis for discrimination and denigration on many levels: subjects did not vote, came under a separate judicial regime allowing arbitrary punishment, and could in some circumstances be made to perform forced labour.[3]

In the aftermath of the Second World War, the situation changed. The reconstituted French government under Charles de Gaulle understood quite well that it had to turn a new leaf in colonial policy. The loss of Vietnam to Japan and Ho Chi Minh's effective takeover of the northern part of that territory in September 1945, violent conflict in Algeria, and fear of strikes and riots in cities across the empire weighed on official minds. At the same time, the fact that French Equatorial Africa had, alone among French overseas territories, remained loyal to the Free French and that African and Maghrebian soldiers had made up the majority of the French troops that had helped to recapture southern France produced a myth of France being saved by the devotion of its empire, and made clear the value of giving subjects a sense of belonging to an imperial France. Leaders knew they had to co-opt some African elites into the governing apparatus and that they had to give peasants and workers some hope for a better future.

The first half of 1946 witnessed far-reaching initiatives on the part of the French government – more far-reaching in effect than in intent as African political and social movements seized and enlarged the opening the post-war conjuncture gave them. The assembly writing a new constitution for the French republic included a small minority of deputies from the colonies, elected by separate voter rolls, one for 'citizens' – mainly Europeans – and the other for subjects. The numbers were absurdly small in relation to population – a mere ten for French West Africa – but their presence shaped the constitutional debate, for the majority realized that if the articles dealing with overseas France were rejected by the representatives of the subjects, the constitution would have no legitimacy. The presence of even a few colonial deputies meant that such colonial policies as forced labour would now have to be defended in public, and reforms soon went into effect. The constitution abolished the status of 'subject', extending the 'quality' of the citizen to all

[3] The historical basis of this distinction is discussed in Blévis (2004), Urban (2009), Cooper (2009), and Saada (2012).

inhabitants of overseas territories, whether or not they came under French civil law or remained under the jurisdiction of Islamic or 'customary' laws governing personal relations and property.[4] A programme of public funding for development that had been talked about since the 1920s and never enacted became government policy in 1946. In addition, a two-month-long strike movement in Senegal at the start of 1946 forced French officials to take the labour situation seriously. Unions were now seen as necessary interlocutors; wages for unskilled workers were pushed upward; and officials began to think that some of the measures used to stabilize labour in France, including minimum wages, career ladders, family allowances, and collective bargaining, would have to be applied to African wage workers too.

All this changed the relationship of individual and state and made identification and registration into issues that could no longer be shunted aside. During the debates over African participation in elections, conservative deputies had argued that without identifying individuals, there was no way of knowing who did and did not belong on a voter roll. Also, it became clear that as some wage workers, at least, were going to acquire family allowances and pensions as a result of their individual status in the workplace, such workers would have to be identified. Those elements in the French government that wished to promote a more inclusive, stable order in the colonies had to answer the objections of defenders of the status quo that both suffrage and welfare benefits did not fit African conditions because of the absence of civil registration.

We need not get stuck with a Foucauldian illusion that 'colonial modernity' or 'colonial governmentality' necessarily implies a state concerned with surveillance and identification; such conceptions have little to do with how colonial – like other – empires actually worked during most of history.[5] The more puzzling and interesting question is why in a *particular* conjuncture, when the utility of tracking individuals and studying populations was recognized, the government was so slow and ineffective in finding a way of following through. French officials hesitated, improvised, and back-tracked on the implications of recognizing the individual citizen as a potential voter and actor in a complex social system. Beneath the juridical question of how and to whom to apply registration was an issue of politics and culture: how to construct a legal order for an empire with people whose relationships with each other were governed by diverse social and legal regimes. And more difficult still, how to connect the *French* character of the political system to the diversity of the people within it, once the dichotomies of citizen/subject, colonizer/colonized, full member/subordinate were no longer acceptable.

Here we come to a framework that had acquired an almost sacred quality in the French secular state – the *état-civil*. From the Revolution, the state sought to keep

[4] The question of citizenship and empire between 1945 and 1960 is the subject of my current research. For a foretaste of where this project is headed, see Cooper (2009).

[5] For a theoretical argument about concepts such as these, see Cooper (2005).

track of its citizens, and to make note of the major events of their life course – birth, marriage, death. With Napoleon's *code civil*, the rules governing those life events were applied to all, at least within an 'inner empire' where departmentalization and bureaucratization, rather than arrangements with local princes and aristocracies, were to be applied.[6] And so the état-civil was not only a record of life events, but a marker of the uniformity of the state-centred framework in which those events took place. What made a marriage legal – and defined its contours – was that it was celebrated before an officer of the état-civil and inscribed in a register, with extracts made available to the individuals concerned and to state officials who needed to know that person's status. The état-civil became, in theory at least, not only a tool of administration, but a marker of the nature of French society: the singularity of the rules governing the life course, from birth through marriage through death, with filiation and inheritance coming under common rules. In practice, as Paul-André Rosental shows in Chapter 5, population registration was more complex than a simple state imposition. But in the colonies, the fiction of a singular population living under a single civil code was not the issue.

Citizenship in the colonial situation[7]

How could the concept of population and the practice of registering individuals apply across an empire, when the art of imperial governance was ruling differently over different people (Burbank and Cooper 2010)? Only to the most French of the French. As jurists assessing the history and status of the état-civil after the Second World War noted, the jurisprudence behind the colonial état-civil was unclear, but generally it was compulsory for French citizens of metropolitan origin living overseas, for people assimilated to such a status, and for people in a few special categories (Gouet 1954). Most court decisions excluded 'subjects' from the état-civil, and for good reason – for them to be inscribed in it, it would record them as if they were citizens. There were complications. In the 'old colonies', especially those in the Caribbean, a law of 1848 freed the slaves and declared them to be citizens. Although of African origin, slaves were considered to have been severed from whatever social arrangements they or their ancestors had once had, and they came under the civil code; so they had their place in the état-civil. Citizenship, the civil code, and the état-civil all underscored ex-slaves' incorporation and effaced

[6] Michael Broers distinguishes the inner empire from a larger outer empire where Napoleon in some cases worked through local rulers, refraining from imposing his civil code where it would ruffle aristocratic feathers (Broers 2001).

[7] The following abbreviations are used for archives cited in this chapter: ANF (Archives Nationales Françaises, Paris), AOM (Archives d'Outre-Mer, Aix-en-Provence), AS (Archives du Sénégal, Dakar), CAC (Centre d'Archives Contemporaines, Fontainbleau), SRASD (Services Régionales des Archives du Sénégal – Dakar).

their history of suffering and exploitation, for they disappeared into the generic category of French citizen.[8]

In Algeria, colonized after 1830, the opposite trend prevailed: a distinction, not fully worked out in juridical terms, between settlers of European origin, who came under the civil code and whose life events were duly and obligatorily recorded, and a Muslim and (until 1870) Jewish population regarded as French subjects, but not citizens. They were not allowed to register births, marriages and deaths in the 'European' état-civil, but from 1882 a separate '*état-civil indigène*' was created for Muslims to use. In many parts of Algeria, the état-civil was little used, but in any case, the existence of two registers marked a dualism in political and juridical practice. The subject–citizen distinction is often seen as of the essence of French colonialism, but recent scholarship has emphasized that it was a contested feature, criticized under the Third Republic by people who felt it a deviation from republican practices, tenaciously supported by settlers who wanted to distinguish themselves from Algeria's Muslim majority, and defended by most officials as a practical necessity for administering – at least provisionally – a population whom they regarded as both different and inferior (Blévis 2004; Héricord-Gorre 2008; Merle 2002).

Senegal represents another possibility in this spectrum. From 1848, the four towns where French presence had been established since the late eighteenth century (the '*Quatre Communes*') were allowed to vote in municipal elections and send a representative to Paris, and there was a debate whether they should be considered French 'citizens' or simply 'voters' (*électeurs*). What distinguished the Senegalese case was that the people in those towns who had at least some of the rights of citizens did not have to come under the civil code. They were expected to bring their civil matters to Islamic courts. No doubt, this apparent exception to the relationship of citizenship and civil status reflected the particular circumstance of Senegal's imperial situation – small enclaves with few metropolitan citizens and little military or administrative support, a situation in which a tiny French establishment needed all the support it could get from people with whom they shared trading interests. When French colonization moved inland in the 1850s and 1860s, something closer to the Algerian model was followed – a sharp distinction between citizen and subject – but the Quatres Communes kept their status, despite misgivings. This status gave the '*originaires*' a mechanism to defend their rights and their cultural distinctiveness at the same time as Muslim citizens of the French empire (Diouf 1998). When their loyalty and support were once again vitally needed during the First World War, their deputy, Blaise Diagne, manoeuvred to deliver manpower to the war effort in exchange for a legislative affirmation that the *originaires* were citizens.

[8] Myriam Cottias (2004) has emphasized this double dimension. On the other hand, Laurent Dubois (2004) found that in the 1790s, after slaves in the French Caribbean island of Guadeloupe were briefly declared free and citizens (before Napoleon restored slavery in 1802), ex-slaves *sought* to be inscribed in the état-civil to mark their membership in the polity.

But their unique status meant that the *originaires*' life events were recorded in the 'European' état-civil, even though the events recorded were not regulated by the *code civil*. Elsewhere in Senegal and French Africa generally, the life course of '*indigènes*' was either recorded on a separate *état-civil indigène*, or most often not recorded at all.[9] Such an *état-civil indigène* was theoretically in existence in French West Africa from 1912, and was the object of a decree issued in 1933, but even in 1950 officials admitted it was little used outside of some towns.[10] The vast majority of French Africans went through their lives without making an appearance in any registration of population.

Citizenship in the post-war conjuncture

So what happened when French politicians decided they had to make empire more inclusive? The issue of the état-civil came up from the very beginning of debates over including at least some Africans in the political process. In late 1945, as government officials concerned with colonial affairs discussed among themselves how Africans could be represented in electoral bodies – including the legislative assembly that would write a new constitution – the Minister of Colonies wrote that non-citizens

> are not always registered by name and the numerical importance of these populations, their dispersion, the state of administrative organization, the insufficiency of the état-civil, and finally the short time before the date agreed upon for general elections make it provisionally impossible to establish electoral lists.

There could be universal suffrage for citizens, but not for non-citizens. For the latter, voting would have to be limited to 'certain categories most representative of the indigenous population'.[11]

The upshot of the initial round of consideration was that a tiny number of Africans voted for a tiny number of deputies to the first post-war assemblies that would legislate and write a new constitution. French West Africa had ten representatives, but five of the seats were for citizens and only in Senegal was there a

[9] The *état-civil indigène* of 1912 was put in place by local decrees without solid foundation in a law voted by the French legislature, was not compulsory, and was largely ignored by Africans. There were more texts on the *état-civil indigène* in 1933, 1950 and 1953, but they were also local '*arrêtés*' (decrees) whose legislative basis was unclear (Gouet 1954, 504–505, 525, 555–560).

[10] Governor General to President of Grand Conseil, 9 May 1950, 23G 34, AS. In 1938, a total of around 42,000 births, deaths and marriages were registered in the *état-civil indigène* – out of a population estimated very roughly to be 14 million. Statistics and the text of the decree (*arrêté*) of 1933 may be found in a little pamphlet, 'L'État Civil Indigene', Gorée, Imprimerie du Gouvernement Général, 1938, copy in 23G 33, AS, statistics on p. 21.

[11] Ministre des Colonies, exposé des motifs for a draft ordonnance on the mode of representation in the Assemblée Nationale Constituante, n.d. [1945] CAB 56–369, AOM.

black majority in the citizens' electoral college. Although French West Africa had a population of around 15–16 million, only about 35,000 citizens and 95,000 subjects voted in 1945. The numbers would rise significantly in subsequent elections: over 515,000 in November 1946 and 1.5 million in 1951 (de Benoist 1982, 519, 524, 526). In 1956, universal suffrage and the single college – ending the system effectively reserving seats for whites – were instituted.

It is hard to tell whether, during the various phases of debate over electoral laws, the absence of the état-civil was an excuse or a reason for restricting voting rights for Africans. One spokesman for white settlers, René Malbrant, argued in the first debates over the constitution that the absence of the état-civil made universal suffrage inconceivable except in those rare instances where it was 'technically possible'.[12] But no less an advocate of the rights of African citizens than Léopold Senghor also admitted that, 'It is impossible, because of the insufficiency of the état-civil, to institute universal suffrage in the overseas territories where it is not yet in place at the time of the next election.'[13] For Adolphe Landry, influential politician and leading demographer during the Third Republic, writing in the newspaper *Le Monde*, the absence of the état-civil was symptomatic of a deeper problem: universal suffrage would be a 'grave error, it being a question of populations that in large part do not have the état-civil, and in large part have no notion of the political and other problems that are debated in our assemblies' (Landry 1946).

I have written elsewhere (Cooper 2009) and am currently writing in more detail about the debate in the legislative bodies writing a new constitution for the post-war Republic, over empire citizenship. In a nutshell, an initial consensus that all inhabitants of the empire should be made into citizens (while electoral laws would temper the full implications of the new status) evaporated after the first draft of the constitution was rejected in a referendum in May 1946.[14] In the second round of constitutional debates, colonial deputies had to briefly boycott the assembly to save the extension of citizenship they had initially won. The constitution that was passed in October 1946 stated that all inhabitants of the overseas territories would have the 'quality' of the citizen, and they could maintain their civil status (under Islamic or customary law) while exercising such rights, unless they chose to renounce that status. How the 'citizens of 1946' would participate in elections would be governed

[12] Assemblée Nationale, Commission de la France d'Outre-Mer, 26 December 1945, C//15293, ANF.

[13] Commission de la France d'Outre-Mer, meeting of 11 April 1951, C//15408, ANF.

[14] Fearing that the first version of the constitution would be defeated in a referendum in which only citizens under the old rules could vote, the Senegalese deputy Lamine Guèye submitted a bill that would convey citizenship as a matter of ordinary law. His bill was passed unanimously and became known as the law of 7 May 1946 or the 'loi Lamine Guèye'. After a tough struggle, the African deputies succeeded in getting the gist of this law inscribed in the constitution that was approved in October. The Ministry started to confront issues raised by citizenship during the interval between the law and the constitution.

by ordinary laws. Although most parties concerned talked a great deal about equality among citizens, neither universal suffrage nor a distribution of legislators proportional to population was for the moment in question. The African deputies had to struggle to prevent the double college from being inscribed in the constitution, but it remained for the time being in effect via ordinary law.

During one of the debates, an influential metropolitan deputy pointed out that if one had a truly egalitarian electoral system, voters from metropolitan France would be a minority and France would become 'the colony of its former colonies'.[15] But a one-person-one-vote system was not what most deputies from Africa wanted, and they were sensitive to French fears of being made into a minority in a state they thought was theirs. What African deputies wanted was a system that was in some sense federal, with each territory exercising significant self-government while remaining part of a France that would provide collective resources and guarantee equal rights to all. Early on, African deputies indicated that augmented powers for legislative assemblies in the territories (compared to those in metropolitan regions) would be a fair trade-off for accepting a disproportionately small representation in the Assemblée Nationale. They also wanted to have a federal assembly where overseas and metropolitan France would have equal representation.

What the overseas deputies got from all the compromises of 1946 was a good deal less than what they wanted: the double college, a restricted franchise, and limited power to the territorial assemblies remained in place for a decade. But they did get citizenship, and juridical authorities soon confirmed that the constitutional provisions meant full equality in all respects except the exercise of the vote, which would be governed by electoral laws.[16] These rights included that of entering any part of greater France, metropole included, and the right to apply to schools, universities, and civil service posts anywhere.[17] It included the usual rights – speech, assembly – and equal protection of the courts in criminal matters. In the overseas territories – but not the metropole – civil matters could be adjudicated under the rules pertaining to the individual's personal status. In respect to most public rights, the citizens with the '*statut civil de droit commun*' (imprecisely referred to as French civil status) and those of '*statut personnel*' were not supposed to differ. But now that everyone concerned was a citizen, it was this distinction in *statut* that determined whether one voted in the first or second electoral college. African politicians quickly tried to make the most of their votes in the Assemblée Nationale and their moral authority as representatives of an important category of

[15] Edouard Herriot, Assemblée Nationale Constituante, *Débats*, 27 August 1946, 3334.

[16] On the application of the citizenship articles, see Minister of Overseas France, circular to High Commissioners and Governors, 13 June 1947, AP 3655, AOM. For a jurist's treatment of the citizenship clauses of the constitution, see Borella (1958).

[17] African citizens turning up in European France, then needing documentation to receive social services or to marry, produced much correspondence between Paris and Dakar and doubts about the accuracy of information available to the state. See numerous dossiers from 1954–1958 in G/13, SRASD.

French citizens, campaigning not only for resources but for remedies to all the defects of the 1946 constitution.

Registering citizens

But how would the state know who had what rights, in which college each person should vote, when a would-be student was the appropriate age, and, with discrimination in benefits no longer legitimate, who was entitled to them – in short, who was who in a continent of people whom the state did not know?

The answer was, in principle, evident. Citizens with their own personal status needed to be in an état-civil. The Minister of Overseas France was adamant:

> While the citizens of the law of 7 May 1946 maintain their personal status, it seems, however, indispensable to organize their état-civil. It would be inconceivable that citizens would not be constrained from now on to make note of and have registered, by an officer of the état-civil, births, marriages, and deaths, on the same basis as any French citizen.

He put this in context of the theme he saw emerging from the politics of constitution writing: 'this law [the citizenship law of 7 May 1946] tends above all to proclaim a principle of equality. But this equality, it is up to us to realize it, to move it from the domain of theory to that of realities.'[18]

Behind the implications of citizenship was the need to underscore a new conception of the African that was entering official discourse – as an individual. Officials had to persuade Africans to present themselves to the state in such a guise, and they had to persuade themselves that they could organize state functions on such a basis, rather than through the vertical channels of European '*commandement*' and 'chiefly' authority, through which the state had long defined its relationship with African collectivities. The concept of individualization was repeatedly invoked:

> French citizens have a right to an état-civil and the right to certain identification; it is necessary for them to have an identification that is not only invariant despite the events that might mark their existence, but transmittable, which is an element of proof of filiation, and hence the individualization of persons.[19]

The état-civil was above all a means 'to prove the identity of a person and register the acts which modify his juridical individuality'.[20] Registering births in the état-

[18] Minister of Overseas France, circular to Governors General, 14 June 1946, AP 3655, AOM.

[19] Minister to Governor General of AOF, 21 September 1951, 23G 6, AS. See also the similar argument in Rapport concernant l'organisation de l'état civil obligatoire au Soudan français, incl. Governor of Soudan to Governor General, 1 December 1948, 23G 33, AS.

[20] Directeur Genéral de l'Intérieur and Directeur Général Adjoint des Affaires Politiques, Rapport concernant la pluralité d'État-Civil en A.O.F., en réponse aux observations faites par M. Monguillot, inspecteur general de la FOM, 6 June 1952, 23G 34, AS.

civil was a prerequisite for establishing identification documents, notably a card which was theoretically – but not practically – required of anyone leaving his or her home district. Such a card, noted one official, would be 'the first identity document delivered, that which must serve as the basis of integration of the individual into a modern society'.[21]

But there were two fundamental obstacles. The obvious one was that it took considerable literate and trained personnel and considerable expense to create and maintain records on every individual in a large and widely dispersed population. Contrary to myths of 'modern' colonial government as bureaucratic and controlling, it was in all but a few areas thinly spread, *ad hoc* in its daily actions, and dependent on African intermediaries generally referred to by the dubious title of 'chiefs'. It remained to bureaucratize the countryside. As the Governor of Senegal put it, 'A compulsory état-civil is a necessity, above all with the new laws on citizenship, but putting it into practice demands means which we do not yet have.' The Governor of the Soudan thought that a compulsory état-civil in his territory of 3.1 million people would generate 312,000 acts each year, and it would have to issue *jugements supplétifs* (retrospective judgments) for the over 3 million acts it had failed to record – a task he decided could only be done for the sedentary part of his population, step by step, and at high cost.[22] Getting chiefs to do the work of bureaucrats would not be simple: most, officials thought, were illiterate.[23]

The other obstacle was even more fundamental. Should there be one état-civil or two, or many?[24] There existed an *état-civil indigène* in Algeria, parts of French West Africa, and a few other places, but – given the idea of unity that lay behind the 1946 system of registration – generalizing a duality seemed to go against the spirit of the times. A 'distinction between two états-civil would only consecrate racial discrimination', wrote the Governor of Senegal in 1951. But others thought a distinction in status was not a distinction of race, and feared that a single état-civil would obscure the rules of marriage or inheritance that particular acts were supposed to represent.[25]

[21] Délégué du chef du territoire du Senegal à Dakar to Chef de la Sûreté locale, Dakar, 27 April 1957, 1D/17, SRASD. The decree instituting an identity card for anyone leaving his district of birth was in theory introduced in 1949, but there is no evidence that its enforcement was taken seriously – except when it was in the interest of the individual to demonstrate his or her entitlement to rights or resources.

[22] Governor of Senegal, Rapport Politique, 1945–1946, AP 2142/3, AOM; Rapport concernant l'organisation de l'état civil obligatoire au Soudan français, incl. Governor of Soudan to Governor General, 1 December 1948, 23G 33, AS.

[23] Governor, Côte d'Ivoire, to Governor General, 17 June 1949, 23G 33, AS.

[24] Both possibilities are brought out in Directeur Général de l'Intérieur and Directeur Général Adjoint des Affaires Politiques, Rapport concernant la pluralité d'État-Civil en AOF, en réponse aux observations faites par M. Monguillot, Inspecteur Général de la France d'Outre Mer, 6 June 1952, 23G 34, AS.

[25] Governor of Senegal, to High Commissioner, 5 February 1951, and Governor General to Governor, Senegal, 2 March 1951, 23G 34, AS; Governor General to Minister, 25 August 1949, 23G 33, AS.

Africa posed a complication that was less salient in Algeria: it was more diverse.[26] Only in some places could a 'Muslim' état-civil stand alongside one for those coming under the *statut civil de droit commun*. And Africans were mobile. People who married according to one set of rules might live in a town where most people followed different ones, and people living under different regimes might even be married to each other. Who would keep the books for each form of marriage and inheritance? Who would know enough to confront the complexities of actual social life that lay behind forms of marriage or inheritance? The alternative to multiple états-civils would be a single one, with a provision that each entry would contain a notation giving the status of the person or persons involved.[27] That would not really solve the problem, since one of the reasons French jurists took pride in the état-civil was that it made no mention of anybody's status, but embraced all citizens. And the practical problem of assuring that each act corresponded to the proper rules of marriage, inheritance, or recognition of children would not be solved by attaching an ethnic name to a personal identification.

Still there was another issue: changing status. The constitution stated that a person could exercise the rights of citizenship without giving up his or her personal status, unless he or she chose to renounce that status. That implied that there needed to be a mechanism for renunciation, an act that would also need to be inscribed in a register and would then imply that one would be using the état-civil in a different way. The question then was whether to treat renunciation as a simple declaration, subject only to verification of competence and absence of fraud, or whether acquiring 'French' civil status required evidence that the person involved lived according to the rules implied by that status.

Difference and the état-civil

What follows is a look at some of the attempts to confront the implications of trying to keep track of an African population that was both 'French' and 'different'. Officials

[26] An official in Dakar complained that the problem of the état-civil in that city was 'very complex because of the particular statuses of inhabitants of the city'. He distinguished citizens under the civil code, '*originaires*' of the four communes who had a special status, and Africans from outside the four communes (former subjects). Different courts had jurisdictions over people in different categories. Originaries sometimes declared their marriages before a *Cadi* (Islamic judge), who kept a register, but it had no legal standing. Délégué du Gouverneur à Dakar (M. Poli) to Governor, 27 June 1956, SRASD, G/13. See also report from Directeur des Affaires Politiques, Ministère de la France d'Outre-Mer, 'Etude en vue d'une réorganisation de l'état-civil dans les territoires dépendant du Ministère de la France d'outre-mer qui connaissent le régime de la pluralité des états-civils', n.d. May 1956, 23G 33; Gouet (1957).

[27] Gouet, who often provided guidance to the Ministry, argued strongly for a single état-civil in which entries would make mention of the status of each individual involved. He also made clear the many obstacles to such an endeavour, including the fact that people following particular marriage rules were often dispersed and any one area was likely to be culturally heterogeneous (1954, 507–510, 518, 551–555).

saw the difficulty of applying a system rooted in France to Africa, even if they could not quite admit that their own conceptions were among the obstacles: 'Socially, the metropolitan état-civil corresponds to a society that is solidly organized and whose evolution has ended, which is not the case in French West Africa, where its [the état-civil's] necessity is barely felt and only by evolved urban populations.'[28]

The French government was able to extend the *état-civil indigène* after 1950, opening up more '*centres secondaires d'état civil*' across West Africa, making use of such centres for compulsory registration of births and deaths (but not marriages – which were seen as too complicated) for citizens living within 10 kilometres of each centre, and getting more people to make use of the état-civil. But the government could not decide whether to have a single état-civil or multiple ones. It could not go beyond the spotty coverage of a vast territory, and it obtained cooperation from African citizens mainly when those citizens had something to gain from their inscription. It did not pass legislation to make clear how renunciation should take place, although legislators and jurists repeatedly proposed doing so. In the end, the French government passed all these questions on to its successors. All this suggests a fundamental ambiguity about the subject, an inability to resolve the basic tensions arising from a stated desire to make empire inclusive, diverse, and egalitarian at the same time. The état-civil was a culture-laden project, not simply an administrative convenience. The imperial government could bring itself to the point of recognizing the importance of remaking the relationship of individual to state, but it proved unable to carry out the task.

The most immediate problem in 1946 was how to figure out who could vote, now that former subjects had political rights. 'Over 90% of our indigènes are not now on the État-Civil', wrote one governor.[29] The Governor General of French West Africa was adamant about the implications: universal suffrage presupposed the identification of each voter.

> This identification is impossible to realize given the current state of the état-civil indigène . . . The état-civil is ignored, I would add *willfully ignored*, by the masses. Any effort to develop it runs into the difficulty of finding officers of the état-civil who can read, write and present the necessary ethical guarantees, and into indifference or hostility in regard to this institution.[30]

[28] Directeur Général de l'Intérieur and Directeur Général Adjoint des Affaires Politiques, Rapport concernant la pluralité d'État-Civil en AOF, en réponse aux observations faites par M. Monguillot, Inspecteur Général de la France d'Outre Mer, 6 June 1952, 23G 34, AS.

[29] Governor of Togo to Minister de la FOM, 20 July 46, AP 3655, AOM. Other references to problems of organizing suffrage in the absence of African participation in the état-civil include Gouvernor, Soudan, to High Commissioner, 17 September 1946, Minister, circular to High Commissioners, 13 June 1947, Governor, Niger, to High Commissioner, 17 August 1946, 23G 96, AS. These arguments blend technical considerations – how lists could be compiled – with cultural conceptions about Africans.

[30] He mentioned other obstacles to organizing voting in remote villages among itinerant people, and concluded on 'the absolute technical impossibility to realize this reform [universal suffrage]'. Governor General to Minister, 3 March 1946, 17G 139, AS.

A jurist justified the restrictive franchise of the early electoral laws by arguing that the special measures had to be taken given 'the non-existence or the insufficiency of the État Civil'.[31]

The provisional solution, used from the first elections to the Constituent Assembly in the autumn of 1945, in effect remained in place for a decade: the designation of voters by 'capacities'. One started with what one knew, and that was in the nature of colonial society itself. Chiefs were supposed to know their people, so forms of indirect suffrage were considered: chiefs would supervise elections in their communities, choosing representatives who in turn would join the more civic-minded citizens who could vote directly. Then there were people whom the state did know: ex-soldiers, trade union officials, members of agricultural or trade cooperatives, merchants, educated people, employees of the state or of French-run corporations (but not '*simples salariés*', who were too numerous). Some people could furnish documents that were alternatives to the état-civil: a worker's registration, a driving licence, a hunting licence. The '*capacitaires*' – the people who met such criteria – could vote directly; others in what was referred to as an election '*à deux degrés*'.[32] The various projects for electoral laws thus generated lists like this, and after 1946 they gradually added categories to the capacities cited.[33] The categories represented people who could present a document, and that document could allow an individual to be inscribed on an electoral roll.[34]

For citizens of the *statut civil de droit commun*, the état-civil – the version that used to be called European – was compulsory, and their identification for electoral purposes posed no problem. But the major trend of the decade after 1946 was the gradual expansion of the number of voters in French West Africa, most of them in the 'second college', where people of particular status voted (except in Senegal, which had the single college): from 790,000 in 1946 to over 3 million in 1951 and 6 million in 1956, after which universal suffrage was implemented and the voter rolls expanded to 10 million (de Benoist 1982, 513). Voter registration until 1956 depended on a mish-mash of documents by which an individual could identify him or herself, but Africans were apparently eager enough – in some cases with the help of political parties – to get themselves registered. But the absence of an

[31] Y. Gouet, Note pour M. Le Directeur des Affaires Politiques, Ministère des Colonies, 13 January 1947, AP 3655, AOM.

[32] Conférence des Hauts-Commissaires et Gouverneurs Généraux, 'Rapport sur l'électorat politique dans certains Territitoires d'Outre-Mer', 16 July 1946, AP 216/1, AOM; Minister to Governor General, AOF, 21 October 1946, 17G 176, AS. See also Decottignies (1955, 59).

[33] See for example the proposals for capacities cited by the Minister of la France d'Outre-Mer in an annex to proposed law No. 934, 31 August 1951, F60/1382, ANF.

[34] See Instructions à M. les presidents des commissions de distribution des cartes électorales, 1955, F/15, SRASD. A person seeking an electoral card could present in addition to a notice from the état-civil or a *jugement supplétif* (see below), documents stemming from military service, regular employment, a university diploma or identification card, a railway pass, etc.

état-civil still allowed conservative deputies to claim that they were all for universal suffrage and the single college – just not yet. Daniel Boisdon, long an advocate of electoral reform, told that body, 'To vote, as you have done in regard to universal suffrage without rules relative to the état-civil is practically, there is no doubt, to vote on nothing at all.' African deputies insisted that the current system allowed French administrators to manipulate registration and that anything other than universal suffrage was 'unjust'. Officials worried about the involvement of African political parties in getting their supporters onto electoral rolls.[35]

By 1949, realizing that generalizing the état-civil was taking a long time, the minister was saying that its absence was not 'an insurmountable obstacle to the registration of voters', but legislators were still trying to get some action on the état-civil (Decottignies 1955).[36] Progressive members of the assembly tried in 1947 and again in 1951 to get their colleagues to vote that a generalized état-civil would be implemented over four years, at which time universal suffrage would be instituted in Africa, but – amidst government insistence that the time frame was impractical – the bill was dropped and the system of capacities kept in place.[37] In the end, once the Algerian war had begun, the government decided that resisting African demands for universal suffrage was too dangerous, and it was put in place in 1956 as part of a wider package of political reforms – without there being a generalized état-civil.

With universal suffrage and the single college, then, the basic problem of identification was still unsolved, and the minister still saw the need to take a 'definitive step' to creating an état-civil.[38] The issue went beyond identifying voters – and that helps to explain why it proved so intractable over so long a time. In 1947, Mamadou Kamara, a member of the territorial assembly in Guinea, submitted a resolution pointing out the need Africans had for birth and marriage registration for numerous acts in daily life, and hence the need for an '*état-civil indigène*'. He pointed out, 'To take account of the polygamy that exists in Africa, [it] should be set up in a manner to permit the registration of acts of the état civil concerning four wives.' But in 1953, the territorial assembly of the Côte d'Ivoire, faced with what members saw as discrimination, voted a resolution calling for Africans to be

[35] See for example the pro-settler deputy René Malbrant, Assemblée Nationale, *Débats*, 24 April 1951, 3846–3847, and Senghor, *Débats*, 3840. Daniel Boisdon's statement was made in the Assemblée de l'Union Française, *Débats*, 29 November 1955, 1025–1026. On the possible abuses in drawing up electoral rolls, see Directeur des Affaires Politiques to Senateur Aarmand Josse, Côte d'Ivoire, 2 November 1955, AP 1082, AOM.

[36] Minister to Minister des Affaires Etrangères, 29 October 1949, AP 3655, AOM.

[37] Report by Commission de la France d'Outre-Mer, Document 2245, 5 August 1947, copy in F60/1399, ANF; Assemblée Nationale, *Débats*, 25 January 1951, 386, 392.

[38] Draft of text for Minister of FOM to deliver to Commission Permanente du Grand Conseil de l'AOF on voyage to Dakar, 21 July 1956, AP 2292/10, AOM. For a jurist's take on the undeveloped state of the état-civil in 1954, see Gouet (1954).

allowed to use the '*registres de l'État Civil Européen*'.[39] It was precisely between these two arguments – one for recognizing difference (through multiple états-civils), the other insisting on equality (through a single état-civil) – that officials in the Ministère de la France d'Outre-Mer and legislators, notably in the Assemblée de l'Union Française, were going around and around, from 1948 to 1956.[40]

The same reformist measure of 1956 that instituted universal suffrage also devolved substantial powers to the legislative assemblies of each territory – including the right and duty to legislate regarding the état-civil. In a report for the Assemblée de l'Union Française, the reporter for a committee concluded that after the government's failure to establish a regular état-civil, 'I fear that progress will be no more rapid than it was in the past'.[41]

What was happening meanwhile was that the indigenous état-civil was slowly becoming more widely used. After a debate in the Grand Conseil de l'Afrique Occidentale Française in June 1950, the government issued, in August, the orders that expanded the centres (adding largely rural secondary centres to the largely urban primary ones) and required people living within 10 kilometres of such centres to register births and deaths. The debate made clear that this was seen as a temporary measure while waiting (in vain) for the legislature in Paris to act.[42] In 1951, administrators reported that there were 1,500 centres recording acts for the état-civil, most kept by canton chiefs. That meant about one centre for every 13,000 people in French West Africa as a whole, but the ratio varied from 30,000 per centre in Upper Volta to 7,400 in Guinea. Officials were trying to get schoolteachers and

[39] Petition from Kamara, 8 November 1947, and resolution of Assemblée Territoriale de la Côte d'Ivoire, 14 August 1953, both in 23G 33, AS. The Governor of the Côte d'Ivoire wrote a long refutation of the latter argument, insisting that the constitution guaranteed the equality of the two statuses and that the use of the European état-civil would necessarily imply the 'brutal' application of the *code civil*. Other officials objected to the Assemblée's resolution, claiming that a single état-civil could be used for births and deaths but not marriages. Governor, Côte d'Ivoire, to Governor General, 27 October 1953, and Procureur Général to Directeur des Affaires Politiques, 28 December 1953, 23G 33, AS.

[40] The attempts and the debate are reviewed in Decottignies (1955) and Gouet (1954). For an early attempt to get legislative action on the état-civil, see the report by the Commissions des Territoires d'Outre-Mer of the Assemblée Nationale, No. 2245, 5 August 1947, copy in F60/1399, ANF. As late as 1955, propositions were made in both the Assemblée Nationale and the Assemblée de l'Union Française for a unified and generalized état-civil. See the latter's approval of a proposal made in the former by René Pleven, Avis No. 23 of 1955–1956, 29 November 1955. This time, the dissolution of the Assemblée Nationale prevented consideration of the proposal. See the reports and correspondence for the Assemblée de l'Union Française, session of 1955, in C//16323, ANF, and the discussion itself in *Débats*, 29 November 1955, 1025–1042.

[41] Alfred Bour for Commission de la Legislation, Assemblée de l'Union Française, session of 1957–1958, C//16350, ANF.

[42] Grand Conseil de l'Afrique Occidentale Française, *Bulletin*, commission reports, 25 and 31 May 1950, and discussion, 9 June 1950, 27–34. The upshot of this effort was the *arrêté* of 16 August 1950. In the absence of a law coming from the Assemblée Nationale in Paris, the juridical standing of this measure was questionable (Gouet 1954, 511).

nurses, as well as chiefs, to staff these centres. Between 1948 and 1953, the annual number of births, deaths and marriages recorded in the état-civil rose from 119,000 to 356,000, but that was not a lot for a region with a population of over 15 million. The overwhelming majority of the registrations were of births – 253,000. Around 23,000 marriages and around 80,000 deaths were registered.[43] Given the disparity of births and deaths, the state could not know how its living population was changing, and it suggests that people's need for documentation for purposes such as schooling and family allowances (see below) – rather than the state's impulse toward surveillance – was driving the way the *état-civil indigène* was actually being used.

The administration was well short of generalizing the system, and facing numerous obstacles, from poor organization to the incongruity of the recording methods with the social life of most people. Procedures were *ad hoc*, depending on local administrators and chiefs who were not properly trained. It also was not compulsory very far from the centres, which were scattered outside of major towns. Officials complained that many acts were registered long after the fact – a sign that people used the état-civil when a reason arose for them to do so.[44] In 1952, to take one example, a local official wrote of the indigenous état-civil, 'implemented in 1951, its introduction has been truly painful'. In 1956, French legislators, despite the increased number of acts recorded, still thought that only 'a very small minority of évolués' were making use of it.[45]

After another constitutional revision in 1958, the territories of French Africa, which had acquired considerable autonomy in the governing of internal affairs in 1956, were renamed 'member states' of the French Community, with enhanced autonomy. The goal of the Community would be to ensure, via conventions, reciprocity among member states, with each recognizing the acts recorded in each other's registers. Officials remarked that the états-civils should respect customary marriage rights.[46] But now the problem of organizing the état-civil, which France had failed to solve, was in the hands of African member states.

[43] Premier Président de la Cour d'appel, chef du service judiciaire pi, A. Laget, to High Commissioner, AOF, 28 February 1955, 23G 34, AS. The ratio of declarations to population varied from eight births and four deaths in AOF as a whole, to thirty-nine and eleven respectively in Dakar. Report from Directeur des Affaires Politiques, May 1956, 23G 33, AS.

[44] Report from Directeur des Affaires Politiques, May 1956, 23G 33, AS.

[45] Directeur Général de l'Intérieur, Service des Affaires Politiques, note sur l'extension et la réorganisation de l'état-civil en AOF, August 1951, 23G 33, AS; Ed. de Larminat, administrateur 4e echelon, Ziguinchor cercle, to Governor of Senegal (via Commandant de Cercle), 12 September 1952, 11D1/173, AS; report for Assemblée de l'Union Française, No. 230, 27 January 1956, CC/16333, ANF. There are comments and data from other *cercles* in Senegal about the implementation of the indigenous état-civil throughout the series 11D1, AS. See also Gouet (1954, 530).

[46] Minister of FOM to Garde des Sceaux, 9 December 1958, and Garde des Sceaux to Secrétaire Général de la Communauté, 10 March 1960, 950236/2, CAC.

Social citizenship and the problem of identification

Meanwhile, during the post-war decade, the absence of the état-civil caused problems in the implementation of social citizenship: to ensure that family allowances would go to people actually entitled to them, to enrol school children of the proper age, and to pay pensions appropriately. Here, too, the preferred solution was *ad hoc*, the *jugement supplétif*. If a parent wanted to register a child to go to school, but there was no record of the child's birth, that person could go before a local administrator, bring witnesses, and obtain a paper that certified the date of birth.[47] Similarly, unregistered marriages could be recorded after the fact when benefits were to be allocated. As a governor noted, provisions being contemplated to pay workers with children an allowance on a per-child basis (to encourage workers' natality and legitimate family formation, as was done in metropolitan France) would require enormous numbers of *jugements supplétifs*, since so few marriages and births had been registered. Their accuracy would depend on the good faith of witnesses and enquiries would have to be made.[48]

Faced with demands for these *jugements*, officials were realizing that Africans were using the état-civil in their own way, when they wanted it, for what they wanted. Registration of a birth for the sake of inscribing an official identity on the child was not the point, but when parents wanted the child to go to school, then the alternative route to inscription had to be taken. Officials worried that the system could be manipulated: what one official tactfully called the 'supple' nature of the *état-civil indigène* gave room for people to adjust their age up or down or even to change names. One cited a case of someone duly inscribed in the état-civil at Saint-Louis who obtained a *jugement supplétif* elsewhere so he could claim to be of a different age.[49]

Between 1952, when a comprehensive labour code for overseas was passed, and 1956, when a programme of family allowances for wage workers went into effect, a debate went on that revealed official ambivalence about the very object that the état-civil was supposed to record, the nature of the African family. Family

[47] An attestation of marriage used to gain a *jugement supplétif* included the names of the concerned parties and their parents and the signatures or fingerprints of two witnesses, done before a chief. Similar certifications were used for births – often long after the fact. See some examples in 11D1/1450, AS.

[48] Governor, Soudan, to High Commissioner, 22 October 1955, 23G 105 (and draft circular to commandants de cercle, with above). On the need for each entering student to provide such a judgement, see Rector of Academy, Directeur général de l'enseignement, note for Directeur Général de l'interieur, 23 June 52, 23G 34, AS, and Governor of Senegal, circular to commandants de cercle, 3 June 1955, 11D1/173, AS.

[49] Mission 1951–1952, Monsieur Monguillot Inspecteur Gen. des Colonies, Rapport concernant la pluralité d'État-Civil en AOF, 14 May 1952; Directeur Général de l'Intérieur and Directeur Général Adjoint des Affaires Politiques, Rapport concernant la pluralité d'État-Civil en A.O.F., en réponse aux observations faites par M. Monguillot, 6 June 1952, 23G 34, AS; Conseiller Technique, Affaires Politiques, Paris, circular to High Commissioners, 22 August 1952, 11D1/897, AS.

allowances had been a standard practice in French labour relations since the 1930s. A demand for them had been one of the prime objectives of African civil servants' unions during the major strike movement of early 1946 in Senegal, and the principle at least of family allowances for civil servants had been won. I have written about these arguments elsewhere, so I will only summarize the main points here (Cooper 1996, ch. 7). Opponents of family allowances for African workers argued that there was no need to encourage natality in Africa – one of the rationales for family allowances in the metropole – and they asserted that Africans would spend the money on marrying more wives and that African families were so varied in nature that identifying eligible children was too hard, not least because of the poor state of the *état-civil indigène*. The argument for family allowances drew on many of the same conceptions of the backward nature of the 'traditional' family: family allowances would allow workers to raise their families without needing resources from their home villages and their distribution could be made subject to the surveillance of children by nurses, doctors, teachers, and social workers. The argument accepted that capitalism was not being generalized in the African countryside, but that a working class could and should be constructed and enabled to reproduce itself, separated from its roots in a backward countryside; such policies sometimes went under the name of 'stabilization'. Officials, based on some rather shaky survey data, presumed that wage workers' families were less likely than others to be polygamous, and it was precisely this sort of family in this sort of economic milieu that the state should encourage and observe.[50]

So alongside a logic of citizenship that recognized that progress toward universal suffrage entailed the identification of an entire population was a social logic that sought to bring a particularly important fraction of the population into a system of registration and surveillance. Here, the administration had positive incentives with which to work – the distribution of family allowances, access to schools, pensions. Local officials could compel individuals who wanted such resources to inscribe themselves or their children in the état-civil corresponding to their personal status, and the records from Senegal from the mid- and late 1950s, for example, suggest that the *état-civil indigène* was indeed being used. But a notion of identification and surveillance that in France was meant to define the unity of a national population had the effect in French Africa of differentiating people.

Changing status

Distinction-making was in part a matter of whether or not one used the état-civil, but also of the status to which one was assigned. In principle, all citizens, regardless

[50] The best study I know of about how stabilization policies played out focuses on British Africa in Lindsay (2003). See also Fall (2010).

of status, had the same rights – including freedom of association and expression, the right to travel anywhere in metropolitan or overseas France, the right to apply for higher education and civil service jobs. The stakes in the distinction between 'common' and 'particular' civil status were clearest up to 1956, when the two-college electoral system meant that people of common civil status had a more heavily weighted vote. After the institution of the single college in French West Africa, that distinction ceased to be meaningful. But the two forms of civil status remained as markers of – depending on one's point of view – the cultural pluralism of the reformed French empire or the existence of two classes of people, one more 'French' than the other. In 1957, the Minister of Overseas France felt he had to remind the High Commissioner of French West Africa that the people in his charge were 'citoyens français'. He went on to emphasize that,

> the autochthonous people of French West Africa have the most absolute right to have on their passports, information cards, and other identity documents the inscription of their nationality, like all French people, and without distinction of origin or status . . . There can remain in this regard no ambiguity, neither in spirit, nor in the labels used in official documents delivered to the people concerned.

Alongside the ambivalence about separate états-civils or unified états-civils with separate statuses distinguished lay this unambiguous assertion that public documents define a person's French citizenship.[51]

The mention in the constitution that people of personal civil status could renounce that status (but not the other way around) pointed to another discussion in which inclusive pluralism and invidious distinction stood in uneasy relation to one another. Officials and legislators agreed that a law was needed to regulate renunciation of personal status, and repeated proposals for such a law were made during the 1940s and 1950s – without getting very far. French leaders saw the adoption of French civil status as a positive move, toward a higher form of social life which it was a duty for the French to promote.[52] As early as mid-1947, the Minister of Overseas France noted that one could be 'very liberal' and give every applicant French civil status on demand, but to do so lacked 'realism'. People were so attached to local customs 'such as polygamy' that were inconsistent with French civil law that there would be a 'very dangerous divergence' between law and practice. Since the French civil code allowed men only one wife at a time, any

[51] Minister of Overseas France to High Commissioner, French West Africa, 26 April 1957, 950236/1, CAC. This was not the first time that such a high official had to be reminded of the equal citizenship status of West Africans. In 1954, the High Commissioner mistakenly called them 'citizens of the French Union', a category intended for inhabitants of the protected states such as Morocco, which had their own nationality; Paris made him send around a correction to his subordinates. Governor General to Minister, 24 February 1954, Minister, Circular, 21 June 1954, and Directeur des Affaires Politiques, Dakar, to Directeur des Services de Sécurité, 2 July 1954, letter circulated to all governors by the Governor General, 3 August 1954, 23G 93, AS.

[52] Note de la Direction des Affaires Politiques, February 1947, 23G 33, AS.

candidate for common civil status would have to be single or monogamous, or else repudiate any wife beyond the first. The implications of renunciation on family members and on inheritance had to be sorted out. So admission to French civil status would have to be regulated, demanding evidence of conformity to the French way of life.[53] The Conseil d'État at the time agreed: to be granted French civil status, one had to exhibit the 'habits and style of life approaching that of people with civil status', that is of French people who already had that status.[54] While retaining personal civil status was not supposed to diminish the rights conveyed by the constitution, some legislators worried that law and practices still made 'distinctions among French citizens of different statuses'.[55] And the constitution seemed to imply that renunciation was a right.

Félix Houphouët-Boigny, then a deputy from the Côte d'Ivoire as well as a member of the legislative council of French West Africa, thought the idea of renunciation was insulting: 'We are Blacks and proud of the colour of our skin. We do not want to renounce our personal status. We have our religion, our customs, which we value greatly.'[56] There were some arguments from Dahomeans in favour of a bill regulating renunciation, but the majority of the Conseil expressed its opinion 'that the proposed law on renunciation of personal status and the acquisition of French civil status for inhabitants of Overseas Territories is pointless, given the possibility of tacitly renouncing the status'.[57]

Proposals to regulate renunciation came up in other forums – it was something of a cause for Daniel Boisdon, at one time President of the Assemblée de l'Union Française – but African legislators again objected. Tiémoko Diarra, for example,

[53] Minister, circular to High Commissioners, June 13, 1947, F60/1401, ANF.

[54] Statement of Conseil d'État in regard to bill on renunciation of personal status, 13 July 1949, F60/1401, ANF.

[55] Assemblée de l'Union Française, Commission de la legislation, de la justice de la fonction publique, des affaires administratives et domaniales, Rapport No. 154, séance of 15 June 1950; Avis de l'Assemblée de l'Union Française, 13 July 1955; Report of commission on legislation of the Assemblée, No. 20, 27 January 1955, Ministre de la France d'Outre-Mer to Secrétaire Général du Gouvernement, 13 June 1949, F60/1401, ANF; Note of C. Deschamps, Chef du Bureau des affaires Admin, 'sur la citoyenneté des ressortissants d'AOF', 14 May 1952; Minister, circular to High Commissioners, 13 June 1947; Note 'sur la citoyenneté des autochtones' by Avocat General, Dakar, April 1947, 23G 96, AS.

[56] Report by Houphouët-Boigny and Almamy Ibrahima Sory on proposed law brought before the Grand Conseil of French West Africa, AOF, *Bulletin du Grand Conseil*, 20 December 1947, 55–56. N'Diawar Sarr argued that renunciation of personal status for a Muslim meant renouncing the religion. *L'AOF*, 6 January 1948. French administrators were sceptical that many Africans would be interested in renunciation. Governor, Senegal, to High Commissioners, 31 May 1952, Governor, Soudan, to same, 3 July 1952, Governor of Dahomey to same, 21 May 1952, Governor, Côte d'Ivoire, to same, 9 June 1952, 23G 96, AS. In partial self-contradiction, most governors worried that renunciation would be disruptive of indigenous social life.

[57] The debate and the reports are in AOF, *Bulletin du Grand Conseil*, 20 December 1947, 52–53, 55–56.

stated in response to Boisdon's efforts in 1950 that renunciation 'favours a tiny minority of people who will separate themselves from the African masses by renouncing their status'.[58] The sceptics had a point. The thinking of proponents of the renunciation law presumed that African notions of personal status did not have the same value as French ones. As Boisdon himself pointed out, the change of status 'is only possible in one direction'. He wrote of his fellow legislators, 'If the diversity of customs is for now respected, it is with the secret hope that, progressively, they will disappear.' He asked critics of renunciation legislation if they wanted to 'wall in' Africans in distinct, often small, traditional social units.

> If you want to raise the level of our autochthonous fellow citizens, give them the possibility to enter the rhythm, the current of modern life by submitting themselves to a status of universal character, and that is precisely the character of French civil status.[59]

The political officers in the Ministry exemplified this point of view: they did not think the statuses equivalent.

> It is by reference to our law that it is possible to encourage the evolution of customs and that has been the case notably, contrary to traditional norms, to favour monogamy, to combat the commercialization of bridewealth, and to recognize the widow's right to dispose of herself. To admit the equality of statuses and the consequences which follow would be to go against evolution, to give up part of our civilizing action and compromise much of the results already obtained.[60]

African deputies objected not only to the clear evidence that advocates of the proposed statute thought one status was superior to another, but to the fact that renunciation under the constitution could only be a one-way street: a personal status could be renounced, but not the supposedly universalistic French one. They saw in this a return to the doctrine of assimilation that they thought had been buried in the Assemblée Nationale Constituante's recognition of multiple status regimes,

[58] Assemblée de l'Union Française, *Débats*, 25 July 1950, 1133. The committee on legislation of the Assemblée de l'Union Française discussed the renunciation question at its meetings of 10, 17, 24, 31 May, 2, 14 June, 22, 27 November 1950 (C//16170, ANF), and the Assembly as a whole debated it on 27 July 1950 (*Débats*, 1160–1169, 1184–1188), without results. There was another try on 7 July 1955, *Débats*, 655–669. René Pleven, who had tried in the Assemblée Nationale in November 1955 to get a bill considered, tried again in October 1956, with equal success. Request to Assemblée de l'Union Française for opinion on bill, 23 October 1956, copy in 23G 96, AS.

[59] Boisdon (1949, 76); Boisdon, statement to Assemblée de l'Union Française, 27 July 1950, *Débats*, 1164. Boisdon added that there were thirty or forty 'customs' in French West Africa alone, in contrast to the French version, which he saw as being 'western' or 'universal' as much as French. *Débats*, 1162, 1165.

[60] Affaires Politiques, Rapport à Monsieur le Ministre, 5 May 1955, AP 492, AOM. Ministry officials thought Boisdon was putting too many obstacles in front of renunciation and did not like his proposal that in limited circumstances people could go back on it. Note d'Études relative au projet de rapport Boisdon sur la renonciation au statut personnel, attached to Note pour Monseiur le Directeur du Cabinet, signed Ralison, 9 May 1955, AP 492, AOM.

turning an ambiguous constitutional provision into a clear demarcation of a 'citizenship of the second zone'.[61] There were objections as well to the government's insistence that it verify that the applicant was actually living a French lifestyle. Opponents thought such a requirement turned the right to renounce personal status into a favour; proponents that letting people come under the civil code whose family life did not conform to it (monogamy, French principles of inheritance) would only produce conflict and unhappiness.[62] The proposals of 1950 were sidetracked; they kept coming back and getting sidetracked again regularly until the advent of territorial autonomy in 1956, increased autonomy in 1958, and independence in 1958 took the entire question out of French hands.

The renunciation proposals thus crystallized a conflict over culture that constitutional compromises had not extinguished. At least some elements in the Paris Ministry maintained their civilizing mission by criticizing African marriage practices: polygamy, bridewealth, the absence of a bride's consent.[63] Africans, now taking active roles in the debate, were defending their right to maintain their own practices. The outcome was that nothing was done: the bills to regulate renunciation – that might encourage it too much or not enough – withered on the vine. However, the constitution did signify, at least, that Africans had an element of choice in the process – they could renounce their personal status (or not do so) – and their representatives had a voice. And if some Africans opposed the very idea of renunciation, at least some others wanted to take advantage of the constitutional

[61] An expression used by Ya Doumbia of the Soudan in the Assemblée de l'Union Française, debate of 27 July 1950, *Débats*, 1166. See also the interventions of Soppo Priso of the Cameroons and Djim Momar Guèye of Senegal, *Débats*, 1167–1169, 1187–1188. The Secrétaire d'État for Overseas France tried to save the day by softening Boisdon's remarks about the universal and modern nature of French civil status, but he could not get around the one-way-street argument. Neither the constitution nor the proposal at hand saw all statuses, including the 'French' one, as equivalent. *Débats*, 1166–1167.

[62] *Débats*, 1162, 1165, 1167. The Commissions de la Legislation of the Assembly also went around and around on this issue in discussions on 2 June, 22 November 1950, C//16170, ANF. For anyone who did change status, there could no longer be a discussion of difference across the French Union, for the civil code was supposed to apply 'uniformly to all French citizens with the *statut civil de droit commun*'. For this reason, some people thought there should be a possibility of partial renunciation – of polygamy only – but that went nowhere either. See the above discussion in Commission, 22 November 1950, and – as the issue kept coming back – Avis No. 266 of the Assembly, 7 March 1957, C//16352, ANF.

[63] See 23G 102 for a large file of official correspondence, from 1945 to 1957, about the possibilities and dangers of regulating marriage in Africa. The problem, some felt, derived directly from the citizenship clause of the 1946 constitution, with its acknowledgement of diverse personal regimes and presumption of equality before the law. If the state was to record marriages, regulate changes of personal status, and pass out benefits on the basis of family status, it had made African marriage its business. The connection with citizenship is made most clearly in an undated note, '*Le marriage entre Africains: aspect juridique*', in this file. The debate brought out what various officials thought of African social practices, as in this remark from the Governor of the Soudan (letter to Governor General, 15 June 1950): 'The African is, by nature, polygamous.' The file reveals little clarity or consensus about how the government should act.

possibility. Some wanted to mark their conversion to Christianity or to get away from indigenous inheritance rules. The dossiers of candidacy for '*statut de droit commun*' contain formulaic expressions to the effect that the applicant 'has approached French civilization by his manner of life and social habits'.[64] The formula was much like that once used by subjects trying to become citizens.[65]

Take the application of Ernest Sampah Kassi, from the Côte d'Ivoire. His form declared, misleadingly, that he was '*citoyen de l'Union française*'. He was monogamously married to a French citizen, probably meaning French citizen of '*statut civil du droit commun*'. His marriage and his children's births were duly registered in the état-civil. Working as a clerk (in the *cadre local des commis-expéditionaires*) he had a salary that allowed him to live 'decently'. He could read, write, and speak French. The report on him commented that he 'lives with his family in an apartment of permanent materials built in European style. The rooms are kept clean and furnished in a European manner. With his family, his style of life and his social habits approach those of French civilization.' He had manifested no hostility to France, had no criminal record, and had been exempted from military service. In short, the application looked as if he was applying for a citizenship he already had.[66] But not many people were following his route: according to Boisdon, there had been only 138 applications to obtain *statut civil de droit commun* in 1954, of which eighteen had received a favourable response, two a negative one, and 118 were pending.[67]

In November 1955 the Conseil d'État reminded everyone that under the constitution, accession to French civil status was a right, not a favour. 'It is self-evident that a recognized constitutional right cannot be negated by the absence of a text of implementation.' Using the methods and criteria intended for citizenship applications before the war made no sense.[68] The Ministry sent around a circular that said that personal status is 'an option available to every citizen who has not put himself in a position that prevents his using it, and an option exercised by declaration'. It admitted that the law was unclear, nor was it obvious what to do when family members were of different statuses.[69] But clarity was not forthcoming. And even on the eve of independence, proposals were being submitted to the French

[64] See the applications in 23G 98, AS.

[65] Applications often followed to the letter the procedures of the decree of 23 July 1937 for obtaining French citizenship, even though the candidates in this instance were already French citizens. See for example the case of Sékou Dabo, 1953, 2D/1, SRASD.

[66] Case of Ernest Sampah Kassi, including report by Commandant de Cercle, Abidjan, 21 October 1955, 23G 98, AS.

[67] Boisdon, Assemblée de l'Union Française, *Débats*, 7 July 1955, 669.

[68] Garde des Sceaux, circular to Procureurs Généraux, 7 March 1957, F60/1401, ANF; see also Urban 2009, 562–568.

[69] Directeur des Affaires Politiques, Paris, circular to High Commissioners in Africa, 25 April 1956, 23G 96, AS.

parliament to codify renunciation procedures, but the entire question of status was by then a problem for the new African governments.[70]

The ambivalence of imperial reformers

So a decade after the constitution of 1946, the question of defining and recording people's personal status was unresolved. Voting, collecting social benefits, and inheritance, in principle, required individual identification; the state's recognition of marriage assumed that people's personal status was known. Yet people voted, worked and collected benefits, married, gave birth, and died – only partially under the eyes of the state.

Why? We keep returning to the basic problem: colonial states lacked the means to insert themselves into the lives of all subjects. They could do so in places where their power was particularly dense (capital cities) and in cases where Africans had some reason to cooperate (collecting family allowances, sending children to school). But the idea of a grid of surveillance over a population was beyond their means, and legislators were not willing to provide the means or the guidelines to undertake the task. Then, too, they had trouble deciding just how they wanted to play the politics of difference. Installing a single état-civil over all of Africa would mean inscribing polygamous Africans on the same lists as monogamous Europeans, while a separate list for people of different statuses would be to admit, a little too publicly, that the supposed singularity of French citizenship did not correspond to the reality of imperial governance in the post-war era. And Africans could, depending on the circumstances, ignore or use the état-civil; some could object to the very principle of renouncing personal status, while others could choose to come under the French civil code.[71]

So the question of the singularity or plurality – of the compulsory or voluntary nature – of the état-civil in French Africa was still unresolved as African leaders began in 1959 and 1960 to negotiate over independence. The issue was soon on the agenda of the new states.

In June of 1961, the Assemblée Nationale of the newly independent state of Senegal passed a law instituting a single état-civil. In introducing the law, legislators and the Minister of Justice described it as putting an end to the 'unacceptable distinction' that had previously existed between people assimilated to European status and everyone else. Insisting that 'a modern state could not dispense with registering these acts [marriage, birth, death] of its citizens', it made the état-civil obligatory. Such registration was necessary 'both for sound family policy and for

[70] Direction Civile, Legislation, to President of Commissions des Lois Constitutionelles, de la Legislation, et de l'Administration Générale, Assemblée Nationale, 8 February 1960, 950236/24, CAC.
[71] For an interesting debate in which multiple attitudes toward equality and difference emerged, see the interventions of Ya Doumbia, Tiémoko Diarra, and Daniel Boisdon, Assemblée de l'Union Française, *Débats*, 25, 27 July 1950, 1122–1124, 1133, 1162.

reasons of health, or at least, in a general statistical and demographic interest'. But Senegal's rulers maintained that they would respect diversity. People could marry in different ways, but they – under penalty of law – had to inform the state that they had done so. If they did not, they would be fined.[72]

Before the bill passed the Assemblée Nationale, a debate ensued which revealed that some of the same questions that paralysed the French government disturbed Senegalese deputies as well. The bill's reporter insisted that the measure was intended to record marriages, not define them. But there was more going on. His committee recommended dropping a proposed article that would make part of the record a husband's declaration – strictly voluntary – that he would not marry a second wife (which would be binding unless the marriage was dissolved). The opponents, who had prevailed in a close vote in committee, argued that this clause could be

> a coercive means at the disposition of future wives to oblige their husbands to contract only one marriage. The temptation of women, if one believes the proponents of this thesis, would be great and with a tendency to generalize, given how true it is that the married woman is the most ferocious adversary of polygamy.

The bill was roundly criticized by the deputy Boubakar Guèye for requiring that, after a Muslim marriage, both partners come before an officer of the état-civil to register the marriage and attest their consent. He thought the bill anti-Muslim, for it required a man who regarded himself as having followed the Koran's rules on marriage to be married twice, the second time 'before someone secular, who moreover might be of Catholic faith'. The bill's defenders retorted that its object was not 'to elaborate Muslim law, but [to enact] legislation that takes account of Senegalese pluralism'. But the proponents had their cultural baggage, too – more was at stake than recording acts in a neutral way. Pressed on why the bill required both parties to the marriage to attest their consent before the official of the état-civil – and that it must be the wife herself, not her father as some self-described Muslims would have it – the Minister of Foreign Affairs said, 'If we have demanded consent, it is from taking account of sociological conditions.' Girls, he asserted, were in fact being married without their consent. Another deputy was even blunter and more sociological: 'our concern is precisely that we do not have confidence in all the fathers'. Insisting on consent came from 'a concern with progress', said the minister. So the act of recording a marriage was also an intervention in the process of marriage.[73]

[72] Projet de loi 17/ANS/61, 'tendant à la création d'un état civil unique et sa reglementation', presented February 1961, VP 121, AS; Garde des Sceaux, circular to Prosecutors and Judges of the Peace, n.d. June 1961, and Report by Khar N'Dofène Diouf on behalf of Commission de la Législation, de la Justice et de l'Administration Générale, Assemblée Nationale du Sénégal, 15 June 1961, VP 226, AS.

[73] Senegal, Assemblée Nationale, *Débats*, 16 June 1961, 458–477. The bill was presented by Khar N'Dofène Diouf, reporter for Commission de la Législation, de la Justice de l'Administration Générale et de la Fonction publique, and its most vocal critic was Boubakar Guèye. Also cited are the Ministre des Affaires Etrangères, Ousmanne Alioune Sylla, and Moustapha Touré.

In the end, concerns were assuaged, with the dropping of the article that some thought threatened polygamy, and the bill was passed. Muslims would have to go through a second process, not a second marriage, but a check by an official of the state on the fact of the marriage and its consensual nature. Failure to do so would not invalidate the marriage, but it would make the couple subject to punishment. Senegalese Muslims, like French Catholics or the defenders of state secularism, were worried that the état-civil might define, not just record, acts like marriage in a manner inconsistent with what they perceived to be their way of life. But the national state, for all the concerns among its legislators, expressed a will to know its citizens that the colonial government did not.[74]

Conclusion

For a long time, French colonial governments cared little who their subjects were, except as members of collectivities whose leaders could be incorporated into the vertical channels of imperial power. The post-war period marked a break, with the French government's embrace of a politics of development and a project of managed political inclusion – a policy shift that soon proved untenable. Yet, the fate of the état-civil reveals an underlying ambiguity about how far an imperial politics of difference could go. That there was serious debate in Dakar and Paris – in which African representatives took part – over the relationship of citizenship and personal status, of equality and difference, itself marks a turning point in the history of French colonialism. But over a decade after the passage of a new constitution for a transcontinental France, it remained an open question whether the state could provide the regulatory architecture for, in the words of a jurist immersed in the état-civil issue, 'the needs of the populations of multiple origin of this great pluricontinental state that France has become' (Gouet 1954, 584). In France, the état-civil represented the deep reach of the state's conception of a singular citizenry. Overseas, this institution sat uneasily with the state's attempt to preserve imperial power by shaping a citizenry that was both unified and differentiated, that could provide some means for satisfying Africans' aspirations for economic, social and political equality with other French citizens, that could recognize the reality of different modes of life across the empire, and that could be both a reflection and an instrument of the government's role as an agent of social progress. In the end, officials did not have enough faith in their own administrative capacity, in their ability to reconcile inclusion and differentiation across greater France, or in Africans' embrace of French conceptions of progress to put in place a consistent policy of identification, registration, and surveillance.

[74] Senegal would go on to adopt a national identity card. Loi sénégalaise instituant une carte nationale d'identité, adopted by Assemblée Nationale, 14 February 1962, VP 121, AS.

References

de Benoist, Joseph-Roger. 1982. *Afrique occidentale française de 1944 à 1960*. Dakar: Nouvelles éditions africaines.

Blévis, Laure. 2004. 'Sociologie d'un droit colonial. Citoyenneté et nationalité en Algérie (1865–1947).' Ph.D. dissertation, Institut d'Etudes Politiques d'Aix-en-Provence.

Boisdon, Daniel. 1949. *Les institutions de l'Union française*. Paris: Berger-Levrault.

Borella, François. 1958. *L'évolution politique et juridique de l'Union française depuis 1946*. Paris: Librairie Générale de Droit et de Jurisprudence.

Broers, M. 2001. 'Napoleon, Charlemagne, and Lotharingia: Acculturation and the Boundaries of Napoleonic Europe.' *Historical Journal* 44(1): 135–154.

Burbank, Jane and Frederick Cooper. 2010. *Empires in World History: Power and the Politics of Difference*. Princeton, NJ: Princeton University Press.

Cooper, Frederick. 1996. *Decolonization and African Society: The Labour Question in French and British Africa*. Cambridge: Cambridge University Press.

—— 2005. *Colonialism in Question: Theory, Knowledge, History*. Berkeley: University of California Press.

—— 2009. 'From Imperial Inclusion to Republican Exclusion? France's Ambiguous Post-War Trajectory.' In *Frenchness and the African Diaspora: Identity and Uprising in Contemporary France*, ed. Charles Tshimanga, Ch. Didier Gondola and Peter J. Bloom. Bloomington: Indiana University Press, 91–119.

Cottias, Myriam. 2004. 'Droit, justice et dépendance dans les Antilles françaises (1848–1852).' *Annales. Histoire, Sciences Sociales* 59(3): 547–567.

Decottignies, Roger. 1955. 'L'état civil en AOF.' *Annales africaines* 44: 41–78.

Diouf, Mamadou. 1998. 'The French Colonial Policy of Assimilation and the Civility of the Originaires of the Four Communes (Senegal): A Nineteenth Century Globalization Project.' *Development and Change* 29(4): 671–696.

Dubois, Laurent. 2004. *A Colony of Citizens: Revolution and Slave Emancipation in the French Caribbean, 1787–1804*. Chapel Hill: University of North Carolina Press.

Fall, Babacar. 2010. 'Sénégal: Le Travail au XXè siècle.' Ph.D. dissertation, University of Amsterdam.

Gervais, R. R. and I. Mandé. 2007. 'Comment compter les sujets de l'Empire? Les étapes d'une démographie impériale en AOF avant 1946.' *Vingtième Siècle. Revue d'histoire* 95: 63–74.

Gouet, Yvan. 1954. 'Remarques sur une réorganisation éventuelle de l'état-civil dans les parties d'outre-mer de la France qui connaissent le regime de la pluralité des états civils et dans les territoires sous tutelle.' *Revue juridique et politique de l'Union française* 8: 492–585.

—— 1957. 'L'Article 82 (paragraphe 1) de la Constitution relatif à l'option de statut et l'élaboration de la "théorie des statuts civils" de droit français moderne.' *Penant* 67: 1–94.

Héricord-Gorre, Alix. 2008. 'Eléments pour une histoire de l'administration des colonisés de l'Empire française. Le "régime de l'indigénat" et son fonctionnement depuis sa matrice algérienne (1881–c. 1920).' Ph.D. dissertation, European University Institute.

Landry, Adolphe. 1946. 'France et l'Union française: il y faut deux citoyennetés.' *Le Monde*, 17 September.

Lindsay, Lisa A. 2003. *Working with Gender: Wage Labour and Social Change in Southwestern Nigeria*. Portsmouth: Heinemann.

Merle, I. 2002. 'Retour sur le regime de l'indigenat: genese et contradictions des principes repressifs dans l'empire francais.' *French Politics, Culture and Society* 20(2): 77–97.

Saada, Emmanuelle. 2012. *Empire's Children: Race, Filiation, and Citizenship in the French Colonies*. Chicago: University of Chicago Press.

Urban, Yerri. 2009. 'Race et nationalité dans le droit colonial français 1865–1955.' Ph.D. dissertation, Université de Bourgogne.

Part IV

REGISTRATION, RECOGNITION AND HUMAN RIGHTS

16

Uruguay's Child Rights Approach to Health: What Role for Civil Registration?

ANNE-EMANUELLE BIRN

> Children have a right to their parents:
>
> Mother: Start raising your children by breastfeeding them. This will bring them health.
>
> Father: Start by registering your sons and daughters in the Office of Civil Registry. This will bring them dignity.
>
> Slogan to mark the thirtieth anniversary of the American International Institute for the Protection of Childhood, May 1957, cover, *Noticiario del Instituto Internacional Americano de Protección a la Infancia* (no. 117)

IN 1934 THE URUGUAYAN LEGISLATURE passed a 'Children's Code', probably the first national code explicitly to stipulate that 'every child has a right to know who are his parents' (Instituto Internacional Americano de Protección a la Infancia 1934a, 83), as part of its larger commitment to 'defend all of the rights of the child' (1934a, 102). Uruguay's formulation, directly linking identity registration to the defence of a child's rights, was a precursor to the language ultimately adopted by the United Nations Declaration of the Rights of the Child in 1959, and which forms the basis for the moral and legal justification of extending such registration systems globally to all populations in the world today. This chapter explores the historical context in Uruguay from which this novel statement of public policy, linking registration to child rights, emerged. It shows how the late nineteenth-century establishment of civil registration was intertwined with child health monitoring and corresponding public policies and institutions as part of a burgeoning welfare state. It draws out the interaction of these domestic approaches with international debates and practices, demonstrating the role played in these developments by Uruguayan public health's established international reputation, recognized by the League of Nations (LN), as the leading Latin American advocate of infant and child health improvement. It also examines how the innovative 1934 code and its associated identity registration features were implemented domestically as an integral part of

Proceedings of the British Academy **182**, 415–447. © The British Academy 2012.

a fully functioning government child welfare programme, and how Uruguay's approach was diffused internationally.

Introduction – the innovative right of registration in the Children's Code of 1934

On 31 March 1933, barely a week after Hitler seized despotic powers through the Reichstag's Enabling Act, Uruguayan President Gabriel Terra orchestrated an internal *coup d'état*, dissolving the Collegiate Council (which shared governance with the Presidency) and the General Assembly (Caetano and Jacob 1989; Oddone 1990).[1] Within a few weeks, amidst dealing with the economic and political crisis, Terra created an honorary commission to prepare legislation for childhood protection and patronage, followed by the establishment of a Ministry of Child Protection (Tomé 1938) – perhaps the first of its kind in the world. In April 1934, even before Terra's dubious re-election two months later, the acting legislature passed – and Terra signed into law – a Children's Code, one of the world's most comprehensive mother and child social protection policies.

The 'Children's Code' coordinated and expanded upon Uruguay's existing child-related legislation and institutions, delineating the juridical and administrative basis for the state's protection of children from the prenatal period to adulthood in the areas of health, education, legal tutelage (of 'delinquents' and abandoned children), nutrition, housing, social services, work (for adolescents), and other aspects of well-being. It established a new interdisciplinary Children's Council (replacing the Ministry of Child Protection) with offices in Montevideo, and eventually, throughout the country, providing services free of charge (Bauzá 1947; Consejo del Niño, Uruguay 1936, 1950). Supported by Uruguayan physicians and social reformers (who were well represented on the legislation's honorary commission), and by Latin American politicians and professionals (who viewed the preliminary legislation at the VIIth Pan American Conference held in Montevideo in December 1933), the main point of contention was financial. During the debate over the Code, parliamentarians expressed concern over implementation costs, especially regarding the new juvenile courts, which went beyond reorganizing and rationalizing existing services. Terra and his Minister of Child Protection fended off concern about new expenditures by deeming them as 'transient, but necessary' in a time of crisis.[2]

[1] The coup, backed by the police and firefighters, was almost bloodless but immediately launched a series of repressive measures including torture of opposition leaders, forced exile, firings, and press censorship.

[2] República Oriental del Uruguay, Comisión Legislative Permanente (1934), 'Debate Código del Niño', *Poder Legislativo*, 3 April (8303), 9–10.

The Code guaranteed working women eight weeks of paid maternity leave (and indefinite unpaid leave), assured poor women prenatal, childbirth, and postnatal care, and granted single mothers full guardianship rights over their offspring (Instituto Internacional Americano de Protección a la Infancia 1934a; Trochon and Vidal 1993). It also stipulated eugenic measures, including Civil Registry advice for couples to undergo prenuptial exams. Promising non-coercion (Chapter V, Article 25), the Code was consistent with the 'preventive eugenics' approaches of other Latin American countries at the time (Di Liscia 2005; Sapriza 2006; Stepan 1991; Stern 1999), despite Uruguay's four-year decriminalization of abortion under Terra (Sapriza 2011; Turenne 1929).[3]

Most pointedly in terms of identity registration was the provision that every child had the right to know his/her parents' identity and that 'natural children' (those born out of wedlock) enjoyed the right to paternal support (Article 173). Not just a theoretical assertion, this measure was backed by a new system of paternity investigation, overseen by the state, from the time the offspring reached 5 gestational months until age 21 (Article 174).[4] The Code's clear articulation of the connection between parental identification and children's rights was premised on the argument that illegitimacy was the 'focal point for all other problems affecting the lives of children and adolescents' (Instituto Internacional Americano de Protección a la Infancia 1934a, 28), including Uruguay's 'population crisis'. Most notably, the Code's preamble asserted, illegitimacy was the largest determinant of infant mortality, with 50 per cent of children born out of wedlock dying in infancy (Instituto Internacional Americano de Protección a la Infancia 1934a, 28) – an erroneous figure – and 90 per cent of 'delinquents' hailing from the ranks of illegitimates (1934a, 29).

At first glance, the Children's Code appears mired in contradictions. A panoply of services provided free of charge was proffered despite declining state revenues. Tutelage measures for children who encountered the justice system were patriarchal, even as legal specialists affirmed broad new rights for children (Casaravilla Estrada 1938). Passed under an authoritarian administration that demanded parents (especially fathers) meet their obligations, it granted a range of rights and protections to mothers and children. Like Uruguay's 1934 Constitution (passed by plebiscite with high abstentions), and akin to other nationalist dictatorships of the time, the Code helped secure state legitimacy through the expansion of a range of social and economic rights amidst ultra-conservative and repressive measures (Ruiz 2008).

In its logistical aspects, too, the Children's Code's connection to identity registration portended the state's expanding population surveillance. To enable the

[3] At the time only the USSR had decriminalized abortion (in force 1920–1936).

[4] The Civil Code and Civil Registry originally banned research on paternal identification; as of 1916 paternal identification research was permitted during the first two years of a child's life, but only with cause (Instituto Internacional Americano de Protección a la Infancia 1934a, 33). The 1934 Children's Code provision contrasted with the situation in Chile, for example, where paternity investigations initiated by children or single mothers were barred from 1857 until 1998 (Milanich 2009).

Children's Council to carry out its responsibilities for children under the age of 3, the Code mandated that Justices of the Peace submit weekly lists of registered births (Instituto Internacional Americano de Protección a la Infancia 1934a, 56). Because Children's Council services for needy children were mandatory, these lists were used to ensure registration, as well as to verify that enrolled children possessed birth certificates.

At the same time, the Children's Council's expansive and expanding services (including via mobile units) offered an unheralded level of protection, making Uruguay a world leader in assuring that children's rights were not only rhetorically invoked but realized through public policies. In just five years the Council director could tout its budget of 1.7 million pesos, comprising almost 2 per cent of total government spending (Berro 1939). Through passage of the Code, the Uruguayan government unambiguously recognized the need to go beyond the growing medical armamentarium to employ both medical *and* social approaches to child well-being. Given its wide mandate, the Children's Council interacted with virtually every Uruguayan child, at minimum through school health check-ups, and far more extensive contact with poor children and their mothers.

In terms of identity registration, the Children's Council's reach grew exponentially. In 1935 its legal office registered almost 250 children previously lacking birth certificates, and legitimized the status of some 200 others through parental recognition, marriages, and other means (Consejo del Niño, Uruguay 1936, 25). By the early 1940s, over 300 children were registered annually with their missing birth certificates, and 1,100 were legitimized. The office also reported initiating approximately 100 paternity investigations per year (Bauzá 1942, 32). All told, the equivalent of 3.5 per cent of all births had their identity status regularized in these years. By the mid-1940s, these figures began to level off, with an average of 265 birth certificate registrations and 450 legitimations in 1945 and 1946. However, paternity investigations rose to 144 in 1946 (Bauzá 1947, 32).

Within a decade, children's well-being improved markedly (Birn 2008a). Illegitimate births (their high prevalence being a long-standing characteristic of Uruguay and Latin America generally), after reaching a peak of 31 per cent in 1936, gradually decreased to under 20 per cent by 1949 (Dirección de Estadística General 1893–1944; Dirección de Estadística y Censos 1945–1953). By the early 1940s Uruguay's infant mortality rate had begun a steady decline, jumpstarted by a small surge in birth registration when family wage legislation was passed in 1943 (making the denominator of births larger) (Berro 1943; Pellegrino 1997). To be sure, by this time both Terra's dictatorship and the economic crisis had passed, with abundant state coffers and a return to social welfare democracy enabling further redistributive social policy (Ruiz 2008), including minimum wages and housing and water improvements. Yet there were more continuities than ruptures with the children's rights approach originally codified under a repressive regime (Berro 1944a, 1944b).

The Civil Registry and the making of the Uruguayan state

Why, in 1933–1934, was Uruguay able not merely to draft and pass into law a precocious statement of children's rights, but to implement it through a highly developed and integrated government programme? And how was it that this legislation came about under a dictatorial, albeit non-military, administration? In fact, Uruguay had been a leading proponent of child-oriented public health measures since the late nineteenth century, entering into a particularly close relationship and dialogue with French models and thinking. As we shall see, its child well-being innovations did not appear out of the blue in the 1930s, but were the fruition of decades of concern, deriving from its earlier accumulation of experiences of successes and subsequent obstacles in improving child health as well as its long-standing international engagement around these issues.

The origins of Uruguay's rights-based approach to child social welfare were inauspicious. The 'Oriental Republic of Uruguay' gained its independence in 1828, reaching relative stability by the 1850s under a livestock-based export economy. Nonetheless, the state remained weak due to marked political divisions between the capital, under the oligarchy-based Colorado Party, and the countryside, dominated by the Blanco Party's ranching interests (Barrán 1994); consequently public institutions were extremely slow to develop.

By the 1870s, in the absence of a central government apparatus and with the urban-rural rift impeding a full follow-up to the country's first census in 1852, there was a near vacuum in state knowledge of populace and economy. The impetus for Uruguayan statistical compilation came from an unlikely source – ranchers: if nothing else, Uruguay had plenty of livestock to count. In 1873 the Rural Association of Uruguay asked statistician Adolfo Vaillant to compile a profile of the country to present at that year's Vienna International Exposition (Vaillant 1873a). As a French immigrant, he was deeply influenced by the French tradition of comprehensive social statistics, epitomized in the Parisian statistical volumes issued under Louis Adolphe Bertillon and, especially, his son Jacques (Rial 1983; Schweber 2006). Vaillant foregrounded 'population movement' as the first 'principle of all statistics' (Dirección de Estadística General 1885; Vaillant 1873b, 2).

Under the entrepreneurial President Lorenzo Latorre (1876–1880), Uruguay underwent an inaugural effort to jumpstart the country's lagging institutional development (López-Alves 2000; Panizza 1997). Latorre oversaw a range of modernizing reforms including the establishment of a civil service. Free and secular public education made primary school attendance mandatory for both boys and girls, leading Uruguay to the region's highest literacy rate in 1900 – a remarkable 54 per cent, and reaching 70 per cent by 1920 (Engerman *et al.* 2000). Latorre also created a rural judicial system and police force to enforce enclosures and end rural banditry (to garner support of the landowning class, albeit a traditionally weaker force than in other countries); and oversaw expansion of the railways (financed through British capital, later ownership), telegraph, and mail service. His administration also supported immigration and modern infrastructural investment in Montevideo, involving sewerage and sanitation systems (taken over by the British company, Montevideo Waterworks, in 1879) (Asociación de Ingenieros del Uruguay 1949), street paving, routine garbage collection, and housing improvements, making it Latin America's urban progress pioneer (Castellanos 1971). Latorre's reforms presaged Uruguay's bona fide state-building efforts in the early twentieth century (Rock and López-Alves 2000), also revealing the complicated possibilities of universalist and protective reforms under authoritarian regimes.

In 1879 Vaillant's aspirations for accurate demographic data were realized when the Latorre administration established the country's Civil Registry as the 'most complete proof of the civil status of persons, carefully and responsibly overseen by civil servants' (Alonso Criado 1880, 1). Evidence of civil status via the existing system of baptism, the decree declared, was 'extremely weak and lends itself to fraud', and moreover 'only indicates religious affiliation, never nationality' (Alonso Criado 1880, 1). From its establishment, the 'urgent measure' of a secular Civil Registry not only mandated the registration by a Justice of the Peace of all births (including foundlings and out-of-wedlock births, whose parentage could not be questioned during the registration act), marriages, and deaths, it also made provisions for the legitimization of children born out of wedlock (who likely would not have been baptized), with implications for inheritance rights and adoption. Reflecting the country's early secularization impulse, which culminated in the 1918 constitutional separation of church and state (Caetano and Geymonat 1997), the timing of the Civil Registry's founding under Latorre suggests the theoretical importance of registration in expectation of a practical set of state entitlements (Szreter 2011), which would complement family roles in the context of the 'rights and obligations' of the Civil Code (Goyena 1900).

The Civil Registry's implementation rules, which remained consistent from the late nineteenth century to the mid-1940s, stipulated that the act of inscription be free in all cases and that the charge for issuing certificates be suspended for the poor. It required births to be registered by parents, or in case of infirmity their representatives, within ten days in urban areas and twenty days in rural regions (Cincinatti Bollo 1894; República Oriental del Uruguay. Dirección General del Registro del Estado Civil 1907).[5] Birth registration was medicalized from 1886, when doctors, surgeons, midwives, and other birth assistants were required to report to the Justice of the Peace all births they attended, as per parental obligations. Given the paucity of doctors in the interior of the country (Legnani 1914) and the lack of medical regulation of midwives and healers (Barrán 1994), medical verification

[5] This contrasted with the situation in Costa Rica, which permitted registration up to twenty-five days after birth, Chile, sixty days, and Cuba, which until 1967 allowed for registration up to one year after birth (McGuire and Frankel 2005).

of births in rural areas was slow to take hold. Further, although baptism was prohibited without presentation of a birth certificate signed by a Justice of the Peace, it would take over a decade before parish registries were displaced (and in the most remote areas, parish and civil registries continued to be synchronized for several decades).

Uruguay was not the only country in Latin America to follow European developments in creating civil registration systems: in the 1850s Peru and Mexico passed relevant legislation, Argentina and Chile set up civil registries in the 1880s, and several aborted efforts preceded Brazil's 1888 law (Loveman 2007; Macchi 1972; Oszlak 1997).[6] By the 1890s, Buenos Aires data were considered reliable, and Brazil published short-lived annuals covering state capitals, but neither country compiled comprehensive national records until the 1940s. Despite their earlier start, Peruvian and Mexican registries, like those of most Latin American countries, did not have reliable national reach until after the Second World War (Hakkert 1996; Agostoni *et al.* 2010). Into the 1960s, leading demographers considered the quality of census data to be superior to vital registries in most Latin American countries (Davis *et al.* 1964; Mortara *et al.* 1964), a situation reversed in Uruguay, given the gaps between censuses (Pellegrino 2010).[7] Experts have deemed Uruguay's vital statistics coverage as of the early twentieth century to be reliable according to international standards (Damonte 1994; Faijer and Orellana 1996; Migliónico 2001).

Unlike in other settings (Corsini and Viazzo 1997; Williams 1996), Uruguay's coverage of deaths was probably more complete than that of births, which were believed to be slightly under-registered (Bauzá 1920; Pereira and Trajtenberg 1966). Deaths in urban areas were to be registered within twenty-four hours (to comply with laws stipulating that burials occur within one day of death), but in rural areas there was a ten-day grace period.[8] In cities, a medical certificate had to be presented

[6] An 1852 popular revolt against mandatory civil registry in Brazil was not repeated elsewhere, but tensions arising from state usurpation of church registration persisted in various Latin American countries well into the twentieth century, limiting the coverage of civil registration (Hakkert 1996; Macchi 1972; Agostoni *et al.* 2010).

[7] In the nineteenth century, weak and unstable national governments made for uneven censuses, conducted nationally only in 1852 and (incompletely) in 1860, and in some departments subsequently. In 1889 there was a very complete census of Montevideo. The seminal 1908 census took place as Uruguay's welfare state was being established. In 1930 a Montevideo census was carried out, but the Depression and state revenue problems, and then the authoritarian period under Terra, impeded a national counterpart. After the Second World War, another census was planned, but the new collegiate (shared) governing structure in the 1950s led to further delays. Since the national 1963 census, which was conducted in the context of state modernization and reform, the census has been carried out more frequently.

[8] Certification of stillbirths offered two options, according to 1892 and subsequent Civil Registry manuals: (a) an infant born without signs of life could be included in a list of stillbirths and not counted as a registered birth; or (b) if an infant died 'moments, hours or days after being born but before the birth was registered' it was considered a live birth and had to be issued both birth and death certificates (República Oriental del Uruguay. Dirección General del Registro del Estado Civil 1892, 30; 1907). This

to register a death, whereas in the countryside certification by a local official or two neighbours was allowed. Moreover, burials were prohibited unless a death certificate (issued free of charge for the indigent) was produced (Cincinatti Bollo 1894). In all likelihood, the death certificate requirement was rarely flouted because in Uruguay, in contrast to other Latin American countries, there is no evidence of clandestine cemeteries (Birn *et al.* 2010; Hakkert 1996; Reis 1997).

By the mid-1890s, the Civil Registry's reach and rules were widely operational, and an aspirational 1838 mandate to register health statistics could finally be fulfilled at a national level (Canabal 1899). In 1895 a National Board of Hygiene was founded to strengthen public health powers amidst the threat of maritime and overland epidemics, and a cadre of medical and public health experts was ready to mine the country's mortality data (Administración Sanitaria de la República Oriental del Uruguay 1896). Given Uruguay's low elevation and mild climate, even remote regions were accessible most of the time, an asset in civil registry terms well before the twentieth-century construction of highways sought to wrest control over ground transport from the British-owned railways. Moreover, Uruguay's late institutionalization carried the advantage of ready adaptation to new approaches in medicine and public administration without antagonizing entrenched interests. Despite limits to national democratic policy making, Uruguayan authorities were poised to know more about their population (particularly in regard to infant health) than did their counterparts throughout the Americas and, indeed, much of Europe.

Demographic conditions, social rights, and the Batllista welfare state

Circa 1900 Uruguay bore certain demographic features that distinguished it from other Latin American countries. The vast majority of the indigenous Charrúa population had been slaughtered or displaced during the colonial era, wars of independence, and early civil wars. Uruguay's population was relatively culturally uniform, consisting of Spanish and Italian immigrants and descendants (the majority), with a small elite from France, mestizos of indigenous and European heritage, and the descendants of African slaves transported under Iberian colonialism, escaped from Brazil, or working as indentured labourers on Brazilian-controlled ranches along the northern border.[9] Uruguay also urbanized early with

differentiated Uruguay's rules – but not necessarily the practice, especially in the countryside – from the French system of classifying early infant deaths as stillbirths (*faux mort-nés*, or false stillbirths) (Birn *et al.* 2010).

[9] A decade after slavery was abolished in 1842, the country's first national census estimated that 9 per cent of the population was of African descent (Andrews 2010). Afro-Uruguayans were not again counted by censuses until 1996. In the nineteenth century, they were (and remain today) the most marginalized group, both in Montevideo and on rural *estancias*, with significant implications for civil registry coverage.

one-third of its population resident in Montevideo, a cosmopolitan capital of over 300,000 people (Anuario Estadístico del Uruguay 1911).

Uruguay's greatest distinction, as an early welfare state, emerged under the 'Colorado' presidencies of José Batlle y Ordóñez (1903–1907 and 1911–1915), who belatedly consolidated the nation and shaped its political and social trajectory along lines Latorre had initiated. Batlle and his broad alliance first had to overcome the city–*caudillo* divide, achieved through a decisive 1904 civil war that all but destroyed the opposition 'Blanco' party's rural power base. Thereafter, the military was subject to civilian control, 'shielding' the country from military coups characteristic of much of Latin America (Rock and López-Alves 2000, 201). Following the civil war, economic conditions improved, with a doubling of hide, wool, and meat exports by 1913, after Uruguay's first frozen meat plant was built in 1905. Democratic politics began to flourish, and unions and an active urban citizenry enabled Batlle (already much admiring of French reforms) to contemplate a larger state role in the economy (including championing the manufacturing sector), and regarding work conditions, maternal protections, and suffrage. But Batlle's administration began more pragmatically, garnering civil servant support through pensions and other benefits (Nahum 1994).

Conservative forces contested this South American 'imitation' of the French Revolution, but the country's secular trend was indisputable, with the 1908 census showing only 70 per cent of the adult population identifying as Catholic (and just 63 per cent in Montevideo), compared to upwards of 98 per cent in Chile, Mexico, and Argentina (Barrán 2004). Further social change was evidenced by the country's first divorce law in 1907; divorce was fully legalized (including unilaterally by women, two decades before women gained the right to vote!) in 1913 (Cabella 1998) – at the time one of the world's most liberal laws.

Claudio Williman, hand-picked by Batlle to succeed him, pursued the Batllista line, most notably through the 1910 establishment of a modern National Public Assistance Agency (APN) to replace the 1889 National Commission of Charity and Public Welfare. Consciously modelled after France's *Assistance Publique*, the APN provided the indigent and resourceless with the 'right to free services provided by the State' (República Oriental del Uruguay. Registro Nacional de Leyes 1911), offering even more expansive protection and centralized control than its French exemplar. Care for all needy persons, including the chronically ill, the aged, poor and abandoned children, and pregnant women and new mothers, was promised through the organization of existing orphanages and foundling homes, maternal asylums, charity hospitals, and other establishments into a coordinated and growing system (República Oriental del Uruguay. Poder Legislativo 1910), though, in practice, the APN's budget never matched its bold agenda, and services expanded only slowly to the country's interior (Anon. 1926).

With a focus more on general provision of services than on selective screening for eligibility (which was defined economically rather than by age or nationality), the APN's interactions with the Civil Registry were limited to the long-time obligation of registering babies abandoned through the anonymous turntable at Montevideo's foundling home (Morquio 1905) and the registration of death certificates for those dying in APN institutions (Consejo Nacional de Higiene 1918).

Batlle spent the period between his two terms in office closely observing social and economic policies in Europe. He returned to Uruguay with grand plans. First, he created national savings, insurance, and mortgage banks, regulated foreign-owned companies, and launched state-owned enterprises (Barrán and Nahum 1983; Finch 1982; Pelúas 2001; Vanger 1980). After an acute economic crisis in 1913 (echoing fears of the 1890 Anglo-Argentinean panic), followed by increased exports during the First World War, his administration passed a series of key worker protections: workmen's compensation in 1914; and in 1915 an eight-hour workday, prohibition of child labour under the age of 13, a mandatory day of rest each week, forty days' paid pregnancy leave, and the lifting of taxes on essential goods. It also funded public school construction across the country, made secondary education free, and expanded the university (Barrán and Nahum 1985). Batlle's ambitious agenda unleashed a decades-long effort at protection and redistribution – undergirded by democratic electoral reforms[10] – that long outlasted his administration: old-age pensions were legislated in 1919, then occupational safety legislation, unemployment insurance, and so on. Together, these measures made Uruguay a welfare state leader in the Americas and beyond.

Tracking infant and child health

As these policy developments were unfolding, doctors and other professionals began to analyse Civil Registry data compiled in statistical annuals, together with census data. They uncovered various demographic phenomena. First, the country was rapidly urbanizing but its population was approximately one-third smaller than expected (Rial 1983), making accurate vital statistics all the more important. Uruguay's urban growth (with a particular acceleration between 1908 and 1930, when Montevideo's population more than doubled to 655,000) was accompanied by early indications of declining fertility. With an economy driven by the export of livestock products, demand for rural labour was limited, while refrigeration plants and the port stimulated urban migration. Moreover, since cattle- and sheep-raising were less labour-intensive than other types of agriculture, large families were unnecessary in the countryside. In Montevideo, as in other cities, birth rates dropped in the context of higher housing and food costs (Pellegrino and Pollero 2000).

[10] The 1918 constitution created a system of executive power-sharing between the president and an elected leadership council, with Batlle's idea of a truly collective, rotating executive (ensuring a democratic role for the opposition) realized in the 1950s (Rodríguez Ayçaguer 2008).

Uruguay's fertility trend, like France's (Klaus 1993), made the survival of children (and complete Civil Registry data) a key public concern.

The news regarding child health was extremely positive at the beginning of the twentieth century. Statistical annuals had been publishing cause-specific mortality data since 1885, adding infant deaths in 1893. Within a decade, health experts were able to track the country's uneven but evident decline in infant mortality from 104 deaths/1,000 live births in 1893 to 90/1,000 in 1901. Not only was it dropping, Uruguay's infant mortality rate was one of the lowest in the world, besting records in France, England, Russia, and Germany (Bauzá 1913; Birn 2008a). The reliability of Uruguay's Civil Registry data allowed its infant mortality statistics to transcend domestic discourse and emerge as a health indicator on a par with European data. Into the 1920s Uruguay was often the sole Latin American country whose data were deemed of a quality to merit inclusion in comparative analyses by international organizations.[11]

Uruguay's interest in infant mortality followed the emergence of European imperial concerns with infant and child health starting in the mid-nineteenth century, at the confluence of Comtian statistical compilation, industrial and military fitness, social Darwinist (later eugenic) anxieties, colonial productivity, and the rising legitimacy of organized public health and urban reform efforts (Armstrong 1986; Fildes *et al.* 1992; Jones 2002; Koven and Michel 1993; Manderson 2002). In Latin America's largely agrarian economies, even inadequate vital registries revealed staggeringly high infant mortality. Concern with child health related to state-building and the under-population of wide swaths of territory and coincided with sizeable waves of immigration from Europe, Asia, and the Caribbean, sparking a range of racialized fears and hopes for demographic destiny (Marko 2006; Stepan 1991; Wadsworth 1999).

As in various other Latin American countries, universalistic French approaches to child health had enormous traction in Uruguay before and under the Batllista welfare state. In the 1890s Dr Luis Morquio (1867–1935), the founder of Uruguayan paediatrics and subsequently a world-famous clinician and child health advocate, trained at the Institut Pasteur and with Paris's leading childhood disease experts (Morquio 1907a). Morquio, together with fellow French *stagier* Julio Bauzá and a handful of other paediatricians, modernized Montevideo's foster care and orphanage systems, founded a Children's Hospital (Morquio 1900, 1907b), and lobbied for, advised, implemented, and operated a series of French-style child health measures, including the APN (Bauzá 1933; Comité Uruguayen 1933). Because they served, simultaneously, as researchers, clinicians, epidemiologists, advocates, and agency administrators, as well as social, political, and scientific elites, this

[11] For example, in a 1925 League of Nations Health Organisation graphic showcasing its work, Uruguay was the only country outside Europe, the United States, and Japan to be included on a chart demonstrating 'The International Incomparability of Mortality Statistics'.

professional cadre was enormously influential (Birn *et al.* 2003). Through the establishment of the prestigious *Archivos Latino-Americanos de Pediatría* (in 1905), and the Uruguayan Society of Pediatrics (1915), Morquio and his colleagues ensured that the puericultural ideas of Adolphe Pinard, Pierre Budin, and other French luminaries became infused into the lexicon and practices of child health in Uruguay (Sociedad de Pediatría de Montevideo 1947; Pan American Sanitary Bureau 1948; Morquio 1906; Pinard 1917).

Thus, in 1908 Uruguay was among the first settings beyond Europe and its colonies to establish a 'gota de leche' (milk station or depot), based on the French 'goutte de lait', to distribute pasteurized milk, furnish dietary and health education, and provide medical attention to needy mothers and their infants (Rollet 1997). By the late 1920s, the *gotas* saw 45,000 annual maternal/child visits, distributing hundreds of thousands of litres of milk each year (Bauzá 1929), and arguably covering the largest proportion of mothers and infants in the world – with the total number of stations (forty throughout the country by the 1940s) exceeded only by France.

The unanticipated challenge of infant mortality

But just as Uruguay's institutional child health framework was becoming a South American showcase, its favourable infant health conditions began to unravel. By the late 1910s, the same health experts who had lauded the country's infant health success were bemoaning the country's failure: the infant mortality rate had risen to 124 deaths/1,000 live births in 1916 (Bauzá 1920) and was at best oscillating around 1900 levels of 100 deaths/1,000 live births and failing to fall any further.[12]

Generating additional controversy was the perceived part played by out-of-wedlock births in infant mortality: in Uruguay's countryside, a high and steady rate of approximately 30 per cent of births took place outside of marriage from 1900 until the late 1930s, and Montevideo's previously lower rate itself doubled to almost 30 per cent between 1900 and 1925 (Morquio 1927). Doctors were divided on how to interpret these figures: Morquio held that illegitimate births were a prime cause of infant mortality, associated with infant abandonment; while Bauzá believed that agnosticism and marriage expenses drove illegitimacy, with poverty as the prime underlying factor (Bauzá 1913; Morquio 1911; it should also be noted that as far back as 1870 Vaillant had argued that the relative sparsity of churches in Uruguay's rural areas was a key factor, limiting access for the populace for regularizing their domestic unions (Dirección de Estadística General 1885, 27–28).

[12] Moreover, Montevideo's infant mortality began to rise above the rural rate, peaking at 140 deaths/1,000 live births in 1916, as Latorre-era urban infrastructure could no longer keep pace with the city's growth (Birn 2008a).

The Batlle administration recognized a role for the Civil Registry in addressing this issue. In 1913 a cadre of mobile civil registry inspectors and sub-inspectors (comprised of rural school inspectors and a new category of civil servants) was created and charged with 'using all the propaganda means in their reach to ensure that people in common-law relationships who have not married regularize their situation and legitimize their offspring' (Ley de 17 de marzo 1913). The inspectors were permitted to carry out household registration, exempt indigent persons from payment, and deliver the acts directly to the Justices of the Peace for official recording purposes, supplementing the 1910 provision allowing for late registration (Uruguay 1927). Despite these measures, after a brief decline, out-of-wedlock births continued to rise, with Uruguay's illegitimacy rate far higher than Europe's at the time and 'even' exceeding published rates for Argentina, Colombia, and Costa Rica (Bauzá 1924).

Simultaneously, the state's role in maternal and child health services expanded. In 1919 the APN established an Infant Protection Service and Wetnurse Office (IPS), with Bauzá at the helm from 1920 until 1943. The IPS centralized services for children under 3, both for those already under state protection and for those 'belonging to the poor class of the population whose parents do not have sufficient resources to nourish them adequately or to avail them of medical attention' (Bauzá 1923). In 1921, the APN's director boasted that Uruguay's social assistance guarantee to the poor was unsurpassed anywhere (Becerro de Bengoa 1922), a claim also made that year for the USSR by the Soviet Health Commissar (Semashko 1990).[13]

By 1923 the IPS was responsible for 'protecting' one-fourth of Montevideo's estimated under-3 population of 28,000 (Bauzá 1929), yet ever new tactics were needed. In order to coordinate women's charities (Ehrick 2005a) and expand the APN's reach, Bauzá helped orchestrate the founding in 1924 of the Uruguayan Association for the Protection of Childhood (AUPI), under the aegis of the APN, as the national counterpart to – and with the active encouragement of – the Geneva-based 'Save the Children' movement (Ferrière 1925).[14] AUPI's senior directors and commission heads included Morquio, Bauzá, and Bauzá's wife, among a 'Who's Who' from Uruguay's medical establishment (Asociación Uruguaya de Protección a la Infancia 1931a).[15] As a charitable-professional partnership, AUPI rapidly mounted an array of APN ancillary activities, including a pre-school

[13] Though Soviet maternal and infant health services were widely praised by visitors, Stark claims foreigners were duped by Potemkin clinics (Starks 2003). Caroli argues that Soviet social protectionism of the 1920s was driven far more by industrial needs than universal rights (2003).

[14] Suzanne Ferrière, 'Comité Uruguayen', 3 February 1924. Archives privées 92.33.65, Save the Children International Union Archives, Archives d'Etat de Genève, Switzerland. Folder: Suisse: Mlle Suzanne Ferrière (1923–1927).

[15] Union Internationale de Secours aux Enfants (1924–1952), 'Statuts de l'Association Uruguayenne de Protection de l'Enfance', Archives privées 92.55.3 (Archives d'Etat de Genève).

nutrition clinic, used clothes depots, a small vocational school, support for formalization of marriage, material aid to poor women and children, and provision of hundreds of thousands of school meals for needy children.[16] AUPI even trained its own corps of several dozen social workers, who carried out over 11,000 home visits in 1928 (Asociación Uruguaya de Protección a la Infancia 1931b; Martirené and Gurméndez 1926).

In the 1920s, health authorities employed ever more protective and patriarchal measures to combat the triad of illegitimacy, abandonment, and infant mortality, including: Civil Registry notification of illegitimate births to APN authorities; mandatory social and health surveillance of illegitimate children unless the family could demonstrate that this was unnecessary; faster paternity investigations; and special homes to enable out-of-wedlock mothers to breastfeed for six months (Bauzá 1924).

Yet the infant mortality situation remained a source of consternation to contemporaries: although still comparatively low, it failed to improve, even as Uruguay's welfare state was burgeoning and French-inspired policies to protect maternal and infant welfare were adopted, adapted, and hailed by European and (Latin) American observers alike (Ferrière 1925).

Looking outwards: towards a children's code of rights

While Uruguayan health leaders were facing this growing domestic conundrum, their international involvement took on new urgency, gradually paving the way for a rights-based approach to child health. In particular it was Uruguay's role in the Pan American child welfare movement that would initially prove pivotal in its development of an incipient notion of 'child rights'.

Starting in the late nineteenth century, Uruguay had one of the highest and most consistent participation rates in international demography, hygiene, and medical congresses in Europe and the Americas, also hosting its share (Anon. 1907; Consejo Nacional de Higiene Uruguay 1913; Bertillon 1900; Birn 2005). Uruguayan efforts and expertise also radiated outwards. Morquio was an elected member of Brazilian and Argentinean medical academies and was widely revered in Bolivia, Chile, Cuba, and elsewhere as the region's leading paediatric authority. Parisian physicians sponsored a Franco-Uruguayan medical fraternity (Duprat 1917), and Morquio was named officer of the Légion d'Honneur, member of the Académie Nationale de Médecine, and lectured throughout Europe.[17] Numerous Uruguayan paediatricians published frequently in leading European journals.

[16] Overseen by APN men but enabled by women volunteers, AUPI services were touted by Uruguayan politicians and even extolled by famed French paediatrician Jules Comby (1931, 18–19).

[17] In 1921, the twenty-fifth anniversary of Morquio's founding of Uruguayan paediatrics was celebrated in France, Italy, and throughout Latin America (see *Archives de Médecine des Enfants*, May 1921).

In 1916, a group of Latin American 'maternalist feminists' organized the first Pan American Child Congress in Buenos Aires, based on the belief that children's well-being was inseparable from the rights of women as mothers. The periodic congresses shaped a larger movement involving reformers, nurses, policy makers, sociologists, physicians, lawyers, and social workers from across the Americas, influencing legislation throughout the region aimed at improving the health and welfare of poor and working-class women and children (Guy 1998a; Netto Nunes 2008).

At the successful second Child Congress held in Montevideo in 1919, Morquio and his colleagues wrested control over the Latin American child welfare movement from its founding feminists (Guy 1998b). Morquio even upstaged Paulina Luisi (1875–1950), Uruguay's first woman doctor and its leading liberal feminist, who in 1916 had launched the Uruguayan National Women's Council, by deftly transforming an elite charity into an important movement for women's equality (Ehrick 1998; Sapriza 1988). At the 1919 congress, Morquio called for an American International Institute for the Protection of Childhood (IIPC) to be established in Montevideo, partially motivated by hopes that it could help Uruguay address its infant mortality problem.[18] In 1924 the proposal was sanctioned by the Uruguayan government and approved by the IVth Pan American Child Congress held later that year in Santiago. Morquio, Bauzá, and other public health elites returned to campaign for their government to pass enabling legislation. Among this group was Morquio's protégé, paediatrician Roberto Berro (1886–1956), who had succeeded Morquio in directing the country's most important child clinics, and, like his mentor, was a close student of French practices. But Berro had a special advantage in advancing the child health agenda: in 1917 he was elected representative to the national legislature and in 1925 became Senator, a position in which he served for most of the next few decades,[19] representing the conservative Blanco Party (a family tradition), while advocating for protectionist, and even redistributive, social policies (Instituto Internacional Americano de Protección a la Infancia 1956). Among his first acts as Senator, Berro presented and secured approval for a decree to found the IIPC (Instituto Internacional Americano de Protección a la Infancia 1925). But then things stalled for two years.

Ironically, it would be Morquio's rival, Luisi, who would facilitate the IIPC's eventual founding in 1927. After having been squeezed out of her leadership role in the Child Congresses, Luisi parlayed her prominence in feminist, scientific, and child welfare circles to become a Uruguayan delegate to the LN – the only woman

[18] Children's health and welfare had been discussed at international congresses since at least 1880 (Rollet 2001), but these efforts were not institutionalized until the 1920s. Two international associations for childhood protection were conceived in Brussels (in 1907 and 1913), but international rivalries meant they had difficulty surviving as permanent organizations and in-fighting continued until after the First World War (Marshall 1999; Rooke and Schnell 1995).

[19] In 1942 he became a Blanco Party candidate for president.

from Latin America to participate in the first LN Assembly. She became an expert member of the LN's advisory commission on 'white slavery', and representative to various treaty, disarmament, and labour conferences. For a decade she was one of only two Latin American delegates on the Child Welfare Committee (Anon. 1925; Scarone 1937) created in 1924 by a complicated constellation of national (Belgian, British, Swiss) and organizational (Save the Children International Union, International Committee of the Red Cross, and League of Red Cross Societies) interests (Marshall 1999).[20]

Luisi vocally advocated for increased Latin American presence in the League's work on children, including surveys of needs and policies, as well as greater representation in governing bodies (Miller 1995; Scarzanella 2003).[21] In 1925 she successfully argued for the yet-to-be established IIPC to have a seat on the Child Welfare Committee.[22] That same year the LN's Health Organization (LNHO),[23] directed by Polish hygienist Ludwik Rajchman, also turned its attention to children, pulling together experts from seven European countries (Austria, Britain, France, Germany, Italy, Netherlands, Norway) to study infant mortality through a uniform survey of urban and rural districts (Campbell 1929). As a way of engaging with Latin America, the LNHO invited several South American delegates to participate

[20] The committee was particularly shaped by the war relief agency 'Save the Children', founded in Britain by social reformer Eglantyne Jebb in 1919 (with an international counterpart, the Save the Children International Union (SCIU), launched in Geneva in 1920) (Marshall 1999). In 1922 Jebb, together with SCIU Secretary General Etienne Clouzot, drafted a Declaration of the Rights of the Child, adopted first by the SCIU and then by the League of Nations in 1924, becoming known as the Geneva Declaration (Veerman 1992). Jebb and colleagues' declaration drew from a variety of European and American child welfare and rights ideas (Mahood 2009), and it was inspired and supported by such luminaries as Janusz Korczak, Polish utopian paediatrician (and later Holocaust martyr). Korczak was perhaps the leading early advocate of child rights, predating the Geneva Declaration in his advocacy, and going beyond its 'plea for good will' to demand concrete rights in his own 1929 pronouncement 'The Child's Right to Respect' (Lifton 1988; Percy-Smith and Thomas 2010).

[21] Erik Ekstrand (1931), 'to Paulina Luisi' (Geneva: League of Nations Archives, Registry No. 11C/34573/322); Luisi, Paulina (1930), 'Memorandum' (Montevideo: Inter-American Children's Institute (hereafter, IIN) archives, Box No. 12-4, Folder C113.A5).

[22] Luisi, Paulina (1930), 'Memorandum' (Montevideo: IIN archives, Box No. 12-4, Folder C113.A5).

[23] The LNHO was permanently established in 1923 as the successor to a post-war Epidemic Commission to control outbreaks of typhus, cholera, smallpox, and other diseases in eastern and southern Europe. Under Rajchman's adept leadership, the LNHO's multinational staff and advisers pursued an ambitious agenda of epidemiologic surveillance, expert committees, and interchange of health personnel, as well as pioneering the collection, standardization, and dissemination of vital and health statistics from around the world, even organizing a Singapore office to this end in 1925. The LNHO oversaw standardization of drugs, vaccines, and biologics, and its health commissions studied everything from medical education and public health reorganization, to the causes and prevalence of chronic and infectious diseases, to housing and rural hygiene, drawing on social medicine precepts that called for the political and structural underpinnings of health to be addressed (Balinska 1995; Borowy 2009; Weindling 1995). Rajchman later helped establish UNICEF.

[24] Societé des Nations, Organisation d'Hygiène (1926), 'Rapport sur les Travaux de la Huitième Session du Comité d'Hygiène. C.585.1926.III' (Geneva).

in discussion of the European studies (Borowy 2009).[24] Pressured by enthusiasm to extend the survey to Latin America, the LN Assembly voted to support both a survey and an LNHO conference on infant mortality, which Rajchman and Morquio arranged to be held in Montevideo to coincide with the inauguration of the IIPC.[25]

This June 1927 'South American Conference on Infant Mortality' was the first LN conference of any kind to be held in Latin America.[26] Hosted by the President of Uruguay and attended by both Rajchman and the LNHO's president, Danish bacteriologist Thorvald Madsen, the conference brought international prestige to Uruguay and its child health experts.[27] The IIPC's official opening, which preceded the conference, also served as a domestic testing ground for rights-based child health policies.

In his speech inaugurating the IIPC, Uruguayan Minister of Education Enrique Rodríguez Fabregat invoked the social solidarity of the moment to propose a concrete set of children's rights to which the IIPC and its member countries should aspire: the right to life (including housing, maternal care, paternity, and state vigilance), education, nutrition, comprehensive economic assistance (via parents or the state), land, human development, social recognition, happiness, and integrated well-being. In the presence of the LN's Rajchman, the minister's 'Table of Children's Rights' went much further than the Geneva Declaration of Children's Rights, which had been penned by Save the Children founder Eglantyne Jebb and endorsed by the LN in 1924, and which was an exhortatory and generalized call to protect children in need and support childhood development. Minister Rodríguez Fabregat's array of rights, which included the right to parents and to 'obligatory paternal recognition' (Rodríguez Fabregat 1927, 1929), foreshadowed Uruguay's Children's Code and its further role in the international child rights movement. Morquio, the IIPC's new director, also made reference to the Geneva Declaration, but it was the minister's 'Table' that caught the imagination of delegates from Peru, Argentina, and beyond (Escardó y Anaya 1927).

Within a few months Gabriela Mistral, famed Chilean poet, educator, diplomat and LN intellectual property expert, echoed the minister's words in her own articulation of child rights, particularly emphasizing the South American child's 'right to be born under respectful legislation' that recognizes the full rights of children born out of wedlock (Mistral 1961); and in 1928 Cuba's First National

[25] Julián Nogueira (1926), 'to Rafael Schiaffino' (Geneva: League of Nations Archives, Box R998, Folder 62772).
[26] Thorvald Madsen (1927a), 'Report on the Work of the Conference of Health Experts on Infant Welfare held at Montevideo from June 7th to 11th, 1927' (vol. 1708; Geneva: League of Nations Archives, Assemblée 8, 1927, Decs. 39–133).
[27] Thorvald Madsen (1927a), 'Report on the Work of the Conference of Health Experts on Infant Welfare held at Montevideo from June 7th to 11th, 1927' (vol. 1708; Geneva: League of Nations Archives, Assemblée 8, 1927, Decs. 39–133).

Child Congress similarly declared children's rights to parents and to paternity and maternity investigation (Instituto Internacional Americano de Protección a la Infancia 1929). By contrast, the comprehensive 1930 United States (US) White House Children's Rights declaration omitted mention of identity rights.

Launched with the support and representation of Argentina, Bolivia, Brazil, Chile, Cuba, Ecuador, Peru, the United States, Uruguay, and Venezuela (by 1949 all Latin American countries), the IIPC served as a library, clearing-house, and policy, research, and advocacy organization that emphasized social approaches to infant, child, and maternal well-being around the world.[28] It sought to [Latin] 'Americanize' the study of childhood so that the region was understood as distinct and not just derivative or reflective of Europe (Birn 2006; Fournié 1934).

The IIPC's first major activity was to oversee the LNHO-funded infant mortality surveys in Argentina, Brazil, Chile, and Uruguay (Debré and Olsen 1930). The results, presented at the VIth Pan American Child Congress in Lima in 1930, called for improvements in vital statistics, centralization of services, and a range of public health, social assistance, economic, and educational measures to reduce infant mortality. In particular, the 'experts insist[ed] on the importance of statistics . . . birth registration should be accurate, secret burials should be prevented' (Debré and Olsen 1931; Morquio 1931; Scarzanella 2003, 604). Conference attendees pressed for a similar study in Peru, but Depression-era budget constraints precluded further LNHO funding. The LNHO continued to invite South American delegates, including founding director of Uruguay's APN, Dr José Scosería, who served in the 1930s (Turenne 1946). But ultimately Geneva had minimal involvement in Latin America and little sway over the IIPC. Still, deeply impressed with the IIPC's work, US and British delegates to the LN's Child Welfare Committee recommended a resolution – passed in May 1933 – paying 'homage to the IIPC, to its activities and its director, and to the influence exercised by Uruguay upon the orientation and progress of its work'.[29]

While its primary purview was the Americas, the IIPC quickly sealed an international reputation, garnering an energetic network of collaborators (Escardó

[28] Dr Gregorio Aráoz Alfaro of Argentina served as President of the International Board for the IIPC's first twenty-five years, with Uruguayan Víctor Escardó as Secretary. In addition to working with an international advisory board, the director, Morquio (later Berro), oversaw a small permanent staff who ran the Institute's library and archive, collected laws, statistics, and reports on child protection from member countries and beyond, sent information to correspondents around the world, and managed the publication of the IIPC's quarterly bulletin. In early years, each member country was represented by a Montevideo-based delegate. After 1936 the IIPC requested two representatives – one technical and based in the home country, the other resident in Montevideo, such as a diplomat. In early years, most operating funds were provided by the Uruguayan government, with intermittent support from other member states.

[29] Anonymous (1933), 'Report of the Advisory Commission for the Well-Being of Children and Youth', League of Nations Archives. Registry No. 8F/18921/321 (Geneva).

y Anaya 1952).[30] Its widely-disseminated trilingual (English, French, Spanish) quarterly *Boletín*, launched in 1927, covered a panorama of topics ranging from the organization of children's social services to summer camps, school health, sports, education, health campaigns, marginalized children, and the causes of infant and child mortality.[31] As one of the period's most international journals, the *Boletin,* through the 1940s, had an authorship that consisted of roughly 20 per cent Europeans or North Americans, and 35 per cent Uruguayans, with the remaining 45 per cent from elsewhere in Latin America. Readership was even more diverse, thanks to the IIPC's periodical exchange service. Some Uruguayan articles described child welfare systems in other countries, but for the most part Uruguayan authors used the *Boletín* to highlight domestic setbacks and promising solutions in infant, child, and maternal welfare.

The IIPC effectively navigated complex waters of autonomy and sponsorship. Initially it acted as a consulting agency to both the League of Nations and the Panamerican Union, and later, in 1949, it was integrated into the Organization of American States.[32] In 1930 Morquio was named President of the Save the Children International Union in Geneva, bringing the organizations closer together.[33] At the 1933 Congrès International pour la Protection de l'Enfance, held in Paris, Paul Strauss – French Senator, former Minister of Health, and author of key child protection reforms – cited Morquio in his inaugural address as an 'indefatigable prophet of maternal and infant protection' (Strauss 1933).

Morquio had patched up relations with Pan American (including North American) feminists (Guy 1998a),[34] and by the 1930s the IIPC operated in close conjunction (and sometimes competition) with the US Children's Bureau's International Cooperative Service. The US was the IIPC's most reliable dues-payer, and prominent Children's Bureau officials attended virtually all IIPC congresses and board meetings as the US delegates.[35]

The Pan American Sanitary Bureau (PASB, established in 1902), meanwhile, was not involved in the IIPC's founding, having eschewed child well-being

[30] Luis Morquio (1933), 'Instituto Internacional Americano de Protección a la Infancia, Organización y Actividades', League of Nations Archives, Registry No. 8F/18921/321 (Geneva).

[31] Interestingly, although the *Boletin* covered developments relating to Herbert Hoover's American Child Health Association and the SCIU's 1931 Conference on the African Child – and IIPC leaders were invited to the conference – (see Chapter 17), there was little direct IIPC contact with these efforts, which were seen as relevant, but not intertwined with the IIPC's mission.

[32] In 1957 the IIPC was renamed the Inter-American Children's Institute (IIN).

[33] W. A. MacKenzie and J. C. van Notten (1930), 'Correspondance avec le Dr Luis Morquio' (Geneva: Archives d'Etat de Genève), Archives privées 92.55.1; Amérique Latine: Uruguay. Dr Luis Morquio (1925–1937).

[34] Similar struggles between physicians and feminist social workers and reformers took place at the Children's Bureau, involving some of the same cast of characters (Guy 1998a).

[35] Most notably Katherine Lenroot until 1940 and then Elisabeth Enochs, who also served as IIPC President from 1955 to 1957.

concerns until its ninth conference in 1934 in Buenos Aires (held together with the Latin American Eugenics and Homiculture Congress) (Birn 2002). The PASB supported the position articulated by Berro, who backed 'positive' eugenics as embracing a 'broad, non-coercive public-health and social welfare approach directed toward the child', in contrast to the US's focus on the 'negative eugenics' of heredity and sterilization (Stepan 1991).

Rights, registration, and the resonance of the Uruguayan child welfare approach

The year 1934 marked a transition in Uruguay's role in the child welfare movement. Until this time, Uruguayan authorities had pursued an adopt-and-adapt approach to policy making and institution-building based on ideas developed elsewhere. Indeed, the IIPC gave Uruguayan authorities even greater access to experiences and policies from overseas.

Continued frustrations with Uruguay's infant mortality stagnation called for a more sweeping approach, and opportunity materialized with Gabriel Terra's March 1933 *coup d'état*. Among Terra's confidants was none other than Roberto Berro. Although Berro was a member of the nationalist Blanco Party, not President Terra's Colorado Party, Terra's conservative *putsch*, and the existing collaboration between the two, induced Berro to join Terra's junta. Berro moved immediately to put children's issues top of the agenda, manoeuvring to get the president to create a Ministry of Child Protection and a legislative commission to review child welfare legislation.

This early move on social policy served to appeal to Batllista, union, and even left-wing party constituencies, showing that despite the political rupture and pro-business economic policy, Uruguay's long-standing protectionist state would continue. In the pro-government newspaper *El Debate*, the Children's Code was heralded as 'Another triumphal step of the March revolution' and 'a magisterial consolidation' of children's rights 'in legal, health, pedagogical, psychiatric, and social spheres', that put Uruguay 'in the vanguard of civilized countries', surpassed only by Mussolini's national maternal and child health masterpiece and Britain's 1933 'Children and Young Persons Act' (Anon. 1934, 1).

Pro-government newspapers[36] commended Berro for his productive (nine-month) administration of the Ministry of Child Protection, during which he oversaw 'passage of the deepest and most transcendental legislation of the entire continent' (Anon. 1934, 1), and the Catholic press cited Berro's 'eminently Christian' legislation (Berro 1934). Berro himself emphasized that although

[36] Other newspapers were muzzled in this era.

Uruguay's Children's Code was predated by Brazil's (enacted in 1927) and Costa Rica's (1932), these were 'largely limited to juridical matters, without taking into account paediatric and sociological aspects of children's social context'.[37] In sum, according to Terra's allies, the Code was a hallmark of 'social prophylaxis carried out by a revolutionary government', affirming the 'right of the child to a home, to his health, to grow up without setbacks, to cultivate his spirit . . .' (Anon. 1934, 1).

Undoubtedly, the Code also revealed a profound state patriarchalism. Its emphasis on out-of-wedlock births as a cause of infant mortality and of broad social ills suggests that the Terra government was motivated by far more than bettering the social conditions of children and families. Its stipulation of the child's 'right to know who are his parents' was not only an enlightened abstraction but the context in which paternal abdication of responsibility was to be reprimanded. As such, this right belonged not just to the child but also to the state, with its power to know the identity of each man responsible for fathering a child. Just as it was repressive, this measure was also fiscally conservative, with state pursuit of fathers who abandoned their offspring also a means of reducing state expenditures. That this policy was passed under an authoritarian regime admiring of fascism (Nahum *et al.* 2007), yet was couched in the language of child rights, reveals both the political opportunism of the Terra regime and of Uruguayan child welfare reformers *and* the paradoxes of early twentieth-century child protectionism, which embraced different guises of eugenic policies in a range of settings (Bashford and Levine 2010).

If Terra's overall effect was to move the country from a cosmopolitan outlook to a nationalist one (Ruiz 2008), the child health arena deviated from this script. Remarkably, Terra came from Uruguay's traditional welfare state party – he was a Batllista, if one for times of crisis – bringing forward the social policies from previous decades (Filgueira 1995) under political conditions that went far beyond dealing with the economic crisis. Terra had partially justified his coup by a supposed need to fore-stall a Communist plot, and he sought to build its legitimacy by returning to the institutional approaches of his predecessors. In employing a rights approach to child well-being, Berro and the Terra administration also appealed to the values and ties shared among Uruguayan child health experts and their counterparts abroad, manifest in the IIPC, the LNHO, and other international players.

The intertwining of national and international platforms was evident in the relationship between Uruguay's Children's Council and the IIPC. The Code granted the Council the ability to propose a shortlist of candidates to serve as Uruguay's representative to the IIPC, ensuring 'an intimate connection' between the two entities (Instituto Internacional Americano de Protección a la Infancia 1934a, 45). The Council was headed by a succession of paediatricians, including Berro (1934–1943) and Bauzá (1943–1949). After Morquio's death in 1935, Berro

[37] República Oriental del Uruguay, Comisión Legislative Permanente (1934), 'Debate Código del Niño', *Poder Legislativo*, 3 April (8303), 13.

became director of the IIPC until his death in 1956 (held simultaneously with his Children's Council role for almost a decade).

Within a decade, throughout the dictatorship and after Uruguay's return to democracy in 1942, the Council extensively implemented the policies Morquio, Bauzá, and others had advocated and campaigned for, including prevention of child abandonment through more generous maternal subsidies and maternity leave, special services for premature infants, and expanded funding for milk stations. Under the Code's family unification policies, families were supported to maintain or regain their offspring, thus leading the number of foster children to plummet from 1,000 per year *circa* 1934 to 150 per year in 1938–1939 (Berro 1939). In 1943 – after Bauzá had headed infant protection services for over two decades – he could finally enjoy the satisfaction of being able to claim a role for them 'in beginning to influence a reduction in mortality' which was occurring by that point (Bauzá 1943).

The Children's Code and work of the Council quickly generated international responses. Uruguay's profile rose ever higher throughout Latin America, as well as in the United States, Belgium, Italy, Spain, and beyond (Instituto Internacional Americano de Protección a la Infancia 1934b). The LN re-endorsed the 'Geneva Declaration' shortly after Uruguay's Code was passed, suggesting that the LN wanted to re-assert its leadership in this arena.

Nowhere were the accolades higher than in France, the very country from which so much of Uruguay's child health approach derived. In 1934 leading French Assistance Publique physician Julien Huber wrote admiringly of Uruguay's child protection efforts in France's *Revue Médico-Sociale de l'Enfance*. He apologized for the lengthy article, which he justified by Uruguay's 'unique' achievements (Huber 1934, 206). In 1936 the International Association of Preventive Pediatrics issued a detailed summary of Roberto Berro's argument about childhood social medicine (International Association of Preventive Pediatrics 1936), and in 1937 a Franco-Latin medical journal outlined Uruguay's foster home programme for 'young delinquents', asking, 'Might it be possible for us [France] to obtain similar results with analogous methods? Assuredly no' (Union Médicale Latine 1937).

The fascist connections of Uruguay's Children's Code also persisted. At the 13th International Congress of Childhood Protection held in Frankfurt in June 1938, Ricardo Jalabert, Examining Judge for Minors in Montevideo, was an invited keynote speaker on the question 'When should legislative measures or public institutions make up for the lack of parental care?' – based on Uruguay's Children's Code and 'the final radical transformation' of the protection and vigilance of child health and welfare.[38] Although many paediatricians boycotted the meeting, two other Uruguayans presented papers discussing the country's child rights agenda.

[38] Ricardo Jalabert (1938), 'When Should Legislative Measures or Public Institutions Make up for the Lack of Parental Care?' XIII Jahrestagung der Association Internationale de Protection de l'Enfance (Frankfurt (Main): Registry No. 8F/18921/321. League of Nations Archives, Geneva).

Uruguay's legacy of child rights and civil registration

Into the 1940s, and as Uruguay's own child health statistics improved, its experience became ever more widely recognized and discussed. After the Children's Code was passed, the IIPC's *Boletín* had started a special section on children's codes, children's rights, illegitimacy, and related legislation and policy making. These policies and practices, cross-fertilized through the Child Congresses and the *Boletín*, rapidly proliferated through the Americas, via national child conferences and a designated day (or week) of the child, and through concrete, often rights-oriented, legislation. By 1945 most of the region's republics, including Argentina, Bolivia, Brazil, Chile, Colombia, Costa Rica, Cuba, Ecuador, Mexico, Nicaragua, Paraguay, and Venezuela, had specific bureaus or agencies dedicated to maternal and child health protection (Aráoz Alfaro *et al.* 1944).

After the Second World War, the international child health field became firmly institutionalized at the World Health Organization and UNICEF. The IIPC's and Uruguay's international moment was eclipsed by donor-driven international development strategies and Cold War exigencies that (at least rhetorically) prioritized political rights over social rights (Birn 2008b). Yet even as the IIPC was lamented for being little known (Enochs 1947), it had one more card to play before becoming a technical arm of the Organization of American States.[39] In January 1948, at the Child Congress held in Caracas, Venezuela, the IIPC shepherded passage of a Pan American Children's Code, and the Declaration of Caracas (a children's health rights addendum jointly crafted by the IIPC, PASB, and US Children's Bureau). The Pan American Children's Code, avowedly adaptable to multiple contexts, expanded on Uruguay's 1927 'Table of Children's Rights', explicitly laying out the right to care, to education, and to be free from exploitation or mistreatment in the workplace, home or judicial system. The Code was anchored in the right to know parental identity, enshrined in Uruguayan law since 1934, offering yet another step in the genesis of the right to identity registration incorporated in the UN's 1959 Declaration of the Rights of the Child (Darbó 1980).[40]

[39] The IIN ceded much of its role regarding child health to WHO/PASB and UNICEF, and child rights became a major focus. From the 1960s to the 1980s one of the IIN's principal activities was improving the quality and comprehensiveness of civil registries in Latin America.

[40] Although tracing a Uruguayan genealogy of the emergence of a UN 'Right to Identity' is beyond the scope of this chapter, a few clues suggest considerable influence. In the 1930s and 1940s, Uruguay was the acknowledged regional Latin American leader (as well as a key international influence) in the development of children's rights. Almost certainly the Chilean jurist and professor, Hernán Santa Cruz, who penned an early draft of the UN Declaration of Human Rights – and who pushed forcefully for the 'indivisibility of rights', that is, the need for *both* political and civil rights *and* economic, social and cultural rights – would have been familiar with Uruguay's Children's Code, which was emulated by Chile. In addition to the large Latin American voting bloc at the 1945 San Francisco meeting that prepared the UN charter and ensured that economic, social, and human rights would be covered, Latin

In sum, Uruguay's child rights approach to health, underpinned by civil registration, the monitoring of infant mortality, welfare state building, and involvement in international child well-being debates, was consistent with 'state-sponsored paternalism', that is, combining protection and obedience via class-based and gendered stratification (Ehrick 2005b), eugenic concerns, and progressive, sometime-feminist, redistributive politics that both predated and endured long past the dictatorship under which child rights were initially codified. Still, the emergence of a child's right to paternity knowledge under a peripheral authoritarian state, bent on addressing illegitimacy to lower infant mortality *and* control wayward fathers, is a jarring reminder of the complex and contradictory origins of the right to identity registration.

References

Administración Sanitaria de la República Oriental del Uruguay. 1896. *Memoria del Consejo Nacional de Higiene y sus dependencias*. Montevideo: Tip. de la Escuela Nacional de Artes y Oficios.

Agostoni, Claudia, Andrés Ríos Molina and Gabriela Villareal Levy. 2010. *Las estadísticas de salud en México: ideas, actores e instituciones, 1810–2010*. México, DF: Universidad Nacional Autónoma de México; Instituto de Investigaciones Históricas/Dirección General de Información en Salud, Secretaría de Salud.

Alonso Criado, Matías. 1880. *Apéndice II a la colección legislativa de la República Oriental del Uruguay*. Montevideo: Ediciones de la Imprenta Rural.

Andrews, George Reid. 2010. *Blackness in the White Nation: A History of Afro-Uruguay*. Chapel Hill: University of North Carolina Press.

Anon. 1907. *Catálogo de la Exposición Internacional de Higiene. Enero-Abril de 1907*. Montevideo: Talleres Gráficos A. Barreiro y Ramos.

Anon. 1925. 'Homenaje a Paulina Luisi.' *Acción Femenina: Revista Mensual del Consejo Nacional de Mujeres del Uruguay* 2(51).

Anon. 1926. 'Reglamento para el funcionamiento de Asilo de Niños de la ciudad de Salto.' *Boletín de la Asistencia Pública Nacional* 16(147): 50–56.

Anon. 1934. 'Un nuevo paso triunfal para la revolución de marzo.' *El Debate*, 4 April.

Anuario Estadístico del Uruguay. 1911. *Censo General de la República en 1908*, 2. Montevideo: Imprenta Juan Dornaleche.

Aráoz Alfaro, Gregorio *et al*. 1944. 'Organización Integral de la Protección a la Infancia.' *Boletín del Instituto Internacional Americano de Protección a la Infancia* 18(3): 345–383.

American countries, including Uruguay, had considerable engagement with the drafting of various UN human rights instruments (Morsink 1999; Waltz 2001; Wright-Carozza 2003). Latin American and Uruguayan participation in the drafting of the 1989 Convention on the Rights of the Child is also evident (Office of the United Nations High Commissioner for Human Rights 2007). As discussed in note 39, improving civil registry coverage for children was a top priority of the IIN, starting in the 1960s, a focus which likely influenced UNICEF's subsequent involvement in this issue.

Armstrong, David. 1986. 'The Invention of Infant Mortality.' *Sociology of Health and Illness* 8(3): 211–232.

Asociación de Ingenieros del Uruguay. 1949. *Síntesis histórica de la Ingeniería en el Uruguay*. Montevideo.

Asociación Uruguaya de Protección a la Infancia. 1931a. 'Asociación Uruguaya de Protección a la Infancia: Autoridades.' *Asociación Uruguaya de Protección a la Infancia Boletín Trimestral* 1(22): 1–2.

—— 1931b. 'Resumen de la memoria del año 1930.' *Asociación Uruguaya de Protección a la Infancia Boletín Trimestral* 1(22): 6–7.

Balinska, Marta. 1995. *Une vie pour l'humanitaire: Ludwik Rajchman (1881–1965)*. Paris: Editions la Découverte.

Barrán, José Pedro. 1994. *Apogeo y crisis del Uruguay pastoril y caudillesco: 1839 – 1875*, vol. 4. Historia Uruguaya. Montevideo: Ediciones de la Banda Oriental.

—— 2004. *Los conservadores Uruguayos, 1870–1993*. Montevideo: Ediciones de la Banda Oriental.

Barrán, José Pedro and Benjamín Nahum. 1983. *Las Primeras reformas, 1911–1913*. Batlle, los estancieros y el imperio británico 4. Montevideo: Ediciones de la Banda Oriental.

—— 1985. *Crisis y radicalización, 1913–1916*. Batlle, los estancieros y el imperio británico 6. Montevideo: Ediciones de la Banda Oriental.

Bashford, Alison and Philippa Levine, eds. 2010. *The Oxford Handbook of the History of Eugenics*. Oxford: Oxford University Press.

Bauzá, Julio A. 1913. 'Mortalidad infantil en la República del Uruguay en el decenio 1901–1910.' *Revista Médica del Uruguay* 16(2): 45–81.

—— 1920. 'La mortalidad infantil en el Uruguay. Sus causas y su profilaxis.' *Boletín del Consejo Nacional de Higiene* 15(161): 167–237.

—— 1923. 'El Servicio de Protección a la Primera Infancia y la Oficina de Nodrizas en 1921.' *Archivos Latino-Americanos de Pediatría* 17(2): 96–118.

—— 1924. 'La situación del niño ilegítimo (trabajo presentado al III Congreso Científico Panamericano, Lima, 1924.' *Boletín del Consejo Nacional de Higiene* 19(218): 821–829.

—— 1929. 'La protección a la primera infancia en Montevideo.' *Boletín del Instituto Internacional Americano de Protección a la Infancia* 2(4): 423–444.

—— 1933. 'La protection à la première enfance dans l'Uruguay en l'année 1932.' *Boletín del Instituto Internacional Americano de Protección a la Infancia* 7(1): 27–47.

—— 1942. *La división primera infancia del Consejo del Niño en los años 1940 y 1941*. Montevideo: Mosca Hnos.

—— 1943. 'Acción futura del Consejo del Niño.' *Boletín del Instituto Internacional Americano de Protección a la Infancia* 17(2): 291–300.

—— 1947. *Síntesis de la gestión desarrollada desde el Consejo del Niño en el período 1943–1946*. Montevideo: Ed. Médica García Morales.

Becerro de Bengoa, Miguel. 1922. *Los problemas de la Asistencia Püblica; Informe presentado a la seccional de Asistencia Pública del Segundo Congreso Médico Nacional*. Trabajos de las secciones de Higiene y profilaxis sexual, Pediatría, Asistencia Pública, Medicina veterinaria, y Farmacia 2. Montevideo: Impr. 'El Siglo Ilustrado' de G.V. Mariño.

Berro, Roberto. 1934. 'Sobre el Código del Niño.' *El Bien Público*, 26 April.

—— 1939. 'Organización y resultados de los servicios de protección a la infancia en el Uruguay. VIII Congreso Panamericano del Niño.' *Boletín del Instituto Internacional Americano de Protección a la Infancia* 13(2): 347–377.

—— 1943. 'Proyecto y exposición de motivos del Señor Senador Doctor Roberto Berro sobre Caja de Maternidad y Asignaciones Familiares, presentado al Senado del Uruguay.' *Boletín del Instituto Internacional Americano de Protección a la Infancia* 17(3): 484–493.

—— 1944a. *Las asignaciones familiares en la protección a la infancia*. Montevideo: Ediciones Ceibo.

—— 1944b. 'Algunos aspectos de la seguridad social de la infancia en la postguerra.' *Boletín del Instituto Internacional Americano de Protección a la Infancia* 18(2): 196–203.

Bertillon, Jacques. 1900. 'Nomenclature des maladies (Statistiques de morbidité-statistiques des causes de décès).' In *Commission internationale chargée de reviser les nomenclatures nosologiques*. Paris/Montévrain: Imprimerie Typographique de l'Ecole d'Alembert.

Birn, Anne-Emanuelle. 2002. '"No More Surprising Than a Broken Pitcher"? Maternal and Child Health in the Early Years of the Pan American Sanitary Bureau.' *Canadian Bulletin of Medical History/Bulletin canadien d'histoire de la médecine* 19(1): 17–46.

—— 2005. 'Uruguay on the World Stage: How Child Health Became an International Priority.' *American Journal of Public Health* 95(9): 1506–1517.

—— 2006. 'The National-International Nexus in Public Health: Uruguay and the Circulation of Child Health and Welfare Policies, 1890–1940.' *História, Ciências, Saúde-Manguinhos* 13(3): 675–708.

—— 2008a. 'Doctors on Record: Uruguay's Infant Mortality Stagnation and Its Remedies, 1895–1945.' *Bulletin of the History of Medicine* 82(2): 311–354.

—— 2008b. 'Health and Human Rights: Historical Perspectives and Political Challenges.' *Journal of Public Health Policy* 29: 32–41.

Birn, Anne-Emanuelle, Wanda Cabella and Raquel Pollero. 2010. 'The Infant Mortality Conundrum in Uruguay During the First Half of the Twentieth Century: An Analysis According to Causes of Death.' *Continuity and Change* 25(3): 435–461.

Birn, Anne-Emanuelle, Raquel Pollero and Wanda Cabella. 2003. 'No se debe llorar sobre leche derramada: El pensamiento epidemiológico y la mortalidad infantil en Uruguay, 1900–1940.' *Estudios Interdisciplinarios de América Latina* 14(1): 35–65.

Borowy, Iris. 2009. *Coming to Terms with World Health: The League of Nations Health Organisation 1921–1946*. Frankfurt: Peter Lang.

Cabella, Wanda. 1998. 'La evolución del divorcio en Uruguay (1950–1995).' *Notas de Población* 26(67/68).

Caetano, Gerardo and Roger Geymonat. 1997. *La secularización uruguaya (1859–1919): Catolicismo y privatización de lo religioso*. Montevideo: Taurus.

Caetano, Gerardo and Raúl Jacob. 1989. *El nacimiento del terrismo (1930–1933)*. Montevideo: Ediciones de la Banda Oriental.

Campbell, Dame Janet Mary. 1929. *Infant Mortality; International Inquiry of the Health Organisation of the League of Nations, English Section. With Statistical Notes by Peter L. McKinlay*. London: HMSO.

Canabal, Joaquín. 1899. *Consejo Nacional de Higiene. Estadística sanitaria del Uruguay, 1887–1896, por Joaquín Canabal*. Montevideo: Tip. de la Escuela Nacional de Artes y Oficios.

Caroli, Dorena 2003. 'Bolshevism, Stalinism, and Social Welfare (1917–1936).' *International Review of Social History* 48(1): 27–54.

Casaravilla Estrada, Rodolfo. 1938. *El nuevo derecho de los hijos naturales: Parte final de un alegato de bien probado presentado ante el Juzgado Letrado de Menores*. Montevideo: Claudio García & Cía.

Castellanos, Alfredo Raúl. 1971. *Historia del desarrollo edilicio y urbanístico de Montevideo (1829–1914)*. Montevideo: Junta Departamental de Montevideo, Biblioteca José Artigas.

Cincinatti Bollo, Luis. 1894. *Manual práctico del Registro del Estado Civil: Dedicado a la Administración Pública*. Montevideo: Librería Nacional de A. Barreiro y Ramos.

Comby, Jules. 1931. 'Un interesante juicio sobre la A.U.P.I.' *Asociación Uruguaya de Protección a la Infancia Boletín Trimestral* 6(22): 18–19.

Comité Uruguayen. 1933. *Protection de l'Enfance à l'Uruguay*. Montevideo: Dornaleche Frères.

Consejo del Niño, Uruguay. 1936. *Consejo del Niño, su organización y funcionamiento, 1934–1946*. Montevideo: Imprenta de A. Monteverde & Cía.

—— 1950. *Guía informativa de las funciones que desarrolla el Consejo del Niño*. Montevideo.

Consejo Nacional de Higiene. 1918. 'Circulares Nros 267 y 268, dirigidas a los señores médicos, relativas al cumplimiento de las disposiciones vigentes sobre la declaración obligatoria de las enfermedades infecto-contagiosas, y expedición de certificados de defunción.' *Boletín del Consejo Nacional de Higiene* 13(138): 179–180.

Consejo Nacional de Higiene Uruguay. 1913. 'El Uruguay en el V Congreso Médico Latino-Americano (VI Pan-Americano) y Exposición Internacional de Higiene anexa. Lima, Noviembre de 1915.' *Boletín del Consejo Nacional de Higiene* 8(84): 515–524.

Corsini, Carlo A. and Pier Paolo Viazzo, eds. 1997. *The Decline of Infant and Child Mortality: The European Experience, 1750–1990*. Cambridge, MA: Kluwer Law International.

Damonte, Ana María. 1994. *Uruguay: Transición de la mortalidad en el período 1908–1963*. Serie Documentos de Trabajo. No. 16. Montevideo: Programa de Población, Facultad de Ciencias Sociales.

Darbó, Adolfo Gaete. 1980. 'El nombre de los hijos ilegítimos en la Declaración de los Derechos del Niño y la legislación latinoamericana.' *Colaboraciones, Boletín del Instituto Interamericano del Niño* 214–215: 171–175.

Davis, Kingsley, I. B. Taeuber, A. Arca-Parró, G. W. Roberts, F. E. Linder and L. J. Reed. 1964. 'The Place of Latin America in World Demographic History.' *The Milbank Memorial Fund Quarterly* 42(2, Pt 2): 19–53.

Debré, Robert and Otto E. W. Olsen. 1930. *Enquiries into Infant Mortality in South America*. Geneva: League of Nations, Health Organisation.

—— 1931. 'Société des Nations. Organisation d'hygiène. Les enquêtes entreprises en Amérique du Sud sur la mortalité infantile.' *Boletín del Instituto Internacional Americano de Protección a la Infancia* 4(3): 581–605.

Di Liscia, María Silvia. 2005. 'Colonias y escuelas de niños débiles: Los instrumentos higiénicos para la eugenesia en la primera mitad del siglo XX en Argentina.' In *Instituciones y formas de control social en América Latina, 1840–1940: Una Revisión*, ed. Jonathan Ablard, María Silvia Di Liscia and Ernesto Lázaro Bohoslavsky. Buenos Aires: Prometeo Libros, 93–113.

Dirección de Estadística General. 1885. *Anuario estadístico de la República Oriental del Uruguay. Año 1884. Libro I del Anuario y XV de las Publicaciones de esta Dirección.* Montevideo: Tipografía Oriental.

Duprat, Pedro Ernesto. 1917. 'Francia-Uruguay: Los médicos uruguayos en París.' *Revista Médica del Uruguay* 20(11): lxv–lxvi.

Ehrick, Christine. 1998. 'Madrinas and Missionaries: Uruguay and the Pan-American Women's Movement.' *Gender and History* 10(3): 406–424.

—— 2005a. *The Shield of the Weak: Feminism and the State in Uruguay, 1903–1933.* Albuquerque: University of New Mexico Press.

—— 2005b. 'To Serve the Nation: Juvenile Mothers, Paternalism, and State Formation in Uruguay, 1910–1930.' *Social Science History* 29(3): 489–518.

Engerman, Stanley L., Stephen H. Haber and Kenneth L. Sokoloff. 2000. 'Inequality, Institutions, and Differential Paths of Growth Among New World Economies.' In *Institutions, Contracts, and Organizations: Perspectives from New Institutional Economics*, ed. Claude Ménard. Cheltenham: Edward Elgar.

Enochs, Elisabeth Randolph Shirley. 1947. *American International Institute for the Protection of Childhood.* Department of State Bulletin. Washington, DC: US Government Printing Office.

Escardó y Anaya, Victor. 1927. 'Instituto Internacional Americano de Protección a la Infancia – Su inauguración.' *Boletín del Instituto Internacional Americano de Protección a la Infancia* 1(1): 29–66.

—— 1952. 'Veinticinco años del Consejo Directivo y de la Dirección General.' *Boletín del Instituto Internacional Americano de Protección a la Infancia* 26(2): 91–105.

Faijer, Dirk Jaspers and Hernán Orellana. 1996. 'Evaluation of Vital Statistics for the Study of Causes of Death.' In *Adult Mortality in Latin America*, ed. Ian Timaeus, Juan Chackiel and Lado Theodor Ruzicka. Oxford: Clarendon Press, 45–68.

Ferrière, Suzanne. 1925. 'Les oeuvres de protection de l'enfance en Amérique du Sud.' *Revue Internationale de la Croix-Rouge et Bulletin International des Sociétés de la Croix-Rouge* 7(79): 453–505.

Fildes, Valerie A., Lara Marks and Hilary Marland. 1992. *Women and Children First: International Maternal and Infant Welfare, 1870–1945.* London: Routledge.

Filgueira, Fernando. 1995. *A Century of Social Welfare in Uruguay: Growth to the Limit of the Batllista Social State.* Democracy and Social Policy Series. Working Paper 5. Kellogg Institute.

Finch, Martin Henry John. 1982. *A Political Economy of Uruguay since 1870.* New York: St Martin's Press.

Fournié, Emilio. 1934. 'Séptima Conferencia Internacional Americana. Capítulo V. Problemas sociales.' *Boletín del Instituto Internacional Americano de Protección a la Infancia* 7(3): 229–249.

Goyena, Pablo V. 1900. *Código del Estado Civil.* Montevideo: Tipografíia y Litografía Oriental.

Guy, Donna J. 1998a. 'The Pan American Child Congresses, 1916 to 1942: Pan Americanism, Child Reform, and the Welfare State in Latin America.' *Journal of Family History* 23(3): 272–291.

—— 1998b. 'The Politics of Pan-American Cooperation: Maternalist Feminism and the Child Rights Movement, 1913–1960.' *Gender and History* 10(3): 449–469.

Hakkert, Ralph. 1996. *Fontes de dados demográficos*. Belo Horizonte: Associação Brasileira de Estudos Populacionais.

Huber, Julien. 1934. 'Protection de l'enfance en Uruguay.' *Revue Médico-Sociale de l'Enfance* 2(3): 206–213.

Instituto Internacional Americano de Protección a la Infancia. 1925. *Antecedentes, publicados por la Comisión Honoraria*. Montevideo.

—— 1929. 'Primer Congreso Nacional del Niño: Habana, Diciembre 31 de 1928.' *Boletín del Instituto Internacional Americano de Protección a la Infancia* 3(2): 332–334.

—— 1934a. 'Código del Niño.' *Boletín del Instituto Internacional Americano de Protección a la Infancia* 8(1): 3–104.

—— 1934b. 'Código del Niño del Uruguay. Juicios del extranjero.' *Boletín del Instituto Internacional Americano de Protección a la Infancia* 8(4): 479–485.

—— 1956. *Roberto Berro (1886–1956)*. Montevideo: Impresora L.I.G.U.

International Association of Preventive Pediatrics. 1936. *Bulletin Trimestriel* III.

Jones, Margaret. 2002. 'Infant and Maternal Health Services in Ceylon, 1900–1948: Imperialism or Welfare?' *Social History of Medicine* 15(2): 263–290.

Klaus, Alisa. 1993. *Every Child a Lion: The Origins of Maternal and Infant Health Policy in the United States and France, 1890–1920*. Ithaca, NY: Cornell University Press.

Koven, Seth and Sonya Michel, eds. 1993. *Mothers of a New World: Maternalist Politics and the Origins of Welfare States*. New York: Routledge.

Legnani, Mateo. 1914. *Apuntes y reflexiones sobre el curanderismo*. Montevideo: Imprenta Artistica.

Lifton, Betty Jean. 1988. *The King of Children: A Biography of Janusz Korczak*. New York: Farrar, Straus and Giroux.

López-Alves, Fernando. 2000. *State Formation and Democracy in Latin America, 1810–1900*. Durham, NC: Duke University Press.

Loveman, Mara. 2007. '"Blinded Like a State": The Revolt against Civil Registration in Nineteenth-Century Brazil.' *Comparative Studies in Society and History* 49(1): 5–39.

Macchi, Manuel E. 1972. *Registros civiles precursores en Argentina: Buenos Aires 1833; Santa Fe 1867; Colón, Entre Ríos 1873*. Santa Fe: Editorial Castellvi.

Mahood, Linda. 2009. *Feminism and Voluntary Action: Eglantyne Jebb and Save the Children, 1876–1928*. Basingstoke: Palgrave Macmillan.

Manderson, Lenore. 2002. *Sickness and the State: Health and Illness in Colonial Malaya, 1870–1940*. Cambridge: Cambridge University Press.

Marko, Tamera. 2006. 'When They Became the Nation's Children: The Raced, Classed, and Gendered Politics of the Foundation of Pediatrics in Rio de Janeiro, Brazil, 1881–1943.' Ph.D. dissertation, University of California, San Diego.

Marshall, Dominique. 1999. 'Construction of Children as an Object of International Relations: The Declaration of Children's Rights and the Child Welfare Committee of the League of Nations, 1900–1924.' *International Journal of Children's Rights* 7: 103–147.

Martirené, José and Carlos M. Gurméndez. 1926. 'Reglamento de visitadoras sociales.' *Boletín de la Asistencia Pública Nacional* 16(150): 580–581.

McGuire, James W. and Laura B. Frankel. 2005. 'Mortality Decline in Cuba, 1900–1959: Patterns, Comparisons, and Causes.' *Latin American Research Review* 40(2): 83–116.

Migliónico, Americo. 2001. *La mortalidad en Uruguay en el siglo XX: cambios, impacto, perspectivas*. Montevideo: Ministerio de Salud Pública – Organización Panamericana de la Salud.

Milanich, Nara B. 2009. *Children of Fate: Childhood, Class, and the State in Chile, 1850–1930*. Durham, NC: Duke University Press.

Miller, Carol. 1995. 'The Social Section and Advisory Committee on Social Questions of the League of Nations.' In *International Health Organisations and Movements, 1918–1939*, ed. Paul Weindling. Cambridge: Cambridge University Press, 154–175.

Mistral, Gabriela. 1961. 'Los derechos del niño, Paris, 1927.' *Boletín del Instituto Internacional Americano de Protección a la Infancia* 35(2): 122–124.

Morquio, Luis. 1900. 'Cuatro años del Servicio Externo del Asilo de Expósitos y Huérfanos (conclusión).' *Revista Médica del Uruguay* 3(8): 201–219.

—— 1905. 'Sobre organización de expósitos.' *Revista Médica del Uruguay* 8(5): 87–99.

—— 1906. 'La pediatría moderna en sus relaciones con la vida profesional (lección de fin de curso).' *Revista Médica del Uruguay* 9(11): 309–342.

—— 1907a. 'La pediatría en París.' *Archivos Latino-Americanos de Pediatría* 3(8): 260–280.

—— 1907b. 'La Cuna del Asilo de Expósitos y Huérfanos. Movimiento de los años 1905 y 1906.' *Revista Médica del Uruguay* 10(1): 1–27.

—— 1911. 'Memoria del Asilo Dámaso Larrañaga correspondiente al año 1911.' *Boletín de la Asistencia Pública Nacional* 1(3): 486–513.

—— 1927. 'La mortalidad infantil en el Uruguay.' *Boletín de la Asistencia Pública Nacional* 22(247): 234–280.

—— 1931. 'Société des Nations. Organisation d'hygiène. Conférence d'experts hygiénistes en matière de protection de la première enfance.' *Boletín de la Asistencia Pública Nacional* 4(3): 535–580.

Morsink, Johannes. 1999. *The Universal Declaration of Human Rights: Origins, Drafting, and Intent*. Philadelphia: University of Pennsylvania Press.

Mortara, Giorgio, P. K. Whelpton, J. V. Grauman, H. Behm, T. H. Montenegro, C. A. Miró, D. Kirk and Kingsley Davis. 1964. 'Appraisal of Census Data for Latin America.' *The Milbank Memorial Fund Quarterly* 42(2): 57–85.

Nahum, Benjamín. 1994. *La epoca Batllista 1905–1929*. Historia Uruguaya 6. Montevideo: Ediciones de la Banda Oriental.

Nahum, Benjamín *et al.* 2007. *Crisis Política y Recuperación Económica 1930–1958*. Historia Uruguaya 7. Montevideo: Ediciones de la Banda Oriental.

Netto Nunes, Eduardo Silveira. 2008. *Os primeiros Congresos Panamericanos del Niño (1916, 1919, 1922, 1924) ea participação do Brasil*. São Paulo: ANPUH/SP – USP.

Oddone, Juan Antonio. 1990. *Uruguay entre la depresión y la guerra, 1929–1945*. Montevideo: Fundación de Cultura Universitaria.

Office of the United Nations High Commissioner for Human Rights. 2007. *Legislative History of the Convention on the Rights of the Child: Volume I*. New York: United Nations.

Oszlak, Oscar. 1997. *La formación del estado Argentino: Orden, progreso y organización nacional*. Buenos Aires: Planeta.

Pan American Sanitary Bureau. 1948. 'Puericultura.' *Boletín de la Oficina Sanitaria Panamericana* 27(8): 557–558.

Panizza, Francisco. 1997. 'Late Institutionalisation and Early Modernisation: The Emergence of Uruguay's Liberal Democratic Political Order.' *Journal of Latin American Studies* 29(3): 667–691.

Pellegrino, Adela. 1997. *Caracterización demográfica del Uruguay*. Serie Documentos de Trabajo. Documento de Trabajo No. 35. Montevideo: Unidad Multidisciplinaria, Programa de Población, Facultad de Ciencias Sociales, Universidad de la República.

—— 2010. *La población de Uruguay: Breve caracterización demográfica*. Montevideo: UNFPA. www.unfpa.org.uy/userfiles/informacion/items/914_pdf.pdf.

Pellegrino, Adela and Raquel Pollero. 2000. 'Fecundidad y situación conyugal en el Uruguay. Un análisis retrospectivo. 1889–1975.' In *Cambios demográficos en América Latina: La experiencia de cinco siglos*, ed. Dora Celton, Carmen Miró and Nicholás Sánchez-Albornoz. Córdoba: International Union for the Scientific Study of Population – Universidad Nacional de Córdoba, 229–249.

Pelúas, Daniel. 2001. *José Batlle y Ordóñez: El hombre*. Montevideo: Editorial Fin de Siglo.

Percy-Smith, Barry and Nigel Thomas. 2010. *A Handbook of Children and Young People's Participation: Perspectives from Theory and Practice*. London: Routledge.

Pereira, Juan José and Raúl Trajtenberg. 1966. *Evolución de la población total y activa en el Uruguay, 1908–1957*. Publicaciones, Universidad de la República (Uruguay). Instituto de Economía 26. Montevideo: Facultad de Ciencias Ecónomicas.

Pinard, A. 1917. 'La mortalidad infantil en Francia.' *La Tuberculosis. Organo de la Liga contra la Tuberculosis en el Uruguay* 15(1–3): 11–12.

Reis, João José. 1997. 'O cotidiano da morte no Brasil oitocentista.' In *História da vida privada no Brasil*, ed. Laura de Mello e Souza, Luis Felipe de Alencastro and Nicolau Sevcenko. São Paulo: Companhia das Letras, II: 96–141.

República Oriental del Uruguay. Poder Legislativo. 1910. 'Ley sobre Asistencia Pública Nacional.' *Boletín del Consejo Nacional de Higiene* 5: 509–514.

República Oriental del Uruguay. Registro Nacional de Leyes. 1911. *Decretos y otros documentos publicados por el Ministerio del Interior*. Montevideo: Diario Oficial.

República Oriental del Uruguay. Dirección General del Registro del Estado Civil. 1892; 1907. *Manual teórico práctico del oficial del Estado Civil*. Montevideo: Talleres A. Barreiro y Ramos.

Rial, Juan. 1983. *Población y desarrollo de un pequeño país: Uruguay, 1830–1930*. Montevideo: Centro de Informaciones y Estudios del Uruguay.

Rock, David and Fernando López-Alves. 2000. 'State-Building and Political Systems in Nineteenth-Century Argentina and Uruguay.' *Past and Present* 1(167): 176–202.

Rodríguez Ayçaguer, Ana María. 2008. 'La república del compromiso, 1919–1933.' In *Historia del Uruguay en el siglo XX (1890–2005)*, ed. Ana Frega. Montevideo: Ediciones de la Banda Oriental, 51–84.

Rodríguez Fabregat, Enrique. 1927. 'Discurso del señor Ministro de Instrucción Pública don Enrique Rodríguez Fabregat y Declaración de los Derechos del Niño.' *Boletín del Instituto Internacional Americano de Protección a la Infancia* 1(1): 37–41.

—— 1929. 'Consejo de Patronato de la Mujer y el Niño. Proyecto de ley presentado al Consejo Nacional de Administración, por el Ministro de Instrucción Pública, señor Enrique Rodríguez Fabregat.' *Boletín del Instituto Internacional Americano de Protección a la Infancia* 2(4): 493–547.

Rollet, Catherine. 1997. 'Le modèle de la goutte de lait dans le monde: Diffusion et variantes.' In *Les biberons du Docteur Dufour*. Fécamp: Musées Municipaux de Fécamp, 111–117.

—— 2001. 'La santé et la protection de l'enfant vues à travers les Congrès Internationaux (1880–1920).' *Annales de Démographie Historique* 1: 97–116.

Rooke, Patricia and Rudy Schnell. 1995. 'Uncramping Child Life: International Children's Organisations, 1914–1939.' In *International Health Organisations and Movements, 1918–1939*, ed. Paul Weindling. Cambridge: Cambridge University Press, 176–202.

Ruiz, Esther. 2008. 'Del viraje conservador al realineamiento internacional, 1933–1945.' In *Historia del Uruguay en el siglo XX (1890–2005)*, ed. Ana Frega. Montevideo: Ediciones de la Banda Oriental, 85–121.

Sapriza, Graciela. 1988. *Memorias de rebeldía: Siete historias de vidas*. Montevideo: Puntosur Editores, GRECMU.

—— 2006. 'La hora de la eugenesia: Las feministas en la encrucijada.' In *Historia de las mujeres en España y América Latina*, ed. Isabel Morant. Madrid: Ediciones Cátedra, 889–913.

—— 2011. 'Historia de la (des)penalización del aborto en Uruguay. 'Aborto libre': la corta experiencia Uruguaya (1934–1938).' In *(Des)penalización del aborto: Prácticas, actores y discursos. Abordaje interdisciplinario sobre una realidad compleja*, ed. Niki Johnson, Alejandra López Gómez, Graciela Sapriza, Alicia Castro and Gualberto Arribeltz. Montevideo: Universidad de la República and Comisión Sectorial de Investigación Científica, 19–64.

Scarone, Arturo. 1937. 'Paulina Luisi, datos biográficos.' In *Uruguayos contemporáneos*. Montevideo: Casa A. Barreiro y Ramos, 91–93.

Scarzanella, Eugenia. 2003. 'Los pibes en el Palacio de Ginebra: Las investigaciones de la Sociedad de las Naciones sobre la infancia latinoamericana (1925–1939).' *Estudios Interdisciplinarios de América Latina y el Caribe* 14(2).

Schweber, Libby. 2006. *Disciplining Statistics: Demography and Vital Statistics in France and England, 1830–1885*. Durham, NC: Duke University Press.

Semashko, Nikolai. 1990. 'Protection of Mother, Baby, and Child in Russia, 1921.' In *Bolshevik Visions: First Phase of the Cultural Revolution in Soviet Russia*, ed. William G. Rosenberg. Ann Arbor: University of Michigan Press, 149–150.

Sociedad de Pediatría de Montevideo. 1947. 'Recordando al Profesor Marfan.' *Archivos de Pediatría del Uruguay* 18(3): 166–167.

Starks, Tricia 2003. 'A Fertile Mother Russia: Pronatalist Propaganda in Revolutionary Russia.' *Journal of Family History* 28(3): 411–442.

Stepan, Nancy. 1991. *'The Hour of Eugenics': Race, Gender, and Nation in Latin America*. Ithaca, NY: Cornell University Press.

Stern, Alexandra M. 1999. 'Responsible Mothers and Normal Children: Eugenics, Nationalism, and Welfare in Post-Revolutionary Mexico, 1920–1940.' *Journal of Historical Sociology* 12(4): 369–397.

Strauss, Paul. 1933. Inaugural Address. In *Congrès International pour la Protection de l'Enfance*. Paris: Comité National de l'Enfance, xlii.

Szreter, Simon. 2011. 'Children with a (Local) State: Identity Registration at Birth in English History since 1538.' In *Children without a State: A Global Human Rights Challenge*, ed. Jacqueline Bhabha. Cambridge, MA: MIT Press, 331–352.

Tomé, Eustaquio. 1938. 'Código del Niño. Anotado con todas las leyes, decretos y acordadas vigentes y con la jurisprudencia nacional.' In *Colección de manuales de derecho y legislación*. Montevideo: Claudio Garcia.

Trochon, Ivette and Beatriz Vidal. 1993. *El régimen terrista, 1933–1938: Aspectos políticos, económicos y sociales*. Montevideo: Ediciones de la Banda Oriental.

Turenne, Augusto. 1929. *La maternidad consciente. Procreación voluntaria de la mujer. Un problema de obstetricia social*. Folleto 33. Montevideo: Sindicato Médico del Uruguay.

—— 1946. 'José Scosería. 1861–1946.' *Apartado de los Anales de la Facultad de Medicina* 31.

Union Médicale Latine. 1937. 'La protection de l'enfance en Uruguay.' *UMFIA CXXI* 11: 508–510.

Uruguay. 1927. *Leyes, decretos y reglamentos vigentes del Registro del Estado Civil*. 2nd edn. Montevideo: C. García.

Vaillant, Adolfo. 1873a. *República Oriental del Uruguay en la Exposición de Viena*. Montevideo: Imprenta a Vapor de la Tribuna.

—— 1873b. *La mortalidad y la población en el departamento de Montevideo*. Montevideo: Estab. Tip. Vapor de la Idea.

Vanger, Milton I. 1980. *The Model Country: José Batlle y Ordóñez of Uruguay, 1907–1915*. Lebanon, NH: University Press of New England.

Veerman, Philip E. 1992. *The Rights of the Child and the Changing Image of Childhood*. Dordrecht: Martinus Nijhoff.

Wadsworth, James E. 1999. 'Moncorvo Filho e o problema da infância: modelos institucionais e ideológicos da assistência à infância no Brasil.' *Revista Brasileira de História* 19(37): 103–124.

Waltz, Susan E. 2001. 'Universalizing Human Rights: The Role of Small States in the Construction of the Universal Declaration of Human Rights.' *Human Rights Quarterly* 23(1): 44–72.

Weindling, Paul, ed. 1995. *International Health Organisations and Movements, 1918–1939*. Cambridge: Cambridge University Press.

Williams, Naomi. 1996. 'The Reporting and Classification of Causes of Death in Mid-Nineteenth-Century England.' *Historical Methods: A Journal of Quantitative and Interdisciplinary History* 29(2): 58–71.

Wright-Carozza, Paolo. 2003. 'From Conquest to Constitutions: Retrieving a Latin American Tradition of the Idea of Human Rights.' *Human Rights Quarterly* 25(2): 281–313.

17

Birth Registration and the Promotion of Children's Rights in the Interwar Years

The Save the Children International Union's Conference on the African Child, and Herbert Hoover's American Child Health Association

DOMINIQUE MARSHALL*

Introduction

TWO INTERESTING CAMPAIGNS for civil registration took place in the interwar years. The first set of efforts towards birth registration during these two decades was that of the American Child Heath Association to standardize and extend states' systems in all the United States. Republican Secretary of Commerce and future President, Herbert Hoover, on his return from massive operations of child relief in Europe after the Great War, and in conjunction with his ascent to political power, directed the efforts of a large private association to build a coherent and extensive network of institutions of child welfare. The American Child Health Association (ACHA) championed children's rights, for which it adopted three successive charters in 1922, 1928 and 1930 (Marshall 2008).

The second set started in 1931, in Geneva, when the 200 participants of the Conference on the African Child, gathered by the Save the Children International Union (SCIU) – the ancestor of one of today's five largest non-governmental organizations, Save the Children – considered that their largest task was to gather vital statistics concerning births and infant mortality, in order to improve the state of children's well-being on the continent. Only this would allow the universal rights

* Thanks to Simon Szreter, Keith Breckenridge, Hans-Martin Jaeger, Dennis Cordell, Martin Klein, Bruce Curtis and to the audience of the Annual Meeting of the Canadian Association of African Studies in 2010, who provided suggestions and revisions to earlier versions of this paper. Funds for this research have been granted by the Social Sciences and Humanities Research Council of Canada, the Leverhulme Trust Visiting Fellowship at Oxford Brookes University, the Gordon and Jean Southam Fellowship of the Association of Commonwealth Universities, and Carleton University.

Proceedings of the British Academy **182**, 449–473. © The British Academy 2012.

granted to children seven years earlier by the General Assembly of the League of Nations (LN), at the instigation of the SCIU, to become a reality in Africa (Marshall 2004, 2009). The League's Geneva Declaration of 1924 had stated in particular that the children, 'above all considerations of race, nationality or creed', 'must be given the means requisite for [their] normal development, both materially and spiritually', and that they should be fed, nursed, helped, sheltered and succoured (Veerman 1992, 444).

While both organizations considered birth registration as an administrative procedure essential to safeguard children's rights (Powell 1980), neither of them included registration at birth in their respective charters of children's rights, in the way the United Nations (UN) would do later, in the Covenant on Civil and Political Rights of 1966 and the Convention on the Rights of the Child of 1989. Why, how, and to what effect, then, did these two associations work for the improvement of birth registration during this same period? How do their efforts compare? How did they understand the relationship between registration and childhood, between registration and the notion of universal right? Why did the American campaign quickly succeed while the African one faltered? And, finally, how do these two episodes help us to make sense of the appearance of an explicit right to be registered at birth in international law only much later in 1966?

This study follows the key moments of this history, first by discussing the goals and assumptions of the Conference on the African Child of 1931, second by comparing them to the interwar campaign of the ACHA – and the earlier efforts of the American Public Health Association (APHA), who had paved the way. It shows how immigration and race were especially significant in determining the extent of registration in both places. The subsequent and related efforts of demographers, philanthropists and politicians are then explored – many of which converged around the British and American work on the population of Africa led by Dr Robert René Kuczynski (who in 1933 fled Germany and worked in England at the London School of Economics (LSE) and for the Colonial Office). Finally, the origins of the UN right to be registered at birth are placed within the context of this interwar account.

The Conference on the African Child of 1931 and the lack of civil registration of colonial populations

Founded in Britain at the end of the First World War to feed children in the nations of the defeated powers, the Save the Children movement believed that the idiom of children's rights would enshrine and perpetuate in peacetime the idea of a common trusteeship for children, which had become important during the war. The SCIU did not consider birth registration as a right, neither in the League of Nations Declaration of the Rights of the Child of 1924, nor in the renewed United Nations

Declaration on the Rights of the Child of 1959 – both of which it helped to write (Veerman 1992, 112, 159–181, 465–467). Nevertheless, the international charity had very early on, in its practical efforts, made registration at birth one of the first conditions of the application of all universal rights, establishing in its practice the link between registration and welfare rights, which appears to be often a crucial element in the history of registration (see Editors' Introduction, p. 16).

To Eglantyne Jebb, the founder of the Save the Children movement in 1919, the relation between information and the welfare of children was paramount (Mahood 2009). The SCIU considered birth registration and the vital statistics it made possible as essential elements 'to carry into effect' its Declaration on the Rights of the Child. In 1925, the compiler of the second edition of its *International Yearbook of Child Care and Protection*, Edward Fuller, wrote that 'Generations yet unborn will profit or suffer by reason of the way in which we have used our knowledge and recorded our experience in efforts on behalf of the world's children.' As the organization wrote to government officials to ask for information about child welfare, it intended to make a '[. . .] first step towards discovering the weak spots in the world's care for its children, and setting foot on remedying such defects as may be found to exist' (Fuller 1925, viii). Fuller called for 'uniformity throughout the world, at least in recording vital statistics and in defining [. . .] terms', arguing that the function of 'a clear and accurate record of vital statistics' resided in its potential to guide legislation (1925, x–xi). Interestingly for later developments, however, in the third edition of the *Yearbook*, published three years later, SCIU officials drew no direct connection between birth registration and 'The Refugee Problem in Relation to Children', to which it devoted one article (Fuller 1928).

The *Yearbook*, which in its attempt at universality systematically discussed the regime of notification of births in the countries and colonies of the world, noted time and again for African territories that 'The registration of births is not compulsory.' As a consequence, the columns for 'infant mortality' and 'birth rate', which occupied pride of place amongst the dozen types of data collated in the 'General Tables', remained empty for most African territories, except for some footnotes on 'European population only'. In 1912, the Special Committee on Infant Mortality appointed by the Royal Statistical Society of London, who had sent to all 'countries and states' a form of enquiry about vital statistics, had received very few replies from Africa (Royal Statistical Society (Great Britain) 1912). In addition, the *International Health Yearbooks*, published by the Health Organization of the LN, during the same period, by the very fact of subversively listing colonies in the same fashion as independent countries, provided an opportunity for exposing the inadequacy of colonial statistics and administration (Borowy 2005). Fuller attributed the problem to European imperial administrations, as his introductory notes underlined the fact that several of the countries in which there was 'no reliable system of computing the most limited vital statistics' were 'under the protectorate of one or the other of the great Powers' (Fuller 1925, ix). Fuller also saw hopes for these countries in the future in the fact that 'even in such an organized community as Great Britain research is much hampered by the fact that what seems to us so elementary a requirement as the compulsory registration of births, marriage and deaths, has been in operation for less than a century' (Fuller 1925, ix).

There existed indeed little detailed knowledge, in Europe, of African infant mortality. In her main book, published in 1929, *Save the Child!*, Eglantyne Jebb had used reports from George Newman, the Chief Medical Officer of the UK Ministry of Health, who in turn had based his knowledge on only a single church report and one report of the Medical Officer of South Africa (Jebb 1929, 15). Colonial administrations were notoriously slow at gathering overseas the kind of information they were assembling at home. What the SCIU was discovering was the kind of 'gatekeeper states', which other contributions to this volume have described, which remained absent from the social and cultural realms of colonial populations and were only present where colonial territory and outside world met. White settlers, like those studied by Szreter in Chapter 2, might have brought registration practices with them for themselves, but the practice was not extended to native populations, only to slave property, as explored in Chapter 12 (see also Editors' Introduction, p. 23). There were a very few exceptions, such as in the unusual interwar Buganda state, documented in Chapter 10. As the Health Organization of the LN and the International Labour Office (ILO) were also realizing in their respective attempts to collect African social statistics, metropolitan powers were also eager to control and retain the little information they had (Borowy 2005, 88, 94; Daughton 2008). This state of affairs might not be unrelated to the fact that, when invited by the leaders of the SCIU to be a patron of the Conference on the African Child, in 1930, George Newman had refused.

Considering that they had finished their work of reconstruction in Eastern and Central Europe, the SCIU called a Conference on the African Child for the spring of 1931, in the hope that 'peoples of the world', when they read 'how the other half lives', 'may be in a better position to help with experience and advice, and, if need be, with tangible succor in time of grave distress' (Fuller 1925, x–xi). Given the apparent general neglect and ineffectiveness of colonial authorities (documented in Kuczynski 1948, 1949), it is not surprising that the only impetus for a widespread reform in vital statistics was coming from private efforts, such as those of the SCIU, which was not closely bound to the colonial authorities. Not only did the SCIU call for the construction of vital statistics by public and private authorities, but it also saw it as its mission to publicize and discuss such figures as were available amongst the public.

The British section of the organizing committee of the 1931 Conference soon confirmed that in most of the British African empire, there was no registration of birth and death on 'native reserves', and 'hospitals were the only places where statistics were kept' (though interestingly Doyle points out in Chapter 10 that some church congregations did keep quite effective parish registers which tended to be overlooked by the secular authorities).[1] Some colonial medical officers were indeed trying to improve registration in isolation, in their effort to promote public health. In 1936, in Asante (Gold Coast), for instance, Dr Selwyn-Clarke of the British Colonial Service was refusing admission to babies whose names had not been entered in the Register of Birth; as a consequence, the number of registrations in the region trebled. Earlier in 1929, entries into the Baby Show had been limited to children whose births had been registered, in an attempt, this time, to appeal not only to parents' wish to see their child cured, but also to their pride and ambitions (Allman 1994, 29–30). Dr J. P. Reinhallt-Jones, founder and director of the South African Institute of Race Relations of Johannesburg, acknowledged the same general unreliability of statistics on all questions related to children for South Africa.[2] The independent state of Ethiopia was no more trustworthy: the organizers lamented the 'complete absence in Abyssinia of anything in the nature of official statistics'.[3]

It had previously been decided that three years of preparatory work would be required to allow the SCIU to gather the information that would become, as the President of the SCIU Executive, Van Notten, declared, 'the starting point for valuable documentation, which at a later date may prove to be the basis – perhaps [the] root – of scientific knowledge and accurate statistics to guide the future of African development' (Save the Children International Union 1932, 4). From their office in Geneva, SCIU workers drafted a lengthy questionnaire, which they sent to 1,500 people. In the end, only 300 answers were collected (Save the Children International Union 1932, xii). In the tradition of international conferences of the day, the information was divided into five regions and by theme, related to the Declaration of the Rights of the Child: 'Education regarded as the preparation of children for life'; 'General conditions of work for children and adolescents'; the 'Protection of children at work' and, 'Still-birth and infant mortality', either 'from the pathological point of view', or 'from the economic and social point of view' (Save the Children International Union 1932). An initial collation of the data was accomplished in London and Geneva, before 'brief monographs' were sent to the experts who were to base their papers on them. Half of the twenty papers presented at the conference concerned infant mortality (Sharp 1931, 109–110). The experts were all Europeans, a fact pointing to the imperial nature of the conference. So the organizers failed to consult either with American experts, or with the International American Institute for the Protection of Childhood, studied in this volume in Chapter 16. The latter omission is especially telling, given the well-established

[1] Thirteenth Meeting, 20 January 1931, Archives of the Save the Children Fund (London) (ASCF), 'British Committee of the 1931 Congress on Children of Non-European Origins', October 1920–June 1931', 251, 252.

[2] Fourteenth Meeting, 3 March 1931, ASCF, 278.

[3] Letter from the British Foreign Office to the SCF, 26 August 1930, mentioned in Tenth Meeting, 30 September 1930, 170.

series of child congresses in Latin America, as well as the close links between Uruguayan or other South American actors and the LN and the SCIU.

'In most of the eight papers contributed on infant mortality . . . stress [was] laid on the impossibility of obtaining exact statistics' (Sharp 1931, 20). The causes of deficient registration resided partly in the undeveloped nature of colonial administration and partly in the lack of understanding of the African population. In the eyes of many assessors at the conference, the habits of the population were not only letting children down, but they were also part of the reason for the poor quality of vital statistics. For one British colonial administrator, Dr Mary Blacklock, the difficulty of gathering numbers

> must necessarily be so in a backward country where medical work is just developing and where, partly from inadequacy of trained staff, partly from lack of education of the people in the necessity of compulsory registration and in the benefit of European medical treatment, the work of keeping accurate records is extremely difficult.
> (cited in Sharp 1931, 21)

To remedy this state of affairs, the Secretary General of the Conference on the African Child believed that it was possible, while respecting natives' knowledge, to transmit to them a technical knowledge which would benefit all.

Curiously, this lack of an effective information system did not stop the participants from concluding: 'On one point the Conference was unanimous, that the loss of infant life, both before and after birth, is not only avoidable but disastrously high.' A letter received in preparation for the conference shows an example of the source of such pessimistic conceptions: a nun from Nigeria, concerned by venereal disease and incest perpetrated on girls as young as 10 years old, quoted a doctor who believed that 'unless they can be protected the race will die out in 30 years'.[4] (See Chapter 10 on the politics of contemporary fears about the scale of venereal diseases in Africa.) When one SCIU worker assessed numbers of births and infant deaths herself in the field, her findings were equally impressionistic, and dark: during a humanitarian aid field trip in Addis Ababa, in 1936, the first of its kind on the continent, Frédérique Small judged that 50 per cent of all infants died in Addis Ababa.[5] Thus, Malthusian fears of over-population did not appear at the conference (Sharpless 1997; Ittmann 2003). Rather, experts such as Hungarian anthropologist and employee of the British Museum, Emil Torday, warned the conference participants about the consequences of depopulation: 'Central Africa offers a wealth to Europe, but this wealth can be realized only if her human wealth is spared. The future of Africa depends on her children, whose place Europeans will never be able to fill' (cited in Sharp 1931, 18). Similarly, alarm at infant

[4] Sister M. Magdalen, St Joseph Convent, South Nigeria, to MacKenzie, 31 March 1930, Archives de l'Union internationale de protection de l'enfance (Archives d'État de Genève) (AUIPE), bundle of documents not catalogued, R 181.

[5] 'Mémoire remis à S.M. l'Impératrice d'Ethiopie de Mme Small', 26 January 1936, AUIPE, 5.2, folder entitled 'Généralités', subfolder entitled 'Mission en Éthiopie de Mme Small'; Marshall 2006.

mortality and optimism about Africa's riches led many, such as John Harris of the Anti Slavery and Aborigines Protection Society, to postulate the under-population of the continent: 'there were ten jobs waiting for any man unemployed' (Save the Children International Union 1932, 40). In these ways, civil registration, if ultimately assisting with child survival, was deemed as a means to sustain manpower, seen by some as a vital resource for exploitation of the continent (Bashford 2008).

Some colonial doctors and administrators had conducted partial experiments in the registration of births, in order to plan their work, which historical demographers have used to interesting avail (Lorimer 1961, 30; Cordell 1993; Gregory *et al.* 1984). In general, however, where some system of registration of the native population existed in the interwar years, it had often come from the colonial state's need to know who qualified for military service, or to provide information for taxation systems aimed at natives which were based on the size of the population. In parts of western and central Africa under French influence, for instance, village registers compiled by headmen listed, in theory, the members of the community. But the lack of literate people and adequate communications hampered the system, and the goals of taxation and recruitment led to 'temptation to fraud'. They also directed their attention to the registration of men, making 'the listing of women, with children, and invalid or aged persons seem relatively unimportant' (Lorimer 1961, 28–29). From 1916, there also existed, in theory, a regime of compulsory civil registration of births and deaths of all populations in French Africa; but it had only been implemented in some cities, and even there, there was never enough information about the entire population to draw any meaningful statistical conclusions (Lorimer 1961, 31; Chapter 15 in this volume).

The appreciation expressed at the quality of the information published in preparation for the conference varied. It was understood that the amount of comparative information now available on the subject represented a helpful precedent; but discussions on methods had not been sufficient, since the people able to collect the necessary data in Africa were few and overworked and solutions to child welfare could not be made with such aggregated information. In other words, the enquiry suffered from being too ambitious given the limited means available to the SCIU.[6]

Observers from the ILO and from the Health Committee of the LN pointed out that they were currently accomplishing a comparable work, which was taking them much longer than the SCIU's enquiry, since indigenous populations did not register births. They were probably referring to the campaign against forced labour and to the *International Health Yearbooks* of these respective organizations.[7]

Over the longer term, however, the results of the efforts of the SCIU might be seen

[6] Lucie Schmidt, 'Note sur la Conférence internationale pour l'enfance africaine', typed document, 2 July 1931, Archives of the International Labour Office, D600/406/9/2, 3.

[7] Testimony of Dr Boyer, AUIPE, 'France', p. 2, folder entitled 'Schlemmer, Raymond. Indigènes. Suisse. II, 1929–1936. (enfance non-européenne)'; Daughton 2008; Borowy 2009.

in a better light. In an indirect way, a conference which had been launched with emancipatory goals in mind – those of children's rights – partly delivered on its promise. The post-war years were a period of development of expert knowledge amongst official bodies, with the appointment of a number of advisory councils, such as the Advisory Committee on Education of the Colonial Office and the British School of Tropical Medicine – the members of which included Lord Lugard, who had been associated with the planning of the Conference on the African Child. Colonial governments had begun to acknowledge that they knew little about the continent, and that knowledge would help the development of resources, which would in turn help finance colonial development. The SCIU benefited from these beginnings by securing the collaboration of some of the experts hired occasionally by the governments, and it helped several such experts in return by providing a tribune and a site of exchange where an institutional basis was missing. The above-mentioned Dr Mary Blacklock, for instance, was a member of the Advisory Medical and Sanitary Committee of the British Colonial Office, and a former Government Medical Officer in Sierra Leone; after she attended the Conference on the African Child for the Colonial Office, she became adviser to the Save the Children Fund 'Child Protection Committee', in charge of non-European children in London. This committee was responsible for the sequels of the conference, such as studies of the 'colour bar' in Britain in the later 1930s, and the construction of a child welfare centre in Addis Ababa in 1936 (Marshall 2006). Another example is the LSE demographer Kuczynski, who collaborated with the Child Protection Committee, and whom we will meet again later, who was employed by the Colonial Office intermittently.

At the conference, the committee in charge of the final recommendations comprised a large proportion of the small contingent of actual Africans who had attended, and its series of recommendations on 'Still Birth and Infant Mortality' bear their mark. The main suggestion pertained to the need for further enquiries on social and economic influences on infant mortality, 'in collaboration with the greatest number of trained Africans'. In addition, there should be some collaboration for drawing up standards 'applicable [to] the whole African continent, but [which] would at the same time be elastic enough for adaptation to the habit, customs, and diseases of different areas'. The second series of recommendations spoke of the need for governments and private institutions to recruit and train doctors, nurses, midwives and health visitors, 'especially amongst Africans', and to maintain contact with them and between them to popularize 'scientific notions on the subject of hygiene' (Sharp 1931, 112–113). In this way, the SCIU was directing its attention to creating a cadre of indigenous African professionals.

A new commission on African children was to meet in Geneva after 1931. It was decided that infant mortality and slavery would become the priorities, but this endeavour was interrupted by the death of the researcher.[8] In addition, from June

[8] ASCF, Child Protection Committee (CPC), Minutes, 9 October 1934.

1932 to August 1934, the SCIU published at least twelve supplements to its ordinary news bulletin entitled *L'enfance africaine*, which mainly informed of the activities of the Geneva office, of its collaboration with the Child Welfare Committee and the Slavery Commission of the LN, and the ILO. Two French doctors, Cazanove and Léger, also promised enquiries into infant mortality, but these do not seem to have materialized.[9] Diplomats and friends of the SCIU spoke of the recommendations at the General Assembly of the League of Nations, and asked countries' members of the Permanent Mandates Commission of the League of Nations for statistics on infant mortality.[10] But the Geneva Bureau had little in the way of resources. In the Save the Children Fund (SCF) offices in London, the new Child Protection Committee published a small *Information Bulletin on Infant Mortality and Allied Questions in Africa*. After a while, it was abandoned for lack of staff and resources, and fear that it might not interest the general public. The mobilization of European public opinion did not happen as the SCIU hoped: in a decade of economic depression in the North, replicating the SCIU European successes of 1919 in Africa was not to be easy.

The London branch also sponsored a series of public events following the findings of 1931. In 1936, Kuczynski spoke on 'Statistics and Child Welfare in African Colonies'.[11] After the lecture, SCF honorary patron, C. R. Buxton, of the famous anti-slavery family, promised 'to arrange for questions to be asked in the House of Commons', where he was a Labour Member of Parliament.[12] From their inception in 1933, such meetings received some publicity from *The Times, The Birmingham Post* and *West Africa*, and the fact that they were attended by some West African students offers a bridge towards the question of civil registration in the history of independent African states, to which we will return.[13]

The SCF movement, like the Rockefeller Foundation who employed Kuczynski later, had offered this proponent of the registration of vital events an early platform from which to denounce the assumption that high rates of infant mortality in Africa were a legacy of the past or a fact of geography. Kuczynski's subsequent comprehensive (but unfinished as due to his death only three of the projected four volumes were published) *Demographic Survey of the British Colonial Empire* combed official reports, legal codes and scientific literature for the whole history of the empire, to unveil a series of failed, repealed or unenforced laws regarding the registration of vital events amongst natives, together with a large number of

[9] De Bunsen to Small, 31 May 1934, and Small to de Bunsen, 5 June 1934, AUIPE, 12.3, file on de Bunsen.

[10] Letter to de Bunsen, 9 February 1934, AUIPE, Great Britain, 12.3, file on de Bunsen.

[11] 'European Civilization and the African. Has It Improved Health Conditions. Dr. Robert R. Kuczynski speaks for the Save the Children Fund.' *The World's Children*, January 1937, 53–55.

[12] ASCF, CPC, Minutes, 10 March 1936.

[13] Series of 'At Home' conferences in London in 1936–1937, summarized in *The World's Children* of the same year. ASCF, CPC, Minutes, 11 May 1933, 10 March 1936.

local medical enquiries into infant mortality, whose data he mostly disqualified as unreliable for serious demographic work:

> If, for example, in an African colony, the birth rate has risen in the course of the last ten years from 10 to 20 per thousand, the conclusion that fertility has increased seems to me quite unwarranted. The only conclusion which may safely be drawn is that ten years ago only a minority of the births were registered and that registration is still incomplete. [. . .] To appraise fertility, morbidity, mortality, or migrations is about as difficult in most African Dependencies as to appraise the frequency of adultery in this country.
>
> (Kuczynski 1948, 1: vi)

The demographer underlined the dilemma of public colonial authorities stationed in Africa in the absence of such information: in the course of their work, they had to 'form an idea' about infant mortality and, in order to do so, to rely on these imperfect enquiries. Moreover, they were asked by the metropolitan governments to provide such numbers. As a result, in imperial statistics 'birth and mortality figures, as well as estimates of overall population growth, were nothing more than educated guesses, made by colonial officials with little or no training in quantitative methods or demography' (cited in Ittmann 2003, 432). Even in the 'most outstanding example of birth and death registration established by native authorities', uncovered by Kuczynski in Uganda for the early decades of the twentieth century (see Chapter 10), the lack of scrutiny by the officials in charge of collecting the data led to defective returns, a weakness about which he commented that: 'nothing is so apt to deteriorate the accuracy of returns, no matter whether they are prepared by the natives of Uganda or of England' (Kuczynski 1949, 2: 113). The training of officials became one of his main suggestions.

Colonial administrations continued to ponder the importance of civil registration for the planning of their welfare and educational institutions with the same unevenness and lack of resources as before. In 1950, a second survey was undertaken by the SCF in Africa, by Dr Leslie Houden, a member of the Council of the SCF and an honorary medical adviser. It focused on Anglo-Egyptian Sudan and British Somaliland, to determine 'how best the Fund may answer calls for aid which have come to it from the respective authorities'. He reported on the same lack of statistical figures, which his predecessors had campaigned to remedy two decades earlier (Fuller 1951, 82–83, 140–141; Freeman 1965, 81). In African colonies, where the purely administrative aspects of registration prevailed, where the scale of welfare and education institutions was small and where there lacked the possibility of such registration being linked to full citizenship, the link between birth registration and welfare rights, which has often been a necessary condition for the success of civil registration (see Editors' Introduction, p. 16, and Chapter 2), was not possible.

The campaign for extensive birth registration of the American Child Health Association, 1921–1939

The Save the Children *International Yearbook* of 1925 praised the US system of 'birth registration areas' of the Census Bureau, established in 1915, which encouraged all states to bring their levels of birth registration to a high degree of accuracy and coverage before they could join, and to adopt a model law (Fuller 1925, x). The remaining problems in the US, Fuller observed, came 'from a vast territory and an exceedingly complex population' (Fuller 1925, xi).

The state of birth registration in the USA in the 1920s was in some parts not very different from that of Africa at the same period (Hetzel 1997, 59). The American Public Health Association, founded in 1872, which had long campaigned for the improvement of registration of vital events, was painfully aware of the 'disgraceful' situation of the country compared to Europe (Wilbur 1912, 999). Its Section on Vital Statistics met annually, composed mainly of the 'Directors of Vital Statistics' of states and large cities, and published at least one paper a year on the issue in the *Journal of the American Public Health Association*, from the start of the publication in 1911. Members of the association retraced the history of registration from the beginning of the colonies, lamented the lack of implementation, and campaigned for uniformity. Combined with the indifference of practitioners and the excessive toil and ignorance of mothers, the invisibility of many births represented one crucial element in the 'annual slaughter of the innocents', the 'yearly toll paid by the baby', who had 'an indubitable right to its natural nourishment' (Mason Knox 1911, 43–45).

The discrepancies with Europe could be partly explained by the difficulties of travelling long distances in thinly populated areas to register people and convince them of the desirability of registration (Dublin *et al.* 1928, 608) – a problem also often noted by students of registration in Africa. In addition, the 'foreign population' of New York, whose births were not attended by doctors, and where midwives and parents were either ignorant of the law or 'fail[ed] to realize the importance of a child's birth being recorded', was described in the APHA records in a similar fashion to the native population of African colonies (Beagle 1911, 362).

> It has been established that about 85 per cent of our unreported births result from this custom [of unlicensed women attending births]. The attendant will not report for fear of prosecution for practicing without a license, and the parent is reluctant to report through fear of involving the attendant.
>
> (Balfe 1918, 777)

Propagandists of the APHA appealed to 'our alien population' by publishing stories of American-born sons of Austrian parents 'arrested as military-service evaders' because their parents were deceased and 'no trace could be obtained of his birth', or that of 'the young Ohio Jew who was caught in Russia at the outbreak of the war and whose privations while awaiting a certificate, reads like a novel' (Manger 1919, 76).

From 1912 to 1918, the APHA collaborated with the Census Bureau, the General Federation of Women's Clubs, the Association of Collegiate Alumnae and the Association of Amateur Genealogists to support and facilitate a vigorous national campaign for birth registration, orchestrated by the newly founded Children's Bureau of the US government. According to Parker and Carpenter (1981), this 'liberal social welfare establishment' thought that, amongst all matters pertaining to the 'right to childhood', the causes of infant mortality and birth registration, by their non-controversial nature, would serve as the main themes for the education of the public and for the strengthening of popular support for the Bureau. This was a necessary condition for the enforcement of child labour, compulsory schooling and inheritance laws, a requirement for the treatment of early diseases, as well as a means to identify the nationality of citizens in time of war. The large voluntary movement, conducted mainly at the local level by means of door-to-door investigations and the publication of results in the newspapers, succeeded in creating enough public interest to enact, change or enforce state laws. By 1918, the new director of the Census Bureau decided to take the lead, in the name of professionalism, and 'the significant part the Children's Bureau played in grass-root organizing faded from memory as this function of local government became widely accepted and routinized' (Parker and Carpenter 1981, 69, 70).

By the mid-1920s, medical experts of the American Medical Association, now claiming the field of preventative health care, and fearing the rise of state medicine, successfully undermined the authority of the Children's Bureau. Herbert Hoover was sympathetic to their cause, and he would eventually use his presidency, from 1929, to curtail the Bureau's prerogatives (Skocpol 1992, 512–522).

It was in this context of the fading leadership of the Children's Bureau that, in 1924, the APHA which had previously collaborated with the Bureau replaced the Bureau in the direction of the next campaign for birth registration. It created a 'Committee to Aid the Completion of the Registration Area Before 1930' and used the slogan 'Every State in the Registration Area Before 1930', which secured funds from private insurance companies and the Rockefeller Foundation. The campaign involved travelling representatives, from state and federal agencies, volunteer organizations, to work with midwives and doctors, and publicity in post offices and newspapers, with the help of Chambers of Commerce and Boy Scouts (Dublin *et al.* 1928, 606–607). In an exercise to create a sense of competitiveness, professionals and bureaucrats from the Federal Census Bureau also appealed to states' pride by comparing their performances. They also insisted on the ways by which doctors, who took the time to fill registration papers, would receive a large compensation for their work in the form of reliable statistics about their area. They discussed the relative merits of various methods in place to punish the delinquent doctors.

In their attempt to convince parents, they persistently emphasized the relationship between registration and the interest of children: 'the children of our land will be able to prove their ages whether the knowledge be necessary to enter school, to go to work, or to prove rights to inheritance', to establish their status in criminal trials, in front of laws on the age of consent, to travel or to be free from enlistment (Anon. 1917, 150; Hemenway 1921, 2). The Director of the Bureau of Vital Statistics of Connecticut, James P. Balfe, reminded his colleagues that registration had been crucial, after the Civil War, for the administration of the system of soldiers' pensions – the first American welfare state (Skocpol 1992). Balfe noted:

> In his annual report for 1863, the State Librarian [of Connecticut] wrote: 'in applications for pensions and bounty lands by the widows and orphans of those who are laying down their lives in efforts to maintain the laws of the land and the unity of our country . . . had our present system of registration of births, marriages and deaths been in operation during the War of the Revolution and that of 1812, some hundreds of thousands of dollars would have been saved to the people of this state, and hundreds of families, which for years struggled with adversity, would have been made comfortable during their lives.'
>
> (Balfe 1918, 776)

Balfe was aware that the existence of systems of public or private (such as insurance) entitlements could be an engine to promote registration, noting 'the tremendous demand for certified copies of birth certificates occasioned by the war and by legislation concerning child-labor, etc.', as well as old-age pensions and private insurance which had increased steadily during the interwar years (Balfe 1918, 778; Deacon 1937, 498). The APHA believed that 'People so registered become apostles of registration' (Manger 1919).

Relying on a strong republican culture of political rights, and in a way that recalls Save the Children's rhetoric, American promoters of public health soon presented registration as a condition for a child's rights: 'Now is the time', read the editorial of the *Journal of the American Public Health Association* of mid-1917, 'for every parent to insist that the rights of his child be safeguarded by a proper birth entry in the official records' (Anon. 1917, 150). Some authors went further, and argued for registration itself as a right: the state of Connecticut 'institute[d] a thorough campaign of publicity with a view to impressing every parent with the idea that one of the first legal rights of a new-born child is to have a certificate of his birth properly executed, filed and preserved' (Balfe 1918, 779). Finally, after the war, the most ambitious apostles of the APHA understood registration to be part of the 'nationalization' of their country, in spirit and administration, brought by the war, which had 'melted these various lines of cleavage' previously dividing the country up 'by sectional, class, religious, industrial and many other interests' (Manger 1919, 77). Their sentiment resembled those of the new countries of Eastern and Central Europe, who were eager to show their capacity by sending statistics to the Health Organization of the LN in the 1920s despite the small scale of their bureaucracy, and those of the French government towards the *état-civil* discussed in Chapters 5 and 15 (Borowy 2005).

From 1918, a new American Child Health Association (ACHA) made many of the American Public Health Association's wishes come true: by concentrating on children; by attracting a wide membership of child welfare reformers and volunteers; and by conducting campaigns on the national scale which were, constitutionally and financially, beyond the reach of states' chiefs of vital statistics. The campaign used the method of publication of national surveys that was later also to serve it well in 1924–1925 on questions of health.

From its creation in 1918 to its demise in 1935, the ACHA used its considerable financial resources, its team of experts in social research, and an exceptional system of publicity, to mount a public campaign in favour of registration of a magnitude and reach the APHA could only dream of. The ACHA was soon presided over by the humanitarian, Republican Secretary of Commerce and future President, Herbert Hoover, whose war relief campaigns in the name of children, and work on behalf of the US government as Food Administrator, were famous for their efficiency and their ability to command public support. Early on, the ACHA addressed the difficulty of establishing knowledge on public health in the absence of civil registration. The federal-based Census Bureau, they lamented, kept much better information on crops than they did on children. The ACHA proceeded to create a Committee on Birth Registration, and began publishing a yearly report on infant mortality statistics, which provided incentives for better record-keeping, including birth registration (Ingen 1935, 157, 183). Amongst a flurry of highly publicized activities, such as community surveys, the nationwide organization of a May Day 'day of the child', and the support work for the White House Conferences on Child Health and Protection in 1930, the American Child Health Association started to publish an annual series of Statistical Reports on Infant Mortality.[14]

The ACHA employed a director of Public Health Relations, S. J. Crumbine, who introduced the 1924 volume by deploring 'the fact that in only 30 out of the 48 states are birth records of such accuracy as to receive the recognition from the U.S. Bureau of the Census, and in only 38 states are the records of such accuracy as to be acceptable'.[15] Poor rates of registration, the ACHA understood, were mainly in relation to the 'Colored population':

> as in 1922, among the Birth Registration States the lowest rates are for Washington, Oregon, Minnesota and California. It is not within the province of this report to discuss the causes of these differences in rates. The colored population influences greatly

[14] Statistical Report on Infant Mortality (SRIM) (1920–1927), Hoover Institution Archives, Stanford University, White House Conference on Child Health Protection, Box 132, Folder 2.

[15] Statistical Report on Infant Mortality (SRIM) (1924), Hoover Institution Archives, Stanford University, White House Conference on Child Health Protection, Box 132, Folder 2, 1.

> the [. . .] rates in the Southern States both by reason of incomplete registration of colored births and because of their higher racial mortality.[16]

The American journalist and communist of African descent, James W. Ford, understood the problems of African American children in the United States to be essentially the same as those of the African children in Africa when he declared to the Conference on the African Child that high rates of infant mortality in Africa were due to imperialism (Ford 1931; Palmer 2004).

In a fashion which recalls the SCIU's *Yearbooks*, the Statistical Reports on Infant Mortality extolled the virtue of information, civic pride and competition for the improvement of children's lives:

> There is reason for believing that a compilation of this character serves a useful purpose in acquainting the country at large with comparative infant death rates, and further that such comparison is a valuable stimulating influence toward betterment in infant welfare work.[17]

In 1920, a large poster ranking states by the rate of registration of births was 'published annually and given widespread distribution for the purpose of acquainting the public with the present status of our infant mortality problem and with the hope that such knowledge may assist in the effort to meet this problem constructively'. The poster listed the record of 519 cities in 1920, and their number had expanded to 716 on the last year of known publication, in 1927.

What was different from Save the Children's approach was that Crumbine presented the poor birth registration records as 'a challenge to the American public'.[18] Graphic summaries of the same numbers were reproduced by the association on propaganda material, to encourage citizens to call for the improvement in birth registration systems. At the top centre of the poster mentioned above, one read: 'Do you know where your city stands? Do you know why? Ask these questions.' The first of these seven questions was: 'Are all births registered?' And, at the bottom of the poster, in an effort to convince citizens of the reciprocal nature of registration, underlined by the editors of this volume, the ACHA explained the use of birth registration in the race to improve one's city: 'The quickest and easiest way to reduce high infant mortality rate recorded against your city is to demand registration of every birth, as required by law.' More energetic and insistent than the SCIU's campaign, such exhortations were aimed at the kind of public of reformists the SCIU envisaged in Geneva, the public who would be moved by the exposition of how the other half lived, and it wished to educate the public about the virtues of registration, again as the doctor of the Colonial Office, Mary Blacklock, had projected.

[16] SRIM (1924), 4; Statistical Report on Infant Mortality (SRIM) (1925), Hoover Institution Archives, Stanford University, White House Conference on Child Health Protection, Box 132, Folder 2, 4.

[17] SRIM (1924), 2; SRIM (1925), Preface.

[18] SRIM (1924), 1.

On the left-hand side of these questions, on the 1924 poster, the interest of children was underlined: 'Commended to the thoughtful attention of mayors, health officers, editors, citizens, taxpayers, in the interest of the 2,500,000 babies born in the United States each year' (Appendix to SRIM 1924). In 1927, the notion of registration as a right for the child appeared explicitly on the poster, as it had done in some of the APHA's articles, at the end of the paragraph on the use of birth registration, now placed on the top right: 'It is also the only fair deal for the baby. His citizenship, his right to go to work and to inherit property, may depend on his birth having been registered. What about your baby's?'[19] In the end, however, Herbert Hoover did not include the right to registration at birth in his three successive charters of children's rights.

In the American campaign of the 1920s, civic pride, the interests and rights of children, and their parents' wish to ensure them, were all likely to help the US system of registration improve, by 'provid[ing] an obvious benefit to the people being targeted' (Editors' Introduction, p. 16). The birth registration area initiative helped many states to raise their rate of notification from half of their population to more than 95 per cent. Still, in 1940, 50 million people in the USA did not have a birth certificate (Hetzel 1997, 55).

Epilogue and conclusion: the United Nations and the right to registration at birth

Article 7 of the Convention on the Rights of the Child of 1989 states that 'The child shall be registered immediately after birth and shall have the right from birth to a name, the right to acquire a nationality and as far as possible, the right to know and be cared for by his parents' (Veerman 1992, 553–573). It was also already part of the United Nations Covenant on Civil and Political Rights of 1966, the American Convention of Human Rights of 1969 and the African Charter on Human and People's Rights of 1986 (Bueren 1995, 117–118). To the interpreters of international law, the right to registration helps safeguard the rights of children, such as a minimum age for labour, and to facilitate effective planning, for school provision for instance (Bueren 1995, 117–118) – a fact which both Eglantyne Jebb and Herbert Hoover helped publicize in their own time. By promoting the rights of children to welfare, education, protection and succour, the ACHA and the SCIU had both come to understand the central importance of birth registration. Why, then, did they not conceive of registration as a right in itself? And how is it that the Convention on the Rights of the Child of 1989 did?

[19] Statistical Report on Infant Mortality (SRIM) (1927), Hoover Institution Archives, Stanford University, White House Conference on Child Health Protection, Box 132, Folder 2, Appendix.

The American campaigns for birth registration had been a domestic matter. The Children's Bureau and Herbert Hoover's Association trusted that the administrative changes required for complete registration to occur would be obtained by citizens' pressures in the name of children's rights, and experts' demonstrations of the usefulness of vital statistics in the attainment of these rights. For the federal institutions involved, such as the Census Bureau, and for the nationwide association that was the ACHA, speaking of registration as an entitlement for children was common practice, but enshrining registration in the American Children's Charter might have provoked states' rigorous sense of their prerogatives. The campaign bore many fruits in any case and, by the time American diplomats faced the proposition of a universal right to registration at birth in the debates at the UN in the 1980s, their preoccupation was no longer influenced by the battle for the registration of their own population. The entitlement now concerned children of newcomers, whose nationality was uncertain, and they feared that 'stateless children' would have a new claim on American citizenship. According to the main analyst of the debates surrounding the Convention of 1989:

> The representative of the United States said in the Open-Ended Working Group that he wanted to prevent difficulties under the immigration and nationalities laws of various States. But his true intentions were revealed when he acknowledged that he especially wanted to prevent a situation where 'stateless children would automatically get the nationality of the state they entered'.
>
> (Veerman 1992, 191–192)

Today, children's rights campaigners eager to see the USA sign the United Nations Convention on the Rights of the Child often return to the republican traditions of civic rights, like the ACHA did, to underline the compatibility of the US legal tradition with the principles of the international instrument, and in order to counter arguments against the encroachment of foreign powers in the country's domestic life. Specific discussion of the right to registration concerns mainly the identity and visibility of refugee children and that of foster children (Woodhouse 2008, 213–233).

The enshrinement of the right to registration at birth in the Convention of 1989 comes largely from discussions about refugees. Close attention to the history of the first utterance of this right in international law, in Article 24 (2) of the Covenant on Civic and Political Rights of 1966, which states that 'Every child shall be registered immediately after birth and shall have a name', shows that children of populations displaced by wars and internal strife were on the legislators' mind (Nowak 2005, 544–545; Ghandhi 1995, 528–529). It is in this spirit that the SCF is currently involved in a joint NGO campaign for the right of registration to birth amongst 'asylum seekers, refugees, internally displaced children, indigenous populations and immigrants, documented or otherwise, as well as stateless children' (Save the Children 2011).

The longer history of this right comes from efforts from humanitarians and reformers of the interwar years to link displaced children and universal rights. In Europe, the question of the welfare of populations of newcomers had arisen in parallel with national protective laws for children, at the end of the nineteenth century. The question had also become more pressing at the same period, because families were replacing young men as the main unit of migration. The Great War and the ensuing transformations of borders and the Russian and Balkan refugee crisis, which entailed the loss of nationality for thousands of individuals, all hit children first. From 1920 to 1926, informed by its discovery of children without nationality, the SCIU made the welfare of minor strangers a priority, and aimed its campaign at the LN in order to promote a common trusteeship in Europe for orphans without a country, who were often overlooked in discussions about the rights of refugees. Their project of conventions in favour of refugee children, based on the universal entitlements promised by the Declaration of the Rights of the Child, which were piloted by the Child Welfare Commission of the League of Nations, was never adopted by the League, because national jealousies were heightened by the Great Depression. They remain, however, of considerable importance in the history of migrations as a factor in the making of social policies (Droux 2011; Baughan 2011, 14–15). The aftermath of the Second World War resurrected the question of refugee children, shortly thereafter to be dominated by the rhetoric of the Cold War, this time to start the round of debates leading to the present conventions.

Herbert Hoover and Eglantyne Jebb first thought of universal rights for children, at the end of the First World War, to establish the moral ground for the relief of children of countries other than those of the publics they addressed. Back in their respective countries, after the war, Jebb and Hoover sought to perpetuate this spirit in their respective ways – Jebb by wishing to use this newfound idea of a world trusteeship for children to avoid a new war; Hoover by ensuring to disadvantaged children at home in America what he had sought for the displaced and hungry children of Europe.

By thinking of the USA as needing a universal minimum for its young as much as the countries of the war-stricken Europe he was returning from, Hoover opened a domestic side to campaigns for rights amongst developed countries, which is still with us. Current international movements for the implementation of the right of registration at birth attract the attention of legislators of the global North to the invisibility of children within various national states. Similarly, Article 24 of the Covenant on Civil and Political Rights was also adopted in the midst of concerns about the rights of illegitimate children, and the rights and duties of unmarried fathers (Ghandhi 1995, 528–529; Nowak 2005, 544–545). More broadly, the new right emphasizes registration as a 'legal technology and resource' available to all (Editors' Introduction, p. 22). Furthermore, as one of the main historians of children's rights has written of the Covenant of 1966,

> The right of each newborn child to immediate registration of his or her name in a State register of births is closely related to the right of every person to his or her own identity, which follows from the protection of privacy, and to the right to *recognition as a person before the law* guaranteed by Art. 16. Only by registration is it guaranteed that the existence of a newborn child is legally recognized.
>
> (Bueren 1995, 117–118)

If the SCIU, for its part, had not included an explicit right to registration at birth in its lists of entitlement, it seems to be because it had to contend with colonial authorities who were jealous of the information about native populations and social provisions to them. Many at the Conference on the African Child of 1931 pointed to the problem of discussing the rights of children at all for populations whose adults were also deprived of fundamental political rights. At a time when American reformers called the expansion of registration a 'challenge to the public', humanitarians and statisticians promoting registration in the colonial world did not envisage a public of African adults claiming civic rights but only a people to be counted (Jaeger 2008; Bashford 2008). Neither did the Save the Children movement invoke a right to registration at birth in their subsequent repeated attempts, from 1945 onwards, to have the UN adopt an updated version of the League of Nations Declaration of the Rights of the Child. In the discussions that surrounded the adoption of such a declaration in 1959, only the new right to a name and a nationality was included, and this with few debates (Veerman 1992, 159–181). The Second World War convinced many colonial authorities of the use of civil registration for the management of labour, as announced at the conference of 1931 by the anthropologist Emil Torday (Hetzel 1997, 55). After the war, when more colonial states sought the help of statisticians in renewed projects of colonial governance, as we have seen, their efforts came not only from an enhanced belief in state intervention, at home and abroad, but also from a wish to counter movements of decolonization. However, they lasted only a short while, because of the success of movements for independence.

After 1960, experts who had been associated with the SCIU, and later with the Colonial Office, now often helped the UN. Many international civil servants continued their predecessors' work at the LN, in an attempt to overcome colonial states' guarded attitude regarding surveys in territories under their administration. From the 1950s, they joined a new school of understanding, that of the 'demographic transition', which associated economic progress with low fertility and low mortality, and blamed colonial administration for only curbing mortality, thus helping what they saw as a population explosion. Many who had previously interpreted the little information there was available as showing undesirable signs of incipient depopulation of the continent, now positively supported international campaigns to reduce birth rates, and their concern for birth registrations remained in the domain of geopolitics rather than individual rights (Bashford 2008).

With decolonization, African claims for birth registration came to resemble the American campaigns of the interwar years. The more aggressive understanding of human rights, that of the 'challenge to the public' of the USA and of France (see Chapter 15), which had previously been limited to national political cultures of the global North, was about to enter inter-governmental and non-governmental international organizations. In 1961, a group of demographers based at Boston University collected '*Demographic Information on Tropical Africa*'. A crucial element, they believed, for the 'development' of independent nation states, 'Adequate information on the status and trends of population is basic to most social studies and essential for planning social and economic development.' They deplored the absence of data on the number of children born to women. For this kind of knowledge, the census method was unreliable: 'it is hardly an exaggeration to say that there is no knowledge about levels of mortality anywhere in Africa – except in some non-African communities' (Lorimer 1961, v, 4–6). African statisticians themselves acknowledged that Ethiopia, the oldest independent nation, was 'the largest terra incognita in Africa'.[20] In 1959, Addis Ababa, which had received the SCIU in 1936, as we have seen earlier, in order to open a child welfare centre, hosted the first conference of African statisticians – a body who would add professional interest to the number of factors militating in favour of civil registration. They underlined the lack of vital statistics whose collection was 'beyond the resources of most of the countries and territories'. African and international experts' call for better data on vital events led, in 1974, to a United Nations World Population Conference, which linked the promotion of birth registration to human rights. It sought to 'identify those human rights that obligate the states to ensure that vital events are registered, as well as those whose realization may depend on civil registration having taken place' (cited in Powell 1980, 1).

Amongst newly independent countries, the need for birth registration was also arising with the requirements of statehood, and the sheer problem of identifying citizens:

> proof of nationality through birth registration has been a problem for many newly emergent independent countries because colonial registration systems often failed to cover the entire population of the country, with the result that births in the dominant native or ethnic group were not registered systematically [. . .] Without certification of birth, such countries were hard pressed, when independence came, to identify nationals, and many began at that time to develop or improve their civil registration systems.
>
> (Powell 1980, 5)

The few Africans who had attended the Conference on the African Child of 1931, those who had helped draft recommendations for the training of native doctors and the education of the population, who had followed Kuczynski's exposition of the ways in which uniform and effective registration of vital events would enhance

[20] Lorimer 1961, entry no. 167 and ch. IV; Gregory *et al.* 1984; Union internationale pour l'étude scientifique de la population 1960, ch. IV.

the quality of colonial governance on the continent, and who had read the international yearbooks that gave an equal treatment to their part of the world, were now embarking on their own campaigns. In the 1950s, during the negotiations leading to the UN Declaration of the Rights of the Child at the Commission on Human Rights, leaders of the new African countries saw in the language of universal rights for children a means not only to mark a visible engagement on their part towards the functions of statehood but also a claim on the international community for help and resources to implement such rights.

This time, it was not in the name of improving colonial trusteeship, but in the name of a common humanity. We have seen that problems of governance and centralization similar to those found in the colonial world existed too in the USA during the interwar years, where the harmonization of methods advocated by the APHA belonged to a larger project of 'nationalization' (Hetzel 1997, 52). Current campaigners for the implementation of the right to registration at birth still underline the importance of registration in the construction of states: 'An effective system of birth registration is fundamental not only to the fulfilment of child rights, but to the rational operation of a humane government in the modern world' (Dow 1998, 5). The inclusion in the 1989 Convention on the Rights of the Child of registration at birth as a right for children has led to the allocation of resources and expertise to study the state of the 'First Right' systematically in all regions of the world. Findings about the political, social and cultural impediments to civil registration often recall those of the interwar years. The discrepancies between North and South have increased and, even more than in 1931, differences in civil registration are 'Intimately linked with rising inequality'. United Nations Children's Fund (UNICEF) literature estimates the number of births which are not registered every year to be 40 million (Dow 1998, 5).

Launched in 2005 under the slogan 'Every Child Counts', the campaign for universal birth registration involving UNICEF and the NGO, Plan International, has exposed major inequalities in registration rates between regions of the world, and insists on the responsibility of all countries to help the low registration regions to improve. With a rate of 37 per cent, sub-Saharan Africa currently has the lowest regional record, while the Middle East and northern Africa have reached 75 per cent (Plan International n.d.; UNICEF 1988, 2002, 2005). Plan International local activities to 'raise awareness' now involve children, in addition to parents, not only in emulation of the Boy Scout of the 1930s, who helped promote the registration of others, but also in the spirit of the Convention, as the active agents of the promotion of their own rights. If these 'calculative practices' of self-interest belong to an ethos of development of a new nature, largely influenced by neoliberalism (Ilcan and Phillips 2010), they can also be seen, in many ways, as inheritances of the interwar years. On the one hand, it has been true in many newly independent states that, 'viewing registration as a colonial custom unrelated to their culture, many citizens [are] slow to accept its benefits' (Dow 1998, 6; see Editors'

Introduction). On the other hand, in their wish to assist disadvantaged states, to enlist the support of the publics of rich regions, to publicize best practices and to produce knowledge that would help these goals in the name of a common humanity, UNICEF and Plan International resemble their interwar predecessors. Thus, the movement to promote birth registration as a universal right for children in the interwar USA and Africa and on the post-war international stage shows that contemporary UN and NGO initiatives today are heir to a complex prior political history in the twentieth century. As is also demonstrated by so many other chapters in this volume, there are few parts of the world, even in those countries where registration systems are currently lacking, where identity registration systems have not in fact already been promoted and in many cases temporarily established at some point in the past. The current international movement to promote registration at birth could benefit from paying close attention to its own precursors in this rich history, especially in Africa where Plan International and UNICEF are active today.

References

Allman, Jean. 1994. 'Making Mothers: Missionaries, Medical Officers and Women's Work in Colonial Asante, 1924–1945.' *History Workshop Journal* 38(1): 23–47.

Anon. 1917. 'The Registration Area for Births.' *Journal of the American Public Health Association* 7: 150–151.

Balfe, James P. 1918. 'Birth Registration in Connecticut.' *Journal of the American Public Health Association* 8: 776–779.

Bashford, Alison. 2008. 'Population, Geopolitics, and International Organizations in the Mid Twentieth Century.' *Journal of World History* 19(3): 327–348.

Baughan, Emily. 2011. 'Building a "True League of Nations": Collaboration between the League of Nations and the British Save the Children Fund in Relief for Russian Refugees and Famine Victims, c. 1920–1930.' Paper presented at conference, 'Towards a New History of the League of Nations', Geneva, 2011.

Beagle, F. D. 1911. 'Registration of Births.' *American Journal of Public Health* 1(5): 359–363.

Borowy, Iris. 2005. 'World Health in a Book – the International Health Yearbooks.' In *Facing Illness in Troubled Times: Health in Europe in the Interwar Years, 1918–1939*, ed. Iris Borowy and Wolf D. Gruner. Frankfurt: Peter Lang, 85–128.

—— 2009. *Coming to Terms with World Health: The League of Nations Health Organisation 1921–1946*. Frankfurt: Peter Lang.

Bueren, Geraldine Van. 1995. *The International Law on the Rights of the Child*. Dordrecht: Martinus Nijhoff.

Cordell, Dennis D. 1993. 'Où sont tous les enfants? La faible fécondité en Centrafrique, 1890–1960.' In *Population, reproduction, sociétés: perspectives et enjeux de démographie sociale*, ed. Joel W. Gregory and Dennis D. Cordell. Montréal: Presses de l'Université de Montréal, 257–283.

Daughton, James P. 2008. 'Documenting Colonial Violence: The International Campaign against Forced Labor during the Interwar Years.' *Revue de l'Histoire de la Shoah* 189.

Deacon, W. J. W. 1937. 'Test and Promotion of Registration of Births and Deaths.' *Journal of the American Public Health Association* 37: 492–498.

Dow, Unity. 1998. 'Birth Registration: The "First" Right.' *UNICEF: The Progress of Nations*. New York: UNICEF Division of Communications, 5–11.

Droux, Joëlle. 2011. 'Les projets de conventions sur l'assistance aux mineurs étrangers (1890–1939): enjeux et impasses de l'internationalisation des politiques sociales (1890–1939).' Paper presented at conference, 'Towards a New History of the League of Nations', Geneva, 2011.

Dublin, Louis I. *et al.* 1928. 'The Growth of the Birth Registration Areas.' *Journal of the American Public Health Association* 18: 606–608.

Ford, James. 1931. 'The International Conference on African Children.' *International Press Correspondence* 39: 39–40.

Freeman, Kathleen. 1965. *If Any Man Build: The History of the Save the Children Fund*. London: Hodder and Stoughton.

Fuller, Edward. 1925. *The International Yearbook of Child Care and Protection*. London: Longman's, Green and Co.

—— 1928. *The International Yearbook of Child Care and Protection*. London: Longman's, Green and Co.

—— 1951. *The Right of the Child, a Chapter in Social History: With a Foreword by Countess Mountbatten of Burma*. Boston: Beacon Press.

Ghandhi, Sandy. 1995. 'Family and Child Rights.' In *The International Covenant on Civil and Political Rights and United Kingdom Law*, ed. David John Harris and Sarah Joseph. Oxford: Clarendon Press, 491–534.

Gregory, Joel W., Dennis D. Cordell and Raymond Gervais. 1984. *African Historical Demography: A Multidisciplinary Bibliography*. Los Angeles: Crossroads Press.

Hemenway, Henry Bixby. 1921. 'Birth and Death Certificates as Legal Evidence.' *American Journal of Public Health* 11: 1–5.

Hetzel, A. M. 1997. *History and Organization of the Vital Statistics System*, 2nd edn. Washington, DC: National Center for Health Statistics.

Ilcan, S. and L. Phillips. 2010. 'Developmentalities and Calculative Practices: The Millennium Development Goals.' *Antipode* 42(4): 844–874.

Ingen, Philip Van. 1935. *The Story of the American Child Health Association*. New York: American Child Health Association.

Ittmann, Karl. 2003. 'Demography as Policy Science in the British Empire, 1918–1969.' *Journal of Policy History* 15(4): 417–448.

Jaeger, Hans-Martin. 2008. 'World Opinion and the Founding of the UN: Governmentalizing International Politics.' *European Journal of International Relations* 14(4): 589–618.

Jebb, Eglantyne. 1929. *Save the Child! A Posthumous Essay*. London: Weardale Press.

Kuczynski, Robert René. 1948. *Demographic Survey of the British Colonial Empire*, vol. 1. Oxford: Oxford University Press.

—— 1949. *Demographic Survey of the British Colonial Empire*, vol. 2. Oxford: Oxford University Press.

Lorimer, Frank. 1961. *Demographic Information on Tropical Africa*. Boston: Boston University Press.

Mahood, Linda. 2009. *Feminism and Voluntary Action: Eglantyne Jebb and Save the Children, 1876–1928*. Basingstoke: Palgrave Macmillan.

Manger, John Emerson. 1919. 'Cooperation of State and Federal Governments in Registration of Births and Deaths.' *Journal of the American Public Health Association* 9: 75–78.

Marshall, Dominique. 2004. 'Children's Rights in Imperial Political Cultures: Missionary and Humanitarian Contributions to the Conference on the African Child of 1931.' *International Journal of Children's Rights* 12: 273–318.

—— 2006. 'The Rights of African Children, the Save the Children Fund and Public Opinion in Europe and Ethiopia: The Centre of Child Welfare of Addis Ababa, Spring 1936.' In *Proceedings of the XVth International Conference of Ethiopian Studies, Hamburg, July 20–25, 2003*, ed. Siegbert Uhlig. Wiesbaden: Otto Harrassowitz Verlag.

—— 2008. 'Children's Rights and Children's Action in International Relief and Domestic Welfare: The Work of Herbert Hoover between 1914 and 1950.' *Journal of the History of Childhood and Youth* 1(3): 351–388.

—— 2009. 'Save the Children International.' In *The Palgrave Dictionary of Transnational History*, ed. Akira Iriye and Pierre-Yves Saunier. Basingstoke: Palgrave Macmillan.

Mason Knox, J. H. 1911. 'The Importance of Birth Registration to Determine Infant Mortality.' *Journal of the American Public Health Association* 1: 43–47.

Nowak, Manfred. 2005. *U.N. Covenant on Civil and Political Rights: CCPR Commentary*, 2nd edn. Kehl: N. P. Engel.

Palmer, Bryan D. 2004. 'Race and Revolution.' *Labour/Le Travail* 54: 193–221.

Parker, Jacqueline K. and Edward M. Carpenter. 1981. 'Julia Lathrop and the Children's Bureau: The Emergence of an Institution.' *Social Service Review* 55(1): 60–77.

Plan International. n.d. 'Facts and Figures – Universal Birth Registration.' *Plan International*. http://plan-international.org/birthregistration/the-campaign/facts-and-figures.

Powell, Nora P. 1980. *Human Rights and Registration of Vital Events*. Bethesda, MD: International Institute for Vital Registration and Statistics.

Royal Statistical Society (Great Britain). 1912. *Infantile Mortality. Report of the Special Committee appointed . . . to enquire into the systems adopted in different countries for the registration of births . . . and deaths, etc*. London: Royal Statistical Society (Great Britain).

Save the Children. 2011. *NGO Position Paper for a UNHCR Conclusion on Birth Registration*. http://resourcecentre.savethechildren.se/content/library/documents/ngo-position-paper-unhcr-conclusion-birth-registration.

Save the Children International Union. 1932. *The Proceedings of the International Conference on African Children*. Geneva.

Sharp, Evelyn. 1931. *The African Child: An Account of the International Conference on African Children, Geneva*. London: Weardale Press.

Sharpless, John. 1997. 'Population Science, Private Foundations, and Development Aid: The Transformation of Demographic Knowledge in the United States, 1945–1965.' In *International Development and the Social Sciences: Essays on the History and Politics of Knowledge*, ed. Frederick Cooper and Randall M. Packard. Berkeley: University of California Press, 176–198.

Skocpol, Theda. 1992. *Protecting Soldiers and Mothers: The Political Origins of Social Policy in the United States*. Cambridge, MA: Belknap Press of Harvard University Press.

UNICEF. 1988. *The Rights of the Child. Selected Proceedings of a Workshop on the Draft Convention on the Rights of the Child: An African Perspective*. Nairobi: UNICEF.

—— 2002. 'Birth Registration: Right from the Start.' *Innocenti Digest* 9(March): 1–21.

—— 2005. *The 'Rights' Start to Life: A Statistical Analysis of Birth Registrations, 2005*. New York: UNICEF.

Union internationale pour l'étude scientifique de la population. 1960. *Problèmes de démographie en Afrique, Colloque de Paris, 20 au 27 aout 1959*.

Veerman, Philip E. 1992. *The Rights of the Child and the Changing Image of Childhood*. Dordrecht: Martinus Nijhoff.

Wilbur, Cressy L. 1912. 'Infant Mortality.' *Journal of the American Public Health Association* 2: 999–1001.

Woodhouse, Barbara Bennett. 2008. *Hidden in Plain Sight: The Tragedy of Children's Rights from Ben Franklin to Lionel Tate*. Princeton, NJ: Princeton University Press.

18

Children, Citizenship and Child Support: The Child Support Grant in Post-Apartheid South Africa

FRANCIE LUND

Introduction

SOUTH AFRICA IS A SIGNATORY to the United Nations Convention on the Rights of the Child, the Covenant on Civil and Political Rights, and the African Charter on the Rights and Welfare of the Child. According to all these conventions, 'all children . . . are entitled to a name, a nationality and immediate birth registration' (Lawyers for Human Rights 2010, 6). In April 1998, four years after the election of the democratic government in South Africa, a new form of state social assistance was introduced for poor children from birth to their seventh birthday, the Child Support Grant (CSG). When the CSG was introduced, a monthly amount of about US$7 was payable to the caregiver of a child up to the age of 7. Twelve years later, the CSG was reaching some 10 million children, which is about 80 per cent of those who had first been eligible, and it is reaching an increasing proportion, annually, of the older age groups to which the grant has since been extended. The extension to the age of 18 will be completed in 2012.

A requirement for receiving this cash transfer was that the adult applicant had to have an identity document – the thirteen-digit ID number which forms the basis of citizen registration in South Africa – and the birth of the child had to be registered. During the twentieth century, a complex system for the registration of adults, especially adult men, had developed, chiefly in relation to the movement of African people for the purposes of employment, to limit the migration into cities of people from rural areas, and to enforce residential segregation in both urban and rural areas. There were different systems for registration of adults of different racial groups, in different regions, and there was very little enforcement of the requirement that births should be registered. Collection of household data, through the census and through household surveys, was notoriously unreliable, and unable (because based on an inappropriate model of family life) to accommodate the complexity of extended household structures, including the mobility of young children between

Proceedings of the British Academy **182**, 475–494. © The British Academy 2012.

kin households. On the other hand, the rapid increase in coverage of state pensions for elderly people (Lund 1993) meant that by the late 1980s, over 80 per cent of the poorest elderly South Africans, the great majority of whom were black, in both urban and rural areas, had the citizen ID, which was a requirement to receive the pensions. They thus laid claim to an entitlement even though, in the pre-1994 regime, they were not yet full citizens.

Since its introduction, the CSG has been the focus of national and international debate and research attention in large-scale surveys and qualitative studies, tracking and analysing the effects of cash transfers on child development, and education, and in mitigating poverty. The evidence for the positive developmental effects of this social programme is strong. It has direct impacts on the reduction of poverty and inequality (Leibbrandt *et al.* 2010, 65, 66). Only four years after its introduction, it had a measurable positive effect on school enrolment in a predominantly rural and poor area of KwaZulu-Natal province (Case *et al.* 2005). Data gathered from approximately 9,000 households enabled a comparison between eligible children who had, and who had not, received the CSG. Those receiving the assistance had an 8.1 percentage increase in school enrolment over those who had not received it, and this in a context where school enrolment rates were already high (Case *et al.* 2005). The CSG's positive impact on child nutrition was established by Agüero *et al.* (2008) – children who had received the CSG when they were very young (first three years of life) had increased height-for-age (a reliable measure of child health) compared to eligible children who did not receive it.

This policy reform has received attention also because of the global shift in social policy towards a more interventionist yet targeted role for the state. The South African CSG is being widely used as an example of good practice in the international campaigns for a 'social protection floor', an idea that has been accepted at the highest level of the United Nations agencies, and driven by alliances between these, and powerful non-governmental organizations. There is wide acceptance of the harm that has been done by structural adjustment policies to many poor people in the global North and global South. Many countries have recently introduced such cash transfers, but the South African CSG is one of the very rare ones that were unconditional when introduced (Lund *et al.* 2009) – in other words, the caregiver did not have to fulfil any behavioural requirements, such as taking the child to a clinic, in order to receive the benefit. It is thus an interesting contemporary case study of a national, unconditional and widely targeted programme that has already in the short term had substantial impact.

This chapter focuses in particular on the role of registration systems in opening up or closing down poorer people's access to state programmes and entitlements. It also explores the recent effects of the new grant on birth registration. The CSG was designed and started to be delivered at the same time as South Africa moved away from apartheid, away from the racially separate political and administrative systems of government, to a unified national system. A prerequisite of transition to democracy was the reunification of the fragmented separate puppet states, at the same time as services had to be racially equalized. The space for the introduction of a new form of support for children was created by the political conjuncture; the possibility of achieving this rapidly was contingent on administrative unification. It also depended on the prior existence of the pension delivery system, partly administered by government but increasingly privatized, which penetrated deep into remote rural areas.

I start with a short overview of the racial and spatial fragmentation imposed by the apartheid government, as well as of the system of limited state assistance that developed even under the apartheid state and its Bantustans. I describe the development of social assistance during the twentieth century, and this provides the context for the introduction, in 1998, of the Child Support Grant, the earliest substantial social policy reform that was implemented in the new democracy. I then focus on issues related to civil registration: citizen identity documents, proof of parental and marital status, and birth registration, as well as other administrative barriers to access to the grants, especially within the Department of Home Affairs (DHA), which is responsible for civil registration. I describe the attempt to legalize the use of alternative forms of identification where original documents are unable to be produced, as well as the access of non-citizens to this and other social security benefits. I also argue, following Goldblatt (2005), that while millions of women and children have benefited directly from the CSG and other state grants, the administrative domain of grants, which includes traditional rural authorities (the chiefs and their headmen) and police stations, involves very masculine, patriarchal and uncomfortable spaces for many of the women – mothers and grandmothers – who apply for the CSG. The chapter concludes with some speculation about how the CSG, as a major post-apartheid policy reform, might have contributed to the consolidation of democracy in the first few years of transition. It did this partly through providing an incentive for the *early* registration of children's births. The CSG has likely also contributed to a heightened consciousness about the rights of children.

Apartheid racial and spatial fragmentation

South Africa is classified as a middle income country, and just more than half of the population of some 49 million is urbanized. A central feature of the apartheid system was the classification of the population in a Population Register with four official 'race groups': African, coloured, Indian and white. This classification was the basis according to which the population was allocated to separate residential areas in which to live, and to the occupations they were allowed to pursue. Under first British colonial domination and then apartheid, there was rigid control of labour mobility, with African people being by and large excluded from free movement in and out of cities, unless they had a permit to work and/or a permanent residence permit. If an African person had ninety-nine-year leasehold rights, and her or his parents had 'section 10 rights' (Section 10 of the Native Laws Amendment Act of 1952, which circumscribed Africans' access to urban areas), she or he could get a work permit. All people who were not white – African, coloured and Indian people – were incrementally and systematically excluded from access to land, the vote, residential areas and choice of employment. Inevitably these policies led to racially and spatially based patterns of poverty, and severe inequality. Poverty was most severe for Africans, especially for African women, and in rural areas.

In order to secure racial separation, the apartheid government set up its grand plan for residential segregation. In urban areas, the townships and suburbs were racially segregated. At the national level, the apartheid state set up different geo-political entities with a pretence of self-administration and independence: the six self-governing homelands and four independent Bantustans, created for different 'ethnic groups'. Each of these entities had its own 'capital' town, and this 'capital' status brought with it some urban infrastructure including electricity, water and communications. At the same time, these far-flung towns and cities did become hubs that enabled the penetration of the delivery of state pensions and grants to very poor black people in rural areas, during the apartheid years. In turn, this was the underlying delivery infrastructure that could so rapidly distribute the new Child Support Grant.

State social assistance

During the apartheid era a set of social pensions and grants (now called 'cash transfers' – see Chapter 19) were set in place, usually established for white people first, then extended to the whole population (Lund 1993; Devereux 2001). In 1990, the Old Age Pension (OAP) for elderly people consumed about three-quarters of all grant money, with a very small additional amount given to a War Veterans Pension for those who had fought in certain wars. The Disability Grant (DG) for people with physical and mental disabilities accounted for about a further 20 per cent of the grant budget. The small (about 5 per cent) remainder of the social assistance budget was allocated to grants for children and families, in the form of a State Maintenance Grant (SMG).

All of the grants were non-contributory and were paid from general revenue. These cash transfers were entitlements in law, for all races, and pertained to the four Bantustans and six self-governing territories as well. White, Indian and coloured people had separate welfare administrations at national level; welfare for African people in the 'common area' (that is, not in the self-governing areas or Bantustans) was delivered through the provincial administrations. Interestingly, these racially separate administrations became strong drivers of upward mobility for civil servants, regardless of race.

The pensions and grants were racially discriminatory both in the amount awarded to each beneficiary, and in the procedures for application and delivery. In 1982 for example the amounts of the OAP and the DG were in the ratio of about 10:5:1 for white people, Indian and coloured people, and African people, respectively. Pensions for white people were paid every month, those for other 'race groups' every two months, and there were many other administrative procedures which disadvantaged those who were not white (Lund 1993). However the cash transfers were *also*, as pointed out by Hassim (2005), a signal of social citizenship for the majority of (poor and black) South Africans.

In order to get a grant before 1995, an applicant had to have proof of identity, proof of citizenship or permanent residence, and proof of age. For the African population this was particularly complex. Proof of *identity* did *not* have to be the identity document ('ID book'). It could be a reference book (a form of identification and mobility control restricted to African people), passport, homeland travel document, or an ID book. Proof of *citizenship* on the other hand required the ID book. Permanent residence could be proved by having the permanent residence permit. Residents of the four Bantustans – Transkei, Venda, Bophuthatswana and Ciskei – had to prove they had been living in South Africa at the date of their 'independence' (Association for Rural Advancement 1990). A section 10 stamp could be used to provide this proof, or a 'Farm Labourer' stamp in an old reference book or ID document, or a letter from a (white) farm owner saying when the applicant had lived on the farm (Association for Rural Advancement 1990). In rural areas where tribal authorities held sway, grant applicants had to obtain a declaration from the local chief that the applicant was a resident of the chief's area.

Proof of age required a birth certificate, or certificate of baptism or marriage, or an ID book. Where there was no documentation, or problematic documentation, then a pension official or district medical officer or two people known to, and older than, the applicant could assess age. Pension officials devised some ingenious locally based timelines for such assessment, based on indigenous knowledge and use. In one remote area, Maputoland in the old Zululand, one such line included 'the Great War' (First World War), 'the German War' (Second World War), 'the year of apartheid' (1948), and 'the time the government started spraying with DDT against malaria' (about 1952).

For individual applicants, it was extremely expensive in terms of time and money to access their entitlements, sometimes involving many visits to pension offices. Forms were complex, in the wrong language, interpreted differently by different officials, and frequently simply not available. Applicants had to supply fingerprints, and a written 'X' could be used in place of a signature. Prospective pensioners could only find out whether their application had been successfully processed every two months when pension delivery took place. If the pension had not been processed and awarded, the applicant was given no reason for the lack of success, and simply told to 'come back next time'.

Even after a pension was awarded, there could be major problems in the system, with a payment failing to appear. The money sometimes ran out. The following extract is taken from the proceedings of the KwaZulu government in 1983, with a senior civil servant accounting to the KwaZulu Auditor General for the overrun in the overall welfare budget, of which pensions comprised the major portion:

> Pensions had always been our lifesaver in the past. Well, it was a quick way of saving. What happened was that a number of pensions were dropped out by the computer and in some way this enabled us to effect some savings. But unfortunately the pensioners are now aware of their rights; thanks to Legal Aid [*sic*: he meant the Legal Resources Centre] and the Black Sash the public is now very well educated on the rights of the pensioner. We faced claims, Sir, and we had to pay. Of course, our Pensions Section, fortunately or unfortunately, has also become much more efficient and it has picked up more pensions that had been dropped by the computer and we had to pay.
>
> (KwaZulu Government 1983)

This pension official was clearly overseeing the misuse of information systems in order to save money, and acknowledging with seeming ambivalence the actions of two human rights organizations, the Legal Resources Centre and the Black Sash, in assisting pensioners to get their correct entitlements.

President F. W. de Klerk announced in 1991 that Nelson Mandela would be released from jail, and that the ANC was allowed to come home from exile and operate legally. Other political parties were also un-banned, and steps were put in place for the move towards a united and democratic South Africa. Some of this change had been anticipated, and the late 1980s had been a time of great policy activity, not least in the social cluster – housing, health, education and welfare. In welfare, as early as 1980 the apartheid government itself had started moving towards racial parity in state pensions and grants. In 1980, the annual value of the old-age pension, at constant 2009 prices, was about R21,000 for whites, compared to R11,000 for coloured and Indian people, and R6,000 for Africans. By 1990, the figure had equalized across all racial groups to about R12,000 (Leibbrandt *et al.* 2010, 61, using data from Servaas van der Berg and from National Treasury). Calculations done by van der Berg for the value of the State Maintenance Grant, which I discuss below, showed a similar dramatic pattern: the SMG for coloured and Indian people held pretty steady between about 1980 and 1990, at around R4,000 annually, whereas that for Africans rose from R1,000 to around R3,000, and that for whites fell from the 1980 approximate level of R6,500 to just less than R4,000. Racial parity in the grants was reached in 1993 (Republic of South Africa 1996, 11). Gradually the other discriminatory procedures such as frequency of payment which worked particularly against the African population were removed. The 1991 national budget speech acknowledged the inevitability of achieving parity in all aspects of the pension system within four years.

Unifying this fragmented administrative state machinery was one of the great achievements of the transitional period (Lund 2008), notwithstanding the failure, identified by Breckenridge (2005), to solve problems with the underlying information systems in order to enable efficient and less corrupt administration. In the early 1990s, nine new provinces replaced and integrated the former four provinces of the Republic, the four Bantustans and six homelands. Their administrations moved to processing the pensions and grants on a non-racial basis, and the vastly improved computer technology enabled better management. The 1994 democratic election itself was an incentive for tens of thousands of formerly unregistered citizens to get their ID numbers and books. The new government then promised a range of pro-poor programmes, including housing subsidies, land restitution and redistribution, and subsidized water tariffs. In order to claim any of these, a citizen would have to have an ID number and book.

The Child Support Grant

Under apartheid there were four main forms of state-administered financial support for children. Typically, these were introduced first for white people, then extended to Indian and coloured people, and finally to African people as well.

First, private parental maintenance was aimed largely at fathers who had left their partner and/or children. This was and is implemented through the judicial system, and a parent, usually the father, has to pay regular maintenance costs. Second, in common with many other countries, South Africa had and has a procedure for the formal fostering of vulnerable children: an adult who is not the biological parent can become the legal foster parent of a child, up to the age of 18, who is deemed to be 'in need of care'. The aim is to enable the child to grow up in a family setting. The state-financed Foster Care Grant is designed to give some financial assistance to this foster parent; it was not designed primarily as a poverty mitigation measure. Third, a Care Dependency Grant is payable to the carer(s) of a severely physically and/or mentally impaired child, ostensibly to avoid the child's admission to institutional care ('ostensibly' because in fact there are virtually no such institutions for African children, especially in rural areas). This grant is replaced by the Disability Grant when the child reaches adulthood.

Fourth and finally, there was a state-financed State Maintenance Grant (SMG). This means-tested grant had been set up to support and protect women and children in cases where the husband and father was missing (through death, abandonment, imprisonment and for various other reasons). It was based on a nuclear model of family life, assuming that 'the norm' for a family was a married couple, with a husband in employment and a wife at home looking after children. These assumptions were similar to those underlying the post-1945 Beveridge welfare state model of British family life. The SMG first excluded African people. Over the years it was extended in law to all South Africans but Africans were *de facto* excluded (Lund 2008, 15–17), and it was received mostly by Indian and coloured beneficiaries, with whites by and large being ineligible because they were too well off.

The Lund Committee of Enquiry into Child and Family Support was set up in 1995 to address issues of child support. I chaired this Committee, and have written an extended account of this policy reform (Lund 2008). The Committee's mandate was to address child support broadly, but embedded in the terms of reference was a most difficult instruction: 'solve the problem of the SMG'. It would have been extremely expensive to have extended this grant to all who were eligible. More important, in my view, was that it was arguably not an appropriate form of support given the realities of family life for the majority of South Africans. The SMG was modelled on a Beveridge-like view of the nuclear family, while the reality in South Africa was different. The following is based on 2005 data, but the basic pattern has existed for decades:

> . . . in South Africa, only about 40 per cent of children live with both their mother and father, while at least an equal number live only with their mother. The majority of women have children, but a large number of them do so outside of marriage, and with different fathers for successive children. Just less than one fifth of children have lost at least one parent. Only about one third of the 12.7 million households conform to the 'nuclear norm' of children and parents, with about one fifth having three generations or more present in one household. Many grandmothers care for their grandchildren, often in the absence of the children's parents.
>
> (Budlender and Lund 2011, 926)

This 'disrupted legacy of family life' (Budlender and Lund 2011, 926) inherited by the new government had been caused primarily by colonial and then apartheid policies and practices of coercing male labour into the mining and commercial agriculture industries.

The core considerations underpinning the child support policy reform were that it had to address child poverty and children's developmental needs. It had to be based on the realities of fractured family life. It had to address apartheid's racial and spatial legacy, and reach the very poor, most of whom were African, and residing in rural areas and informal settlements. It had to anticipate the alarming increase in the number of young children who would be orphaned through HIV/AIDS. It had to be administratively feasible, taking into account the lack of capacity in the new government. And to get through the Fiscal and Financial Commission, the Budget Council, and the Cabinet, in particular the Treasury, it had to be 'fiscally sustainable' – in ordinary language, not cost too much, and designed in such a way that costs could be managed over time.

The main recommendation of the Lund Committee was for a very modest unconditional cash transfer to go, in the first instance, to children up to their seventh birthday. Most on the Committee wanted a universal grant: one that went to *all* children, rather than targeting only poorer children through a means test. This was an issue of solidarity and inclusiveness in 'the new South Africa'. There were also sound administrative and financial reasons: it is well known in the social security literature on targeting, that focusing on excluding the (fewer) wealthy people can instead lead to the exclusion of those poorer people who are in fact eligible (Barr 1995). The government, however, insisted on an income-based means test.

The government did, however, accept linked innovations that shifted the underlying principles of support for children. The SMG and other child-oriented grants were all premised on the relationship between the child and the biological parent(s). The new policy took into account first the high levels of mobility of very young children, and second that many are taken care of by kin, especially by grandparents or aunts. So, first, the principle of 'follow the child' was accepted, rather than the focus being on whether the biological parent was present; second, 'reach the child through the primary caregiver', and allow the entitlement to go to the person who bears daily responsibility for the care of the child. It was hoped that this would indeed be the biological parent, and probably would be the mother, but if the child was not with the mother, the access to the entitlement should not be refused or delayed. This significant shift – that the applicant did not have to be the biological mother or father – broke with the convention that the biological status of the parent automatically is the pathway to entitlement to a child-oriented benefit.

Some at the time, and since, saw this aspect of the Child Support Grant as an 'anti-familist' reform, or as one that de-links children from their families. On the contrary, it can be seen as a way of accommodating the realities of African family life, of confronting the inappropriateness of an essentially European or Beveridgean model of the family. It can be seen as precisely focusing on the family, though not on biological parenthood as such, in order to protect the child.

The acceptance by government and its legal advisers of the status of 'primary caregiver' as a basis for receiving an entitlement for a child clearly held potent implications for systems of defining access to entitlements. Access to state entitlements depends on identification as a citizen, and that identification is embedded in who one's biological parents are or were.

Registration, and parental status

As noted, application for the CSG requires both that the adult applicant (the primary caregiver) has an ID book, and that the birth of the child has been registered. Under apartheid, the ID book was a political instrument of the government's repressive control apparatuses, and one could have anticipated some resistance to the idea that the primary caregivers applying for the CSG would need to have an ID book. With regard to registration of births, the Medical Research Council estimated that in 1994, fewer than 20 per cent of all births were registered during the first year of a child's life. The Birth and Death Registration Act No. 51 of 1992 had been a first step towards trying to achieve comprehensive and free registration for all South

African citizens, but it retained the old rule that births had to be registered within seven days of the child being born – extremely difficult, especially for new mothers, in rural areas where registration offices are scarce. Subsequent amendments, starting in 1995, have extended the time period for registration to thirty days; late registration can be done, but needs additional and more complex documentation (Skelton 1998, 53, 54). With late registrations, although the list of documents required is long, officials may vary this requirement and tend to insist only on the ID of the caregiver and birth certificate of the child (Hunter and Adato 2007, 15, 16). As will be discussed below, however, obtaining a birth certificate has been far from straightforward for many.

When the new CSG policy was introduced, there was some resistance to these requirements from non-governmental organizations (NGOs) such as Access of Children to Economic and Social Security (ACESS). This was because the responsible Department of Home Affairs was incompetent in the extreme, and it cost hours in time and money for very poor people to get their documentation in order. However, overall there was an acceptance that an ID system is a 'normal' requirement in a democracy, as it is also for sound planning. The NGOs later played an important role in assisting CSG applicants to assemble and deliver their papers.

A policy issue in the design of the CSG was whether all eligible children up to the age of 7 should have immediate access, or whether there should be a phased year-by-year introduction as children were born. Equity and racial redress arguments favoured the former option, driven by the overall political climate towards inclusiveness as soon as possible. Administrative considerations would have favoured the latter, as it would have spread the burden of administration over a longer period. The government opted for the former, 'everyone-eligible-at-once', approach.

As is to be expected at the start of any new programme of intervention, the take-up rate was initially slow. Progress was closely monitored by numbers of human rights, child welfare and other non-governmental organizations such as the Centre for Applied Legal Studies at University of the Witwatersrand, ACESS, the University of Cape Town's Children's Institute, CASE (the Community Agency for Social Enquiry), and the Legal Resources Centre. They ensured that the results of their research were shared with those in government. Take-up rapidly improved as the systems settled down, and by about 2001, 400,000 new beneficiaries were being added each year. However, there was patchy delivery, with some bleak spots where no grants were being distributed. Nevertheless, by 2010, just over 10 million children were getting the grant.

Not all prospective caregivers hasten to get the grant when a child is born. One major barrier to receipt is not in the welfare department at all, but is in the infamous DHA. Of all South African ministries and their departments, this one has appeared to be most impervious to attempts at improved administration. In an early study of barriers to getting the CSG, a child rights NGO canvassed other organizations assisting children to obtain the CSG. The most common problems were that application forms were simply lost; there were long delays in processing applications for identity documents; where information was missing, applicants would only be told of this when they returned months later to receive, they hoped, the document itself. There were difficulties getting death certificates of dead parents; it was especially difficult to obtain a death certificate if the deceased parent had a Pauper's Burial (ACESS 2003).

In a recent household survey those who were eligible for the CSG but had not applied for it were asked why they had not applied. Over a fifth of the respondents – 22 per cent – cited problems with documentation (Leibbrandt *et al.* 2010, 58). This finding comes up repeatedly in studies about access to the CSG (Goldblatt *et al.* 2006, 24–32; Hunter and Adato 2007, 15, 16; Leibbrandt *et al.* 2010, 58). Unfortunately, many studies do not ask respondents exactly which of the documents cause the greatest problems. An exception is the finding from a large UNICEF-supported survey which established that it was the birth certificate, rather than 'other documents' (Delany *et al.* 2008, 48). CSG applicants cite long delays experienced in getting the birth certificate processed; this stands in stark contrast to the 'same-day service' advertised on the DHA website (accessed 2 October 2011). Health facilities are now able to issue maternity certificates after the birth of the child, and these are used in the registration of births; this should be viewed as a constructive step that will have facilitated easier access for many people. However, maternity certificates are not uniformly distributed; some clinics do not have the maternity certificate, instead using the Road to Health Card; babies born in informal facilities, or in their own homes, do not have access at birth to this early step in the procedure. The caregiver applying for the CSG then confronts problems when presenting at the DHA (Lawyers for Human Rights 2010).

For most of the period that the SMG was in place, only the biological mother could apply (although for a few years before it was phased out, biological fathers were also eligible to claim maintenance). Marital status had to be proven, and the onus was on the mother-applicant to do the administrative work regarding identification of the father and his employment status. Soon after the CSG was introduced, some of the bureaucratic requirements from the SMG crept back in, including this insistence on proof of marital status, and on proof that the father has tried to find work. Both of these were supposed to be irrelevant to eligibility for the CSG, and both involve heavy transaction costs, in time and in money, for the poorer women who apply.

The vast majority of primary caregiver applicants are the biological mothers of the children being applied for. When the CSG was introduced, in cases where the primary caregiver died, the CSG was automatically stopped. Another person then had to be designated to be the primary caregiver, and start the process of application anew. If this new caregiver had no ID book, this meant that there could be a delay of many months before the child would again be awarded a CSG, exactly those months in which, for children whose main carer has died, they are very vulnerable and need all possible support and protection. In response to demands for change from the NGOs, an improved procedure was introduced which allows the CSG to continue to be paid while the new caregiver is going through the formal procedure of being designated.

Early research on the CSG (Case *et al.* 2005) showed that maternal orphans were less likely to get the CSG than non-orphans. In other words, the biological mother's presence was an important factor determining which children, in complex households, would have the CSG. Murray Leibbrandt and his colleagues specifically cite, as a problem, the 'complex documentation required without the child's mother as caregiver' (Leibbrandt *et al.* 2010, 55). Both Hunter (2004, 28) and Hunter and Adato (2007, 15, 16) identify as a particular difficulty the situation where a mother is missing (she may have left the child in the care of a grandparent, or she may be dead) and has not left the birth certificate of the child being applied for with the caregiver.

There have been improvements to some of the bureaucratic requirements of the system, many of which resulted from vigorous campaigning by civil society organizations. Some of these actions have involved documentaries on national television, submissions to parliament, and litigation through the courts. In 2002, ACESS, a child rights organization, initiated a court case against the welfare department. The organization argued that as documentation presented the major barrier to access to the CSG, the department should allow alternative forms of identification for the applicant and the child, for example a letter from a local leader such as a school principal, or an affidavit from a police station. ACESS won this case only six years later. Since 2008, the regulation allows CSG applicants to apply without an official ID book or birth certificate. Sworn affidavits, stating the name, age and parentage of the applicant, and signed by commissioners of oaths, are accepted. To date there has been little progress, however, with actually implementing such alternative identification procedures. Some (for example Mirugi-Mukundi 2010) have expressed concern that such alternative identification might open up the citizen identification system to further corruption.

There have been quiet initiatives where collaboration has been built between government facilities, private individuals, and NGOs. Box 18.1 is drawn from Durban, KwaZulu-Natal province, and shows a remarkable – because in fact remarkably simple – instance of cooperative work which has little cost to any single party, but is to the great benefit of the CSG applicants.

The elements that contributed to the success of this intervention were that someone had the facts about the problems with access; someone cared enough to intervene; an official acknowledged there was a problem, and made himself available on a regular basis; the clinic had the capacity to process documents; and a person was willing to bridge the spatial and institutional distance between the clinic and the DHA.

Box 18.1 Informal collaboration to improve access to the CSG

The Cato Manor Development Project, in the Durban Metropolitan area, is an integrated urban planning organization serving some 100,000 Cato Manor residents. *Ithemba Lethu* is a project there that focuses on the well-being of local children. A staff member working with an AIDS prevention project saw that although a large number of local children qualified for social grants, they were not receiving them. This was mainly because of the caregivers' inability to access identity documents for themselves, and birth registration for the children. The forms and other supporting documents required to register births were often missing. The staff member set up a meeting with the DHA in Durban to explore ways of ensuring that all new births at the local clinic were registered. The DHA allowed the clinic to become a site for birth registration after an official had provided training for the social worker and the research clerks based at the clinic. Mothers with newborn babies arrived at the clinic within a few weeks of the baby's birth and as part of the process of providing primary health care services to these babies, their birth registration applications were processed. A staff member or a volunteer then delivered the documentation to the DHA, in the centre of the city, where an official informally agreed to be waiting for her. At the same time she collected completed birth certificates, and discussed and tried to resolve 'problem cases'. The week's new certificates would be returned to the clinic and issued to the mothers when they next came to the clinic.

Through this system it is estimated that almost all babies born to families living in Cato Manor had their births registered within the first few months of being born.

(Compiled by child rights activist Shirin Motala based on an interview with Darlene Menzies, of NGO *Ithemba Lethu*, on 5 August 2005)

Notwithstanding the bureaucratic barriers to access to the CSG, the speed with which it reached large numbers of children and indeed some of the attempts made by the bureaucracy to introduce alternative more flexible systems are remarkable. It is very clear that the CSG had a positive impact on birth registrations. The democratic elections in 1994 had caused more adults to get their ID books (and an ID as we have seen was a necessary requirement for the caregiver applicant for the CSG); and the new National Health Information System (NHIS) initiated after 1994 embarked on vigorous attempts to increase registration of births and deaths. It was estimated that only about a quarter (24.7 per cent) of births were registered in 1998, the year the CSG was introduced. By 2005, the proportion had increased to 72 per cent, and by 2008 to over 90 per cent (StatsSA 2009). Without detracting from the NHIS's own efforts, it must be the case that the CSG played a significant role in this increase. Of perhaps even greater significance is the shift, in proportions of births registered, between those registered within thirty days (called 'current registrations') and those registering later.

The percentages of late birth registrations, as compared to current registrations, have been declining since 1998. During 1998, over three-quarters (77.5 per cent) of birth registrations were late, whereas just over one-quarter (28.3 per cent) were registered late in 2008. From 1991 to 2004, the number of late birth registrations was higher than the number of current registrations. This pattern was reversed in 2005, when most births were registered during the year of birth rather than later (StatsSA 2009, 2). This trend from late to current registrations must be related to access to the CSG, as well as more simplified procedures for current registrations.

Non-citizens and social security

Civil registration systems are frequently used to enforce national boundaries around social welfare benefits. With increasing migration worldwide, a policy issue that is growing in importance at the global level is that of the rights of non-citizens to state support in a country in which they may have temporary or permanent resident rights, and rights to employment. During the last century, many people, especially from Mozambique and Zimbabwe, crossed the border into South Africa, primarily for economic reasons (see Chapter 9 on the longer-term history of the permeability of South African borders). People also crossed in order to consult with traditional leaders. For example, in Maputoland (in what is now KwaZulu-Natal province), the British colonial government had drawn the border between South Africa and Mozambique straight through the territorial area of the Tembe-Thonga people, with Chief Tembe living on the South African side, while people and lands governed by him also existed in Mozambique. In the 1970s and 1980s, the South African police would detain people they thought were from 'across the border', who were indistinguishable from local South Africans in the way they spoke and dressed. The police looked on the upper arm for the vaccination mark, which was different in pattern and place for Mozambicans compared to South Africans. Those carrying the foreign stigmata, as it were, were arrested and deported. This practice of deporting border-crossers continued into the 1990s.

The public debate in South Africa about foreigners' access to welfare is shaped by a history of regional solidarity and cross-border movement. During the struggle against apartheid, the ANC was given significant assistance by a number of African countries in the form of safe political space, and material and political support to those in the resistance movement in exile. At the political transition, there was strong popular political sentiment that one way in which South Africa could repay this large political debt would be through giving access to state grants to those from other countries.

In the late 1990s the Legal Resources Centre started a series of court cases arguing that permanent residents had the right to be included as beneficiaries of state social assistance. Most of the grants, including the CSG, are now available to permanent residents and, for the most part, to documented refugees from other countries (most of whom are from African countries). A study in rural Agincourt in Limpopo Province found that, although the mostly Mozambican permanent residents in that area had a right to grants, far fewer of those eligible actually applied for this financial support compared to South African citizens (Case and Menendez 2007). In that area, 92 per cent of South African households who had a member eligible for the old-age pension received the pension. Twenty per cent of households in the area were Mozambican, but only half of all Mozambican households with a pension-age-eligible permanent resident received the pension (Case and Menendez 2007). Case and Menendez suggest that it is more difficult for Mozambicans to access South African government grants, largely because of documents. One could also speculate further about the reasons: foreigners from other African countries have frequently been victims of South Africans' violent xenophobia, and have been accused of 'taking jobs away from South Africans'. Even those with welfare rights, such as the permanent residents, may nevertheless feel vulnerable and wish to stay away from engaging with state bureaucracies and police.

Gendered access to social security

State social assistance has made a material difference to millions of poorer South Africans – both those who directly receive the grants, and those in their households. There are interesting gendered dimensions (Lund 2006), which first became clear in research over the pension for elderly people. In the past, in common with the situation in many developed countries, women received the pension earlier than men, at 60 years of age compared to 65. As women on average live longer than men, they receive it for more years overall. They also use it differently: there is ample evidence that where the pension goes to an older woman in the household, it has a larger difference on overall household welfare than when the pension goes to an older man. Where women receive it, school-going children in the household stay in school for more months, with the effect being greater for girls than for boys. At present the age discrimination against men is being incrementally removed, and men and women will be eligible for the OAP at age 60.

The overwhelming majority of applicants for the CSG have been women. A KwaZulu-Natal study for example found that 87 per cent of CSG applicants said they were the biological mother of the child being applied for, 11 per cent were the grandmother or aunt, and fathers made up only 0.2 per cent of applicants (Case *et al.* 2005). Nevertheless, the state pension domain is masculine and patriarchal. In rural areas, the 'traditional authorities' (chiefs, almost exclusively men) have the power to endorse or dismiss claims about age and residential status of those who live in their areas; this opens up or limits access to registration required to access the grants. Furthermore, while there have been great improvements in grant procedures, the punitive bureaucratic spirit prevails in both rural and urban areas. Reports from watchdog NGOs describe the embarrassment endured by younger unmarried women applicants as older male or female officials question their morality. In both rural and urban areas, where there are problems with documentation, an affidavit from a police station will suffice for evidence about for example how much income there is, or how many children. The police station domain, however, is also masculine and patriarchal – uniforms, guns, forms, stamps. There is typically no private space in the crowded offices; scarcely literate police will not allow the applicant to fill in the forms for herself, and publicly question the applicant about the events leading to her application for the CSG. It can be a frustrating, time-consuming and humiliating procedure (Goldblatt 2005; Lund *et al.* 2009).

Conclusion

With the complexity of South African family structures, fluidity of household boundaries, and mobility of children in their youngest years as they move between different kin-households, the driving idea for implementation of the CSG was 'follow the child', and award the grant to the person who in fact is the main care-giver. This innovation attempted to indigenize a social policy that had previously been built on a model of family life constructed in England, and imported into South Africa before the apartheid government came to power in 1948.

The CSG has been widely assessed as being the policy reform of the post-apartheid era that has done most to contribute to a decrease in income poverty. This chapter has cited research that captured CSG impacts on child and household welfare. Measuring such impacts is never simple, but was relatively easy early on when the grant was awarded for a defined few years in a child's life (0–7 years old). The subsequent age extension process makes it much more difficult to isolate the effects of the grant *per se*. Of course, cash on its own is not enough for robust child development; cash is a necessary but not sufficient condition for enhancing the well-being of children. Particularly in the light of the rampant AIDS epidemic, a range of health, education and welfare services for children are needed in addition to the CSG. The CSG was not the only mechanism available to the state, and other major attempts at reform have failed or lagged behind for a variety of reasons, including poorly formulated initial policies, poor technical and design inputs, and lack of state capacity.

One of the reasons that the CSG was accepted, even in the face of the rapid appearance of a conservative macro-economic policy, was – obviously – the political will in the space created by the transition from apartheid to democracy. In this sense the political circumstances for the creation of the CSG closely resemble those for the US Children's Bureau in the early twentieth century. There, a substantial extension of the franchise to a previously excluded majority (women in the historical US case) created the opportunity for a successful policy of Child Support to be implemented, as Skocpol has shown. The final outcomes of the grant, in South Africa and elsewhere, seem likely to be very different, however, from the very constrained forms of welfare that followed in the USA (Skocpol 1992). As in the early twentieth-century USA there was also a national focus on children as a policy issue, strongly endorsed by President Nelson Mandela. Further, there was a familiarity with the idea and practice of cash support as a response to poverty. Other critical factors in getting the recommendation for the CSG through the political process were that the welfare minister and director-general were both convinced of the merits of a cash transfer. A body of research had proved that the cash transfers to both elderly people and people with disabilities had marked social and economic *developmental* effects, in line with national development goals.

However, a substantial difference between the two cases, as Chapter 17 in this volume shows, was that in the USA, despite an extant late nineteenth-century public health campaign to extend vital registration on public health grounds, this pre-Great War Child Support movement was not initially closely associated with a successful push for universal registration of children at birth. In the USA a distinct post-war campaign was instigated in the 1920s by Herbert Hoover and the American Child Health Association.

At a fundamental level, the delivery of the CSG would simply not have been possible without the existing administrative systems and technological development in the pensions and grants system developed under the apartheid regime. The policy reform depended vitally on building on the administrative structures that were already in place. A number of members of the Lund Committee were familiar with how the existing cash transfer system worked administratively. We could thus convey a realistic and authoritative assessment to the new parliament and cabinet of how and whether the administrative system could bear the weight of the introduction of a new form of support (Lund 2008).

Colonialism and then apartheid had systematically disenfranchised the African population, and then, in the late 1970s and early 1980s, a limited form of political representation was given to people classified as Indian and coloured, through the tri-cameral parliaments. However, the pre-democracy system of grants, and in particular the pensions for elderly people, was widely known about, and the idea that this was a citizen's entitlement, rather than a passing political favour, was widely accepted. Hassim (2005) puts forward an interesting variation on T. H. Marshall's influential explication of varieties of citizenship. Marshall held that social citizenship *follows* political and civil citizenship. Hassim points out that in South Africa 'social assistance was already inscribed as state responsibility, albeit in a racially discriminatory form, prior to the creation of apartheid' (Hassim 2005, 624). She suggests that, through the state grants, most South Africans (i.e. those who were not white and who were receiving grants) 'achieved a level of social citizenship *before* being formally recognized as citizens' (Hassim 2005, 624).

What role might this CSG policy reform have played so soon after the introduction of democracy in South Africa? First, this chapter has described how the policy process took place in the immediate post-apartheid space in which NGOs learned how to exercise their new watchdog role on the new government: monitoring, providing feedback on implementation, sometimes going all the way to litigation on specific issues. The lack of consultation about the phasing out of the SMG, as well as about the low level of the CSG at introduction, marked, for some, the first signs that government and the ANC were closing down spaces for citizens' participation (see Lund 2008, 97–105). This was a highly controversial, contested and, for many, bruising terrain.

Second, under apartheid, the registration and identification systems had been used primarily as part of the state apparatuses of control and repression. With the transition to democracy, there was a new emphasis on inclusive systems of registration. The CSG certainly contributed to the rapid increase in birth registrations, especially early birth registration, and may have contributed more broadly to normalizing the idea of a registration and identification system as relating to positive entitlements of shared citizenship.

Third, and related, systems of registration may be important in their own right, but they also form the information basis for other economic and social programmes with different purposes. For the CSG to be effective, it had to have a relatively good underlying information system, and also an effective system for delivery of the grant. This already existed, in the form of the pension delivery mechanisms. Up until the mid-1980s, pension payments were in the main organized by the racially separate welfare administrations, some of which used the state-owned Post Office. Towards the end of the 1980s, the state increasingly contracted private companies for delivery, many of these having been set up by the large banks and finance houses in order to capture this growing market. The objective of the delivery system is to get small sums of money to very poor people, on a regular and reliable basis, at an affordable rate, with a built-in planning and monitoring system to assist government with management and budgeting. The addition of some 10 million new CSG grantees over a decade has made the delivery of state social assistance an increasingly lucrative proposition. Firms are eager to extend their services to, for example, the massive monthly salary payments to civil servants. A careful eye needs to be kept on how much of the state expenditure on social assistance grants directly reaches the beneficiaries, compared to the amounts paid to private companies for the delivery service.

Finally, the policy reform was consciously in line with then-President Mandela's 'First Call for Children'. It rapidly inserted into the society as a whole, into public consciousness and public discourse, the constitutional rights of children to access to social security. It is in line with Szreter and Breckenridge's formulation, in the Editors' Introduction to this volume, of 'registration as recognition'. In the past, research had shown how children in the households of pensioners and persons with disabilities benefited through the pooling of pension income of these *other* groups. With the CSG, children now have access in their own right, albeit through the primary caregiver. In a way that has yet to be fully understood, the CSG may have contributed to giving children a new form of social and civil recognition.

References

ACESS. 2003. Submissions from ACESS Members in KZN with respect to problems with Social Security delivery. Submission from ACESS to the Provincial Welfare Department of KwaZulu-Natal.

Agüero, Jorge M., Michael R. Carter and Ingrid Woolard. 2008. *Do Unconditional Cash Transfers Enhance Human Capital Accumulation? Analysis of the South African Child Support Grant*. Working Paper. Durban: School of Development Studies, University of KwaZulu-Natal.

Association for Rural Advancement. 1990. 'A Guide to Pensions/Ezimpesheni.' Association for Rural Advancement.

Barr, Nicholas. 1995. 'On the Design of Social Safety Nets.' ESP Discussion Paper No. 65. Washington, DC: World Bank.

Breckenridge, Keith. 2005. 'The Biometric State: The Promise and Peril of Digital Government in the New South Africa.' *Journal of Southern African Studies* 31(2): 267–282.

Budlender, Debbie and Francie Lund. 2011. 'South Africa: A Legacy of Family Disruption.' *Development and Change* 42(4): 925–946.

Case, Anne and Alicia Menendez. 2007. 'Does Money Empower the Elderly? Evidence from the Agincourt Demographic Surveillance Site, South Africa.' *Scandinavian Journal of Public Health* 35(69): 157–164.

Case, Anne, Victoria Hosegood and Francie Lund. 2005. 'The Reach of the South African Child Support Grant: Evidence from Kwazulu Natal.' *Development Southern Africa* 22(4): 467–482.

Delany, Aislinn, Zenobia Ismail, Lauren Graham and Yuri Ramkissoon. 2008. *Review of the Child Support Grant: Uses, Implementation and Obstacles*. Braamfontein: Community Agency for Social Enquiry.

Devereux, Stephen. 2001. *Social Pensions in Namibia and South Africa*. IDS Discussion 379. Brighton: Institute of Development Studies. www.ids.ac.uk/files/Dp379.pdf.

Goldblatt, Beth. 2005. 'Gender and Social Assistance in the First Decade of Democracy: A Case Study of South Africa's Child Support Grant.' *Politikon: South African Journal of Political Studies* 32(2): 239–257.

Goldblatt, Beth, Solange Rosa and Katherine Hall. 2006. 'Implementation of the Child Support Grant: A Study of Four Provinces and Recommendations for Improved Service Delivery.' Children's Institute, University of Cape Town. http://wiredspace.wits.ac.za/handle/10539/4683.

Hassim, Shireen. 2005. 'Turning Gender Rights into Entitlements: Women and Welfare Provision in Post-Apartheid South Africa.' *Social Research* 72(3): 621–646.

Hunter, Nina. 2004. *Welfare Grant Administration in Kwazulu-Natal: Looking at the Child Support Grant*. School of Development Studies Research Report No. 62. Durban: University of KwaZulu-Natal.

Hunter, Nina and Michelle Adato. 2007. *The Child Support Grant in Kwazulu-Natal: Understanding Administration and Household Access*. School of Development Studies Research Report No. 72. Durban: University of KwaZulu-Natal.

KwaZulu Government. 1983. *Minutes of the Meeting of the Sessional Committee on Public Accounts of the Kwazulu Legislative*. Ulundi: KwaZulu Government Service, 11 April.

Lawyers for Human Rights. 2010. 'Towards Universal Birth Registration in South Africa.' www.lhr.org.za/sites/lhr.org.za/files/briefing_paper_towards_universal_birth_registration.pdf.

Leibbrandt, Murray V., Ingrid Woolard, Arden Finn and Jonathan Argent. 2010. *Trends in South African Income Distribution and Poverty since the Fall of Apartheid*. Organisation for Economic Co-operation and Development Social, Employment and Migration Working Papers, No. 101. Paris: Organisation for Economic Co-operation and Development. www.oecd-ilibrary.org/social-issues-migration-health/trends-in-south-african-income-distribution-and-poverty-since-the-fall-of-apartheid_5kmms0t7p1ms-en.

Lund, Francie. 1993. 'State Social Benefits in South Africa.' *International Social Security Review* 46(1): 5–25.

—— 2006. 'Gender and Social Security in South Africa.' In *The Development Decade? Economic and Social Change in South Africa, 1994–2004*, ed. Vishnu Padayachee. Cape Town: HSRC Press.

—— 2008. *Changing Social Policy: The Child Support Grant in South Africa*. Pretoria: HSRC Press. www.hsrcpress.ac.za/product.php?productid=2213&freedownload=1.

Lund, Francie, Michael Noble, Helen Barnes and Gemma Wright. 2009. 'Is There a Rationale for Conditional Cash Transfers for Children in South Africa?' *Transformation* 70: 70–91.

Mirugi-Mukundi, Gladys. 2010. 'Reaffirming the Social Security Rights of Children in South Africa with Particular Reference to the Child Support Grant.' *ESR Review* 11(1): 7–9.

Republic of South Africa. 1996. *Report of the Lund Committee on Child and Family Support*. Pretoria: Government Printer. www.info.gov.za/otherdocs/1996/lund.htm.

Skelton, Ann, ed. 1998. *Children and the Law*. Pietermaritzburg: Lawyers for Human Rights.

Skocpol, Theda. 1992. *Protecting Soldiers and Mothers: The Political Origins of Social Policy in the United States*. Cambridge, MA: Belknap Press of Harvard University Press.

StatsSA. 2009. Recorded live births 2008. Statistics South Africa Statistical Release P0305, October. www.statssa.gov.za/publications/P0305/P03052008.pdf.

19

What Comes After the Social? Historicizing the Future of Social Assistance and Identity Registration in Africa

JAMES FERGUSON

IT WAS IN ITS ANALYSES of systems of distribution that a classical social anthropology made some of its most memorable contributions to broader discussions in social theory and political economy (Malinowski 1984; Mauss 2000; Polanyi 2001). Today, when questions of distribution are more likely to take us into the intricate mechanisms of modern state bureaucracies than into the means by which chiefs divide up piles of yams, the topic of distribution seems to have faded from the anthropological agenda. But this can hardly be because the issue of distribution has become less important in the societies we study. On the contrary, in these times of unprecedented inequality (both within and among national societies) questions of distribution would seem to be more pressing than ever. Perhaps, then, it is time for a new anthropology of distribution.

Such an anthropology will have to give a central focus to modern states and their institutions of distribution. There is, of course, an extensive scholarly literature on the role of modern states in effecting various, as Seekings and Nattrass (2005) have put it, 'distributional regimes', and an impressive body of work on the topic of welfare states in particular (where the issue of distribution looms especially large). But this is a literature to which anthropologists have had remarkably little to contribute. The old division of labour between anthropology and sociology that left the modern industrial societies of Europe and North America to the sociologists while bequeathing the rest of the world to anthropology no doubt has much to do with this. But even if we accepted this division of labour, leaving welfare to the sociologists seems problematic on the face of it. After all, programmes of social assistance today are not only to be found in Western liberal democracies. On the contrary, they have long been quite central to the lives of poor and marginalized people in many areas of the global South. What is more, fascinating new developments (some of which I will briefly note at the end of this chapter) are bringing new kinds of social assistance into the lives of increasing numbers of people, creating both new dangers and (I will suggest) possibilities for new forms

Proceedings of the British Academy **182**, 495–516. © The British Academy 2012.

of politics. I am particularly interested here in the increasingly important role of what are termed 'cash transfers', and in the way that new forms of welfarism are popping up in the very midst of macro-economic contexts that are often (and not without reason) termed 'neoliberal'.

The proliferation of such large-scale systems of social assistance in the global South, and particularly in my area of special concern here, southern Africa, raises issues of documentation and registration that are very relevant to the concerns of this book. In Europe, as several of the contributors to this volume note, systems of civil registration (indeed, parish registration in the case of early modern England) were a crucial foundation for the emergence of rights-based claims to the collective's resources and to both political and social citizenship. The absence of such robust systems of registration in most of Africa has often seemed to consign any plans for far-reaching welfare schemes to the domain of wishful thinking. In this view, it can only be *after* African states build up their informational and documentary capacities, just as European states did before them, that a strong, welfare-based, social citizenship has any chance of being established. Yet the material I will review in this chapter shows two things: first, that a robust social citizenship in some sense already exists in much of the region, notwithstanding the significant informational limitations; and second, that the formation of 'the social' that supports such claims to entitlement is, and long has been, significantly different from the better-known Western European cases. If that is so, then it may be useful to consider whether the creation of systems of identification, documentation and registration in the future (in southern Africa and elsewhere) might not also take forms quite different from those we are used to associating with the 'advanced' welfare states of the North. This issue of identity documentation, including some novel technical means through which it can be linked to social entitlements, is an issue I will return to at the end of the chapter.

In approaching the question of social assistance today, I take as a starting point the important literature on what Jacques Donzelot has termed 'the invention of the social' (see also Foucault *et al.* 2003). As Nikolas Rose has observed, many of the issues and 'problems' that would be identified in twentieth-century Europe as 'social' were previously understood as moral problems that might best be addressed through some combination of religious institutions and what were known as 'the moral sciences'. Problems such as vagrancy, idleness, thieving, or prostitution, in this optic, were the result of the faulty 'character' and 'morals' of the poor. This was partly a matter of good old-fashioned sin, of course, the responsibility of the Christian religious institutions that had dealt with such matters for centuries before. But the response to such 'problems' had also come, by the early nineteenth century, to include a host of scientifically-informed disciplinary 'moral technologies' whose purpose was to improve the moral hygiene and character of the poor. Pauper schools, reformatory prisons, lunatic asylums, public baths and wash-houses – these 'great machines of morality', Rose has argued, 'took the characteristic form of enclosed sites for the manufacture of character' (1999, 103). Such things as thievery, vagrancy, and prostitution were forms of immorality, and remedies were aimed at this fundamental cause.

Over the course of the nineteenth century, however, it became possible to pose the problem in a fundamentally different way. Thanks to the emergence of an idea of 'society' as a natural system with regular and even calculable properties, it became possible to reinterpret what had been understood as moral failings as instead (in Durkheim's famous phrase) 'social facts'. Early socialist thinkers were already stretching the notion of 'character' in ways that foreshadowed the late nineteenth-century notion of social causation. Already in 1813, Robert Owen wrote:

> In those characters which now exhibit crime, the fault is obviously not in the individual, but the defects proceed from the system in which the individual was trained. Withdraw those circumstances which tend to create crime in the human character, and crime will not be created. Replace them with such as are calculated to form habits of order, regularity, temperance, industry; and these qualities will be formed.
>
> (Owen 2004, 30)

But this vision was given real substance only following the nineteenth-century 'avalanche of numbers' (Hacking 1990) that revealed astonishing regularities in a broad range of observable and enumerable phenomena, once sufficiently large samples were acquired. For 'vices' such as crime and vagrancy (once properly documented and compared across time and space) could be shown to follow, like suicide rates, their own predictable and determinate laws. No longer would it be necessary to see the cause of the crime in the moral failing or innate traits of the criminal, for crime rates were demonstrably caused by (again Durkheim) 'other social facts' and not by underlying factors of character or psychology. Crime, then, was not a matter of immorality or the 'criminal types' of criminological anthropology, but rather a measurable social phenomenon whose rate varied in a more or less determinate correlation with other measurable social facts (e.g. unemployment, family structure, etc.). In this sense, crime is no longer principally a moral or biological problem; it is precisely a social problem. And if social problems have social causes, they must also have social solutions. A host of new institutions and occupations arose during this period to observe, measure, manage, and correct this new object – social work, social statistics, social reform, the social policy expert, and, of course, the social scientist.

A key focus for 'social' intervention, from the very start, was the family. Social reasoning, of course, required a whole new level of interest in childhood, upbringing, and 'social background' as causal 'factors', and anxieties over the pathologies of 'society' quickly settled on the family as both blameworthy cause and supremely valuable solution (Donzelot 1979). It would not be enough to morally correct the prostitute, or even to re-educate her; it is the social milieu that produced her that is the problem: the deficient family structure, the alcoholic mother, the absent father – all this would have to be corrected. Thus was born an extraordinarily ambitious project (uniting the 'social' and the 'psy') of surveillance and correction of intimate life, what Donzelot (1979) famously described as 'the policing of families'.

A crucial additional development, according to most accounts, made it possible for the regularities of social phenomena to be turned into institutionalized solutions to social problems. This was the development of techniques of social insurance. As François Ewald (1986) argued in a ground-breaking account, the regularities that had been discovered in such things as accidents, illnesses, and life span created the possibility of what he termed a new 'political technology', the technology of risk. Starting with wage labourers in large firms, measures began to be taken to calculate risks (especially the risks of workplace accidents), and to socially distribute them via pooling. An early emphasis on 'prudence', which encouraged workers to voluntarily join associations provided by trade associations or friendly societies, started to give way (around the turn of the century, in most European countries, following Bismarckian Germany) to national schemes of compulsory social insurance (Ewald 1986; Defert 1991; O'Malley 1996; Horn 1994; Dean 1992). These schemes applied only to formal-sector workers (who made contributions to the system via their pay-cheques); others were included (if at all) via their status as 'dependants' of recognized workers (i.e. wives and children). The family thus becomes a key relay or point of conjunction, linking institutions focused on wage labourers with the larger urban population via the construction of the recognized dependant.

The workplace accident (like the crime) was now not principally a moral or legal problem (who is at fault? what is the wrong, and who is responsible for it?) but a social one (what is the risk, and how is it insured?), requiring a social solution (compensation, not justice). Like life expectancy or the chance of going blind, the accident is probabilistic and calculable – and therefore manageable via institutions for pooling risk. The social thus becomes available for a new kind of intervention that would be principally technical, rather than moral. The poor child needs educating not because we feel sorry for him, but because it is good for society, just as the Keynesian economist argues that laid-off workers need unemployment insurance not because they deserve it, but because the economy needs their economic demand to offset a dip in the business cycle. At the same time, such technical interventions relied on, and helped to buttress, a new moral sentiment, which takes many names, but is probably most recognizable under the label, 'solidarity'. If honesty, thrift, and so on are 'bourgeois virtues' (McCloskey 2006), then it is solidarity that is surely the first among what we might call 'the social democratic virtues'.

The welfare state was therefore founded on a set of techniques for managing 'the social' that depended for their efficacy on a refusal to reduce social problems to either morality or the market. In this way, new circuits of distribution became possible. At the same time, it became possible for such circuits of distribution to be justified and legitimated in radically new ways. In the new dispensation, a disability pension or a free education was neither the price of a commodity (like a wage) nor a religiously inspired gift or donation (like charity). It was a social intervention (understood technically) and an expression of social solidarity (understood normatively).

In recent years, a number of authors have suggested that this conception of the social, along with the institutions based upon it, has weakened or broken down. Peter Miller and Nikolas Rose, for instance, have suggested that recent years have seen something resembling 'the death of the social' (Miller and Rose 2008). In this account, neoliberal restructuring has not only (or even principally) been about 'rolling back the state' or opening a path for 'free markets'. Rather, what has occurred has been the development of new rationalities of government that make it possible for 'the conduct of conduct' to be guided in ways that rely on market mechanisms to achieve governmental ends. Individuals are increasingly induced to take responsibility for managing their own risks (what Rose has termed 'responsibilization'), while an 'enterprise model' is increasingly applied not only to capitalist firms, but to government agencies, non-profit entities such as universities, and even individuals (now conceived as the proprietors of their own 'firm' or promoters of their 'brand').

Along with this, Miller and Rose argue, comes an increasing value placed on 'community'. In place of a 'society' governed by social forces, an alternative conception gains traction, within which communities are composed of individuals who share certain attributes ('identity', 'culture', sexuality, a disease status, etc.) and associated interests (against the solidarity of 'society', we have the fragmentation of 'interest groups'). 'Communities' are charged with attending to those responsibilities that the state and its taxpayers cannot or will not continue to accept (thus voluntary 'community safety programmes' etc.), while marginalized populations (who cannot or will not be 'responsibilized' and who evade being governed via 'affiliation' with a 'community') are increasingly relegated to a zone of abjection: dispersed, invisible, and cared for only by privatized and re-moralized 'programmes', fragmented by niche (drug treatment, homeless shelters, etc.) – if not actually incarcerated in the rapidly expanding prison system that Loic Wacquant (2001, 404) has argued is an integral part of contemporary neoliberal governance.

An anthropology of contemporary social assistance will have to address two questions about all this. First: is this whole discussion not hopelessly Eurocentric? Much of the conceptual and institutional apparatus of 'the social' that this literature describes was never well established in the global South, where neoliberal restructuring represents not a 'rolling back' of a Keynesian welfare state but the very context within which new forms of social assistance have been pioneered. Given the importance of institutions of social welfare in the global South, and the inapplicability there of much of the account provided by Rose, Donzelot, and Ewald, do we not need new sorts of historical narratives to understand contemporary struggles around distribution? And second: if the sort of 'social' that this literature describes is in fact going through fundamental changes (if not – as Rose *et al.* hyperbolically put it – facing 'death'), then what comes after it? That is a question that is being addressed, at least to some extent, for the so-called 'advanced liberal' countries of the global North, but one that few have yet begun to think about in the post-colonial South. And the word 'neoliberalism' is hardly an answer – particularly when (as I have elsewhere argued – see Ferguson 2010) neither neoliberal economic policies nor neoliberal techniques of government are by any means incompatible with certain forms of social assistance.

The African social

We might begin by asking whether 'the social' (in the sense intended by authors such as Rose and Donzelot) ever really existed in the colonies. I treat here only the case of Africa, with a special focus on the anglophone countries of southern Africa. In this context, it is clear that as 'social' techniques swept across Europe – starting in the early twentieth century, and with much greater intensity after the Second World War – there were attempts to introduce them in the African colonies. Such projects were sharply limited, though, by a number of factors.

First, the populations of the African colonies were overwhelmingly rural, with land generally abundant, and small-scale agriculture the main source of subsistence. Under these circumstances, it was easy for colonial officials to imagine that social security was 'naturally' provided by what they conceived of (usually in highly idealized terms) as 'the extended family'. Rural kin did, of course, do most of the heavy lifting when it came to assisting the sick, the injured, the disabled, and the destitute. But there was also evidence all around of the limits of such provision. Rural famines revealed stark limits to kinship-based sharing even in the countryside, while colonial towns quickly became peopled with ragged beggars, vagrants, 'delinquents', and so on (i.e. precisely the undesirable and potentially destabilizing social phenomena which the Tudor state had effectively sought to counter through the parish Poor Law of collective, trans-familial provision – see Chapter 2 in this volume). Yet such manifestations of need were determinedly interpreted as signs of the 'breakdown' of 'traditional' institutions.[1] This is empirically dubious – as John Iliffe has noted, 'there was nothing new either in the fact that families did not always care for everyone or in the fact that most families did care for most of their unfortunate members most of the time' (Iliffe 1987, 213). But the caring 'traditional

[1] On the idea of 'breakdown', see Iliffe (1987), Moore and Vaughan (1994) and Hunt (1999).

African extended family' was a powerful imagined reality that shaped the whole discussion of social security in the post-Second World War era.

If people were left in acute need only through the 'breakdown' of old institutions, then what might have been identified as urban 'social problems' could be seen instead as pathologies of 'urbanization' requiring not the new institutions of 'the social', but rather projects of restoring rural 'tradition'. Again and again, as one reads the discussions and debates from the period, one finds that attempts to extend the sorts of projects of 'social' reform that were flourishing elsewhere in the empire were countered by strategies that sought to reduce the problem of security to the need to restore and revitalize what was imagined as a degenerated rural society.

The result is that what looked like it might become a project for encompassing African poverty within the terms of 'the social' became something rather different, namely: 'rural development'. Strategies of restoring and developing peasant agriculture were here tightly bound up with fantasies of a communal and caring rural sociality that had to be restored. And the solution this implied for problematic 'lumpen' urbanites such as beggars, the handicapped, thieves, and prostitutes was that they should be restored to the countryside, under the care of 'their people'. In this way, urban poverty came to be a problem not of social assistance and welfare, but of 'development'. Rhodesia, following the international trends, had created a team of African 'welfare officers' after the war, but by 1950, they had their titles changed, tellingly, to 'district officers – rural development' (Seekings 2005, 54), just as the Tanganyika Social Welfare Department became the Social Development Department, charged principally with rural 'community development' (Iliffe 1987, 204).

But the project of creating an African 'social' encountered another problem that was perhaps equally fundamental, for the sorts of moralizing understandings of poverty and crime that Miller and Rose argue were displaced by 'the social' in Europe continued to hold a much more central place in the southern African colonies. The power of the Christian missions (together with the relative weakness of the state) meant that institutions like education and health care were never really secularized, and explicitly moral and religious ideas remained considerably more prominent than they did in Europe (Iliffe 1987).

The result was that the prostitute and the beggar did not (with a few exceptions) become the charges of the social worker, but remained (to the extent that they were attended to at all) a problem for the church (as a matter of sinfulness and bad character) and a problem of urbanization (insofar as urban 'hangers-on' could be dealt with by sending them 'back to their people' in the countryside). Thus, the dominant formation for dealing with the problematic urban classes was not 'the social' at all, but what we might call the 'moral-developmental'.

But if 'lumpen' urban hangers-on required removal or moralization, proper workers required something more, and this is where something like 'the social' did manage to obtain a small foothold. Workers, according to dominant colonial conceptions, ought to become civilized, live in proper families, learn the dignity of labour, and so on. But how could they live proper urban lives, without the incomes, housing, and social security that would support this? The circular migrant labourer might be cheap, but he could never become modern (and disciplined, stabilized, skilled, etc.), and this was seen to be problematic by industry leaders and colonial planners alike (Cooper 1996). But in the absence of the social security that would enable continuous urban residence, even in retirement, how could migration cease to be circular? In this context, a range of 'social' institutions were created for relatively small groups of formal-sector workers in many African colonies. Probably the most ambitious of these was the system of family benefits introduced in the French colonies during the 1950s, which provided cash allowances to workers' families for the support of children (Cooper 1996, 318–321; see also Iliffe 1987). Southern African examples were less ambitious, but still important. The major mining companies on the Zambian Copperbelt, for instance, provided modest pensions to mineworkers (Ferguson 1999), while Union Miniere in Katanga went further by providing a broad package of social support meant to encourage the 'stabilization' of the workforce (Perrings 1979; Higginson 1989).

Such provisions were linked to a colonial vision that African workers (or at least some 'advanced' subset of them) might become what were sometimes termed 'proper workers' – and part of being a 'proper worker' was living in 'proper', 'European'-style nuclear families (cf. Ferguson 1999). An ideology of familism was thus central to all of these schemes, which were meant to support not just a worker, but also the recognized dependants of that worker (the latter Eurocentrically understood as 'wife' and 'children'). The wider population (i.e. beyond the formally-employed, recognized workers) was therefore provided for only via the relay of an idealized nuclear family. Thus, the French family allocation system involved payments to parents to help support the raising of children – but the funds were dispersed not to mothers or children, but as a supplement to the father's pay-cheque (Cooper 1996, 319).

The functioning of such systems (let alone their extension to a broader population) was sharply constrained by a paucity of social and demographic documentation. Family-based schemes, for instance, required documentation of births, and reliable ways of assigning particular children to particular families and a single, bona fide wife to each wage earner. Even among the 'advanced' formal-sector workers that these schemes targeted, such information was rarely complete or accurate enough to inspire confidence (Cooper 1996, 334). The near-absence of such documentation for much of the wider population posed an informational barrier that made it difficult even to imagine how 'social' schemes could be generalized to an entire society, leaving the question of 'the social' very much a question of the formal wage labourer.

In this context, 'social' institutions were not so much about taking care of the needy as they were about trying to solve what Frederick Cooper (1996) has described as 'the labour question'. Thus 'social welfare' work (sometimes styled urban community development) tended to be focused on such things as setting up recreational activities and adult education classes for workers in privileged industries and occupations – among the most (rather than the least) secure sections of the urban population. A Nyasaland provincial commissioner tellingly complained in 1952 that local Social Welfare Committees were not looking after the needy at all, but instead 'organizing "snob classes" among the "intelligentsia" and their wives, such as knitting classes, basket-ball classes, football teams, and such like' (Iliffe 1987, 205). Yet such a focus on recreational and social activities for the better-off was found across the region (cf. Ferguson 1999), reflecting the fact that 'social welfare' had become a way not of helping the poor or insuring against risk, but of providing 'modern' facilities to a small and privileged minority of recognized, formal-sector workers.

The ironic fact that the apparatus of the social was most available not to the destitute, but to a kind of elite, reminds one of T. H. Marshall's famous definition of 'social' citizenship as entailing 'the right to live the life of a civilized being' (1987, 8). While Marshall intended this as an argument for universal social rights (since all British citizens were entitled to live the life of civilized beings), under colonial conditions the association of the social with the civilized had the opposite implication. 'Civilization' was not a universal entitlement, but the property of a privileged minority, and the association of 'social' rights with this attribute was precisely a principle of restriction, so that social assistance was available only for the 'civilized', the 'stabilized', the 'évolués' (with 'the African extended family' the imagined remedy for the less civilized rest).

'Social' provisions were obviously important for those few who held the most securely institutionalized formal-sector waged employment, but the effect on the wider society was far more limited. Formal-sector workers were everywhere a small minority of the population, so 'social' institutions that were restricted in this way never had any chance of approaching full 'coverage' of the society. On the contrary, as Cooper has noted (1996, 283), what colonial attempts to 'stabilize' the working class reveal most starkly is 'a desire to treat it as a wholly different world from rural Africa'. Fundamental obstacles, prominent among which were the paucity of funds and the lack of an adequate informational basis, meant that the generalization or universalization of 'the social' under colonial conditions could be neither achieved, nor even convincingly advocated. As a British Colonial Office specialist on social security put it bluntly in 1961, 'Obviously a genuine insurance scheme is out of the question' (Cooper 1996, 333).

In the settler colonies, however, a much more fully realized 'social' was established, the history of which sheds much light on the nature of the systems of social assistance that now play such a prominent role in the region's political economy. South Africa, with by far the largest population of white settlers on the continent, led the way. Starting in 1928, a non-contributory social pension was introduced for white 'Europeans' and mixed-race 'Coloureds', conditional on age (men over 65, women over 60) and means-testing (Devereux 2001; Seekings 2007). 'Natives' (also known as 'Africans') were excluded since they were supposed to be able to rely on their 'Native custom which makes provision for maintaining dependent persons' (Pienaar Commission, cited in Devereux 2001, 2). In addition, white settlers in the 1930s came to enjoy a range of other social protections, including unemployment benefits, job programmes, farm assistance, child welfare, invalid and blindness pensions, and public health provision (Seekings 2008). By the late 1930s (even before the substantial expansions associated with the 1940s and the worldwide post-war boom in welfare states), the foundations had been laid for what Seekings has described as 'a remarkable welfare state', one which, already in 1938, was budgeting some 20 per cent of total public expenditure on 'services of an essentially social welfare nature' (Dept of Social Welfare, cited in Seekings 2008, 515). Indeed, the University of the Witwatersrand's Professor of Sociology, J. L. Gray, could boast (with only a little exaggeration) that 'today the provision for [the] European population . . . is scarcely less complete than that of Great Britain' (cited in Seekings 2008, 516).

What motivated this extraordinary development? The coalition ('Pact') government that came to power in 1924 was based on an alliance between the National Party (NP), representing largely poor rural Afrikaners, and a smaller socialist Labour Party, with its base among white workers in the gold-mining towns on the Rand. And its principal purpose in pursuing social protection was to protect the 'civilized standard of living' of whites, especially the 'poor whites' whose racial privilege was endangered by the economic conditions they increasingly shared with blacks. As Seekings has put it,

> [. . .] the most important factor was the imperative – for the NP – of raising its 'poor white' supporters out of poverty and the attendant risks of becoming subordinate to or intermingling with African people. Old-age pensions constituted one cornerstone of the 'civilized labour' policies by which the Pact Government sought to raise all white people to 'civilized' standards of living, above rather than below or alongside the 'native' (African) population. South Africa's welfare state thus has its origins above all in the Pact Government's general strategy of racial segregation (and discrimination) in response to the *swartgevaar* (black peril).
>
> (Seekings 2007, 378)

While these early forms of social assistance and social protection explicitly excluded 'Africans', this began to change starting in the 1940s, as South Africa joined much of the rest of the world in seeking to expand and rationalize its various programmes of social assistance. In this 'radical moment', as Seekings (2005) has called it, key features of the South African welfare state were extended to include all South African citizens. The 1944 Pension Laws Amendment Act, crucially, extended disability grants to Coloured, African, and Indian people, and extended the non-contributory old-age pensions (already enjoyed by whites, coloureds and

Indians) to include Africans as well (Seekings 2005, 47–48; see also Posel 2005; Iliffe 1987; Devereux 2001). But while this involved a kind of universalization of the social, it operated explicitly according to what the government called 'a principle of discrimination' (Devereux 2001, 4). From the beginning, benefits were pegged to a starkly unequal racial scale, and benefits for Africans were never more than a small fraction of what they were for whites – indeed, in 1965, the ratio of white pensions to Coloured/Indian and African pensions was 11:4:1 (Devereux 2001, 4). While welfare states in the North are generally thought to be committed to a kind of citizen-egalitarianism (such as we might associate with a country like Sweden), South Africa shows us a very different formation of 'the social', universal in its reach, but specifically designed to support and maintain an explicit racial hierarchy.

Similar trajectories unfolded in the other settler colonies in the region. In the South African trust territory of Southwest Africa (which would become the independent state of Namibia), pensions and other benefits for whites were introduced in 1949, on the South African model. They were later extended to 'coloureds' in 1965. Finally, an African pension was introduced in 1973 (presumably motivated in part by the need to win 'hearts and minds' during the national liberation struggle) (Devereux 2001). As in South Africa, the system had grown to address the entire population in some minimal sense, but again social expenditures were overwhelmingly focused on maintaining white standards, and the allocation of benefits was highly unequal and explicitly racialized. Even by the time of independence, the ratio of white pension benefits to African benefits was still as high as 7:1 (Devereux 2001).

In Southern Rhodesia (later to become the independent Zimbabwe), too, a quite ambitious welfare state was constructed for 'non-Africans', starting in the 1930s. The provision of old-age pensions (along with widows', orphans' and war pensions), public assistance for the destitute, free public education, and a state monopoly providing subsidized meat (Kaseke 2002; Iliffe 1987; Henderson 1972), all meant that by the end of the Second World War, Rhodesia's European settlers 'had little to complain of', as Henderson has put it, enjoying 'a welfare state with comprehensive social services at little cost' (Henderson 1972, 398). Africans, however, were entirely excluded from these schemes, on the grounds of their allegedly 'simple needs' and the idea that the rural reserves 'provided a form of indigenous pension which enabled them to support the aged and destitute Africans' (Kaseke 2002, 222–223; see also Iliffe 1987, 206). For Africans living in town, therefore, destitution, far from triggering access to benefits, 'became a justification for the colonial regime to remove them from urban areas' to the supposed sanctuary of the rural reserves (Kaseke 2002, 222). Attempts in the 1940s to expand welfare services to urban Africans did not get far. African urban welfare was generally left to municipalities or voluntary organizations, 'both of which concentrated on recreation', according to Iliffe (1987, 206). The isolated progressive experiment of the city of Bulawayo in providing more comprehensive urban services to Africans (Brokensha 2007) did not survive the 1965 unilateral declaration of independence (UDI) which, as Iliffe put it, 'subordinated everything to white survival' (1987, 206).

In the southern African settler colonies, then, in matters of social policy as in so many other domains, there were two governmental systems, not one. For the whites, a genuine (and in some ways quite robust) version of the Beveridgean 'social' was established. Blacks were able to participate only marginally in this, and on decidedly unequal terms. They were, however, included (though unequally) in a few significant programmes of social support. In particular, the extension of key social benefits to black South Africans in 1944 must be regarded as of enduring significance. While some such gains (e.g. unemployment insurance) were reversed by the reactionary triumph of the Nationalist Party in 1948 which inaugurated an explicit policy of apartheid, the NP never abolished the non-contributory old-age pensions and disability grants, a fact that would come to be highly significant for post-independence developments (see Chapter 18).

Given all of this, it seems necessary to shift our question: it is no longer a matter of what comes after 'the' social, but of what comes after *this* 'social' – that is, the historically particular, and decidedly non-egalitarian 'social' of white settlers and black labour aristocracies in southern Africa.

What comes after the southern African 'social'?

The most interesting place to explore this question is surely South Africa, where a racially highly unequal system of pensions and grants dating from the 1940s was deracialized, and benefits equalized, in the years leading up to the transition to majority rule in 1994. That was already a huge expansion of social assistance, since the new, racially equal rates were far higher than the old, racially-discriminatory 'African' rates had been. The years since 1994 have seen continued enormous expansion, both in terms of amounts of money distributed and numbers of recipients (see Chapter 18). According to South African government figures, social assistance programmes today pay grants to nearly 15 million South Africans, some 30 per cent of the entire population. Of these, 9 million are caregivers of children (who receive a child support grant), while most of the rest are recipients of old-age pensions and disability grants. In 2010/2011, the government spent R89 billion on social grants, raising expenditure on social grants to 3.5 per cent of gross national product (South African Government 2011). In the poorest regions of South Africa, such as the rural Eastern Cape, fully 75 per cent of all households now receive some sort of grant (Bank 2009).

Given this extraordinary expansion of pensions and grants to the entire population, one is tempted to say that the black South African majority got 'the social' at just the moment when it was being declared dead in the West. But that is not quite right. As argued earlier in this chapter, the old European 'social' was based most fundamentally on wage labour and insurance rationality. But in contemporary South Africa, grants are mostly not based on insurance mechanisms, and they are most significant as means of support for individuals and communities that lack wage labour altogether.

This combination of society-wide social assistance and staggering levels of mass unemployment is something that the engineers of Europe's systems of social assistance could never have imagined. Indeed William Beveridge, in his world-conquering 1942 report on social insurance, regarded it as obvious that 'a satisfactory scheme of social insurance assumes the maintenance of employment and the prevention of mass unemployment' (1942, 163). This was so for technical and fiscal reasons (having to do with the insurance mechanism that was central to his scheme), but also on grounds of first principles (since, for him, the battle against what he called 'Want' had to be complemented by coordinated attacks on the other 'giant evils', among which Idleness stood co-equal with Disease and Squalor (Beveridge 1942, 170).

Colonial officials in southern Africa were likewise unable to imagine any applicability for widespread social assistance in circumstances where earning a decent wage was an exceptional circumstance rather than the general rule. Southern Rhodesia's social security officer, F. T. Russell, explained clearly why Beveridge's ideas of social security could not be applied in southern Africa:

> The Beveridge Committee dealt with a radically homogeneous community in which three-quarters of the existing poverty was due to the interruption of normal earning power by sickness, accident and unemployment, and its termination by old age or premature death. Most of the remaining poverty in Great Britain was found in families too large for the breadwinner to support adequately on normal earnings; low earnings as a cause of poverty were relatively of minor importance. In Southern Africa, on the other hand, it is not so much the interruption of earning power as the inefficiency of earning power which causes poverty. The great majority of the population is in poverty, in work and out of it.
>
> (cited in Seekings 2005, 55)

What has changed? How is it that a massive apparatus of social assistance that was never regarded as a serious possibility in the days when welfare states ruled the roost came to be considered (under 'neoliberal' conditions supposedly antithetical to welfare) not only thinkable, but practical, and even necessary?

A difficult question, to be sure. But we can at least start to answer it by pointing out that the South African state's willingness to expand the system of social support so substantially is surely linked to two quite fundamental predicaments. First, post-apartheid planners have had to come to terms with the radical deterioration of agrarian livelihoods in the old 'native reserve' areas of South Africa. In earlier decades, dreams persisted (however unrealistically) that black poverty could be contained (if not actually overcome) through strategies of 're-agrarianization'. By 1994, the decisive political defeat of apartheid's 'Bantustan' project (and the forced removals it had entailed), together with the grim economic state of the reserves, made it only too clear how limited were the possibilities for a rural 'fix' to the problems of poverty and unemployment. At the same time, though, another fundamental predicament appeared, which was the failure of the new ANC regime's economic policies to produce robust employment growth. Neoliberal restructuring did bring some economic growth, but it was largely 'jobless growth', and unemployment rates (especially among poor and low-skilled blacks) rose to alarming levels (sometimes reckoned at 40 per cent, though official figures are lower).

The conjuncture of these two crises has yielded a fairly abrupt, and more or less simultaneous, end to *both* of the great fantasies of familism that long sustained social policy in Africa: the rural 'extended family' (based on an agricultural rural homestead), and the urban 'nuclear family' (based on the 'breadwinning' male wage labourer).[2]

Importantly, in current policies on social assistance, we see not only expanded levels of assistance and increased 'coverage', but at the same time a questioning of traditional ideas of 'the family' as a basis for calculating eligibility for grants. Since 1998, the huge programme of child support grants has had no requirement that the recipients of the grants be in any prescribed familial relation, either conjugal or filial (see Chapter 18). The recipient need not be married, may reside with or without a partner (of either gender), and is not required to be a parent, or even a relative, of the supported child. All that is necessary is that the person receiving the grant be recognized as the 'primary caregiver'. In contrast with older forms of social assistance (such as the old State Maintenance Grants), there is no longer any attempt to identify the 'real parents', to impose responsibilities on fathers, or to impose 'proper' family forms.[3] Poor women, for their part, have become increasingly reliant on child support grants, and are increasingly unlikely to see any benefit in marriage (Hunter 2010).

An even more radical break with welfare familism is represented by the recent campaign for a 'Basic Income Grant' (BIG). This proposal would ignore all distinctions of family status (and indeed, of every other sort as well), and simply provide a minimum monthly cash payment (of about US$15) to each and every individual. There would be no means-testing of any kind, so all South Africans would receive the grant (though the better-off would have their $15, and more,

[2] I say that these fantasies have come to an 'end' only in the sense that they can no longer provide a serious basis for social policy. In the wider society, however, both conceptions have a powerful nostalgic afterlife. An idealized rural patriarchal family, especially, seems to be a touchstone for a certain kind of 'Africanist' cultural politics, even as such family forms in their actuality become ever harder to locate.

[3] See Lund for a thoughtful discussion of how and why policy makers moved away from policies based on 'an outmoded model of family life . . . based on the model of the nuclear family' (2008, 80).

recouped through the tax system). The BIG campaign illustrates with special clarity something that is also evident in many other areas of social policy, which is a new willingness to contemplate decoupling assistance for the poor from calculations about wage labour and family structure alike. In such conceptions, what we used to call 'social assistance' starts to look like simply 'assistance' (just as cash payments themselves, in technocratic discourses, are increasingly described not as 'welfare' but simply as 'transfers').

Nor is this only a matter of South Africa. Old-age pensions on the South African model have recently been introduced into several other African countries, and a pilot Basic Income scheme has been established (with international funding) in Namibia, where discussion of the BIG remains lively and serious. What is more, what are known as 'conditional cash transfer' schemes have flourished all across the world (especially, but not only, in Latin America). The 'conditions' usually involve an income cut-off, and a requirement that recipients' children attend school and make regular visits to the clinic, as with President Lula's Brazilian Bolsa Familia, where the child's vaccination is also a condition. Unlike the Basic Income Grant, there is here an explicit aim to govern behaviour in some minimal sense, usually justified to external bodies such as the World Bank in terms of the need to 'enhance human capital'. But it is noteworthy that the ambition to mould or discipline recipients remains much scaled back from 'the social' of old. And as in the South African examples, these policies of cash assistance make no reference to particular configurations of employment (the wage labourer, the breadwinner) or family structure (the 'proper family', marriage, the father). A recent major World Bank report (Fiszbein *et al.* 2009) assesses such schemes in twenty-seven countries, and makes a vigorous argument for their expansion as a central part of any strategy for fighting poverty.

This raises a number of questions, which I am hoping to address in a larger project. First: why is it that the fear of 'handouts' seems to be abating? Twenty years ago (or forty years ago), mainstream development institutions would have reacted in horror to any proposal to 'just give money to the poor', citing a familiar litany of dangers that would have included 'dependency', misuse of resources ('they'll just drink it away'), and (above all) a potential reduction of the incentive to work. Today, however, the World Bank is a leading advocate of expanded cash transfers to the poor (Fiszbein *et al.* 2009), while a new book by an eminent group of development studies academics is titled precisely, *Just Give Money to the Poor* (Hanlon *et al.* 2010). What has changed? Part of the answer must be the massive contemporary over-supply of manual labour, which means the age-old bourgeois task of getting the poor to make their labour available on the market no longer appears especially pressing. The problem is rather what to do with the surplus millions who would be only too happy to work for wages, but for whom no jobs can be found. Here we find a new governmental interest in vernacular ways of surviving that do not involve wage labour ('livelihoods', the 'informal economy'), and a new appreciation of the virtues of cash as a 'flexible' resource that can 'catalyze' other economic activities. Emergent in all this, perhaps, a new rationality of poverty is becoming visible.

Second: why the new openness to questions of family and household composition? If the welfare state of old was based on the figure of the family, quite as much as that of the nation state and the wage labourer, the disappearance of that figure in the new welfare states of the South seems striking. Again, the declining role of wage labour seems crucial. With the figure of the male wage-earner or 'breadwinner' displaced, the very idea of 'dependants' becomes artificial. Increasingly, 'society' comes to be imagined not as an assembly of families, each with a 'head', but as a network of flexible individuals, where few have 'real jobs', and all are opportunistically adapting to changing conditions. There remain crucial domestic alliances and commitments, to be sure, but planners increasingly ask themselves if it is wise to pre-judge their nature. In the most ambitious rethinkings, the flexibility of cash is matched by the flexibility of unqualified eligibility (thus, any care-taker gets the South African child support grant, and every individual would be eligible for the BIG), and recipients are then free to use their 'transfers' to make whatever domestic and intimate arrangements they wish.

Third: what possibilities and challenges does this raise for progressive politics? It would be easy enough to label these new developments as 'neoliberal' and then (with a great 'Aha!') denounce them. But, as I have argued elsewhere (see Ferguson 2010), such easy denunciations do not really get us any further in thinking about progressive possibilities, and may even blind us to recognizing some of the more hopeful forms of new thought and practice that are emerging in new welfare states like South Africa. Instead, we need more engaged and pragmatic analysis of what strategies might be effective on this new terrain. What are we to make of things like the Basic Income Grant campaign? Does the increasing reliance on cash transfers (with its implicit acceptance of decommodified livelihoods that do not depend on an exchange of labour for wages) simply acquiesce in the failure of the state to pursue job creation more effectively? Or might it create openings for new sorts of political strategies, strategies that might go beyond the twentieth-century horizon of 'full employment' to pursue goals that would be both more realistic and, in some sense, more radical?

Historicizing the future

The project of historicizing 'the social' cannot only be about the past. To say that something has not always existed implies the possibility that what once appeared may also one day disappear. If there was a time before 'the social', that is, it may also be possible to imagine a time when that same figure fades into obscurity, or mutates into something different altogether.

If 'the social' was constructed on such pillars as the male wage labourer, the nuclear family, and the interventionist, social-engineering state, the contemporary southern African scene gives us reason to take such a possibility seriously. In South Africa, long the African site where conditions came closest to approaching the Western ideal of social inclusion via formal-sector employment, mass unemployment remains stubbornly entrenched, and young black men in much of the country see slim and declining prospects for the sorts of formal-sector jobs their fathers and grandfathers held or aspired to hold. Marriage is also a radically diminished institution, as poor and working-class women (often receiving child support or other grants from the state) see little to gain from bringing an unemployed man into the household. Elsewhere in the region, formal employment plays a far smaller role, while the rural livelihoods that once supported the largest part of the population are in sharp decline. The result is the emergence of massive urban populations that lack formal (and often even much informal) employment, while increasingly lacking meaningful rural connections as well. Such people were once designated as 'the lumpen', and understood (by colonial officials and Marxist theoreticians alike) as a small and dangerous residuum. Today, they may well constitute the majority of the population in most African cities.

Historicizing helps us to see this circumstance as something other than simply decay and degeneration (*à la* Davis 2006). The idea that Africans leaving agricultural village life for the city would be incorporated into a stable, Fordist industrial working class, where unemployment and destitution would be atypical conditions, stabilized through insurance mechanisms, is increasingly implausible. But if we make ourselves aware that what is being lost is not any possibility of a decent future, but instead just one very particular formulation of what such a decent future might look like, then we can perhaps learn to free ourselves from a politics of nostalgia, and see new sorts of futures, and new sorts of politics, that only a properly historicized sense of the future might be able to detect.

In a world of urban dwellers increasingly unanchored to either subsistence farming or the certainties of formal-sector wage labour, what sorts of demands for economic inclusion and assistance are likely to emerge? What sorts of strategies for governing such populations will prove viable? As my brief discussion of cash transfers (above) was meant to imply, social assistance, in some form or other, seems to be emerging as part of the answer to both questions.[4] But it will be a very different sort of 'social' that will be in play, one whose dangers and possibilities, for the most part, remain to be mapped.

[4] The humanitarian and the medical also appear to be key sites – but that is another discussion. See the dissertation of Ramah McKay (2010).

Recognition beyond documents

Finally, let me conclude by bringing all this to bear on the topic of this book, the question of documentation and registration. Like 'the social' itself, we must think of documentation as having not only a past, but also a future. The social implied a whole range of other institutions, which constituted its conditions of possibility, and on which all 'social' technologies depended (the shortlist would include widespread regularized wage labour, the male-headed family, insurance mechanisms, and the nation state as bounded membership group). All of these had documentary entailments (attesting to where one was born, when, to whom, to whom one was married, when one died, whose children belonged to whom, and especially, of course, to membership of the bounded entity – parish, town or state – providing the vital entitlements). Pushing this observation into the future, then, we might ask, what would be the documentary entailments of possible future forms of assistance?

Is it the case that social assistance in Africa must wait on the development of the economic, political, and documentary institutions that enabled it in the West? Does effective social assistance in fact require the kind of state that knows things like how old every citizen is, who lives in which house, what each household's income is, and which children belong to which parents? It is not possible to say for sure, but the present holds some clues. Promoters of the idea of a 'basic income grant', for instance, make interesting arguments about the reduced need for documentation entailed by unconditional social transfers, and the role that new technologies might play in providing new kinds of bureaucratic recognition. In an ideal system, in some of these accounts, a monthly BIG payment could be obtained by any recipient simply by being biometrically recognized (e.g. through a retina scan) as a unique individual at any ATM cash machine. Instead of all the paperwork, files, and social workers that conditional schemes require to sort out who qualifies and who does not (what's your name, where were you born, how many children do you have, are they really yours, what is your income, etc. etc.), the BIG and its biometric recognition scheme would only have to answer one question: have you already been paid yet this month, or not?[5] Thus is a radically stripped-down form of recognition envisioned, one that requires far less from the state (in informational and registration terms) than the 'social' of old.

There are ample reasons to be sceptical of such proposals, given both the poor record of the general tendency of our time to seek reductive technological solutions to complex political problems, and a more specific South African history of hyped claims for the efficacy of biometrics (Breckenridge 2005). But the idea that biometrics can facilitate the delivery of services to marginal and geographically

[5] Restriction of the benefit to citizens, of course, would require a second – and extremely difficult – question: are you [really] a citizen?

remote people is not just a fantasy, either. Pensions and other social grants are being paid quite effectively in Namibia, for instance, through a network of mobile pay stations with fingerprint readers that allow people in even the most remote parts of this vast and lightly populated country to receive payments each month. India, another state with a large rural poor and a chequered history of identity registration systems (see Chapter 11 in this volume), has pioneered the use of biometrics (using a combination of iris, face, and fingers) for establishing unique IDs for purposes such as distributing ration cards, and is now rolling out a comprehensive scheme for a nationwide biometric identification scheme that proponents claim will improve service delivery to the poorest while reducing opportunities for corruption (Lakshmi 2010). Breckenridge's recent review of Ghana's current effort to introduce what has been called 'the world's first biometric money supply' has highlighted the dangers of such schemes, and the likelihood of their being deployed in ways that respond principally to the needs of banks and wealthy depositors (Breckenridge 2010). But at the same time, Breckenridge acknowledges 'that these systems of biometric registration can, as has been the case in South Africa, serve as technologies of inclusion, working, very efficiently, to provide the old, infirm and the young with a measure of social security' (2010, 656).

Biometrics are often imagined as scary instruments of control at the disposal of a potentially totalitarian state. But, in the context of new thinking about social assistance in Africa, more effective techniques for identifying biological individuality have some attractive political features, and could even facilitate forms of social transfers that would require less, rather than more, intrusive surveillance. To appreciate the case for biometrics, it is useful to remember that current regimes of (paper) documentation in Africa have some quite obvious and severe problems. First of all, it is well established that the burdens of obtaining and retaining documents fall hardest on the poorest and most marginal members of society (just those who are most in need of social assistance), who often fail for this reason to qualify for schemes ostensibly meant to benefit them. In addition, widespread fraud (through forged documents etc.; see Chapters 9 and 10) wastes resources from both the state's and taxpayers' viewpoints, which, importantly, can undermine political support for social assistance programmes. Reliance on local officials to issue or certify documents creates vast opportunities for corruption, while linking benefits to the holding of specific cards or identifying documents allows social stigma to be attached to the receipt of payments. In contrast, the mechanics of bio-recognition appear to fit well with the universality of unconditional cash transfers, where everyone with a retina is entitled to get a transfer once a month. In this scenario, many of the identity-related documents the 'social' state has always needed can be dispensed with, and resources that would otherwise be spent tracking down who really qualifies for the income cut-off or who really lives at what address could be used instead to provide benefits. Critical scepticism toward such ideas is of course important, but I am increasingly convinced that it is equally important to allow ourselves to be open to the political possibilities that such new 'techniques of the social' might enable.

It would be easy to say that what the 'lumpen' masses of Africa's cities really need is 'proper jobs', and the whole range of 'social' rights, state protections, and documentary entailments that (at least in European welfare states) have long been understood to come with them. But such a demand seems increasingly irrelevant in places where state capacities are extremely limited, where a formal-sector job is a distant rumour, and informal hustling the dominant livelihood. To find forms of social assistance and state services – and perhaps also forms of political mobilization – that can be effective in such circumstances, we may require both a historically-informed sense of the future and its possibilities, and a willingness to envision new forms of legibility that might correspond to new forms of social and political recognition.

References

Bank, Leslie. 2009. 'Land and Livelihoods in Southern Africa.' Paper. Center for African Studies, Stanford University, 24 April.

Beveridge, William. 1942. *Social Insurance and Allied Services: Report by Sir William Beveridge*. New York: Macmillan.

Breckenridge, Keith. 2005. 'The Biometric State: The Promise and Peril of Digital Government in the New South Africa.' *Journal of Southern African Studies* 31(2): 267–282.

—— 2010. 'The World's First Biometric Money: Ghana's e-Zwich and the Contemporary Influence of South African Biometrics.' *Africa: The Journal of the International African Institute* 80(4): 642–662.

Brokensha, David. 2007. *Brokie's Way: An Anthropologist's Story: Love and Work in Three Continents*. Fish Hoek: Amani Press.

Cooper, Frederick. 1996. *Decolonization and African Society: The Labor Question in French and British Africa*. Cambridge: Cambridge University Press.

Davis, Mike. 2006. *Planet of Slums*. New York: Verso.

Dean, Mitchell. 1992. 'A Genealogy of the Government of Poverty.' *Economy and Society* 21(3): 215–251.

Defert, Daniel. 1991. 'Popular Life and Insurance Technology.' In *The Foucault Effect*, ed. Graham Burchell, Colin Gordon and Peter Miller. Chicago: University of Chicago Press, 211–234.

Devereux, Stephen. 2001. *Social Pensions in Namibia and South Africa*. IDS Discussion Paper 379. Brighton: Institute of Development Studies.

Donzelot, Jacques. 1979. *The Policing of Families*. New York: Pantheon Books.

Ewald, François. 1986. *L'État providence*. Paris: B. Grasset.

Ferguson, James. 1999. *Expectations of Modernity: Myths and Meanings of Urban Life on the Zambian Copperbelt*. Berkeley: University of California Press.

—— 2010. 'The Uses of Neoliberalism.' *Antipode* 41: 166–184.

Fiszbein, Ariel, Norbert Schady, Francisco H. G. Ferreira, Margaret Grosh, Nial Kelleher, Pedro Olinto and Emmanuel Skoufias. 2009. *Conditional Cash Transfers: Reducing Present and Future Poverty*. Washington, DC: World Bank.

Foucault, Michel, Mauro Bertani, Alessandro Fontana, François Ewald and David Macey. 2003. *Society Must Be Defended: Lectures at the Collège de France, 1975–76*. New York: Picador.

Hacking, Ian. 1990. *The Taming of Chance*. New York: Cambridge University Press.

Hanlon, Joseph, David Hulme and Armando Barrientos. 2010. *Just Give Money to the Poor: The Development Revolution from the Global South*. Sterling, VA: Kumarian Press.

Henderson, Ian. 1972. 'White Populism in Southern Rhodesia.' *Comparative Studies in Society and History* 14(4): 387–399.

Higginson, John. 1989. *A Working Class in the Making: Belgian Colonial Labor Policy, Private Enterprise, and the African Mineworker, 1907–1951*. Madison: University of Wisconsin Press.

Horn, David. 1994. *Social Bodies: Science, Reproduction, and Italian Modernity*. Princeton, NJ: Princeton University Press.

Hunt, Nancy Rose. 1999. *A Colonial Lexicon of Birth Ritual, Medicalization, and Mobility in the Congo*. Durham, NC: Duke University Press.

Hunter, Mark. 2010. *Love in the Time of AIDS: Inequality, Gender, and Rights in South Africa*. Bloomington: Indiana University Press.

Iliffe, John. 1987. *The African Poor: A History*. New York: Cambridge University Press.

Kaseke, Edwin. 2002. 'Zimbabwe.' In *The State of Social Welfare: The Twentieth Century in Cross-National Review*, ed. John Dixon and Robert P. Scheurell. New York: Praeger, 217–231.

Lakshmi, Rama. 2010. 'Biometric Identity Project in India Aims to Provide for Poor, End Corruption.' *The Washington Post*, 28 March. www.washingtonpost.com/wp-dyn/content/article/2010/03/27/AR2010032701460.html.

Lund, Francie. 2008. *Changing Social Policy: The Child Support Grant in South Africa*. Pretoria: HSRC Press.

Malinowski, Bronislaw. 1984. *Argonauts of the Western Pacific: An Account of Native Enterprise and Adventure in the Archipelagoes of Melanesian New Guinea*. New York: Waveland Press.

Marshall, Thomas Humphrey. 1987. 'Citizenship and Social Class.' In *Citizenship and Social Class*, ed. Thomas Humphrey Marshall and T. B. Bottomore. London: Pluto.

Mauss, Marcel. 2000. *The Gift: The Form and Reason for Exchange in Archaic Societies*, trans. W. D. Halls. New York: W. W. Norton.

McCloskey, Deirdre N. 2006. *The Bourgeois Virtues: Ethics for an Age of Commerce*. Chicago: University of Chicago Press.

McKay, Ramah. 2010. 'Post-Social Prescriptions: Medical Welfare in Mozambique.' Ph.D. dissertation, Stanford University.

Miller, Peter and Nikolas S. Rose. 2008. *Governing the Present: Administering Economic, Social and Personal Life*. Malden, MA: Polity.

Moore, Henrietta L. and Megan Vaughan. 1994. *Cutting Down Trees: Gender, Nutrition, and Agricultural Change in the Northern Province of Zambia, 1890–1990*. London: Heinemann.

O'Malley, Pat. 1996. 'Risk and Responsiblity.' In *Foucault and Political Reason: Liberalism, Neo-Liberalism, and Rationalities of Government*, ed. Andrew Barry, Thomas Osborne and Nikolas Rose. Chicago: University of Chicago Press, 189–208.

Owen, Robert. 2004. *A New View of Society or Essays on the Principle of the Formation of the Human Character and the Application of the Principle to Practice*. Whitefish, MT: Kessinger Publishing.

Perrings, Charles. 1979. *Black Mineworkers in Central Africa: Industrial Strategies and the Evolution of an African Proletariat in the Copperbelt, 1911–1941*. London: Holmes and Meier.

Polanyi, Karl. 2001. *The Great Transformation: The Political and Economic Origins of Our Times*. Boston: Beacon Press.

Posel, Deborah. 2005. 'The Case for a Welfare State: Poverty and the Politics of the Urban African Family in the 1930s and 1940s.' In *South Africa's 1940s: Worlds of Possibilities*, ed. Saul Dubow and Alan Jeeves. Cape Town: Double Storey Books, 64–86.

Rose, Nikolas S. 1999. *Powers of Freedom: Reframing Political Thought*. Cambridge: Cambridge University Press.

Seekings, Jeremy. 2005. 'Visions, Hopes, and Views about the Future: The Radical Moment of South African Welfare Reform.' In *South Africa's 1940s: Worlds of Possibilities*, ed. Saul Dubow and Alan Jeeves. Cape Town: Double Storey Books, 44–63.

—— 2007. '"Not a Single White Person Should Be Allowed to Go Under": Swartgevaar and the Origins of South Africa's Welfare State, 1924–1929.' *Journal of African History* 48(3): 375–394.

—— 2008. 'The Carnegie Commission and the Backlash against Welfare State-Building in South Africa, 1931–1937.' *Journal of Southern African Studies* 34(3): 515–537.

Seekings, Jeremy and Nicoli Nattrass. 2005. *Class, Race, and Inequality in South Africa*. New Haven, CT: Yale University Press.

South African Government. 2011. 'About SA – Social Development.' *South African Government Information*, 20 July. www.info.gov.za/aboutsa/socialdev.htm.

Wacquant, Loic. 2001. 'The Penalisation of Poverty and the Rise of Neo-Liberalism.' *European Journal on Criminal Policy and Research* 9(4): 401–412.

Index

abolitionism 90, 324, 325, 327
absconders 121–2, 341
Abul Fazl Allami 302
Access of Children to Social Security (ACESS) 484, 486
access to documentation 160–1
Acemoglu, Daron 359
Act of Toleration (1689) 74, 77
Adato, Michelle 486
Addison, R. H. 369
address books 106
adoption: Athens 173; France 144n15, 146, 149; Japan 119, 124, 125, 127; Uruguay 420
affidavits 486, 490
Africa xii, 2, 3, 25, 30, 358, 496; children's rights 26, 449, 450–8, 467–9, 470; Conference on the African Child 26, 371, 433n31, 449, 450–8, 467, 468; disillusion with the state 10; 'gatekeeper' states 10; governmentality 6; highland peoples 9n1; infant mortality 463; names 278; non-literacy based methods of registration 27; pan-Africanism 293; the 'social' 500–7; stigmatization of Africans 200; tax 359; unregistered populations 1; *see also* French Africa
African Americans 462–3
African Charter on the Rights and Welfare of the Child 475
agents 262–4, 266, 271
agriculture 50, 500, 501
Agüero, Jorge M. 476
AIDS 357–8, 482, 487, 490
Ain-i-Akbari 300
Ake, Claude 11
Algeria 386, 389, 394, 398
Ali, Mehmed x, xii, 335, 338–40, 341–3, 344–5, 346–7, 351
Allgemeines Landrecht 96–8, 100, 108
Aly, Gotz 13–14, 94
American Child Health Association (ACHA) 25, 433n31, 449, 462–4, 465, 491
American Public Health Association (APHA) 459–61, 469
Amin, Idi 280
Amsterdam 214, 217–18, 241, 242; births and baptisms 215, 216; citizenship 221–2; documents 223–4; guilds 226; Orphan Chambers 227; poor relief 227–30, 232; punishment of criminals 236–7; sailors 233
Anderson, Benedict 71n5
Anderson, Clare 312
Anderson, Ross 255
Angola 2
anthropology 495, 499
Antigua 85
apartheid 16, 360, 375, 491, 492; regional solidarity 488; Shepstone's method of indirect rule 363; social assistance 476, 477–81, 482, 506
Archias 181, 182, 184n48
archives: England 69; South Africa 256–7; Spain and Spanish America 202
Argentina 421, 423, 432, 437
Aristogeiton 175
Aristotle 172–3
Arthashastra 300
Aryanism 94, 98
assimilation 289, 290, 405
Athens xi, 16, 170–6, 177, 181, 187–8
attestaties de vita 224–5
Augustus Caesar xi, 169–70, 176–8, 185, 186–7
Austria 95, 105

al-Bakrī, Muhammad ibn Abī al-Surūr 337
Balfe, James P. 459, 461
baojia system 53, 60–1, 63n27
baptisms: Dutch Republic 214–16, 230n34, 240, 242; English parish registers 71n3, 72, 75n11, 76; English settlers in the Caribbean 87; France 141n10; Germany 95–6, 97; Spain and Spanish America 196, 200–1, 202, 203; Uganda 280, 280n7, 282, 284, 285,

289–90, 291; Uruguay 420; *see also* births
Barbados 82
Basic Income Grant (BIG) 508–9, 510, 512
Batlle y Ordóñez, José 423, 424, 425, 427, 434
Bauzá, Julio 425, 426, 427, 429, 435–6
Bavaria 97, 98, 100
Bayly, C. A. ix–xiii
Bayly, Susan ix, 300
Berro, Roberto 429, 434–6
Beveridge, William 507
Biet, Christian 159n33
bigamy 141, 149, 217
biometrics 2, 28, 292n18, 512–13; Africa 11; France 138n4; Germany 107; India 317; South Africa 362, 375, 377, 512, 513; Uganda 277, 278, 291, 294
biopower 3, 18, 71n5
Birn, Anne-Emanuelle 26, 415–47
birth certificates: France 140, 141, 144, 149; French Africa 401; South Africa 479, 484, 485, 487; Uganda 292; United States 464; Uruguay 418, 421
births 1–2, 72; Africa 358; children's rights 432, 449–73, 475; Dutch Republic 214–16; English parish registers 67, 75, 76, 89; English settlers in North America 78, 79–81; English settlers in the Caribbean 83, 84, 85; France 144, 146, 148, 151, 152, 154; French Africa 389, 390n10, 393–4, 396, 398, 399–400, 401; Germany 93–4, 95–7, 100, 101, 106; India 307–9, 314, 316, 318; Japan 118–19, 129; South African Child Support Grant 475–7, 483–4, 487–8, 491, 492; South African civil registration development 361, 363, 364–6, 367–9, 370, 371–4; Spain and Spanish America 200–1, 202; Uganda 277, 278–9, 280–1, 282–3, 286, 292; United States 25, 459–64, 465, 491; Uruguay 418, 420–1
Blacklock, Dr Mary 454, 456, 463
body marking 15
Boisdon, Daniel 398, 404–5, 406n61, 407
Boisseau de Mellanville, Paul 142, 144, 146, 148, 150n23, 155, 160, 161
Boisseau, Robert 140, 141, 151, 152, 152n25, 157, 158, 158n32, 159, 160
Bolivia 432, 437
Bombay 270, 304, 308, 310
Bonneuil, Noël 154
border controls 260, 488
Botswana 359
Bourdieu, Pierre 160n35
Bowker, Geoffrey 12
branding 236–7, 238, 247, 341
Brazil 421, 432, 435, 437, 509
Breckenridge, Keith 1–36, 357–83, 480–1, 493, 513
bribery 253, 266–9
British East India Company 303, 306
British Empire 6, 21, 87, 457–8; Africa 452–3; India xii–xiii, 303–14; origins of the 77–8; slave trade in the Caribbean 323–33; Uganda 287, 288; *see also* Great Britain
Broers, Michael 388n6
Brubaker, Rogers 5
Brunt, Peter 177, 182
Buchanan, Francis 306
Buckingham, James Silk xiii
Budlender, Debbie 482
Bueren, Geraldine van 467
bureaucracy 9, 12; bureaucratic rationality 360–1; Egypt 352, 353; Germany 107; Japan 123
burghers: Dutch Republic 212–13, 220–1, 222–3, 225–6, 241–2, 243; Germany 98
burials: Dutch Republic 214–15, 216–17, 240, 242n58; Egypt 337; English parish registers 67, 72, 76; English settlers in North America 78; English settlers in the Caribbean 82, 83, 84, 85, 87; France 141n10; Germany 95, 97; Japan 129; Uganda 280n7, 282; Uruguay 421–2; *see also* deaths
Burley, Henry 265, 268, 269
Buxton, C. R. 457

Cadir, Abdul 253, 267
Cairo 336, 338, 342, 343, 345, 349–50, 351–2
Calvinism 96, 216, 218, 240
Canada 89n23
Caplan, Jane 21
Caribbean: English settlers 81–7; slavery 90, 323–33, 388
Carmille, René. 147n19
Caroli, Dorena 427n13

Carpenter, Edward M. 460
Case, Anne 489
cash transfers 476, 478–80, 496, 509, 510, 512, 513; *see also* Child Support Grant
caste 300, 302, 311–12, 313, 314, 318, 319
Catholicism 17, 18; baptisms 71n3; Dutch Republic 214, 215, 228–9, 240, 243; English parish registers 68, 70, 73, 77; France 141n10; Germany 94–5, 96, 97, 99–100; godparents 69n2; Spain and Spanish America 200; Uruguay 423; *see also* Christianity
Cato Manor Development Project 487
censuses ix, 18, 30; British Caribbean colonies 324, 325; China 47–8, 54, 58; Dutch Republic 219–20; Egypt 338, 344–6; France 154; Germany 93–4, 101, 106, 107; India xii, 303, 306–7, 311–12, 318; Japan 116, 118, 126; Roman Republic 169, 176, 177, 178–81, 182, 183, 184–7; South Africa 475; Uganda 280, 281; Uruguay 421; *see also* enumeration
Central America 27
Ceylon 325
Chamney, Montfort 253, 262, 268–9, 270
chancellery registers 4–5
Charles I, King of England 74
Charlesworth, Lorie 75n11
Child Support Grant (South Africa) 11–12, 475–7, 481–93, 508, 510
children 1, 25–6, 449–73; China 40, 41, 46n10; Conference on the African Child 26, 371, 433n31, 449, 450–8, 467, 468; Dutch Republic 226–7, 229, 242n58; France 149, 160, 161; French Africa 401; Germany 97; illegitimate 149, 160–1, 202n31, 417, 418, 426–8, 435, 438, 466; Japan 117, 118–19, 120–1, 128, 129–30, 132, 133; orphans 149, 226–7, 239, 425, 482, 486; Roman Republic 178, 185; South Africa 362–3, 475–94; Spain and Spanish America 202n31; Uganda 279, 284, 290, 293–4; Uruguay 26, 415–47; *see also* infant mortality
Chile 417n4, 421, 423, 432, 437
China xi, 3, 24, 30, 39–66, 300, 361, 420n5; Equal Field system 48–51, 52, 62; household ranking system 51–5; immigrants to California 261; IT registration systems 27; *lijia* system 56–61, 62–3; as model for Japanese state 114; origins of household registration 43–7; types of registers 4; village lineages 5
christenings: English parish registers 67–8, 72, 76; English settlers in North America 78, 79; English settlers in the Caribbean 82, 83, 84, 85; *see also* baptisms
Christianity x, 5, 496; French Africa 407; Japan 116; missionaries in Africa 501; South Africa 362; Spain and Spanish America 204; Uganda 282, 285; *see also* Catholicism; Protestantism; the church
the church 14, 18, 20, 361; Dutch Republic 214–19, 220, 240, 241, 242; English parish registers 67–8, 69–70, 72–3, 76; German shift from ecclesiastical to civil registration 95–102; Spain and Spanish America 200, 204; Uganda 280; *see also* Christianity
Church of England 72–3, 76, 77n13; *see also* Protestantism
Cicero, Marcus Tullius 179n30, 181, 183, 184n48
citizenship: Athens 171–2, 173, 174, 187–8; 'documentary' 255; Dutch Republic 219–22, 231, 242–3; France 139; French Africa 385, 386, 388–95, 401–2, 403, 406–8, 410; Germany 94; India 317; Indian merchants 258; link with registration 496; Roman Republic 171, 176–7, 180, 181–3, 185, 186–8; social 401–2, 492, 496, 503; South Africa 362, 479, 492; Spain 193; Uganda 289, 291; United States 464; varieties of 491–2
civil society 22, 137, 148, 149, 157
civil status 16, 17; France 139, 140–3, 144, 146–7, 149, 150–61; French Africa 386, 391, 395, 402–8; Uruguay 420
Clanchy, M. T. 4, 5, 7
clans 287, 289
Clarke, W. J. 369, 370, 373, 375
Clarkson, Thomas 324
classical world 16, 169–90
clerks 80–1, 262, 264–5; *see also* officials
Clot, Antoine-Barthélemy 341–2
Cohn, Bernard S. ix, 14
Colombia 437
colonialism ix, 14, 467; Africa 10, 359,

451–3, 454–6, 457–8, 468–9, 491, 500–2; Dutch Republic 234; English settlers in North America 77–81, 88–90; English settlers in the Caribbean 81–7, 88–90; French Africa 385–412; governmentality 6, 257; India 14–15, 258, 299, 301, 302, 303–14, 317–18; slave trade in the Caribbean 323–33; South Africa 361, 362, 363–4, 375; Spanish America 193, 195–206; Uganda 277–91; *see also* British Empire
communism 10, 21
community 17, 499
Conference on the African Child (1931) 26, 371, 433n31, 449, 450–8, 467, 468
confirmations 214, 216, 241
Confucianism 49, 52, 62n26, 123
consent 16, 29; English parish registers 74; France 154, 157, 161
Cooper, Frederick ix, 5, 10, 16, 19, 23, 358, 385–412, 502–3
Cornish, W. R. 311
corporate lineages 59n24, 61, 63
corporatism 240
Corrigan, Philip Richard D. 7–8, 358
corruption 265, 513; *see also* fraud
Costa Rica 420n5, 435, 437
Côte d'Ivoire 398–9, 407
Cottias, Myriam 389n8
Council of Trent 71n3, 200, 214
courts: Dutch Republic 224; France 152, 157; Spain and Spanish America 193, 202
Cousins, Wilfred 266, 267–8
Crais, Clifton 360–1
crime and criminals ix, 28, 255; Dutch Republic 233, 236–8, 247; Egypt 346, 347, 348–51; France 160n36, 161; Germany 104, 105, 106; Japan 113, 120–1, 126; social causes of crime 497; *see also* forgery and false papers; fraud
Cromwell, Oliver 74
Cromwell, Thomas 67–8, 70–1, 72–3, 90
Crozes, Paul 153n28, 157–8, 159n33, 161n37
Crumbine, S. J. 462, 463
Cuba 420n5, 431–2, 437
Cuno, Kenneth M. 344
Curtis, Bruce 301
Curtis, Lionel 260–2, 263, 271, 362
customary law 376–7, 386, 387

al-Damurdāshī Katkhudā 'Azabān, Ahmad 337
databases 27
de Becker, Joseph 127
de Gaulle, Charles 386
de Klerk, F. W. 480
de Witt, Johan 242
deaths: Dutch Republic 216–17, 242n58; English parish registers 67, 76, 89; English settlers in North America 78, 79–81; English settlers in the Caribbean 82, 83, 84, 85, 87; France 70n3, 146, 149, 151, 152; French Africa 389, 390n10, 393, 396, 399–400; Germany 93–4, 95–7, 100, 106; India 307–9, 314, 318; Japan 118–19, 129; modern civil registration systems 72; South Africa 361, 363, 365–6, 367–9, 370, 371–2, 373, 374, 485; Spain and Spanish America 202; Uganda 277, 278–9, 280–1, 282, 283, 285, 292; United States 461; Uruguay 420, 421–2, 424
debt 155–6
decentralization: Dutch Republic 240, 241; Japan 123, 124; South Africa 258
decolonization 467–8
Dekker, Rudolf 244n63
Delhi 307
'demes' 172, 173, 174, 187
Demetrius of Phalerum 175
democracy xi–xii; Athens 172, 175n18, 176; India 316, 319; South Africa 476–7, 481, 491, 492; Uruguay 423; *see also* politics; voting
Denis, Vincent 142n12
Department of Home Affairs (DHA) 477, 484, 485, 487
development 9–10, 11, 387, 468, 491, 501, 509
Dhupelia-Mesthrie, U. 257, 263
Diarra, Tiémoko 404–5
diasporas xiii, 254, 256
Dionysius 179n30
Dirks, Nicholas B. ix, 14, 311
disability 478, 481, 491, 493, 504, 506
discrimination: French Africa 386, 394; South Africa 479, 480, 492, 505, 506
disease: Egypt 336–7, 338–9, 342, 343; Germany 108; League of Nations

Health Organization 430n23; South Africa 357–8, 371; United States 460
disinheritance 113, 114, 120–1, 129–30
'disowning' of children 120–1, 129–30, 132
displaced children 465–6
divorce: France 146, 149; Uganda 285, 293; Uruguay 423
'documentary citizenship' 255
documentary government 8, 9
documents: Dutch Republic 212–13, 222–5; Egypt 170, 353; France 141, 143, 153, 161; French Africa 394, 397, 403; Roman Republic 181–2; social assistance in Africa 502, 512, 513; South Africa 475, 479, 485, 486, 487; Spain and Spanish America 205; *see also* birth certificates; identity papers; passports
Domesday Book 4, 20, 73n7
domicile, certificates of 105
Donzelot, Jacques 496, 498, 499
double counting 100–1, 131
Dow, Unity 469
Dower, Edward 369
Doyle, Shane 10, 20, 277–96, 452–3
drivers' licences 16
Dubois, Laurent 389n8
Dubow, Saul 360
Duncan, Alice 371
Durkheim, Émile 497
Dutch East India Company (VOC) 232, 234, 244–5
Dutch Republic 211–51; church registration 214–19; criminals 236–8; factors shaping registration 239–41; guilds 225–6; identity documents 222–5; Indonesia 6; limits to registration 241–7; migration 213; Orphan Chambers 226–7; paternal identity 238–9; registration of the poor 227–32; sailors and soldiers 233–6, 244–6; *see also* Netherlands
Dutch West India Company (WIC) 234
Dutt, R. C. xii
Dutton, Michael 63n27

East Germany x
Eastern Europe 21, 461
Ebrahim, Mohamed 266
economic development 40, 359, 468; Africa 358; China 42, 52, 64
economic information 157, 160
Ecuador 432, 437
Edge, Granville 68n2
education: Africa 501; French Africa 401; Japan 133; South Africa 476, 490; Uganda 289, 292, 293; United States 460; Uruguay 419, 424
Edward VI, King of England 68
Egypt x, xi, xii, 25, 335–55; British colonialism 361; census 344–6; medical and public hygiene establishment 341–4; military conscription 339–41; Ottoman rule 336–7; quarantines 338–9, 343; role of law 346–52, 353–4; Roman Empire 169–70, 177
elites: China 39, 53, 56, 61; Dutch Republic 242; Japan 122, 124; Ottoman Empire 347; Roman Republic 178, 186–7; South Africa 377; Uganda 278, 289, 291; *see also* nobility
Elizabeth I, Queen of England 68–9, 71, 74, 77, 86
Elton, Geoffrey 72
'encarding' 138–9, 143, 149
Engerman, Stanley ix, xiii, 23, 90, 323–33
England x, 12, 15–16, 18, 67–92, 358; chancellery registers 4–5; creation of civil registration system 68–77; Cromwell's founding injunction 67–8; English settlers in North America 77–81, 88–90; English settlers in the Caribbean 81–7, 88–90, 328; eugenics 13; land-labour ratio 24; laws 21–2; purpose of registration 20–1; state-making 7–8; *see also* British Empire; Great Britain
Englund, Harri 11
Enlightenment 71, 354
entitlement 476, 483, 496, 512; *see also* welfare and poor relief
enumeration 7, 18, 19, 30; Athens 172n8; India 300, 301–3, 306–7, 317–18; *see also* censuses
Equal Field system 48–51, 52, 62
equality: China 44–5, 48–9, 51, 55; Egypt 354; French Africa 392, 399, 405, 410
errors 150–3, 156n31, 157, 158–60, 161
état-civil 16, 387–91, 393–400, 402, 408, 410, 462
Ethiopia 468
ethnicity: South Africa 256; Spain and

Spanish America 203; Uganda 286, 287–8, 289; *see also* race
eugenics 13, 417, 425, 434, 435, 438
Europe: civil registration systems 496; distinctiveness claims 8; governmentality 6–7; religious registration 5; surveillance 361
Ewald, François 498, 499
exclusion 17, 19, 277, 292; biometrics 294; South Africa 254, 256, 261, 478

Fahmy, Khaled x, xi, xii, 19, 335–55
Fahrmeir, Andreas 12, 93–112
familiarity 150–1, 153
family: Africa 500–1, 502, 508; China 64; France 158–9; French Africa 401–2; Germany 101, 102, 107; head of the 124–5, 127–9, 132, 133; Japan 117, 124–5, 127–9; social reasoning 497–8; South Africa 482, 483, 490; welfare state 510; *see also* paternal identity
famines 308, 310, 336–7, 500
fascism 435, 436
fathers *see* paternal identity
fees: Dutch Republic 220–1; English parish registers 76; English settlers in North America 81; English settlers in the Caribbean 83, 85–7; slave registration in the British Caribbean 327; South Africa 365, 373, 375; Uganda 292
feminists 13, 429, 433, 438
Ferguson, James 11, 24, 377, 495–516
fertility 424–5, 458, 467
field measurement books (FMBs) 304, 305
fines: English parish registers 76; English settlers in North America 79, 81; English settlers in the Caribbean 83, 84, 86; France 148; South Africa 363; Uganda 279, 282
fingerprinting 28, 513; Germany 107; India 14–15; South Africa 256–7, 260–6, 268, 270–1, 359, 362, 369, 375, 377, 479
Flemming, Rebecca xi, 16, 19, 169–90
flogging 237, 247
Fontaine, Laurence 153
Ford, James W. 463
forgery and false papers 4; Dutch Republic 246, 247; Indian Ocean migrants to South Africa 254, 255, 258–72; Spanish America 196; *see also* fraud
foster children 425, 436, 465, 481
Foucault, Michel 17, 21, 139, 301, 345, 358–9, 361; biopower 71n5; governmentality ix, x–xi, 3, 6–7, 18, 339; 'problem of population' 336, 340, 353; 'reason of state' 337; sciences of government 360
France 16, 17, 21, 137–65; birth records 101; civil status errors 150–3, 156n31, 157, 158–60, 161; civil status policies 153–7; influence on Uruguay 425–6, 436; limits of civil status 140–3; monitoring 143–50; property registration 25; Roman Catholic Church 18; tradition of social statistics 419; Villers-Cotterêt Ordinance 70; *see also* French Africa
fraud 513; Dutch Republic 230n35, 244, 245–6, 247; Indian Ocean migrants to South Africa 254, 255, 258–72; South Africa 255, 369, 370, 373, 375; *see also* forgery and false papers
freedom of movement 105–6, 191–2, 194, 198–9
French Africa 16, 23–4, 385–412, 455; ambivalence of imperial reformers 408–10; changing status 402–8; difference 395–400; family benefits 502; legislative assemblies 390–3, 399; registration of citizens 393–5; social citizenship 401–2
Freund, Bill 358
Fuller, Edward 451–2, 459

Gandhi, Mohandas K. 262, 266, 362, 367
'gatekeeper' states 10, 358, 376, 452
gender issues: access to social security in South Africa 489–90; disguising of gender 243–4; Japan 129; women's marital status 155–6; *see also* women
genocide 14
Germany 18, 93–112; lists of travellers 102–4, 106–7, 108; Nazi 13–14, 16, 21, 94, 108; registers of residents 105–6; shift from ecclesiastical to civil registration 95–102; social insurance 498
Ghana 2–3, 358, 513
Giddens, Anthony 1
Gilbert, Sir Humphrey 78
Gluckman, Henry 374
godparents 68, 214

Goldblatt, Beth 477
Goody, Jack 4, 6, 17, 25
Gopinath, Ravindran x, xi, 299–322
Gorski, Philip S. 5
Gouet, Yvan 395n27, 410
governmentality ix, x, 3, 6–7, 18, 24, 257, 301, 339, 387
Gray, J. L. 504
Great Britain: abolitionism 23; Beveridge Committee 374, 507; General Register Office 101, 142; urban associational society 28; *see also* British Empire; England
Grenada 324–5
Groebner, Valentin 5, 14, 361
group membership 17
guardianship 227
Guerre, Martin 247n70
Guèye, Boubakar 409
Guèye, Lamine 391n14
guilds 196–7, 225–6, 240, 241
Guinea 398, 399
Gutman, Robert 79, 80
Gypsies 138, 193, 194–5, 237–8

Habermas, Jürgen xiii
Habib, Irfan 300
Hacking, Ian 71n5
Han dynasty 45–7, 62
Harris, John 455
Hassim, Shireen 479, 491–2
health: Africa 456, 501; Egypt 335, 336–7, 338–9, 341–4, 345–6; Germany 97, 99, 108; India 310–11, 318; South Africa 358, 359, 361, 364–5, 371–5, 490; Uganda 279, 280, 292; United States 461; Uruguay 415, 416–19, 422, 424–8, 434–8; *see also* infant mortality
Hébert, J. B. 144, 146, 147, 148
Henderson, Ian 505
Henry VIII, King of England 21, 67, 73n6, 358
Herzog, Tamar 8, 13, 19, 20, 28, 191–209, 247n70
Hesse-Kassel 106
Higgs, Edward 16
Higman, B. W. 327
Hindus x
Holland 22, 28, 70, 213; census 219–20; land-labour ratio 24; marriage 217, 218; migration 232; *see also* Netherlands
Hongwu, Emperor 55–6, 58–9
Hoover, Herbert 433n31, 449, 460, 462, 464–6, 491
Houden, Dr Leslie 458
Houphouët-Boigny, Félix 404
household registration: China 4, 39–47, 52–5, 57, 59–60, 61–4; Japan 24, 114, 116–22, 123–6, 128–31; Uruguay 427
Hsiao Kung-ch'uan 61
Hu Yaobang 361
Huber, Julien 436
hukou (household registration) system 4, 39–47, 52–5, 57, 59–60, 61–4
Hulett, Liege 364, 365
human rights 11, 26, 27, 30, 292, 467–8; English parish registers 71, 91; legal personhood 22; Uganda 293; *see also* rights
Hunt, Lynn 71
Hunter, Nina 486
Hunter, W. W. 311

Ibrāhīm, Nāṣir Ahmad 336
identity 19–20, 25; ambiguities of the word 5; children in Uruguay 417, 418; classical world 187, 188; Dutch Republic 211–47; Egypt 335, 347–8, 349–50, 352, 353; India 299, 301, 311–14, 316–17; right to an 29, 291n17, 292, 417, 437, 467; Uganda 283–90, 291–2
identity cards 16, 394
identity papers: France 137–8, 139, 147, 154; South Africa 475, 479, 481, 487; Spain and Spanish America 203; *see also* documents
identity politics 291–2, 317, 319
identity theft 29, 141, 155, 159
ideology x, 22–3, 26, 182, 304
Iliffe, John 500
immigration: 'documentary citizenship' 255; Dutch Republic 213, 221–2, 231; France 149; Indian Ocean migrants to South Africa 253–76; Spain and Spanish America 191, 192–3, 194, 196–7, 200, 201, 203; Uganda 278, 281, 287, 288–9, 290; Uruguay 422; *see also* migration
inclusion 17, 19, 289, 292, 410
indentured labour xiii, 256, 364, 422
indexing 101, 106, 261
India ix, x, xii–xiii, 3, 30, 299–322, 361;

absence of individual identity registration 301, 311–14, 317, 318; biometrics 2, 513; births and deaths 307–9, 314, 318; census 306–7; earliest registration practices 300–1; early British presence in 82n16; fingerprinting 14–15; governmentality 6; health issues 310–11; migrants to South Africa 20, 253–76; *panchayats* xi; post-colonial period 314–17, 319; pre-colonial period 301–3, 314, 317; property registration 303–6; rejection of nationalism 10; Sample Registration System 315–16, 319; seamen xiii
Indians (Spanish America) 198–9, 203–4
indigenous people: Africa 386, 455; Spanish America 198–9, 203–4; Uganda 280
individuals: absence of individual identity registration in India 301, 311–14, 317, 318; concept of the individual 335, 348, 352; individualization in French Africa 393; 'individuating logic' 335, 346, 354; relations between 155
Indonesia 6
industrialization 40, 42, 131, 132
inequalities 41, 42–3, 469, 495
infant mortality: Africa 451–2, 454–5, 456–7, 463; Egypt 342; League of Nations Health Organization 430–1, 432; Uganda 279, 280, 283; United States 459, 460, 462–3; Uruguay 417, 418, 425, 426–8, 434, 436, 438
informal economy 255
inheritance: Athens 173n9; China 44n6, 55n18; English parish registers 70, 71, 72; France 156–7; French Africa 394–5, 407, 408; Germany 101, 102; Japan 113, 114, 126, 128, 129; Spain and Spanish America 200; Uganda 277, 282, 290; United States 460; Uruguay 420
initiation rites 17
insurance: Dutch guilds 226; social 498, 507
International Institute for the Protection of Childhood (IIPC) 429–34, 435–6, 437, 453–4
International Labor Office (ILO) 452, 455, 457
international law 464
Ireland 23, 72n6, 142n13
Islam x, xii; *see also* Muslims
Italian states 183–5, 201

al-Jabartī, 'Abd al-Raḥman 338, 339
Jalabert, Ricardo 436
Jallād, Filīb 351
Jamaica 83–5
Japan xi, 3, 113–35; household registration 114, 116–22, 123–6, 128–31; *koseki* 24; land registration 114–16, 126–8, 129, 132–3; local imperatives 18; purpose of registration 20; religious surveys 5
Jebb, Eglantyne 371, 430n20, 431, 451, 452, 464, 466
Jews: Dutch Republic 215, 221, 225n27, 238, 240, 243; France 138, 141n10; French Africa 389; Germany 99, 107, 108; Nazi genocide 14; Spain 194, 200
John, A. Meredith 323–4, 327
Johnson, Simon 359
Jones, Gareth Stedman ix, 13
Judaea 169
judicial records 146, 150
Julius Caesar 185, 186
Junod, Henri 371
Justices of the Peace: England 71, 72, 75, 76; Massachusetts 81; Uruguay 420–1, 427; *see also* magistrates

Kafka, Franz 12, 374
Kamara, Mamadou 398
Kamerling, Johannes Cato 104, 211–12, 246–7
Kenya ix
Khamissa, Ali Mohamed 268
Khan, Ali Muhammad 302
kings of arms 202–3
knowledge, and power 7
Korczak, Janusz 430n20
koseki 24
Kosovo 155n30
Kuczynski, Robert René 26, 82, 87, 89n23, 456, 457–8, 468

Labbé, Morgane 155n30
labour: Africa 502–3; China 40, 42, 46, 55, 58, 60, 62, 63; French Africa 386, 387, 401–2; land-labour ratio 24–5, 318; male wage labourer model 510, 511; over-supply of 509; South Africa 15, 477–8, 482, 511; Uruguay 424

Laferté, Gilles 139
Lambton, William 303
land-labour ratio 24–5, 318
land ownership: China 44n6, 48–51, 54, 59, 62; India 305, 313; Japan 115, 116, 126–8, 129, 132–3; South Africa 359; *see also* property
land registration: France 145; India 303–5; Japan 114–16, 126–8, 129, 132–3; *see also* property
Landry, Adolphe 391
language issues 203
Latorre, Lorenzo 419–20
law: Anglo-Indian 305; customary 376–7, 386, 387; Egypt 335, 346–52, 353–4; English parish registers 70, 73–4; French Africa 387, 391–2, 393; international 464; legal empowerment 21–4; Roman 191, 201; South Africa 376–7; Spain and Spanish America 202; *see also* regulation
League of Nations (LN) 415, 425n11, 429–30, 433, 436, 449–50, 457, 466, 467
League of Nations Health Organization (LNHO) 430–2, 435, 451, 452, 455, 461
van Leeuwen, Marco H. D. 20, 22, 70, 96, 211–51
legibility 8–9, 18, 191, 204, 257, 360–1, 514
Legrand, Henry-Léopold 144n15
Leibbrandt, Murray 486
Lenoël, Albert 141, 143, 145–6, 147, 152, 153, 156–7
Leroy, Reine 157n32
Lesotho 9n1
letters of recommendation 222–3, 225, 258, 259
letters of surety 230–1, 232, 241
Levivier, Édouard 147, 148
Lewis, Mary D. 139n5
licensing: Dutch Republic 229; Spanish America 196–7, 198
life certificates 224–5
lijia system 56–61, 62–3
lineages 59n24, 60, 61, 63
Linehan, Peter 68n2
list-making 4
literacy: China 57n21; England 74; Japan 118; Uganda 282; Uruguay 419
'*livret individuel*' 147
Livy 178, 179n31, 180, 181, 183, 184
London ix, 8, 13
Looijesteijn, Henk 20, 22, 70, 96, 211–51
Lorimer, Frank 455
Lugg, Harry 371–2, 373, 375
Luisi, Paulina 429–30
Lund Committee 482, 491
Lund, Francie 10, 11, 12, 15, 377, 475–94
Lutheranism 96, 97, 215, 216, 240
Lyon, Raymond 140n8

MacDonald, Andrew 12, 20, 28, 253–76
Madras 304, 306, 307, 308, 310, 311, 314
Maggaris, Abraham 247
magistrates 236, 237–8, 240; births and baptisms 215, 216; burials 216–17; citizenship registers 219–22; documents 222–3, 224; marriages 217, 218–19; poor relief 230; population movements 231–2; South Africa 258, 261, 363, 365, 367, 368; *see also* Justices of the Peace
Malbrant, René 391
Mamdani, Mahmood 363
Mandela, Nelson 480, 491, 493
maps 303, 304, 305, 313
Marquant, Robert 158
marriage: bureaucratic paperwork 247n71; China 4; Council of Trent 71n3; Dutch Republic 212, 213, 214–15, 217–19, 240, 242, 243; English parish registers 67, 72, 75, 76, 89; English settlers in North America 78, 79–80, 81; English settlers in the Caribbean 82, 83, 84, 85, 87; France 140, 141, 144n15, 146, 149, 151n23, 155–6, 160, 388; French Africa 389, 390n10, 393–5, 398–401, 403–4, 406, 408–10; Germany 93–7, 100, 106; Japan 118–19; Roman Republic 178–9; South Africa 15, 362n1, 371, 511; Uganda 282, 283, 285, 292; United States 461; Uruguay 420
Marshall, Dominique 25–6, 449–73
Marshall, T. H. 491–2, 503
Marshall, William E. 313
Mary I, Queen of England 68
Massachusetts 78–81, 89
maternity certificates 485
maternity leave 417, 436
Mauritius 324
McKeown, A. 261

medical statistics: Egypt 341–3, 345–6; Germany 97, 99, 108; India 310–11; South Africa 374; Uganda 279, 280; Uruguay 420–1, 422; *see also* health
Meiji era 113, 114, 117, 123–32, 133
Menendez, Alicia 489
Mennonites 215, 221, 225n27, 240
Mersier, Émile 156n31, 158, 160
Mesopotamia 25
metics (resident aliens) 171, 173, 174–5, 176
Mexico 421, 423, 437
Meyer, E. A. 181n38
Middle Ages xi, 5, 195, 237
midwives 239, 342–4, 420–1
migrant labourers: China 42–3; Dutch Republic 219n15; South Africa 15; Spain 193–4; Uganda 288–9
migration: China 40, 41, 42; displaced children 465–6; Dutch Republic 213, 222–3, 228, 230–2, 241; Egypt 351–2; France 139, 143–4, 154; Germany 102–4, 106–7; Indian Ocean migrants to South Africa 253–76; Japan 119–20, 121–2, 130–1; non-citizens' rights 488; Roman Republic 183, 184; South Africa 475, 477–8, 488; Spain and Spanish America 191–9, 203
Mikhail, Alan 336n1, 337
military service: Athens 171, 172, 174; China 44, 45, 46, 49, 52, 61, 62; Dutch Republic 234–6, 245–6; Egypt 339–41; France 161; French Africa 385; Roman Republic 170, 171, 179, 183–4, 186; *see also* soldiers
Miller, Peter 499, 501
Ming dynasty 55–60, 62–3
missionaries 116, 282, 501
Mistral, Gabriela 431
modernity xi, 24, 128, 360, 387
monitoring: France 139, 140–1, 143–50; Uganda 277, 283; *see also* surveillance
morality 496–7, 501
Morquio, Dr Luis 425–9, 431, 432n28, 433, 435–6
Mozambique 488
Mughals 302, 303, 305, 314, 318
Museveni, Yoweri 277, 291–2, 293, 294
Muslims: China 41; Egypt 353, 354; French Africa 389, 395, 404n56, 409–10; South Africa 262–3; Spain 194, 200
muster-rolls 233–4, 235, 245

Nainsi, Munhata 302
names: China 4; Dutch Republic 229n33; Egypt 348–50, 353; France 152, 153–4, 158; Jews 238; right to a name 1, 292, 475; Roman Republic 178, 185; slaves in the British Caribbean 326n3; South Africa 366; Spain and Spanish America 199–204; Uganda 160n35, 278, 283–6, 287–8, 289–90, 291
Namibia 505, 513
Naoroji, Dadabhai xii
nationalism 10, 290
Native Affairs Department (NAD) 357, 362, 363, 369, 370, 371–5
Nattrass, Nicoli 495
Nazi Germany 13–14, 16, 21, 94, 108
negotiation 19, 20
neoliberalism 317, 496, 499, 500, 507, 508, 510
Netherlands (Dutch Republic) x, 3, 211–51; church registration 214–19; congregational denominations 18; criminals 236–8; factors shaping registration 239–41; guilds 225–6; identity documents 222–5; Indonesia 6; Jews 14; limits to registration 241–7; migration 213; non-state registering bodies 22; Orphan Chambers 226–7; paternal identity 238–9; population registers 19; registration of the poor 227–32; sailors and soldiers 233–6, 244–6; slave trade 325
New England 79
Newman, George 452
Nicaragua 437
Nietzsche, Friedrich 7
Nigeria 2–3, 358, 454
nobility: China 43, 44, 48; France 159; Germany 98; India 302; *see also* elites
Noiriel, Gérard 101, 138, 142n12, 149n21, 153n29, 160n36
non-governmental organizations (NGOs) 470, 484, 486, 490
Northern Wei dynasty 49
notaries 21; Dutch Republic 217, 224, 225; England 71n3; France 144–5, 147, 156n31; Spain and Spanish America 203, 205; *see also* officials
'notes in the margin' 141, 149, 150

occupational groups 56–7, 170
officials: China 47, 53, 55; corruption 513; France 147, 152, 153; French Africa 385, 395–6, 400, 401, 410; India 307, 309; Japan 115, 118; Roman Republic 179; South Africa 262, 269, 271, 363, 375, 480; Spain and Spanish America 205; *see also* notaries
Oloka-Onyango, Joe 11
Ong, W. J. 4
Ooms, Herman 113, 116, 120–1
oral methods 3, 4, 6, 27, 191, 205–6
Orphan Chambers 226–7
orphans 149, 226–7, 239, 425, 482, 486
Ottoman Empire xi, 335, 336–7, 338, 346–7
van Oudtshoorn, William van Reede 265, 267–8, 269
Overy, Richard ix, 13
Owen, Robert 497

pan-Africanism 293
Pan American Children's Code 437
Pan American Sanitary Bureau (PASB) 433–4
panchayats xi
Paraguay 437
parishes: English parish registers 20–1, 67–77, 88–91; English settlers in the Caribbean 82, 83, 84–5, 86, 328; Germany 95–6, 97; Uganda 285–6
Park Ross, Dr George 371–2, 373, 375
Parker, Jacqueline K. 460
Pasha, Ibrahmim xii
passes 4, 26, 364
passports 29; Dutch Republic 222–3, 225, 246; Egypt 351–2, 353; French Africa 403; Germany 102, 103, 104, 107, 108; Spain 195, 205; Uganda 292
paternal identity 238–9, 417, 418, 435, 438
peasants: Egypt 337, 340, 351; Japan 114–15, 118, 119, 126
penalties: Roman Republic 180–1; South Africa 363; Uganda 277, 290; *see also* fines
pensions: French Africa 385, 387; Namibia 505, 513; Rhodesia 505; South Africa 357, 358, 375, 476, 477, 478–81, 489–90, 492–3, 503–6, 509; United States 461; Uruguay 423, 424
performativity 19, 20, 28, 176, 247n70
permits 254, 255, 257–61, 270, 271–2, 477–8, 479
Peru 421, 432
photographs 263
phrenology 312–13
Piazza, Pierre 138, 139n6, 143, 144n15, 154
Pillet, François 138n4
plague 336–7, 338–9, 343
Plan International 1–2, 469–70
Plowden, W. C. 312
van de Pol, Lotte 244n63
Pole, Cardinal 68
police and policing: China 53, 60–1; Egypt 350; France 138, 139n6, 143, 155; Germany 103; India 14–15; South Africa 265, 359, 362, 488, 490; Uruguay 419
political suspects 41, 104
politics 26; French Africa 387, 390–3, 410; Roman Republic 186; South Africa 361, 488–9, 491; Uganda 282; *see also* democracy; voting
polygamy 398, 402, 403–4, 406, 408, 409–10
Poor Laws: England 23, 68, 71–2, 74–6, 77, 86, 88, 90, 500; Jamaica 85; *see also* welfare and poor relief
population growth: China 50, 52, 61; England 77; India 309, 315; Roman Republic 177
populousness/population distinction 301, 336
port sheriffs 233–4
Posel, Deborah 15
poverty 507, 509–10; Africa 501; England 74; India 310, 319; Japan 131; South Africa 476, 478, 482, 490, 491, 504, 507–8; Uganda 277; *see also* welfare and poor relief
Powell, Nora P. 468
power 7, 14, 361
priests 21; Dutch Republic 214–15; France 145; Germany 97, 98
prisoners 138, 146, 351
'problem of population' 336, 339, 340, 341, 344, 353
property: ascendancy of property rights 358; Athens 173n9; China 4, 44n6, 46, 54, 57, 59n25, 63; Dutch Republic 219; England 20, 70–3, 74–5, 88, 90; France 21, 25, 144–6, 158; India 303–6, 318;

Japan 127–8, 129; Roman Republic 179, 185, 186; South Africa 362, 377; Spain and Spanish America 200; United States 464; *see also* land ownership; land registration
Protestantism 5; Dutch Republic 211, 216; English parish registers 72–3; France 141n10; Germany 94–5, 96, 97, 99; Scotland 73n6; *see also* Christianity; Church of England
provocatio 182
Prussia 12, 93, 96–8, 100, 101, 102, 105, 107
public health: Egypt 335, 336–7, 338–9, 341–4, 345–6; Germany 97, 99, 108; India 310–11, 318; South Africa 358, 359, 361, 364–5, 371–5; United States 461; Uruguay 415, 416–19, 422, 424–8, 434–8; *see also* health
public sphere xiii, 28
punishment of criminals 236–7, 247, 347

Qin dynasty 45
Qing dynasty 60–1, 63
Quakers 18, 22, 77
quarantines 338–9, 343

race: French Africa 390–1, 394; Germany 93–4, 95; India 313, 318; Jamaica 83; Namibia 505; South Africa 15, 360, 376, 476–82, 492, 504–5, 506–7; United States 462–3; *see also* ethnicity
racism 376
Rajchman, Ludwik 430, 431
rationality, bureaucratic 360–1
recognition, right to 467
rectification of errors 152–3, 156n31, 157, 158–60, 161
Reformation 214–15, 217, 227, 240
refugees 465, 466
registers 3–5; Africa 452–3; Athens 173–4, 175, 176; China 39, 44, 46, 54, 57, 58, 60, 63; Dutch Republic 215–16, 218, 220–2, 226, 227, 229, 240, 241–2; Egypt 341, 344; English parish registers 20–1, 67–77, 88–91; English settlers in North America 78, 80–1; English settlers in the Caribbean 82, 83, 86–7; France 141n10, 142–6, 148, 151–2, 159, 159n33, 160–1; French Africa 400; Germany 93–4, 95–102, 103, 105–6, 107, 108; India 258, 309, 310; Japan 113, 115, 116–22, 124, 130–1; refusal to certify 113; Roman Republic 169–70, 184n48; slave 323, 328; South Africa 253, 262, 365; Spain and Spanish America 68n2, 202, 205–6; Uganda 280n7, 285; of visitors and travellers 103
registration: concept of 30–1; crisis of 28–30; definition of 3–5; in history 13–16; legal empowerment 21–4; modern state 24–6; and recognition 16–21; technologies of recognition and representation 26–8; in theory 5–13; universal 1–2, 10–11
'registration cultures' 28
regulation 28–9; Dutch Republic 217; Egypt 338, 350, 351; French Civil Code 143, 149, 152, 158–60, 386, 388–9, 403–4, 406n62, 408; Germany 100; India 314; Japan 119, 120, 123–6, 127, 128–9; slave trade in the Caribbean 324, 325; South Africa 256, 261, 362–3, 364–6, 369, 370, 483–4; Spanish America 195–6; Uruguayan Children's Code 415, 416–18, 434–6, 437; *see also* law
Reimer, Michael J. 344
Reinhallt-Jones, Dr J. P. 453
religion 5, 71; Dutch Republic 227–8; English parish registers 72–3, 74; Germany 107; India 311, 313, 318; Japan 116, 117; Spain and Spanish America 199, 204; Uganda 282; *see also* Christianity; the church
religious groups x, 98, 299–300
Rennell, James 303
repression: France 139, 148; South Africa 255, 257, 492; Uruguayan Children's Code 417, 435
residence permits 254, 255, 257–61, 270, 271–2, 477–8, 479
residents, registers of: Dutch Republic 222; Germany 105–6, 107; Japan 131n16
'responsibilization' 499
Rheinallt-Jones, J. D. 371
Rhodesia 501, 505–6, 507
Richards, Audrey 288, 289
rights 1, 6, 11–12, 26, 29, 30; children in Uruguay 415, 416–19, 420, 428–34, 435–8; England 21, 71–2, 75, 90;

French Africa 16, 392, 393, 402–3, 407; Germany 105–6; Japan 115; landownership in China 59, 60; legal personhood 22; non-citizens 488; promotion of children's 449–73; Roman law 182, 191; social 503, 514; South Africa 257, 493; Uganda 291, 293; *see also* human rights
Risley, H. H. 313
rituals 17, 58–9, 173, 176
Rituals of Zhou 46–7
Robinson, Hercules 363–4
Robinson, James A. 359
Rodríguez Fabregat, Enrique 431
Rodseth, Frank 375
Roman Catholicism *see* Catholicism
Roman Republic 16, 169–71, 176–88; Roman law 191, 201
Rose, Nikolas 496–7, 499, 500, 501
Rosental, Paul-André 16, 17, 21, 137–65, 388
Roth, Karl Heinz 13–14
Rowe, William 61
Roy, Ram Mohan 312–13
Rudolph, L. I. and S. Hoeber 300
rule of law 22, 27
rural areas: Africa 500, 501; China 40, 41, 42, 54, 56; Egypt 344; South Africa 370–3, 376–7, 477–9, 482; Uruguay 419, 421–2, 426; *see also* villages
Rusnock, Andrea 154
Russell, F. T. 507

Sadiq, K. 255
sailors xiii, 223–4, 232, 233–4, 241, 242–3, 244–5
Saito, Osamu 5, 8, 18, 113–35
Sample Registration System (SRS) 315–16, 319
samurai 114, 115–16, 118, 122, 123–4, 129
Santa Cruz, Hernán 437n40
Sato, Masahiro 5, 8, 18, 113–35
Save the Children Fund (SCF) 457, 458, 465
Save the Children International Union (SCIU) 371, 430, 431, 433n31, 449–57, 459, 461, 463, 464, 466–7
Saxony 105
Sayer, Derek 7–8, 358
Schlumbohm, Jürgen 102
Schneider, Michael 102
Scotland 72n6, 73n6, 142n13
Scott, James 6, 8–9, 10, 17, 21, 360
scribes 57n21, 205
secularism: Egypt 354; England 71, 72; Germany 95, 100; Uruguay 420, 423
security: China 24; Egypt 335; Uganda 277, 294; *see also* police and policing
Seekings, Jeremy 495, 504
segregation 13, 360, 475, 478, 504
Sekiyama, Naotaro 122
self-registration xi–xii
Selwyn-Clarke, Dr 453
Sen, Amartya 11, 12
Sen, Sukumar 316
Senegal 387, 389–91, 394, 397, 402, 408–10
Senghor, Léopold 391
separations 219
Servius Tullius 180
Setel, Philip W. 12
Shachar, Ayelet 1
Shang Yang 44–5, 300
sharīʻa law 347–8, 350, 353, 354
Sharp, Evelyn 454
Shepstone, Arthur 369
Shepstone, Theophilus 362, 363, 364, 365
ships, listing of 325
siyāsa 346–50, 352, 353–4
Skinner, G. W. 60–1
Skocpol, Theda 13, 491
slavery ix, xiii, 23, 90, 456–7; Athens 171n6, 174, 175, 177; British Caribbean 323–33; China 45n7; French citizenship 388–9; Roman Republic 176–7, 183; Uganda 287; Uruguay 422n9
Small, Frédérique 454
smallpox 342, 343
Smith, Richard Saumarez 305
Smuts, Jan 360, 362, 364, 367, 369
the 'social' 496–9, 500, 512; African 500–7; historicizing 510–11; new techniques of 514
social citizenship 401–2, 492, 496, 503
social class: France 159–60; Germany 104, 108; India 304, 316–17; Japan 124; Roman Republic 179–80, 182, 186–7; Uganda 289
social control 24; China 39, 40, 44, 54, 60, 62, 64; Uganda 277, 294; *see also* surveillance
social engineering 108, 360

social institutions 61, 63, 359, 497, 502
social insurance 498, 507
social mobility 62
socialism 63–4
sociology 495
soldiers 232, 234–6, 244–6; Dutch Republic 242; Egypt 335, 339–41; French Africa 385, 386; India 302; United States 461; *see also* military service
solidarity 482, 488, 498, 499
Somaliland 458
Song dynasty 51–5, 62, 63
South Africa 4, 15, 23–4, 357–83, 453; Basic Income Grant 508–9, 510, 512; biometrics 512, 513; border towns 269–70; bribery cases 266–9; Child Support Grant 11–12, 475–7, 481–93, 508, 510; clerks and agents 262–5, 271; customary law 376–7; development of civil registration 367–70; fiscal retrenchment 370; gendered access to social security 489–90; Indian Ocean migrants to 20, 253–76; legal reforms 362–6; migrant associations 265–6; as modernist state 360–2; non-citizens 488–9; permit markets 257–61; post-apartheid problems 507–8; public health challenge 371–5; racial fragmentation 477–8; racism 376; state social assistance during apartheid 478–81, 503–5, 506–7; uncertainty about population 357–9; unemployment 508, 511
South America 27
South Asia 1, 2, 26, 27
Southeast Asia 8–9
Soviet Union 21, 27, 39, 40
Spain 3, 18, 20, 68n2, 191–209
Spanish America 193, 195–206
spelling of names 152
St Kitts and Nevis 82–3
St Lucia 324
St Vincent 86–7
Stanford, S. H. 367
Stanziani, Alessandro 157, 160
Starks, Tricia 427n13
Starr, Susan Leigh 12
state x, xiii, 1, 3, 10, 29; China 61, 63; civil society and 22; control 150; disciplinary systems 23; England 69–70; *état-civil* 16, 387–91, 393–400, 402, 408, 410, 462; France 139, 143, 147–8, 155, 387–8, 410; 'gatekeeper' 10, 358, 376, 452; Germany 93–4, 100, 102; identity papers 137, 138; India 305, 314, 317, 319; IT registration systems 27; Japan 114, 123; literacy bureaucracy 6; modern 24–6; power 7, 14; reduction of market uncertainty 157; Roman Republic 176; South Africa 357, 359, 360–2, 376; Uganda 291
State Maintenance Grant (SMG) 478, 480, 481–2, 483, 485, 492, 508
Stephen, James 323, 324–5
stillbirths 279, 280, 283, 421n8
Stoler, Ann Laura 6, 257, 361
Strauss, Paul 433
subject-citizen distinction 386, 389
Sudan 394, 458
Sui dynasty 49–50
Surinam 325
surnames: Dutch Republic 229n33; France 153, 158; Jews 238; Spain and Spanish America 200–4; *see also* names
surveillance 7, 361, 513; China 41, 44, 45; colonial states 387, 408; France 137–8, 139, 147, 148; French Africa 402, 410; Germany 107; India 319; South Africa 257; Uruguay 417; *see also* social control
surveys: China 57; India 304, 305n1; Japan 114–15, 124
Swaziland 9n1, 271
Sweden 154
Syria 169, 186
Szonyi, Michael 59–60
Szreter, Simon 1–36, 67–92, 282, 358, 452, 493

Table of Heraclea 185
Tang dynasty 50–1
tax xi; Africa 359; Athens 171, 172, 174–5; Caribbean colonies 86; China 4, 46–7, 49–53, 55–6, 58–60, 62–4; Dutch Republic 217, 219; Egypt 170, 337; English parish registers 71n4, 76; France 145; French Africa 385, 455; Germany 101; India 305, 314; Japan 114, 115, 120, 126; Roman Republic 170, 171, 179–80, 186, 187; slave trade in the Caribbean 325; South Africa 363, 364, 365–6; Uganda 282

teachers 367, 399–400
technology 26–8, 319, 481; *see also* biometrics
telephone directories 106
Terra, Gabriel 416, 418, 434, 435
terrorism 28, 294, 319
testimonials 223, 259, 263
Thier, Andreas 101
Thomas, Louis 140, 141
Thurston, Edgar 313
Tinker, Hugh xiii
Tobago 87
Togukawa era 113, 114–22, 123, 127, 128–31, 133
Torday, Emil 454–5, 467
Torpey, John C. 21
touts 253, 254, 255, 261, 264–5, 266, 272
transparency 160–1
transvestites 243–4
travel papers 101, 102–4, 106–7, 108; *see also* passports
Trinidad 87n22, 323–4, 326–8, 329–30
Turkey xi
twins 285–6

Uganda 20, 160n35, 277–96; demographic crisis 283; early attempts at civil registration 278–83; fixing of identities 283–90; Kuczynski's work 458
Ukraine 9n1
unemployment 108, 508, 511
Unique ID (UID) programme (India) 317, 319
United Nations (UN) 26, 467, 476
United Nations Children's Fund (UNICEF) 437, 438n40, 469–70, 485
United Nations Convention on the Rights of the Child (1989) 1, 291n17, 438n40, 450, 464, 465, 469, 475
United Nations Covenant on Civil and Political Rights (ICCPR, 1966) 26, 450, 464, 465, 466–7, 475
United Nations Covenant on Economic, Social and Cultural Rights 71–2
United Nations Declaration on the Rights of the Child (1959) 26, 415, 437, 450–1, 469
United States 3, 25; children's rights 432, 433, 453–4, 459–64, 465–70, 491; Chinese immigrants 261; English settlers in North America 77–81; eugenics 434; racialized government 376; slave trade 325–6; welfare 13, 491
universal registration 1–2, 10–11
urban areas: Africa 501–2; China 40, 41–2, 54; Egypt 344, 345; Japan 131; South Africa 370, 376, 478, 511; Uruguay 421–2
urbanization: France 150; Japan 131; pathologies of 501; South Africa 477; Uruguay 422–3, 424
Uruguay 26, 415–47; challenge of infant mortality 426–8; Children's Code 415, 416–18, 434–6, 437; Civil Registry 420–2, 424, 425, 427, 428; demographic conditions 422–3; IIPC 429–34, 435–6, 437; Latorre's reforms 419–20; legacy of child rights 437–8; tracking infant and child health 424–6; welfare state 423–4

vagabonds 351
vagrants: Africa 500; Dutch Republic 213, 232, 237; France 138; Germany 104; Japan 121; 'moral technologies' 496–7; Spain 193–4
Vaillant, Adolfo 419, 420, 426
Veerman, Philip E. 465
Venezuela 432, 437
Verwoerd, Henrik 360
Vichy government 138, 148n20, 149, 154
Vietnam 386
villages: China 5; Egypt 340, 341; French Africa 396n30; India 300, 304–5, 310, 313–14, 318; Japan 115, 116, 118, 119, 120, 126; *see also* rural areas
Virginia 78
visas 103
Vitoria, Francisco 193, 195
Voigt, Wilhelm 105
Völk, Joseph 100
Von Glahn, Richard 4, 5, 8, 12, 24, 39–66
voting: France 141; French Africa 387, 389, 390–3, 396–8, 403, 408; Germany 106; India 316, 319; Roman Republic 180, 182; South Africa 362; Uganda 294; *see also* democracy

Wacquant, Loic 499
Wagle, Narendra xi
Wagner, Patrick 101
Wales 20–1, 72n6

Walter, Henry 306
Washbrook, David 305
Weber, Max 5, 360
welfare and poor relief 3, 25–6, 495–516; Africa 11, 496, 502–14; China 61; Dutch Republic 220, 227–32, 240; family allowances in French Africa 401–2; France 142n12; Germany 101n8, 105, 107; India 316–17, 319; 'invention of the 'social' 496–9; Japan 131; link with registration 358–9, 451, 458; South Africa 358, 377, 475–94, 503–5, 506–9, 510; United States 13, 25; universalist social security 90–1; Uruguay 416–17, 418, 423–4, 427–8, 438; *see also* Poor Laws; poverty
West Africa, French 390–1, 394, 396–7, 399, 403
Western Jin dynasty 47–8
Wheelwright, C. A. 370
Whitehead, D. 172n7, 175n17
widows 217, 218, 226
Wigmore, John Henry 118–20
Wilbur, Cressy 25
William the Conqueror 73n7
Williman, Claudio 423
Winther, Jennifer A. 127
witnesses: Athens 174, 181; Dutch Republic 224–5, 229, 230, 239; Egypt 335, 347–8, 349, 352; France 151; French Africa 401; South Africa 259, 365, 369, 370, 373, 375; Spanish America 197
women 13, 18; Athens 171, 174; China 58n22; disguising of gender 243–4; Dutch Republic 238–9, 243–4; Egypt 342, 343–4; English Poor Law 75; France 155–6; French Africa 455; Japan 117, 129; patriarchal restriction of 293; Roman Republic 177, 185; South Africa 362, 368, 477, 478, 485, 489–90, 508; Uganda 279, 283–4, 285, 293; Uruguay 417, 429
Wordsworth, William 6
World Bank 509
World Health Organization 437
Wright, Marcia 364
writing 5–6, 7–8, 9
Württemberg 98, 106–7

Xiaowen, Emperor 48
Ximenes, Archbishop 68n2, 70

Young, J. M. 372–3
Yuan dynasty 55

Zambia 502
Zhou dynasty 43
Zimbabwe 488, 505–6